THE
EUROPEAN
EXPERIENCE
SINCE
1815

THE EUROPEAN EXPERIENCE SINCE 1815

Peter N. Stearns   RUTGERS UNIVERSITY

HARCOURT BRACE JOVANOVICH, INC.

NEW YORK / CHICAGO / SAN FRANCISCO / ATLANTA

PICTURE CREDITS

The Ben Roth Agency: 371

Culver Pictures: 44

FPG: 400

Historical Pictures Service, Chicago: 4, 22, 25, 58, 64, 75, 99, 112, 124, 142, 155, 171,
193, 198, 199, 211, 236, 249, 252, 304, 309

Magnum, Bruno Barbey: 418

The Museum of Modern Art, New York: 262

The National Gallery, London: 29

Wide World Photos: 321

The Phillips Collection, Washington: 389

Photoworld: 104, 223, 268, 297, 323

Pix: 449

Private Collection, San Francisco: 152

Radio Times Hulton Picture Library: 45, 139

Sovfoto: 285

Wil-Jo Associates, Inc. Copyright 1963 by The Chicago Sun-Times and reproduced
courtesy of Wil-Jo Associates, Inc. and Bill Mauldin: 378

PREFACE

Students frequently ask why they should study European history. It is a good question, but difficult to answer, for many traditional assumptions about the teaching of modern European history no longer fully apply.

The history of Europe during the last two centuries is above all the history of how a group of societies became modern. Its study is the study of the transformation of traditional values and institutions—not only political structures but personal values, family patterns, indeed the whole range of human activity. The historian of modern Europe must try to convey the sense of a basic and ongoing process; in this way modern European history can help illumine the study of other areas of the world.

Europe's patterns of modernization, which involved the displacement of deep-seated traditions, provide at least partial models for understanding the emerging Third World and offer a vital supplement to the study of America's past. Only by examining the establishment of modern civilization in Europe can we judge what is distinctively American about America. An earlier generation of historians, writing from the 1930s to the 1950s, found the study of Europe a useful way of pointing up America's strengths, in contrast to Europe's agonies of political instability, class conflict, and war. Today an examination of the stages of Europe's modernization, including the contemporary stage, may well suggest some desirable alternatives to the American experience. Furthermore, an understanding of Europe is important for its own sake, and even here the essential theme of modernization, the ongoing process of transformation, deserves primary emphasis.

The reader will find such an emphasis in *The European Experience Since 1815*. Indeed, my principal reason for writing the book has been to show the significance and distinctiveness of Europe's patterns of modernization. In concentrating on this theme the book does not ignore the standard landmarks in European history but it minimizes their detail and places them in proper context. It covers a broad range of factual materials, combining facts with analysis and the posing of interpretive questions. The book thus reflects many of the exciting new lines of inquiry that have been opened up by historians of Europe in recent years. Social developments and the evolution of popular culture receive particular stress because of their fundamental importance in the modernization process. My purpose here has been to outline what the people of Europe have been and what they have become.

To this end the text focuses on movements and processes that affected all or most of Europe. Hence, wherever possible, my approach has been supranational, emphasizing comparative history rather than giving a nation-by-nation capsule summary. The underlying assumption of this book is that it is important to learn about liberalism, for example, before learning the details of French or Italian liberal parties or policies. National and regional peculiarities are not neglected but are treated in a comparative context—which is, after all, the only means of determining what is in fact distinctive. By the same token the text deals with some of the larger periods in modern European history, concentrating on the essential characteristics of these periods instead of giving a strictly chronological account of events.

No book can ever be completely up to date, but in writing *The European Experience Since 1815* I felt that considerable attention should be given to the most recent decades of Europe's history. I have not only devoted several chapters to the post-World War II period but have undertaken a serious assessment of it, with all the risks this entails. The text takes the view that a major new period of European history opened up after 1945 and that its characteristics can be at least roughly determined. I saw no need to limit these chapters to a description of leading institutional developments, as many surveys, even those on the twentieth century alone, are prone to do. This postwar vantage point gives us an opportunity to seek in Europe's past more than the seeds of decay and failure that quite understandably preoccupied an earlier generation of American historians.

The European Experience Since 1815 is a fairly short text, given the span of time covered, and requires no particular background or prior knowledge in the field. It can be used in a general survey of western civilization, in combination with materials on other periods, or as a core text in a modern European history course, around which supplementary readings can be developed. It is my hope that the questions raised in this book will spur student interest and stimulate additional reading and discussion.

I am grateful to many people for their assistance in preparing this book, not the least of whom are the many students who have helped teach me how to teach European history. My father, the late Raymond P. Stearns, first proposed the book and reviewed a number of the chapters. Professor J. Kim Munholland of the University of Minnesota read the manuscript and made many useful suggestions. The editorial and production staffs at Harcourt Brace Jovanovich were extremely helpful. Karen and Peter Meyers assisted in several aspects of the manuscript's preparation, as did my wife, Nancy.

Finally, uncertain as I must be of the book's reception by students and teachers, I still acknowledge the great pleasure I derived from writing this survey. The range of issues demanding interpretation is endlessly fascinating. I can only hope that readers will share some of this fascination and will be encouraged to carry the process of inquiry still further.

PETER N. STEARNS

CONTENTS

8

WAR, REVOLUTION, AND THEIR AFTERMATH   *222*

Battlefronts of the War / The War's End / The Impact of the War /
Wartime Government / The Russian Revolution / Versailles / Postwar
Unrest / World War I: A Watershed?

9

DEMOCRACY PARALYZED: WESTERN EUROPE 1920–1939   *251*

Stability and Depression / Economy and Society / European Culture
Between the Wars / Politics and Diplomacy in the 1920s / Economic
Collapse / Politics in the Depression / Toward a Brighter Future

I O

THE AUTHORITARIAN REGIMES   *281*

The Nature of Totalitarianism / Communism in Russia / The
Authoritarian Regimes / Fascist Theory / Nazism / The Origins of
World War II

I I

WORLD WAR II AND THE DECLINE OF EUROPE   *305*

Axis Victories / The Invasion of Russia and War in the Pacific / Europe's
People at War / Great-Power Diplomacy and the War's End / Economic
Collapse / The Postwar Settlement / Development of the Cold War /
Decolonization

I 2

POLITICS AND THE STATE IN CONTEMPORARY EUROPE   *335*

The New Europe / The Authoritarian States / The Communist States:
Stalinism / Post-Stalinist Communism: The Smaller States / Western
Europe: The Political Spectrum / New Regimes / The Formation of the

Welfare State / The Nature of the Welfare State / European Diplomacy / Politics and Dissent in Western Europe

13

SOCIETY AND CULTURE IN CONTEMPORARY EUROPE   382

Ideas and Styles / The Arts / Science and Social Science / Economic Development and Population Growth / Social Structure / Stability and Protest / New Stresses in Society / Popular Culture: The Modernized European

MAPS

INTRODUCTION

In Europe, the modern age began to take shape well before the end of the eighteenth century, yet by 1800 the European was still a largely premodern man. Herein lies the principal fascination of recent European history, indeed the chief reason for its study. Within less than two centuries Europe has undergone a profound transformation: it has become modern—one of the relatively few areas of the world to do so. Modernization involved more than changes in the functions of states or even the advent of industrial technology. It required a new way of thinking and behaving on the part of ordinary people, in family and sex life as well as in politics and work. Recent European history provides a laboratory in which modernization can be studied historically. Modernization has not been uniform. The process has taken different forms within various areas of the continent, and Europe generally has developed a somewhat different style of modern life from that in North America.

Some of the principal themes of modernity were visible in Europe even in the seventeenth century, which is why certain parts of Europe could lead the way to the new age. The powers of the sovereign state had been increasing since the late middle ages and the modern state would build upon this base. The hold of religion had been shaken by the bitter legacy of the religious wars following the Reformation. Secular rulers gained greater control over church affairs, while philosophers wondered whether there was an absolute religious truth or, still more boldly, whether it mattered much one way or the other. Concurrently the interest in science and in the powers of man's unaided reason grew, though neither was new in the European tradition. Europe had also steadily elaborated its technology since the Middle Ages. There were few startling advances, but in most aspects of manufacturing Europe led the world technologically by the seventeenth century. Capitalism, yet another product of the Middle Ages, had also won a firm hold, particularly in overseas trade and related banking activities. Capitalism entailed not just a method of ownership and a system of business organization: even more important was its spirit, its belief that increased wealth and improvements in material comfort were good things and that individual economic efforts should focus on achieving such goals.

These, then, were the foretastes of modernity, and their evolution is the basis of European history after 1800. The expansion of the state, the decline of religion, the rise of science and rationalism, the spread of capitalism and its economic ethic—such were the building blocks of a new society.

During the eighteenth century the pace of change quickened in Europe. Science moved to the center of the intellectual stage. Newton's laws, capping a century of scientific discovery, revealed man's power to understand the physical universe. Eighteenth century Enlightenment thinkers, building on this foundation, hailed the power of man's reason and castigated faith and most other aspects of religion as mere superstition. Their universe was orderly and rational, operating on simple, regular laws such as those Newton had developed; society was or ought to be organized in the same manner. Enlightenment thinkers sought clear, universal political principles. Tradition was not enough—indeed it was more than likely evil. The state should be judged by reason with constitutions devised to set forth its functions rationally. The state, moreover, should leave free play to man's powers, should not interfere with free thought, and should cease trying to impose religious orthodoxy. For the most part, the political theory of the Enlightenment linked society to nature, claiming that each individual had natural rights by virtue of his innate rationality, which should not be tampered with. Most theorists stressed property rights as well as the right to freedom of thought. In Scotland Adam Smith, building from this base, formulated an economic theory that individuals should be left free to follow their own economic interests, which in turn would lead to the greatest possible general economic advance. Finally, the Enlightenment believed in progress. With man rational and nature beneficent, things should get steadily better. There poured forth a steady stream of proposals designed to improve all aspects of life including politics, technology, prison management, and education.

The organization of the state changed less decisively than did the intellectual life during the eighteenth century. The term "enlightened despotism," which describes the most prevalent form of government during the century, is in many ways exaggerated. Nevertheless a number of monarchs began to justify their functions in terms other than their God-given right to rule. They talked of the good they could do for their subjects and many began to sponsor economic improvements. For example, Frederick the Great of Prussia, who ruled from 1740 to 1786, encouraged the cultivation of the potato in order to increase agricultural production. Defense of religion declined, and many states granted religious toleration. The enlightened despots worked to improve their governments by developing better training for bureaucrats and by introducing increased specialization in their functions. The chief goal of most of these activities was military strength. Economic improvements, for example, were sought less to benefit the population than to provide a better tax base for the royal coffers. Here, clearly, the motives of the modernizing state changed far less than the functions. Unhappily this, too, foreshadowed the future.

The most profound change in the eighteenth century was remote from the world of kings and philosophers. Beginning about midcentury the population in most areas of Europe started to soar after centuries of scant growth. In England, in Spain, in Prussia it doubled during the second half of the century, and in many other countries it increased rapidly. One of the chief causes of this population explosion was the introduction of new crops, notably the potato, that greatly increased the available food supply. Another was the decline of epidemic disease, a worldwide phenomenon at this point (as was population growth itself) because of a cyclical lull in plagues. Europe benefited also from the better border controls that the more efficient states could now impose over the movement of people and livestock, particularly in the traditional plague route from the Middle East to central Europe. Unusually warm weather during much of the century also helped reduce death rates and heighten agricultural production. Finally, although in some parts of Europe the birth rate rose, the main factor in population growth was the decline in the number of deaths caused by famine and disease.

Such a massive demographic revolution inevitably had profound effects on all aspects of society. Europe's population grew more rapidly than that of most other areas of the world, which was one reason for the continued colonial expansion during the eighteenth century and beyond. Within Europe many people had to seek new ways of doing things. Since further agricultural improvements were considered vital, landlords discussed the planting of nitrogen-fixing crops, which would allow them to stop the age-old practice of leaving a third to a half of the land fallow each year. Manufacturing expanded providing new products for the rising population and new work for the growing labor supply. From Britain through central Europe hundreds of thousands of peasants became full- or part-time weavers and spinners in their own homes. Often individual families had to make painful decisions when they found themselves with an unexpected number of surviving children. What would the younger sons of aristocrats do, excluded as they were from the family's main inheritance? Similarly, younger peasant sons had to seek new work. Though a distressful situation, it proved an important source of innovation.

Spurred by the population advance, capitalism spread during the century. Peasants who manufactured textile goods became part of a capitalist system, for they received their raw materials and sold their finished product to urban merchants. Other peasants and many aristocratic landlords produced food for sale at distant markets. Factories were established in the cities, and while they were as yet without advanced machinery they provided increased specialization of labor and heightened the production of goods as diverse as rugs and pins.

Better food, new economic opportunities, and the disruption caused by the population explosion prompted even more profound changes in society. Younger peasants—and peasants were still the vast majority of the population everywhere—began to think of themselves in new ways. They sought new satisfactions and developed a greater sense of individualism, a certain freedom from group controls traditionally enforced by family and the village. The most striking illustration of this change was a marked increase in the desire for sexual pleasure. Illegitimacy rates rose rapidly, while at the same time people were marrying younger. With better food, the average age of puberty began to drop to fifteen from the traditional age of eighteen, a process that has continued to the present day. The modernization of sex was clearly underway, and it involved new attitudes as well as physical changes.

Still, by 1780, most of these developments were just beginning. The spread of capitalism, for example, had not created a capitalist middle class. In cities like Paris, most businessmen feared risky investment and instead put their money into real estate, which was respectable and safe even though it gave them a return of little more than two percent on their capital. There were far more landlords who talked of new agricultural methods than who put them into practice, and many more were not aware of them at all. Peasants planted some new crops, including the potato, but their methods and their goals changed little: they thought in terms of subsistence, of maintaining what they had, instead of striving for more. Changes in the state were also limited. Bureaucracies, though slightly better trained and more specialized, were still largely drawn from the aristocracy, which saw its public service as a traditional obligation and a means of preserving its social supremacy rather than an opportunity for professional competence. Frederick the Great of Prussia, the leading enlightened despot, actually increased the aristocracy's political role. Enlightenment ideas had a limited clientele. Religion, though under fierce intellectual attack, still maintained its hold on the common people. New religious movements such as Methodism in Britain revealed widespread popular piety.

Furthermore, the changes that had occurred were spread unevenly. Demographic and economic change was concentrated in western Europe, and the impact of the Enlightenment was far greater in France than elsewhere. New state functions developed particularly in central Europe, but they were notably absent in southern Europe as well as in England.

Thus the forces of change had yet to be fully combined. The preconditions of modernization were set, but the process itself had barely begun. Two revolutions after 1780 ushered in the modern age in history: the political revolution in France and the industrial revolution in Britain, both of which resulted from the less decisive changes of previous decades.

British industrialization clearly began about 1780. Ten years earlier James Watt had invented the first steam engine that could effectively power machinery. With the substitution of power from carbon fuels for human and animal power, the central feature of industrialization came into being. Inventions earlier in the eighteenth century had already altered key manufacturing processes, particularly in textiles. The spinning jenny, though operated by hand, wound fibers into thread semi-automatically. Looms were developed to reduce the manual labor needed in weaving. After 1780, first spinning, then weaving machines were linked to the new motors. Textile manufacturing was gradually taken out of the home and put into factories. At the same time metallurgy was transformed by the use of coal and coke instead of charcoal to smelt and refine iron. Coal was cheaper than charcoal and it allowed the creation of larger blast furnaces. Coal mining expanded rapidly, as did factories and the new industry of machine building. British manufacturing soared, filling the needs of the increased population at home and leaving substantial margin for trade abroad. Industrialists, many of whom were from humble social origins, sank their capital into machinery that was costly and committed British industrialization to the capitalist ethic. They thought in terms of risk, growth, and of course, profit.

Before 1815 only a small portion of British society was involved with the new industries. The main impact of industrialization was yet to come, and in the rest of Europe the process had not really emerged at all. Industrial society was now possible, however, indeed it was inevitable as British competition started to be felt throughout Europe. But its history had only begun.

The French Revolution, which burst forth in 1789, was less profound in its implications than the industrial revolution, which would require a total reordering of society and of human outlook. But the upheaval in France was a major development and, because it was far more visible than industrialization, it created a greater initial shock. France was Europe's leading country, its greatest military power, and the center of its culture. The tumult that engulfed France fascinated Europe's statesmen and intellectuals long after the revolution had ended. Opposition to or support of the principles of the revolution were the defining factors in European politics as late as 1870.

The revolution produced a wide variety of political ideas and tested most of them at one point or another. In its first phase it was a constitutional monarchy with a strong parliament. Then, after the execution of the king, it became a republic and a democracy, though this phase lasted but a short time. Under Napoleon it developed into a dictatorship, reminiscent of enlightened despotism but vastly streamlined and at the same time suggestive of modern totalitarianism. A few socialist movements arose during the revolution, though these were repressed. More important was the emergence of French nationalism. The revolution proclaimed that the state belonged to the people and that the people owed loyalty to the state.

As the French warred against the rest of Europe, initially in defense of the revolution, nationalist and revolutionary fervor intermingled.

The revolution molded a political consciousness both within and outside France. The rural population was largely immune, but in the French cities people felt intense political loyalties. In Britain and elsewhere, political interest heightened as various groups favored one faction or another in France. The revolution, therefore, not only produced a variety of political formulas but developed supporters for them as well. English artisans were drawn to republican democracy; German students were fascinated with nationalism. Later on there would be ample opportunity for these loyalties to spread further.

Under the revolution the power of the central state was greatly extended as many competing bodies were abolished or reduced in power. The Catholic Church in France was put under state control, guilds were abolished, and the political prerogatives of the aristocracy, as well as the traditional powers of provinces and cities, were destroyed. The state bureaucracy expanded and bureaucrats were promoted because of their talent, not their birth. Laws were codified by the central state, which now kept records of births, deaths, and marriages and extended its power to tax and to recruit. Mass conscription was one of the key inventions of the revolution and it illustrated the new power of the state to reach individual citizens.

The revolution also had the effect of advancing capitalism. The abolition of manorial obligations for the peasantry had ambiguous implications. It increased the potential mobility of the labor force, free from legal restrictions, but it created a mass of small peasant proprietors who resisted agricultural change. The revolution also seized land from the Church and from aristocrats who fled its onslaught. Most of these lands passed to middle class owners who might exploit them in new ways. By abolishing guilds, which had long resisted technical innovations in urban manufacturing, the revolution helped set the stage for industrialization on the continent; because it also forbade labor unions, manufacturers could do their work without much interference. The new law codes confirmed rights of private property and favored manufacturers over workers in the courts of law. The abolition of internal barriers to trade and the standardization of weights and measures were vital preconditions to economic development. France lagged economically during the confusion of the revolutionary years, but the legal framework was set for change thereafter.

The revolution severely weakened religion by taking away Church lands and thereby tying the Church to state support and control. It also introduced full religious freedom. Catholic opposition to the revolution came quickly, setting the stage for a war between Church and modern politics that would last for more than a century. The revolutionaries responded by reducing the powers of the Church still further, and for a time they undertook an active program of deChristianization.

Thus did the revolution further most of the currents of modernization that had been gradually developing before. Under Napoleon, who came to power in 1799, most of the central achievements of the revolution were confirmed. The liberal element was suppressed, as parliament was reduced to a rubber stamp and dissent repressed by a powerful political police. But Napoleon maintained the revolutionary principle of equality under the law, regardless of birth, with but few exceptions. He strengthened the bureaucracy by continuing to open it to men of talent, and by creating a centralized secondary and university school system largely to train his bureaucrats. In 1801 he signed a concordat with the Church that officially ended the state's attack on religion but confirmed the Church's loss of land and extensive dependence on the state.

Napoleon's impact on the rest of Europe was greater than on France. The armies of the revolution had already conquered considerable territory in the Low Countries, Italy, and western Germany. Napoleon extended direct French rule in these areas and, following the revolutionaries' example, applied most of the new French legislation to the conquered territories. Manorialism was abolished, guilds destroyed, Church land seized, equality under the law established. In his more distant conquests, such as Spain, Italy, and Poland, revolutionary laws were less rigorously enforced and had little lasting impact save in the example they provided for subsequent political movements.

The major states of Europe were bitterly hostile to the French revolution, particularly after the execution of the king, and their hostility extended to Napoleon. But many of them had to copy certain features of the revolution simply to oppose it. They realized that France had strengthened its state and raised a military force of unprecedented size. Hesitantly, some of them began to follow suit, most notably Prussia. Under the leadership of Baron von Stein Prussia tried to improve the bureaucracy and liberalize commercial legislation. Prussia granted peasants personal freedom and allowed non-nobles to buy land, though it did not abolish manorialism. Universal military service was also established, education improved, some Church lands seized. The result was far from revolutionary, at least by French standards, but it opened the way for further possible change. In Russia, Michael Speransky improved the bureaucracy and expanded university training, though his more sweeping reform ideas came to naught. Only Austria, of the major continental states, stood pat.

In 1814 Napoleon was defeated by a coalition of Prussia, Austria, Russia, and Britain. This raised the immediate problem of what to do with the territories he had conquered. Italy and Germany demanded particular attention, for Napoleon had obliterated most of the small states and principalities that had flourished before. As a result, the year 1815 was dominated by diplomacy as the victorious powers sought to remake the European map in their own way. This in itself was significant but more was involved, for diplomacy could not be divorced from internal political change. Prussia had

to decide what to do about the war-induced reforms that had been introduced. Decisions had to be made about French-sponsored legislation in all
the states near France, while the new rulers of France had to determine
what they would do with the enactments of the previous twenty-five years.

The revolutionary and Napoleonic years had aroused new emotions.
Most obvious, and dominant in 1815, was revulsion. The bloodshed caused
by the revolution, the aggressive wars that resulted, and the whole defiance
of established institutions had nurtured an articulate conservatism on the
part of most statesmen, church leaders, and numerous others. Yet the
revolution's example had also inspired many people, not only in France.
Even some of the resistance to Napoleon had been phrased in terms of
liberalism or nationalism rather than conservatism. Moreover, the revolution
had largely moved with the current of European history rather than against
it—which is what a successful revolution has to do. In many ways it extended the more hesitant initiatives of enlightened despots and applied
some of the lessons of the Enlightenment. For this reason too the revolution's
effects could not be swept away by even the most determined conservatives.
1815 thus launched a new era in Europe, in which the revolution and the
established order would be tested not on the battlefield but in normal political life.

THE
EUROPEAN
EXPERIENCE
SINCE
1815

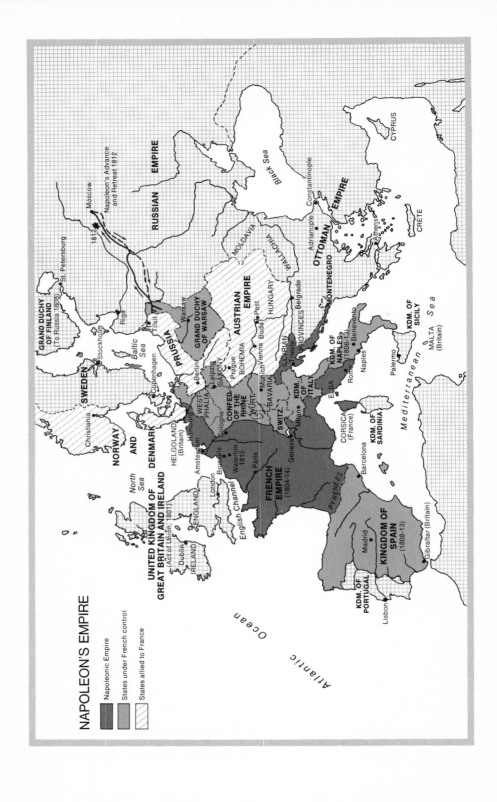

NAPOLEON'S EMPIRE

Napoleonic Empire

States under French control

States allied to France

I THE CONSERVATIVE REACTION

After a quarter-century of revolution and war in which so much in the old order had been overturned or challenged, Europe in 1815 was on the threshold of still further change. The idea of persistent change, though foreign to many people accustomed to the virtues of stability, had filtered far down in society, at least in western Europe. Artisans, for example, were beginning to believe that political reforms would benefit them. Businessmen in France and elsewhere came to realize that they had to alter their methods to match Britain's industrial advance. Change had certainly reached intellectuals, both those in the Enlightenment tradition who believed in planned progress and the newer Romantics who believed in more spontaneous evolution.

RESPONSES TO CHANGE

This sense of change was one of the underlying elements of the first half of the nineteenth century, giving some unity to developments in such diverse fields as art and business. But it should not yet be equated with an overall belief in progress; rather, there were three general reactions to the prospect of change: one welcomed it, a second simply admitted its inevitability, while a third sought to resist it as long as possible.

Apart from the most basic forces like population growth that were beyond immediate control, enough people in various fields of activity believed in fruitful change so as to make it highly probable. Yet the number of conscious innovators was small. For example, in manufacturing, where the

3

Confronting Innovation: In 1783 a balloon launched in Paris landed in the village of Gonesse. The terrified peasants attacked it, believing it was a monstrous animal.

monetary risk was great, merely a handful of industrialists really welcomed the chance to lead in technological improvements. In the most rapidly developing regions, at best, three or four individuals typically brought in not just the first new engines and machines but also later sponsored innovations such as local railroads. Only in the realm of thought did conscious innovation come to dominate, though not without dissent. These were the decades in which virtually all political "isms" were born in the minds of men, but as yet were not always political realities; these were the decades in which an unprecedented challenge was mounted, again more in theory than in practice, against centuries-old canons of artistic and literary style. Many people felt that change could not be resisted, but they were fearful of its consequences: this was a dominant mood in France after 1815. Many Romantic intellectuals like Chateaubriand or Lamartine, conservatives at the beginning, hostile to the revolutionary upheaval that wracked their country, could never shake the sense that further change would come. The career of one of the founders of liberal Catholicism, Félicité de Lamennais, illustrates this perfectly. By 1820 he had emerged a brilliant defender of conservatism, but his premonition of change was too great to allow him to remain a true conservative. Haunted by the realization that, with the old order gone, further instability was likely, he soon moved to liberalism, then to democracy and socialism (and out of the Catholic Church in the process). He saw the direction of a changing society and thought that the only recourse was to move with it. This belief, which was widespread not only in France but in other countries in Europe, went far beyond the field of political thought. A French business group, contemplating the advent of industrialization, expressed the mood perfectly: "Progress, were it not inevitable, might best be avoided altogether."

The sense of change also produced a counterreaction that gave rise to a formal conservatism. Conservative thought and action were not new to politics or any other field, but an organized and articulate movement had not been necessary until the concept of change had become pervasive and the possibility of it vividly illustrated by the French Revolution. Prince von Metternich, the leading practitioner of conservatism, believed that gradual change was a normal condition of society; he contended, however, that for the present all major change had to be resisted, lest the gates be opened to those who wanted to overturn everything.

Did the conservatives think they could prevail, or were they simply trying to hold on as long as they could? Certainly the intellectual basis of the movement proved shaky. Conservative political thought blossomed as part of Romanticism, itself a new cultural force that was striving for innovation in diverse ways. Many Romantics would abandon conservatism in their search for individual expression, while many more would seek to link it to some idealized past that would really be new. But the tenuousness of the link between conservatism and the intellectual community, coupled with the fact that conservatism so often seemed on the defensive after 1815, should not deceive us into underestimating the strength of the movement.

The fear of change led some to join progressive political movements in an attempt to recapture the past, but this association could seldom endure. Rather this fear of change led many people to exaggerate the changes that were actually occurring and prompted them to seek defenses. Many people resisted mechanization before machines had touched them directly. Many claimed that immortality was growing and society was on the verge of collapse. Fear of change created widespread potential support for conservatism, which thus proved one of the most durable and successful products of these confusing decades.

Above all, formal conservatism suited the mood of Europe's ruling classes. Though many had dabbled in new ideas during the previous century, the political and economic elite, almost all of them aristocrats, had been taught by the French Revolution to defend all aspects of the established order lest their own power be eroded. This reaction gave conservatism powerful support. Conservatism was not merely a passive effort to stem the tide of change. It was an active force whose triumphs, in the political arena, outweighed its losses even after 1848.

The belief that unprecedented change was occurring or might occur

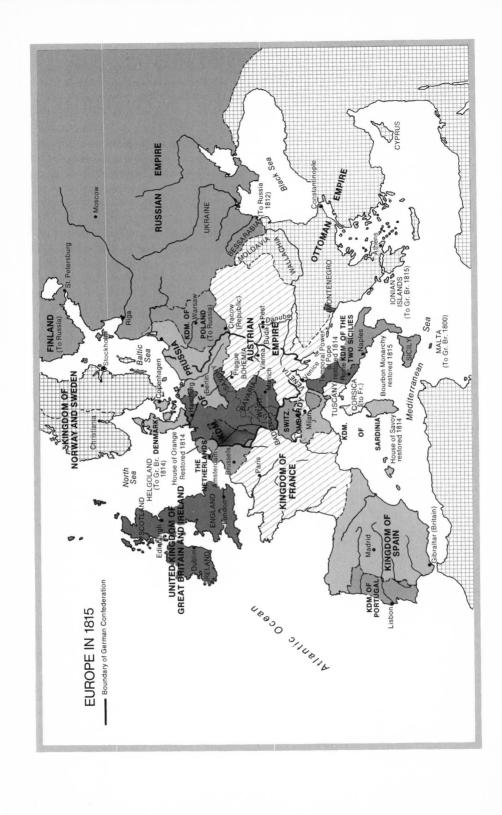

EUROPE IN 1815

— Boundary of German Confederation

helped to make the years between 1815 and 1848 markedly unstable, despite the fact that European society changed less in this period than in the politically less volatile 30 years that followed. Not only the sense of change but the diversity of reaction to it created the instability. Ultimately there had to be a showdown between the newly conscious conservatives and the advocates of progress. The showdown was delayed by the new methods the conservatives devised and by the continuing divisions among the progressives. It was delayed also by the confusion of the large middle group who feared change but were also afraid to resist it, or who sought novel political remedies to combat social change. It was delayed above all by the more immediate emotional reaction to 25 years of chaos. Europe was tired. That she reawakened so quickly was a remarkable testimony to the forces that the eighteenth century had unleashed.

THE CONGRESS OF VIENNA

The statesmen who gathered in Vienna in 1814–1815 to pick up the pieces after a generation of war were conservatives of varying stripe, but the settlement they produced cannot be labeled so easily. They were eager to restore as much of the old order as possible, but they recognized that they could not turn the clock back to 1789. They were still worried enough about France to make a special effort to hem her in; in addition, they hoped to acquire important spoils for their own countries. Above all, however, they were eager to avoid further war, which was the main reason the Vienna settlement proved so durable and so successful.

The Vienna settlement demands attention for several reasons. It launched a period of conservatism that extended for decades, setting the basis for internal resistance to the tide of revolution as new conservative regimes were established, as old ones gained new strength, and as diplomacy became allied with the defense of the status quo. Also, by what it failed to do, it encouraged some forces to attack conservatism. On the purely diplomatic front, the Treaty of Vienna was most remarkable for its success in keeping the peace. The territorial settlement established was not fundamentally shaken until the 1860s and there was no European-wide war until 1914. The Treaty represented the greatest triumph—perhaps the final triumph in a traditional European sense—of the principle of balance of power. But the settlement was not static—it would not have been so successful if it had been. Rather, it suggested a new method of diplomacy, the congress system, and altered the position of all the major European powers. Two or three states gained particular advantage from the Treaty of Vienna, a power shift that could hardly have been avoided but that ironically, in the long run, helped to undermine the settlement itself.

Provisions of the Treaty

The conservative interests of the diplomats in Vienna were most evident in the restoration of several dynasties that had been deposed. The Bourbons were returned to Spain, southern Italy, and France. It was hoped, however, that they would not ignore the changes that had taken place during their absence. The new king in France, Louis XVIII, granted a constitutional charter that confirmed the major gains of the Revolution: equality under the law, religious freedom and the concordat with the Church, the Napoleonic law codes, and eligibility for public office regardless of class. In addition the charter established a parliament based on very limited suffrage. Clearly, restoration of the monarchy could not be equated with a return to the old regime. It was assumed that restored monarchs would be equally sensible, though this assumption proved false particularly in Spain and southern Italy. The diplomats at Vienna tempered their attachment to the old order with an understanding of what was practical. Viscount Robert Stewart Castlereagh, the British representative, knew well the benefits of parliamentary government. British conservatism was perforce different from the continental variety; indeed it was under British sponsorship that the Congress of Vienna abolished the international slave trade. The French representative and even the still-idealistic tsar of Russia also encouraged the congress to balance its restoration of old dynasties with a recognition that times had changed.

In its territorial settlement the treaty was neither reactionary nor punitive. The tiny states of pre-Napoleonic Germany and Italy were not reinstated but many other changes were established. France was cut back to her boundaries of 1790, with a few minor exceptions in her benefit. The principle of balance of power demanded that France still be able to play a role, and even at the congress itself her skillful representative, Talleyrand, was able to take a significant part in negotiations. But Britain led in seeking buffer states on every side of France that would discourage renewed French expansion. On the north was Holland, now a kingdom that included Belgium. On the east, Prussia was given holdings on the Rhine and medium-sized states were confirmed in the rest of Germany. Northern Italy was divided between a reconstituted Piedmontese state and Austria, for Austria held Lombardy and Venetia outright and dominated a few smaller states between these and the Papal States.

The other main element of the territorial reshuffling was a simple land-grab by the major powers. Conflicting ambitions were balanced out to a considerable extent, so that the state that lost in one area usually was compensated in another. Prussia and Russia nearly came to blows over the division of Poland, but Austria and England, who feared too great an extension of Russian power, joined with France to force a compromise. Russia managed to retain Finland and Bessarabia, which it had occupied while fighting Sweden and Turkey when both were allied with France.

Russia also got the lion's share of Poland, which was made a separate king-dom under the tsar. Prussia gained part of Saxony as well as the Rhineland and continued to hold a portion of Poland. The British, peacemakers in continental squabbles, reaped their harvest in the rest of the world. Only one of the colonies seized during the war—the Netherlands Indies—was re-turned to its previous owner. The British refused to discuss their other gains, which included new holdings in India, the island of Ceylon, Malta, the Cape of Good Hope, several West Indian islands including Trinidad, and a few other areas.

New Alliances and the Congress System

Less concretely, the diplomats in Vienna suggested a new mechanism for future diplomatic relations. Napoleon's escape from Elba in 1815, which forced renewed fighting that culminated in the Battle of Waterloo, prompted the Quadruple Alliance among Britain, Austria, Russia, and Prussia; this alliance pledged the powers to maintain the treaty arrangements, including the exclusion of the Bonaparte dynasty from the throne of France, for 20 years. It was a novel agreement for peacetime, at the least an unusually formal pledge to maintain the balance of power against the most obvious threat. Moreover, a number of countries wanted to extend mutual agreement still further. Tsar Alexander of Russia urged that the Quadruple Alliance pledge intervention to maintain Louis XVIII and his constitutional charter, but Britain refused. Alexander did manage to get most of the powers—Britain, the Ottoman Empire, and the papacy expected—to sign a document called the Holy Alliance, which promised devotion to the Christian prin-ciples of charity and peace. It had no direct influence on diplomacy, where charity and love rarely have a place, but it came to symbolize the coopera-tion of Russia, Prussia and Austria in maintaining conservative regimes in various parts of Europe. The two alliances, which were quite different, both suggested cooperative action among the powers—one to uphold the terri-torial status quo, the other, more vaguely, to uphold the internal status quo. Although the Congress of Vienna showed real flexibility in redoing the European map, it clearly intended to defend its work against future change, and thus became part of the conservative current.

Many historians have suggested that the two alliances and the congresses that followed must be viewed as an important departure in European diplomacy. While it is true that there were a number of congresses during the next eight years, mainly to deal with unrest in Southern Europe, and occasional ones throughout the 1880s, nevertheless a congress system in the sense of frequent meetings among the powers was dead by 1823. There-after, congresses settled no major issues, at least in Europe proper, and, after 1815, they played no role in keeping the peace. Vienna did not change the methods of diplomacy.

The Treaty's Results: A Scorecard

Why, then, was Europe able to maintain the peace for so long a time? How, to ask the obvious and important question, did the statesmen at Vienna manage to settle a world war so much more successfully than those of the twentieth century have managed to do? At Vienna all the victors gained some spoils but none gained too much, while the loser was not forced into defiance by a punitive settlement. Here is the answer; it is simple only if one compares paper treaties from one century to the next. France was not unduly punished because diplomats still believed in the balance of power. The distribution of spoils could roughly satisfy everyone because appetites were still restrained by a sense of what was reasonable and, moreover, there was still so much territory in Europe and around the world to be distributed. The diplomats at Vienna were polished aristocrats, some of them clever and many of them witty, but not all were extraordinarily talented. It is clear, however, that between 1815 and the twentieth century the motives and methods of diplomacy changed. Hence neither the principles nor the success of the Vienna settlement have been reproduced after more recent great wars.

Furthermore, one need not attribute undue credit for the subsequent peace in Europe to the Treaty of Vienna. The succeeding decades were filled with internal political strife and, in some countries, unprecedented economic changes and opportunities. With the exception of Austria, governments and leading social groups turned away from diplomacy for 40 years. When they turned back, the Vienna settlement was quickly undone.

Not surprisingly, the Congress of Vienna failed to take into account certain new political principles that were just beginning to emerge. Nationalism was ignored and liberalism given short shrift. Insofar as the diplomats were aware of nationalism they feared it. Metternich in particular was cognizant of the damage nationalism could do to Austria's interests in Italy and Germany. But the Vienna settlement must largely be explained not by conscious opposition to nationalism but by the weakness of national sentiment and the commitment of the diplomats to older principles of monarchical legitimacy and balance of power. It is easy to point to the evil, callous manipulations of people and territories without consultation: Catholic Belgians being given over to a Protestant Dutch king, or the Poles being handed back once again to their enemies. But this sort of judgment is more moral than historical; it suggests a behavior that was incomprehensible in the early nineteenth century, a foresight that would have had no precedent. Moreover the forces that Vienna neglected did not rise up quickly. There were stirrings in Germany but no nationalist revolts against the settlement until 1830, after an additional 15 years' experience. We must often ask how strong nationalism was during the nineteenth century; we can begin by saying it could quite safely be ignored in 1815.

The guiding assumptions of the diplomats of the major powers, general fatigue with war, and subsequent preoccupation with internal developments were all factors that combined to make the Treaty of Vienna a good peace settlement. The diplomats succeeded in what they most hoped to accomplish: to give Europe a new map that would largely confirm the positions of the five great powers. Their success should not conceal the extent to which the balance among the powers was changing; there were, though it is too seldom noted, winners and losers at Vienna. Britain was the clear winner, the only large and expanding imperial power in Europe. Her gains were relatively inoffensive because they were not in Europe, but Britain was well on the way to her next great spurt of empire-building. France, her traditional rival, now hemmed in, was on the decline. To be sure, France was not severely treated; for over half a century her power was overestimated by diplomats who, like most of their kind, relied on traditional evaluations. It was of great importance to European stability that the French leaders implicitly recognized that their country's relative strength was reduced, at least until 1850.

Prussia was the other clear winner at Vienna. Its territorial gains were not as great as Austria's or Russia's, but they brought Prussia into a new and more advanced part of Germany; this was a source of new prestige in Germany and new vigor for Prussia itself. Austria on the surface gained a great deal, both in territory and in the broader conservative principles of the settlement. But the gains soon overburdened the government and helped wed it to diplomatic maneuvers to preserve its power rather than to internal reforms. To a lesser extent the same was true of Russia, whose appetite was drawn again to the Near East while the newly absorbed peoples, like Finns and Poles, added to the country's internal difficulties. In these aspects, as much as in its neglect of newly born "isms," the Treaty of Vienna, like all treaties, helped fuel new tensions.

INTERNAL POLITICS

The outstanding development between 1815 and 1825 was the rise of a new conservatism,—more precisely, *conservatisms,* because each country developed its own version as the conservative trend extended from Britain through Russia. In the broad sense, the most important division was between those countries that sought to defend an unchanged and inefficient old regime and those that could innovate while preserving the essentials of the old social and political order. In any of its versions, conservatism was new. Conservatives are as old as human society, but modern conservatism needed the French Revolution as the focus of its opposition. It was *for* what the Revolution had been *against:* aristocracy, monarchy, Church; it was *against* what the Revolution had been *for:* individualism, rationalism, egalitarianism.

The Pillars of Conservatism

Nineteenth-century conservatism drew the aristocracy and the established churches together. This was not a new or surprising alliance, but it put an end to the flirtation with religious indifference that some aristocrats had engaged in during the eighteenth century. The aristocrats, so severely challenged during the Revolution, had everything to gain from their alliance with religion. In retrospect, we can see that the churches may have suffered from their entanglement with the old social order. Peasants blamed them for siding with landlords, while elements of the middle classes resented churchmen and nobles indiscriminately. At the time, however, the alliance was as inevitable from the churches' point of view as it was from the aristocrats'. The leading churchmen were mainly aristocrats themselves or the protégés and appointees of aristocrats. The churches were appalled at the forces the Enlightenment and Revolution had unleashed. They too believed their very survival was at stake and that their defense in turn required the defense of the old order. Thus they continued to guard the traditional social hierarchy. The archbishop of Paris, himself an aristocrat, tried to prove that the mother of Jesus had noble lineage, which indicates how far the association of Christianity and aristocracy could go. Throughout most of the nineteenth century clergymen from the established churches—not only Catholic but Anglican and Lutheran as well—provided powerful support and advocacy for conservative causes.

The key to nineteenth-century conservatism, and in many ways its most novel element, was the monarchy, an institution that had been attacked by the Revolution along with church and aristocracy. The alliance among the three made sense. It meant that the aristocracy had to drop most of its traditional objections to a strong central ruler. There were still hints of the old aristocratic preference for decentralized rule, particularly in eastern Europe where the threat of revolution seemed most remote. But the whole position of the aristocracy, its economic as well as its political base, now depended increasingly on the central government's support. The jobs the government provided and the subsidies it gave to agriculture were vital to the survival of the aristocratic class. In return the aristocracy lent their great influence and their often considerable talents to the support of the monarchy.

The alliance of the church with the monarchy was, if not new, at least more intense than ever. Even in Prussia, where the Lutheran and Evangelical churches had long been under state control, the state began in the 1790s to try to extend its power in order to improve the quality of the clergy, to the mutual benefit of religion and the state. The drawing together of church and monarchy was most novel in the Catholic countries, but the church believed it needed any support it could get. Its loss of land, in the German and northern Italian states as well as in France, heightened its financial dependence on the state, for few churchmen could imagine a system of voluntary contributions. As a result, the church firmly defended existing states—even when they were not Catholic. The pope condemned the 1830 rebellion by Catholic Poles against a Russian Orthodox tsar and long refused to recognize the successful revolt of Catholic Belgians against the Protestant Dutch king. Again, from the standpoint of most churchmen, all established institutions had to be defended at once. This was, after all, the essence of the conservative mood. Monarchs, who had long sought to extend their powers in the religious sphere, could only welcome the churches' new support.

Conservatism, then, merged three great institutions, with the monarchy at the center. In the churches, for example, loyalty to the monarch was increasingly urged and spread widely among the common people. Peasants still proclaimed their allegiance to their sovereign even when they were rebelling. The monarchical focus of conservatism in many ways continued the expansion of the powers of kings and central governments that had been going forward during the previous two centuries. There is no label so catchy as absolutism or enlightened despotism for the monarchies of the nineteenth century, and the personalities of the kings often seem less striking. But the alliance with church and aristocracy removed much of the traditional opposition to the monarchical powers, and by using some of the methods introduced by the French Revolution—in taxation and conscription, for example—the kings and their subordinates greatly enhanced their strength.

The Functions of the Conservative State

Conservatism meant strong government. Conservatives argued and believed that government had a prime responsibility for keeping order and promoting the well-being of its subjects. We should not let our attention to apparently modern movements such as liberalism and republicanism, which attacked many of the powers of kings and governments, distract us from what was really happening to most governments in the first half of the nineteenth century. Their budgets were expanding and only in two countries—Britain and Norway—did liberals ever manage to hold down per capita expenditures. Bureaucracies grew. Just as Napoleon had established a new school system for training bureaucrats (which subsequent French governments carefully protected), states like Prussia and Russia now expanded their universities to increase their bureaucratic cadres. We must remember that governments did not yet have their twentieth-century powers. They were limited still by slow transportation and communication and, in most countries, by the important local rights held by aristocrats, guilds and other traditional elements. Nevertheless, the functions of governments were expanding and conservatism was attached to this real and important trend.

An important characteristic of conservatives, particularly in their belligerent, defensive mood after 1815, was their desire to extend the repressive apparatus of government, including the political police and the army. But conservatism was not merely a defensive movement. Conservatives also urged that the government perform many positive functions: to intervene in the economy by means of tariffs, subsidies and regulations; to assume a greater role in higher education, if only to train its own bureaucrats; to promote the general well-being as well as defend the established order. It was the conservative Prussian state that first passed a child labor law *before* industrialization had begun, rather than after its abuses became agonizingly clear. Prussia enforced this law with unusual vigor.

Conservatism was not a brief episode in European history soon to be crushed by the forces of modernity. Conservatives were powerful enough in many places to defeat challenges to the established order. One question that must be asked repeatedly in studying nineteenth- and even twentieth-century history is: when and in what ways, did conservatives really lose out? Despite all the unrest of the nineteenth century, no major monarchy was overturned outside France and Spain, and many durable new ones were established. Furthermore, as conservatives contributed to a strong state, they could promote a development that was part of modernization itself. This process too demands consistent attention.

This is as far as a general definition of nineteenth-century conservatism can take us. Conservatives were everywhere dominant in 1815, but their subsequent success varied greatly from place to place. Conservatism also evolved within its basic framework until the revolutions of 1848 provided a clear break; this is one of the principal reasons that the three decades after 1815 form a coherent historical period. Conservatives ruled in most countries after 1848 as they had before, but their methods changed significantly. The men who ruled between 1815 and 1848 had been born before the French Revolution. They knew what the old society was like and, even when they recognized that they could not fully bring it back, their policies were colored by a reverence for the past and a fear of the forces that had proved capable of destroying it.

THE METTERNICHIAN ORBIT

The symbol of the conservative reaction and the author of many of its policies was the Austrian foreign minister, Prince von Metternich. Like all conservatives he believed that the state's first duty was to ensure order and, again like all conservatives in 1815, he realized that the forces of revolution could still thwart this purpose. Metternich rejected any notion that society could ever be reformed by a rational plan or that men could govern themselves through reason. A strong state was needed by everyone, not just the privileged classes, and any method could be justified to protect this state. But Metternich did not exclude the possibility of gradual change, particularly in economic policy.

Metternich did not control the internal policies of the government in the sprawling Hapsburg empire. Here Francis I held sway until his death in 1835, and he was more conservative than his foreign minister. Francis summed up his own approach in 1831: "I won't have innovations. Let the laws be justly applied; they are good and adequate." Conservatism within Austria meant preservation of an inefficient political and economic order, coupled with severe restrictions on potential political opposition. Internal tariffs still hampered the economy. Since there was no financial reform, the imperial debt mounted steadily. The huge bureaucracy was headed by an indolent aristocracy and divided into so many conflicting agencies that its operations were severely hampered. Only in the army administration was there any degree of improvement. To defend this system two characteristic conservative devices were employed. The regime reached a compromise with the Catholic Church, whose powers had been limited in the eighteenth century; in return for active support, the hierarchy was given substantial powers in education and censorship. The government also built up a political police system throughout the empire. Even Metternich's correspondence was opened by police spies and many presumed subversives were often arrested. The police kept a careful eye on teachers and students at the universities, and students were forbidden to attend foreign institutions, lest they be infected with dangerous ideas. The press was rigorously censored.

Here, then, was a standpat conservatism embellished only by new repressive agencies. Internal measures could not alone maintain it; Metternich's foreign policy was a vital supplement. The policy had two purposes: to repress political dissent wherever it might spread and to maintain Austrian preeminence in Germany and Italy. The survival of the Hapsburg monarchy was henceforth linked to its diplomacy, with grand results until 1848 but recurrent disaster thereafter. In the absence of internal reforms the state had to guard against subversion from the outside and it needed a prestigious foreign policy to enhance its position at home. But there was yet another motive behind Metternich's diplomacy: Austria also had to guard against nationalism. Metternich saw that nationalism had been part of the revolutionary impulse and opposed it as such. He was well aware that nationalism could corrode the multinational empire and could drive Austria out of Germany and Italy, where its diplomatic power lay. He therefore created a system to fight diplomatic as well as political change all over Europe.

Metternich's influence extended throughout the continent. He had spies everywhere and his advice was heard in France and Russia. But the Metternichian system applied chiefly to Italy and Germany. Austria's own holdings allowed her to dominate the Italian peninsula. The two principal independent rulers, the pope and the king of the Two Sicilies, were as conservative as Francis I; they resented Austrian power but could not object to the policies Metternich urged. Germany was more troublesome. The states were more powerful and their conservatism was, as we shall see, different from that of Austria. But the Treaty of Vienna had joined the 39 German states into a loose confederation, of which Austria was president and the most powerful member. Metternich was careful also to treat Austria's potential rival in Germany, Prussia, with great respect; the conservative German rulers willingly accepted many of Metternich's directives.

Hence throughout central Europe a common repressive apparatus prevailed. In Germany, nationalistic university students, began to form political clubs, the *Burschenschaften,* to protest the Vienna settlement's neglect of nationalism and the disunity of their country. A nationwide congress was held in 1817. Two years later, the political assassination of a Prussian agent gave Metternich his chance to introduce repressive legislation; in the Carlsbad Decrees of 1819 the principal German rulers pledged to disband the *Burschenschaften* and to impose strict censorship on the press and universities. Alarmed by liberal agitation after 1830, the diet of the German Federation in 1832 further decreed that no representative assembly could limit the power of its prince. Similar policies were pursued by the Italian governments. In the Papal States the religious orders supplemented the powerful political police by reporting any subversive elements they encountered. Every year thousands of suspects were jailed or kept under house arrest.

Conservatives in Germany and Italy were faced with one problem that Austria lacked: what to do about the reforms that Napoleonic governments (or, in Prussia, reformers like Baron Stein) had introduced. These reforms, which had reduced the position of both church and aristocracy, could not be ignored by the new or restored regimes. The three leading independent Italian states rescinded almost all the Napoleonic measures. The Papal States, for example, repealed everything from compulsory vaccination to the secular law court system. Church power was restored in both Piedmont and the Kingdom of the Two Sicilies, while in the latter state the large landholders regained manorial rights over the peasantry. Ferdinand I in the Kingdom of the Two Sicilies pledged in a secret treaty with Austria not to introduce liberal reforms. He repealed the liberal constitution that had been introduced in 1812 and restored many church lands. Opposition soon developed particularly through the *Carbonari,* a growing secret society. A revolution in 1820 was suppressed only through the intervention of Austrian troops operating with the approval of the Holy Alliance. Ferdinand thereafter was free to restore his repressive policies in full. The Piedmontese government differed from its southern counterparts only by being more efficient. Ironically, the policies in Austrian territory in the north were relatively enlightened—not only was the government honest, but many Napoleonic measures, including freedom of commerce and the abolition of serfdom, were allowed to stand. With these exceptions, however, Italy turned back the clock to the eighteenth century.

The situation in Germany was somewhat different, for here Napoleonic measures were modified but not eliminated. None of the states restored lands to the Catholic Church but followed the general conservative policy of seeking close cooperation with the leading churches. Southern German states signed concordats with the Catholic Church granting it substantial rights over education and censorship. The Prussian government by fiat united the Lutheran and Evangelical churches to bring them under greater control, and tried without complete success to maintain friendly relations with its new Catholic minority. But on the whole relations with the churches did not return to past patterns and the state retained the upper hand.

On a somewhat similar basis previous land reforms were sufficiently undone to return power to the aristocracy, and in some cases even increase it, but without completely restoring the arrangements of the old regime. Prussia, for example, continued to allow peasants to rid themselves of manorial obligations, but to do so they were required to give up a third to a half of their land to their lord. Clearly, this modification of old regime policies would benefit few peasants and harm many, but it did allow some measure of economic and social change. It encouraged the Junkers, the Prussian aristocrats, to expand their estates and introduce new agricultural methods, and it facilitated the expansion of the propertyless manufacturing labor force. Most German states also did not restore all the traditional rights of guilds. This meant that artisans suffered from growing competition, but it also meant that new manufacturing techniques could be introduced.

Finally the German states took some further new initiatives. In the south and the west, German rulers, after 1815, allowed the formation of parliaments. These bodies had highly limited powers and were based on a narrow suffrage, but they did exist, in defiance of Metternich's wishes. In the 1840s the new Prussian king, Frederick William IV, who believed firmly in his divine right to rule as he pleased, called a joint meeting of provincial diets to discuss financial matters. This fell short of being an actual parliament but there was at least the suggestion of change. More important, the Prussian state continued to improve upon its already efficient bureaucracy. The university system was expanded and training generally improved. The German states, most of which took an active hand in encouraging economic growth, were among the continental leaders in railroad development after 1830, spurting well ahead of France and certainly of Austria. All the states provided capital and direction for the railroads and some owned and operated them directly. The Prussian government also extended roads and canals and constructed model factories with British machinery. Prussia also led in major tariff reform. The tariff of 1818 was carefully designed to promote all aspects of the economy; unlike most continental governments at the time, Prussia believed that moderate tariffs brought the greatest revenues by facilitating trade. Other German states imitated this measure and some united with the Prussian system. Almost all the major states joined Prussia in a national customs union, the *Zollverein*, in 1833. Austria was excluded, which was the first real jolt to Austrian preeminence in Germany and symbolized the gap between Austrian and German conservatism. The *Zollverein* spurred the entire German economy and ultimately played an important role in drawing Germany together.

The German states were undeniably conservative. They adopted all the standard conservative measures and defended the traditional social order. The concessions in some states toward political reform were invariably weak and were often emasculated as rulers grew increasingly fearful of unrest. Important initiatives such as railroad construction were undertaken for highly traditional purposes: the enhancement of the military power of the state. In all matters the difference was in method, not goal. For German conservatism was not the standpat type. Although the German rulers fully belonged to the Metternichian system, they were not bound by the Austrian model.

CONSERVATIVES
IN THE EAST AND SOUTH

Spain rivaled Italy in its zeal to restore the past, while Russia had never left it. Both states were part of the Metternichian system although outside Austria's control. Russia, indeed, played a European role in defending the established order. Russian troops had helped restore conservative leadership to Germany and the tsar had used his influence and occasionally his armies to protect legitimate monarchy for many decades thereafter.

Ferdinand VII returned to Spain in 1814 amid great popular rejoicing. He immediately undid both the measures the Napoleonic government had introduced and those that the opposition to Napoleon had established. He ignored the constitution that the liberals had formulated in 1812, arrested many prominent liberals, and disbanded the parliament. He restored all church property, outlawed foreign books and papers, and reestablished the Inquisition. As in Austria and much of Italy, this brand of conservatism did not permit improvements in government service or an extension of positive government functions, for to do so required innovations in bureaucratic training and personnel and the Spanish government resisted innovation in every sphere. Hence public services deteriorated, the economy lagged, and Spain's finances were in constant disarray. Led by discontented army officers, a liberal revolution broke out in 1820, and was only put down three years later by French troops sent in by the Holy Alliance. The restored monarchy promptly reestablished its earlier policies.

In Russia, the idealism of Alexander I, which had led the tsar to a genuine interest in reforms, quickly dwindled after 1815. Far from dealing with the issue on which all else in Russia depended, the treatment of the serfs, the tsar simply and brutally put down peasant agitation whenever it cropped up. His successor, Nicholas I, came to power in December 1825 on the heels of a rebellion by a handful of army officers. This abortive uprising, known as the Decembrist Revolt, served to heighten Nicholas' fear of insurrection. Thereafter his preoccupation in internal affairs was the development of the

Third Section of the Imperial Chancery, a vast network of uniformed political police, spies, and informers. Religion, as always, was employed to support the state, and church schools were required to stress loyalty to the tsar. As a result, Orthodox religion suffered and educational standards, outside the universities especially, visibly declined.

Russia, then, fits the general model of a largely defensive conservative regime. There were, however, some special features of Russian policy that deserve mention, for although it was vastly less efficient than the German states, the Russian regime proved more durable and successful than those of Spain, Italy, or Austria. First, the government undertook some expansion of the central bureaucracy and reforms of its procedures, but not on as extensive a scale as the earlier Speransky reforms. Universities grew, laws were codified, and finances stabilized. Second, the privileges of the Russian aristocracy, though extensive, were state-created and the class was unusually dependent on the government. Indeed the state was still creating new aristocrats, mainly from the bureaucracy, throughout most of the nineteenth century. Because of this close connection, the government, albeit cumbersome and inefficient, was less impeded by local resistance than was a regime such as the Hapsburg monarchy, where the great nobles were traditionally independent and very powerful. Finally, the Russian government added a mildly adventurous foreign policy to its domestic conservatism.

Most of the diplomatic developments after the immediate postwar period (that is, after 1823) involved Russia and often were a result of Russian initiative. The focus was the Near East, which was the only area resembling a diplomatic troublespot until after 1848. Even here, the level of tension was rarely high, for the interests of the powers balanced each other and no one, including Russia, wanted to risk a war. Still, some of the ingredients of future trouble were beginning to form. The Ottoman Empire, whose weakness had long drawn Russian attention to the south, continued to decay. Now, internal revolts against Turkish authority gave the Russians new causes to champion in the area—above all, the defense of Orthodox coreligionists.

The Serbian rising of 1804 had already challenged the Ottomans. The revolt had been suppressed in 1813 but renewed rebellion won Serbian autonomy in 1826. No foreign help was involved in this victory, but Serbian autonomy was placed under a Russian protectorate. None of this attracted general diplomatic notice, though it was really the first step in the creation of the modern Balkans.

Far more significant was the Greek rebellion that began in 1821, led by nationalistic businessmen and scholars. This was the great diplomatic issue of the 1820s, which indicates how inactive diplomacy was under the Metternichian system. Still, the Greek uprising did create an interesting dilemma. Conservatives were opposed to rebellion in principle. Led by Metternich, who was also opposed to nationalism and further territorial changes, the powers, including Tsar Alexander, initially refused all help to the revolutionaries. As the revolt continued, amid great bloodshed and cruelty on both sides, Europe became aroused. England, and to a lesser extent France, were sympathetic to the aims of liberal nationalism in Greece, but the most decisive change in policy was that of the Russians. Nicholas I had no intention of taking orders from Metternich and was actively interested in improving Russia's position in the area. Russia, England and France insisted that the Greeks be given self-government and Russia declared war on Turkey in 1828. In the Treaty of Adrianople in 1829, the Turks lost some territory to the Russians and granted the Russians a protectorate over the principalities of Moldavia and Wallachia—the area now known as Rumania. Here was the suggestion (and only a suggestion at this point) of another Balkan nation, and again, as in the case of Serbia, Russian sponsorship was involved. Finally, the Greeks gained their independence, and Russia's prestige was greatly advanced.

The area cooled down after this, but Nicholas maintained his interest in extending Russia's influence there. In 1833 Russia sent troops to help the sultan against an attack from Egypt and won an alliance in return. Another Egyptian attack in 1839 raised the prospect of further Russian gains. Faced with Austrian and British opposition, the Russians agreed to a general guarantee of Turkish independence instead of the Russian protection established six years before.

To Russia's internal conservatism, then, was added an opportunistic and occasionally aggressive foreign policy. In this respect Russia differed from Austria, which adhered to the diplomatic status quo. Ironically Russian conservatism was just as vulnerable to diplomatic setbacks, for the internal order could be threatened when foreign adventures failed. During the first half of the nineteenth century, however, Russia's goals remained modest and her regime was thereby secure. Russia was the only great power to avoid internal unrest in 1848.

CONSERVATISM IN THE WEST

The conservative trend in western Europe was just as real as it was elsewhere, but it was uniquely shortlived. Outright conservative reaction lasted less than a decade in Britain, while in France it was shaken from below in 1830. Furthermore, even while it held sway, conservatism in the West was diluted by concessions to parliamentary forms. Nonetheless, its development shows the sweep of reaction to the French Revolution, for with all their peculiarities Western policies shared many of the features of conservatism elsewhere. At the same time the concessions that were made to liberal forces suggested patterns that conservatives in central Europe would later follow. Finally, the conservative impulse became a recurrent part of the political spectrum in France, and even in England it survived in modified form.

Thus despite its fragility, conservatism in western Europe deserves attention. Not the least of the questions to be asked is: how much was changed or really abandoned even after the old line conservatives had passed from power?

The British Reaction

Both Parliament and the bureaucracy in Britain were in the hands of the Tory party, the beneficiaries of the patriotic sentiment for national unity during the long wars. Because the Whig party was weak and inactive, parliamentary opposition was at an unprecedentedly low ebb. Conservatives in Britain did not support a strong monarchy; indeed the monarchy was weakened by the madness of George III and the dandyism of his son. Nor were structural changes introduced in the relationship between the established church and the state; conservatives were content, now and later, to resist efforts to extend religious toleration to Catholics and to maintain the Anglican monopoly on public offices. But in 1818 Parliament granted a million pounds to build new churches, as the best way to halt social unrest. There were specific efforts to support the aristocracy. George III had created numerous new peerages that helped confirm Tory political dominance. The passage of the Corn Law of 1815, which virtually excluded foreign grain, was a piece of obvious class legislation designed to benefit large landowners at the expense of a growing urban population which, as a result, was forced to pay high food prices.

The principal manifestation of conservatism in Britain, however, was outright political repression. As Britain's war-based prosperity collapsed in 1816, widespread unemployment was exacerbated by bad harvests and high prices. Bread riots and strikes were the inevitable result. Britain was convulsed by violence in the cities, burning and machine-breaking in the countryside. Added to this were the plots of small radical groups, some of which led to conspiracies and assassination threats. The conservatives grew hysterical, particularly as the government seized every chance to stress the dangers to religion and the state. The army was used as a repressive force, and there is little doubt that sheer physical coercion was greater in Britain at this time than in any other country. Spies and agents provocateurs spread throughout the land. Parliament responded by passing the most repressive legislation that Britain had known for over a century. In 1817, the government suspended the Habeas Corpus Act, allowing imprisonment without trial, and banned public meetings and unlicensed associations. In 1819, some 50,000 people gathered in St. Peter's Fields in Manchester to hear speeches demanding government reform. When troops were called in to disperse the crowd, 11 people were killed and hundreds were injured in what was promptly labeled the Peterloo Massacre. Following this, Parliament voted the Six Acts that limited public meetings and newspaper circulation still

The Peterloo Massacre,
1819: Soldiers
attacking the crowd.

further. Britain did not establish outright censorship, but the press was severely restricted by frequent trials of opposition editors, and, under the Six Acts, heavy stamp taxes on all publications, as well as punishment for seditious or blasphemous libel. Wellington wrote of his hope that all these measures would allow Britain to "escape the universal revolution which seems to menace us all."

By 1820 the wave of repression began to recede. Increasing Whig success in parliamentary elections showed that even the upper classes were not united in adamant conservatism. Tory policies were moderated as younger members of the party began to advocate reforms. The government lowered many duties and taxes and simplified the whole tariff system. Under Robert Peel the criminal code was simplified and made more humane as well, and the death penalty was removed from almost 200 types of crime. Prison reform was undertaken. Peel also established a new police force both to prevent crime and to help maintain order without resort to clumsy military forces or amateur spies. Most interesting of all were the measures taken to extend religious liberty. In 1828 the Test and Corporation Acts were repealed, which had required every state official to receive sacraments in the Anglican Church; although the acts had not been rigorously enforced for a century, they had annoyed dissenters. At the same time, agitation for full rights for Catholics arose in Ireland in protest against the legal exclusion of Catholics from major political office. Even Wellington urged concessions as an alternative to civil war, and in 1829 full legal equality was granted to Catholics.

Britain was still ruled by conservatives, and some in the government vigorously objected to the reforms that were enacted. But the leading conservatives had changed. Like certain ones on the continent, they realized that conservatism could be compatible with improvements in administrative procedures, as in matters of taxation. They learned, before their continental counterparts did, that protest could be headed off by concessions instead of repression, without abandoning anything of substance. For example, full rights for Catholics were offset by a new voting law that cut the Irish electorate by over 80 percent; in actuality, therefore, Ireland had really gained very little despite reform. British conservatives were groping toward a realization that even liberal measures could be introduced without a great deal of change in internal affairs.

The Restoration in France

For a time after 1815, it appeared that French conservatives around the monarch knew the potential benefits of flexibility too. Louis XVIII hoped to reconcile all elements of French society. He wanted to solidify his regime if only because he was weary of exile and knew that a reactionary approach would not work. There were, from the first, aristocratic conservatives who advocated a return to the old regime pure and simple, and they dominated early elections. But until 1820, the policies of the Restoration government were moderate. Unlike most continental countries, France did not roll back the major revolutionary reforms. While the Church was treated with great courtesy and state financial aid was increased, freedom of religion was maintained. Louis rejected a papal effort to negotiate a new concordat more favorable to the Church, so there was no structural change in the Church's position. Freedom of press and thought was also protected, and there were few arrests of former revolutionaries and Bonapartists. The government also put its finances in good order, a remarkable accomplishment after the Napoleonic wars. The Revolution and Napoleon had set up a governmental apparatus of extraordinary efficiency that the new regime did not alter, except for adding a parliament. France in 1820 was the most flexible, intelligently run, and perhaps the most popular state in all Europe.

Ten years later the regime had collapsed, pushed aside by a minor uprising in Paris. Within a decade it had turned to the conservatism that was prevalent in other continental countries. The conservatives in France, headed by aristocrats and churchmen, had never been any different from their counterparts elsewhere. It was the king who had held them back. But Louis XVIII grew steadily older, a tired man, burdened with the daily pain of gout. The assassination of his nephew in 1820 doomed his effort to reconcile liberalism and monarchy. His successor in 1824, Charles X, was an unreconstructed advocate of the old regime. Now there was no bar to the most conventional sort of conservatism.

The monarchy gained in power over parliament by a new system of elections. The voters—already restricted to the very affluent, particularly the landed elements—chose electors from the wealthiest of their number, who actually selected parliament. This system gave the government much more opportunity to influence elections. Charles also tried to embellish the monarchy with a variety of ceremonies, including his elaborate coronation. The aristocracy was also strengthened. In 1825 the *émigrés*, those aristocrats who had fled France during the Revolution, were awarded a billion franc indemnity for the land they had lost, and some were able to repurchase estates. The election procedure assured aristocratic control of parliament, and the government proposed the reestablishment of primogeniture. The support given to the Church was even more dramatic. Churchmen controlled the higher education system, though it remained a state monopoly. Religious orders, including the Jesuits, were brought back and Catholic influence was strong in all areas of government, particularly in appointments to important positions. In return, the clergy supported the government in countless sermons and by serving as virtual election agents. In 1825 a law was passed decreeing the death penalty for sacrilege, the theft of sacred objects from churches. Here was eloquent testimony to the union of throne and altar in France.

This edifice was capped by growing repression. Liberal teachers were expelled from the schools and several history and philosophy courses at the University of Paris were suspended when their professors were suspected of subversion. Issues of opposition newspapers were often seized before they went on sale. No new paper could be founded without the government's consent and no issue could appear without the censor's permission. Efforts in 1830 to tamper still further with the rights of press and parliament brought about revolution.

The Restoration government in the 1820s remained efficient. Finances were in good order and, behind a high tariff wall, some encouragement was given to new manufacturing. Roads and canals were rapidly extended. In 1829 Charles launched an invasion of Algeria, in an effort to gain popularity in yet another way. This was an isolated diplomatic effort, however. Furthermore the time had not yet come when an imperialistic foreign policy could win support for conservatism.

Although the Restoration regime turned out to be conservative in the

A Caricature of Reaction:
Charles X of France
portrayed as a crab
moving backwards.

continental sense, the situation in France was distinctive. There was a hollowness to the government's measures long before the regime collapsed. The sacrilege law was not really enforced. The indemnity did not abrogate the revolutionary land settlement; indeed it confirmed this settlement by eliminating aristocratic claims to most of the land and was, in itself, a constructive measure. Churchmen held the top offices in the educational system but the system was still secular in its conception and many professors were religiously indifferent. At the height of the apparent Catholic domination, a vote was taken among the students in one secondary school on the question of the existence of God. God won, but by a single vote. The press was hampered but opposition newspapers actually won increasing attention. Votes were limited to the upper class but, as in England, the upper class soon tired of repression and began returning opposition deputies. Thus conservatives could not undo the effect of the Revolution on the French social order or on French politics. Unlike their counterparts elsewhere on the continent, they failed very quickly—but not before ten years of conservative rule ruined any chance for a reconciliation of diverse political elements and subsequent political stability in France. One is tempted to speculate: Was this historical course inevitable, or would ensuing events have been different if, for example, a healthier Louis XVIII had managed to restrain the conservatives long enough for a healing of wounds and a cooling of passions?

2 EUROPEAN SOCIETY AND CULTURE
1815–1848

The energy that had been aroused by revolution and then poured into war was turned, after 1815, to economic and cultural pursuits. Instead of considering a military career as the path to success, an increasing number of men now joined the ranks of journalists, doctors, teachers, and clergymen and also flocked to the business professions, including banking, shopkeeping, and manufacturing. The guidelines for this cultural and economic upheaval had been set in the eighteenth century with the launching of industrialization in Britain and Romanticism in Germany. Both movements were extended in their respective countries of origin and began to be adapted elsewhere.

This new direction of energy indicated that what was happening in culture and in the economy was more important and more innovative than concomitant political developments. Indeed the closed character of the conservative political establishments was one of the reasons innovators turned to other fields. New energy had been roused most fundamentally by population growth, which increased the competition in all areas of endeavor. Whereas before only one, possibly two, sons in a family reached adulthood, now the average rose to three or more—all of whom were compelled to seek new ways of earning a living. So, often, was their father, if he was concerned about giving all his sons something to inherit. Camille Schlumberger, for example—a good but not an extraordinarily imaginative bourgeois in eastern France—found himself with 12 children to provide for; he therefore set about expanding a small textile operation, creating the basis for one of the first modern factories in the area, and in the process giving good jobs to all his sons and ample dowries to his daughters. For some groups, particularly in western Europe, the Enlightenment's erosion of old norms and the Revolution's encouragement to more equal opportunity enhanced this restless vigor.

Innovation, restlessness, and energy were the pervasive themes of the period. The debate between reason and emotion, which has been basic to western intellectual life ever since, was at this time firmly established. So was the framework for industrial society, and along with it, even before industrialization was well launched, the modern class structure. Romantic intellectuals, many of whom were inspired by the prime example of the conquering will, Napoleon I, stressed the will over the mind; in business the leading manufacturers were men of undoubted willpower. Although businessmen and intellectuals often had scant contact, and no one can pretend to find unity in all the cultural and economic developments of the time, in both fields there was a common preoccupation with what the individual human will could achieve.

The creation of a new intellectual outlook and a new social order had important implications for politics. Aspects of each supported the conservative approach, but it became increasingly clear with time that the basic thrust of Romanticism and certainly of industrialization had to undermine conventional conservatism.

ROMANTICISM

The decades between 1815 and 1848 saw Romanticism at its height in Europe. Romanticism was a new movement and the Romantics gloried in their novelty. Yet in a broader sense they were restoring in a new way a traditional balance to Western intellectual life. After a century of emphasis on the head, Romantics stressed the heart. They did not revive the debate between faith and reason, but they did challenge the total adequacy of reason, just as many Christian theologians had done previously. The Romantics did not halt the advance of rational thought, which remained the principal current of modern European intellectual life. Never again, however, would rationalism seem so facilely triumphant as it had been during the Enlightenment; never again would it lack fundamental criticism.

The Romantic Impulse

One way, perhaps the easiest way, to approach Romanticism is to identify what it was against. The Romantics did not see man governed by his reason, but by his emotions; they wanted him to develop his instincts and his passion for beauty. Their novels and poems fairly dripped with sentiment, designed to evoke an emotional, often tearful, response from the reader. The Romantics saw the universe not as a rational plan but as un-

tamed nature. They liked tangled mountain paths and the ocean's roar, not
a nature disciplined by man. The Romantics did not reject the past but
gloried in it; they saw time as a continuum, its movement governed by
forces that reason could not fully grasp. Above all, they exalted the Middle
Ages and its art because it symbolized man's striving for something higher.
Many believed in progress as well, but not a progress that could be rationally planned and calculated; their progress would evolve, unfold, happen.
For the Romantics, the Enlightenment was wrong about man's nature,
wrong about the universe. Some found it dangerous, others simply dull
and petty.

Precisely because Romantics rejected reason and gloried in the individual emotion, they resist the attempts at rational categorization that historians tend to apply to movements in the past. There may have been not
one but many types of Romanticism. Certainly there was no single Romantic approach to politics. Nor could Romantics agree about religion or
philosophy. And while many were profoundly pessimistic, others were
boundless optimists.

One kind of Romanticism was a stylistic movement in opposition to classical standards. The Romantics revived interest in writers like Shakespeare
and Dante who had defied all the rules of Aristotle. They hoped to go even
farther themselves. Victor Hugo trumpeted this note in the preface to his
play, *Hernani:* "The principle of freedom in literature has advanced a step."
Poets—and Romanticism produced an abundance of poetry—abandoned the
formalism of the eighteenth century, seeking a flexibility that could convey
the personality of the poet. The style of Romantic writing, however, was less
daring than the attacks on the principles of classicism might imply; later
writers would go much further. But the themes of Romantic literature were
much more vivid: the exotic; the medieval (as in the work of Sir Walter
Scott); soaring nature; and intense personal emotion. The Romantics' self-
proclaimed innovations were clearly attacking centuries-old conventions.
French classicists howled, "Romanticism is not merely ridiculous, it is a
disease, like sleepwalking or epilepsy," and they rioted at the first showing
of *Hernani*. Romanticism gained ground steadily despite the opposition.

The stylistic expressions of Romanticism were most pronounced in the
arts. Painters and musicians had to be innovative to convey and arouse emotion. Delacroix painted wild landscapes and exaggerated figures. John Con-
stable revived the importance of landscape painting while Joseph Turner
went farthest of all in his free handling of light, color, and movement. Romantic composers rejected the pure, mathematical forms of the eighteenth
century, in favor of music that created a mood. They used new instruments
such as the tympani and developed bigger orchestras in an effort to achieve
rich harmonies and new musical effects in symphonies and operas. Beethoven
made the transition from classic to Romantic, followed, among others, by
Schubert and Wagner in Germany and Berlioz in France. Only in architecture did the Romantic impulse misfire. Romantic architects restored medi-

The Art of Romanticism: A seascape by J. M. W. Turner.

eval buildings and designed new ones in exaggerated Gothic style—which was one of the main reasons the nineteenth century failed to develop a new architectural style.

In all the artistic and literary forms, Romanticism generated amazing creativity all over Europe. Wordsworth, Byron, Keats, and Shelley experimented with new poetic themes in England. No period produced more first-rank novelists—Scott, Balzac, Dickens, and the young Dostoevsky were just a few. Central Europe abounded in composers, western Europe in painters. This burst of creativity, together with the innovative style of the Romantics, was one of the most important, certainly the most durable, legacies of Romanticism to later periods.

The writing of history was another major beneficiary of the Romantic impulse. Spurred by their fascination with the past, Romantics everywhere collected legends and folk tales. Germans led in the development of the history of law and economic history, in opposition to the Enlightenment-derived effort to deduce general economic and legal principles from reason.

Leopold von Ranke laid the foundation for modern historical criticism by stressing that historians should write history "as it really happened." He and others opened the attack on dusty archives which has since characterized the historical profession.

During this period a new philosophy was developing, particularly in Germany. Philosophers groped for a higher principle, an almost mystic entity, which would transcend the individual and, often, the rational. They were essentially developing the idealism of Immanuel Kant, who had stressed spiritual qualities and phenomena that could not be grasped by reason alone. Friedrich Hegel, though he believed both in reason and in rational patterns, looked for an all-encompassing unity that governed the world and the unfolding of history. A world spirit, a fate, determined historical evolution by means of a dialectic process in which the spirit of one people clashed with the spirit of another to produce a new civilization; a new, disciplined Germany would be the final product of history.

Others, in Germany and elsewhere, sought a higher principle in traditional religion. Friedrich Schleiermacher, the leading theologian of the nineteenth century, stressed that religion was an inner, emotional experience, not a rational system of thought. The many Romantics who embraced Catholicism found in it authority, beauty, and tradition.

Romanticism and Political Theory

Many Romantics were politically conservative and led in developing various conservative political theories after 1815. They reacted to the chaos of the Revolution, which could so easily be blamed on false rationalism. Fascination with the past led many Romantics to defend tradition, while an interest in the process of history induced others to place emphasis on the organic nature of social development, the constant links between present and past. Romantics who saw man as primarily emotional could seek political restraints on his passions. And the search for a higher authority—such as a German state for Hegel—could easily reinforce conservatism, for here man was part of a collective whole and subject to its guidance, not an individual free agent.

Romantic conservative theorists agreed on the importance of order, religion, and a strong state. Joseph de Maistre, the leading reactionary philosopher in France, preached the absolute sovereignty of the Pope as the guarantor of order. Friedrich Savigny in Germany, claiming that reason could create nothing new, emphasized the historical basis of law and institutions.

Romanticism was also compatible with liberalism, radicalism, and socialism. After 1825 most of the Romantics who had political interests were hostile to the status quo. The passion for individual creativity and the attack on classicism's rules led to a defense of political liberty and an attack on political conservatives; Hugo made this connection specifically in his preface to *Hernani*. Lord Byron, the English Romantic writer, died defending the Greek revolution. Love of adventure led many Romantics to take up similar causes. The Romantics' interest in the common people and their lore brought about an attachment to democracy and social reform. Few Romantics, certainly, could sympathize with the rising capitalist order, with its prosaic, money-grubbing goals. Finally, the Romantics' fascination with the peculiarities of national traditions had an influence on the rise of nationalism, and in the Metternichian age nationalism, if it was political at all, had to be radical.

Romanticism, then, had a host of diverse and even contradictory implications, apart from its central contributions to Europe's intellectual life and to the arts. Furthermore, Romanticism differed from one country to the next. In England and France the movement was primarily artistic and literary. Early Romantics in both countries were usually conservative; some were interested in the Germans' efforts to find a new principle of authority, but the mood quickly switched to political radicalism. Romanticism was more tenaciously conservative in Germany, though there were individual exceptions such as the poet Heinrich Heine. The movement may also have penetrated German intellectual life more fully, so that the quest for higher authority and abstract ideals has been seen as an enduring German characteristic. This we shall examine later.

Did Romanticism, which was so interested in national characteristics, produce or at least exaggerate such characteristics? Unquestionably its heritage was mixed. From a long range perspective, Romanticism's affirmation that man was not primarily rational must be viewed as conservative. But in these first generations of Romanticism, when energy ran high and the implications of basic assumptions were confused, Romantics struck out boldly in all possible directions.

RATIONALIST CURRENTS

Even at its height, Romanticism did not exhaust Europe's intellectual fertility. The rationalist tradition continued, particularly in western Europe. Most of the political isms, such as liberalism and socialism, embodied a faith in man's reason. Liberals and socialists believed that a rational ordering of human society was possible and, further, that rationally derivable rules could describe human society. In abandoning the eighteenth century belief in natural rights of man, liberals pulled back from an association of orderly, beneficent nature and social life. They stopped arguing, also, that primitive man was spontaneously good. But the fundamental belief in reason remained. Liberal economists like J. B. Say in France claimed that individual competition automatically produced maximum public good; in this sense they directly carried on eighteenth-century beliefs in a rational order.

Rationalists were active in many fields besides political theory. They wrote histories, often good ones, celebrating the rise of liberalism and the middle classes. Science, which most Romantics ignored, continued its advance. German universities made extraordinary progress in scientific work, particularly in chemistry, an increasingly important field; exact quantitative analysis was developed, while Justus von Liebig and others applied chemistry to industrial and agricultural uses. In physics, André Ampère measured the effects of electric current on magnetism, and Sir Humphry Davy and Michael Faraday founded electrochemistry. By close observation of geological processes, Sir Charles Lyell, in England, concluded that the present form of the earth resulted from a continuous operation of these processes since a remote past; he thus contradicted the Biblical account of the earlier formation and ascribed a much greater age to the earth than was conventional in Christian accounts.

The list of scientific accomplishments could be expanded indefinitely, but the main point is clear. Scientists abounded who continued to believe in the operation of constant, discoverable physical laws, and the advance of quantification beyond physics made this belief ever more precise. Moreover, the growth of practical applications of science confirmed for many laymen the importance of science and practical reason. Research societies like the Royal Institution in Britain specifically furthered applied science by calling on leading scientists to improve soil testing or develop new farming processes. The association of science and technology furthered the optimistic rationalism of many agriculturalists and manufacturers.

It was in this period, in fact, that positivism, a major new formulation of rationalism, was begun. The French philosopher Auguste Comte, founder of positivism, held that social laws were directly analogous to the physical laws of nature and that society could therefore be studied scientifically. It must be stressed that while positivism was intensely rationalistic it could reject part of the traditional rationalist's creed. Comte noted that man's inherent reason was not an empirical fact. Positivism ultimately produced social scientists who rationally studied other people's irrationality, but this was not significant until later.

Romanticism, then, did not have exclusive reign between 1815 and 1848. There were two distinct approaches, the Romantic and the rationalist, and the existence of the two has been decisive from this time onward. Their basic assumptions would invariably clash in a recurrent battle that has not ended; at the same time, their effects could oddly blend. Both rationalists and Romantics were, for example, moving toward a theory of evolution. The Romantics, whose interest in an unfolding past permeated the intellectual atmosphere of the age, believed in evolution already, though they did not apply this theory to natural processes. During this same period rationalists like Lyell were building the scientific foundations of an evolutionary theory, while liberal economists, who saw life as continual competitive struggle, suggested another dimension of the theory. Charles Darwin, whose work began in the 1830s, would in a sense merely formulate the obvious. Appropriately, the heirs of both Romanticism and rationalism would make use of his theories.

Political theory was another area, more immediately important, in which the work of rationalists and Romantics could merge. There was an extraordinary outpouring of new theoretical isms derived from both approaches with the result that the isms conflicted with each other and were often internally contradictory as well.

THE ISMS

Liberalism, nationalism, and socialism all had roots in the eighteenth century, but each became much more explicit after 1815. Liberalism and nationalism were also becoming political movements, blending theory and political action. We will deal with the political movements later, but first it is important to look at the theoretical underpinnings.

Liberalism

Liberalism, as we have seen, drew support from the Romantics, but formal liberal theory had a rationalist base. Even so, it was diverse. Following the lead of Adam Smith, liberal economic theory flourished during this period, marked by a belief, often more rigorous than Smith's, that the state should be inactive, a mere policeman, and that individual initiative should guide the economy. As liberal theory became more refined and was supplemented by some empirical observation, it tended to take a pessimistic tone. Malthus in England had claimed that population was outstripping productive capacity, while David Ricardo now reasoned that landlords alone were benefiting from economic advance, their rents sucking profits from manufacturers and workers alike. These were the years when economics came to be known as the dismal science. For according to liberal economic theory, there was little that could be done. Any state intervention to improve the lot of the workingman would simply encourage him to have more children, which would worsen conditions through the competition of excess workers.

These refinements of liberal economic theory were exceedingly important, particularly in France and England where they contributed to public policy. They spurred rebuttal from men who would not endure such cold calculations; Marx would be one of these, though he too accepted certain aspects of the liberal description of the economy. But it is wrong to take too much of liberalism's tone from these economists. There were many liberal economists who differed. English pessimism, for example, did not spread widely on the continent. J. B. Say in France was blissfully optimistic. Many liberal theorists quickly came to advocate new state intervention—for example, in the matter of child labor. Friedrich List, in Germany, adapted Smith's doctrines to include an active, efficient—and, for Germany, united —state.

The main thrust of liberal political theory differed from liberal economics. It agreed on the importance of limiting the state and protecting individual freedom; it agreed too on many specific economic policies. But most liberal political theorists were not very interested in the economy, looking instead to the political structure and the area of civil rights. They believed profoundly that man was rational and improvable; they had little in common with those economists who saw man the animal reproducing whenever he could. And they were optimistic.

Liberal Political Thought

Under the influence of Jeremy Bentham, the utilitarians increasingly dominated liberal theory in England, and their influence spread to the continent. The utilitarians judged political arrangements not by abstract rights but by practicality. Whatever worked, whatever was conducive to the happiness of the greatest number, was good. Liberty worked, liberty developed the best in man and in society as a whole, so it was good. The utilitarians also produced, in John Stuart Mill, the most eloquent formulator of political liberalism. His *On Liberty*, written in 1859, stressed the importance of intellectual freedoms and their utility on grounds that individual self-development was the true goal of society and the basis of society's progress. Few liberal theorists would have disagreed.

Indeed even in the 1820s liberals concurred in their basic political formula. Benjamin Constant, a leading French liberal, defined liberty as "the right to pursue our own ends unimpeded, so long as they do not interfere with the equally legitimate activities of others." Continental liberals shared much of the pragmatic tone of the English, but they were more concerned with constitutional structure. They wanted the government's limits defined and they wanted a representative parliament to enforce them. Authority had to be limited—this was the watchword of moderate liberals in France, known as the Doctrinaires, who were to guide the founding of a new regime in 1830. It dominated German liberal thought as well, for there were many who attacked conservative traditionalism and urged that the present could improve upon the past.

During the 1820s liberal Catholicism emerged in France, Germany, and Belgium. Many Catholics held that liberalism was bound to triumph and that the Church should come to terms with it as a matter of self-interest. Catholicism could survive amid religious toleration and parliamentary politics; indeed it might gain in strength. Some liberal Catholics claimed that freedom of thought and expression was a good in itself, advancing civilization and Christianity to a new level. The most vociferous liberal Catholic, Félicité de Lamennais, urged the Church to welcome not only liberalism but also democracy and social reform. Because of his extreme views, boldly proclaimed in a daily newspaper, liberal Catholicism was explicitly condemned by the pope in 1832, but it survived as an important minority movement within the Church.

Radicalism incorporated most of the basic assumptions of liberalism but carried them farther. In addition to constitutions and effective parliaments, radicals advocated a much broader suffrage, possibly even a democracy, and in France, after 1830, they wanted a republic. They also favored some government action to aid the poor. They remained, however, essentially liberal, and they differed more in their vocabulary and methods of agitation than in their goals. William Cobbett, in Britain, was a typical example. He addressed his newspaper and his speeches to the lower classes and suggested that political reform would bring social change. But he did not believe in universal suffrage and preached gradualism instead of any revolutionary effort.

Nationalism

Nationalism stemmed primarily from Romanticism, for the rational tradition stressed universality; but like liberalism it easily attracted support from the other camp. Two types of nationalist theory, cultural and liberal, developed before 1848. Cultural nationalists believed in a distinct and definable national tradition but they did not necessarily claim that a nation should have political identity. Cultural nationalism spread steadily eastward, where the upper classes had long looked to the West for their identity, speaking French or German—indeed often being ignorant of their native language, which only peasants used. Vuk Karajich published the first Serbian grammar in 1814; two years later George Lazar began to teach, in Rumanian, about the distinctiveness of Rumanian history. Native-language schools and newspapers were founded for most of the Slavic groups, including the Croats, the Bulgarians and the Czechs. Jan Kollár, a Czech nationalist, tried to promote Slavic culture in general, urging the establishment of Slavic bookstores and education in the major Slavic languages.

Liberal nationalists accepted the principles of cultural distinctiveness but they wanted a politically distinct nation as well. They are called liberal for two reasons, both of which differentiate them from later varieties of political nationalists. First, they expected that the national state would have a constitution and parliament and often a laissez-faire economic structure. Second, while they were devoted to their own nation, they held that other nations had equal rights and equal contributions to make. Joseph Mazzini, the leading nationalist writer of the period, saw mankind as a common family with each nation devoting its peculiar talents to the general good. Liberal nationalist theory was not, however, simply liberalism with an additional emphasis. Nationalists found it difficult to avoid special claims for their own nation; Mazzini, for example, referred vaguely to restoring the primacy of ancient Rome, though he did not mean this in a territorial sense. More important, the nationalist saw the nation as an entity above the individual. Mazzini believed in liberty but he criticized individualism and stressed that duty to the nation came before any rights that the nation might grant. This distinction in theory does not mean that many liberals were not nationalists and vice versa. It does suggest the difference in origins between rationalist liberalism and Romantic nationalism, a difference that would become important, in practice, when ordinary politicians had to decide in 1848 and thereafter whether the nation or liberty came first.

Utopian Socialism

A flurry of socialist theories completed the spectrum in this formative period of modern political ideologies. There was a variety of approaches. Charles Fourier and others in France and Robert Owen in England wanted society to be grouped in small cooperative communities, with each individual working freely and being rewarded equally. Saint-Simon proposed a technocracy in which the state, run by industrial experts, would work to advance production and improve the conditions of the poor. Louis Blanc also wanted state help, but his main goal was the establishment of small, cooperative workshops.

For all their diversity, the socialist theorists had several points in common. As socialists they attacked capitalism and wanted communities or the state, not the individual, to guide the economy. As socialists they believed that this would not only create economic justice and equality but would enhance true individual freedom. These theorists are also called utopian, a term coined by Marx to mean fundamentally that, since socialist ideas before 1847 differed from his, their proponents were unscientific and starry-eyed. The term is useful even though Marx used it derisively, for the utopian brand of socialism was in several respects distinct from later, more scientific varieties of socialism.

The utopians eschewed revolution, always hoping for some gradual, non-violent installation of their system. Most of them, too, were utopian in their dislike of industrialization as well as of capitalism. Except for Saint-Simon they did not plan to include factories and machines in their system. Socialism at this point and later united the rationalist and Romantic impulses more clearly than any other ism. Socialists believed that man was rational and they delighted in planning rational rules for the new order; Charles Fourier saw society mathematically divided into communities of 1620 people each, no more and no less. But many socialists shared the Romantics' commiseration with the poor. They too sought, though through material arrangements, a renewal of society's spiritual purpose.

The theories that emerged after 1815 were sufficiently diverse to represent a variety of interests and purposes. They all reflected, in different combinations, rationalist and Romantic elements that still comprise Europe's intellectual makeup. The theories themselves would change and evolve further in succeeding decades, but it is significant that except for fascism, which was in part a blend of nationalism and socialism, no fundamentally new political theory has arisen since the early nineteenth century. Here is another indication of the creativity of this period.

Enunciation of a political theory is not the same thing as the foundation of a political movement. With socialism, particularly, there was a considerable gap between ideological formulation and significant political action. As the three major isms became part of the political scene, they inevitably became more complex. This process, harder by far to define than the evolution of theory itself, demands particular attention.

After the brief blaze of conservative theory that occurred before 1825, political theory was on the side of dissent against the established order. Only English liberals could be content with their political and social framework. Neither liberals nor socialists advocated revolution to achieve change; both hoped for rational persuasion. But the spokesmen for nationalism, with Romantic zeal for action, could preach revolution; socialist and liberal theorists would be drawn to it in the excitement of the moment. The new ideologies frightened the conservatives and brought new measures of repression that would heighten discontent. None of the ideologies remained theories alone. The years of rapid intellectual change were also years of intense economic dislocation. Inevitably, the two currents would unite and the mixture would be explosive.

FORCES FOR ECONOMIC CHANGE

The most basic cause of economic expansion and innovation was population growth, just as it had been in the eighteenth century; but this growth now reached new heights, and a variety of other factors combined with it to change the economy. Only southern Europe was exempt from the demographic surge. During the first half of the nineteenth century, Britain's population was rising by 1.5 percent per year, 50 percent more rapidly than during the last half of the eighteenth century, while Germany's growth rate more than doubled to 1.25 percent per year. Russia and Austria touched similar rates, and most other major states were growing at a rate that doubled their population within 50 years. Only in France did the pace of population increase show any sign of slackening. This factor, which contributed to France's decline as a power, seems to have resulted from an unusually widespread desire for security, as peasants and bourgeois alike limited their birth rate in order to protect their land or their fortune against the demands of too many children. But even the French population continued to expand, rising by about 50 percent during the first half of the century.

The reasons for this demographic vitality were much the same as in the eighteenth century, with the added fact that eighteenth-century growth bequeathed a rising number of women of childbearing age, so that rapid population gains were almost inevitable. Moreover, many of the people who were being crowded off the land, including those who entered factories, actually began to marry earlier than before, which helped maintain if not increase the birth rate. There was a slight recrudescence of epidemic disease, notably a cholera epidemic in the 1830s, and mortality rates increased in some growing cities, particularly in Britain. These developments, however, did not offset the effects that improved production of foodstuffs (like the potato) had in curbing traditional mortality rates. Now, too, medical advances in western Europe, particularly the smallpox vaccination, had some bearing in reducing the death rate, and new industrial products, such as easily laundered cotton clothing, helped to limit disease. At the same time, outside of France, few people were sufficiently shaken from traditional habits to limit their birth rates.

As a result of this demographic expansion, a tremendous new market and new labor force were being created. Although the process was dynamic, it also proved profoundly upsetting, and everywhere caused great disruption. Not the least of the sources of disorder in this period was the jostling of unaccustomed numbers of people and the presence, in an expanding population, of rising numbers of the young. At every level, parents were faced with decisions about what to do for and with unexpected numbers of surviving children. Younger sons, excluded from the principal inheritance, had to find some source of income and plunged into new occupations. Finally, the new numbers of people strained every established institution—from the university, whose enrollments rose from a few hundred to several thousand reflecting larger families among the upper classes, to the peasant village, which for the first time was faced with large numbers of landless residents.

Other factors contributed to economic change. Government bureaucracies, now expanding, continued generally to take an interest in the economy. Governments from Naples to Russia tried to import and introduce some new techniques in agriculture and manufacturing and many set up pilot factories. This policy did not necessarily result in actual industrialization but it could help. From Prussia west, from Scandinavia through northern Italy, reforms of manorialism introduced during the revolutionary and

Napoleonic eras, even if now modified, freed at least a portion of the labor force from traditional ties to land and lord.

Social and economic rivalry between old and new elements of society encouraged economic change. In Russia, suggestions of a class of independent rural merchants, visible in the eighteenth century, were now abandoned as the aristocracy resumed complete control of the rural economy. But in central and western Europe, competition between the aristocracy and the middle class was stepped up. The aristocracy, which relied heavily on its political power, also tried to increase its social exclusiveness. French aristocrats began in the Restoration to use their full titles regularly, while English aristocrats founded clubs where they could be alone with their kind. Economic weapons, particularly new agricultural methods, were vital too. In France some aristocrats who had regained their estates led in introducing fertilizers and new farm implements. Many Prussian Junkers began to grow sugar beets and constructed their own refineries. Most aristocrats lacked the knowledge or capital to make innovations, but although the class did slip economically there were enough resourceful aristocrats to alter agricultural patterns and even to contribute to new factory industry.

Far more evident were the efforts of new elements of the middle class who sought to use economic initiative to gain a higher place in society. At the top, bankers who invested in heavy industry might hope to rival the aristocrats, while many factory owners, more modest in their goals, wanted to buy a bit of land to demonstrate their gentility. Throughout western Europe men from the lower reaches of the middle classes—small merchants or artisan masters—saw new economic opportunities and sought to establish a firm economic basis and a higher social status for their families. They wanted better housing, better schooling for their sons, and a more ample dowry for their daughters. Some relied on traditional business and manufacturing methods, but there were those who were willing, sometimes eager, to effect innovations.

Most of these forces for economic change had been at work before, though the reforms in manorialism were new in many areas and population growth and social rivalry were now far more intense. There was one clearly new element: the incontestable fact of British industrialization. Britain's success in bringing down Napoleon drew the attention of continental states to her economic strength, and manufacturers eager for higher profits studied her methods. But Britain was by now more than a mere model for study; British competition was cutting into traditional industries all over Europe. British capital, built up by industrialization, began to seek foreign investments, and British manufacturers used their technological superiority to set up operations on the continent—for example, in Belgian metallurgy, in French machine building and in the mines of the Ruhr. British labor crossed too, selling their new skills for high wages. Up to 20,000 came to France during the Restoration, though some quickly regretted giving up their English beer for French wine. It was no coincidence, then, that industrialization spread first to those countries nearest Britain. Britain's industrial lead, however, also guaranteed that no industrial revolution on the continent would follow the British pattern exactly.

COMMERCIALIZATION

Although historians have often tried to show diverse relationships between the political disorders through 1848 and the industrial revolution, most of them have scant basis in fact. At this point, western Europe was not galloping into a fully emerged industrial world. Rather, the most general economic development before 1848 was the spread of commercial or capitalistic practices to traditional activities. Industrialization did touch the continent after 1820, and its effects undeniably reached many more people than the small numbers actually employed in factory industry. But these developments should not overshadow the far more pervasive spread of capitalist practices that helped prepare the continent for extensive industrialization. By 1848 most of Europe was still pre-industrial, undergoing changes that in many ways were more disrupting than industrialization itself.

Eastern and southern Europe was largely exempt from even the commercialization process. Southern Italy and southern Spain remained locked in an essentially manorial system and the landlords were not active in using this system to increase production. Eastern Europe did take advantage of the growing market for grain in the cities of the West. Landlords in Hungary and Russia exported increasing amounts, but they did so without introducing new methods or altering the social structure. They relied on the peasants' manorial obligations, particularly the work service they owed on the lords' estates. In Hungary some even increased this service, from four days a year to eight or ten. Some landlords in Russia also spread cottage manufacturing among their serfs. All of this was important, but it did not alter basic social relationships. The social and economic differences between eastern and western Europe grew steadily greater, even as common intellectual currents spread.

From Prussia west, with the exception of southern Europe, agricultural economy became increasingly commercial. Landlords and peasants alike had to produce for the market. In the case of the landlords, it was because they were deprived of all or part of their manorial dues and their expenses were rising as they strove to make their style of life more elegant and distinctive. Peasants had to produce for the market in order to redeem their manorial dues, a situation that existed in much of Germany, and to meet new taxes that the states there and elsewhere imposed. Dues and taxes required cash. Furthermore, faced with growing families, many peasant landowners had to adopt new methods to compensate for divided land holdings, while those who were absolutely landless were available for hire as wage laborers.

Large landowners, seeing the growing markets, introduced new crops and methods and tried to acquire more land. Aristocratic landlords in England won legislation requiring all landowners to enclose, or fence in, their property—a procedure so expensive that many small farmers sold out to the large landlord, who then used his great estate to produce for the market. This enclosure movement continued until 1830. Prussian Junkers gained more land when peasants redeemed their manorial obligations by surrendering a third of their property; it was precisely for this purpose that Junkers often pressed peasants to buy out of the manorial system. Although most peasants in East Prussia remained serfs and were exploited in their labor services to gain marketable products, even here wage labor was found to be more productive and was increasingly used. Aristocrats moved only slowly toward more commercial agriculture. Many, in fact, went bankrupt and their estates were purchased by successful businessmen or bureaucrats. But this development, too, increased the commitment of large estates to production for the market.

Changes were less striking where peasants controlled the land. French peasants, for example, ignored new methods and equipment. Lack of education and capital certainly prevented many peasants from taking advantage of market opportunities, even when they desperately needed to increase their cash income. Gradually, however, the simpler work-saving devices came into use, such as a scythe instead of a sickle for harvesting, which improved productivity up to 50 percent. Peasants increasingly specialized in a few crops that could be sold and bought foods they did not produce. Small shops began to spring up in the larger villages, for peasants could no longer rely on itinerant peddlers and occasional fairs for their purchases. In this respect the rise of the commercial system was evident. But the most general sign of the peasants' new economic system was the growing division between those who had enough land to farm for the market and were acquiring more and those who had too little land to subsist and were likely to lose even this. Peasants had rarely possessed equal plots of land, but traditional village agriculture was designed to limit extremes and protect the middling peasant who had enough land for subsistence but not more than he could farm himself. Now a minority of peasants bought land from the majority and the middling peasants declined in numbers. Those who had too little land might sell out and go to the city, but many stayed behind as agricultural laborers, working not only for the big estates, but for the successful peasants. Production for the market and a wage labor system—two hallmarks of capitalism—spread rapidly in the countryside.

Until the 1840s, cottage industries also increased on the continent. Rising population meant new markets for traditional cottage products, particularly textiles. Even when spinning processes were mechanized, the need for hand weavers rose. Within this putting-out system, capitalism gained ground. Fewer and fewer rural manufacturers worked on their own, but rather for a wage, under a merchant who bought raw materials and sold the finished product.

The spread of cottage industries was a vital aid to the growing rural population, for it allowed survival even for those with little or no land. But the system was doomed to a tragic end. Local mechanization (and even before that, British competition) forced rural manufacturing workers to endure growing unemployment and falling wages. After long agony they had to quit altogether; the number of rural manufacturing workers began to fall in France in the 1830s and in Germany in the 1840s. But many workers remained in this system, willing to accept capitalism if they did not have to leave their homes.

In the cities, the most notable extension of capitalistic motives and methods was in the crafts. The growth of cities created many new opportunities for such urban artisans as bakers, shoemakers or construction workers. Very few of the major crafts were yet threatened by machine competition, and even in Britain the number of artisans rose steadily until well after mid-century. But the nature of artisan employment changed. Masters began behaving like small employers, treating their journeymen as wage laborers. Most important, masters guarded their positions jealously, so that while the number of artisans grew the number of masters remained the same. This meant that many masters now employed four or five workers instead of one or two. The chance to become a master, long a goal in the crafts, was virtually eliminated for most journeymen. At the same time the artisans' traditional protective group, the guild, had either been abolished outright, as in France, or was severely weakened.

Trade in the cities was increasingly carried on by a shopkeeper, another sign of expanding commerce. Shopkeeping was a great opportunity for a petty capitalist, and many peasants who came to the city with a bit of money set themselves up in this way. In addition, many cities became centers of capitalism on a far larger scale as factories, banks, wholesale trading operations and insurance companies expanded.

The general spread of capitalistic production and exchange was a vital development, but ironically it resulted in a diminution of the number of people who had property. Many peasants lost their capital in land, while many journeymen were denied traditional opportunities to acquire shops of their own. The possession of capital is not, however, the distinguishing feature of capitalism. Rather the spread of capitalism meant a gradual change in the motives of those who owned capital, namely, an interest in increasing production and sales in the hope of receiving greater reward. It meant too a change in the relations between owners and nonowners, in which the money wage, not obligations in kind and service, was the key connection.

INDUSTRIALIZATION:
GREAT BRITAIN

Britain became the first industrial society during the decades between 1815 and 1850. Britain had long since set out on this path, but there is a significant difference between a society that has begun to industrialize and one that has reached a certain industrial maturity. By 1850, one-half the British population was urban—the first time in human history that this had occurred anywhere. British industrial production rose far above agricultural production in value, which meant, among other things, that leading entrepreneurs could for the first time rival the top aristocrats in their wealth and lavish standard of living. Factory workers outnumbered artisans in the manufacturing labor force. Many of them were now of the second or third generation in the factories and were relatively attuned to the steady and rapid pace of industrial labor, and to city life. Entrepreneurs, for their part, were no longer pioneers, but had increasingly assumed managerial functions. Industrial maturity meant that a large percentage of the population was now involved in factory production and related distribution and clerical work; that the leading branches of production were mechanized; and that those involved in the industrial economy at any level were not new to their work and way of life.

Mechanization was applied to a number of new economic activities after 1820. Transportation was mechanized for the first time with the introduction of the railroad in 1829 and the development of steam shipping, which came into heavy use after about 1827. Mechanization had its usual effects here, as the cost of transportation dropped and its speed and capacity rapidly increased. Weaving, printing and other production processes were newly mechanized as well. Equally important, the techniques in industries that had been mechanized earlier were steadily elaborated. For the first time, steam engines were applied to metallurgy to run bellows in blast furnaces and to operate hammering and rolling devices. Spinning machines became ever larger and faster.

As mechanization expanded, production increased rapidly. Britain's per capita output of pig iron, which had not quite doubled during the whole eighteenth century, more than tripled in the first three decades of the nineteenth. Internal and foreign trade multiplied with extraordinary speed. These were the peak years of British industry, before any significant rivals had emerged. The nation had pinned its future on industry, becoming increasingly dependent on agricultural imports to feed its population.

Such rapid industrial growth naturally imposed great strain on many people. With the continued improvement in agricultural methods and the virtual destruction of cottage industry because of factory competition, hoards of workers were driven out of their traditional occupations and habitats. The rate of urbanization reached its highest point between 1820 and

Mechanization: A woolen spinning mill in England.

1850, and British cities were ill-prepared to handle the new influx. Many were still governed by aristocrats or churchmen and municipal governments in England traditionally shunned responsibility for such necessities as the provision of roads and sanitary facilities. With little or no regulation, slums developed in British cities the like of which would never be seen on the continent. Mortality rates, which had been falling in the 1790s, rose again after 1820, an indication of the plight of the urban poor. Only in the 1840s were the rates reversed again, as cities began to pay some attention to medical care and recreational facilities.

Work grew more rigorous within the factories. With bigger machines the pace of work increased. Families were now separated on the job, whereas before they had been allowed to work together. Also, British manufacturers developed a new attitude toward the labor force. In the early period of industrialization, workers were looked upon as part of the traditional poor, to be treated with both condescension and charity. Now the ruling ethic, clearly related to liberalism, viewed each worker as an individual responsible for his own fate. This new attitude was in a way optimistic, holding that men could improve themselves and could earn the right to be treated with respect. If a man worked hard he deserved high rewards; but if he did not succeed it was his own fault. If, for example, he lost his hand in an unprotected machine he deserved no compensation. In a period when so many workers were new to their jobs and confusion was so great, the effects of this new outlook were undeniably harsh.

Were these hardships mitigated, at least in part, by higher earnings and improved standards of living? This is a question that historians continue to debate. It is important not only in formulating a moral judgment of industrialization but in trying to understand what the reactions of the workers themselves must have been. Unquestionably, some workers, particularly the skilled labor in factories, gained an advantage; it is also true that the far larger number of unskilled workers, those not in factories and particularly those who were being displaced from cottage industry, lost ground. For the ordinary urban worker, however, the situation is more complex. Housing deteriorated with the crowding of the cities, but clothing, which dropped in price, became more abundant and stylish. Food prices probably rose more rapidly than wages, which meant that workers consumed less meat, less wheat and more potatoes than before, though consumption of some peripheral items like tea and sugar increased. Many workers, furthermore, fell victim to the frequent economic slumps of the period, for British industry, dependent on exports, was particularly vulnerable to severe depressions and to resultant unemployment. Rising mortality rates suggest that these were bleak years for most urban labor.

Industrial society was thus installed in Britain. It brought unprecedented prosperity to the nation and to the property-owning classes. It had yet to fulfill its promise to the poor.

Exploitation of Child Labor: Children hauling coal in a British mine.

INDUSTRIALIZATION:
THE CONTINENT

Belgium took the lead in industrialization outside Britain, with the aid of British and French capital and her own substantial coal resources. Significant factory development occurred also in France, Switzerland and Germany. Nowhere did industrialization proceed beyond rather early stages, and then only a small minority of the population was involved. By 1848, less than 2 percent of the population in France was employed in factories, which was less than 10 percent of the manufacturing labor force. Industrialization was visible enough, however, to be noticed and often feared by many people not directly involved in it, particularly because it was so clearly the wave of the future. It must then be discussed even though its extent must not be exaggerated.

The basic characteristics of industrialization were everywhere similar, resembling the early stages in Britain a few decades before. More advanced techniques could be borrowed, but the steam engine remained the foundation for huge gains in productivity and production, and cotton textiles, coal, and metallurgy led the way as they had in Britain. Continental industrialization reproduced other earlier British developments, such as rapid urbanization, the rise of new entrepreneurs, and the creation of a factory labor force subject to a radically new discipline and pace of work. Also like the British, continental industrialization was in part a response to a rising population which provided new markets and new workers. It developed most rapidly in regions rich in coal or iron, most notably the belt that ran from Belgium and northern France through the Ruhr. Clearly we are dealing with a broadly common process.

Yet it was evident, even by 1848, that continental industrialization was not going to be exactly the same as British and that there were important differences within the continental states. The relationship of industrialization to the broader society and to the state was different, in both cause and effect, and some of the characteristics of the new industrial classes were different also.

The dependence of rapid industrialization on coal and iron was one of the reasons Britain had soared to the lead. No continental country had resources that were both so abundant and so easily combined. France, for example, had less than a fifth of Britain's coal supply and less than a tenth of Germany's; although by 1848 France was exploiting the highest percentage of its coal resources, it was beginning to be clear that the country could not industrialize as rapidly as her neighbors. Germany, on the other hand, had abundant coal but lacked natural waterways in key places; the coal, therefore, could not be used effectively until railroads were introduced to move iron to it.

But resources alone did not determine the timing and pace of continental industrialization, as witness Spain, which had ample resources. One factor was the mountainous terrain, which was a barrier to effective transportation, but there were human factors as well. All continental industrialization relied significantly on the state for the introduction of new technology and for the amassing of capital. All continental governments planned and at least partially financed their railroad systems, and in some cases they operated them outright. Dynamic governments like the Belgian or the Prussian were most active in railroad building and in other innovations; hence their countries led or would soon lead in industrialization. A traditionalist country like Spain obviously lagged, but so, to a lesser extent, did the French state, which was controlled by rural, socially conservative middle-class elements.

The state's role in industrialization followed from continental traditions of government activity, but it resulted also from two, possibly three, newer factors. None of the continental countries, save France, was nearly as rich as Britain in the amount of capital potentially available for industrialization. Hence capital had to be more centrally organized and the financial power of the state invoked. Thus, the role of the state was greatest in the countries that were poorest, which meant that the government loomed larger in industrialization the farther east one went, in Germany more than in France, in Russia (at a later time) more than in Germany. All continental states, when they seriously resolved to sponsor industrialization, were painfully aware that they were behind England and that catching up was important diplomatically and economically. This was the second reason they intervened ever more actively. Finally, continental governments had to supply some of the dynamism that private entrepreneurs had provided in England.

There were vigorous, risk-taking entrepreneurs in France and Germany. One need only mention the Krupps, who began to build their metallurgical firm in this period. But none of the continental states had a pre-industrial business group as accustomed to commercial motives and initiatives as Britain had in the eighteenth century, from whom industrial pioneers could be drawn. None had an aristocracy so committed to capitalism and therefore ready to tolerate industrialization—in some cases actively to participate in it.

Thus, whereas industrialization was spontaneous in Britain, on the continent it was, in a sense, artificially induced, either by the state or by direct British involvement. In France, the state was not active enough to compensate for a majority of routine-minded entrepreneurs, which was certainly one reason French industrialization was slow. But induced industrialization did not have to be slow, as Germany was soon to prove. Even there, however, most elements of the population were hostile to industrial society and its goals. The result of this would be felt in 1848 and for a hundred years thereafter.

For the people directly involved in industrialization, conditions on the continent before 1848 were far better than they were in Britain. Material standards had improved for factory workers, who in France and Germany were among the best-paid among the lower classes; it must be remembered though that traditional living standards were lower to begin with and that hundreds of thousands of displaced cottage workers were suffering on the continent as in Britain. Continental manufacturers did not fully adopt the British approach toward labor, another sign that they were a somewhat different breed. They were more paternalistic, surrounding many workers with company housing and sickness insurance that aided them materially while increasing their dependence on their employers. Also, it was harder to recruit workers for industry, even in Germany where the population was growing rapidly. Partly because there was nothing on the continent like the enclosure movement in Britain but also because potential workers were more tradition-minded and clung to the countryside whenever they could, relatively high wages were necessary to attract the new labor force.

FORMATION OF CLASS STRUCTURE

The spread of capitalism and incipient industrialization completed the process begun in the eighteenth century throughout western and central Europe—that is, the substitution of a society founded on class for one founded on status groups technically known as "orders." No longer were social groups identifiable primarily by birth and legal privilege; rather social classes were based on money, with type of occupation and level of education related criteria. How much a man earned, what property he possessed if any, now increasingly determined his social station and how he would see himself.

This transition was of fundamental importance but it was not yet complete. Legal definitions of social groups continued. By the mid-nineteenth century only Norway had abolished aristocratic titles by law; elsewhere, governments not only tolerated but defended them in law. In many places the position of artisans was still defined by law. Great importance was still placed on birth, regardless of a person's earnings. Not only aristocrats but traditional merchants, professional people and artisans tried to shun newcomers who might earn as much as they but who could not claim the proper family origins. Newcomers themselves adopted the same criteria, inventing a family tree and excluding the latest arrivals. The marks of a status society would persist well into the twentieth century.

But in a capitalist society, money could not be denied. Aristocrats saw their distinctive style of life increasingly imitated by rich businessmen or, perhaps even worse, attacked as immoral. Reforms in voting systems, wherever they were introduced, recognized the new social structure, with the right to vote now being based on property not birth. Moreover, it was no longer possible, at least in the cities, to identify a man's precise station by the clothes he wore. Aristocrats gradually adopted long trousers and abandoned their wigs. Artisans, particularly where guilds had been abolished, laid aside the distinctive costumes of their craft. New earnings and cheaper cotton clothing allowed many workers to imitate middle-class styles in their Sunday dress.

The new society was by no means homogeneous. The divisions among classes were great because of the vast differences in earnings and property ownership. In the cities, social groups for the first time began to separate by place of residence, as the wealthy now moved away from the poor. But the substitution of a class structure for the previous status grouping involved not only new criteria to measure social divisions but criteria that were qualitatively different. The old signs of social position were rather rigid. Birth was the key, and birth usually determined the type of economic activity one could engage in, even the type of costume one could wear. Class criteria were more flexible. New wealth could be acquired, and with it new social position. Social mobility, the passage from one social level to another, was not new, but it inevitably increased as classes emerged.

By 1848, social classes as we know them today had emerged. Aristocracy and artisanry remained distinct, partly on the basis of wealth and occupation and partly through traditional status. The peasantry had some overall unity but this class tended more and more to be divided between owners and workers. In the cities, the industrial working class was the newest and most rapidly growing group, while the middle class was becoming increasingly well defined.

THE MIDDLE CLASS

What did a social class mean? Could it be defined simply by level of wealth and type of job? What internal unity did it have by the mid-nineteenth century? Because social classes were now becoming so important, we must try to understand their complexity.

A social class was a group that shared a common range of wealth and type of occupation, was recognized as distinctive by other elements of society, and shared some common values and behavior patterns, even if its members did not explicitly acknowledge class unity. At this point, none of the social classes was united by common organizations. Membership in a social class did not dictate precise behavior patterns. The farther one gets from values close to day-to-day activities, above all from economic activities, the more class unity tends to dissipate. Members of a given class could differ in culture, particularly in politics; in the middle class, the most important of the new social classes, they might even oppose each other.

The middle class was nontitled and its richest members—big bankers and manufacturers—were still less wealthy than the leading aristocrats; this defines its upper limit. At the bottom, most urban shopkeepers owned property and lived in apartments at least four times as valuable as those of the highest-paid journeymen and workers. Although the lines on both ends were fuzzy in detail and not always easy to define, it is possible to identify the middle class and to see its growing strength in western Europe. In the expanding cities this class constituted at least 20 percent of the population; it was no small elite.

The middle class was the sponsor and leading beneficiary of the spreading commerce and industry. Because of its economic success, it was able to exert a profound influence on politics and culture. Members of the middle class led all the political revolutions of the period, gained power in all the new regimes that were established, and set the tone of formal culture. In music, its wealth and numbers allowed the creation of the first professional symphony orchestras. The press and theaters catered to a middle-class audience.

The culture sought by the middle class was a culture that was respectable, moral and suitable for the family. Sentimental novels with happy endings and virtue triumphant, theaters with comfortable seats, furnishings that were useful, solid, and not too imaginative (like those of the Biedermeier style in Germany)—these were among the products of the growing cultural dominance of the middle class. Even more broadly the middle class began to shape, or try to shape, the values of society generally, railing against idle aristocrats and lazy workers. Its preaching of hard work, saving, family unity, and the importance of material progress influenced many people beyond the class itself.

This all sounds familiar and is vitally important—but it is too simple. Because the term middle class is so widely used (everyone knows something about it), the class is more often stereotyped than studied. Three types of differences within the middle class must be briefly suggested, for otherwise the curious, often contradictory role the class played in its growing ascendancy cannot be understood.

The middle class differed from area to area. Germany's middle class, generally unconcerned with politics, gave little basis for a strong liberal movement; France's timid, individualistic middle class shunned rapid economic modernization. Thus many characteristics of modern nations derived in part from peculiarities of the national middle class.

The middle class in any country was composed of at least two distinct occupational groups, whose interests could be quite different. Professional people—lawyers, doctors, teachers and the like—generally owned property, but their rising status was based on education, not financial capital. More than businessmen, they were interested in ideas and in politics. They could of course represent the interests of businessmen, especially in politics, and any claim that there was a broad middle-class political approach derives from this kind of representation. But businessmen could easily ignore or even resent the theorizing propensities of professional people, who in turn could easily neglect or dislike the mercenary interests of businessmen.

It is most important to note that during the first half of the nineteenth century the middle class throughout western and central Europe was divided between old and new elements. In talking of the rise of the middle class and its association with economic and political change, we naturally think of dynamic, forward-looking men who were willing to innovate, who parlayed personal advancement in business and the professions into an insistence that society in general be remade in a middle-class image. Such men existed, but they were undoubtedly a minority of the people in the middle layers of European society. Most property owners resented change. Far more manufacturers persisted in employing cottage workers than in setting up factories. Even newcomers to the urban middle class, such as many of the shopkeepers, often thought in traditional terms about their own goals and the way society should be constituted. Hence many members of the middle class were filled with anxiety in these years of rapid change. They feared social mobility and complained about the upstarts from the lower classes who imitated their style of dress. They also feared being crushed by the businessmen who had adopted new methods and motives; indeed resentment of "big business" was born with industrialization itself. A feeling that somehow modern life was going astray and that immorality was spreading reflected their general uneasiness. As a whole the middle class cannot be linked with a progressive or capitalistic spirit. Many of its members were repelled by the very developments that marked the growing ascendancy of the dynamic elements of the class.

Did a middle class exist at all, save as a group that can be statistically defined in terms of range of income? To the extent that its members shared vital personal values about the sanctity of property and the family and, further, that it was conscious of being separate from the aristocracy and the lower classes and superior at least to the latter—in these important areas the middle class was real. The marked differences within the class, however, not only point up the complexity of the new class structure but reveal how some of the greatest tensions in the new society were occurring within the middle class. Well into the twentieth century the middle class would oscillate between competition with other classes and bitter if not entirely explicit internal warfare.

CONCLUSION: SOCIETY AND CULTURE

A student of European history cannot expect to find ready coherence in the vastly dynamic period between 1815 and 1848, for the social and intellectual trends both complemented and contradicted each other.

Romanticism appealed to many of the new elements of society, particularly within the middle classes. Sentimentality pervaded the most popular stories and novels of the period, appealing to the newly literate who were joining the "reading public" for the first time, notably the wives of business-men and shopkeepers. The more formal Romantic styles served the middle class in its attack on aristocratic prestige. Because aristocrats tended to prefer and defend classical taste, new middle-class patrons of art or music were inclined to favor Romantic forms. The Romantic interest in novelty and in individual forcefulness corresponded in many ways to the motives of the men who were rising within the middle class.

Yet the basis of society was becoming increasingly materialistic. Al-though most people had always, of necessity, devoted most of their attention to coping with material problems, the spread of capitalism meant that a greater number of them were concerned with material advancement, not simply with preserving the status quo. And whether motives changed yet or not, most men had to think in new ways about assuring their livelihood. The extension of material criteria as the basis of social structure was a function of these changes. Romanticism, on the other hand, scorned the material. It was not born in protest against economic and social change but it easily led to such protest. Romantics could find little appeal in the motives of capital-ism or the ugliness and squalor of new industry. They too normally defied the status quo, but they took a different direction. Here was yet another conflict that arose with the new society—a conflict that has yet to be re-solved.

3 FORCES OF REVOLUTION

Because of the unsettled state of European society and culture during the first half of the nineteenth century, challenges to the conservative political order were inevitable. These grew increasingly intense in western and central Europe, culminating in the final wave of revolutions in 1848. Yet almost everywhere the challenges failed. While the proponents for change were divided by ideology and by social position, the conservatives enjoyed not only the control of the state's repressive force but also the implicit support of many segments of the population.

The intellectual bases of conservatism were rather quickly eroded, particularly outside of Germany. The new generation of Romantics who began writing after 1825 largely rejected conservative political theory, while some earlier Romantic writers abandoned their conservatism. The area of political doctrine, therefore, was wide open to attacks on the status quo. Advocates of reform and protest also proved most adept at making use of the newspapers, where they had freedom to do so, whereas conservative and religious journalism developed haltingly.

Even the religious revival, which had been an important part of Romanticism in the first decade after Napoleon, showed some signs of slackening. In France particularly, missions that had been established to arouse religious piety in the countryside and had proved a great success in the early 1820s, declined by the end of the decade; despite all the government's support for the Church, and in some cases because of it, the number of Easter communions fell by two-thirds between 1820 and 1829. In England the great upsurge of Methodism, which had been aroused by John Wesley and his followers, was coming to an end, while in Italy and Spain many poor people were beginning to turn against the Church, though not necessarily against religion, because of its association with the wealthy.

Hence some of the gains the conservatives could claim after 1815 proved transitory. But intellectuals by themselves had only limited power, and if religion was not gaining it retained much of its traditional hold, particularly among the vast rural population; this was one of the surest guarantees of the conservative order. The churches received new or renewed support from the aristocracy and from the many businessmen who came from pious families. Societies arose, whose purpose was to spread the Bible and religious pamphlets, and church-building increased at an unprecedented rate. In countries like Britain the nineteenth century can be rated a great age for religion in terms of the financial support given to the churches and their influence in politics and education.

It is true that much of the new religious enthusiasm was confined to the upper classes and part of it was self-consciously defensive, an effort to spread religion to quell the lower classes. Not only conservative aristocrats but industrialists as well realized that a firm belief in heavenly rewards could distract from suffering on this earth, and most of the schools set up for the lower classes stressed piety accordingly. These efforts won some converts but the sheer persistence of traditional faith was even more significant. In France, despite the fact that institutional religion had been interrupted for 25 years and religious practice had become increasingly lax, most people retained some Christian belief and some loyalty to the Church. In central and eastern Europe the influence of religion was scarcely shaken at all. Some peasants in Prussia and especially in Russia resented their churches' attachment to the landlords, but they expressed their grievance by seeking a purer, more traditional religious practice. By mid-nineteenth century possibly one-fifth of the Russian peasantry had turned to the Old Believers, a sect that rejected the changes introduced in the Russian Church from Peter the Great onward. This was a sign of discontent, but at least for the time being it turned peasants away from violent protest, for the Old Believers pinned their hopes on a life after death. Religious faith confirmed and supported the traditional resignation of most people in Europe.

SOCIAL BASES OF CONSERVATISM

The social structure, for all its changes, also helped maintain conservative regimes in many ways. There are three points to be considered here. First, aristocracies everywhere retained important powers and resisted challenges to their preeminence. Second, many common people were as yet untouched by social changes sufficient to arouse them to protest. And, finally, some of the new elements of society quickly found reasons for supporting the established order.

We can see in retrospect that the power of the aristocracy was declining. From Prussia west the class had lost important legal privileges. The spread of commercial agriculture put most aristocrats at a disadvantage, for they could not adapt to it quickly. Many sank deeper and deeper into debt and had to sell their lands outright. But the aristocracy tenaciously resisted any inroads into its power and its decline was very slow. Some aristocrats gained new wealth by modernizing their agricultural methods, while others pressed their peasants harder than ever, either their serfs where the manorial system was still intact, or their sharecroppers or wage laborers where it had been modified or destroyed. Supplementing their economic power, aristocrats still dominated local government in most rural areas and gained new positions in the central government. They were, finally, adept at winning the support of some members of the rising middle classes. Businessmen who bought landed estates and middle-class bureaucrats or army officers who worked alongside aristocrats quickly adopted opinions that were indistinguishable from those of the aristocracy. The aristocracy was undeniably under new attack, but it had powerful weapons for its own defense.

Many peasants and artisans—still the vast majority of the population everywhere—had not yet been shaken from their traditional ways or, if they were, had no clear idea of what they could now do. Capitalism was spreading in town and countryside, population pressure was intense, and industrialization was underway. But many peasants could still rely on most of their traditional methods of work and took comfort from a village structure that continued to function as a political and recreational unit. This was one reason that German peasants remained calm throughout the period and stirred only modestly in 1848. Enough French peasants owned land, the panacea for all ills in the peasants' eyes, that rural disturbances were insignificant even in most years of revolution, save for a few regions. Many artisans, for their part, clung to their customary skills and to what remained of their guilds. In France, where there were no longer any guilds, some craftsmen joined groups that maintained elaborate secret rituals and provided facilities for young men to wander over the country from job to job; these groups fought among themselves but they threatened the established order not at all. And this leads to another point. Many people who were damaged by the spread of capitalism—from peasants to traditional elements of the middle class—could see no remedy in sight. In particular, they lacked political consciousness, a sense that protest against the state and for political rights might benefit them. Political consciousness was itself new for most people and it often had no appeal for men who looked to tradition above all.

The groups that benefited from economic change, and they existed in most social classes, were rarely explicitly conservative but seldom saw much reason to challenge the existing order. Peasants who were buying more land and converting to market agriculture were a stabilizing force from this time onward. In France and Germany, factory workers whose standards of living were among the highest in the lower classes were usually calm; no significant number of them played a role in revolution. Most advancing businessmen, finally, concentrated on their businesses. Some had no interest in politics, others gained a large enough role at least in local government to content them, and very few were willing to risk disorder that might threaten their own property. It might be logical to assume that unrest was caused by businessmen whose political rights and social position lagged behind their growing wealth, but this has rarely happened in European history. Only in England, in this period, did many businessmen strive for political power directly, and their efforts were brief and, in some ways, without much effect.

Although the currents of social change persisted, only a minority of the European population were willing and able to challenge conservative regimes. In eastern and southern Europe, where economic changes were slight, this minority was too small to cause much trouble after the brief revolutionary flurry of the 1820s. In western and central Europe the ranks of the discontented were large and growing larger. It is well known that only a minority is needed to start and even win a revolution. Still, as we turn to the forces of disorder, the existence of important positive support for conservative politics and even more widespread apathy must not be forgotten.

BASES OF PROTEST

In several countries, particularly in France and Italy, small numbers of dedicated revolutionaries began to emerge in the late 1820s and early 1830s. These men were different from mere conspirators or from dabblers in plots like the Decembrists in Russia. They believed that revolution was the highest good, an absolute necessity, and they devoted their lives to bringing it about. They began also to develop new types of revolutionary organization. Filippo Buonarroti, called the first professional revolutionary, tried to work through the *Carbonari*, but the large, highly ritualistic societies increasingly lost favor. In Italy Giuseppe Mazzini formed the Young Italy movement specifically to work for national unification; he stressed the need for small numbers of dedicated nationalists who would be capable of direct paramilitary action.

In France Auguste Blanqui began a 40-year career as an advocate of revolution almost for its own sake. While his ultimate goals were fuzzy, his contributions to revolutionary organization were considerable. His organizations were small and secret, designed for direct action.

Ironically, however, the dedicated revolutionaries rarely had much to do with starting revolts or even maintaining them. Blanqui tried to launch a number of uprisings without success, while Mazzini attempted a comic-opera invasion of Savoy. Most revolutionaries were either in jail or in exile much of the time and they were unable to recruit widely. They symbolized the extreme of discontent, and contributed to the development of revolutionary organization in the later nineteenth century. In their own lifetime, revolutions were still largely unplanned, partly spontaneous mixtures of accidental provocations and diverse grievances. The actual leaders of most revolutions normally took advantage of situations that they themselves had not created and often feared.

The force of numbers for revolutions and other protests was provided for the most part by those whose economic position was being damaged or whose values were threatened by the spread of capitalism. Artisans were the key revolutionary class everywhere. They had some education and a certain tradition of organization. Where their guilds had been abolished many artisans formed societies to provide insurance for sickness and burial and, to a lesser extent, organized early trade unions. Few of these groups were initially designed for protest, but they could be turned to such ends. At the same time, many journeymen possessed little or no property and they were willing, on occasion, to risk violence. They had obvious grievances. They resented the legal prohibition of guilds or other associations and being treated as simple wage earners. They feared outright displacement not only by machines but by the hordes of people who flocked to the cities seeking jobs. Long periods of unemployment and frequent recessions, though by no means new, caused great hardship. However above all it was the long-term threat of the erosion of the traditional way of life that spurred the artisans. If artisans differed from the propertied classes in their willingness to take violent action, they differed from the very poor in their ability to organize and to formulate goals. As such, they were an ideal revolutionary group. Peasants who feared population pressure and commercial agriculture and rural manufacturing workers who faced machine competition directly also participated in disorder, though less frequently than urban artisans.

The great strength of these lower-class groups, aside from sheer numbers, was their consciousness of a past, however idealized, by which they could judge the present. They generally thought in terms of a precommercial, premachine age. In some cases they had a political ideology that was forward-looking but they did not have to have a political ideology at all. The great wave of revolutions that ended in 1848 was in a real sense a final protest of precapitalist Europe. It failed to head off the advance of capitalism and industry and its failure was no doubt inevitable.

The grievances of artisans and others were more commonly expressed in riots and strikes than in outright revolution, though revolutions in turn were partly composed of such disorders. Three kinds of popular protest can be distinguished, but in general none was explicitly political and none depended on very formal leadership. Together, they left few countries in western and central Europe free from an undercurrent of unrest even aside from revolution.

The most common form of disorder was the bread riot, the protest

Ned Ludd: The mythical leader of the machine breakers, disguised as a woman, incites his followers.

against a shortage of food and high prices. Peasants, factory workers, and artisans participated in these riots, which were directed against bakers, merchants, employers, tax collectors—anyone who seemed to be responsible for hardship. Though usually small and local, the riots could turn quite violent. They were most widespread in recession years, such as the late 1820s or the late 1840s, but local shortages occurred at other times and provoked isolated riots.

Another, less frequent type of protest took place when artisans and rural manufacturing workers struck for the return of small shops or against the introduction of new machines. More important were recurrent efforts to destroy machines directly, such as the Luddite riots that broke out in Britain between 1811 and 1816. Claiming inspiration from a mythical leader, Ned Ludd, artisans and rural textile producers smashed machinery in protest against low wages and unemployment. Agricultural workers in southern England attacked machines in 1830, this time invoking a Captain Swing. French artisans engaged in sporadic Luddism, and rural Silesian weavers rose against machines in 1844.

In this period some urban artisans, construction and factory workers, coal miners, and others began to use the strike to demand better material conditions. Most strikes—and they were rare outside of Britain, in part because they were illegal—occurred in recessions and involved the same motives of desperation as the bread riots, with which they were sometimes associated. A few durable craft unions were formed and some were even able to bargain directly with employers. This approach was not typical before 1848 because it required workers to think of themselves as workers and to seek positive goals within the new commercial system, rather than striving to recover what once had been.

Popular disorders occurred in all European countries, particularly in cities where population was expanding. Britain, however, was a special case, because of its unique social and economic structure. Popular unrest was more common in Britain, its forms and participants more diverse. The outbreak of Luddism and many strikes against economic recession between 1815 and 1820 led to the formation of a large number of trade unions, among miners and cotton spinners as well as artisans. A law in 1824 permitting trade unions—revised the next year to outlaw strikes—encouraged this development, but the fundamental cause was the growing hardship of life in the British cities. The early union movement, which led to many strikes, culminated in an effort to form national unions. Under the influence of the socialist Robert Owen, a Grand National Consolidated Trades Union was set up in the early 1830s, which aimed to establish cooperative production units and bypass capitalism altogether. Here, clearly, the artisans' resistance to capitalism was expressed, but on a scale no other country could match. Added to the union effort, which collapsed in 1835, was a variety of rural unrest and political protest involving the lower classes. Small wonder that continental as well as British conservatives feared the turbulent society that industrialization could create.

None of the three most common forms of lower-class protest, even in Britain, involved political demands. Some of the most elaborate visions of a just society ignored the government altogether. The followers of Robert Owen had little use for politics, while the more articulate Luddites had dreamed of a machineless, egalitarian utopia with no government at all. In sum, popular grievance, though it normally ignored the state, always worried governments and so had political repercussions.

POLITICAL CONSCIOUSNESS

Revolutions, in a formal political sense, challenge the existing governmental structure and envisage taking over the state, either to use it or to abolish it. The revolutions between 1830 and 1848 occurred because some elements of the lower classes were becoming politicized and because politically conscious members of the middle class sometimes used lower-class protest whether it was political or not.

Political Demands

A growing belief in political rights, combined with a desire to use the state to win economic reforms, was one of the leading developments of the nineteenth century, but it did not occur rapidly. The lower classes traditionally looked to small, political units within their proximity, such as the village, and only gradually did they turn their attention to the larger, more abstract and remote unit called the state. Before political parties emerged and actively sought mass support, only a few agitators went to the people to tell them to try to use the political process. In his speeches and pamphlets William Cobbett in England, though not a democrat, reached small towns and villages to urge the importance of political reform and political petitions even for the countryside. A few republicans in France sought some popular support. But far more reformers assumed that the people had a political sense instead of trying actively to create one.

The politicization that did occur was confined to the cities and to groups that were literate. Again, among the lower classes, artisans led the way, particularly in the larger cities of western Europe. Parisian craftsmen in the revolution of 1830 spoke clearly of the importance of political liberties. The next year weavers in Lyons rioted solely for a raise in pay and a minimum wage scale. But after the outburst was put down, political agitators began to win converts, so that renewed unrest in 1833 included demands for a republic. In other words, the earlier economic demands of the weavers had turned into political ones.

Politicization went still further in England. Many lower-class elements supported suffrage reform after 1815, attending meetings such as the one that ended in the Peterloo massacre. Disappointed by the 1832 Reform Bill that denied votes to the lower classes, a group of London artisans began the Chartist movement, which advocated universal suffrage. The Chartists assumed that democracy and a reform of parliament would bring vast improvements in the education and the economic condition of the common people. The movement reached its peak in 1842, when the Chartists obtained over three million signatures on petitions for universal suffrage. It is doubtful, however, that all the signatories were actively interested in gaining political rights. Many rural manufacturing workers saw Chartism as a protest against factory industry, while many factory workers were angered by economic recession. Hence when the Chartists' final effort failed, in 1848, there was no widespread renewal of political agitation for two decades.

The very fact that political consciousness spread most widely in Britain shows its ambiguous relationship to outright revolution. There was no revolution in Britain, despite the fact that the British lower classes were the most aggrieved and best organized of any in Europe. It is idle to pretend, at this point, that the British lower classes were imbued with the characteristic British sense of compromise and muddling through, though it is true many of their leaders, particularly in the Chartist movement, were mild men who discouraged revolution. Britain avoided a revolution because the British middle class did not need one. Moreover, the lower class was not sufficiently experienced in politics to provide the political ingredient that a revolution requires. On the continent, revolutions depended on lower-class participation, but it was invariably the middle class the provided the key political element.

Most of the formal isms of the period had little meaning for the lower classes, both because of their position and their general lack of political awareness. There was no sign, before 1848, of any significant lower-class interest in nationalism. Nationalist revolutionaries tried in vain to arouse the Polish peasants in 1830 and the Irish in 1848. Outside of Britain there was little interest in socialism. Socialist agitators in France were ignored by the workers; only in Paris were some artisans drawn at least to socialist slogans. A few German journeymen in exile formed socialist groups in the 1840s, but they were out of touch with most of their class. Both socialism and nationalism were to gain mass support, but only later and in different circumstances. Nor were many in the lower classes drawn to liberalism, except briefly when liberals seemed to promise revolutionary change, as was the case in the first half of 1848, and in this case the antipathy of the masses proved more durable.

The only ism that was capable of attracting lower-class interest was radicalism. When artisans turned to politics at all, they wanted a democracy and, often, a republic, which alone would overturn the existing political order to their benefit. With this important exception, the interests of revolutionary ideologists and those of the masses remained largely distinct. Since revolutions require an ideological element, this was yet another reason that aggrieved segments of the lower classes could not on their own foment a revolution. It was a reason also that most revolutions failed, for lower-class participants were quick to see that most of the formal leaders of revolution would soon betray their interests.

THE MIDDLE CLASS AND REVOLUTION

The middle class, on the other hand, wanted political rights and many of its members were drawn to one or another of the isms. Even socialism received much of its formal support from the middle class; socialist propagandists in France who toured factory centers were welcomed by some manufacturers even as they were rebuffed by the workers. But this support was too limited to make socialism any more than an embryonic movement before 1848. Liberalism (which in some cases shaded into radicalism) and nationalism attracted significant numbers, drawing on both the "new" segment of the middle class—those who sought a greater voice and a political structure attuned to a capitalist economy—and the more traditionalist segment that sought to defend its position by new political means. Much of the middle class, however, was only sporadically interested in politics; although politicization was incomplete, it was sufficient for grievance to become revolution.

Professional people, including government bureaucrats, were most likely to be wholehearted converts to liberalism and/or nationalism. Their education gave them a taste for formal ideas and also experience with the repressive hand of the state in the schools and universities. Through student groups and then professional societies they had a chance to discuss politics with some regularity. New regimes, and particularly an active parliament, would obviously provide new importance for the professionals. With the growth and specialization of bureaucracies, together with the new work that rising commercial wealth gave to lawyers and doctors, professional people were rapidly advancing in status and undoubtedly sought a commensurate political position. At the same time increasing university enrollments may have made some professionals fearful for their future. By the 1840s there was a tendency to overproduce educated people, and those forced into employment beneath their expectations were greatly aggrieved. Not surprisingly, political unrest among professionals mixed idealism and immediate self-interest. Businessmen, though rarely active fomenters of political agitation, were also often drawn to liberalism and countenanced, if they did not encourage, actual revolutions. Rarely committed to a thoroughgoing economic liberalism, these businessmen certainly stood to gain from an increase in internal free trade and in the abolition of manorial and guild restrictions on the mobility of labor. They too wanted political representation for themselves and a reduction of aristocratic power, particularly when existing regimes seemed to favor agriculture over industry and commerce.

For the middle class, nationalism could easily be linked with liberalism, particularly since national unifications could facilitate trade. German businessmen learned of the importance of a nation from the benefits they gained in the *Zollverein;* Italian economic journals vigorously urged unification as the basis of economic modernization. Bureaucrats, too, realized that a strong and unified nation would enhance their own importance.

But nationalism meant more than this. The middle class could not accept justifications for the state that relied on traditional legitimacy and religion alone. Yet they could not accept popular sovereignty, which they interpreted as the rule of the mob. The state as representative of the nation was justified in a new way but did not have to be democratic. National loyalty was also an alternative to aristocratic cosmopolitanism. Finally and more personally, certain growing elements in the middle class sought some means of identifying themselves and proving their worth in terms other than sheer self-interest. For all the presumed brashness of the new middle class, there was a profound need for self-justification. Hence businessmen delighted in showing how their new factories made the nation strong, while bureaucrats too felt that the work they were doing was in the national interest. Nationalism came to be a genuine loyalty with the rising middle class. In established countries it was not a revolutionary force, but elsewhere it was inevitably so.

The middle class had sufficient opportunity to keep new political ideas under discussion and to seize direction of most revolutionary unrest. In France and England newspapers not only disseminated ideas but provided journalists who actually led the agitation. In Italy the economic journals helped to keep liberal nationalism alive when the outright revolutionaries were arrested or expelled. The Vienna Chamber of Commerce discussed modest reforms before 1848 and was helpful in advising the revolutionary government once it had been installed. Unlike the lower classes outside of Britain, the middle class had some room to maneuver, and even in central Europe it could circulate ideas. Leading businessmen and bureaucrats were close to governments despite being denied formal political rights. Their contact with the state and their experience with business and professional organizations enabled them to form governing bodies of their own when the existing state was attacked.

Yet in many ways the middle class was ill-prepared for revolution, aside from its political divisions and the split between progressive and traditionalist elements. The class shunned violence, for in disorder it could lose property and position. Only a handful of agitators and students went into the streets in the revolutionary outbursts, yet the streets were where revolutions were made. At the least, the middle class needed allies for a revolution; more often than not it quickly discovered that it did not care for revolution at all.

1830: THE RENEWAL OF REVOLUTIONARY AGITATION

Revolution has been one of France's most successful exports. The uprising that began in Paris in July 1830, reverberated in Belgium, Italy, and Poland and encouraged significant agitation in Britain and Germany.

The July Revolution:
A barricade in Paris
in 1830.

The year 1830 was preceded everywhere by two years of bad harvests and a manufacturing recession; as a result, the poor were becoming increasingly restive. In France the growing tension between liberal elements and the conservative regime of Charles X came to a head at the same time.

The Outbreak in France

Despite the very limited suffrage in France, liberal deputies were being returned to parliament in increasing numbers after 1825, while the liberal press grew more and more active. The liberals resented the government's favors to Church and aristocracy. Charles experimented with a moderate government in 1828, offering, as one of his concessions, to prohibit Jesuits and other nonauthorized religious orders from teaching. But the liberals, now a majority in parliament, were not satisfied and the king, who had never been wholeheartedly conciliatory, was now determined to defy parliament.

In 1829 Charles appointed the ultra-conservative Prince de Polignac as his chief minister, knowing that it was impossible to obtain parliamentary support for such a ministry. Only a handful of extreme conservatives supported the king in his belief that he had the sole right to govern and, in a crisis, could rally the country behind him. The liberals grew more angry and excited. When the king seemed to threaten parliament, parliament replied by insisting that the king govern in accordance with its majority. Charles dissolved parliament, but in the elections of July 1830 the liberals gained an even greater majority than before—despite the news that France had captured Algiers, which Charles had hoped would increase his popularity. The government then decided on a *coup d'état* and issued five ordinances on July 25 that dissolved the new parliament, reduced the electorate from 100,000 to 25,000 voters, and forbade any publication without government authorization. The king took no military measures to forestall possible trouble. Polignac assured him that the nation cared nothing for politics and told him of repeated visions of the Virgin Mary who always promised success.

Liberals in Paris moved quickly to protest. The issues could not have been better drawn for liberal resistance: freedom of the press and a strong parliament responsible at least to an upper-class electorate were two goals that liberals could always agree upon, whatever their differences on other matters. Most French liberals were characteristically moderate, but they did want a genuine constitutional regime in which the king could not act according to whim. The liberals were led at this point by Parisian journalists, who were of course directly threatened by the government's new measures against the press, but they had wide backing among intellectuals and the most prominent bankers of Paris.

The July Revolution of 1830 was the most purely liberal rising in European history, but the liberals had no intention of starting it; they merely set the stage for a revolution and then took it over. Liberal newspapers proclaimed resistance, hoping simply to force Charles to rescind his ordinances. Liberal placards, plus the closing of newspapers and shops, brought many artisans into the streets on July 27. With the help of some republican students, barricades were erected. Then clumsy intervention by government troops turned milling people into a revolutionary crowd, and by July 29 Paris was in their hands. The republicans had hoped to abolish the monarchy and make the aging Marquis de Lafayette president, but once again the liberal deputies and journalists took over. Believing in monarchy as a vital defense against democracy, they persuaded the Duke of Orléans, Louis Philippe, to become king. The duke in turn talked to Lafayette, who was a fine symbol as a hero of the American Revolution but not too perceptive, speaking vaguely of his own republicanism. Taken in by his praises Lafayette embraced the duke before a large crowd. Parliament then revised the charter slightly and proclaimed Louis Philippe "King of the French people," which sounded a bit more democratic than "King of France." The revolution was over.

The July Monarchy

In its results, the revolution was hardly revolutionary. Under the modified charter there was a new king but the monarchy still remained, only it was slightly relabeled. Catholicism was now called the religion of the majority of Frenchmen instead of the religion of state. Suffrage was expanded to about 250,000 people. These changes, plus the new king's promise to rule according to the charter, were sufficient to provide for the possibility of a genuine if very moderate liberal regime, the first ever in Europe. It is as such that the July Monarchy can be assessed to find out what liberalism-in-practice really meant. But it should not spoil the otherwise dull story of this regime to note that its principal innovation turned out to be a new dynasty only slightly less unrealistic than the last.

On the other hand, the people who were actually in the streets—the workers and the students—had wanted more, but they were confused about their political goals and were badly led. The revolution was certainly accidental in the sense that Charles could have suppressed it if he had tried, instead of fleeing to England as soon as he spotted the tricolor flag flying from Notre Dame. But the discontent of the artisans was real. Religious buildings and even priests themselves were attacked by crowds for over a year, while strikes and riots persisted in various parts of France until 1834. An undercurrent of revolutionary if vague aspirations, compounded by a regime that only briefly pretended to be revolutionary, would prove an explosive combination.

AGITATION OUTSIDE FRANCE

However historians dissect their real nature, at the time the July Days sounded like a revolution and were hailed by liberals throughout Europe. A number of revolts broke out in Italy in 1830 and 1831, aided by French-based Italian exiles. The revolt in the Papal States was particularly severe, but the new French government refused to intervene. Austria was gradually able to put down the risings. The policies of the Italian governments remained unchanged and a new pope, Gregory XVI, condemned liberalism and revolutions more vigorously than ever before. Outbreaks in Switzerland and Germany met with greater success. Swiss liberals won reforms in a number of cantons. In Germany liberal sentiment had been building up for several years, most notably in the revived *Burschenschaften.* Disturbances erupted when the news from Paris spread and a number of smaller German states were forced to grant constitutions. Twenty-five thousand people from all over Germany met at Hambach in 1832 to denounce the principles of the Holy Alliance.

The Belgian Revolution

More serious revolutions occurred in Belgium, Poland, and the Iberian peninsula. Since 1815 Belgium had been ruled by William I of Holland, who managed to offend Belgian liberals though he actively and successfully encouraged Belgian manufacturing. Belgians were not given equal representation in the parliament; they resented the predominance of the Dutch in the government, as well as the fact that the Dutch language gained sole recognition for official use. These grievances, it should be noted, were more nationalistic in nature than specifically liberal. In addition, Belgian Catholics were growing restive under Dutch Protestant rule, particularly when the king tried to regulate the training of priests. This religious unrest reflected a widespread current of liberal Catholicism, which was unique in Europe at the time. In August 1830, a student-led riot broke out in Brussels. As in France, the leading liberals hoped mainly for concessions from the king, but once again the riots could not be contained and compromise proved impossible. Artisans in Brussels, who joined forces with the students, successfully beat off Dutch troops in September; by November Belgian territory was practically free from Dutch control.

As a result of this revolution—the most successful in Europe in the nineteenth century—Belgium not only achieved national independence but enacted the most liberal constitution in all of Europe. Property qualifications for voting were set low; freedom of press, assembly, education, and religion was guaranteed; a powerful parliament was established to balance the new Belgian monarchy. For a time the conservative European powers threatened intervention against Belgium, but neither Britain nor France would support such a move. Aided by Britain, the Belgians chose Leopold of Saxe-Coburg, a minor German princeling, to be their new king.

The Polish Revolution

Poland also experienced revolution but it was of a different type from Belgium's and proved to be abortive. Here the aristocracy, motivated almost solely by nationalist reasons, led the revolt against Russian rule. Among the Polish intellectuals were liberals, even radicals, whose secret societies helped to trigger the 1830 revolt. But these intellectuals had little power; moreover, there was no real middle class and only a small urban artisanry. The peasants, who properly realized that their rebellious landlords intended no substantial manorial reforms, stayed out of the quarrel. So the Polish army, led by aristocrats, stood alone against the Russians and, partly because of inept leadership, the revolt was brutally crushed.

Agitation in Spain and Portugal

Disorders in Spain and Portugal were tied to dynastic confusion, not to nationalist issues. Here, as in Poland, native liberalism was weak, owing to the absence of a significant middle class; only a continuing interest among some Spanish army officers kept liberalism alive. Occasionally the urban lower classes rose up, notably in 1835 when many church buildings were attacked in the cities. A new queen of Spain, Isabella II, came to the throne in 1833 and proposed a constitution similar to the French charter. She was opposed by an ultraconservative pretender, Don Carlos, and civil war raged for seven years. By 1840 the dynastic war had abated and Spain emerged as a constitutional monarchy, at least in form. Portugal also established a nominal constitutional monarchy after a period of struggle between rivals for the throne. But since there had been no real revolution in either country, there could now be no real guarantee for parliamentary government.

Agitation and Reform in Britain

Liberal British historians were fond of saying that their country proved its political genius by adopting revolutionary changes peacefully. True, Britain avoided a formal revolution but there was a revolutionary scare. By the late 1820s demands for reform of parliament, led by the Whig party, became increasingly intense. The rapid growth of new urban centers in northern England revealed the absurdity of an electoral system that allowed small towns or even villages—the rotten and pocket boroughs—to send representatives to parliament while centers like Manchester were unrepresented. Reformers demanded a redistricting of seats while radicals called for a wider extension of the suffrage. In the election of 1830, the Tory majority was greatly reduced. As in France, even elements of the established upper classes voted for the liberals. At the same time, the example of the July Revolution, combined with recurrent urban unrest and the Captain Swing rising in the countryside, created an undercurrent of popular discontent, which, though not for the most part overtly political, convinced even some Tories that change was essential. Whigs gained control of the House of Commons in new elections in 1831 and passed a reform bill. When the House of Lords rejected it, riots and demonstrations broke out in various parts of the country. Finally, the Reform Bill became law in June 1832.

The bill redistributed 143 seats in the House of Commons, which removed the most flagrant disparities and granted some representation to the large urban centers. Property qualifications were lowered, increasing the electorate by 50 percent. One out of 30 inhabitants could vote, compared to one out of 200 in France in the July Monarchy. This, then, was the "revolutionary" aspect of the Reform Bill: in broad terms, the bulk of the middle class was given the vote. Yet the implications of the Reform Bill must be treated warily. Quite clearly, the lower-class elements that wanted the vote had been ignored. Furthermore, electoral constituencies still varied greatly in population, a situation that benefited the rural districts. It is evident that the Tory country gentry countenanced or even encouraged the reform, being willing to grant minority representation to the cities where the Whigs would dominate in return for the Tories' continued hold on the countryside. The British "revolution" was indeed fairly peaceful, but like the French it may not have been very revolutionary. Only subsequent acts of government could definitely reveal how much had changed.

THE NEW REGIMES

In those countries where revolutions had failed, governmental policies remained virtually the same over the next two decades. The tsar pretended to grant new constitutional guarantees for the Poles, but in practice Poland was governed by the most ruthless military methods. Universities were closed, thousands were killed or exiled. German rulers, frightened by liberal agitation, punished many of the leaders of the Hambach meeting. The Diet of Frankfurt passed the Six Acts of 1832, which assured that rulers in states that had parliaments could veto any legislative act. When Frederick William IV came to the Prussian throne in 1840, he offered some hints of liberalization in his country by allowing provincial assemblies to send delegates to Berlin, but this in no way resembled the kind of parliament that liberals wanted and it therefore satisfied no one. These were years of great change in Germany: the government participated in forming the *Zollverein* and in building the railroads, but German politics seemed static.

Major Diplomatic Issues

With conservatism unaltered in central and eastern Europe, Europe was divided into two camps. There were some signs that diplomacy would reinforce this division, that Europe would drift into a sort of cold war between east and west, between reactionary and constitutional regimes. The rulers of Austria, Prussia, and Russia signed the Convention of Münchengrätz in 1833, which recognized the right of any sovereign threatened by revolt to call upon these three countries for aid; the convention also defined the treatment of the Poles and measures of repression within the German Confederation for the future. The Holy Alliance seemed renewed, and Metternich rejoiced, writing that "So long as the union of the three monarchs lasts, there will be a chance of safety in the world." Britain and France specifically rejected this pact and warned against interference in Belgium, Switzerland, or Spain.

Despite these rhetorical flourishes, diplomacy had not really changed much. The new regimes in the West were not interested in protecting liberalism beyond their own borders. The leading diplomatic clashes of the 1830s and 1840s occurred between France and Britain over the extension of their influence in Spain and in the Near East, not over the forms of government that existed there. Even these clashes were moderate, however, mainly because the regime of Louis Philippe needed a period of calm in order to build its strength internally and win respectability abroad—above all to gain recognition as a valid dynasty from the dynasts of eastern Europe. This was not a time for a bold French policy—in fact, the government pulled back whenever serious trouble threatened. Louis Philippe sought instead to slake his subjects' thirst for glory by bringing Napoleon's body back to Paris, finishing Napoleon's Arch of Triumph, and even refurbishing Louis XIV's Palace of Versailles.

The diplomatic split in Europe was, then, more superficial than real. What diplomatic activity there was occurred mainly beyond the borders of Europe and had little to do with the regimes at home. France quietly continued her conquest of Algeria, though it had been started by the reactionary regime of Charles X. Britain continued to expand abroad despite the liberals' sincere abhorrence of empire. Liberalism did have some impact on formal policy, however. In 1833, parliament abolished slavery within the colonies as well as most of the preferential systems for colonial trade. Between 1839 and 1854 Canada gained substantial autonomy, as the executive governor appointed by the Crown began to accept policies formulated by a cabinet responsible to an elected legislature. These developments were exceedingly important, but of equal significance was the incompatibility between what liberals said about empire-building and what was actually done. The secretary of state for the colonies summed up a common sentiment in 1846, writing against the acquisition of African land which would be "not merely worthless, but pernicious—the source not of increasing strength, but weakness." Yet the empire grew, as local trading posts expanded their influence in Africa and Asia. The first war between Britain and China began in 1839 to protect British traders, and it ended with Britain's taking over Hong Kong and gaining entry to many Chinese ports for trade. The growing European advantage in armaments and trade continued colonial expansion even when it was unfashionable at home.

Liberal Regimes

Internally, the Western monarchies did change under the new regimes. The gap between East and West, already suggested even under conservative rule, grew greater. Still, questions remain. How new were the new states? How much difference did constitutional change make? Were liberals installed in power, and what did they do that was distinctively liberal?

In the case of Spain these questions are largely academic. Liberal rule during the period of civil war produced just one important step, the seizure of much Church property. This failed to destroy the Church's power, however, and in the long run caused it to draw closer to a conservative state. Furthermore, liberal rule was overturned in 1843. The members of the upper house of parliament were now named by the monarch, the sale of Church property was halted, and clergymen were granted salaries from the state. Spain was a constitutional monarchy in name only.

At the other extreme, liberals remained in power in Belgium. Aside from maintaining its parliamentary structure, Belgian liberalism aimed to balance state and Catholic influence in education and to expand the manufacturing economy. State aid to railroads and encouragement to business continued unabated, and public expenditure per capita increased by 50 percent.

New Regimes in Britain and France

The genuine newness of the regimes in France after 1830 and in Britain after 1832 can be assessed by examining three related areas: changes in governing personnel, new factional splits, and new government policies.

During the 1830s and 1840s, landed aristocrats still predominated in Britain. Parliament assumed a larger role and considered a wider range of subjects, but the type of people within parliament remained about the same. This does not mean that the 1832 reform was hollow or that the same type of people necessarily pursued the same policies. It does reveal the limitations on the reform and the fact that most new voters were not eager to cast aside their traditional social leaders. Elections, furthermore, were not free from intimidation and corruption.

The situation was more complex in France. Many supporters of the Restoration monarchy (called legitimists because they maintained that the expelled Bourbon dynasty alone had proper claims to the throne) retired from government service and the military. New men came in. Although the power of parliament increased, particularly in the 1830s, the ruling class in France, which filled most positions in the bureaucracy and parliament, was still largely landed, partly aristocratic, with a leavening of influence from big bankers and merchants in Paris. This bourgeois monarchy, as it has been called, did not admit most of the middle class to its ranks. Thus in neither Britain nor France was the ruling class decisively altered.

The Revolution of 1830 forced a new split among political factions in France, for the liberals of the Restoration were now in power and they were clearly distinct from the legitimists. This moderate liberal group, now known as Orleanists for their support of the new dynasty, was to remain a permanent element of French politics into the twentieth century. To their left, radicalism became increasingly coherent and specifically republican. In this sense the revolution created new political alignments; within the political process, however, they had little influence, for the legitimists stayed out of politics and most of the radicals lacked a vote. Parliamentary divisions were built around personalities and fluctuated frequently.

The same situation prevailed in the British parliament. The 1832 reform succeeded in creating a wider political spectrum, with Chartist demands for democracy emerging on the left, but the fuzzy structure of British politics in parliament was not clarified. The Whigs ruled between 1832 and 1841. They represented liberal interests for the most part, as opposed to the Tories who defended strong government and the traditional social order. But neither faction was firmly organized. Within parliament the Whigs were unable to enforce discipline and were often defeated on specific issues even when they had a majority. Elections to parliament were locally run without reference to national leaders. Finally, even the ideological split between the Whigs and the Tories was not clear. Sir Robert Peel began a modernization of the Tories that stressed the possibility of reform. Hence, particularly after 1840, the Tories periodically produced proposals for legislation that were essentially liberal.

In sum, the new regimes in France and Britain suggested new political alignments but did not make them firm. Most notably, although the parliament increased in importance in each country, modern political parties did not emerge. For both countries, this was a golden age of factions and political clubs without formal organization or national base.

Policies of the British Government

After the passage of the great Reform Bill, the internal policies of the British government were largely liberal. Government expenditures were cut. Municipal government was reformed through the institution of local elected councils, which, in a broad sense, gave town government to the middle class for the first time. The liberals' greatest success came in the removal of trade restrictions. English liberalism owed a great deal to the Corn Laws, which had first aroused businessmen to political action to combat the obvious discrimination against their interests. Agitation by the Anti-Corn Law League finally bore fruit in 1846, when the laws were repealed. Liberal economics and industry were together triumphant.

Liberalism did not adhere to a neat, absolute formula for the functions of government. This was true even in Britain where in actual operation the government was the most liberal in all of Europe. Precisely on this account, some of the ambiguities of liberalism are readily visible. The government, never as omnipresent in Britain as on the continent, retrenched in certain ways. It ignored the worsening plight of the lower classes and even added to their misery with the harsh Poor Law Reform of 1834 that forced recipients of relief to enter dreary workhouses where they were separated from their families. This was a characteristic liberal measure. Its purpose was to make relief as unattractive as possible, thus saving the taxpayers money and avoiding malingering among the poor—a dual result eminently satisfying to the liberal middle class. When famine hit Ireland after 1846 the government did almost nothing, though perhaps because it was British as much as because it was liberal. All of this fits the nasty stereotype of nineteenth-century liberalism.

On the other hand, paradoxically, the government tentatively assumed some new functions. In 1833 it began very modestly to fund the building of schools and then it embarked more vigorously on a program of prison reform. Both these efforts reflected the liberal interest in improving men's character. At this time too the government refrained from political or religious repression. More confusing perhaps was a new kind of government intervention in the economy. A law regulating the hours and conditions of child labor was passed in 1833, and in 1847 the Ten Hours Act restricted the working hours of women as well as of children. These laws admittedly indicate that liberals did not rule Britain alone; conservatives, hostile to industrialization, also played a role in their passage. But the laws expressed genuine liberal humanitarianism as well. Also in this period town governments in Manchester and other cities, impelled by the liberal middle class, rapidly expanded their functions to include rudimentary sanitation measures and the building of parks.

The Evolution of the July Monarchy

Many of the leaders of the July Monarchy in France longed to follow Britain's footsteps. One of the leading politicians, also a prominent historian, François Guizot, wrote that the triumph of middle-class parliamentary government constituted the final glorious stage of human history. He thought this stage would long endure and, like most historian-prophets he was wrong. The July Monarchy pursued some policies that, by English standards, were undeniably liberal. Guizot sponsored a primary education act, in 1833, that went much further than anything in England; the English lagged in this field less out of a liberal reluctance to use government to educate than because of rivalries among the various Protestant churches for influence. In typical liberal fashion, the French government did little for the lower classes. Yet with the help of some liberals it passed a child labor law in 1841. It did not leave railroad building to private hands, but unlike any other continental government it at least hesitated before committing the state to railroad sponsorship; the main result of this was that France ran badly behind in railroad building until after 1848. The July Monarchy defended religious liberty, yet in France, as in most Catholic countries, liberalism in practice meant hostility to the Church, which liberals felt was too powerful to be left free in the American sense. Hence Church schools were closed, government supporters appointed to bishoprics and some monasteries attacked. The association between liberalism and anti-clericalism, launched in the Great Revolution, was clearly resumed, in part because most churchmen were demonstrably unenthusiastic about the new regime.

The July Monarchy shunned some policies that were gaining ground in Britain, an indication that French (and as it turned out, continental) liberalism was different from the English variety. Tariffs were kept high and there was no serious move to adopt free trade. Nor was there a move to decentralize the government. The Napoleonic administrative structure remained intact.

Finally, the nature of the July Monarchy changed, even in its short 18-year lifetime. Some of its liberal supporters, like Guizot, found that they would rather defend the government than defend liberalism. The king himself was no liberal at all, but a man eager to establish his dynasty while salting away as much money and property for his family as possible in case he failed. Repression against lower-class agitation increased steadily after 1833. In 1835 the press' freedom to criticize the regime was curtailed by threats of heavy fines and imprisonment; subsequently, the government forbade all unauthorized assemblies of more than six people. So much for devotion to the principles on which the Revolution of 1830 had been launched. After 1840, with Guizot as prime minister, the government increasingly controlled parliamentary elections and created a docile body through bribes and the placement of state officials in the parliament. The regime grew more friendly to the Church as well.

In sum, the July Monarchy came more and more to be dominated by the dynastic conservatism of Louis Philippe. It succeeded in winning some liberals to its moderately repressive policies, the first of many conversions of liberals to conservatism. For a short time the regime managed to keep down disorder, in part because of economic expansion and relative prosperity. But it was not too long before the regime also produced the next great wave of European revolutions.

The Great Sea Serpent of 1848: Old-regime monarchs terrified by the wave of revolutions that at first seemed irresistible.

1848: THE LAST YEAR
OF REVOLUTION

In 1848 revolution spread like wildfire across the European continent. From Sicily in the south to Denmark in the north, from France to Hungary, major uprisings occurred. In Britain the Chartists made their final appeal in this year and there were stirrings in Ireland.

What caused the eruptions of 1848? There were particular causes in any given revolt and we must not make the mistake of thinking that all the revolutions were basically the same. Still, two general factors were the underlying causes of discontent almost everywhere. First, a major economic recession began in 1846, the most severe in the nineteenth century. Grain harvests were bad and potato blight ruined the staple on which millions of the poor depended. In the cities food prices doubled or tripled and unemployment mounted. As many businesses failed, businessmen as well as the poor were affected, and it was easy to blame governments for insufficient aid. This economic unrest was compounded by the ideological ferment of the times. The ideas of liberalism and nationalism had spread widely, particularly in the middle class. Britain managed to avoid revolution despite massive suffering because the political system satisfied liberal standards. Russia avoided revolution because dissident ideologies had not widely penetrated; moreover, the economic crisis was not severe since Russian manufacturing was ill-developed and the potato had not been widely introduced. Elsewhere economic collapse and ideological ferment, in combination, paved the way for revolution. Paris, again, was in the forefront.

Revolution in France

Discontent with the government of Louis Philippe mounted steadily in France in the 1840s. Radical ideas spread widely: newspapers preached republicanism and social reform, a number of historians revived memories of the democratic aspects of the Great Revolution, and a new generation of socialist writers attacked the evils of early industrialization. Louis Blanc advocated cooperatively run workshops, established with government assistance; his aim was to replace capitalism with what he called the organization of labor. A movement grew among Catholics against the government monopoly of the schools. Some aristocratic observers claimed that Frenchmen were bored with Louis Philippe's timid foreign policy. The nephew of Napoleon, Louis Napoleon, had tried to arouse enthusiasm for a Bonapartist coup, though without success.

There was, in sum, a welter of political currents hostile to the existing regime. Only in 1847, however, did political opposition develop clear focus. A banquet campaign—dinners followed by rousing speeches—was begun to demand an extension of suffrage and greater power for parliament. Its sponsors combined genuine liberals who were opposed to the whole tenor of the July Monarchy and opportunists who resented being kept out of power by Guizot. The movement was especially popular among professional people. Few of the banqueters really wanted a revolution. They hoped merely to correct the existing system, but they lost control of events.

A banquet was scheduled in Paris for February 22 1848. The previous day the government issued orders forbidding it, but radical students and artisans gathered in the streets anyway and, in an ensuing clash with police, several demonstrators were killed. Riots continued for three days but Louis Philippe offered little resistance. Like his predecessor, he abdicated the throne and fled to England. On February 25 a republic was proclaimed and a new provisional government was installed under the Romantic poet, Alphonse Lamartine. The government was run by political radicals committed to the establishment of a democratic republic; to this end they pressed for a popularly elected assembly to draw up a new constitution. They were determined that the revolution would go no farther than this, which put the government on a collision course with the Parisian artisans who had actually made the revolution. The artisans shouted for what they called "the organization of work"; some doubtless hoped for a socialist order but many more simply insisted that the government set up national workshops, which sounded very progressive but in practice just gave some outdoor relief to the Parisian poor. Louis Blanc was put in charge of a commission to investigate working conditions but with no power to enact reforms. The government sought only to hold out until the new assembly was elected. Parisian radicals, realizing that a popularly elected assembly would be moderate at best, led a number of riots in the spring, though without success.

The new assembly, elected in April, reflected the interests of the small towns and countryside of France, not of Paris, the birthplace of the revolution. The vast majority of deputies could countenance a republic and accept democracy because most Frenchmen could be counted upon to vote conservatively, but they could tolerate no social change. In June the assembly ordered the closing of the National Workshops as a danger to public order. Fifty thousand Parisian artisans tried a last, desperate resistance to this destruction of their vision of what the revolution meant. After three days of fighting in the streets—the bloody June Days—they were crushed. The revolution was now effectively over. In order to prevent further unrest, the assembly went on to establish a strong presidency and the people of France then elected Louis Napoleon Bonaparte, as a symbol of a family that knew how to keep order.

The structure of the Second Republic was vastly different from the July Monarchy. Abolition of the monarchy and the creation of a democracy were two important achievements. But social policies remained unchanged and, in Louis Napoleon, the French had chosen a man who would quickly try to distort the political achievements to his own ends.

Revolution in Central Europe and Italy

The revolution of 1848 was much more important in central Europe, particularly in Germany, than it was in France. From a progressive point of view, there were, quite simply, many more issues to be attacked. Liberals had to seek not a better parliament, but the establishment of a parliament in the first place. They also had to combat manorialism and the guild system. Nationalists pursued their own demands for national unity or independence. Artisans were aroused not only by hunger but by changes in their status, which were newer and therefore more disturbing than those in France. Peasants had to contend with a manorial system or remnants of one. The issues and the potential social composition of the revolutions in central Europe were much more like those in France in 1789 than in 1848. If the revolutionaries had triumphed, political and social structures would have been fundamentally altered. In fact they failed, and so helped solidify a modified old regime.

Revolution broke out in Vienna in March 1848, soon after news of the Paris uprising had arrived. Business and intellectual groups circulated petitions that demanded economic reform, an effective parliament, and an end to censorship, but the government rejected them all. Student demonstrations led to clashes with the army, and artisans joined in. At this point the emperor backed down, dismissed Metternich and summoned a united diet to draw up a new constitution. In April the government abolished serfdom throughout the empire. This was a vital accomplishment of the revolution but it also turned the peasantry, now satisfied, into a conservative force.

Revolution then spread to Hungary and Bohemia. Stirred by the leader of the radical party Louis Kossuth, the Hungarian Diet demanded and won a new constitution that guaranteed civil liberties, abolished serfdom, established a parliament based on wide suffrage, and permitted autonomous Hungarian ministries within the empire. These political reforms were liberal, but the tenor of the Hungarian revolt was basically nationalist. Of the many revolutions in 1848, only in Hungary did the aristocracy take the lead. It adopted the new doctrines of nationalism but its goals were in many ways traditional—the desire for aristocratic, Magyar control. Although the Magyars opposed rule from Vienna, they sought to subject Slavic minorities within Hungary. Even during the revolution this aroused great protest, particularly by Croat nationalists, and weakened the Hungarian cause.

Revolts in Prague and in Italy were also mainly nationalist rebellions against Austrian rule. The Czechs demanded local autonomy, civil liberties and a Czech parliament. Rebellion in Italy centered at first in the Austrian territories, though an earlier uprising in Sicily had won constitutional concessions from the southern Italian monarch. In Milan and Venice, middle-class nationalists concentrated on the expulsion of Austria. They were supported in this effort by volunteers from other areas, while the armies of Piedmont—whose ruler, though no revolutionary, wanted to profit from the situation—also entered the fray. A subsequent insurrection in Rome, led by the nationalists Mazzini and Garibaldi, focused on demands for a democratic political structure and social reform, as well as ultimate national unity; in the uprising the pope was chased from the city.

Because the rebellions within the Hapsburg empire were nationalist first and foremost, they weakened each other rapidly. In Vienna, the moderate, middle-class elements, frightened by the prospect of further lower-class disorder, were quickly satisfied by the government's promise of a constitution, even though the army and other key institutions of the old system remained intact. Nowhere could the various national movements come to each other's aid, with the result that the Hapsburg army was able to pick them off one by one. Repression of agitation in Bohemia, Hungary, and Italy actually pleased many Viennese revolutionaries, whose nationality and language were German. The Czechs were put down in June 1848. The Italian nationalist armies were attacked in July and then finally defeated in October 1849. Venice was subdued by Austrian troops, while the pope was restored in Rome by an army from the new conservative French government. Earlier, in October 1848, the Austrians regained Vienna. Hungary held out longest, but in 1849, aided by Russian troops, they put down the rebels there. The Constitutional Assembly, which the emperor had summoned in 1848, continued its work into the next year, drawing up an admirable document that fulfilled liberal demands. It provided for a parliamentary, liberal monarchy and also granted considerable autonomy to the provinces and towns to give each nationality local self-government—the most generous and sensible approach to the nationalistic problem devised during the nineteenth century. The government, now in full command, ignored this whole effort.

Revolution in Germany

Revolutions in Germany foundered in much the same way as in Austria. There was the usual split between middle and lower classes, and the problem of nationalism, though different here, distracted the revolutionaries from needed internal reforms. Indeed the Germans failed, in a sense, to attempt a revolution at all, in that they did not displace the existing governments or seriously try to seize military power for their own use. No revolution has a chance unless it develops its own armed force. Italians and Hungarians naturally had set up their own armies, for they were fighting foreign rule. The Germans, like the Viennese Austrians, had no foreign rule to fight. Their nationalism made them pause before they weakened national strength by attacking existing armies. Beyond this, they thought that revolution was a simple matter, perhaps in part because the French had made it look simple, at least in 1830; it is also possible that not enough Germans wanted internal reforms badly enough to take the trouble to stage an all-out revolution.

Demonstrations occurred in many German cities in March 1848. In the south, several rulers granted constitutional reforms before violence broke out and appointed moderate liberal ministries. In Berlin a more serious uprising took place. Large demonstrations were met by clumsy military intervention, which led to the erection of barricades by artisans and some students. The Prussian king, fearful of bloodshed, restrained the army, assembled a Prussian parliament, and appointed liberal business and professional people to government offices. In most German states during the following year, liberal ministries and parliaments tried to draft new and effective constitutions. As in Paris, they worried about preserving order, for artisans, and in some areas peasants, continued to agitate for reforms. Peasants in southwestern Germany seized land and burned manorial records. Artisans rioted frequently and also met in many congresses, to demand jobs and better education from the government. Artisan masters wanted full restoration of the guilds and insisted that they be treated with greater respect, while journeymen talked of a more modern form of association to maintain their rights. There was little socialist agitation in Germany. Karl Marx hurried to Cologne to set up a newspaper, but he stressed mainly political reforms. Lower-class agitation, though rarely ideological in operation, was intense. This led the liberal revolutionary governments to use newly expanded civil guards to repress disorder by force and, when this failed, to call on the troops of the old regime.

At the same time, the German revolutions operated on a second, national plane. To establish real German unity nationalists in southern Germany summoned a national assembly in Frankfurt. The Frankfurt parliament, which met in May 1848, devoted eight months to elaborate discussions of the basic political principles involved in drawing up a national constitution. Their first draft called for a federal Germany under the Prussian king, from which Austria would be excluded. It set forth rules for parliamentary governments in the individual states and guaranteed civil liberties for all Germans. The Frankfurt assembly showed that German liberalism commanded significant albeit verbose support. The decision to exclude Austria from a united Germany, taken after much debate, was obviously important for the future. But the actions of the assembly were hollow, for it created no government. It called on Prussian armies to attack Denmark, for the assembly considered some of the territory under the Danish king as German and wanted to regain it. It appealed to an existing ruler, Frederick William IV, to head the new Germany, and when he turned this offer down—saying that he would not pick up a crown from the gutter—the Frankfurt assembly collapsed.

The assembly delegates, like most German middle-class revolutionaries, had also thoroughly antagonized the lower classes. Artisan demands were ignored, for the assembly insisted on a regime of economic liberalism in which worker associations, and certainly guilds, would be banned. This clash was perhaps inevitable. But the politicians in Frankfurt rebuffed the peasants as well, maintaining that manorial rights were based on property rights and property had to be protected. Here, quite clearly, the German liberals were less revolutionary than their French counterparts a half century before. So the lower classes either lost interest in the revolution or tried further uprisings. The middle class became increasingly frightened. The Prussian king sent troops back to Berlin in November 1848, to preserve order and suppress the parliament. The following year he put down insurrections elsewhere in Germany, often at the request of the Frankfurt assembly.

PATTERNS OF REVOLUTION

Everywhere the revolutions of 1848 began with a bang but ended, within a year and a half, with a whimper. The collapse took on a common pattern, which had already been suggested in 1830. Once the revolution was underway, the leaders no longer were revolutionaries. They accepted the upheaval that had brought them to power, but they wanted no further disorder. Lamartine, who can be seen as a starry-eyed Romantic idealist, did have visions of a better world. But he had not even been a convinced democrat before the revolution and became one only as he sought both legitimization and a conservative social orientation for the new regime. Leaders of the new governments in central Europe were still more respectful of orderly political process. Everywhere there were real revolutionaries, and in the Frankfurt assembly there were ardent democrats, but they were in a small minority and were easily crushed when they tried to carry on the revolution after the assembly's collapse. Leading revolutionaries in Paris were in jail during many of the key riots.

In orientation, the de facto guides of the revolution were all liberal. Many historians have seen 1848 as the point at which liberalism had a final idealistic fling before becoming pragmatic and venal. There is some truth in this, but even before 1848 liberals petitioned and assembled in parliaments rather than organizing the forces of revolution.

In many countries liberals also had won some of their goals, and so their rebellion against the old order was limited. In France, the July Monarchy had departed from liberal principles, but it was not a conservative regime in the Metternichian sense. Most of the deputies elected to the parliaments of the Second Republic did not want a government that was much different, though they did accept the abolition of monarchy. There was even an effort to restrict the vote once more, by eliminating about three million people who did not maintain a fixed residence. The political notables of France, who were not yet dislodged from power, wanted a slightly reformed, more genuinely parliamentary July Monarchy.

The case of Prussia is even more interesting. The old regime had not offered liberals a genuine parliament or constitutional rights; liberals therefore had great cause for discontent. But the government was efficient; it encouraged some economic modernization, spread education widely, offered opportunities to middle-class bureaucrats, permitted a considerable degree of religious freedom, and granted substantial powers to city governments. This was not, then, an old regime of the pre-1789 French variety. German liberals have been greatly criticized for their lack of success in 1848. Some historians take 1848 as a sign that liberalism never had a chance in Germany, while others accuse liberals of a failure of nerve. It is unquestionably true that the collapse of the revolution left in power an authoritarian government and an aristocratic upper class. It is also possible to see why liberals did not feel a need to press too hard.

Given the nature of liberalism everywhere, the most potent revolutions were those with a nationalist element. The Belgian revolt of 1830 triumphed, while revolutions in Italy and Hungary were crushed, often with the aid of armies from other great powers. Where there was foreign rule to be driven out, revolutionaries—even liberals—had a clear goal that was lacking elsewhere and that induced them to take up arms. Revolutions without such a goal usually faded quickly or, like the French revolution of 1830, managed to change very little.

Another factor was that the national enemy had to be clearly identified. Vigorous nationalism was present in Austria and Germany but it lacked focus since there was no foreign rule involved. Nationalists were tempted to protect the established order as part of national strength, which distracted them from fomenting revolution, consolidating internal reforms or forming alliances with other nationalist revolutions. This very obviously weakened the revolutionary cause in the Hapsburg empire. By 1848 revolutionaries in central Europe had already begun to make a choice: to put the national cause ahead of purely liberal goals. This was the choice made by the Frankfurt assembly that offered a crown to the Prussian king and by the Austrian liberals who cheered the army's victory in Prague.

All the major revolutions were, moreover, divided by class conflicts—a circumstance that made failure inevitable. In France after 1789 there were early signs of potential conflicts, but they became explicit only slowly. Middle-class leaders of the revolution preached a stirring rhetoric that promised gains to all citizens; although these same leaders introduced class legislation such as property qualifications for the vote, they believed in what they said. The lower classes, without much experience politically, believed in the rhetoric as well. There were at least four years of grace, sufficient time for substantial changes, before class hostilities helped bring the revolution to an end. In 1848 middle-class leaders offered fewer promises; from the first they feared lower-class demands and the lower classes were quick to realize that they had been betrayed. Since the middle classes could not accept the vague socialism of Parisian artisans or the reactionary demands for guilds by German craftsmen, they concurred in the suppression of the lower classes by force. At the same time, the lower classes were incapable of revolution on their own, for they lacked the firm organization and political experience necessary for success. In addition, there was internal friction, as in France where most peasants were either apathetic or hostile to the revolution or in Germany where peasants sought their own goals, separate from those of urban revolutionaries.

Thus were the revolutions doomed to failure. Apart from England, Europe was caught in a network of political repression more severe in 1850 than it had been in 1820. Nevertheless, some positive measures grew out of the abortive revolutions of 1848. Universal manhood suffrage was established in France, never seriously to be questioned thereafter. This was the first time democracy had ever been established in a major European power for more than a few years. The abolition of serfdom in Germany and Austria helped the existing political regimes in both countries—for peasants were now a satisfied and conservative force—but it opened the way to great economic and social change. These were the immediate, and not inconsiderable, results of 1848.

Furthermore, within two decades most of the leading demands of the revolutions had been achieved. By 1871 Germany and Italy were unified and Hungary had achieved substantial autonomy. Parliaments with some real powers had been established in Germany, Austria, Italy, and France. Germany adopted universal suffrage of sorts, and France was a republic once more. Liberal civil rights and economic legislation were spreading rapidly. Hence, though the revolutions were at the time unsuccessful, they helped start forces in motion that quickly gained victory. Liberals and nationalists set about to achieve their goals by more practical means. Conservatism changed even more significantly, for the fall of Metternich was not merely symbolic. Almost immediately conservative leaders changed their tactics and accepted a variety of reforms that did not seem to touch the essence of the established order.

Yet the aura of failure lingered, even as many of the goals of 1848 were being realized. The idealistic fervor that had been associated with liberal goals took new directions, either toward socialism or away from politics altogether. It would be several decades before idealism again entered the mainstream of politics. As liberals turned to compromise they won increasing success, but because they knew (or thought they knew) that revolution was impossible, they did not seize the bases of power. After 1848 the structure of society changed more rapidly than before, but in politics the conservatives were triumphant, so long as they proved a bit flexible.

4 TWO DECADES OF TRANSITION
1848–1870

The years 1815 to 1848 constitute one of the most clearly marked out periods in European history. It began and ended with striking events, which pleases historians who seek neat boundaries. We have thus far considered the period in part by chronology but even more by topic, yet the essential unity of these decades must be discussed before we turn to the quite different Europe that emerged thereafter.

MAJOR THEORIES: 1815–1848

Both the politics and the diplomacy of the period were reasonably coherent and different from what came before and after. Conservatism varied somewhat from country to country, but in essence changed very little. It was preoccupied with the task of avoiding revolution and only in England, France, and Belgium did it yield to any extent. The forces that challenged conservatism were generally constant, though they tended to pick up momentum with time. Radicalism and, far more modestly, socialism gained ground, but liberalism and liberal nationalism remained the principal challengers. Hence the issues in political conflict were the establishment of parliaments, constitutions, and civil rights. These issues, plus the current of popular, particularly artisan, protest that ran beneath the surface of politics, created the amazing proliferation of revolutions with which the period was so obviously marked. Diplomacy was largely the handmaiden of internal politics, both in the sense that conservatives used diplomacy and military force to quash rebellion, and that in their preoccupation with internal unrest they were distracted from serious outside diplomatic conflicts. The

brief flurry of European concert with which the period began did not endure, but diplomacy thereafter was in sufficiently low key that there were
no serious threats to the Vienna settlement.

In essence, the 30 years after 1815 saw the working out of the previous
quarter century of upheaval. Diplomacy was calm because the Vienna settlement recognized enough of the territorial changes forced by Napoleon—
but not too many—to content the leading powers; also, two decades of war
inevitably produced fatigue. The challenges to internal conservatism came
from political movements that sought to introduce or restore the leading
principles of the Great Revolution.

A period that has a reasonably neat political unity does not necessarily
have a similar unity in other types of development, but in this case certain
claims can be made. Romanticism began well before 1815, particularly in
Germany, but it gained its widest appeal thereafter and spread over the
whole of Europe. The second generation of Romantics, who had begun
their work in the mid-1820s, began to fade from the scene after 1848. The
failure of the revolution had something to do with this: liberal Romantics
were disillusioned or, like Victor Hugo, were even driven into exile. Such
younger men as Charles Baudelaire in France and Richard Wagner in Germany turned away from politics in revulsion after their brief enthusiasm
for the revolution. But the end of Romanticism was not owing to political
events primarily. Writers and artists of the new generation either rebelled
against Romantic sentimentality or sought to carry the stylistic freedom
preached by the Romantic much farther than the Romantics themselves
had done.

As in culture there was no sudden change in the economy in 1815. From
the late eighteenth century on, industrialization and capitalism had been
spreading, respectively, in England and on the continent. The three decades
before 1848 saw an intensification of these developments, while in the years
after 1848 there was a distinct change. Between 1815 and 1848 capitalist
forms and motives directly touched most people in western and central
Europe for the first time, attracting some and disturbing still more in each
social class. A new, dynamic middle class arose as part of this movement.
From Paris to Vienna, new families took over the upper positions in manufacturing and commerce and they brought a new spirit with them. Yet
older groups with a more traditional outlook were not dislodged, either
within the middle class or outside it. Much of the protest in the period came
from groups that still had some hope of preventing the spread of capitalist forms.

Europe after 1848

After 1848 western and central Europe became industrial as well as
capitalist. The new middle-class elements that were now entrenched worked

to consolidate their power in politics and culture. Preindustrial social groups declined and the forms and methods of protest that had expressed lower-class grievances since the Middle Ages now began to vanish. The revolutions of 1848 did not cause these basic changes but they are more than a convenient signpost. They helped teach many artisans that the old forms of protest were no longer valid and, in some cases, that industrial capitalism had to be accepted. By discrediting the idealism of intellectuals, the revolutions gave businessmen greater prominence in middle-class politics and, in addition, taught conservative leaders that more active sponsorship of economic change was a concession that might usefully be made in the interest of preventing further revolt. The 60 years of recurrent revolution before 1848 had been nurtured by the birth pains of a new economic order. This order had now triumphed. Capitalists old and new were free to run the economy, usually with government aid. Although defenders of traditional economic values abounded, they lacked the vitality to engage in revolution.

In sum, for much of Europe after 1848 the transition to modernity was completed. The issues that next emerged are with us still: the "social question"—that is, the question of how to help make the lower classes content—mass political consciousness, the role of Germany, the expanding bureaucratic state, the gap between artist and society. The era that took shape in the third quarter of the nineteenth century continued in many ways until World War II.

The Nature of the Transition

Between 1848 and 1875 the character of European politics was altered fundamentally. The basic political questions raised by the French Revolution or by the rise of the middle class were settled to a sufficient extent that political divisions based upon them began to decline though they did not disappear. Liberalism and conservatism both changed greatly in the process, as did diplomacy, for diplomatic initiatives were a vital part of the new political picture. The Vienna settlement was disrupted and Europe was set on a new diplomatic course. These developments gave the quarter century after 1848 a real unity. For those who like to close off the period with a great event, the Franco-Prussian War of 1870–1871 will serve the purpose. It may make more sense, however, to end the period with a nonevent, the haphazard foundation of the Third Republic of France, which completed the formation of new regimes in western and central Europe.

In economic or cultural spheres, the decades after 1848 do not form a distinctive period. The rise of big business and heavy industry began during these years but continued to develop thereafter. The Franco-Prussian War imposed great economic losses on France and caused a stagnation in industrial development that lasted until the 1890s. The war encouraged the

German economy, though it had already been booming. These developments, and the more coincidental faltering of British industry after the mid-1870s, are important, but they do not add up to a major break in economic history. The principal distinctive characteristic of the period 1850–1875 was the relatively uninterrupted prosperity for both agriculture and industry, marred by only a few short slumps. Only in the mid-1870s did a new round of industrial recessions begin; more significantly, there was a collapse in European agriculture. If the basic character of the economy did not change in the 1870s, its impact on society did, and with important implications for politics. Between 1850 and 1875 the transition to a new political framework was greatly facilitated by the absence of extensive economic discontent. Real wages, profits, and agricultural earnings were all generally rising.

In European culture the 1870s brought no significant break at all. Darwinism, Marxism, and aestheticism had already changed European culture fundamentally, and they were not superseded or altered in the 1870s. Some historians have made a case for a distinctively "realistic" tone to European culture between 1850 and 1870, which fits in nicely with tough-minded politics and diplomacy. The notion of a pervasive realism ignores the heritage of Romanticism in the arts, which formed one of the leading cultural currents in this period and long after. During the eighteenth and early nineteenth centuries the intellectuals had reached a high point of influence in politics, particularly the politics of dissent, but now this influence receded. Hence the periodization of political and of cultural developments cannot be the same. The cultural trends that emerged after 1850 became significant political factors only after 1880.

The period 1850–1875 was a period of transition. A new political structure was being forged. Somewhat separately industrial society and a very new version of the "reason-heart" controversy in culture also arose. From these developments in turn came two of the three leading challenges to the new political order after 1875.

THE CONSERVATIVE REACTION

One of the more significant results of 1848 was the emergence of conservative groups and movements in most continental countries, eager to ensure that revolution would not recur. In Prussia, most notably, some of the Junkers founded a conservative newspaper, the *Kreuzzeitung*, and acted as a pressure group on the monarchy both during the revolution and afterwards. In France conservative newspapers were not new but journalists, such as Catholic Louis Veuillot, tried to increase their bite and their popularity. There were signs, in other words, of conservatives defending old principles with new methods.

Policies of Reaction

More important initially were the defensive policies of most continental governments. Prussia reestablished the guilds in an obvious effort to hamper capitalism and win the support of artisans against the dangerous middle class. Several south German states and Spain signed concordats with the Catholic Church that gave the Church economic support and control over educational systems and censorship.

In France the parliament of the Second Republic became increasingly monarchist in tone. It not only tried to limit the vote but also, with the passage of the Falloux law, greatly increased the role of the Church in education, particularly at the primary level. Many of the leading dissidents had been killed or arrested following the suppression of the June Days. Then in 1851 Louis Napoleon, who had been barred by the constitution from succeeding himself as President and opposed by the largely monarchist parliament, seized full power by a *coup d'état*. This occasioned another round of repression. Parliament was disbanded and its leaders arrested or driven into exile. Radical papers were suppressed and 27,000 potential dissidents arrested. Following this the government established a rigorous censorship, expanded the police force, and widened the major streets of Paris, in part to facilitate the movement of troops against riots. A year later, Louis Napoleon established a new imperial regime called the Second Empire, titling himself Napoleon III.

Reaction was even more clearly the rule in the Hapsburg monarchy. Guided by his forceful minister, Prince Felix Schwarzenberg, the emperor promulgated an illiberal charter but even this he rescinded in 1852. However, the pre-1848 regime could not be completely restored; new institutions were essential because manorialism had been abolished. Under Alexander Bach, a former liberal, the state bureaucracy was rapidly enlarged to replace local manorial administration. Local police and administrators were brought under central control, which facilitated repression of potential disorder. But the increased efficiency of the bureaucracy, combined with greater official support for economic development, helped break down local barriers to trade and pleased many Austrian liberals. The Bach system revived some of the reformist principles of Joseph II. At the same time, to solidify its repressive policies, the government signed a concordat with the Catholic Church.

The most important and durable reaction to 1848 occurred within the Catholic Church itself. Pius IX brought a somewhat liberal reputation to the papacy in 1846 and proceeded to introduce a few modest reforms in the administration of the Papal States. Driven from Rome by the revolt in 1849, Pius came back an embittered conservative determined on a policy of alliance with conservative regimes through the new concordats. In return for protection of Rome by French troops and for a Catholic role in the French educational system, the church backed the repressive policies of Napoleon III. When the Papal States were lost through the unification of Italy in 1860, Pius grew still more hostile to the modern world. He issued the Syllabus of Errors of 1864, which condemned liberalism, socialism, science, and any belief that the church should tolerate change. Pius later summoned a solemn assemblage of churchmen, the First Vatican Council, which proclaimed the doctrine of papal infallibility in 1870. At a time when limitations on authoritarian rule were gaining support in many secular states this doctrine seemed another clear defiance of the tenor of the modern world.

Pius IX was not simply a blind reactionary. Papal infallibility was in part the culmination of an effort to strengthen church government to compensate for the loss of close ties with many secular states. Nor did the Pope speak for all Catholics in his politics. A number of French churchmen tried to soften the impact of the Syllabus of Errors; in Germany and elsewhere there was substantial resistance to the proclamation of papal infallibility by liberal Catholics who believed in religious liberty and parliamentary government. Nevertheless, Pius encouraged Catholics to remain traditional political conservatives as he successfully defied most of the opposition to his policies. This maintenance of pre-1848 conservatism in a new era contributed to the decline of religion and to new attacks on the political position of the Church.

Liberals were naturally appalled by the papal policies. The pope's hostility to Italian unification, though understandable, virtually forced Italian liberals to be hostile to the Church. Catholic support for Napoleon III cemented the bitter anticlericalism of liberals in France. The Church had shown many signs of disaffection for the July Monarchy, notably in the movement for "free" schools; liberal republicans who were opposed to the regime grew less antagonistic to the Church as a result. Priests joined in welcoming the revolution of 1848, planting trees of liberty and singing Te Deums. But most Catholics soon feared that the revolution would go too far. Catholic deputies led in suppressing the National Workshops. The Falloux law proved that the Catholic hierarchy wanted a share in the state education system, not free schools. A brief hope for a truce between liberals and Catholics in France had been wiped out. In France and elsewhere, the Church's gains from its conservative stance were short-lived, for liberals advanced once again and were bent on attacking the Church. As liberalism and now socialism won new adherents, religion declined.

Equally important, Pius IX's brand of political conservatism did not keep pace with the changes in the leading conservative states. Within a decade the Church's position was being attacked by governments in all the leading Catholic countries. In part, to be sure, this was owing to the need to conciliate liberals. Full support for the Church could be sacrificed in the interest of preserving political stability. But conservative governments themselves wanted to gain new powers and to use some of the new isms that the pope had condemned. The Church's policies worked smoothly only with states such as Spain whose conservatism had changed very little. After Pius' death in 1878 Catholic politics would be altered; however, because of the Church's virtually complete failure to adapt in a formative political period, it had lost ground that could not be regained.

Policies of Reform

In most countries the period of unqualified reaction was short-lived. The Bach bureaucratic system had already brought important reforms to Austria; Napoleon III quickly did the same for France. Prussia in 1849 tried to use German nationalism, rather than simply to ignore or repress it. Frederick William IV proposed a union of German princes under Prussian leadership that excluded Austria. With Russian backing Austria forced Prussia to abandon this scheme in 1850, but a precedent had been set for Prussian policy. More important was a modification of Prussia's own governmental structure. A new constitution was issued guaranteeing certain liberties to the Prussian people and establishing a bicameral legislature that would meet annually. The upper house had few elected members and was a bulwark of the landed aristocracy. But the lower house was elected by an ingenious system that gave every adult male a vote while protecting the conservative interest. A three-class voting system graded the voters by the taxes they paid. Although the lowest class contained 83 percent of the population, each class elected the same number of delegates to a district convention, which then chose the parliamentary representatives.

One conservative state, Piedmont, went still further, actually converting to a moderate liberalism in its effort to prevent revolution while harnessing some of the forces that 1848 had released. Realizing that it could gain internal strength and enhance its prestige elsewhere in Italy by a progressive policy, the government granted a constitution and a parliament, proclaimed equality under the law and, after a bitter battle, abolished the church courts. Under the leadership of Count Cavour, it adopted a policy of economic modernization that stressed lower tariffs and railroad construction and established links with liberal groups in other parts of Italy. In essence, Piedmont had introduced a regime similar to that of the July Monarchy in France, with greater stress on economic advance and on an adventurous foreign policy. Ministers of government were responsible to the king, not to parliament; suffrage was very limited; and while the power of the church was reduced and religious freedom assured, there was no desire to destroy Catholicism. Piedmont created some genuinely liberal institutions instead of making cautious concessions in the Prussian manner. Both countries, however, groped toward a combination of the new and the old, and both were on the verge of still more daring ventures.

THE NEW CONSERVATISM

Dangerous as it is to generalize about the policies of many different governments, one can discern a roughly common pattern in the evolution of the governments of central and western Europe by the 1860s. The evolution began at somewhat different times in each country and policies differed in emphasis. The net effect was a new conservative stance.

Conservative leaders took the offensive. No longer content simply to repress disorder, they sought to come to terms with many of the new, potentially unsettling forces of the nineteenth century. Conservative governments now wholeheartedly supported economic modernization. Economic development was vital to the diplomatic and military strength of the state; it thus appealed to a traditional conservative goal and helped to keep the middle class content. Increased governmental efficiency and opportunities for bureaucrats to advance on the basis of talent also served to satisfy the middle class and, more important, to advance the power of the state. Austria and then Italy worked to develop a competent, centralized bureaucracy, while Prussia and France, which already had the basic framework, added new functions and, through the use of civil service examinations, tried to improve training and recruitment. As a result of this improved efficiency, the repressive and manipulative capacities of conservative governments were greatly enhanced. All the states expanded their police forces and trained them in riot control. French prefects became reasonably proficient in controlling elections even under universal suffrage. The chronic financial weakness of Austrian and Italian governments was at least modified.

Conservative sponsorship of economic development and of administrative efficiency was by no means new. Napoleon I and the Prussian state had suggested both policies before. Even in France and Prussia, the policies were carried further than before and government power increased markedly. More novel were conservative efforts to come to terms with the two major industrial classes. Conservative leaders tried to conciliate the lower classes with some economic reforms. Their efforts were limited, for they did not want to disturb the social hierarchy, and their success was at best incomplete. But to counterbalance the power of the middle class, the new conservatives hoped to gain some positive support from the lower classes, not just traditional apathy. Some of them were willing to introduce universal suffrage as part of this tactic.

A compromise with liberalism came harder and usually later than the first approach to the lower classes, but conservatives began to realize that they could introduce some liberal institutions without destroying the conservative state. Finally, conservative leaders began to use an active diplomacy to win widespread support. This policy, too, had been suggested before—by Charles X of France for example—and the desire to enhance their power had long been a traditional goal for European states and monarchs. Consistently active diplomacy was new to the European conservatism that had developed after 1815, however, and it had a new purpose: to win nationalist sentiment to the defense of the existing order and to spread national loyalty as widely as possible.

Conservative leaders began, then, to sponsor industrialization, to introduce new political forms, and to toy with the map of Europe. In view of these policies, should they even be called conservatives? Possibly a different term would be clearer, for these conservatives were obviously not bent on retaining the status quo in all respects. Nevertheless they did defend the traditional social hierarchy and the power of the aristocracy. They were essentially trying to modernize the economy without modernizing society, and in Germany at least they pulled off the trick. They defended a monarchical form of government and they never did give sovereign power to the people or to parliaments. They believed in strong government, in firm suppression of disorder, and even in religion, though they reduced the power of the churches. Their basic goals, then, were conservative in the pre-1848 sense, but they knew the strength of the modern isms. None of the new conservative leaders had been born before the French Revolution; none was wedded to an ideology of the old regime. Although they sought to use the new isms, often with great success, they did not actually believe in them.

The changes in conservative policy were directed in most cases by a few men at the top, and initially without very clear political support. Ordinary conservatives were slow to follow the innovations. Catholics in France and Italy and Junkers and other conservative Lutherans in Germany opposed many of the new initiatives. Bismarck, for example, often had to rely mainly on liberal support though he, and leaders like him, were never comfortable with it. Here again, the labels are confusing. By 1870 there were three major political forces in Europe: traditional conservatism, liberalism and a new conservatism somewhere in between.

At no point between 1815 and 1914 were there so many striking personalities in European politics as between 1850 and 1875: Napoleon III, at least a glorious failure after stodgy Louis Philippe; Léon Gambetta and Adolphe Thiers who founded a new regime, compared to the opportunist politicians who followed them in the Third Republic; Cavour, the author of unity in Italy; and Bismarck who dominated nineteenth-century German history during 28 years in office. Here were men who could accommodate old and new political forces and, in two cases, create new nations. Were these great leaders inevitable products of the age, responses to the new opportunities that opened up in politics and diplomacy after 1848? Or were they the motivating forces without whom the transition to a new politics would not have been made?

THE SECOND EMPIRE

Napoleon III in France was the first new conservative. His was a new regime, free from some traditional restraints. Napoleon had to be innovative in order to establish the Bonapartist dynasty and to vindicate the ideals of national and social justice that he vaguely and mistakenly thought his uncle had stood for. Though he believed in social hierarchy, Napoleon was not devoted to the existing aristocracy and other notables as were conservatives elsewhere. He tried to get along with them because of their political power, but he knew that their loyalty was not firm. He therefore worked to undercut their political hold over the masses in the countryside and toyed with building his own elite in the glittering, gaudy social whirl of imperial Paris. Napoleon, then, was at an extreme of the new conservatism. Some of his policies, particularly his plebiscitary appeals to the people, have been called prototypes for fascism—an observation worth considering but one that exaggerates the political changes Napoleon wanted to introduce. More important was the fact that, being the first new conservative, Napoleon helped force changes in other countries. Bismarck, as ambassador to Paris, learned from Napoleon's example how democracy could be manipulated. More important, the diplomatic initiatives that were fundamental to Napoleon's policy made diplomatic experiments in central Europe inevitable; these, in turn, required internal political adjustments. They also, ironically, toppled Napoleon III.

After the empire was established in 1852 Napoleon maintained only the facade of liberal, parliamentary institutions. Parliament was a rubber stamp, with an upper house that was appointive and a lower house that had almost no functions. Government agents actively repressed political opposition and only official candidates were nominated for election to the lower house. The empire thus operated under essentially authoritarian rule. Napoleon later said that when France was ready he intended to restore political liberties; there was little suggestion of this until after 1860.

From the first, however, Napoleon tried to develop active political support among the masses, though he relied heavily on the Catholic Church and local notables—the landlord, and others with political experience and influence—for more conventional conservative support as well. Each major political move, including the establishment of the Empire, was confirmed by a democratic plebiscite. There was no real alternative in these elections; one voted simply for or against what Napoleon proposed. But Napoleon did not rely solely on official pressure to gain his ends. He campaigned actively among the masses, particularly among the peasantry, trying to win direct backing for his regime and to woo voters away from support of the local notables. Here was a clear clash between traditional and new versions of conservatism.

Napoleon also worked to modernize the economy and spread prosperity to the lower classes. To spur economic development he established new investment banks for industry and agriculture. After 1860 he lowered tariffs to force French industry to become more competitive and technically advanced. At the same time he speeded up railroad construction and port development; expanded public works to improve urban facilities and employment opportunities; and, as an aid to French farmers, reclaimed wasteland and provided technical information. Some of these policies, such as free trade, annoyed routine-minded businessmen. Napoleon favored dynamic entrepreneurs with visions of rapid industrial progress and a zeal for speculation, some of them partisans of the doctrines of Saint-Simon. The economy advanced more rapidly under Napoleon than in any other period of the nineteenth century. With a rise in real wages, the position of the lower classes improved. In the 1860s Napoleon loosened the restrictions on strikes and trade unions in a further effort to aid the workers. Napoleon enjoyed claiming at times that he was a socialist, which was clearly nonsense. He was, however, sincerely eager to advance the economy for the general welfare and he had his greatest success in this field.

As soon as his regime was well established Napoleon embarked on an active foreign policy. His basic goal was to enhance the glory of his rule and his dynasty and to undo the Vienna settlement that he viewed, with good reason, as an insult to the Bonapartes. He was not a French nationalist, but he appealed to French nationalism both by seeking additions to French territory and by espousing a Europe organized on national principles. His vague hopes for a better Europe, and particularly the advancement of the Latin peoples, coincided to an extent with the tradition of revolutionary nationalism in France, which also claimed an interest in the liberation of all peoples. Napoleon's sponsorship of Italian unification especially appealed to this distinctive nationalist sentiment. His support for an independent Rumania, his effort to form a Latin monetary union, his attempt to gain new territory in the Low Countries and his costly, abortive conquest of Mexico were other facets of his policy.

THE CRIMEAN WAR

Napoleon's first diplomatic initiative came in the Near East. It was a probe designed above all to shake up diplomatic alignments, and it worked. Nicholas I of Russia had long been interested in gaining influence in the Ottoman Empire and one of his favorite ploys was to claim protection over the Orthodox Christians there. In the 1850s an obscure quarrel arose between Orthodox Christians and Roman Catholics over rights to churches and other holy places in Palestine. Napoleon, who was particularly eager to win Church support at this point, championed the Catholic cause, which brought him into conflict with Russia. Britain was drawn in on France's side, despite considerable suspicion of the new Napoleon. The British were as concerned as ever to mantain the integrity of the Ottoman Empire, to avoid any great power influence near its routes to India. Russia had long been the principal danger to British interests in the area. The British were anxious also to make sure that France did not act alone, lest she gain all the benefits of intervention. Furthermore, Palmerston, the British prime minister, supported an active foreign policy and British public opinion, tired of the long decades of peace, delighted in a war that was safely remote.

The Crimean War, which began in 1854, was in many ways a farce. It took place in southern Russia, far from Palestine where the quarrel had started. It was full of tragic-comic episodes, as the western powers tried to storm Russian fortifications. British cavalry columns, such as the famous Light Brigade, charged artillery with great bravery and utter folly. Supplies were in chaos. At one point the British sent out a shipload of boots for left feet only. But France and Britain finally won and in 1856 Napoleon, at the height of his power, hosted the peace conference, the Congress of Paris. Both the war and the settlement shook up European diplomacy fundamentally and Russia's defeat forced equally fundamental internal reform. This war was the first conflict among major European powers in 40 years and as such it was bound to have important repercussions.

The Results of the War

The Hapsburg empire, though a noncombattant, was in many ways the biggest loser from the war. Its internal stability had long depended on diplomatic success and its diplomatic success depended on alliance with Russia. This was now lost. Russia had expected Austrian aid during the war, in return for Russia's assistance in Hungary in 1849. Owing to a longstanding fear of Russian influence in the Near East, Austria remained officially neutral though Austrian troops did occupy Moldavia and Wallachia, which had been under Russian protection. Because of its hesitance, Austria gained no sympathy from Britain and France and, having alienated Russia, Austria stood alone for the first time since 1810. It was no accident that Austria became the focus for most of the diplomatic offensives of the next decade or that these offensives were successful.

The Holy Alliance, that dam against change, was now broken, and this was the most important result of the Crimean War. The war settlement weakened and angered Russia, for the Ottoman Empire acquired Bessarabia and the Black Sea was neutralized. The settlement also created a new Balkan state, for Moldavia and Wallachia were granted autonomy and were united two years later as Rumania. Finally, the war helped create appetites for further diplomatic change as Napoleon wanted to continue his remaking of the European map. He hoped to do this peacefully, by discussion, for the Congress of Paris superficially revived great power talks. But none of

the other powers wanted further discussions; even Britain, France's erstwhile ally, grew hostile to Napoleon's plans. More concretely, Piedmont resolved to profit from the new diplomatic atmosphere. Cavour led Piedmont
into the last stages of the Crimean war in the hope of raising the question
of Italian unity at the peace settlement. Raise it he did, but without result;
Piedmont decided on direct action.

NATIONALISM

The great events of the period 1850–1870 were the unifications of Italy
and Germany. The dreams of 1848 seemed fulfilled. Nationalist intellectuals
in Rumania, thwarted in an abortive revolt in 1848, gained national independence just ten years later. The more moderate Hungarian nationalists,
who sought autonomy rather than independence, won their goal in a major
constitutional reform in 1867.

The tone of nationalism also changed after 1848. The decline of Romanticism and the experience of failure robbed many nationalists of their
enthusiastic if naive idealism. Nationalist theorists now preached the use of
practical, forceful diplomacy. There were already hints of the adaptation
of the Darwinian notions of survival of the fittest to nationalism. Walter
Bagehot, in England, taught that only strong nations could prevail and that
those that prevailed were best. Without any question, the way national
gains were made in the period taught still more nationalists that diplomacy
and force were the keys to success. The leading Italian nationalist organizer,
Daniel Manin, decided that liberal goals and methods were less important
than Italian unity, and so pinned his hopes on Piedmontese diplomacy.
Piedmont's success roused German nationalists to look to Prussian leadership. South Slavic nationalists began to turn to big brother Russia.

Yet the importance of nationalism must not be exaggerated. Nationalist
movements were confined to elements of the middle class and, especially in
eastern Europe, to landholders chafing under foreign rule. There is no sign
that nationalist loyalties gained lower-class adherents until after 1870, when
new regimes began consciously to inculcate the sentiment. Hence where nationalism triumphed, most people did not greatly care or, because of older
religious or local loyalties, some were actively hostile.

Nationalist sentiment played a role in Italian unification, but its limitations were also clear there. Manin's Italian National Society was formed in
1856 to agitate for unification under Piedmont. Nationalist uprisings in
north-central Italian cities, after the war with Austria began, contributed to
the formation of Italy. But the enthusiasm had not spread to the south.
Garibaldi's famous campaign was manned by northern volunteers and supported by northern funds. Some local support developed but seldom for
nationalist goals; Sicilians, for example, abandoned the campaign when

they realized that Garibaldi did not intend to free Sicily from the mainland. In the early 1860s anti-national insurrections in the south had to be
put down by force.

Nationalism played an even smaller role in Germany where there was no
particular enthusiasm for the nationalist cause in the 1850s. Hopes arose
after Italy's success and the *National Verein* was formed in 1859 in imitation of Manin's group, to work for German unity. There was certainly
enough nationalist sentiment in Germany to applaud unification, but it had
little to do with the process. There was also significant opposition, particularly among Catholics in the south and west.

Furthermore, nationalism was not the motivating force for the diplomats
who were most responsible for national success. Despite Cavour's nationalist
background he worked primarily for the advancement of Piedmont. Historical accident, not intentional policy, allowed him to unify Italy when he did.
Bismarck sought above all to protect Prussian interests and never even contemplated the unification of all racial Germans, thus the new Germany,
which Bismarck had not initially planned on anyway, left out the Germans
in Austria and other areas.

The idealism most relevant to the unifications was Napoleon III's, but
even his was not conventional nationalism and it certainly worked to the
disadvantage of France. Bismarck and Cavour were aware of nationalism
and used it, without becoming its creatures. Modern, mass nationalism and
its influence on diplomacy were the products, not the causes, of the formation of new states. Only in France in 1870—that is in an existing state with a
nationalist tradition dating back to the 1790s—did nationalist "public opinion," in the press and among politicians, actually determine diplomacy when
it drove France to war.

Finally, outside the mainstream of diplomacy, cultural nationalism continued to spread much as it had before, often in association with liberal
aspirations. There were stirrings of nationalism in Bulgaria and Albania.
Finnish, Ukrainian and Lithuanian movements began in Russia. Catalonian
and Provençal separatist sentiment arose in Spain and France respectively.
Various Slavic nationalisms, particularly the Czech national movement,
spread in the Hapsburg Empire and stressed cultural identity at least as
much as political goals.

ITALIAN UNIFICATION

Napoleon III had long been sympathetic to the Italian cause, partly because he had spent much time in Italy. He resented Austrian influence in
the peninsula, considering it a slap at France and the Bonapartes. By the
late 1850s, when it became clear that nothing would change through discussion, Cavour was able to seal an alliance with Napoleon. Napoleon

planned a federated Italy consisting of an expanded Piedmont in the north, the Papal States, and Naples; as a reward for his help, he would gain Savoy and Nice for France. Cavour's plans were more general; he wanted whatever he could get for Piedmont. With expert staging by Cavour, war between the allies and Austria was declared in 1859. France could not drive Austria out of Italy, but Austria, fearful of disorder at home, ceded Lombardy to Piedmont. Following this, Cavour helped foment disorders in central Italy, including the Papal States, and annexed these territories after plebiscites indicated popular approval. In 1860 Garibaldi and a small band of volunteers, aided by Piedmontese funds and weapons, moved through the kingdom of Naples and then, under some pressure from Piedmontese troops, joined southern Italy with the north. A united Italy had been achieved.

Venetia was still in Austrian hands, while French troops protected the pope's hold on Rome. Napoleon's plans had clearly gone awry. He had helped create a far more powerful state to the south than he had intended.

Italy Unified: Garibaldi, having conquered southern Italy, is courted by King Victor Emmanuel of the north.

THE MAN IN POSSESSION.

V—ʀ E—ᴍ—ʟ. "I WONDER WHEN HE WILL OPEN THE DOOR."

ITALIAN UNIFICATION

- Piedmont-Sardinia on the eve of war in 1859
- Acquired in 1859 through war with Austria
- Additions in 1860
- Addition in 1866
- Addition in 1870

Catholic sentiment in France was outraged at the loss of the Papal States. To conciliate the Catholics, Napoleon at least had to defend Rome; this infuriated his Italian allies. Napoleon gained only Savoy and Nice. His star was waning. Napoleon, the first of the new conservatives, was also the first to reveal one of the key weaknesses of the system: it depended on diplomatic success.

The Nature of the New Italy

More important, the new Italian state was born dissatisfied. Nationalists wanted Rome, their natural capital, and complete expulsion of Austria. But when these goals were achieved, they wanted still more. Italian diplomacy was far more cautious than the nationalists wished, but it too remained opportunistic. Not only a new nation but a new source of disturbance had been added to Europe's diplomatic spectrum.

Internally, the new Italy was essentially the Piedmontese government writ large. The king of Piedmont, Victor Emmanuel, became king of Italy.

Piedmontese officials dominated the major posts of government. The state on the whole fit the new conservative pattern, though with a greater admixture of genuine liberalism than was then the case in France or, later, in Germany. It was highly centralized, copying the French administrative system of departmental prefects for regional administration, though the economic backwardness of the country made central control less extensive in practice than it was on paper. The state did not hesitate to repress with force, as it quickly demonstrated in dealing with uprisings in the south. It encouraged economic development, particularly the building of railroads, and extended to the whole peninsula legislation that was favorable to capitalism. Not surprisingly, significant industrialization began in Italy soon after unification. Whenever possible the new state maintained an active diplomacy and sought to come to terms with the Church. Like new conservatives elsewhere, Italian leaders wanted no outright war with Catholicism though it could not grant the Church its old position in Italy. Cavour and his successors tried to negotiate the cession of Rome, promising the pope control over the Vatican and some other enclaves and a large financial indemnity.

The Church refused any concessions. The pope did not recognize the Italian state and forbade Catholics to participate in it. Hence the most traditional and powerful conservative force in Italy stayed out of politics. This fact, and the genuine strength of liberalism in Italy, encouraged the liberal aspects of the new state. Civil rights were guaranteed, including freedom of religion, and Piedmontese legislation restricting Church courts and religious orders was extended to the rest of the country. Parliament had important powers, particularly over the budget. It was elected by a very limited suffrage, for only 2 percent of the population could vote. There were no experiments with democracy in Italy and the state did little to aid the lower classes. In these respects, the regime was shaped more by moderate liberalism than by new conservatism. On the other hand parliament was restricted also, for the king retained substantial power independent of it, including the choice of ministers. In this sense the Italian state exemplified the compromise with liberalism that conservatives in other countries were undertaking. During the 1860s parliament was controlled by men who supported the existing political structure and wanted no further change.

GERMAN UNIFICATION

Suggestions of a new conservatism had abounded in Prussia even before 1848. In the 1850s rapid economic development was encouraged by government aid to investment banks as well as to railroads. The state extended technical assistance to agriculture and helped some peasants, now freed from serfdom, to acquire land. Restoration of the guilds satisfied most

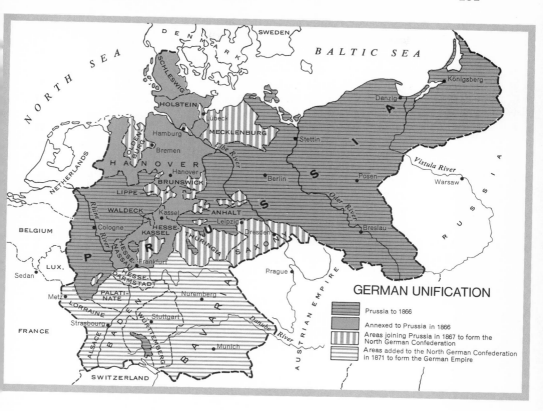

GERMAN UNIFICATION

Prussia to 1866

Annexed to Prussia in 1866

Areas joining Prussia in 1867 to form the North German Confederation

Areas added to the North German Confederation in 1871 to form the German Empire

artisans, while factory legislation in the 1850s gave Prussian workers the most complete protection for health and safety of any country in Europe. Finally, the new Prussian parliament gave at least some solace to liberals though censorship and the political police were rigidly maintained. The 1850s were calm.

Political Crisis

In 1861 William I became king and promptly precipitated a major political crisis. By relaxing government pressure during elections, he opened the way for a liberal majority in parliament. But William was a conservative of the most traditional sort, who believed in the Crown, the State, Protestantism, the aristocracy, and the military. He would stand for no reduction of the monarchy and saw the enhancement of the military character of Prussia as his main duty. He wanted a larger, more efficient army. To acquire the necessary funds, he was obliged by the constitution to win parliament's approval; parliament, reluctant to encourage the conservative Prussian military, refused. The battle was on. The liberals formed a political party, the Progressives, and managed to increase their majority in the new elections of 1862, despite great government pressure. William considered abdicating in this impasse but one of his ministers sent an urgent message to Otto von Bismarck: "Danger in delay. Hurry."

Bismarck saw no reason to bow before a liberal parliament. His immediate solution was simple. He collected taxes and financed an expanded army without parliamentary authorization. As he noted, "Might goes before Right." Bismarck was firm in his defense of the king's rights and the privileges of the Junker aristocracy of which he was part. Yet he was no traditional conservative and was not content merely to defy liberalism. Even as he battled the liberals he resisted advice to abolish parliament. Within a few years he was ready to make concessions to liberal political and economic interests and also to conciliate the lower classes. He discussed social problems with the socialist Ferdinand Lassalle. Bismarck's willingness to grant universal suffrage showed his faith that the masses could be guided and trusted. But initially his weapon was diplomacy. He was angered by Austria's influence in Germany and Prussia's lesser role, so he wanted Germany restructured. He recognized also that a successful foreign policy could soothe many domestic hurts and that Prussia had a chance to win support by championing nationalism. Bismarck probably had no thought at first of unifying Germany. He was an opportunist, in many ways a cautious one, but his opportunities proved extensive.

Prussia of course had great strength on her own: an expanding industrial economy together with a well-trained and well-equipped military drawn from widespread conscription. Prussia benefited also from the distraction of the three powers really capable of opposing her. Russia was indebted to Prussia for assistance in putting down a Polish insurrection in 1863 and was ill-disposed toward Austria or toward foreign adventures of any sort. France was distracted by the effort to conquer Mexico and by Napoleon's vague feeling that German nationalism might be justifiable too. Napoleon also hoped to benefit by assisting Prussia's advance. Britain, a sea power anyway, was above all afraid of French ambition. Like all the powers, Britain failed to appreciate Prussia's strength. This accounts for the otherwise amazing fact, in view of the impact of German unification, that there was no coordinated resistance among the great powers and little resistance at all from some of them.

War Against Denmark

In 1864 Prussia went to war against Denmark over the old issue of Danish possession of Schleswig-Holstein, territories with a partially German population. Here was a way for Bismarck to win land for Prussia and prestige among the nationalists at little cost. Denmark was beaten easily. Austria feared Prussian gains and obtained the administration of one of the duchies, while Prussia controlled the other. This set the stage for Prussia's next advance.

Throughout 1865 Bismarck raised a number of objections to Austrian policies in Holstein. He met with Napoleon III to win a promise of French neutrality in case of a war with Austria and he vaguely promised French gains in the Rhineland to repay Napoleon for his help. Napoleon in turn helped arrange a Prussian-Italian alliance, with Italy obtaining Venetia as a reward for a new war on Austria. Napoleon was confident that any war would be prolonged, weakening all parties and allowing France to arbitrate a settlement. Bismarck had more trouble persuading his own William I to go to war against a fellow monarch and member of the German Confederation than in preparing the diplomatic conditions for the war. But Bismarck was adamant that Austria's power in Germany had to be eliminated.

War Against Austria

The Seven Weeks' War of 1866 was an extraordinary demonstration of Prussia's military power, for Austria was easily crushed along with the several German states who had been Austria's allies. Bismarck wisely refrained from humiliating Austria in the peace settlement, thus minimizing future friction between the two powers. Austria lost no territory but did lose her position in Germany. Prussia united all the German states north of the Main River into the North German Confederation, under Prussian domination. Italy, which had also attacked Austria, finally gained Venetia.

Bismarck had won a great triumph but his work was not done. His victory made it tempting to think of further gains but this was not his main motive. He was convinced that France would inevitably attack the rising power to her east and that Prussia had best prepare for a conflict on the most favorable possible terms. Napoleon had won nothing from the Seven Weeks' War. Prussia's swift victory enabled Bismarck to ignore French pleas for territory in the Rhineland or in Luxemburg; in fact, Bismarck cleverly publicized the French request, thus maintaining British hostility to Napoleon since the British wanted no French expansion so near the Low Countries. The French were vividly aware of the threat that Prussia's expansion posed to their own status in Europe. Bismarck was correct, then, in assuming France's growing hostility, though war became inevitable only when he provoked it. He was worried also about those states in South Germany that were tied to Prussia only by new military alliances and had been traditionally open to French influence. Whatever his plans before, Bismarck now began to think of completing German unity through a war with France.

Paris in 1871, after the Siege: The Champs Elysées and the Arch of Triumph.

War Against France

Napoleon III, now aging and ill, was increasingly distracted by liberal opposition. He tried to improve France's military power but without great success, partly because the liberals refused to cooperate. He tried to form alliances but again without success. Russia remembered the Crimean War; Britain continued to harbor suspicions of Napoleon's ambition. Austria showed some interest in revenge against Prussia but refused a formal alliance until it was clear that France could defeat Prussia. Italy also declined to help, for France as the defender of papal Rome was now her principal enemy. France was ill-prepared when Bismarck engineered the incident that led to war.

Spain, the victim of a new military revolt in 1868, was looking for a new king. Bismarck worked vigorously to induce the Spanish to offer the throne to a Prussian prince. When this offer was made public in 1870, the French were outraged, for they obviously could not tolerate Prussian influence on their southern border. Their protests led King William to withdraw the candidacy of the Prussian prince, but French insistence that the king promise further never to raise the candidacy again saved Bismarck's scheming. Napoleon's wording of the telegram to William at Ems conveying the French demand easily made the French posture seem insulting; William refused to promise. The French, their politicians excited and thirsting for a fight, declared war.

Again Prussia won handily, though Paris long resisted a siege. During the Franco-Prussian War, Italy seized Rome and Russia unilaterally abrogated the neutrality of the Black Sea. Napoleon was overthrown in France when he was captured by the Prussians, and republicans gained control of the French government during the war itself. Most of them were eager to continue the war, but French voters, called to elect a new assembly in 1871, voted for peace. Bismarck was able to impose the terms he wanted. Convinced that France would be an enemy regardless of what he did, Bismarck was not as forbearing as he had been with Austria. Germany acquired Alsace and most of Lorraine and further demanded a large financial indemnity from France. The territorial gains were designed to please generals who insisted on a more easily defended border with France, as well as the nationalists who wanted the inhabitants of these provinces, who were ethnically Germans, to be united with the fatherland. Most important of all, however, Bismarck's overwhelming success broke down the resistance of the south German states to a united Germany. In January 1871, William I of Prussia was crowned emperor of Germany in the Palace of Versailles.

The Nature of the New Germany

Bismarck's victories in 1866 and 1871 reconciled most liberals to the Prussian state. Their enthusiasm for national gains led them to agree to compromise their demands. In 1866 the Prussian parliament voted a Bill of Indemnity that legitimized the state's expenditures since 1862. Bismarck promised not to defy the constitution again, but he had proved the monarchy's supremacy over parliament. The structure of the Prussian state was not changed.

Bismarck did not rely on nationalist enthusiasm alone to resolve the conflict with the liberals, nor were the liberals without genuine gains of their own. A new government had to be established for the North German Confederation, and its institutions were extended in 1871 to the whole of Germany. The institutions were granted from above and Bismarck made sure he would not lose control of them. The king selected government ministers, and members of the upper house of parliament were appointed by the German states, with Prussia in effective control of that body. The powers of parliament as a whole were carefully limited; in particular, it had no direct control over the military. Military and diplomatic functions were centralized in Prussia's hands. With all this assured, Bismarck granted important concessions to liberals and radicals, confident that the masses were fundamentally conservative. The lower house of parliament, now called the Reichstag, was elected by universal suffrage. Parliament was given considerable power over the national budget, and liberals enacted a number of important reforms. Guilds were abolished in Prussia and liberal commercial codes were developed for the new nation. Jews were granted full legal equality. Bismarck had established institutions that could attract liberals, allowing them to work for further change. During the 1870s he relied in fact on liberal support in parliament, for conservatives were suspicious of the new institutions and of united Germany itself. Yet the liberal institutions could not touch the essence of power in Germany. Sovereignty remained with the king. With Bismarck, the new conservatism reached its greatest triumph.

THE HAPSBURG MONARCHY

The Hapsburg monarchy lacked a statesman with Napoleon's innovative power or Bismarck's cunning talent. Diplomatic setbacks, not conscious political leadership, gradually forced the government to retreat from the conservatism of the early 1850s. Austria's defeat in Italy in 1859 brought concessions to the liberals. The government reestablished provincial diets and created a two-chamber parliament for the whole empire. During the next six years further constitutional reforms were promised repeatedly, including decentralization. The emperor resisted however, for he was particularly eager to preserve a strong central bureaucracy.

Moreover, the type of concessions that flexible conservatives made in other countries were unusually complicated in Austria. Liberal pressure came mainly from German Austrians, particularly in Vienna. Yet discontent was spreading also among non-German nationalities, for the centralized government established by Bach was administered by German bureaucrats bent on "Germanizing" the whole empire. The modest liberal reforms of the early 1860s did nothing to conciliate the non-German nationalities: the central German bureaucracy remained untouched and the electoral system assured German control of the new national parliament. At the same time, the revived provincial diets were given very limited powers. The non-German nationalities resisted, though only passively. They refused to send representatives to parliament, which meant that the government could not function effectively. Even before the war with Prussia, reform measures had been discussed, particularly with representatives of the Magyars, the second largest ethnic group in the empire and bitterly opposed to German centralization. Yet the government was cautious. It feared that too many concessions to the various nationalities would dissipate the power and the diplomatic stature of the Hapsburg empire. It was also aware that the liberals, who were German nationalists as well, would resist undue conciliation.

Austria's defeat by Prussia compelled the government to reduce the grievances of both liberals and nationalists. The *Ausgleich* of 1867 created a dual monarchy. Austria and Hungary each had a substantially autonomous government, including a separate parliament. Thus the Magyars now ruled Hungary while the Germans retained predominance in Austria. The imperial government was charged with the conduct of foreign affairs, finance and miltary matters, and there was a single army. Other common interests, such as currency and tariffs, were regulated by treaties between Austria and Hungary, renewable every ten years; each parliament sent delegations to decide such matters.

In other words, this was no mere gesture to the Magyars. The structure of the empire had been profoundly altered and the most vigorous national protest appeased, at least for a time. No solution, however, was offered to the problem of nationalities as a whole. Slavs in Hungary as well as in Austria remained subject to rule by another people and in many ways the Magyars proved to be tougher masters than the Germans. Together, Germans and Magyars comprised less than 45 percent of the total population of the empire. German Austria faced the largest Slavic minority—the Czechs were over 12 percent of the empire's population—but Hungary had a substantial number of Croats, Serbs and Slovaks. Almost inevitably the *Ausgleich* heightened the self-consciousness of the Czechs and other nationalities, for it proved that concessions might be made if demands were pressed vigorously enough. At best the reform bought only a decade or so of relative internal peace.

Within the Austrian state, substantial new concessions were made to the liberals. Though suffrage was limited and districts were gerrymandered to assure German control, the power of parliament was increased. The government granted guarantees for civil liberties, admitted liberals to the ministry, virtually abolished the concordat with the Church, and gave full legal equality to the Jews. As in Germany, liberals viewed these measures favorably even though the essentials of the emperor's rule were not sacrificed. Liberals became vigorous supporters of the state. As German nationalists, they had the additional motive of wanting to assure continued German preponderance in Austria. With the Magyars bought off and the liberals largely satisfied, it seemed for a brief time that the Hapsburg empire, like its sister states, could achieve political stability.

RUSSIA

Government policy in Russia remained much closer to the traditional conservative mold than was the case in central Europe, with only the slightest hint of concessions to liberalism. There was no strong demand for liberal institutions in Russia, and nothing so bold as a parliament was introduced. Nevertheless the policy of sheer repression was modified and the government undertook a fundamental change in Russia's social structure.

Abolition of Serfdom

Serfdom was abolished in 1861 and with provisions far more humane than those in many other European countries. The government made a genuine effort not simply to emancipate the peasantry in a legal sense but to provide most peasants with land. There were a number of reasons for this. Alexander II, who became tsar in 1855, was no ardent reformer but he was considerably more flexible than his predecessor. Many of the bureaucrats around him wanted to modernize the Russian economy and saw that serfdom prevented mobility of labor and also impeded the contact between government and subject. Some landlords, too, realized that serfdom was an inefficient form of labor and welcomed a more productive system. Moreover the government and upper classes alike were fearful of peasant disorder. Finally, the Crimean War forced the government to try to balance defeat by a new approach at home. The war had revealed how badly Russia lagged behind the industrial powers of western Europe, thereby increasing the possibilities of unrest. Veterans returning to the countryside did indeed stimulate a rising rate of rural disorder.

The emancipation did not satisfy the peasantry however. Indeed, by arousing unfulfilled expectations, it made matters worse in many ways; recurrent rural protest was much more severe after 1860 than before. The aristocracy was allowed to salvage as much as it could from the reform. Hence, though peasants received most of the land, landlords retained the best land. Moreover the peasants had to pay redemption for the land they received, often in amounts far greater than the land was worth. Since the state paid off the aristocrats right away, the peasants became debtors to the state, with payments to extend over the next decades. Many aristocrats squandered their money quickly and the economic decline of the class continued; but peasants were left with great and annoying new burdens.

Furthermore the state could not bring itself fully to free the peasantry in the western sense. New institutions partly replaced aristocratic control, and the peasant was still not fully equal to other subjects in law. Village governments were established with extensive powers, primarily to make sure that peasants paid off their redemption dues. Peasants could not move or sell land without village permission and in some villages land was periodically redistributed so that there was no real private ownership at all. Regional councils, the *zemstvos,* watched over village decisions and in these bodies local aristocrats had the predominant voice.

The emancipation of the serfs was unquestionably the most substantial reform undertaken by any government between 1850 and 1875. It was followed by other important measures—notably a revision of the judicial system that made procedures more uniform. Also the Russian army began to pay more attention to its common soldiers, giving many of them a primary education within their period of service. Yet with all these changes Russia remained an old regime in a sense that was not true even of Bismarck's

Germany. The aristocracy dominated both government and the social structure. There were no political institutions capable of limiting the tsar and his bureaucracy. Hence the reformist tone of the 1860s was easily reversible, in contrast to developments in most of the rest of Europe. The state could quickly undermine promising experiments such as the regional *zemstvos* that initially provided some genuine representation through a three-class voting system. Even during the reformist years, when attempts to conciliate Poland collapsed in the revolt of 1863, the Russian government responded with bitter repression.

GREAT BRITAIN

In Britain, at the other extreme of Europe geographically and politically, the dominant patterns of the continent also did not fully apply, for liberals, not conservatives, ruled during most of the period and conservatives had long since adapted to liberal institutions. Even here, however, there were some analogies to continental developments as conservatives tried to modernize their political approach and a definite national party system took shape.

Whigs versus Tories

The Whigs controlled the government during most of the years from 1846 to 1874. They were not yet a modern political party nor were they fully committed to liberalism. Their leading figure until his death in 1866 was Palmerston, who was interested more in foreign than in domestic policy. He thought of politics in traditional British terms: political clubs as the basis of parliamentary factions and local electioneering, which included bribing and pressuring the voters, as the means of choosing members of parliament. However there was a liberal tone to most of the measures of legislation. Duties on foreign trade were reduced still further and in 1860 the Cobden Free Trade Treaty was signed with France. Governmental expenses were kept low. At the same time, municipalities were encouraged to develop new services, notably in the field of health and sanitary inspection.

Tories, for their part, began to grope for an alternative to liberal rule. They founded a central political office in 1852 and then, in 1867, a national party association. During the 1860s Benjamin Disraeli assumed leadership of the party and actively sought new issues that could gain popular support. Like the new conservatives on the continent, Disraeli used nationalism and tried to establish a positive contact with the masses to further his cause. He suggested an interest in social reform. In 1867, as prime minister, Disraeli tried to steal the liberals' thunder by sponsoring a further electoral reform that gave most urban workers the vote; property qualifications were greatly reduced and the electorate was doubled. Parliamentary seats were also redistributed so that for the first time the cities had more representation than the countryside. Not surprisingly the liberals won the first elections under the new act, in 1868, but the conservatives did not do badly. More important the new suffrage forced further changes in the structure and platform of both political parties.

REVIVAL OF LIBERALISM

During the 1860s and 1870s liberalism made its greatest gains throughout much of western and central Europe. Admittedly the concessions granted to liberals in Germany and the Hapsburg monarchy came from above, but they were great gains nonetheless. Nor were the concessions to liberalism neatly planned by conservatives like Bismarck. For example, because of continuing liberal pressure, the powers given to the Reichstag, including a guarantee of regular meetings, and the liberal economic legislation, exceeded what Bismarck had intended.

Further Liberal Gains

Liberals grew in strength through the early 1870s. The German Progressive party split in 1867, with a minority refusing to accept Bismarck's political system. But the majority National Liberals remained the leading party through the next decade. Austria's chief minister after the *Ausgleich* was Count Beust, a man devoted to the interests of the empire but undeniably a moderate liberal. In both countries, also, liberals were able to support measures that reduced the role of the churches, particularly the Catholic Church, in public life. In Austria the concordat was rescinded in the early 1870s, and the government secularized the school system and introduced civil marriage. Much the same process occurred in Germany under the grandiose title *Kulturkampf*, or battle for civilization. Bismarck led the fight largely because he suspected Catholics of disloyalty to united Germany. Liberals backed him—both to guarantee national unity and to serve the specifically liberal concern for a secular society. The government expelled the Jesuits, increased state regulation of clerical education, and made public education more secular.

Moderate liberals served as chief ministers in Spain during the decade before the interregnum in 1868. They lacked widespread support, however, and were hampered by their inability either to come to terms with the Catholic Church or to combat it vigorously. Hence they were easily displaced after 1868.

A far more significant liberal advance occurred in Italy. Parliament became increasingly divided between the *Sinistra* and the *Destra,* the Left and the Right. The divisions were modest since both parties shared something of the liberal tradition, but the Left stood in opposition to the moderation, not to say inactivity, of the government's internal policies of the later 1860s. Led by Agostino Depretis, the Left urged extension and reform of the state educational system, more public works and government encouragement to the economy, a more vigorous, nationalistic diplomacy, and an extended suffrage to enable greater representation of the Italian middle class. The Left was also harsher toward the Church, resembling the liberals of Germany and Austria in the same period. When the Left gained a parliamentary majority in 1876, it succeeded in expanding state education, restricting religious orders, and increasing the suffrage (to about 7 percent of the population).

Liberals in Power in Britain

In Britain the electoral reform of 1867 added to the urban vote, thereby strengthening the Liberal party and encouraging it to improve its organization. In Birmingham, for example, party leaders learned that by careful planning they could capture all three of the city's parliamentary seats and to do this they formed a liberal "caucus." The party was becoming increasingly institutionalized. More important, under the first ministry of William Gladstone, from 1868 to 1874, major reforms were undertaken, which at the same time completed the liberalization of British political structure and set the basis for the modern state in Britain. In 1870 the government abolished patronage in the choice of government officials and established compulsory competitive examinations for civil service posts. The judiciary was also remodeled. In the army, recruitment was improved, the purchase of commissions eliminated and punishments scaled down. In all the main branches of government the liberal principle of efficient administration, with careers open to talent (so long as the talent was suitably educated), was being increasingly realized. At the same time the government moved more actively into the field of education. The Education Act of 1870 set up locally elected school boards that could compel school attendance to the age of 13. Fees could be waived for poor parents. Government requirements for local supervision of sanitary facilities were also increased and local government boards were set up to supervise all such work.

French Liberalism

If liberal legislation progressively changed British society, the liberal revival in France achieved more fundamental gains. French political structure was returned to a liberal basis—a process that began in the 1860s when

The Defeat of the Commune: Summary executions of suspected agitators.

a handful of liberal republicans began to be elected to the parliament of the Second Empire. As Napoleon III's foreign policy faltered and his popularity among Catholics declined, he, like so many new conservatives, tried to win liberal support. The powers of parliament were increased and deputies had some control over the choice of ministers and the imperial government. Catholic influence in education was reduced and the minister of education strove to create new secular educational institutions. For French liberals these measures posed a dilemma similar to that faced by German liberals at the same time: should they accept important reforms that were granted from above but left them without full power? A minority said yes. The liberal Émile Ollivier agreed to become prime minister in 1870. In May 1870 a plebiscite was held to approve the liberal reforms and reaffirm support of the Empire: 7,336,000 citizens voted for the government and 1,572,000 against. The majority of French liberals, however, could not accept a mongrel regime of this sort. They wanted a republic and they wanted full power in their own hands. In contrast to their liberal counterparts in Germany, the French worked actively for popular support, converting many voters to republicanism, particularly in the cities; hence the million and a half votes against Napoleon in 1870.

Then came the war and with it France's defeat. The Empire was abolished but what would replace it? At first the republicans were at a disadvantage, for they had championed the war and opposed the peace, contrary to the wishes of most Frenchmen in 1871. The majority of new parliament members elected that year was monarchist and during the next four years monarchist leaders strove to set up a new regime. Furthermore a new revolt in Paris threatened to discredit radical forces still further. Exhausted by months of German seige, angered by the peace settlement and the conservative parliament, artisans and small shopkeepers expelled the national army and set up their own Parisian government—the Commune. The Commune was inspired by the Parisian revolutionary tradition and aided by socialists of various stripes. It undertook a few small social reforms but had to devote most of its attention to maintaining its claim for local autonomy that would isolate Paris from the rest of France. After assembling a sufficient armed force, the national government put down the Commune with great brutality and subsequently jailed or exiled many radical leaders.

Ironically the suppression of the Commune was one of the stepping stones to the formation of a new republic. The chief executive of the government, Adolphe Thiers, was now a moderate republican. Thiers' political principles had not changed much since the days when he helped establish the July Monarchy but he was now convinced that his principles could be realized in a republic. Many others came around to the same view. Moreover Thiers' suppression of the Commune was proof that being a republican was compatible with being a social conservative. At the same time, the monarchist parliament was hopelessly divided between supporters of the Bourbon house and supporters of the Orleanist cause. Precious time was lost in negotiation between the two camps, while the Bourbon pretender made things worse by refusing to compromise with any liberal institutions, in the characteristic but now futile ploy of the traditional conservative.

Republicans were quick to revive. Under the leadership of Léon Gambetta they campaigned actively for popular support. As a young politician during the Second Empire, Gambetta had resisted the temptation of compromising with the regime; he, and many liberals like him, wanted a parliamentary, democratic republic. During the war with Prussia Gambetta escaped from besieged Paris in a balloon to organize resistance in the provinces; afterwards he was long associated with nationalist resentment against the German victory. So in Gambetta the liberal republicans had a dedicated, flamboyant leader. Ironically Gambetta's real contribution to French politics involved compromise rather than devotion to high ideals, patient campaigning rather than spectacular gestures. Gambetta was convinced that a new social layer, the small town and rural middle class, could be won over to support of the republic and the leadership of France. He and his followers addressed themselves mainly to landowning peasants and small-town shopkeepers, people who were socially conservative, anxious to defend their property, but at the same time were interested in political rights and suspicious of the Church. The republicans argued that a republic already existed in fact and that it would carefully preserve private property and the existing social order.

The anomaly of a government without permanent institutions became increasingly obvious. The republicans gained ground in by-elections and in 1875 the assembly agreed to establish a presidency chosen by parliament; by one vote it passed an amendment designating this office the presidency of the republic. Republican institutions were further defined during the next four years, though a formal constitution was never enacted. A two-house parliament was established in which the senate, at first partly appointed by the assembly, was intended to be a conservative body; the chamber of deputies was elected by direct, universal suffrage. The president was given almost monarchical powers to direct the military, to name the ministers and in case of dispute to dismiss parliament. The royalists, still powerful, hoped to control the presidency until a king could be chosen. The first president, Marshall MacMahon, was an ardent royalist, but parliament was becoming more predominantly republican and in 1877 forced the president to yield in a test of power; two years later MacMahon resigned. This established de facto that government ministers were responsible to parliament and that presidents could not dismiss parliament.

With parliament supreme, France had the most liberal political structure on the continent, and with the republic firmly proclaimed it had the most radical system of any major European power. Following their triumph in political forms, liberal republicans went on during the 1880s to enact the usual sorts of liberal legislation: curtailment of the powers of the Church, particularly those of religious orders, and expansion of secular education.

LIBERALISM: THEORY
AND MOVEMENT

Liberalism was unquestionably the most important new political current in Europe through the first three-quarters of the nineteenth century. The term is constantly used by historians who trace the triumphs and tragedies of liberalism in the major countries, citing when liberals were in power and what they tried to achieve. But it is important also to analyze liberalism as a political movement and to ask a basic question: to what extent can liberalism be defined?

Any definition of liberal theory must be approached with caution. There is always a gap between the idea basic to a political movement and the activities of practical or even impractical politicians. In liberalism the gap was heightened by the vagueness of the theory itself. The definition of the boundaries between government and individual was extremely flexible and liberals were constantly changing the boundary line. German liberal theorists in fact tended to argue that rights themselves came from the state and that it was up to the state to define them. Furthermore liberalism as a political theory lost ground after 1848, precisely as liberalism as a political movement became more important. There were no schools of thought as important as the utilitarians or the doctrinaires had been, or as the Marxists were becoming. John Stuart Mill's *On Liberty* was still to come in 1859, but on the continent, particularly, liberal ideology waned. Some liberal intellectuals, like the historian Heinrich von Treitschke in Germany, turned to an aggressive nationalism led by an authoritarian state; others, including Mill, moved increasingly toward socialism.

Liberal Political Goals

A limited definition of liberalism in practice is possible and is clearly related to liberal theory. First, liberals believed in parliaments that would effectively represent some segment of the population and limit the powers of the executive to some degree. They varied, of course, on how much power they thought parliament should have. German liberals did not necessarily want parliament to be supreme over the monarch, lest this unduly weaken the state. Second, liberals wanted individual freedoms of speech, press, and religion. When a group or a regime abandoned civil rights and some parliamentary independence, it was no longer liberal. Such a transition occurred rather clearly in at least two regimes—the July Monarchy in France and the Italian government of the 1890s—and in the National Liberal party in Germany after 1880. It is possible to define liberalism sharply enough to recognize when liberals became conservatives.

But to go beyond this is difficult, for liberalism varied greatly from country to country. We have already seen the difficulties in defining a liberal position with regard to revolution before 1848. Liberals, who believed in some human rationality, preferred persuasion and evolution to revolt but they could advocate and certainly make use of revolution. Only after the failures of 1848 was this ambiguity cleared up, for major liberal movements everywhere renounced revolution as impractical and damaging to liberal goals. Liberals in most countries supported nationalism well beyond the point at which nationalism began to compete with the liberal goals of a small state and harmony among men. In Germany, and to an extent in Italy, nationalism would lead liberals to abandon their liberalism altogether in the advocacy of big armies and forcible expansion. In the established countries, notably Britain and France, liberals held out longer against the illiberal aspects of nationalism. But in both countries important groups of liberals led in the building of empires. Jules Ferry in France and Joseph Chamberlain in England wanted greater national glory but they also saw the empire as a way to extend liberal values of peace and education to native peoples—albeit by force. Again the protean quality of liberalism. French republicans had no qualms after 1870 in rapidly building up the French army by extending military conscription, among other ways.

Initially liberalism was not democratic. Liberals believed in rule by an elite, which was defined by property and education. Before 1848 a democrat was a radical though he might believe in liberal goals in other respects. But liberals had a hard time resisting democracy, for their own slogans held that men should be equal under the law and that men were improvable. Hence it is often argued, with some justice, that the Reform Bill of 1832 in Britain, clearly a liberal measure, had to lead to democracy. Liberals could not, in other words, put up convincing arguments for stopping electoral reform within any group. After 1851 French liberals had no trouble adapting to universal suffrage. Their campaigns in the 1860s and 1870s represented the first cases in which they campaigned for mass support and showed it could be done. British liberals urged the electoral extension of 1867 and by the 1880s led also in developing mass campaign techniques. Elsewhere the conversion to democracy was slower. Universal suffrage was imposed upon German liberals and they were long suspicious of it. Italian and Belgian liberals accepted universal suffrage only after 1900. Again there was no common pattern; there were elements within the liberal impulse that could explain a number of different positions.

Liberalism and the State

Liberalism was more ambiguous in regard to the functions of government than to its forms. On the continent, particularly, liberalism cannot be viewed as a movement to scale down the functions of government. Even in Britain, where liberals through Gladstone worked hard to reduce government expenditures, new government activities were developed. This was noticeable first on the municipal level. When liberals gained control of the cities through the municipal reforms of the 1830s, they invariably worked for city park programs, sanitation measures, and other urban concerns. The main contribution of the first Gladstone ministry was not the attention paid to the budget but the development of new state responsibility for education and health. On the continent the pattern is still clearer. Most liberals wanted the government to take an active role in economic development and education. It is true that liberals were suspicious of state power especially when they did not control it; it is also true that they did not seek to expand the power of the state indiscriminately. But liberals balanced their fear of the state by their desire to make the state more efficient—for example, through an expanded civil service system—and to use the state as an agent for progress. Hence, as they attacked some of the functions of the mercantilist state, they added new ones. The liberal state as a mere policeman existed only briefly as a historical reality and then only in Britain. Liberalism's real contribution to the history of the state was to open the bureaucracy to new talent and to make the state responsible for education, for record-keeping, and for marriage law. As critics of liberalism pointed out at the time, the state moved closer to the individual.

Liberal Social Policy

By the same token, liberal economic and social policy cannot be summed up easily. It is true that liberals did not want too much interference with individual economic freedom as they defined it. Liberals were not socialists. But liberal policy extended over a wide range. Only in Britain did liberals consistently defend free trade; in France they almost never did. Liberals tended to be suspicious of trade unions for imposing the will of the group over that of the individual. But liberal governments in both Britain and France legalized strikes and trade unions. Liberals can be accused of great indifference to the poor, as witness the inactivity of the British government during the worst miseries of industrialization and the harsh Poor Law Reform that was so clearly a liberal measure. Yet in these same years the first factory laws were passed, with liberals arguing on both sides of the issue. Again liberals had no uniform position on how far the state should interfere to protect the unfortunate or the extent to which poverty was the fault of the poor themselves.

National Varieties of Liberalism

These ambiguities within liberalism are complicated by national differences. In a very real sense there could be no liberal movement or government on the continent of the type possible in Britain. It is very easy to adopt Britain as criterion and point out all the ways in which the continentals fell short. All continental liberals faced central governments whose functions were already extensive and which possessed substantial military and police forces. None managed to reduce police surveillance of political meetings or avoid police violence in repressing disorder to the level normal in Britain, where the police grew up with liberalism itself. All continental liberals, but particularly those in France, Italy, and Spain, were preoccupied with the power of the Catholic Church to an extent unnecessary in Britain. Many were ardent anticlericals and some even sought to use the government to repress Catholic activities. As already indicated, no continental movement was able to reduce government expenditures, as British liberals managed to do briefly, and few seriously wanted to.

Yet liberalism did exist on the continent. Political parties in France that were primarily liberal outlasted their British counterparts, remaining important elements of the political structure until after 1918. French and even

Italian liberals were slower than the British to compromise their traditional principles in the face of new social pressures. French liberals were anti-clerical and tolerant of a highly centralized state but their policies fit a definition of liberalism that must, as we have seen, encompass a broad range of policies even within a single country.

Was liberalism stillborn in Germany or did it somehow sell out? Historians, with an eye cocked to the horrors of Nazism, have combed German history to find out what happened to liberalism. Did the statist emphasis of German liberal theory and the obvious attraction to nationalism mean that German liberalism was not liberal at all—by any definition? Possibly, but German liberals advocated and achieved many reforms of government structure and function. They renounced revolution when only revolution would have allowed them to capture and remake the state. They betrayed their cause perhaps less by timidity than by undue confidence in further reforms and in continued popular support. Compared to liberalism in the West, German liberalism differed less in its goals than in the inability of its leaders to win support from the lower classes or even much of the middle class. Here Bismarck's gamble with universal suffrage paid off. But only in France and the Anglo-Saxon countries were liberals clearly more successful.

Liberalism was, then, something of a will o' the wisp. It cannot neatly be associated with a particular type of government or voting system or with laissez-faire economics. Though it cannot be identified with any one national tradition, nowhere did liberals manage to overcome preestablished national political patterns. Nor can liberalism be linked with a particular social class. Liberal policies encouraged capitalism; liberal political structure increased middle-class influence in government. Yet many of the middle class in Germany rejected liberalism because it was associated with economic change, or accepted it, as in France, because its economic individualism could protect small proprietors against larger, more modern business forms. Precisely because it could mean such diverse things, liberalism served many different interests and survived many apparent deaths.

THE NEW REGIMES

Throughout western and central Europe an implicit compromise had been reached between leading liberals and conservatives by the end of the 1870s. Outstanding questions of political form and the relations between Church and state were on their way to settlement. The nature of the settlement differed significantly from one country to the next. The German regime was conservative in base; the French liberal and the Italian hovered in between. Yet even in Germany the structure of politics had greatly changed. The combination of conservative flexibility and liberal concessions had ended the period of intense political unrest that had begun in 1789. Economic prosperity and the decline of Romantic political idealism had aided this transition, but by the 1870s the new regimes could survive renewed hardship and attack. Only defeat in war could dislodge them, in fact, as happened in Germany in 1918 and France in 1940.

Political quarrels continued. Traditional conservatives in many countries remained suspicious of the new political process; liberals generally sought further reform. But the strength of each movement now lay within the political system, one symptom of this being the spread of formal political parties.

The extent to which old issues had been resolved led to a blossoming of the political manipulator—a man who could juggle various factions without great concern for ideology or principles. The leaders we shall encounter when we return to political history were all men of this type. Politics, during the 1880s especially, seemed dominated by deals rather than ideals but this is simply another way of saying that the political structures were now widely accepted.

Elements of the politics of compromise spread beyond central and western Europe. New states established in the Balkans set up parliaments and developed political factions as a matter of course. The Spanish state returned to conservatism in the 1870s but it too had a parliament and political parties that it juggled in power at least for show. Only Russia stood apart from even superficial innovations in political structure and only Russia, as it turned out, risked revolts in the name of liberalism.

In western and central Europe the settling of old disputes helped clear the way for a new set of problems to dominate the political scene. The settlements were not designed to solve a number of new issues and they raised important problems of their own.

With the steady advance of industry the social question—that is, the question of what to do with and for the workers—came to the fore. Neither liberals nor conservatives could meet workers' demands, yet several of the new political systems gave workers a direct political voice. Socialist movements were in fact taking shape before 1870 though they had nowhere achieved great importance. Continued missionary activity, the rise of big business and a new round of periodic depressions soon changed this situation. By the 1890s the social question had become the basis for the most important political divisions.

The new regimes had in many ways less relationship to leading cultural trends than they had to social developments. There was a superficial correspondence between pragmatic political policies and the decline of Romanticism. More important was the fact that compromise politics easily disgusted intellectuals of many persuasions, precisely because compromise seemed to ignore high principles. Furthermore, developments in both the arts and in science tended to undermine assumptions of human rationality on which even qualified parliamentary democracies were based. In short, the new regimes were soon in trouble with intellectuals and the intellectuals could arouse other groups to complain.

Finally, the new regimes depended rather obviously on diplomatic success, a key ingredient of the new conservatism. Governments had learned that an active foreign policy was a great help in winning popular support; some degree of popular support was now essential to rule. This development, plus the huge shift in Europe's balance of power with the uniting of Germany, assured a troubled period of diplomacy. Governments sought to gain or regain position and delight their citizenry. The amazing extension of European empires was the first fruit of these policies, but when empire-building was exhausted, the states returned to a focus on Europe. Diplomatic problems, entwined with internal social and cultural malaise, finally destroyed the stability that the new political systems achieved for a few decades.

5 THE RISE
OF INDUSTRIAL
SOCIETY

1848–1914

During the last half of the nineteenth century, most countries in western and central Europe reached industrial maturity—a goal Britain had achieved by 1850. Their economies continued to develop, but the bases of industrialization were well established and the vast majority of the population was involved in the industrial process, either as industrial employees, as consumers of industrial goods, or as producers of food or services for a capitalistic market. Most factory workers were familiar with their jobs and the tempo of industrial work. Entrepreneurs became managers of established processes, including the process of invention itself, rather than daring pioneers. Industry vastly overshadowed agriculture and at least half the population lived in cities. Industrial maturity meant that new techniques and forms of organization could now be applied to any branch of production, including agriculture and the crafts.

The pace of industrialization still varied significantly. Germany's rise, like that of the United States, was extraordinarily swift; German rates of heavy industrial production soared massively. Britain's economic supremacy was correspondingly challenged. After two final decades of untroubled prosperity, between 1850 and 1870, the British economy began to falter. Production rose far less rapidly than in other countries and both management and labor became increasingly resistant to innovation. France, following rapid gains under Napoleon III, lagged behind after 1870, owing to the loss of industrial territory and capital in the Franco-Prussian War. But a new industrial spurt began in 1895 that continued for more than 30 years. These and other national differences were extremely important. Nevertheless the most important economic and social developments spread over national boundaries. France, England, Germany, Scandinavia, the Low

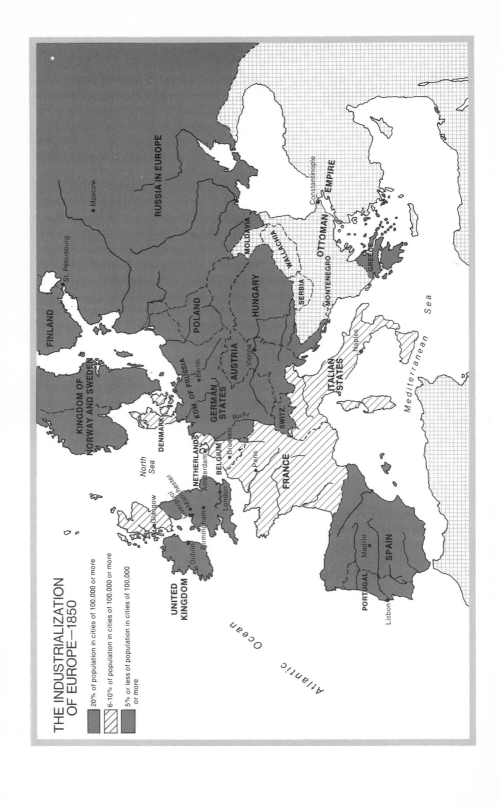

THE INDUSTRIALIZATION
OF EUROPE—1850

20% of population in cities of 100,000 or more

6-10% of population in cities of 100,000 or more

5% or less of population in cities of 100,000
or more

UNITED
KINGDOM

Glasgow

Dublin

Birmingham

London

Mersey

Manchester

Leeds

NETHERLANDS

Amsterdam

BELGIUM

Brussels

Paris

FRANCE

North
Sea

DENMARK

KINGDOM OF
NORWAY AND SWEDEN

FINLAND

St. Petersburg

Moscow

RUSSIA IN EUROPE

POLAND

KDM. OF PRUSSIA

Berlin

GERMAN
STATES

Ruhr

SWITZ.

AUSTRIA

Vienna

HUNGARY

MOLDAVIA

WALLACHIA

SERBIA

MONTENEGRO

OTTOMAN EMPIRE

Constantinople

GREECE

ITALIAN
STATES

Naples

Mediterranean   Sea

SPAIN

Madrid

PORTUGAL

Lisbon

Atlantic Ocean

Countries, and to a lesser extent northern Italy, Austria, and Bohemia, had become part of the same industrial system.

Beyond this zone, important economic changes were also taking place. Not only in Russia and Russian Poland but in Spain and the Balkans as well, industrialization began during the final decades of the century. It copied technology and business forms currently being introduced in countries like Germany, but remained far short of industrial maturity. In many ways the spread of capitalism and market production, particularly to the countryside, overshadowed the importance of industrialization in this outer zone of Europe. Certainly it affected more people. Finally, demographic vitality, waning now in western Europe, forged ahead in the east and south. The outer zone of Europe was undergoing a number of changes that had occurred earlier in the west, changes that in many respects were more sweeping than the industrial development in the west. They produced far more unrest.

INDUSTRIAL EUROPE: TECHNOLOGY

Manufacturing techniques improved steadily during the last half of the century. New textile equipment, for example, contributed to greater productivity. By 1900 the most efficient weaving establishments required workers to man 12 or more mechanical looms instead of the two that had been standard at mid-century. New techniques were also used to produce new consumer goods, such as artificial fibers, bicycles, and automobiles.

Although steam engines still dominated factory production, other sources of power were being developed. Electrical engines allowed areas that had a poor supply of coal, such as northern Italy, to compensate in part by the use of hydroelectric power. Both electrical motors and internal combustion engines, which burned petroleum rather than coal, facilitated the use of power outside factories, since steam engines were too large for use in small shops or on farms.

With the development of new products and new power sources, major new industries emerged. Manufacturers of chemicals and electrical equipment were added to the list of industrial leaders, chemical production now involving not only dyes but also fertilizers, explosives, medical drugs, and synthetic fibers. Germany's rise to industrial prominence included an early lead in both these new industries.

The Rise of Heavy Industry

The most striking development in industrial technology occurred in heavy industry. By 1850 the demand for metallurgical products was rising

The Apotheosis of Materialism: The main hall of the Crystal Palace at the Great Exhibition of 1851, where the latest industrial products and techniques were displayed.

rapidly, particularly because of the expansion of railroad networks. The invention of the Bessemer converter in 1856 was the first of several innovations that permitted a massive increase in metallurgical production. The Bessemer process, as well as the open hearth process that developed soon after it, removed impurities in iron ore chemically, rather than by skilled labor. Much bigger blast furnaces could be constructed. Furthermore carbon could be automatically reintroduced to the smelted metal, making the mass production of steel possible for the first time. Finally, the invention of the Gilchrist-Thomas process in the 1870s allowed the processing of iron ore that was heavy in phosphates, thus opening the massive ore fields of

Lorraine to industrial exploitation. Germany, which had just taken over much of Lorraine, was the first beneficiary, but by the 1890s French Lorraine also forged ahead.

Toward the end of the century power machinery was gradually introduced for the mining as well as for the hauling of coal, but the expansion of coal production continued to depend primarily on the growth of the labor force in the mines. More important technical strides were made in machine-building, where power machinery increasingly displaced skilled workers in lathing, riveting, and the like.

With its new technology, heavy industry quickly dominated the economies of all the industrial countries, a development that had a number of implications beyond the purely technical or economic. Heavy industrial firms had to be large since the new blast furnaces required massive capital and a large labor force. Here was one of the key causes of the rise of big business and the consequent, relative decline of the small entrepreneur. The manufacture of artillery and warships improved along with the production of motors and bicycles; as a result, the ties between industry and the military inevitably increased. These developments occurred throughout Europe, but they were most evident in some of the newer industrial countries such as Germany and, more tentatively, Russia.

The pattern of industrialization had now changed. Almost any country that began to industrialize after 1840 first started by building railroads and then heavy industry. Textiles and other highly individualistic and competitive industries were of relatively little interest to the state and failed to achieve the importance that they had in England and France. With the rise of heavy industry, the tone of the industrial economies of England and France changed but never matched that of the industrial newcomers.

Machines in Craft Industries

The expansion of heavy industry can easily obscure another aspect of late nineteenth-century technology, one that affected more people more intimately. Machines were now introduced in almost all the light industries. The key single invention, along with the spread of electric power, was the sewing machine, which rapidly transferred the manufacture of clothing and shoes from artisan shops to factories or sweatshops. But no traditional industry was immune. Printing presses grew larger and automatic typesetting machines were introduced. Cranes and electric saws altered construction work. Canning changed the nature of the food processing industry. In other words, many traditional branches of production were put on a factory basis while those that remained in smaller shops were also transformed by new methods and equipment.

New machines meant a rapid increase in production. Output soared in goods as diverse as newspapers and steel ingots. Between 1850 and 1870 alone, heavy industrial production rose 600 percent in Germany and 300 percent in France. Gains of this sort, impelled by rapidly rising productivity per worker, were quickly translated into improved standards of living. Manufacturing and commercial profits continued to advance more rapidly than any other form of earnings, but wages now were also clearly on the rise. In Britain, for example, real wages increased by a third between 1850 and 1875 and by almost 40 percent from 1875 to 1900. Similar gains occurred in the industrial countries on the continent, as prices fell and money wages advanced.

New horizons opened for many in the lower classes, particularly in the cities. Diets improved as the lower classes were able to purchase more meat, milk products, sugar and coffee, and at the same time the percentage of the budget spent on food declined. Only 60 percent of earnings, instead of approximately 80 percent, went for food. There was a chance for more varied and abundant clothing and, in some cases, better housing as well. The lower classes could also regularly afford expenditures on non-necessities —insurance, newspapers, union and party dues, recreation, and even bicycles—something they were not able to do before. For the first time in human history, absolute poverty—life on the margins of subsistence—was confined to a minority of the population.

The growth and sophistication of industrial technology brought suffering as well, for many people were displaced or subjected to a new pace of work by machines. Naturally, too, improvements in living standards were spread very unevenly. Many were still desperately poor, and disparities of income tended to increase. Nevertheless, by expanding production and facilitating the movement of goods, advancing technology brought a new freedom to most ordinary people—the freedom from want. This historic change was in turn the source of new ideas and new vitality among the common people.

Toward a Consumer Ethic

The new technology also transformed the central focus of the economy. Production was no longer the key problem. In a mature industrial economy, even a somewhat laggard one such as Britain had by the end of the century, there were no technical barriers to expanding production. Organized industrial research virtually guaranteed continued technical innovation. Rather, the key problem was assuring consumption of the new goods now available. Because of the class structure of industrial society, it proved harder to distribute purchasing power equitably than to produce goods that had to be purchased if the economy was not to falter. The new stress on distributing goods was evident in the development of mass commercial outlets, such as department stores, and in the rapid expansion of advertising. Problems of distribution were reflected in recurrent economic slumps and in the growing fear that constricted markets could be broadened only with the government's help through imperial expansion, armament purchases, or other artificial stimuli.

The change in economic orientation from production to consumption challenged the prevailing economic ethic. Symptomatic of this change was the fact that socialism, which focused on the proper distribution of goods, increasingly displaced liberal economic theory, which focused on expanding production. Relatedly, the economic ethic of the middle classes began to erode. In a society whose principal economic problem was expanding consumption, the virtues of hard work and restraint became less relevant. A change of values was also necessary for the lower classes, who had traditionally stressed equilibrium, the balance of both production and consumption. The imposition of industrial capitalism had already forced many of them to expand production; now they were called upon to expand consumption as well. This could be learned, of course, though not always so rapidly as we in the twentieth century might assume. Again it involved a historic change of outlook.

The industrialization of much of Europe by 1900 was a technological revolution, which, in the whole sweep of human history, was matched in importance only by the transition from hunting to agriculture in the Neolithic age. Achieved in less than a century, this technological revolution altered not just the political or social structures but the very way men thought about life.

NEW ECONOMIC FORMS

From the beginnings of industrialization, technical innovation had an immediate impact on economic organization. The rise of capitalism posed a threat for traditional, small units of economic activity such as guilds and peasant villages, but at first new factory groupings, though far more powerful and tightly disciplined, were relatively small themselves. After 1850 industrialization created the large, impersonal economic unit. The age of big business was born.

Big Business

Technical requirements encouraged the development of big business. Entrepreneurs had to amass huge sums of capital to afford the new machines in heavy industry. But companies grew well beyond the levels required by new technology. The chemical industry, for example, developed gigantic firms at least a decade before expensive equipment was introduced. Big firms arose primarily because capitalists learned to modify competitive pressure through large-scale operations. A big firm could diversify its products, afford a research staff to seek out new methods and influence its market for supplies and sales, in some cases dictating terms to both buyers and sellers. Small wonder that the number of big firms increased rapidly. By the 1890s well over half the entire labor force in the industrial countries was employed in companies with over 20 workers, while in the most modern industries, such as the electrical equipment industry in Germany, two or three firms controlled virtually the entire output.

The corporate form of business and the industrial investment bank were the twin companions of mature industrial capitalism. Both changed the nature of ownership in addition to encouraging larger business units. Most countries eased the restrictions on corporate formation between 1850 and 1870. Beginning in Britain in the 1850s corporations spread rapidly, not only in manufacturing but in insurance and other sectors. The corporation divided ownership among a number of shareholders, whose responsibility to the company was limited to the percentage of their share. Stock exchanges, previously concerned mainly with government securities, now flourished with the buying and selling of private shares.

With the expansion of railroads and heavy industry, the financial resources of banks had to be opened to industry. During the 1850s both the French and the Prussian governments encouraged the formation of investment banks. Huge firms, like Krupp in Germany, were intertwined with giant banks.

The growth of big business and the diffusion of ownership were heightened by combinations among business units. Lobbying associations were formed, like the *Comité des forges* in France, to influence the government, while other groups tried to coordinate policies toward labor. Of greater importance was the formation of cartels, which first arose in response to the slump of the 1870s to restrict competition within an industry. A cartel was an association of individual firms that set market or production quotas for each member, or determined prices. In Germany, where the movement was particularly strong, there were 300 cartels by 1900 and many similar groups had arisen elsewhere. The power of cartels and other groups should not be exaggerated, for they often could not enforce their own policies and in no sense did they run the whole economy. Still the movement toward association in industry was yet another sign that the individualistic ethic was fading among the bigger businessmen, while their ability to maintain profits, even during recessions, increased.

The trend toward big business was not confined to manufacturing. Large shipping firms and wholesalers increasingly controlled the movement of goods, while retail department stores spread in all the major centers, putting considerable pressure on smaller, more specialized shops.

The implications of this spread of big business were far-reaching. The political power of the leading firms increased greatly. One of the reasons for the relative weakness of liberalism in Germany was the ability of businessmen to win the legislation they sought directly through pressure groups; they did not need liberal parties or political structures to serve their interests. The economic power of many middle-class sectors was greatly enhanced not only by the huge profits business accrued but by the distribution of its earnings to a number of shareholders. Many big firms also extended benefits to labor through company-sponsored hospitals and welfare schemes. Despite such paternalism, big companies exerted pressure on workers as well, forcing them to become accustomed to greater coordination and discipline on the job, speeding up the pace of work in the interests of efficiency, and removing any opportunity for personal contact with owners. As a result, many workers came to look on capitalists as an enemy class.

Industrial Unionism

With the rise of trade unions, the principle of big organization was extended to yet another facet of the economy, in part as a response to the growth of business. This development should not be exaggerated, however, for in no sense did "big labor" rival the economic and political power of "big business." Many unions were small, and as a whole, they nowhere won the majority of the manufacturing labor force. Mass unionism evolved slowly. The movement failed significantly to penetrate some of the strongholds of big business, such as French and German metallurgy. Nevertheless unions were gaining in strength because of their ability to organize many people and build up large funds.

The specific pattern of unionization varied, in part according to doctrinal influences. Where Marxism was strong, as in Germany, unions were at first distrusted and kept under party control. Here they stressed strong central organization, but revolutionary syndicalism in France encouraged very loose organization with a small union bureaucracy. Despite these differences, industrial unions tended to move in the same direction and characteristically grew impatient with formal doctrines of any sort. Many craft unions imitated them as well.

Membership in the union movement rose rapidly around the turn of the century. By 1914 there were about four million union members in Britain and about two million in Germany. Along with the cooperative movement that spread at the same time, these were the largest private organizations ever developed. Their powers were great. In most countries they succeeded in having laws passed that regulated working conditions. Through strikes and other pressures they fostered collective bargaining in many branches of manufacturing, a sign also of how rapidly the power of giant organizations could increase. Now, for example, the head of the 100,000-member miners' federation, founded a scant decade before, would discuss with the president of the mine owners' association, scarcely older, conditions that would affect not just a single industry and its workers, but the entire economy.

BOOM AND BUST

Major recessions occurred in the mid-1870s and the mid-1890s, with smaller ones every five to ten years. These slumps were not as damaging as the preindustrial recessions nor were they caused in the same way. The trigger was now a bank failure—not a crop failure—which dried up investment funds and thereby forced a slowdown in manufacturing. Since food prices did not rise, unemployed workers did not suffer nearly so much as before, and business combines helped manufacturers survive. Still the recessions caused great hardship.

After 1900, though there were no major slumps, certain other disquieting signs began to appear in the manufacturing economy. In key industries, such as mining, the expansion of production slowed down and in much of western and central Europe annual economic growth dropped. Unemployment rose, most notably in Britain. Furthermore, real wages fell in some countries for the first time in over half a century, while elsewhere they rose much more slowly than before. Partly because of the discovery of new gold supplies, but also because of tariffs and other restrictions on production or trade, prices advanced rapidly. This was the longest period of inflation since industrialization had begun, for during most of the nineteenth century increased production had tended to drive prices down.

There were, then, signs of structural weakness in the economy, particularly after 1900, despite the advances in technology and business organization. This explains the rising tide of industrial unrest, and also forces a closer look at the economy itself.

Limits of Economic Growth

There was a persistent danger that purchasing power would lag behind production. The poorer classes, who were likely to spend their money most rapidly, received a decreasing share of the national product. In Britain, the workers' share of the total national income fell by 26 percent between 1870 and 1900, while in Germany it dropped by 55 percent. The rich, getting richer, were unable to spend fast enough to keep pace consistently with the growth of production. Moreover in all the industrial countries they were increasingly tempted to withdraw some of their funds from the national economy. Interest rates were higher in less developed areas, not only in the colonies but also in industrializing countries like Russia. Foreign investment burgeoned: by 1900 Britain had invested over a quarter of her assets abroad, France 15 percent. Foreign investment could produce new income and new orders for products of the investing nation, but it tended to exacerbate the problem of recurrently insufficient demand at home. It also reflected some sense on the part of investors that opportunity at home was drying up. The patterns of income distribution and investment threatened the basis of the new industrial economy. Europe had developed mass production without an adequate base in mass consumption.

Obviously, production continued to increase and, for many groups, so did prosperity, up to 1914. Foreign as well as internal trade increased rapidly, aided by new methods of transportation and communication such as steamships and the telegraph. One major sector of the economy, however, was not simply threatened with trouble: agriculture faced a long-term crisis from which it has yet to extricate itself fully.

Agricultural Crisis

The blow came in the 1870s, after two decades of good harvests and prosperity. Progress in shipping enabled farmers in North America, Australia, and elsewhere to ship grain to Europe at a price lower than Europeans—whether landlords or peasants—could match. For two decades European agriculture struggled to adapt to this foreign competition. New equipment and fertilizers spread more rapidly than ever before on both peasant holdings and large estates. But this situation only heightened the problem of overproduction and falling prices for grains. More successful was an attempt to turn to truck or dairy farming or meat raising, for demand for these products was rising and competition from outside Europe was less severe. Such conversions were very difficult and required capital and new knowledge. Many peasants proved more adaptable than estate owners, but there were failures everywhere. The growth of cooperatives, which provided capital and market facilities, aided rural adaptation, particularly in Denmark, the country that met the crisis most successfully.

The agricultural crisis severely restricted rural income, which now lagged greatly behind urban levels; here was a clear structural weakness in the market for industrial production. Nevertheless many rural producers were able to weather the crisis by yet another stage in agriculture's adjustment to capitalist market conditions. But adaptation was not the only response. Estate owners, with peasant support, called for protection from the government. After a period of growing freedom in international trade, tariff barriers were erected anew—at the expense of urban groups. Germany's tariff on agricultural products in 1879 was matched by similar restrictions in almost all the continental countries. By the 1890s food prices rose behind the tariff walls. In Germany, protection of Junker estates, where rye could best be grown, prevented the conversion to a white bread diet that had become standard fare among urban lower classes in the West. Yet with all this protection many agriculturalists were severely pressed—rural debt rose greatly everywhere—and many were seriously aggrieved.

DEMOGRAPHY

A historic change took place in the demographic patterns of western and central Europe after mid-century, though it had already been foreshadowed in France. The rate of population growth took a downward turn as birth rates dropped farther and farther below their traditional levels. Only a continued decline in the death rate allowed population to expand at all.

In a sense, the fall in the birth rate was a belated reaction to a century or more of population growth and to the dramatic decline in infant mortality rates. People realized that to have the number of children living to maturity they wanted, they had to limit the number of children born. But to accept this required a new mentality, one at least partially removed from the grip of custom and of religion. The limitation of birth was now largely achieved by artificial devices, knowledge of which spread rapidly among the lower classes. The marriage age continued to drop, with a consequent increase in the rate of marriages; hence one traditional way of limiting births was ignored.

From the standpoint of the twentieth century, it is perhaps natural to judge the demographic slowdown as a good thing, a necessary adjustment lest the number of people outrun the space available. But there is another side to this. Population growth, historically, is a creative, unsettling development; a slowdown can have the reverse effect. For the first time in two centuries, western Europe's population was growing less rapidly than that of the rest of the world. One might suggest that, in this final age of imperialist expansion, the basis for a reduction of Europe's influence was being set. More immediately, with both birth and death rates declining, western Europe's population was aging. The problem of old people became acute and, perhaps, the vitality of the whole population declined.

And what of the motives for a family's deciding to limit the number of children? Was this decision based on new expectations for a higher standard of living and greater resources for each child? Or was it the product of insecurity, a sense that conditions were so uncertain that a family could not risk having more than one or two children? The answer, probably, is a bit of both. Workers restricted their birth rate because they wanted more for themselves and their children and because they also found life a great burden that too many children would make worse. Middle-class people, who limited their births far more rigorously, wanted to assure their children's future status but they were not confident that this would be easy.

Both the causes and effects of the new demographic stage in western

Europe had ambiguous implications. They reveal a mentality and ability to innovate, coupled with a new timidity. At the time, the decline in population growth was a cause for alarm, for nations continued in the mercantilist tradition of judging their strength by the numbers they could command, among other things. France was particularly nervous as her population fell below the levels of Britain and Germany. It seems obvious, though immensely difficult to explain, that the decline of demographic vitality in Frence was linked to a decline in vitality in other fields. As demographic vitality began to ebb elsewere, albeit more slowly, was a more general vigor to be lost?

A FEELING OF CONSTRICTION

In regard to the economy, the mood of Europe around 1900 was decidedly ambiguous. This mood was clearly related to the new demographic situation and in part helped create it. People in various social classes were aware that great economic advances had been and were continuing to be made. We can certainly see, in retrospect, the huge innovations in technology and business organization. Prosperity spread and the traditional misery of even the lowest classes was mitigated. Famine had ceased as rising agricultural production and, especially, more efficient transportation freed the poor from the tyranny of crop failure. Relatedly, the most common forms of popular protest, riots stemming from hunger or rising food prices, disappeared in western and central Europe.

Yet, despite all these gains, there was an overall sense of uncertainty, in part owing to the real structural weaknesses in the economy. The rise of new industrial nations brought on fear of international competition. Trade unions, craftsmen, farmers, and most obviously big businessmen increasingly claimed the need for government help. Tariffs spread, at first mainly for agriculture but then for industry as well. France passed a very high tariff in the early 1890s, while in Germany the Bülow tariff of 1902 placed a 25 percent duty on many foods and metal products. Only Britain resisted this wave of protectionism, but even there many groups wanted help. In all countries, associations sprang up to urge the need for larger empires to bail out the faltering domestic economy. These and other groups also urged the need for increased military spending, ostensibly to protect the nation but more patently to provide greater markets for heavy industry.

The combination of growing power and a pervading sense of nervousness that characterized the economy around the turn of the century was to prove dangerous. Diplomacy became more and more intertwined with the economic mood. Internally, the rise of huge economic organizations and the new claims on the state decisively ended the liberal phase of

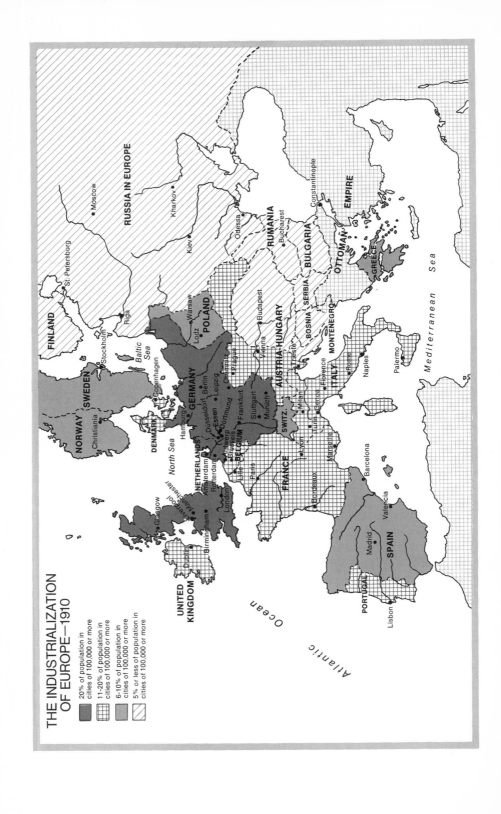

THE INDUSTRIALIZATION
OF EUROPE—1910

20% of population in
cities of 100,000 or more

11-20% of population in
cities of 100,000 or more

6-10% of population in
cities of 100,000 or more

5% or less of population in
cities of 100,000 or more

RUSSIA IN EUROPE

Moscow

Kharkov

Kiev

Odessa

St. Petersburg

FINLAND

Riga

Stockholm

Baltic
Sea

NORWAY

SWEDEN

Christiania

Copenhagen

DENMARK

North Sea

Hamburg

GERMANY

Berlin

Leipzig

Düsseldorf

Dortmund

Essen

Frankfurt

Stuttgart

Munich

Chemnitz

Prague

Warsaw

Lodz

POLAND

AUSTRIA-HUNGARY

Vienna

Budapest

Prague

Trieste

SWITZ.

Milan

Turin

Genoa

Florence

ITALY

Rome

Naples

Palermo

RUMANIA

Bucharest

SERBIA

BOSNIA

BULGARIA

MONTENEGRO

OTTOMAN
EMPIRE

Constantinople

GREECE

Mediterranean
Sea

NETHERLANDS

Amsterdam

Rotterdam

BELGIUM

Antwerp

Brussels

Lille

Paris

FRANCE

Lyon

Marseille

Bordeaux

UNITED
KINGDOM

Glasgow

Liverpool

Manchester

Birmingham

London

Dublin

SPAIN

Madrid

Barcelona

Valencia

PORTUGAL

Lisbon

Atlantic Ocean

Europe's economic history. Economic liberalism had never been fully put into practice and its reign had been brief. It could not survive in an age when the powerful decided they could not stand alone and the weak, who had been forced to rely on themselves, also learned through association to demand some share in state protection.

THE TRIUMPH OF THE MIDDLE CLASSES

Not surprisingly, the leading social developments of the last half of the nineteenth century reflect the same blend of vitality and uncertainty that we have found in the economy. This is particularly true of the middle classes, who increasingly set the tone of "public opinion" by dominating the press and the school systems. The power of the middle classes grew in all spheres. One group achieved an old middle-class goal: it became a true ruling class. Yet, in their triumph, the middle classes split apart and many became resentful. In short the mood of the middle classes changed during the half century and by 1900 there was scarcely a common outlook at all.

The middle classes gained steadily in position and in confidence until the economic crisis of the 1870s. Rising profits gave a firm economic base, and for the first time in western Europe the middle classes controlled most of the capital wealth. Opportunities increased in the professions, and secondary and university education expanded to meet them. The middle classes grew in numbers and many individuals could take advantage of new social mobility. With the growth of parliaments and reform of the civil service, government too created new opportunities. The middle classes became the dominant patrons of theater and the arts. Their tastes, however, were often rather ostentatious and they sought a culture that would bring social prestige; for example they preferred older styles in art and architecture because the social value of classical pillars or Gothic arches was well established. Middle-class culture antagonized many leading artists, for the class tended to regard them as dangerously Bohemian. But the new resources and interests of the middle class contributed to the further development of opera houses and symphonies, the restoration of many architectural monuments, and the introduction of science, modern languages, and history into the curricula of the upper schools.

Confidence in middle-class values was at its height. In Britain the "self-help" writings of Samuel Smiles expressed middle-class belief in the power of the individual to better himself and in the progress of society through industrial and scientific advance and humanitarian legislation. In Germany the magazine *Gartenlaube*, which reached thousands of middle-class homes, praised the ethic of hard work and self-restraint and criticized the idle, parasitic aristocracy. Middle-class values spread well beyond the class itself, to artisans and aristocrats alike. The New Model Unions of skilled workers in Britain really tried to institutionalize the values of self-help and restraint by promoting education, savings, and temperance among their members.

Toward a New Upper Class

In these same decades the upper segment of the middle class, the wealthiest businessmen and the leading professional people, began to separate themselves from the rest of the class and merge with the aristocracy as dominant partners in a new upper class. The process occurred first in education. The upper middle class sought admission to the most fashionable schools and shouted loudly that the schools' curriculum and exclusiveness needed reform. But in the 1850s and 1860s, after their children had been admitted and curricula partially modernized, the cries for reform diminished. Educated in the same schools as the leading aristocrats, the upper middle class increasingly shared in the patronage of prestigious cultural events. After 1870 it began to intermarry with the aristocracy and often gained or invented aristocratic titles. Despite traditional divisions, a common political stance developed. The upper middle class and aristocracy cooperated in resisting socialism; jointly supported imperialism, which brought economic gains to industry and gave administrative jobs to aristocrats; and combined to back a high tariff policy. The Bülow tariff reflected the careful merger of the two groups, as Junkers and big industrialists supported each other's interests in return for support for their own. A new upper class had been created, the product of the power of the upper middle class and the tenacious adaptability of many aristocrats. Known as the Establishment in Great Britain, it dominated most aspects of social life and would not easily be dislodged.

The rest of the middle class, by far the largest segment, suffered from this spinoff of its leading element. Advancement to the upper class from below probably became more difficult. Big business certainly made it hard for a newcomer to build a commanding position in the established industries, while the top posts in the bureaucracy were largely reserved for the upper class. Here was one reason for uneasiness and resentment in middle-class ranks.

General Middle-Class Gains

Yet there were gains for the remaining middle class too, until 1914. Few segments of the class failed to share in rising prosperity, though recessions hurt small businessmen and financial collapses harmed small investors.

New business opportunities developed. The growing importance of huge firms should not conceal the continued vitality of smaller units. The number of small factories and shops increased steadily and new industries, such as automobile production, provided important opportunities for smaller entrepreneurs. Social mobility was still possible. The expansion of state educational systems benefited the middle class, who were able to take advantage of new secondary schools. The middle class was not educationally submerged to the level of the masses; with superior education many could enter state or business bureaucracies or the professions. Big business created a vast array of opportunities for managers and technicians, and, as management functions became separated from ownership, many of these people rose from below.

The later nineteenth century also saw the creation of the lower middle class, the white-collar class—people without much property who nevertheless aped middle-class values and remained carefully distinct from manual laborers. This became the most rapidly growing social group—rising from 7 percent of the British population in 1850 to 20 percent by 1900. Expansion of state and private bureaucracies created the need for clerks and secretaries, and the now familiar range of service jobs—teachers, sales personnel, telephone operators—was clearly developing. The lower middle class was a distinctive group in many ways: its earnings were below middle-class standards and it generally lacked property. But the lower middle class tried to associate itself with middle-class status. It typically shunned the labor movement and active trade unions and valued social mobility and education. Its members devoted unusual amounts of money to housing and clothes, both of which could distinguish them from manual laborers. The lower middle class, in sum, displayed the continued attractiveness and power of middle-class values. It could also be a vital numerical addition to the political strength of the middle classes.

Hence though the middle classes became more disparate and challenges to middle-class values assumed greater importance, neither the broad grouping nor elements of its distinctive spirit had disappeared. There was ample evidence, in 1900, that a large segment of the middle classes continued to believe in the old virtues and still thought that science and industry guaranteed steady progress in the future, for themselves and for all of society.

THE LOSERS

The gains of the middle classes and the very persistence of middle-class aspirations not only created new insecurities but supported the fears of modernity that traditional property-owning groups had developed earlier in the century. Although many small shopkeepers were thriving, the rise of department store competition seemed menacing. Artisan masters, accustomed to running their own shop with one or two helpers, were now directly threatened by factory production in several industries. Tailors and shoemakers in particular had to limit themselves to luxury production or repair work if they were to survive as artisans. Another disturbing element was the increased number of working women. Male clerks and teachers feared future competition and declining status as women entered their ranks. Still another, more general ground for discontent was the fact that professional people were being educated at a faster rate than the economy could absorb them. In France in 1901 only half the doctors were in any sense prosperous and a large number could not practice medicine at all. In Germany trained lawyers had to take work as clerks in the bureaucracy. It was small wonder that professional people and students aspiring to become professionals grew increasingly restive.

Many in the middle classes thus feared that their status was deteriorating, as no group could keep pace with the earnings and prestige of the new upper class. Some individuals held jobs that were beneath their expectations. A good share of the new industrial managers were downwardly mobile, in the sense that they were now paid employees whereas before they, or their fathers, had been independent entrepreneurs. Periodic economic crises added to the economic woes. Many small investors were vulnerable to bank failures and speculative scandals—for example, thousands in France lost their savings when a Panama canal investment scheme fell through. Rising rents and a growing shortage of servants put yet another pressure on the middle-class standard of life.

Challenge to Traditional Values

The traditional middle-class ethic was eroding in many ways at the same time. The relationship between the class and capitalism, never entirely firm, grew increasingly ambiguous. Big business, by restricting competition and separating ownership from management, made a mockery of economic individualism. It was harder now to claim that hard work and savings were the basis of success. Speculative finance indeed could bring wealth or ruin without productive work at all. Without any question, many businessmen, particularly those who associated their family with the firm, failed to adopt the newest business forms, while others, including many new shareholders, were uncomfortable with the direction the economy was taking. Combined with this was the threat of organized labor, whose expensive demands and strikes added to costs and pressed some of the smaller and weaker manufacturers severely. Trade unions also shook the traditional middle-class belief in a social hierarchy in which the lower orders had no direct voice in the activities of the higher orders.

The Bicycle Craze: Cyclists in Hyde Park, London, 1895.

More generally still, the work-production ethic of the middle class was increasingly inappropriate in an economy geared for high rates of consumption. From the mid-nineteenth century onward the middle classes had more time and resources for leisure, supporting their schools' formal sports, such as soccer football, subscribing to recreational magazines, and leading the craze for bicycles after 1880. At the turn of the century a still greater enthusiasm for sports and recreation developed among middle-class youth. This can be seen as a rebellion against the materialism and rationalism of middle-class society, but it continued a trend apparent in the class itself for several decades.

In many ways the middle classes adapted surprisingly fast to new leisure and consumption. Their magazines pointed out that leisure and exercise improved the quality of work, that sports encouraged some of the same virtues of character as work did—all of which aided the transition. But the decline of the work ethic was troubling, for it brought with it the decline of other traditions. The bicycle craze, for example, encouraged changes in women's dress toward looser, less voluminous coverings, and in courting patterns, since chaperonage became increasingly difficult. The role of women was clearly changing. Whether actual sexual morality was changing or not, there was no question that topics were being discussed with a freedom inconceivable at mid-century. The rights of prostitutes were defended—by a woman—before the British parliament, while plays in Paris advocated pre-marital sexual relations.

These trends were disconcerting to members of the middle classes who held to their traditional values. Writers who lambasted modern life, like Julius Langbehn in Germany, won a wide readership. A revival of religious piety in some French provincial centers was another expression of dismay. The most widespread symptoms of malaise, however, were nationalism and anti-Semitism. Nationalism allowed discontented members of the middle class to feel they shared a broader purpose, that they were participating in the dynamism of the state. By advocating tariffs and imperial gains in the interests of their country, they hoped to improve their own economic security directly. Anti-Semitism, which spread in central Europe and in France, could serve as a more general protest against the modern world. The Jews represented new competition. They were entering the professions in increasing numbers, particularly in Central Europe, thanks to the full legal equality they had won by 1870. They were involved with banks and department stores and also, ironically, were associated with socialism. They were the personification of much that seemed menacing.

It is hard to measure even the most overt symptoms of uneasiness among the middle classes. The most fervently nationalistic groups, like the German Navy League, were not massive, though they could be very influential. When anti-Semitic papers were at their peak in France, they reached perhaps a hundred thousand people, an impressive figure but only a tiny minority of the middle classes. Anti-Semitic rioting in France, drawing mainly on students, artisans, and shopkeepers, attracted many thousands, but it was episodic and trailed off almost completely after 1900. An anti-Semitic political party in Germany, led by Adolph Stöcker, won over three hundred thousand votes in the 1890s, but again this was a small minority of the total vote.

It is important not to exaggerate the crisis of the middle classes before 1914. We know why a sense of crisis existed and we know some of the actual symptoms. But most members of the middle classes were adapting satisfactorily, often very profitably, to the new social order. Their response even to the lower-class threat was, as we shall see, on the whole constructive, certainly not pathologically repressive. There was a basis for a more massive reaction to modern life, if conditions for the middle classes should worsen sharply. Some individuals rejected modernity already, providing a certain audience for pessimistic and anti-rational intellectuals. But more broadly there was at most a certain ambiguity in the outlook of the middle classes. How many gained satisfaction from attacks on Jewish speculators while investing regularly in stocks and bonds? How many urged the traditional virtues on their wives and daughters while shifting their newspaper reading to the sensationalist mass press? The middle-class world was still intact by 1914, which is why its later collapse was such a shock.

The Lower Classes

There were also ambiguities in the position and outlook of the lower classes in industrial countries. This was an age of increasing protest through socialist voting and strikes. Certainly there were massive reasons for lower-class discontent and it is tempting to dwell on these aspects alone. But there were also many reasons for positive satisfaction, in terms of lower-class expectations. Hence aspects of the industrial structure were attacked, but there were few who rejected the structure itself. Most obviously, there was no revolution in these decades in industrial Europe, at a time when apparently revolutionary ideologies were spreading ever more widely. The repressive apparatus of the state, particularly its trained and well-armed police, inhibited revolution; but even aside from this there was no social basis for it, despite the rising tide of protest.

Protest

Workers had a multitude of grievances. Even before 1900 their wages were not rising as rapidly as profits and everywhere their share of national income was down. After 1900 they suffered more directly as inflation slowed the increase of real wages, and in some cases purchasing power actually declined. The most serious labor protest, which occurred in Britain after 1910, was in direct response to diminishing standards of living. After 1900 also, Britain suffered from some continuing unemployment, even among skilled workers and during otherwise prosperous years. On the job, workers everywhere were pressed to work more rapidly. As hours of work declined and international competition increased, manufacturers tried to speed up production. A few began to introduce the time and motion studies of the American engineer Frederick Winslow Taylor. For workers, the speed-up meant increased nervous tension, exhaustion, and frequent clashes with foremen who enforced the new pace. Workers' concerns were not just material. They had to worry also about the growing size of business units, which exposed them to an impersonal management and decreased their chance for any real voice in their own working conditions. Artisans were particularly sensitive to this problem, whether they were thrown directly into factories by the spread of new machines to their trade or, like most construction workers, simply employed in bigger and bigger work crews.

Between 1880 and 1914, strikes became a normal part of industrial life. By 1900 hundreds of thousands of workers struck each year in the major countries. Coal miners and artisans had the highest strike rates, but virtually every type of worker was involved and every kind of strike was attempted —even national general strikes in Belgium, Holland, and Sweden. Most notable was the advent of protest by the unskilled. In 1889 London dockers

A Violent Strike: Scottish railway workers attacking a station, 1891.

struck—and won—after massive demonstrations that were surprisingly well organized and peaceful. Similar dock strikes took place in Hamburg, Marseilles, and elsewhere on the continent during the 1890s. Here was proof that the unskilled working population was becoming an active force in the labor movement.

Most of the thousands of strikes that were occurring annually by 1900 were entirely peaceful, but the threat of violence was rarely absent from the more serious protests. Some workers attacked their employers directly

—miners in one French town, for example, dropped their hated manager from a factory window—but far more commonly workers battled with non-strikers and with police. Strike demands were often more moderate than the tactics employed. Workers sought wage raises, reductions in hours of work, and other improvements in conditions. The strikes directed at foremen and managers, however, reflected the anger that was building up against problems as diverse as unemployment and the loss of dignity on the job.

On the heels of the strike wave came the new forms of trade unionism. Until about 1890 craft unions, usually small and conservative, had predominated, leaving most of the new industries completely unorganized. British artisans and skilled workers developed national federations after 1850, in a movement known as New Model Unionism; but usually their organizations were reluctant to strike or to use political action. Instead they stressed self-reliance and respectability. The industrial unions that arose in the 1890s were different. They found strength in numbers, not in special skills, and sought to organize as many workers in as many industries as possible. Moreover they were willing, even eager, to battle employers. Many craft groups copied some of the new union forms, notably in the building trades, by organizing unskilled workers and engaging more readily in massive strikes. The power of the new industrial unionism was enhanced by the creation of national confederations of the leading trade unions, like the *Confédération générale du travail* in France.

Limitations on Protest

Yet the picture of class conflict cannot be left unqualified. Most of the industrial unions turned out to be not as different from the craft groups as their founders had intended. Benefit funds and bureaucracies enhanced their caution and the strike movement itself, for all its extraordinary vigor, was not an all-out war on the existing order. Workers soon learned not to strike too often but rather to bargain and compromise. By 1900, and even earlier in Britain, a network of collective bargaining was developing in almost all the major industries. By negotiation employer and union representatives resolved many grievances without a strike and reduced the anger and violence in strikes that did occur. The advent of collective bargaining was a milestone in industrial history, but it suggests also the moderation of most workers. Along with negotiation came some recognition of employers' authority, which meant that workers rarely obtained their full demands. Nor did collective bargaining prevent the stagnation in standards of living after 1900 or the growing inequalities in the distribution of national income. Yet only in Britain after 1910, when massive, nation-wide strikes spread in most of the major industries, was there even a hint of rebellion against the new collective bargaining system.

Workers were still restrained by fear. Although strikes and unions had been legalized in all the industrial countries by the mid-1880s, clashes with the police were likely to occur during a strike. Even more inhibiting were the loss of earnings and the possibility of employer reprisals against labor protest. As a result most workers stayed away even from moderate trade unions—nowhere did the union movement recruit a majority of the labor force—and those who participated in protest did so with some caution. But fear alone cannot explain the position of labor. Workers were deriving some positive satisfactions from the industrial order; they did not see the need for all-out protest.

We cannot blithely assume that all workers felt as deeply about their grievances as might be expected; socialists, in fact, often complained of the difficulty of arousing their audience. Inequality of income distribution, for example, may have been a rather remote issue. Various social scientists and political agitators since the later nineteenth century have written of workers' alienation. Marxists have stressed the workers' alienation from the products of their work in the factory system, while others have cited the impersonality of urban life, the remoteness of government and big business bureaucracies. But how acutely did workers sense these problems? Many workers took pride in the giant machines and big firms with which they were associated. Responses to the industrial economy varied with the individuals involved, but by 1900 more workers were adapting to it successfully than ever before.

Working-Class Gains

The key to the adaptation was improvement in living standards after 1850, an improvement sufficiently great that even recessions did not bring about the stark misery so prevalent in human history. Workers took pleasure in their improved diet, better clothing and increased opportunities for recreation. Many ambitious individuals could improve their lot still further by advancing to jobs requiring higher skills or even to supervisory positions. The pace of work might be heightened, but the steady reduction of working hours in part compensated for this. Most important was the fact that more and more workers learned to make the basic bargain of industrial society: acceptance of changing work techniques and even increased boredom on the job in return for higher earnings and consumption standards. This bargain kept workers from an all-out attack on industrial society.

The worker's life was improving in less material ways as well. Neither industry nor the big city was as confusing as in the very first generations of industrialization. Workers made friends on the job and with their neighbors; they were no longer surrounded by strangers. Family life probably improved, partly because of better housing. Fewer wives had to work and those who did found their jobs were less strenuous than before. As workers rapidly learned to limit the size of their family, they gained more opportunities to care for the children they had. The labor movement itself created new social outlets for workers, who could use trade union libraries and go to socialist picnics. Certainly some of the symptoms of isolation and confusion began to fade as workers developed values and social contacts appropriate to the new life. One indication of this was the decline in the rate of alcohol consumption.

On a broader level, workers no longer felt shut off from society. Giant factories provided benefit programs and governments, fearing the labor protest, made unprecedented efforts to assist the working man. The social insurance programs against illness and accident and the vast increase in factory inspection made it difficult for workers to regard the state as totally hostile. State education not only encouraged greater literacy and new ideas, which in turn aided the labor movement, but also inculcated national loyalty. Military service, which touched a growing number of workers, had a similar effect, as did the nationalistic newspapers that most workers read in preference to socialist journals. In 1914, when workers responded to each nation's call to arms, the extent of their involvement with larger loyalties was revealed. But the involvement had long existed and was yet another limitation on labor's protest.

Industrial Protest Defined

Industrial protest, as it had developed by the turn of the century, was quite different from traditional forms of protest. Better organized and occurring far more frequently, it concentrated on strikes and political action instead of on riots. It looked more often to new gains than to past rights, but was not necessarily as menacing to the existing order as preindustrial protest had been. Because industrial protest had to be better organized, it created bureaucracies, as in the trade unions, which had an interest in ensuring that the protest did not get out of hand. It depended on a desire for improvement, yet collectively workers had not developed a strong belief in progress. Only economic disaster would spur them to a thorough-going attack on the existing order. In this sense the traditions of lower-class protest still applied. Between 1850 and 1914 there was no economic collapse severe enough to cause a revolutionary challenge.

The impact of protest was limited also by the lack of unity among the lower classes in industrial Europe. In addition to many workers who resisted the new labor organizations, peasants and the lower middle class were rarely ripe for agitation. Clerks and shopkeepers were frightened by the labor movement, which seemed to threaten their superior social status; if they organized at all they were careful to refrain from strikes and socialism. Only after 1900, and mainly in France, were there any signs that white-collar people like postal clerks and teachers might turn to leftist agitation. The peasantry suffered from the prolonged agricultural slump but it suffered in silence. Most peasants heeded conservative political leaders who told them that their hopes lay in higher tariff protection and other stop gaps. Many were delighted with their ownership of the land and willing to accept a low standard of living. After 1900, and again mainly in France, a new mood began to develop as agricultural laborers started to strike for higher wages. In general, however, the countryside was calm.

Governments in the industrial countries faced an unprecedented amount of revolutionary rhetoric in the later nineteenth century, and in socialism they had to contend with a very new type of political movement. There was no real threat of revolution, however. It was not long, in fact, before the ambiguities of the working-class outlook—the mixture of discontent, satisfaction, and resignation—left their mark on socialism itself and tamed it.

EASTERN AND
SOUTHERN EUROPE

The gap between the societies of industrial Europe and those of the east and south was never wider than in the last decades of the nineteenth century. Russia, Italy, Spain and the Balkans were beginning to undergo the transformations western Europe had experienced a century earlier, but in circumstances far less favorable. All were confronted with recurrent revolutionary agitation. If outright revolution was less common than in western Europe a century before, it was owing to the superior weaponry of the state and the absence of a large middle class to provide political guidance. The social order was fully as troubled.

The Pressure of Modernization

The people of eastern and southern Europe were less attuned to the demands of economic modernization than were those of the west, even in the eighteenth century. Prior to industrialization, the dearth of large business and absence of artisanal classes made it difficult to find the necessary talents and motives for economic change. This was one reason the state, particularly in Russia, had to play a large role in arranging for investments and in introducing new techniques. Still more basically, the common people of these areas were loathe to depart from their traditions and had little interest in acquiring material objects. Well into the nineteenth century the typical peasant's home in the Balkans contained at most 50 objects, fewer than ten per person. It was not until the later nineteenth century that Balkan peoples began to increase their acquisitions and only slowly abandon their religious veneration of the customary tools they used. Industrialization would come hard to such people—and at a great psychic cost.

Well into the twentieth century, the vast majority of the populations of eastern and southern Europe remained agricultural, but the rural world was in agony. The agricultural slump that hit western Europe affected the more backward regions too. Prices fell and, lacking the necessary capital and training, these countries found it difficult to respond to the crisis with improved methods. Russia instituted very high agricultural tariffs, but this was at best a palliative.

Population pressure mounted steadily in eastern and southern Europe. In Russia the peasant population rose by one-third after 1870, without any increase in available land. Domestic manufacturing, the recourse of excess rural labor, declined at the same time under local and foreign factory competition. Emigrants poured out from Eastern Europe, Italy and the Balkans. Other millions flocked to the growing cities, but there were still too many left on the farms.

The effect of land reform completed the tragedy. Spain abolished the last remnants of manorialism in 1855, leaving peasants free to buy and sell their land. Italian unification brought Piedmontese commercial law to the southern countryside. Russia's great emancipation of the serfs occurred in 1861, while Rumania abolished manorialism in 1868. As in western Europe earlier, agricultural reforms brought hardship to many peasants. Now that they were free to sell their land, many yielded to temptation, only to deprive themselves of their livelihood. The state treated the peasant as a citizen, at least for tax purposes, and taxes rose steadily in Russia, Italy, and elsewhere. The money that governments began to pour into new industry came mainly from the peasantry. At the same time the freedom from manorialism was often illusory. In southern Spain and southern Italy landlords continued to own most of the land and millions of peasants served as their sharecroppers, turning over half or more of their harvest each year. Spanish peasants were further brutalized by local bosses employed by their landlords to keep order. Rumanian peasants lost most of their land by their "emancipation," aristocratic landlords taking over in their stead. Russian peasants were treated somewhat better. Landlords retained about one-seventh of the arable land, including some of the richest plots, but the average peasant held 20 acres of his own. Yet he owed redemption payments on this to the state in addition to regular taxes; he could not leave his land without village permission, for the village was collectively responsible for redemption payments; and he was often limited in the improvements he could introduce on his land. In Russia, but still more so in other countries, restrictions of peasants' freedom further reduced the opportunities for new and more profitable techniques and crops. The peasants grew steadily poorer.

Early Industrialization

Industrialization began seriously on the European peripheries before 1900. Factories sprang up even in the Balkans, though there was no rapid development. Two industrial zones arose in Spain, with the concentration of textiles in the Barcelona area and heavy industry around Bilbao. Italian industry, centered mainly in the north, advanced still more rapidly. Most important, Russian industrial production began to rise at an extraordinary rate after 1890, by as much as 8 percent a year. S. Y. Witte, minister of finance after 1892, guided this process, convinced that Russia's great power status depended on government-sponsored economic modernization. He stressed the rapid expansion of railroads and heavy industry, relying heavily on foreign loans for the necessary equipment. With her vast population and resources, Russia ranked among the world's leaders in some branches of industrial production by 1914. Overall, however, Russia remained in an early stage of industrialization; there were only three million factory workers in a population of 170 million.

The initial decades of industrialization were painful, as they had been earlier in western Europe. Cities grew rapidly. Moscow expanded by four hundred thousand in the last three decades of the century; Warsaw by half a million. Such growth meant crowding and misery. Workers endured long hours and low wages, though Russia and other countries enacted some protective factory legislation. Adjustment to factory life was difficult because of the rural traditions to which most workers were attached. Furthermore factory machinery was complex and the factories themselves were often large. Russian factories were the biggest in Europe; over half of them had more than 500 workers each because the government encouraged concentration. Hence workers were exposed to impersonal, bureaucratic controls and were therefore easy to organize despite legal barriers.

By 1900 strike rates were far higher in the newly industrializing areas than in western Europe. Unions were illegal in Russia, save for a brief period after 1905, and were severely repressed in Spain. The police often used brutal tactics to counteract strikes, which only inflamed the workers. Russian workers struck over 1700 times between 1895 and 1904. They conducted a spontaneous general strike, which was the basis for the Revolution of 1905, and averaged 2000 strikes a year thereafter until World War I. The Italian rate was still higher, and in a major uprising in 1898 workers seized Milan for five days. A bloodier strike occurred in Barcelona in 1909. Even the less important strikes raised political demands in these countries, again in contrast to western Europe where economic issues predominated. Workers asked for strong parliaments, civil rights, and the vote. Small wonder that socialist and other radical ideologies spread rapidly among them.

Rural Revolt

Rural unrest was less political and more episodic, but it had as great an impact as the turmoil in the cities. Indeed the workers' radicalism was in large part founded on the intense grievances that young peasants brought with them as they entered the factories. Rural disorder, ranging from banditry to outright rebellion, was endemic to southern and eastern Europe by the later nineteenth century. Peasants in Bosnia rose up against their Moslem landlords in 1875. Rumanian peasants, starved for land, rebelled several times, and in their 1907 uprising thousands were killed. From 1860 onward peasants in southern Spain revolted about once every ten years, seizing land and attacking government officials. Sicilian peasants briefly took over the land in the Fasciti uprising of 1893; subsequently peasants in various parts of Italy attacked grain dealers and tax offices. The tide of rural unrest increased sharply after Emancipation in Russia, during the depression of the 1870s, and again in the first years of the twentieth century. In 1905 and 1906, peasants in many areas of Russia seized land and forests and burned tax and redemption records.

Only rarely was the peasant protest ideological. Radical students in Russia, the Populists, tried to spread socialism in the villages in the 1870s, but without success. Some Balkan peasants expressed their discontent through nationalism. Still others, in Italy and especially in southern Spain, were won over to the vague doctrines of anarchism, which condemned state and society and advocated the destruction of existing systems. But large numbers of peasants were not swayed by an ideology with precise political goals, for these were not germane to their grievances. Yet the badly organized, apolitical protests called the basic social order into question. No regime could survive the level of rural protest that had built up by the turn of the century. During the next 30 years new governments would arise—sometimes offering reforms and always more efficient repression.

Middle Classes and Intelligentsia

The overwhelming discontent of the lower classes was the basic historical force in eastern and southern Europe after about 1870. Other social groups added to the furor, however. Industrialization brought something like a middle class into being. Most businessmen were preoccupied with their economic effort and were often closely linked to the state, though in Barcelona many participated in separatist protest against the Madrid government. Members of the liberal professions were far more politically aware. They wanted genuine constitutions and civil rights, and in most eastern and southern European countries these liberal demands were still potentially revolutionary. Many professional people in Italy turned to socialism in their political frustration, while those in the Balkans looked to radical nationalism. In Russia liberal professional men played a vital role in the Revolution of 1905.

A radical intelligentsia, composed of students and writers of various backgrounds, also arose in many of these countries. Many shared similar ideologies, such as Marxism, and similar grievances that could be found in western Europe, although nothing quite like an intelligentsia ever developed there. Intellectuals in Russia, particularly, were profoundly concerned about their country's backwardness. They wanted rapid change but they also wanted to avoid the evils they saw in western society. At the same time they felt isolated in their own country, repressed by the government yet shunned by the common people. They suffered directly from the government's heavy-handed control of the schools. Hence they churned out the most extreme ideologies of protest and occasionally produced tactics to match. Russian nihilists urged the renunciation of all traditional values and institutions. A Russian, Michael Bakunin, fathered the doctrine of revolutionary anarchism. Ideas of total upheaval arose elsewhere as well, notably in Italy under the banners of Futurism. Terrorist acts and assassinations, launched first by Russian intellectuals in the 1870s, colored the political life of eastern and southern Europe for many decades and, in 1914, triggered a ghastly war.

The ferment on Europe's peripheries could not be controlled by the largely traditional governments that still ruled these countries. Here was the most basic contrast between these areas and the industrial nations, where protest was limited and governments adopted new means of conciliation. We can no more present a unified political history of Europe before World War I than we can a united social history. Yet there were vital contacts between eastern and western Europe. A sense of cultural malaise, variously expressed and varying in intensity, was all pervasive. Neither the workers nor the burghers of the European world could unite, for their situations differed too greatly. But intellectuals and artists in all countries, with widely divergent views, implicitly agreed that there was something basically wrong in the modern world. How much did their gloom reflect—or cause— fundamental difficulties? Europe remained a diplomatic entity also; this was the second and more obvious contact between east and west. Ironically and tragically, the unstable nations on the peripheries had seized the initiative by 1914. Through this, their social ferment changed the face of the world.

6 CULTURE AND SOCIETY

1850–1914

The second half of the nineteenth century was as fertile in ideas and artistic styles as in economic and social developments. This period of great diversity saw the birth of modern art, of modern social science, and of one of the most compelling political ideologies—Marxism. Formal Romanticism had ended, but its spirit continued to do battle now not just with the rationalist tradition but with the materialism of industrial society. Rationalism lived on too, but the conclusions of scientists and social scientists increasingly modified, if they did not undermine, the premises of the Enlightenment. A growing pessimism was nurtured by both the post-Enlightenment and the post-Romantic currents.

Despite their importance, intellectual trends must not be examined for their own sake alone. The crucial questions concern the effects of intellectual developments. The political implications of innovations not just in political theory but in social science and art were great: what political influence did the ideas actually have? What impact did new styles and ideas have on broader social groups? To what extent did intellectual malaise reflect or encourage more general unrest? These questions, legitimate for any historical period, are particularly difficult for the last half of the nineteenth century. For in many ways a gap was developing between intellectuals and the broader society that demonstrably contributed to the intellectuals' distress. It may also have reduced their historical importance.

REALISM AND SCIENCE

Most of the great Romantic writers and artists had passed from the scene by 1850. Later nineteenth-century poets like Charles Baudelaire pushed stylistic innovation further than the Romantics had ever done, experiment-

Realism in Art: *The Man with the Hoe,* by Jean Millet.

ing with exotic themes and new forms of verse. Against the growing materialism of industrial society they maintained the primacy of "art for art's sake." But their principal influence was felt later, at the end of the century.

Realism was the dominant theme in novels and the fine arts in the 1850s and 1860s. Writers Gustave Flaubert and William Thackeray shunned the more exotic themes and heroes of the Romantics and preferred close observation and description of ordinary people in ordinary pursuits. In Russia Feodor Dostoevski and Leo Tolstoi portrayed emotional and psychological conflict with particular skill.

Painters sought to rival the camera in capturing reality. They too took their scenes from daily life and conveyed the ugly as well as the beautiful. The French were preeminent in realist art, with Gustave Courbet and Jean-Francis Millet among the outstanding painters. It was Courbet who said of one of his paintings: "I have invented nothing. I saw the wretched people in this picture every day as I went on my walks."

The realists fit nicely into Europe's mood. They corresponded to the no-nonsense attitudes that were converting the continent to industrialization and developing the tough-minded diplomacy of Cavour and Bismarck. The relationship was partly coincidental, born of the artists' rebellion against ethereal Romanticism, for neither industrialists nor diplomats had been starry-eyed idealists before. But for two decades, until the realist current subsided, European culture knew a certain unity.

The Sciences

Science benefited from this new intellectual atmosphere and scientific discoveries confirmed the value of the realistic approach. Romantics had been hostile to science, but now science caught the public eye once again. Basic discoveries were made in most of the physical sciences and some of them had immediate practical consequences.

During the first half of the century most common chemical elements were identified and the modern notational system was introduced. In the 1860s the Russian Dmitri Mendeleev classified all the known elements according to their atomic weights and other characteristics and predicted the existence of other elements that were then unknown. His "periodic law" showed that the properties of elements were functions of their atomic weights. The world of chemistry seemed as rational, as classifiable, as that of physics.

Chemists also learned how to synthesize organic compounds and in so doing gradually resolved an old controversy about organic matter. Many scientists had held that life processes did not obey the same laws that governed inorganic matter and that some inexplicable "vital principle" was involved. As chemists learned that organic compounds contained a relatively small number of elements and could be synthesized in laboratories, they once again revealed the orderliness of nature. From their discoveries came artificial fertilizers vital to agriculture, new dyes for industry, new pharmaceutical drugs, and the development of anesthetics for surgery. Science was becoming increasingly useful and this, more than its rationalism, enhanced its importance in the public's mind.

In France, Louis Pasteur propounded the germ theory of disease. He himself devised a host of practical applications of his theory, including cures for diseases afflicting vineyards and silkworms, sterilization procedures known as pasteurization, and improvements in the brewing of beer. Joseph Lister, a Scottish doctor, introduced antiseptic surgery in the 1860s, using carbolic acid. This, along with anesthesia, constituted a revolution in medical technology and greatly reduced the mortality rate in childbirth and surgery.

Physicists continued to reduce more and more natural phenomena to uniform, sometimes quite simple, laws. Research on steam engines and the energy equivalents of heat led to the First Law of Thermodynamics, stated by Hermann von Helmholtz in 1847. The total energy in the universe is constant, according to this law, while a second law added that the sum of useful energy is diminishing by conversion into dissipated heat. Here were great generalizations of Newtonian scope, uniting various facets of nature into a few fundamental laws.

The science of electricity arose in the nineteenth century, as researchers in many countries worked on batteries, electrolysis and electromagnets. In the 1860s James Clark Maxwell deduced mathematically the velocity of electromagnetic waves. Maxwell's theories seemed to show that electricity, magnetism, and even light were essentially identical.

The practical applications of the discoveries in electricity included the telegraph and the electric motor. Physicists, like scientists in other fields, now directly contributed to technological advance. The relationship between science and invention was changing: the role of the dabbler-inventor declined; the prestige and impact of science rose. It was a physicist who discovered radio waves, in 1885, and another physicist, Guglielmo Marconi, who developed the wireless radio a decade later. These same discoveries fulfilled Maxwell's predictions about the behavior of electromagnetic waves. Science continued to advance knowledge of an orderly universe. Joseph Thomson and Hendrick Lorentz, near the end of the century, independently discovered that electricity was composed of particles, called electrons, which existed in all atoms. Different kinds of matter have a common basis; the simplicity of nature was again revealed. Thomson and Lorentz assumed also that the behavior of electrons was regular, thus supporting Newtonian laws of the regularity of motion. In this they were wrong, but their error shows the power of the classic, Newtonian assumptions of physics. Near the end of the century a renowned scientist claimed that the secrets of the universe had been unraveled and that physicists had only to make more precise measurements of the operation of nature's laws.

THE THEORY OF EVOLUTION

The most important scientific development of the century was the publication in 1859 of Charles Darwin's *On the Origin of Species,* which enunciated the theory of evolution. Darwin held that members of every species must struggle for survival, because each species gives birth to more individuals than the means of subsistence can support. In this struggle variations or mutations occur among individuals (Darwin did not say why), which make some better able to survive than others. This process of natural selection means that the fittest reproduce, the unfit perish. When characteristics change substantially, a new species may gradually emerge. Man, thus, had evolved from earlier and simpler forms of life and was descended from the apes.

Here, on the face of it, was another great triumph for rationalism. Darwin utilized the scientific method, relying on extensive observation and some laboratory work. He confirmed discoveries made in other sciences, notably geology, which revealed that the earth was far older than had been believed and that it, too, had undergone great change in the past. Darwin's theory opened a new round in the conflict between rationalism and religion. Christians, particularly Protestants, were appalled at the challenge to the Bible. If Darwin was to be believed, nature's creatures, including man, had not been created *de novo* by the hand of God. Biblical chronology, which had been worked out in the seventeenth century to reveal that the earth was created in 4004 B.C., was undermined. Ardent Darwinists, though not Darwin himself, carried forward an active attack on religious obscurantism. The theory of evolution was widely popularized, contributing to the decline of religious belief. This decline was encouraged also by a new spate of historical criticism of the Bible, which focused on claims that Jesus could be understood as purely human being.

Social Darwinism

The theory of evolution was quickly applied to society, notably by Herbert Spencer. Social Darwinism confirmed much of the rationalist tradition and bolstered the idea of progress. Men and societies steadily improve by means of competition. Natural selection occurs in human development, leaving the fittest individuals and institutions triumphant.

Comforting as Darwinism was to many rationalists, the theory of evolution had a darker side. Indeed the theory was the first of many cases in which science in the later nineteenth century began to undermine key assumptions of the rationalist order. It was no coincidence that Darwin actually developed his theory during the heyday of Romanticism, even though he published later, for Romantics talked of the wildness of nature, the links of man to history, and the importance of struggle. Darwin's nature was neither beneficent nor orderly. If progress occurred, it resulted not from reasoned planning and education but from conflict and, for some, extinction.

Evolution Caricatured: How a mug of beer evolves into a beer drinker.

Darwin's man might be rational, but his origins were animal. Darwinism obviously encouraged studies of man's nature that sought traces of animal passions.

Some pseudo-scientists used Darwinism as a basis for racism. Houston Stewart Chamberlain, for example, wrote of the differences between inferior and superior races and of the inevitable struggle to assure the purity of the superior races and the proper subordination of the inferior. In the racist view, Anglo-Saxons and Germans were popular candidates for the superior races, while the Slavs, Latins and Semites vied for the inferior positions. Racist thinking and the idea of struggle for survival of the fittest easily carried over into imperialist arguments. Native peoples were judged to be obviously inferior, and therefore in need of guidance and control; the most superior European races considered it their duty to make sure that they and not some inferior people assumed the obligations and benefits of empire.

Racist thinking spread widely. Darwinism did not cause it and a proponent of the theory of evolution did not have to be a racist. But it was tempting for the evolutionists, starting with Darwin himself, to divide men into higher and lower categories, to see some groups as less evolved and fit than others. The new attack on the rationalist idea of the fundamental equality of man was in many ways more important than the earlier blasts from Romantics and conservatives because it seemed to be endorsed by the prestige of science.

MARXISM

The principal innovation in political theory after mid-century was also ambiguous in its implications about man and his reason. Karl Marx thought himself a scientific realist. He wanted to dedicate the first volume of *Das Kapital* to Darwin, but the latter prudently declined. Marx was beyond question a pioneer in social science, yet Marxism was also an amalgam of Romantic and rationalist elements.

Karl Marx and Friedrich Engels published the *Communist Manifesto* in January 1848, but Marx's more extensive writings appeared in the 1860s and 1870s. Marx and Engels were both offspring of German middle-class families; both spent most of their lives in England. Marx was a devoted family man and a diligent scholar. The "ism" that bears his name was not concerned with political theory alone—it was a new approach to history.

Marxism rested on the belief that all human activity was determined by the means of production and classes were based, most simply, on whether people owned or did not own the means of production. All human endeavor, therefore, was based on class struggle. The ruling class exploited everything, including government and morality, to perpetuate its own power, yet it would be shoved aside when technology advanced to a new stage. Thus had the feudal aristocracy been displaced by the bourgeoisie; in like manner the bourgeoisie itself would be overthrown by the proletariat.

In western Europe, Marx saw the bourgeoisie using government, art, and religion as weapons in the class struggle. The bourgeoisie had also launched industrialization, and this was to be its undoing. Capitalist industrialization created a larger and larger propertyless class, the proletariat. Workers were paid only enough to subsist, not in proportion to what they produced. Their production, which was far greater, went into profits and this was the basic immorality of the system. But with advancing technology, production increased even as the bulk of the population was at subsistence level. Markets would become harder to find, and most businessmen would be reduced to proletarian status. Marx pointed to the frequency of industrial slumps as a sign that the bourgeoisie had lost control of the economy. A new, socialist society was inevitable. But because of the power of the big capitalists, revolution was essential. The proletariat would rise and form a transitional dictatorship to purge society of its bourgeois trappings. Then the laws of history would lapse because classes would be eliminated. With class struggle over, the government would wither away and men would live in harmony, producing what they could and taking what they needed.

The Implications of Marxism

Marx's utopian vision was very much in the Enlightenment tradition. His men of the future were spontaneously good and rational. His vision of history, however, was far different. Men were trapped by material forces superior to their wills. Change occurred not by persuasion or conscious planning, but by struggle and, sometimes, violence. To be sure, Marx was not always as strict as his doctrines implied. Though he insisted that capitalism was an inevitable stage in history and that capitalists could not avoid behaving as they did, he often condemned the system as if it were at fault. Though he held that the proletarian revolution was inevitable, he nonetheless urged Communists to work to ensure it. Nor did he necessarily believe that revolution in a literal, violent sense was inevitable; rather, revolutionary change might come in some other way. Most Marxists were rationalists, for they had to believe that progress was feasible and that men *could* be rational; otherwise communist society was impossible. This is one reason that many Marxists in practice could make concessions to liberals and liberal institutions: they both shared some common beliefs about the nature of man. At the same time, Marxism was not the unambiguously rationalist doctrine that liberalism had been. Its ascendancy in political theory, together with the concomitant disappearance of significant classical liberal theory, was another sign of the growing complexity of the intellectual spectrum.

SOCIAL SCIENCE
AND PSYCHOLOGY

The social sciences emerged as distinct disciplines in the last decades of the nineteenth century, though they built on the earlier work of Marx, Comte, and many others. Even older disciplines such as history acquired a new methodology. Social scientists believed firmly in the possibility and utility of a rational study of man and society. They were divided somewhat on how to approach the study, depending on what signals they picked up from the physical sciences. Some stressed empiricism, and in all fields masses of data began to be accumulated during the second half of the century. Others emphasized general theories or laws; still others combined the two approaches. But a significant tension remained. The problem was that empiricism did not lead so easily to overriding generalizations when man rather than nature was the subject. Certain disciplines tended to stress one approach, some another. History, for example, turned primarily to empiricism. But the tension existed within all disciplines. It has colored the development of the social sciences ever since.

The rise of the social sciences had broader implications too. The social scientists were firmly in the rationalist tradition, in terms of their method of study, but their work often led them to the conclusion that men were primarily irrational.

Enduring characteristics of the historical discipline were established in these decades. Leopold von Ranke in Germany insisted that historians portray events as actually happened. This led him and many others to detailed perusal of dusty archives, from which they emerged to write multivolume works, elaborately footnoted. Fact and exactitude became the stuff of history. Bias was supposed to be put aside.

A new generation of biblical scholars added facts and another breath of scientific skepticism to the study of the Christian past. Renan's *Life of Jesus*, a somewhat popularized work, portrayed Christ as a rather ordinary, if unusually naive, person, with "no knowledge of the general state of the world." Archeology became a major interest as well, again corresponding to the growing desire to have more facts about the past. The site of Troy was discovered and excavated. By the end of the century it was possible to trace the history of the Aegean lands, Egypt, and Mesopotamia back several thousand years before Christ.

Non-Marxist economics continued to develop. One branch of the discipline, particularly in Germany, turned to empiricism, investigating problems in economic history and current economic development. But the interest in theoretical description of economic activity remained high. In 1862 Stanley Jevons deplored the fact that commercial trends had not been investigated "according to the same scientific methods with which we are familiar in other complicated sciences." Statistics steadily gained in importance as government agencies and private sources like the London *Economist* began to produce statistical data on all sorts of economic activity. This added greatly to the accumulation of empirical information, but the leading statisticians and economists sought more. The German statistician Georg von Mayr stated the scientific intent: "Statistical science is the systematical statement and explanation of actual events, and of the laws of man's social life that may be deduced from these, on the basis of the quantitative observation of mathematical aggregates." Indeed the promise of the marriage between statistics and economic theory was great, though it had some amusing false starts. Jevons, for example, used the new approach to demonstrate a correlation between economic crises and sun spots.

Historians provided information and insight into the nature of man, but they had no overall approach. Economists largely continued to assume man's rationality, at least as an economic being. Alfred Marshall, the leading conservative English economist at the end of the century, elaborated the older liberal statements about the workings of the marketplace. Man, he said, would continue to respond rationally, if rather mechanically, to changes in wages and prices.

The Newer Disciplines

It was the newer social sciences that provided the most novel suggestions about man and society. Political science began to emerge as a discipline, combining empirical studies of existing political processes with an interest in theory. Gaetano Mosca mercilessly dissected the workings of the Italian state, showing the importance of a corrupt political elite. On a somewhat more theoretical level, Robert Michels questioned the reality of a pure democratic process even in institutions such as socialist parties; again he pointed to the role of elites.

Anthropologists had no direct political comment to make, but their approach raised questions about human nature. Many, in the Darwinist tradition, busily tried to classify the "races" of mankind by skull shapes and other anatomical features. Others studied primitive tribes all over the world, related their data to European history and produced facile outlines of the evolutionary stages of man's cultural advance. Their prognosis was often optimistic, but they too pointed to man's irrational, animal origins.

Sociologists included a number of pure empiricists. Frédéric Le Play in France gathered data on family structure and working-class life. Charles Booth and others in Britain produced massive studies on the conditions of the poor. But the more theoretical approach had greater importance. Emile Durkheim established sociology as an academic discipline in France, carrying forward Comte's desire to subject society to scientific study. Durkheim sought an extensive empirical base formed by detailed observation and factual research, but generalization was always the goal. He applied

his techniques primarily to irrational aspects of human behavior and produced important theories about social phenomena such as suicide and
religion. Led by Max Weber, a number of German sociologists used historical materials as their source for generalization, though they also sponsored
elaborate investigations of German society. Weber developed major theories
about the relationship between religion and the rise of capitalism, the nature of cities, and the characteristics of bureaucracy.

Many of the new social scientists were democrats or socialists in politics,
believing that political reforms were possible and desirable. Many of the
empiricists, like Booth, were rightly convinced that their investigations
could shock the public into demanding social reforms. But, particularly
among the theorists, there was less facile optimism about reform than there
had been in the days of Comte or even Spencer. Social scientists could rationally understand how man behaves, but correcting the behavior was another matter. They were obviously affected by their growing realization of
the irrational in human nature. Furthermore their very method raised
questions. If man behaved in predictable ways, how rational, or at least how
creative, was he in fact?

Some social scientists took their conclusions directly into the political
arena. Gaetano Mosca, disgusted by the corruption of liberal politics, called
for a frankly elitist rule. His compatriot Vilfredo Pareto, a sociologist with
a background in mathematical economics, claimed that his scientific, un-
biased study of human relations led him to the conclusion that liberalism
was impossible because of the irrational in human nature. He admitted a
rational element, but his main interest was in classifying rationalizations of
unconscious impulses. Using general historical materials for the most part,
he traced the various expressions different societies have worked out which
derive essentially from the same impulse. Religions are one such expression.
According to Pareto, religion or other similar forces make almost no difference in human behavior. What are important are permanent, abiding
sentiments in men, which have almost no intellectual content in themselves.
Man's rationalizations may change; his nature, which is primarily irrational,
does not. From his theory of sociology Pareto was led, not necessarily
logically, to a belief in a strongman rule, for the skilled political leader may
be able to manipulate man's irrational impulses to good ends. Late in life
Pareto accepted an honorary position in Mussolini's government, which at
least symbolized the uses to which his theories could be put.

Growing numbers of psychologists studied human nature directly. One
important group was directly experimental. The clinical psychologists based
their work on the assumption, which followed from Darwin, of the affinity of
human minds to those of the lower animals. Wilhelm Wundt opened a
famous psychological laboratory in Leipzig in 1875, in which knowledge of
human behavior was deduced from experiments on a variety of animals. A
whole generation of younger psychologists from all over Europe began conducting similar experiments. Ivan Pavlov, in the 1890s, dealt with condi-

tioned reflexes that operated entirely beneath the conscious level. He worked with such phenomena as salivation in dogs, which he proved could not be rationally controlled. His work supported the idea that the mind of man, as well as that of animals, consisted of matter and was governed, in a machine-like way, by physical laws.

Sigmund Freud, by far the most influential student of the human unconscious, was trained in clinical psychology but did not employ the methods or all the conclusions of this school. He too was an empiricist of sorts, but less rigorous because he sought to understand the whole of the human mind, not just its mechanistic components. He generalized, then, from a series of case studies. He posited that a vast unconscious segment of the human mind, the id, determined a great deal of human behavior. Traumatic experiences, particularly in early childhood, could be harbored in this unconscious, disturbing an adult's mental balance without his having any awareness of what was wrong. Civilization had to control man's basic animal instincts; this process began with parental discipline. But when the control went too far, when it repressed rather than sublimated man's primitive drives, mental illness could result.

Freud produced a complex view of human nature in which reason had a definite role. It was in fact through reason that mental illness could be cured. What was new in this picture of man was the importance of the unconscious, the nonrational, and this aspect of Freudian psychology had the greatest impact.

Freud's influence came primarily after World War I, but well before this intellectuals outside the social sciences had grasped the message of man's irrationality. Some turned it into a virtue. The most popular philosopher in France before the war, Henri Bergson, dismissed conscious thought as superficial, finding man's vital spirit, his *élan vital*, in deep-seated instincts that could lead him to greatness. For others the message was more troubling, particularly in its political implications. This springtime of the social sciences set important and enduring themes for the later development of every major discipline. It also contributed powerfully to the intellectual *malaise* that arose around the turn of the century.

REVOLUTION IN SCIENCE

The end of the nineteenth century witnessed vast changes in both physics and biology, all of which further undermined the foundations of the rationalist tradition. Biologists in 1900 rediscovered the experiments of Gregor Mendel, which pointed to the transmission of fixed hereditary characteristics from one generation to the next. The carriers of these characteristics were genes.

The new science of genetics brought biology much closer to the more precise physical sciences, for mathematical theories could now be developed to predict inheritance and to guide laboratory experiments. At the same time genetics provided yet another link between man and insensate nature. Darwin had not described exactly how evolutionary change took place. Many popularizers wrote as if adaptation to nature, though involving struggle, was a basically rational process; good traits would be carried on when they proved useful. Genetics showed how far evolutionary change was from rational choice, for its basis lay in mutations occurring in submicroscopic elements in the reproductive cells.

Physicists began to cast doubt on the simplicity of the Newtonian universe. Research on the atom and on radiation led to the conclusion that atoms are not necessarily stable or indivisible and that their particles do not always behave in a regular manner. Work by Max Planck and others undermined the classic separation of matter and energy. Planck discovered that radiation takes place not continuously but in discrete units or quanta. Quantum theory held that energy consists of particles that have weight while mass itself represents bundles of energy.

Building on this, Albert Einstein's theory of relativity, first sketched in 1905, overturned the classic separation of space and time. Space and time exist on a continuum; there are four dimensions, not three. Time is not an absolute; *when* something takes place depends upon the observer. We see events "now" in outer space that took place millions of years ago. Einstein's theories explained phenomena that the Newtonian system could not account for. His most important contribution to general intellectual history was his rejection of the traditional belief in inexorable natural laws that determine all events by cause and effect. Events take place in accordance with the laws of statistical probability, in more or less random fashion.

By no means did all the innovations in science and social science have immediate impact. Freud and Einstein gained their main audience after World War I. But many developments pointed in similar directions, and added up to a major change in the rationalist tradition. Did they really end it?

The Impact of the New Physics

No longer was the Enlightenment's friendly view of nature evident in the work of the leading rationalist intellectuals. Nature was incredibly complex. Old absolutes like cause and effect had disappeared, and science, among other things, was becoming immensely difficult and specialized. An intelligent layman could not now claim to "know" physics. Einstein contributed doubts to the intellectual community, along with catch words like relativity; Newton had offered a whole system of thought. Furthermore, nature was now considered either hostile—as implied by the struggle for survival image, or neutral—as implied by the random behavior that both physicists and geneticists were studying.

Rationalist views of man were less completely overthrown. Some social scientists stressed man's irrationality, while they were definitely raising the prospect of human control through the unconscious in a way that had implications for political theory and ultimately political practice. If dogs could be taught through conditional reflex to salivate automatically at the sound of a bell, what could man be taught to do without thinking? Genetics suggested the possibility of selective breeding to produce predictable people and a predictable society. Some scientists and social scientists were enthusiastic about the progress that would result from elimination of the unfit, but again the notion showed how far individual men were from improvement through their own reason.

Use of rational, scientific methods greatly expanded knowledge of man and the possibilities of social control, but seriously weakened the notion that man, ordinary man, is rational.

Although greatly modified, the rationalist tradition lived on. Its view of man became more complex but remained recognizable. Freud believed in human reason. Most people, in his opinion, were not mentally ill; through reason they could control and sublimate their passions. Those who were ill could be cured by understanding, by bringing their childhood traumas to the conscious level, to the attention of their reason. Freud believed in a rational civilization despite the strains it caused, and he thought that men could arrange to abolish war. In this belief Freud was not typical of the social scientists of his period. But with all the new doubts and complexities, most social scientists continued to believe in rational aspects of human behavior that could be rationally studied.

LITERATURE AND THE ARTS

Radically new styles developed in both art and literature at the end of the nineteenth century. Realism was not dead. Joseph Conrad and other novelists used realistic settings, while the leading playwright, Henrik Ibsen, employed a stark realism. But a rebellion against realism dominated painting, music, and poetry. This rebellion owed much to the earlier declarations of stylistic freedom by the Romantics, and also to the new discoveries in science and in psychology. Insofar as many of the rebels were interested in their art alone, they resembled some of the Romantics. But the stylistic rebellion inevitably had broader impact. By creating a new picture of man and the world it supplemented developments in science and contributed to a growing attack on rationalism.

Symbolism is the best single term to describe the new styles. Artists and writers sought to alter the usual means of expression to communicate with the intuition—not the reason—of the viewer and to convey their own mood and spirit. Literal representations were dropped, for they assumed an orderly environment.

Impressionist painters applied new scientific knowledge of light and optics to portray the reality of nature in a nonphotographic way. Beginning in the 1860s, Edouard Manet and others developed the characteristic impressionist style with patches of color and blurry outlines. Their links to Romantic painters, notably Turner, must not be ignored, but it is fair to say that the impressionists launched the most important stylistic shift in art since the Renaissance. They held the belief that truth lay in the artist's capturing an impression of his subject, not a realistic outline. Later impressionists such as Claude Monet drifted ever farther from literal portrayals.

New schools in art multiplied with dizzying rapidity. Postimpressionists like Vincent Van Gogh made one further innovation in their imaginative use of bright color: they were more concerned with suggesting their own feelings and personality than the scenes they painted. Art became increasingly a communication between the psyches of artist and of viewer. Early cubists such as Pablo Picasso were much more restrained in mood, but they abandoned representation altogether. Abstraction spread also to sculpture, furniture design, and even to architecture.

Romanticism had continued unabated in music, as in Richard Wagner's dramatic operas. Even at the end of the century such major composers as Tchaikovsky and Grieg tried to evoke powerful emotions, usually in association with nationalist themes and folk music. A symbolist current arose as well. Stravinsky, Bartók and many others sought a "pure" music by the use of atonality, twelve-tone scales, and many other radical innovations.

Poetry and Novels

Symbolist poets similarly violated all the stylistic conventions of their genre. They blithely disregarded meter, rhyme, and often punctuation. They chose words and images for their evocative value and did not hesitate to experiment with new meanings for words. There were no direct statements, for every effort was bent to suggest impressions and feelings. Stéphane Mallarmé was the first specifically symbolist poet, but the movement influenced almost all major poets thereafter.

Novelists were far less daring in their stylistic initiatives, but they too experimented with new images. They also became increasingly interested in writing from a psychological standpoint, drawing forth, rather than dryly discussing, the moods of the individual. The "stream-of-consciousness" technique, developed by James Joyce in A Portrait of the Artist as a Young Man in 1916, was the most startling product of this twin devotion to stylistic innovation and the often irrational workings of the individual man.

By 1900 the artists, in their own way, were suggesting a world not too dissimilar from the one physicists were beginning to study. The key word was "relative." Sights, sounds, and words themselves were no longer fixed quantities but rather impressions to be interpreted by the individual. Many of the new artists, like the musicians experimenting with atonality, were coldly logical. The symbolist movement had none of the exuberant emotionalism of Romanticism. It was, nevertheless, a profound attack on rationalist assumptions of an orderly relationship between individual man and the world outside.

THE POLITICS
OF ANTI-RATIONALISM

Direct attacks on the idea that man is primarily rational and on the political and progressive corollaries of this were certainly encouraged by the varied artistic and scientific movements of the period, but the association was not close. Many of the new artists and scientists remained in the rationalist political tradition while others had no politics at all. Anti-rationalists often despised the new art and science, being far more directly linked to Romanticism than were the new artists. Their rebellion against the heritage of the Enlightenment was far more direct and simple.

The philosophical framework of anti-rationalism was sketchy. A Romantic philosopher of the early nineteenth century, Arthur Schopenhauer, belatedly gained attention with his profound pessimism and his stress on will and striving, as opposed to human reason. Friedrich Nietzsche, one of the leading thinkers of the century, agreed that human life was a profound tragedy. At the same time he insisted on the necessity of struggle and combat and rejected Christianity and rationalism as handicaps. What was needed was implacable will. Struggle should produce a new race of supermen impelled by their desire for power. The weak should perish. Nietzsche's thought was taken up after 1900 by the French philosopher Georges Sorel, who preached the virtue of violence.

A variety of second-level thinkers translated some of these notions into political theory. In the process they distorted Nietzsche (a common phenomenon in intellectual history) and the distortions generally have more historical importance than the original. In most countries diverse authoritarian-nationalist tracts poured forth from the 1880s onward, penned by writers profoundly critical of modern society—among them, Julius Langbehn in Germany, Maurice Barrès in France, and Enrico Corradini in Italy. They attacked society's selfishness and materialism, its absence of belief, its class divisions and injustice, and ridiculed the ineffectiveness and corruption of parliamentary governments. Seeking scapegoats, many of them pinned the blame for the modern decline on the Jews, but more basically, they attacked key assumptions of rationalist liberalism. In their opinion man could not stand alone, he was not primarily rational, he needed leadership and collective loyalties, and he pined for action, not thought. Nor did they believe that men were equal.

Some of the anti-rationalists just expressed their despair with modern society, but others groped for remedies. They preached a racist, aggressive nationalism. The nation was the higher unity men needed. It should be ready for war, not just to advance its own interests but because violence brought out the best in men. The state should be strong, authoritarian and capable of stilling divisions among classes and individuals. The anti-rationalists sought some alternative to capitalism and talked vaguely of a corporate society that would unite men of different classes along professional lines. Far more clearly they looked toward a strong leader who could impose his will on the nation. Corradini urged a new Caesar to lead his people to war, while others considered a Nietzschean superman as their only hope.

A few groups managed to reconcile some of the diverse strands of cultural activity at the end of the century. A movement called Futurism arose in Italy and won wide popularity among intellectuals elsewhere. The Futurists vaunted perpetual revolution in the arts. Their own styles were abstract and stressed motion and energy. They believed that politics also should have no rules or moral codes and considered both liberalism and socialism dull and timid. For them, the essence of politics was aggressive motion: the state should be organized for war. The Futurists, in other words, managed to unite anti-rationalism in the arts and in politics.

This was atypical, however. Intellectual activity grew increasingly compartmentalized and diverse forces were at work. If there was a general intellectual mood at the turn of the century it was one of confusion and uncertainty. Dissatisfaction with nineteenth-century standards was widespread, in science as in the arts. The boundless optimism of some earlier rationalists and Romantics alike was a chief victim of the new questioning, but the very relativism that emerged in so many fields inhibited a new synthesis. Hence, among other things, neither contemporaries nor subsequent historians have devised a single term, like Romanticism, to describe the period in even rough terms. The lack of common assumptions from one area of cultural activity to the next was one of the most important features of the age.

THE SPREAD OF IDEAS

It is far easier to discuss intellectual trends than to assess their historical importance. A case in point is racial Darwinism, the use of evolutionary theory (which Darwin himself mildly suggested) to posit the superiority of some peoples over others and the struggle for power, if not for survival, among them. Anthropologists elaborated on racial differences and French and German historians began to argue whether feudalism, with its warrior virtues, was of Germanic or Roman origin. Anti-Semitic writers and apologists for imperialism applied the racial-struggle notions to the events of the day. The very use of the word "race" to describe Englishmen or Germans or Jews stemmed from the desire to apply Darwinism to current events. The idea, then, had wide currency, but did it spread widely beyond the intellectuals? On first glance, yes. Popular magazine articles on imperialism certainly assumed the racial inferiority of native peoples. Anti-semitism was widespread among shopkeepers and other groups who feared big business competition. For many people nationalism suggested both the virtues of one's own race and the validity of struggle and war for national goals.

Despite the evidences of racial-Darwinist influence, we cannot assume too quickly that most literate people absorbed these doctrines very deeply. We do not know how many people in Britain or Germany were seriously interested in imperialism at all. Historians have written about imperialism's role in distracting the humble clerk from his dull and insignificant daily life, but there is little evidence to prove that most clerks cared—or did not care—about imperialism. Imperialist organizations were mostly upper-class affairs. Major political parties rarely talked about empire and there were few demonstrations over imperial questions. The popular press—and by the 1890s newspapers had developed an audience of millions in the big cities—played up imperialist excitement, but even this is not absolute proof that the ordinary newspaper reader was deeply concerned. Moreover, most of the popular-press arguments about imperialism did not invoke Darwinism very vigorously. In advocating empire they stressed the excitement of exploration, the fervor of Christian missionary work, and the desirability for the home country and the natives alike of bringing trade and other trappings of civilization to the backward world. Imperialist rhetoric was definitely racist in that it assumed natives were inferior, perhaps permanently so; but it did not argue in terms of struggle and certainly did not advocate the extinction of inferior peoples. The rhetoric probably owed more to Christianity and even to liberal humanitarianism than to any of the doctrines developed in the second half of the nineteenth century.

Similar questions can be raised about anti-Semitism. Christian Europe had long been anti-Semitic, so where the sentiment existed it was not necessarily new. Shopkeepers who protested Jewish merchants and bankers had new economic grievances, but their choice of scapegoat may have owed less to new ideas than to the traditional suspicion of the Jew as a usurer and clever trader. We can also question the virulence and persistence of anti-Semitism before World War I. Except in Vienna, specifically anti-Semitic political movements drew only scattered support, and everywhere anti-Semitic riots and propaganda declined after 1900.

We are left with problems that are difficult to resolve. We know that the formal intellectual climate had changed, and we can see traces of this change in more popular attitudes. We can see contrary evidence as well. At this point the historian cannot produce a neat formula. Yet the topic is so vital to an understanding of the period and of intellectuals themselves that it cannot be ignored.

Popular Outlook

The key issue is whether the central ideas of the Enlightenment were gaining or losing favor among the general populace. To what extent did the various critics of rationalism, who admittedly were not challenged in the intellectual community, find an audience? To what extent can we translate the undeniable cultural malaise as a crisis in European society?

There was an audience for the attacks on rationalism, as is evident from the fact that books by Langbehn and others in Germany went through many editions. Bureaucrats and professional people who were frustrated by their decline in status, small-town notables who were left behind by the new world of big cities and big business—these were probably the main constituents of the audience.

Larger segments of society showed a new interest in physical activity that perhaps paralleled the intellectuals' attack on reason and the mind. Organized sports gained unprecedented popularity. Rules were formalized for most of the great European team sports, especially soccer football, and professional teams arose. A worship of athletic prowess spread from the schools of the upper classes. The newly affluent middle classes learned that athletic recreation had virtues along with hard work. Women as well as men enjoyed one fad after another, from croquet to bicycle riding. Workers followed suit, spending considerable sums to watch and to bet on team sports and to organize their own games after work. The establishment of the Boy Scouts and, on the continent, smaller groups of nature-lovers and hikers, was yet another sign of the new interest in physical skills.

None of this bears any necessary relationship to intellectual developments. Increased leisure time and higher living standards—the basis for a new consumer society—can account for the widespread interest in sports. Certainly few bicycle addicts read Freud and decided to sublimate their unconscious desires by pedaling furiously. Yet if there was a broad revulsion against a culture that preached rational restraint and planning, the intellectuals echoed and furthered this revulsion.

Popular Nationalism

Nationalism spread to the masses for the first time in the later nineteenth century. It replaced, to some extent at least, many traditional loyalties that eroded as people moved to the cities: loyalty to church and loyalty to village and region. Nationalism was urged on the citizens by the state, through the schools and the military by a number of political parties that were now forced to woo the masses, and by the newspapers that had wide circulation. Socialist parties, which opposed nationalism, had to soft-pedal their arguments as they realized that most workers accepted national loyalty.

But what was the full significance of mass nationalism? At the level of formal ideas, it was without question hostile to the rationalist tradition. It denied the universality of mankind and in its later nineteenth-century versions preached violence and struggle. Some groups, such as the anti-Semites, used nationalism as a vehicle for attacking socialism, big business and parliamentary corruption—all apparently the products of a belief in human reason—while remaining respectable. Even for people not so completely at odds with their society, nationalism could provide the comforting feeling that they belonged to a larger community, which in itself corresponded to the intellectuals' claim that the individual could not stand alone. Nationalism could, moreover, be a respectable outlet for the violent impulses of people frustrated by the dullness and regimentation of urban life.

The beginning of World War I was greeted with wide popular enthusiasm in the industrial countries. Admittedly, everyone thought it would be a short war, but people were stimulated by the prospect of excitement and violence, by the chance to attack a hated enemy across the border. French socialists decided to view German workers as Germans rather than as fellow workers and human beings; the Germans reciprocated. Here may be the clearest proof of the impact of new ideas of action and violence.

The Rationalist Current

Yet this is at best an incomplete picture. Many of the forces shaping popular attitudes had little to do with the new attacks on reason. Most obviously the newest political force, socialism, preached a belief in progress and in man's ability to improve himself by reason and education. State school systems stressed nationalism and, often, religion, but they also taught the importance of science and education. Popular magazines and newspapers were generally nationalist, but few advocated war or violence. They paid great attention to progress in science and technology and to other apparent gains in human enlightenment.

In 1900, as attacks on the rationalist framework were mounting, the popular press took a look at the century that had passed and the one that was to come. They found virtually uninterrupted progress and anticipated steady advance in the future. Among the criteria they used in making this judgment were: improvements in human knowledge and education and the concomitant decline of superstition; advances in material well-being; humanitarian gains, ranging from abolition of the slave trade to better treatment of children; increased political freedom and participation; and peace. The optimism rivaled that of the most extravagant enlightenment optimist and it had the same roots in a firm belief in human reason.

The popular press is not the only measure of popular attitudes, yet it is clear that most of the formal ideas that had wide influence in the later nineteenth century derived from the rationalist tradition. The audience for the new ideas was limited and anti-rationalist political theory received just slight attention. Georges Sorel preached violence but was largely ignored— until after World War I when Italian fascists paid him heed. Einstein and Freud would not be popularized until later. The new styles in painting only slowly attracted the interest of leading patrons and then against the opposition of more conventional art academies. There was a gulf between formal culture and the culture of the middle and lower classes. Popular culture was not neatly consistent. Most people blended nationalism with Enlightenment ideas (as many intellectuals had done in the early nineteenth century). Their brief excitement over war was due less to new ideas, less even to nationalism, than to a much older human impulse. None of this should blind us to the real gains that Enlightenment-derived ideas had made. The intellectuals' attack on these ideas was partly caused by their realization that the ideas had triumphed, at least in the bourgeois world they so detested.

MASS CULTURE

During the nineteenth century, and particularly in the century's last decades, there were enormous changes in the outlook of most people in the industrial areas of Europe. The history of these changes has little to do with the rationalist versus anti-rationalist framework that dominated formal intellectual activity. Rather, the transition was from traditionalist to broadly rationalist assumptions about life.

The spread of the idea of progress is the easiest measure of the great change that was taking place. As late as 1850 few people in Europe believed in progress, including successful businessmen who, ironically, were slow to accept the general concept. The revolutions of 1848 showed that the lower classes still looked to the past for their standards in protest. By 1900 acceptance of the notion of progress was still limited, particularly among peasants and the very poor. A Prussian worker's wife, for example, who refused to see a doctor, offered the explanation: "God is the best doctor. If He wishes, I'm healthy; otherwise not." Labor leaders found it difficult to persuade many workers to strive for positive improvements in their lot. Yet the experience of material gains and the constant preaching of the idea of progress from many quarters gradually convinced most people in the cities that things could get better. Never before in history had masses of people believed in progress on this earth and through the agency of man alone.

A Day at the Beach: Railroad excursions gave working-class families new recreational outlets, though swimming became popular only later, after World War I.

The New Approach to Life

The idea of progress involved a variety of new concepts. Declining death rates, the cessation of public executions, and the prohibition of such traditional urban spectacles as cock-fighting made the sight of violence and death far less common than before. The poor, long attuned to accepting and ritualizing death, gradually altered their culture accordingly. Early factory workers first joined together in groups in order to provide adequate burial funds; later labor unions concentrated on other goals. As child mortality declined, workers and peasants could afford to be more affectionate with their children; it was emotionally less risky to love a child who was almost certain to live to maturity than to love one who was likely to die by the age of two. Desire for material improvement and for a better future for the children—the idea of progress in the most direct sense—encouraged the lower classes to reduce their birth rate by artificial means. For many people this was another decisive break with tradition. Yet the marriage rate continued to rise as workers and peasants now felt free to seek the pleasures of wedlock without waiting for any inheritance or, often, even parental consent.

Workers and peasants were, in fact, gaining a new idea of themselves as individuals. In the later nineteenth century the Balkan peasants shed traditional beliefs in the religious character of key tools and natural phenomena. An ax was no longer regarded as an object of ritual but simply an instrument to be used for its wielder's benefit. Common people in western Europe had made this transition earlier, but they also gained a new sense of their power over nature. Locomotive engineers were enthralled by the monsters they piloted through the countryside. The widespread use of the bicycle by the 1880s gave millions of people in various social classes a new sense of freedom. Technological change continued to cause disruption and hardship, particularly by speeding up the pace of work. Yet few of the workers most affected tried to protest technological change directly. This was partly because they knew opposition was fruitless but also because they had learned to exchange annoyance on the job for greater leisure and earnings. Many of them joined the rising tide of working-class discontent, asking for new gains—for progress—within the industrial system. Changes in popular culture thus altered the nature of protest. More generally workers increasingly focused their life on consumption of goods and services and on freedom outside the job. The rise of recreational outlets, including sports, responded to this new orientation.

The desire for individual enjoyment extended to sex. We know far too little about the history of sex, but it is becoming clear that sometime in the eighteenth century a new attitude toward sex began to arise among the common people in western and central Europe. One sign of this was a marked rise in number of illegitimate births, in the countryside as well as in the cities. The rate dropped a bit in the later nineteenth century, but it was still high by traditional standards. In the nineteenth century the steadily rising marriage rate, together with the lowering of the marriage age, was another indication of new attitudes toward sex and love. The artificial birth control devices that became widely known in the later nineteenth century simply furthered the trend. Sex was no longer primarily for procreation. It was no longer tied to and restrained by the property arrangements of peasant society, but was to be enjoyed by individuals, as individuals.

Lower-class women, particularly in the cities, won new freedom. In the villages and in families, women had wielded considerable power, some of which they now lost as outside agencies took over such traditional functions as the education of children. But as women gained employment and earnings outside the home, as they were protected from biennial childbirth, many new opportunities evolved. In the later nineteenth century there was a visible change in costume, and not only in the upper classes. Women's dress became less rigid, less restrictive and less somber. Salesgirls and cannery workers alike began to follow fads and fashions, at least while they were in their teens.

Clearly a massive change in outlook as well as opportunity was developing, and whether it was good or bad, the change was fundamental. Traditional attitudes toward protest, toward marriage, toward most aspects of life gave way to a new belief in progress and in individual self-expression. Ordinary Europeans were redefining their purpose in life.

The Transition to New Ideas

Occasionally the shift was startlingly quick. A young German worker, fresh from the countryside, was taught by his factory-mates to substitute socialism for religion, to agitate for higher pay instead of gratefully accepting traditional levels, and to use contraceptives (which the Germans called "Parisian articles") instead of burdening himself with a huge family. In 1899 the miners in Montceau, an isolated French town, who struck against poor conditions, were harangued by socialist and radical propagandists from the big cities. The strike freed the miners from decades of employer domination and also from a traditionalist outlook. Hence workers not only flocked to the socialist party and the new trade union movement, but largely abandoned the Church and altered their family structure in the interests of greater material well-being. By 1910 church attendance and baptisms had dropped over 50 percent and the birth rate was down by almost 75 percent. In general, of course, changes did not occur so dramatically or so rapidly. It took generations for old beliefs to be abandoned. Even in western Europe the transition was not complete by the end of the century, but its dimensions were clear.

The Decline of Religion

Decline of religious faith was an inevitable part of the development of the new popular outlook, and in the second half of the nineteenth century this decline shifted from the intellectuals to the masses. Attacks on traditional theology by evolutionary biologists and by the new biblical critics contributed to the process, but the key development was the loss of faith by the growing urban lower classes. New workers could not identify with the urban churches: they were too big and too fancy and lacked the familiar ritual of the village church. Moreover priests and ministers offended workers by their conservative social views. Many workers found it easy to believe the socialists who attacked Christianity as a tool of the established order. Most basically, the new outlook that was developing among workers ran counter to traditional Christian doctrine.

The decline of religion came slowly. Most peasants adhered to traditional religious practice, though there were large de-Christianized areas in France; in southern Europe peasants attacked the Church, but not religion, in their massive uprisings at the end of the century. Possibly as a reaction to these attacks, piety actually increased in some small towns and villages such as Brittany where devotion to the Virgin Mary spread among lay groups. Strengthening this popular devotion were reports of miracles at La Salette in 1846 and at Lourdes in 1858. Missionary activity burgeoned as well, as churches sent thousands of priests and ministers to all corners of the globe. Here popular piety was supplemented by the continued support of the churches by the wealthy classes. Many rich businessmen found that support of religion helped to establish themselves socially, and the upper classes saw how vital religion was in maintaining social order. In several countries there was a pronounced upsurge in support for religion after the upheavals of 1848.

But the decline of religion was irresistible and the more sensitive churchmen saw what was happening. Protestant churches tried to accommodate their theology to the new scientific discoveries and also attempted to reach the workers by establishing settlement houses and other urban institutions. Following the issuance of Leo XIII's encyclical *Rerum novarum,* which urged social justice and reform while attacking socialism, a variety of Catholic trade unions were founded. These won support from a minority of workers, and converted few who had already lost their faith. Moreover, the unions were hampered by the fact that most of the hierarchy found them dangerous to the traditional social order. As a result, the churches continued to lose ground in the growing cities.

Some people found in socialism or nationalism a new, religious-like faith. Socialism had many religious attributes: It had a bible in the writings of Marx, a heaven (albeit here on earth), and many saints and martyrs. The most fervent socialists undoubtedly achieved a religious intensity in their belief. But for most people the loss of religion was above all the loss of ritual and of a few key assumptions. These people had never required a full theology and were not interested in the overall doctrines of socialism or nationalism. Did the decline of religion increase the tension and isolation of modern life? Or were adequate substitutes found in the new "isms" and in the new outlets for personal pleasure?

The people of Europe were divided in their outlook at the end of the century, in some ways more than they had been before. The population of eastern and southern Europe was still locked in largely traditional beliefs, which even their rising protest reflected.

In the industrial countries there were signs of increasing standardization of popular culture, associated in some cases with centralized direction from business and government. The masses were now given a common education by the state. Newspapers with a circulation in the millions, like the *Daily Mail* or the *Petit Parisien,* guided and reflected popular tastes while responding also to the wishes of rich advertisers. The papers stressed excitement, action (including sports) and human interest against the older press tradition of elaborate political and cultural news. Closely reasoned editorial comment gave way to a superficially objective reporting style. Closely typed pages were replaced by big print and screaming headlines. In this might be summed up much of the culture of the newly articulate masses. Cheap and sensationalist, it could be manipulated from above, as, for example, when the popular newspapers with their conservative big-business outlook distracted attention from internal problems by playing up imperialist adventures. Above all the culture was monotonously the same. Even the wealthier classes, as they turned more to recreation and pleasure, were attracted by many aspects of the new mass culture. They shared the masses' growing interest in sports, often bought the same papers, and hesitantly developed a more open interest in sexual pleasure.

Yet against the elements of uniformity the significant, growing political and social divisions must be stressed. "The masses" might read the same papers or even learn a common basic nationalism, but they were not lured into political unanimity. Life styles varied widely, despite some common recreational interests. Workers tended to look more for immediate enjoyments, spending increased earnings on food and sometimes on gambling, while clerks who earned similar wages appreciated more durable status items such as clothing and housing. If there was a common popular culture it derived most basically from the general conversion to belief in progress and in individual enjoyment. Yet even this conversion was incomplete by 1914, and there were important segments of society—most obviously, those faithful to traditional religion—who resisted conversion outright.

INTELLECTUALS
AND SOCIETY

It is impossible to define a common outlook either for intellectuals or for the masses of people. But if we take the dominant trends in each camp we can suggest a further barrier to any simple summary: intellectual attitudes and popular attitudes were drifting apart. On the whole, intellectuals were becoming increasingly skeptical of, or hostile to, the Enlightenment heritage, while the masses in the industrial countries were being won over to generally progressive assumptions. Although there was some audience for attacks on rationalism among more traditional middle-class elements, most of the clientele for the intellectuals' new styles and ideas at the turn of the century came from other intellectuals and groups, such as students, who were close to them.

The fact that many intellectuals—the symbolist poets, for example—explicitly produced for themselves and for each other was a new and perhaps disturbing phenomenon. The vital slogan "art for art's sake" came to mean art for the artists' sake. Scientists did not so deliberately push in the same direction, but push they did. By 1914 the forefront of science was well beyond the understanding of the educated layman. This too was new, a dramatic contrast not only with the age of Newton but with that of Darwin.

Intellectuals of many types disdained the society they saw rising around them. Many of them railed against the materialism and sensationalism of the bourgeois culture. They noted the middle classes' unwillingness to accept new styles, for indeed businessmen who purchased art tended to stick to established modes to be sure that their purchases would be socially acceptable. Again the contrast with the eighteenth and early nineteenth century was marked, for then elements of the middle classes had comprised much of the audience that was open to new ideas and supported the intellectuals who produced them. In the later nineteenth century the middle classes tended to reciprocate the intellectuals' scorn, regarding artists as morally degenerate "bohemians" and political theorists as dangerous radicals. Only scientists seemed useful, and then mainly as they contributed to improved technology.

Intellectuals grew suspicious of the masses too, and certainly there was relatively little direct interaction between the two groups. According to many of them the masses could easily vaunt mediocrity and stifle the creative individual.

Clearly, then, by the end of the century, intellectuals on the whole felt apart from, sometimes violently hostile to, the society around them. The basic problem was this: no institutional relationship between intellectuals and society had arisen that could fully replace the old system of church sponsorship and upper-class patronage—the system that intellectuals had led in tearing down. (In traditional society most intellectuals were priests, though not all priests were intellectuals. Their activities had, through religion, some clear relationship to the broader society.) Politics was the most obvious modern counterpart to religion. Intellectuals set forth all the great isms but then tended to lose control of them. For three decades Marxism had been largely a movement of intellectuals. The role of intellectuals diminished as Marxist parties worked out their bureaucratic structures and attended to the concerns of their constituency. Not surprisingly the process disgusted many intellectuals. Finally, with the expansion of wealth and of educational opportunities, the number of intellectuals grew steadily. This made it easier for intellectuals to define their distinctiveness as intellectuals by the presence of so many similar people around them. At the same time it made it more difficult to find suitable jobs, which increased the intellectuals' disenchantment.

Hence the mood of intellectuals at the turn of the century cannot be taken for the mood of society as a whole. Many intellectuals delighted in speaking about society in general, but their testimony should not be taken too literally. They responded to different causes from those that motivated most other groups. At the same time, the efforts of intellectuals were not entirely removed from broader events. They did not immediately shape popular values but since they were articulate spokesmen they were read, particularly by elements of the ruling elite who had their own uncertainties about the modern world. The bulk of the German middle classes, for example, read stories and essays that reflected ideas of progress and individualism. But many German bureaucrats, both middle-class and aristocratic, were more open to the writings of intellectuals who attacked rationalism and industrialism. Many had been educated with and by these intellectuals; many felt shunted aside by the modern world. A gap between intellectuals and society can always be dangerous, and in Europe, at the turn of the century, new intellectual currents may have affected politics and diplomacy. To what extent can one trace a link between the growing uncertainties about rationalism and the immense irrationality of World War I?

7 POLITICS, DIPLOMACY, AND WAR

The advent of parliamentary government in western and central Europe by 1871 had one clear effect: it created an impression of persistent political effervescence. Party and factional alignments changed often. Ministries rose and fell. France was already staking her claim to primacy in ministerial instability, but Italy and, after 1890, Germany offered competition. One could dwell at some length on the permutations of politics, stressing the peculiarities of each nation, yet in terms of basic political forces the pattern is not complex.

For a decade or so after the establishment of the new regimes there was little fundamental political change. By the end of the 1880s socialism was broadening the political spectrum on the left, the principal fruit of the workers' challenge to the status quo. There were more diffuse challenges on the right, some of which reflected the discontent of the intellectuals. But despite occasional appearances to the contrary, the regimes of western and central Europe remained stable. The principal result of the new political forces was to broaden the powers of the sovereign state.

This pattern, however, cannot be applied to southern and eastern Europe; the states in these areas were unstable and some of them perhaps doomed to collapse. In Russia and Spain, particularly a new, more flexible conservatism had not penetrated.

To what extent did internal political stability depend on a vigorous, successful diplomacy? There is no question that the governments in southern and eastern Europe tied their domestic fortunes increasingly to the success of their diplomacy. Western diplomats also were extraordinarily active and skillful from the 1870s on, and they were certainly aware that diplomatic triumphs could be used in diverting unrest at home. The explosion of imperial expansion in these decades gave clear evidence of the great diplomatic vitality of the European states. This same vitality, however, may also have proved a fundamental weakness, for turned inward to Europe itself, it produced within a few years one of the most dreadful wars in human history.

CONSERVATIVES AND LIBERALS

In the last two decades of the nineteenth century liberals in Europe were on the defensive. There were three basic reasons for this attitude. First, liberals had won many of their demands and had trouble finding new issues. Some wanted largely to conserve what they had gained. Second, the structure of the economy had outstripped the vision of conventional liberalism. Liberals could not deal easily with big business pressure groups or fierce international economic rivalry. Some tried to hold out for pure principles, as in Britain where liberals fought successfully against tariff demands until after 1914. Others yielded. The National Liberals in Germany, for example, became spokesmen for big business and urged high tariffs. Third, liberals had great difficulty expanding their electorate. As liberals they could not respond positively to lower-class demands for social legislation, and they were hampered also by their reluctance to establish firm political parties and campaign organizations.

Liberals in Germany and Britain

Bismarck broke with the liberals in 1879. He had never been comfortable with them and now sought repressive laws against the socialists, which the liberals would not approve. He drew the *Kulturkampf* to a close, rescinding the harshest measures against the Catholic Church, and passed a high agricultural tariff in 1879, thus gaining support from conservatives and the Catholic Center party. Although the liberals' electoral strength actually began to dwindle even before this, for they could not win the working classes, they still remained a political force. Their influence was felt in the 1890s, for example, when the government passed a reform of the system of military justice that allowed soldiers to have legal advice in courts martial, and again when the government was prevented from passing harsh restrictions on strikes and labor unions. But the liberals were not dominant. They continued to accept the existing regime, which was far from liberal, and their ties with big business drew them away from economic liberalism and from the possibility of alliance with socialists for genuine political reform.

In Austria liberalism declined still more drastically by the 1880s. Liberals could not win even lower-middle-class voters, who were granted the suffrage in this decade. Moreover, as German nationalists they could not cope with the disputes that arose among the various nationalities in Austria.

British liberals did not fade so badly, but they too lost control of events. They had gradually developed a party structure and in the 1879 election campaign Gladstone displayed new tactics to win a mass electorate, making frequent and impassioned speeches. But the Liberal Party emerged more slowly than did the Conservative. Election appeals were still largely personal, rather than the pronouncements of an organization. Liberals themselves were still divided between Whigs and Radicals. Of overriding importance was the fact that they had accomplished about all they could as liberals. Gladstone's second ministry, from 1880 to 1884, put a few final touches on the liberal structure, notably by making primary education compulsory in 1880. Beyond this Gladstone seemed chiefly interested in keeping the budget low. The Liberals had a foreign policy that was full of pious statements but in actuality they were unable to stop the drive for further imperial acquisitions. They could not settle the Irish question either, as Irish demands for political autonomy became steadily more intense. A new expansion of the suffrage in 1884, which gave the vote to many rural workers, hurt the Liberals who could not appeal to these groups. Toppled in 1884, the Liberals returned only briefly to government during the next decade; beginning in 1895 the Conservatives had a decade of uninterrupted rule.

When they won the election of 1906, the Liberals could no longer be considered "liberal" in the nineteenth-century sense. They had now embraced the principle of social intervention by the government and cooperated with socialists in parliament. In the interests of retaining working-class support, Liberals passed laws limiting the hours of work for miners, as well as many other factory and insurance acts. The National Insurance Act of 1911, funded in part by new taxes on high incomes, insured workers against accident, sickness and unemployment. For the workers it covered, this legislation provided the most advanced system in Europe—a clear sign of the continued flexibility of British politics. The Liberals' evolution foreshadowed similar changes elsewhere, but involved substantial revisions in the liberal approach. The Liberals' success in Britain was at best incomplete as workers turned increasingly to the Labour party and after 1910 conducted strikes of unprecedented ferocity.

Liberals in France and Italy

Liberals fared better in Italy and France. In Italy they were cushioned from possible defeat because of the country's limited suffrage and their leaders' rigging of elections. Their true strength then cannot be fully determined, but they controlled the government most of the time until 1914. French liberalism went far deeper. The vast array of small property owners, both rural and urban, had been converted to republican liberalism. The republicans also managed to preserve a sense of the republic in danger, which gave them an issue their counterparts elsewhere lacked. Their enemies were partly contrived, but against them they could still appear active and radical even when they were defending the status quo. They were also willing to work with socialists when possible and necessary. Liberals were an ill-organized group that developed into loose political parties only after 1900; they embraced many shades of political opinion, but they largely controlled the government in the pre-war decades.

In the 1880s the French government made a concerted effort to weaken the Church by expelling the Jesuit order, requiring state authorization for all teaching orders, and reestablishing civil marriage and divorce. Most important, the government made primary education compulsory and created a system of secular state schools to compete with church schools. Little was done about France's growing social problems, though trade unions were legalized in 1884. A group of radical republicans, who advocated more social legislation, arose during the decade, but they did not come to power until the end of the century. France in 1890 combined the most radical political structure and the most rudimentary social legislation of any major industrial country in Europe.

Conservatism

The difficulties liberals encountered in most countries gave renewed opportunities to conservatives. Conservatives drew support from the lower middle class, which was growing in size, and, except in France, from the rural vote. Conservatives were successful in developing political parties and were willing to use the state to sponsor social reform, if only to reduce the appeal of socialism.

In most western and central European countries, the rise of conservative forces was aided by the policies of Leo XIII, who became pope in 1878. Except in Italy, where he adamantly refused to compromise with the government, Leo urged sensible accommodations with existing regimes, even when they had diminished the Church's power. This was one reason for the end of the *Kulturkampf* in Germany. In 1890, following the same basic policy, a leading French cardinal appealed to Catholics to accept the Republic—a *ralliement* that had only partial success, but that did induce many Catholics to work within the existing regime. Leo also wanted Catholics to support social reforms. His encyclical *Rerum novarum*, issued in 1891, condemned socialism and defended private property, but urged governments to contain the abuses of the industrial system. Here, too, Church policy paralleled some elements of the new conservative approach.

Leading conservative groups now accepted the parliamentary structure and other liberal institutions. In this they followed the example of conservatives like Bismarck. Though still somewhat suspicious and wanting no further political change, they could accept the new political order. This change was marked in Germany, where conservatives remained suspicious of Bismarck through the 1870s. They yielded only at the end of the decade when they had learned that the new regime did not threaten their basic interests and they needed government support for agriculture. With conservative backing, the regime became more repressive in the 1880s. The anti-socialist law, passed in 1878, forbade all associations and publications with socialist tendencies. Freedom of the press declined as the government used secret subsidies to influence editorial opinion. But the 1880s also saw the passage of the first great social insurance laws covering accidents, illness, and old age. The Bismarck government intended these measures primarily as a means to win workers away from socialism, but they also appealed to the paternalistic social consciousness of many conservatives and Catholics.

Conservative ascendancy in Britain did not bring repression, but it did bring some social reforms. Under Disraeli the Conservative government of 1874–1880 liberalized trade union laws and introduced government inspection of housing and public health. Conservatives added further reforms after 1900, notably a system of old-age pensions.

There was no formal conservative party in France or Italy. The Church's prohibition of Catholic participation in Italian politics inhibited what was potentially the most conservative element. Many French monarchists and Catholics similarly refused to participate in the political system of the republic. But gradually some former monarchists, seeing that their cause was hopeless, converted, and some of the Catholic population rallied to the republic as the pope advised. At the same time some republicans shifted slightly to the right. Conservative republicanism dominated the 1890s. Its advocates did not sponsor significant social reform, but, like conservatives elsewhere, they were sympathetic to religion and to agriculture, relaxing some of the anti-clerical laws of the 1880s and establishing high protective tariffs.

Conservative politicians made one other important change by the 1890s: they became the leading supporters of nationalism. Many liberals and others were still nationalist, but conservatives increasingly took over the cause. Disraeli claimed credit for Britain's imperial gains. German conservatives stressed defense of the nation's strength in arguing for agricultural tariffs and other goals. French conservatives were less vocal on this subject, in part because nationalism was so firmly identified with republicanism; however, in their adamant support of the army during the Dreyfus affair it became clear that their vision, too, was nationalistic. The movement of conservatives toward nationalism was extremely important, for the cause had been liberal or radical from its inception. Now nationalism was turned to defense of the status quo, while the conservative cause depended on a vigorous diplomacy.

What statesmen like Bismarck had learned before 1871—namely, that a successful foreign policy could disarm internal dissent—conservatives now generally realized as they regularly urged national strength and imperial expansion in their election campaigns.

Political Harmony

The changes in conservatism and liberalism reduced the differences between the two forces. Conservatives could accept liberal institutions. Liberals began to accept increased state activity in the economy. Thus the two groups could and did cooperate on many matters. The Bülow tariff, for example, was the product of horsetrading between liberals who wanted protection for industrial goods and conservatives who sought still greater protection for agricultural interests.

This growing harmony was the basis of the political stability of the last decades of the nineteenth century. The clash of ideals in the political arena was reduced, at least until socialism became a serious political force. These were golden years for the political manipulator who could win support from various factions and groups. Bismarck became adept at shuffling his parliamentary coalitions. In Austria, after the emperor broke with the liberals in 1879, Count Edward Taafe ruled until 1893 with the support of Catholics, German conservatives, Slavs, Poles and Czechs. He wooed the minority nationalities by local concessions, such as granting a Czech section of the University of Prague, but he avoided any sweeping reforms. Italian politics, from Agostino Depretis onward, was dominated by a process called "transformism," which meant that, regardless of their campaign promises, once deputies were in Rome they were transformed into giving full support to the existing system. French republican deputies similarly switched their allegiances from faction to faction in return for political office; they were known, in the 1880s, as Opportunists. Cases of bribery and corruption were common, particularly in France and Italy. Obviously, this sort of politics was uninspiring, even disgusting, but it reflected a substantial degree of consensus among those who participated in the political process. Basic issues were ignored, for neither conservatives nor liberals sought fundamental change.

Only in France was there significant political disruption between 1875 and 1890. Frenchmen of various political opinions were angered by the dullness of the republican Opportunists and by frequent financial scandals involving politicians. The government's failure to deal forcefully with Germany was condemned by ardent nationalists, who were mostly former republicans. Monarchists and Catholics still hoped for a chance to overturn the regime. Artisans and others in the lower classes sought a state truly committed to social reform. In the late 1880s, the discontent of many disparate elements focused on the cause of General Georges Boulanger, the enigmatic minister of war, a popular though weak leader who appeared to be different things to different people: for the nationalists, he was a strong enemy of Germany; for the radicals, a dashing reformer; for the conservatives, a vigorous anti-republican. Boulanger won a number of elections to parliament, and many street demonstrations championed his cause. But in 1889, having been accused by the government of conspiracy, he fled, and his movement dissolved. The Boulanger affair revealed diverse opposition to the republic; its collapse testified to the strength of the republic, if only as the regime most Frenchmen found least annoying.

UNRECONSTRUCTED CONSERVATISM

The governments of Spain and Russia remained conservative in the early nineteenth-century sense. With the establishment of a parliament, Spain had a facade of modern institutions, and, after 1885, it instituted universal suffrage, but the combination of police intimidation of voters and the government's outright rigging of elections made suffrage practically meaningless. When the government needed ballots, votes of the recently deceased and even not-so-recently deceased were counted. Bureaucratic positions were obtained by bribes and used for personal profit. The church controlled education and censorship. The regime, weak and corrupt, was attacked by peasant and worker uprisings. It lost important colonies to the United States in the 1898 war, but it stumbled along in power, meeting lower-class unrest with police spies and bloody repression. Liberalism had lost in Spain.

The Russian government also tried to turn the clock back, after its reform efforts in the 1860s and early 1870s. When the populist intellectuals failed to win peasant support, they turned to terrorism. Many secret cells were set up after 1878 with the goal of political assassination. After several abortive bombing attempts, one group succeeded in killing Tsar Alexander II in 1881.

Repression was the government's answer to terrorism and to the growing agitation of the lower classes and minority nationalities. The chief minister, Pobiedonostsev, a firm believer in an absolute monarchy linked with the Orthodox Church, actively persecuted ethnic and religious minorities. He increased the Church's role in education, augmented the secret police, and set up military courts to deal with political crimes. In Russia at this time there was no national assembly at all and Pobiedonostsev severely limited the powers of the local *zemstvo* assemblies. Only Count Witte's encouragement to industrialization qualified this reactionary policy, and it too was resisted by many conservatives at the Court.

The Russian system allowed no channels for the expression of grievance or for compromise, which differentiated it from conservative regimes in central Europe. It encouraged a test of will. But the day of reckoning had not yet come. Repression was hard to circumvent and the prosperity of the 1890s reduced lower-class agitation.

DIPLOMACY
OF ALLIANCES

In many ways the diplomacy of the 1870s and 1880s enhanced the impression of European stability. As in internal politics, many traditional issues seemed largely resolved. Italy and Germany were no longer power vacuums inviting intervention and war. The rise of Germany proved to be fundamentally unsettling, but its effects were not immediately felt. Germany, under Bismarck, proclaimed herself a satisfied power and behaved as such. Of the two powers directly harmed by Germany's rise, Austria wisely swallowed her pride and posed no threat while France, already isolated by Bismarck's diplomacy, also showed no real desire to prepare for attack. The French army was strengthened and, as the Boulanger affair revealed, there was vigorous anti-German nationalism in France; but the government turned its diplomatic attention elsewhere and the bulk of French public opinion quickly forgot France's humiliation. Even the "lost provinces" of Alsace and Lorraine received little attention. There was a war scare between France and Germany in 1875, but it faded quickly.

Diplomatic stability was also enhanced by the diversity of interests, indeed of enmities, among the great powers. Britain, the traditional opponent of any dominant continental power, was disturbed by Germany's rise, but also continued to harbor an abiding fear of the French. She found the French, and particularly the Russians, to be her principal opponents in the race for empire. As a result Britain did not work to undo the new continental map. Nor did Russia, which saw as its main opponents Austria in the Balkans and Britain in the Far East.

Out of the confusion of interests and hostilities, Bismarck managed to divise an alliance system by 1882 that was designed to keep the peace and to isolate France. Even in the early 1870s Bismarck formed loose links with Austria and Russia, but the cause of the full-blown alliance network was renewed trouble in the Balkans after 1875. This was the one unsettled area in European diplomacy, the one large vacuum of power, and its internal instability made it still more vulnerable.

Balkan Unrest

In 1875 Bosnia and Herzegovina rose up against Turkish rule, and insurrection spread to Bulgaria. Serbia and Montenegro declared war on Turkey, and Russia joined them in 1877. Having won a rather painful victory, Russia set claim to large Ottoman holdings on the Black Sea and established a new Bulgarian state, one powerful enough to dominate the Balkans yet serve as a vehicle for Russian influence. Understandably, neither Austria-Hungary nor Britain stood idly by. Bismarck, anxious for peace, convened the Congress of Berlin. In trying to settle the issue, he called for a plan that would give something to everyone, which was easy enough from his standpoint since nothing German was involved. The congress reduced the size of Bulgaria, enlarged the territory of Serbia, and declared full independence for Serbia, Montenegro, and Rumania. To offset Russian influence in the area, Britain acquired Cyprus, while Austria assumed the administration of Bosnia-Herzegovina. France was given tacit permission to take over Tunisia.

The Congress of Berlin did not settle the Balkan question. The Bulgarians lamented territories that had been taken from them, the Serbs objected to Austrian control of Bosnia, and the Greeks resented British takeover of Cyprus. A measure of peace had been restored to the area, however. Fearful of her new Bulgarian neighbor, Serbia entered into a defensive alliance with Austria in the 1880s. With both Austria and Russia working for Balkan stability, and Russia turning her expansionist interests elsewhere, isolated unrest in the Balkans could not disturb European harmony.

Bismarck's Allies

Cognizant of Russia's resentment at the setback it had received from the Berlin congress, Bismarck entered into the Dual Alliance with Austria. This alliance, which guaranteed mutual protection against attack by Russia and benevolent neutrality in case of attack by France, was the foundation of German policy through 1914. Bismarck was also eager to avoid possible trouble with Russia. In 1881 he was instrumental in having the three emperors of Germany, Russia, and Austria-Hungary pledge their neutrality in case of war with an outside power and provide for consultation in Balkan affairs. Finally, in 1882, Italy joined Austria and Germany in what was to become the Triple Alliance. Italy, though no friend of the Hapsburgs and in fact seeking some of Austria's Adriatic territory, was still more interested in making inroads in North Africa, where France was her enemy. In particular, she objected to the French acquisition of Tunisia, an area with many Italian settlers. She therefore joined France's enemies. Germany was now the focal point of all European diplomacy. Even Britain had a loose naval agreement with Germany's allies, Italy and Austria, and France, which was adroitly isolated, was not in a position to disturb the European peace.

There were several novel, potentially troublesome, elements in this new diplomatic system. Most obviously it violated the principle of balance of power that Europe had followed in most peacetime decades since the seventeenth century; Germany, the most powerful state, was the sponsor of all the principal pacts. The French inevitably wanted to alter this system but remained fearful of German designs. The system required extraordinary agility from German diplomats, particularly keeping Austria and Russia in uneasy amity. Moreover, the whole notion of enduring alliances, based on secret terms, was new for Europe in peacetime. Though the alliances were defensive they almost anticipated trouble and thereby reduced diplomatic flexibility. At the time, however, given Germany's self-restraint, European peace seemed secure.

IMPERIALISM

Most of the great powers were in fact looking beyond Europe's borders by the 1880s. Imperialism was a vital if temporary contribution to the lack of tension in continental diplomacy.

The last three decades of the nineteenth century capped the long process of Europe's expansion in the world. It was a grand finale. Britain had added to her empire earlier in the nineteenth century. France had taken Algeria and, in the 1860s, began to stake claims in West Africa and Indochina. Russia had been creeping east and south for over a century. For these old hands at imperialism the wave of expansion was not entirely new, but in magnitude it was unprecedented. The new imperialism also differed from traditional colonialism in that it sought from the first to extend full governmental controls over the native peoples even where, as was usually the case, substantial European settlement was impossible. The imperialists intended, then, much more than a network of trading stations. Finally, the imperial game had a large number of new players: Germany above all, but also Italy, Belgium, Japan, and the United States. More than ever before, possession of an empire was seen as a vital attribute of great power status.

The drive for empire quickly penetrated all corners of the world. Outright intervention in Latin America was left mainly to the United States, but there was substantial European economic control. The Near East was not fully carved up because its closeness to Europe presented the possibility of all-out war if one power advanced to any great extent. Beyond the Ottoman Empire Britain acquired Kuwait and other east Arab territories, while Britain and Russia strove for dominant influence in Persia.

Imperialism in Asia and Africa

The European powers proceeded to divide the Far East more thoroughly, starting with the peripheries. Russia extended into central Asia and vied with Britain for control of Afghanistan. France completed its takeover of Indochina in the 1880s, a move that alarmed Britain. Anxious to protect

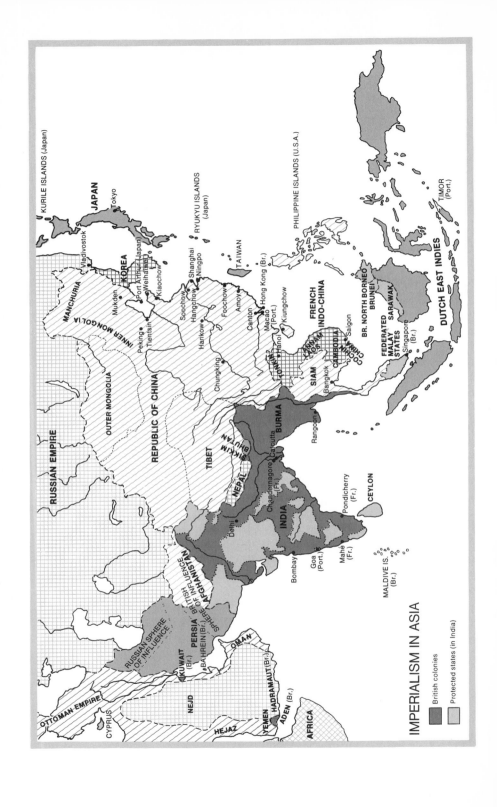

IMPERIALISM IN ASIA

British colonies

Protected states (in India)

India, Britain acquired Burma as a buffer state in 1886. France, Britain, Germany, and the United States all competed for the Pacific Oceania, with Germany and the United States dividing control of Samoa, and France developing its Polynesian holding.

In the 1890s imperialist rivalries reached as far as China, although Britain had established interests there many years before. Now Russia precipitated the scramble for territory. In order to shorten the route of the Trans-Siberian railway, the Russians had designs on part of Manchuria. Their pressure on China aroused the Japanese, who sought territory in return. Russia managed to acquire railroad concessions in Manchuria, while in the Sino-Japanese War in 1894 Japan defeated China and gained Formosa. The gate was now open for the great powers to take action. For the

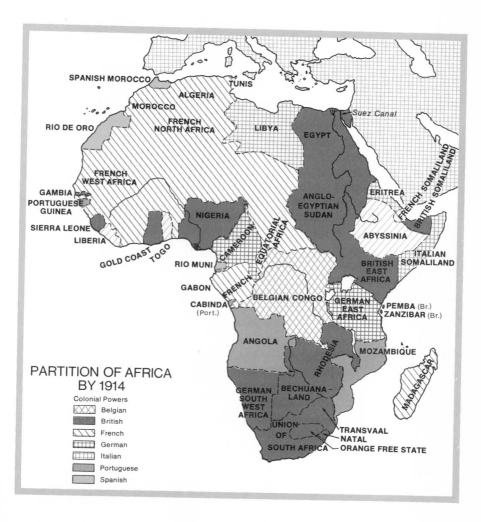

PARTITION OF AFRICA
BY 1914

Colonial Powers

- Belgian
- British
- French
- German
- Italian
- Portuguese
- Spanish

most part they did not assume territory outright but forced the Chinese government to grant 99-year leases and ran their areas as virtually sovereign governments. Germany leased Kiaochow in 1896; Russia, Port Arthur in 1897; Britain, Weihaiwei in 1898; and France, Kwangchowan in 1899. Only Italy was refused the territory it requested. By the end of the century Russia had occupied Manchuria without benefit of a lease, and the full partition of China seemed to be only a question of time.

Africa was gobbled up even more thoroughly. With British protection, Portugal increased its control of Angola and Mozambique; the giant Congo fell into the hands of Belgium; and Italy gained part of Somaliland. From the standpoint of European diplomacy, Germany's entry into the continent with the acquisition of Tanganyika and Southwest Africa was of great significance. Britain and France, however, obtained the major new holdings. French territories ran from west to east and included most of west Africa, the Sahara, Algeria and Tunisia, and part of Somaliland. British holdings, except for a large section in west Africa, ran from north to south, from South Africa through Rhodesia, Uganda, Kenya, the Sudan, and Egypt. By 1900 the only country that remained completely free of imperial control was Ethiopia, while Liberia, Morocco, and Tripoli were partially independent.

CAUSES
OF IMPERIALISM

It is far easier to describe imperial expansion than to explain it, for this was an unparalleled development in the history of the world. Not surprisingly, contemporary and later historians have argued vigorously about the causes of the new imperialism. Even in this brief survey we must suggest a number of factors.

Imperialism was a massive demonstration of Europe's great strength. The unprecedented speed of expansion was the result of a mature industrialization that created the new wealth and produced the necessary ships and arms for such ventures. Imperialism followed also from the political stability most European countries had gained by 1880, which allowed statesmen to turn their attentions elsewhere. Confidence in European values was an equally important factor. The sense of Christian mission, though not new, played a major role in imperialism. Europeans could also boast now—whether accurately or not—of their superior humanitarianism. They killed and tortured as they hacked their way to empire but they tried to stop slave trade and cure native diseases. Certainly the imperialist self-image was fed by appeals to humanitarianism; Europeans assumed the duty of bringing their superior civilization to peoples they considered inferior. Imperialists argued whether native peoples could rise to European levels, but there was no question that by European standards such peoples would be inferior

for some time and therefore had to be controlled. It came down to a question of race: Europeans were fittest and should therefore rule. It was a
white man's burden. Finally, this confidence in Europe's superiority was
more narrowly channeled into confidence in national superiority. British
apologists, for example, vaunted the special virtues of English civilization,
the aptness with which Anglo-Saxons ruled. Imperialism flowed from the
achievements, real and imagined, of Europe at the end of the nineteenth
century. It fit the sense of confidence with which liberals and conservatives
viewed the European order.

Economic Factors

However, imperialism was also a sign of weakness. The British economist
J. A. Hobson in 1905 put forth the argument that imperialism resulted from
the weaknesses of industrial capitalism, and this was taken up subsequently
by Lenin and many other Marxists. Capitalism had reached a point where
it could not survive without exploiting other people. Capitalists could not
find sufficient investment outlets at home; to preserve their profits they
needed new territory, new markets and new supplies, which only the
colonies could provide.

These arguments were at least partially wrong. Foreign investment rose
rapidly but not primarily in the empires. The new colonies offered scant
opportunities for industrial sales; expanding world trade went mainly from
one industrial country to another. Raw materials were provided by some of
the colonies, such as the Congo, and it is true that many individual companies profited greatly from their imperial operations. But there is little
question that most of the colonies cost more than they returned to the
mother countries.

Yet whether correct or not, many people believed the economic arguments for empire and were convinced that their country needed to control
new markets and resources. Imperialism resulted in part, then, from the
growing sense of economic restriction and competition, and business groups
took a lead in advocating colonial gains. Imperialism was also a vital source
of jobs for bureaucrats, including many aristocrats whose economic and
political position was eroding at home and Christian missionaries who grew
ever more doubtful of the validity of industrial civilization. Imperialism was
created in part by losers and misfits in European society. Ironically they
usually preached Europe's superiority to the natives nonetheless.

Mass Culture as a Factor

Some historians have argued that imperialism was the product of more
general strains in European culture. As society became more complex, so the
argument runs, the restraints of civilization grew too galling, forcing Euro-

peans generally to seek satisfaction, if only vicariously, in the violence and excitement of empire. Clerks and workers, bored with their jobs, might find joy in the imperial exploits that the most popular newspapers touted so highly. Here too, Europe's sense of superiority was less a fact than a psychological necessity to people who were pathetically unsure of their own worth.

The arguments that imperialism stemmed from the defects of European civilization deserve serious consideration. Two warnings are in order, however. Several countries that were not yet industrialized participated fully in the race for empire, notably Russia and Italy. Here the causes must have been somewhat different from those operating in the mature industrial societies. More important, public enthusiasm for empire-building did not come until after the first decade or two of expansion. Portions of the public in Britain and Germany became excited about their respective empires, but only in the 1890s. Even the sense of mission developed partly after the fact, as publicists sought to explain and justify what had already happened. Nor has it been proved that most ordinary people cared very much about imperialism—even by 1900. Where it was a serious electoral issue the advocates of imperialism almost always lost. Imperialism ultimately aroused a mild public interest, in part because it flattered the public ego, in part because of a general sense of economic insecurity, but it did not stem from public support.

The Role of Leaders

Imperialism in the 1870s and 1880s often resulted from the activities of a few adventurers or missionaries. For example, the ardent nationalist Karl Peters went to east Africa and conducted negotiations with native chiefs on Germany's behalf. With support from nationalist groups and business organizations at home, he pressed for German recognition of his holdings and ultimately Bismarck took action. Savorgnan de Brazza, an explorer, staked out France's claims in the French Congo with only vague government authorization. Cecil Rhodes, spurred by nationalism and a desire for personal profit, was instrumental in pressing the British government to expand northward from South Africa.

Diplomatic Factors

Rather traditional diplomatic motives supplemented the efforts of individuals. France sought to find in an empire the glory that now eluded her in Europe, but the thirst for glory was not new. Britain acquired new imperialist holdings, but largely in reaction to the efforts of other states;

Imperialist Rivalry:
Britain, watching other
powers seize territory,
stands ready to claim her
own share.

she was constantly picking up just one more colony to defend what she already had against interlopers. When Germany took over Tanganyika Britain had to get Rhodesia and Uganda, fearful that the Germans would move on toward South Africa. The imperialist decisions of Germany and Italy were more novel, in that they came to the realization that colonies were an attribute of a great power and they were great powers. This conclusion on the part of Germany and Italy stepped up imperial rivalry immensely. But once Germany decided that she deserved the same powers that Britain had, the motives were in many ways prosaic. Germany moved into China because Russia had done so. Nationalism heightened the diplomatic rivalry, as did the growing belief that great nations were great because of their large navies and, further, that these navies were in need of coaling stations throughout the world. But even without these arguments, traditional desires for aggrandizement could produce startling results when Europe was closed to expansion and when technological and organizational superiority made it so easy to move throughout the rest of the world.

It is doubtful, therefore, that imperialism was the product of a new, fundamental, and profoundly disturbing change in European civilization. The motives if not the means involved were more traditional, even sometimes accidental. The most important new factors were the rise of new contestants for empire and the undeniable desire of conservative politicians and journalists to include imperial gains in their campaign pledges to counter the growing challenge of socialism. The explanation of imperialism is not easy; it involves a general understanding of Europe at the end of the century. It also contributes to an understanding of the impact that the loss of empire had a mere half-century later, for the deeper the roots of imperialism in modern European society, the more traumatic its uprooting.

Effects of Imperialism

Imperialism had the greatest impact on the native peoples subjected to it. By arousing them to new motives and expectations it would ultimately diminish Europe's world role. Even by 1900, Europe had been profoundly affected.

Imperialism undoubtedly encouraged belligerent nationalism at home. It taught people to expect diplomatic success, by force if necessary. Tolerance of diplomatic failure, even compromise, decreased. In 1907 a French foreign minister who reached a successful settlement of the Moroccan question with Germany was forced from office because he had made a few concessions to Germany.

Still more directly, imperialism changed the outlook of diplomats and military men themselves who now thought in terms of redividing whole continents. German leaders by 1914 could contemplate redoing the map of Europe. British statesmen during and after World War I tossed huge chunks of the Near East and Russia from one power to another—if only on paper. Bluntly stated, the sense of diplomatic realism was severely weakened.

Imperialism also brought the great powers into renewed conflict. By 1900 virtually all the available territory had been taken. Confrontations which in themselves were dangerous increased in Asia and Africa. Imperialism also encouraged renewed diplomatic interest in the European continent, but after three decades of expansion and conquest, what form would this interest take?

SOCIALISM

By 1890 the three great weaknesses of Europe's political order were becoming increasingly visible. The first, growing diplomatic adventurism, was the most serious, but growing social tensions and the disaffection of the intellectuals posed major challenges as well, contributing ultimately to the diplomatic collapse.

Socialism was a significant political force by 1890. More than 40 socialist deputies sat in the French parliament. The party in Germany not only survived the anti-socialist law, which severely limited propaganda and campaigning, but after 1881 had actually increased its electoral strength. The law was abandoned in 1890 when the new emperor, William II, forced Bismarck from office; William believed that he could conciliate the working classes. The socialists in fact gained ground ever more rapidly, regularly winning a million and a half votes by the middle of the decade. Socialism was also winning converts in Scandinavia and the Low Countries, while parties were forming in Italy and the Hapsburg monarchy. Here was a major addition to the political spectrum.

Socialism had influenced politics even earlier, chiefly by provoking countermeasures from the established authorities. The repression after the Commune and Bismarck's attacks on socialism were overreactions, in terms of the strength socialists had at the time. The sometimes unintentional ability of socialists to frighten conservatives was not the least of their contributions to history. Elements of the middle class trembled at the idea of a propertyless society. Governments reacted instinctively to a movement that preached subversion and revolution.

These reactions were an important element in the early history of socialism. Repression convinced most socialists of the need for strong organization and encouraged their distrust of the existing order; in both respects repression furthered the Marxist impulse. It was no accident that in those few countries that avoided a period of repression, notably Britain and Scandanavia, socialism was largely immune to revolutionary sentiment, in contrast to most continental socialist movements.

Socialism in France and Germany had undergone internal evolution in those formative decades before it became a political force. During the Second Empire, Proudhon and his followers were the leaders of French socialism. They shunned politics and revolution, looking toward the dissolution of the state and capitalism into small, producer-controlled units. The native brand of socialism in Germany was far different. In 1863 Ferdinand Lassalle formed the General German Workingman's Association, which was largely a political party. Lassalle also eschewed revolution, but he looked to control of the state as the precondition for a new industrial order.

At about the same time, in 1864, Marx took a hand in socialist political organization by forming the International Workingmen's Association (the First International). This group had little practical influence, but it sponsored organizers who set up branches in France and Germany by the end of the decade. Marx's principal concern was to establish the doctrinal purity of the International. He successively expelled British trade unionists, Proudhonists, and anarchists. The International, thus weakened, expired in 1876.

Marxists in Germany and France could not worry about doctrinal purity alone, though this was an enduring concern. Wilhelm Liebknecht and

August Bebel, the German leaders, merged with the Lassalleans to form the German Social Democratic party in 1875, on a compromise platform that Marx bitterly condemned. Then ironically, Bismarck's persecution of the socialists convinced many Lassalleans that revolution was the only way to the new order. The party platform in 1891 was almost undiluted Marxism.

The repression of the Commune severely weakened the Proudhonist forces in France. When French socialism revived it was under Marxist banners; the Marxist party was established in 1879. But unity was not long preserved in France, though the Marxists fought for socialism on their terms alone. Tentatively reunified in 1895, French socialism split apart over the Dreyfus affair. Only in 1905 was the party united, on a largely Marxist platform.

Marxists directly founded socialist movements in most other countries, though in Italy and Spain they had to compete with anarchists and syndicalists. In Belgium and Austria, particularly, parties of the German type developed and quickly gained strength.

Only in Britain and Scandinavia did Marxism fail to take significant hold. The British Fabian Society was organized in the 1880s partly in opposition to Marx. Its theorists urged peaceful social reform through gradual nationalization of industry. The actual Labour party was formed only in 1906, as a merger of various socialist groups and, primarily, the political representatives of the trade unions. It did not commit itself to a socialist program until 1918, though socialists, particularly of the Fabian type, steadily gained influence. Its trade union origins guaranteed that the party, whether socialist or not, would be gradualist rather than revolutionary, seeking major but piecemeal reforms. The Scandinavian parties adopted a similar approach because of their close alliance with the trade union movement.

Characteristics of the Socialist Movement

The diverse origins and national patterns of socialism make generalization difficult, but there are some general points that should not get lost in the array of detail. Marxist parties had a number of features in common, and by the 1900s all socialist parties in industrial countries came to share important characteristics, whether they were Marxist in origin or not.

Marxist parties preached the doctrine of class war and revolution. Their goal was to overturn the state, set up a proletarian dictatorship, and through this establish a completely new society. Party congresses and pamphlets condemned all aspects of the existing order, not only capitalism but the system of justice, the military, and imperialism.

In parliament, Marxist deputies could be a recalcitrant group, voting against army budgets and against welfare measures that in their eyes did not go far enough, and refusing to cooperate with other political parties. Though a minority, they could upset normal political calculations.

Decisions on programs and tactics were made at the top, through the party congresses. Marxist parties had a bureaucracy and were relatively well organized; in fact, they were the first really well-organized political units in France and Italy. In Germany and Belgium, where they were still more highly structured, socialist parties were not merely political organizations. They sponsored elaborate social and cultural functions and set up cooperative stores. The socialists' organizing ability, along with their announced programs, frightened their opponents. They also encouraged other political movements to develop more formal structures.

Marxists participated in the political process when they could, that is, in all the parliamentary countries. They talked revolution but did not directly foment it in western and central Europe. With time, even the talk became less fierce.

REVISIONISM

At the end of the 1890s Eduard Bernstein, in Germany, developed the doctrine called revisionism. He said that Marx had been wrong about several aspects of capitalist development: the workers were not getting poorer; the middle class was growing, not shrinking; the "bourgeois state" was gaining strength as it became more democratic. Revolution was neither necessary nor possible. Socialists should therefore cooperate with other reformist parties, further democracy and peaceful social reform, and broaden their appeal to many social groups, not just the proletariat.

The Social Democratic party debated the revisionist doctrine extensively but finally voted it down. Yet after 1900 the party behaved as the revisionists had wished. Its parliamentary deputies voted for welfare legislation. They cooperated with "bourgeois" parties to press for suffrage reform. They voted against the general strike as a means of toppling the government and tried to hold their followers back from more limited strikes and violence against the inequitable class voting-system.

This evolution was repeated in all the parliamentary countries. Austrian socialists followed the German pattern almost exactly. Because they were also hostile to quarrels among nationalities, they supported the Hapsburg empire against many attacks, while wanting major reforms from within. In Belgium, socialists conducted two general strikes against the class voting-system that prevailed, but they too were essentially revisionist. Italian socialists oscillated but became increasingly revisionist before 1911.

Even before Bernstein spelled out the revisionist doctrine, many French socialists had split away from the Marxists. A group called the Possibilists was formed in the mid-1880s and, as its name implied, supported the idea of piecemeal reforms. The major figure in French socialism, Jean Jaurès, was a revisionist. His group even provided a minister in the government of 1899, when the republic seemed threatened by the Dreyfus affair. This was the first time a socialist held a major position in any government, an experiment that was not repeated in France after 1905 or in other countries until World War I. Eager to unify French socialism, Jaurès accepted the Marxist platform of 1905, which among other things pledged nonparticipation in bourgeois governments. But as in Germany, formal allegiance to Marxism proved compatible with revisionist behavior in practice. French socialists voted for such reforms as the eight-hour-day for miners. They did not normally seek to obstruct parliamentary functions.

Throughout western and central Europe, the socialist parties voted the necessary military budgets when war broke out in 1914. Many participated in wartime coalition governments. Here was proof of the extent of socialist involvement with the existing order.

The rise of revisionism was an extremely important development. If it blunted the all-out attack on the status quo, it allowed socialists to push for major reforms.

The Spectre of Socialism: Socialism is here seen as a threat to everyone's property.

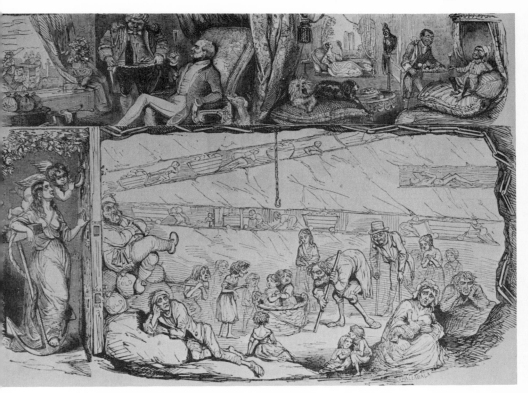

The Necessity of Socialism: Capitalists living off the labor and misery of the workers.

Revisionism developed for four reasons. First, there was genuine ideological inspiration. Bernstein, Jaurès, and indeed the Fabians in Britain
believed in the truth of their message. They were passionately devoted to
social justice as they saw it, convinced that society could be improved if
socialists were realistic in their tactics.

Second, growing party bureaucracies encouraged revisionism in practice.
The administrator of a big campaign fund or the director of a socialist
theater was unlikely to jeopardize his job by active service to the cause of
revolution. Trade union leaders played a major role in the conversion to
revisionism. Marxists had always been suspicious of trade unions, which so
easily distracted workers from revolution, but they had to allow them as a
means of protecting workers in day-to-day economic life and of drawing
them to the socialist movement. Socialist unions in Germany, long held
back, began their rapid growth in the mid-1890s. Within a decade union
leaders were preventing the party from adopting any radical measures that
might jeopardize union funds and organization.

Third, most supporters of socialism undoubtedly wanted reforms here and now, whatever their interests in ultimate revolution. Despite its rapid advance, socialism never captured the whole working class. Many workers were frightened by radical ideas. Given the socialists' commitment to the parliamentary process, they needed as many votes as they could get. They therefore steadily modified their tone and worked for immediate gains. This was one reason they came to support trade unionism. In addition, even bolder workers were rarely revolutionary; the restraint of the strike movement in the industrial countries revealed their commitment to limited gains. And nowhere was socialism simply "working class." In France and Italy it long had as much support from radical middle-class elements as from workers. Middle-class voters in several areas of Germany turned to socialism as a protest against the class voting-system. This sort of support increased the socialist involvement with political methods and reforms.

Finally, the socialists were able to win reforms. They found they could cooperate with some liberal groups for welfare legislation. Their gains at the local level were particularly striking, for in industrial towns they gained political power quite early. They worked for better schools, better sewers and better streets in working-class districts. Here, even more than on the national level, was confirmation of the revisionists' lesson.

In most countries a minority rebelled against the prevalence of revisionist tactics. Under Rosa Luxemburg a group within the German socialist party fought for genuine revolutionary activity after 1907. Syndicalism in France served much the same sentiment, though it was outside the party and in opposition to it. The syndicalists urged destruction of the state, not its capture, through a general strike. Their importance should not be exaggerated, however. Though they controlled the principal trade union federation, they did not win over the majority of union members. In 1910, before their strength began to wane, they nevertheless served as an outlet for those who found revisionist socialism intolerable. No formal rebellion against the pragmatism of the Labour party arose in Britain, but the workers' radical strikes after 1910 suggested widespread discontent.

Only in Italy, of the parliamentary countries, did revolutionary socialism win out, as Benito Mussolini led the party away from revisionism in 1912. Only the Italian party voted against entry into World War I. Italian workers and peasants, just entering the industrial system, were unusually aggrieved. Many of them had sought a political voice long before universal manhood suffrage was established in 1912. Elsewhere in western and central Europe, workers had a vote of some sort and they had made their peace with industrialization. Hence revisionism made sense to most of them.

In most European countries, then, the socialist challenge was somewhat muted. It altered the political spectrum and forced changes in the functions of governments and the conduct of politics. But it supported parliaments and democracies. Even revisionist socialism, however, could shake the defenders of the existing order. The more conservative defenders had after all barely accepted parliaments and democracies themselves. Now they were being asked to undertake substantial social reform as well. It was no accident that conservatives became much more reluctant to sponsor modest welfare legislation after 1900 than they had been before, lest they appear to be yielding to socialist pressure. Moreover, socialist rhetoric, which usually remained revolutionary, differed from actual socialist practice, and this could be confusing. The socialists gained ground rapidly, and by 1912 theirs was the largest party in both Germany and Austria. There were more than 100 socialist deputies in the French parliament.

This history of socialism in the prewar decades is one of growing moderation. The history of socialism's political impact is different, for the socialists aroused fears. Even as they became increasingly revisionist their growing strength and the concomitant wave of strikes after 1900 caused uneasiness in most countries. Employers became harsher toward strikes. The British government used troops against workers more freely, while the Germans talked of new laws against strikes and political agitation. Nonsocialist voters in France and elsewhere turned more conservative.

THE RADICAL RIGHT

Movements to the right of the established political framework developed in the 1880s and 1890s. They had no common inspiration such as Marx, but they, too, shared many similar ideas and tactics. The radical right was against parliamentary government, democracy, and capitalism. It held that men were not primarily rational and that self-interest led only to corruption and chaos. Hence democracy was stupid and parliaments petty and impotent. Capitalism was wrong because it was based on selfishness and led to a class war that paralyzed society. Socialism, the product of class war, was evil.

The radical right wanted authority and a higher unity to replace the existing order. They longed for strong-man leadership. Their devotion was to the nation, which could provide inspiration and purpose far above the individual. They sought an active, even violent nation, which would express the irrational will of man and give meaning to his life. Their alternatives to capitalism were vague at best, but they talked of a corporative economy that would eliminate greed and give each economic group a collective voice in economic policy. Most radical rightists were anti-Semitic.

Few radical rightists participated in the political process, which was consistent with their principles. In Austria, the Christian Socialist party developed in the 1880s with a program of German nationalism and practical welfare legislation, anti-Semitism and anti-Marxism; it won massive sup-

port from the Viennese lower middle class and, later, the Austrian peasantry. In control of the government of Vienna, however, the party forebore
from attacks on the Jews and concentrated on an extensive and effective
urban welfare program. In the Austrian parliament the party supported the
Hapsburg monarchy. Here was a suggestion of "rightist revisionism," but it
remained an isolated case. Even in Austria a group arose still further to the
right, blasting all cooperation with parliaments and castigating the Jews.
Among the people it interested was a young construction worker and
would-be architect named Adolf Hitler.

Most radical rightist groups concentrated on extra-parliamentary agitation, and many of them were skillful propagandists. In newspapers, pamphlets and speeches they played on many popular economic and social
grievances. Their attacks on individual politicians or on Jews in general
took on a sensationalist tone. In other words, the radical right strove for a
mass audience, even if it did not usually reach one. The radical right also
organized demonstrations and violent attacks on political meetings. Some
had bands of strong-arm toughs for this purpose.

The *Action française* was the leading radical rightist group. Not surprisingly it arose in France, which had the most democratic political structure of any major European power. Formed in 1899 during the Dreyfus
affair, it professed to be monarchist and Catholic but in reality sought an
authoritarian regime that would use religion to keep order in society. It
was vigorously nationalist and anti-German. It maintained a lively press,
and tried to seize on potentially explosive issues, such as leftists in the
University, to mount demonstrations. It organized a group of young men to
attack political opponents and break up meetings. Never very large, *Action
française* nevertheless offered a haven to people who rejected the whole
political system in France, for the group resolutely stayed out of electoral
politics. Its skillful tactics and publicity, combined with the history of extra-
parliamentary attacks on the republic, made French politicians wary of a
threat from the right.

In France and elsewhere, the radical right appealed to a number of different groups. It attracted members of the lower middle class and even
government bureaucrats who were worried about their status and hostile to
big business. It drew some disgruntled aristocrats and appealed to many
university students. But in terms of numbers the radical right was not important. It touched on some common grievances but did not yet reach most
of the groups that felt these grievances.

A radical right developed in most countries. Britain was largely immune, though the formation of Primrose Leagues within the Conservative
party, vigorously nationalist and addicted to parades and uniforms, suggested a search for new tactics. Extreme nationalist groups in Russia had
many of the goals of the radical right. But serious movements developed
only in Germany, France, Austria, and Italy, and in Germany the most
specifically radical rightist groups declined after 1900. Few rightist groups

in these countries had more than two or three thousand members. Their press might reach thousands more, but the effect was still limited. Moreover, nowhere, save in Italy, were the radical rightists able to disrupt the political process directly.

In a sense, then, the rightists must be chiefly regarded as forerunners of movements that arose after World War I, suggesting many of the tactics and goals that fascists were to use. Europe had to change greatly before either the tactics or the goals would become overwhelmingly significant.

Yet the importance of the radical right in the prewar years cannot be entirely dismissed. The movement was part of the broader cultural currents of violence and of rebellion against rationalism and individualism. It appealed to certain groups, including many intellectuals and men in positions of authority who had importance beyond their numbers. Moreover, the radical right shaded off into other groups that shared some similar programs but did not go as far. The Pan-German League, for example, which included large numbers of government bureaucrats and military men, promoted imperialism and German expansion in Europe. Its internal political goals were unclear, but it leaned toward authoritarian rule. This was not a full radical rightist program, but it came close.

Socialism and the radical right attacked some of the same aspects of the existing order. They were both hostile to excessive individualism and to capitalism. They both looked to higher unities—the class or the nation—and talked of violence, either in class war or national war. Wanting a strong state, at least in the short run, both were part of an attack on liberalism. Although the movements helped change the political climate, they were profoundly different and not simply because they opposed each other. Socialism stemmed from the rationalist tradition and drew most of its support from people who had accepted the industrial order. The radical right was anti-rationalist and appealed to people bewildered by modern industrial society.

THE EUROPEAN STATES

Most of the states of western and central Europe became less stable after 1890 than they had been during the previous decade or two. Socialist and, to a lesser extent, rightist attacks contributed to this instability, as did the recession of the 1890s and the leveling off of lower-class earnings after 1900. There were more particular problems as well. Yet one general point is clear: the industrial nations, though sorely troubled, remained far more stable than did the agrarian nations. From this observation two separate questions arose: were the industrial nations so severely shaken by 1914 that their leaders' judgment might be clouded by fear of internal upheaval? Could the regimes in the agrarian nations survive at all?

FRANCE, BRITAIN,
AND GERMANY

In the Dreyfus affair the French government faced a major crisis at the end of the 1890s. In 1895 Captain Alfred Dreyfus, a Jewish army officer, was falsely condemned for treason. There were growing doubts of his guilt, but the army refused to grant him a retrial. When the case came to the public's attention in 1898 it split France's intellectual and political elite. Rightists took the side of the army, the symbol of authority, against a Jew. Most Catholics did the same. Among the anti-Dreyfusards were many who opposed the republic and supported an abortive nationalist coup. But the anti-Dreyfusards also numbered conservative republicans as well. The partisans of Dreyfus consisted of liberal and radical republicans and the more revisionist socialists. It appeared for a brief time that the divisions would threaten the regime, but in 1899 the supporters of Dreyfus gained control of parliament and a new government was established.

The Dreyfus affair led to a more formal division between conservative and liberal republicans. Each group formed a political organization, the Independent and Radical parties respectively; both were so loosely organized, however, that frequent factional realignments continued. Both parties accepted the republican framework, the Independents appealing to Catholic and agrarian interests and favoring laissez-faire economics.

The Radicals, with socialist support, remained in control for six years. They introduced some new factory legislation and social insurance programs. Their liberal inspiration was clear, for the social insurance programs were voluntary and France lagged behind all other industrial nations in welfare legislation. The Radicals paid more attention to a traditional issue: the Church. Seeking to punish the Church for its support of the anti-Dreyfusards and to remove it as a hostile force once and for all, the Radicals began in 1902 to subject religious orders to stiff controls; then in 1905 the government in an unprecedented step declared the separation of Church and state. This meant that the Church was deprived of state financial support, and the state could no longer nominate Catholic prelates. This measure caused great consternation in the Church, but on the whole the country accepted the principle of separation. Thus a perenially disruptive problem was removed from French politics. The Radicals also tried with some success, to republicanize the army officer corps.

The regime was now firmly established, with only the small radical right and the syndicalists completely rejecting it. Governments changed with bewildering frequency, but the regime was never as unstable as it appeared. Key ministries often remained in the same hands from one government to the next. The highly centralized bureaucracy imparted still greater stability; for the most part it was more conservative on social issues than the parliamentary majority. Syndicalist-led strikes peaked in the years 1906 to 1910 but the government replied firmly, sending in troops and police freely. Even this agitation receded after 1910. Partly because of the labor agitation, partly in response to diplomatic developments, the government and public opinion became more conservative and nationalist in the years before the war. Military budgets rose and military service was extended from two to three years.

Unrest in Britain

Britain was less stable than France in 1914. Three groups, none political parties in the conventional sense, were working outside the parliamentary system. Workers, goaded by inflation, struck with unprecedented vigor. Impelled by rank-and-file pressure, the leaders of the miners, the dockers and the railroad workers formed a Triple Alliance in 1913, apparently in an effort to launch a paralyzing national strike the following year.

Militant feminists were demanding the vote in these same years. They had forsaken the respectful petition in favor of huge demonstrations and passive resistance.

Finally, Ireland was becoming a much more intensive problem. Gladstone had tried on two occasions to introduce home rule for Ireland but failed; between 1895 and 1905 the Conservatives talked of "killing home rule with kindness," but there was no substantive reform. The Liberals pressed for home rule again in 1912, arousing great opposition from Protestants in Northern Ireland who would be submerged in a separate Irish parliament. Civil war threatened as private militias formed in both Ulster and the south.

To some, Britain seemed to be on the verge of revolution in 1914, from which the war alone saved her. It is doubtful that the crises were that severe, for the three political parties remained loyal to the regime and commanded the support of most of the populace. Much constructive legislation had been passed in the preceding decade, including firmer protection for the rights of trade unions and many social insurance measures. But there was little question that Britain would have faced continued strife in 1914 or that her statesmen were confused by the un-English unrest that had already occurred.

German Politics

Germany faced nothing like the syndicalism of France or the feminism of Britain after 1890. Repression, including a prohibition on political speeches in their native tongue, kept Germany's principal ethnic minority, the Poles, in line. Socialism reflected great discontent but it worked largely within the legal order. Germany's most troublesome political problem, at least superficially, was Emperor William II, an erratic leader at best. The political leaders under him, often mediocre, were unable to provide the needed balance. William dropped Bismarck in 1890, largely because he wanted to rule on his own. Bismarck's departure and William's headstrong qualities were felt primarily in foreign affairs. Yet the absence of firm leadership was clear at home. The Reichstag was frequently at odds with the emperor's ministers. It was able to prevent some legislation the government desired, such as a revival of the anti-socialist laws. It extended the social insurance laws to new categories of workers and passed other factory legislation. But it was unable to respond to the growing demand for electoral reform, as Prussia retained its class voting-system and several other states restricted their suffrage in the 1900s. With the emperor in control of the ministers and substantial political power in the hands of the states, the Reichstag was indeed severely limited. At the same time it continued to vote greater sums for the army and navy. Even the socialists by 1912 supported tax measures necessary to expand the military forces.

Nevertheless the very existence of the Reichstag, elected by universal suffrage, inflamed many elements of the bureaucracy and upper classes. There were recurrent rumors in the 1890s of a *coup d'état* in which the emperor and the military would abolish the whole system. Nothing of the sort occurred, but it was small wonder that the military and civilian bureaucrats ignored parliament in setting their policies. Growing socialist strength frightened them particularly, for many of these men, whether aristocrats or not, thought in terms of fixed social hierarchies, with workers and peasants irrevocably at the bottom. Germany's ruling elite, in other words, was far less adaptable than that in Britain and France, where the upper classes had largely come to grips with democracy and social change. This, rather than overt protest or disorder, was Germany's political weakness in 1914.

A NEW STATE

Amid the welter of political forces, a new kind of state was emerging in the industrial countries at the turn of the century. All the major political forces contributed to it. Socialists, though never in power at the national level, pressed for state-sponsored social reform, and many new state functions were adopted in response to the socialist threat. Conservatives favored a strong state. Nationalists supported state action not only in diplomacy but in the interests of a healthy and united populace at home. Liberals were more hesitant in supporting new state functions. Some, as in Britain, converted to advocacy of social insurance and imperial expansion. Even aside from this, one part of the liberal impulse had always favored state action in education, commercial inspection, and the like.

The result was a state far more active than the mercantilist state had been. It preserved order with much larger police forces than ever before. It collected taxes directly from each citizen; income taxes were levied in most of the industrial countries around the turn of the century. It conscripted most eligible males into a period of military service. In essence, the state had vastly extended most of its traditional functions. While it had lessened or abandoned its religious role, it now assumed direct responsibility for education, instilling in individuals (or so it hoped) love of country along with basic skills. Without laying down detailed edicts in the mercantilist fashion about how goods were to be manufactured, the state was an active agent in the economy. Its purchases, particularly for the military, took a substantial share of industrial production. Except in Britain it ran at least part of the port and railroad network. Its regulations on factory conditions were backed by growing inspection personnel. All this meant that the state was in more intimate contact with private individuals than ever before, except in city-states. Most citizens, including those who voted for revisionist socialism, seemed largely to approve, as the state tried to teach them to do.

Government bureaucracy expanded rapidly, even aside from the military forces. Teachers, inspectors, colonial officials, and others swelled the ranks of government employees.

There is no special name for the type of state that emerged at the turn of the century and we need none to describe it. In a sense, it was a state in transition, moving toward the twentieth-century forms we can define more precisely as totalitarianism or the welfare state. Both these forms, however, imply a change in the motives as well as in the functions of the state. The late nineteenth-century state had not clearly broken with traditional motives. Despite the liberal influence, it was still primarily devoted to preservation of internal order and diplomatic strength. Motivated mainly by these purposes it encouraged industrial growth and offered protection to the lower classes. World War I was to reveal the new power of the state. It would also reveal that basic goals had changed little from the eighteenth century.

THE UNSTABLE STATES

Popular rebellion forced a suspension of parliamentary government in Italy at the end of the 1890s. Peasant and worker uprisings prompted the government to limit socialist activity and jail many leaders, which only aroused further anger. The virtual revolution that had broken out in Milan in 1898 led to military rule for three years. Thereafter, under Giovanni Giolitti, the normal political process seemed restored. "Transformism" continued and deputies were bribed to support the government. Giolitti moved

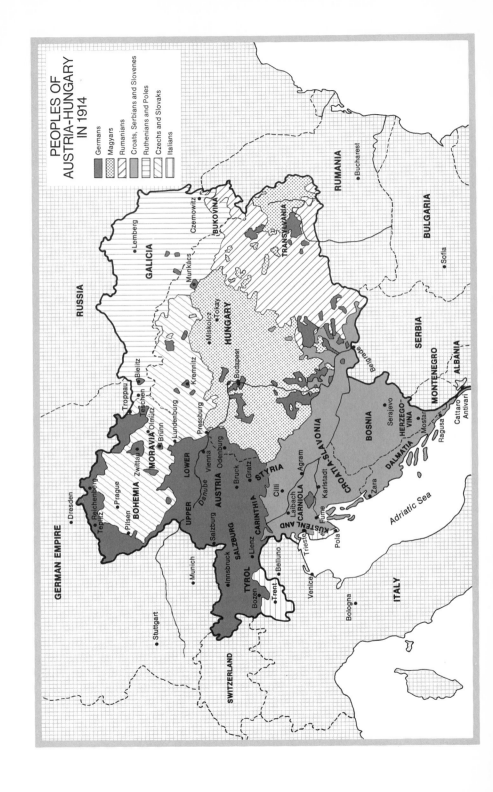

PEOPLES OF
AUSTRIA-HUNGARY
IN 1914

Germans
Magyars
Rumanians
Croats, Serbians and Slovenes
Ruthenians and Poles
Czechs and Slovaks
Italians

RUSSIA

GERMAN EMPIRE

GALICIA

Lemberg

Czernowitz

BUKOVINA

Munkács

Miskolcz

Tokaj

Kremnitz

HUNGARY

Budapest

TRANSYLVANIA

RUMANIA

Bucharest

BULGARIA

Sofia

SERBIA

Belgrade

MONTENEGRO

ALBANIA

Antivari

Cattaro

Ragusa

Mostar

HERZEGO-
VINA

Serajevo

BOSNIA

DALMATIA

Zara

CROATIA-SLAVONIA

Karlstadt

Agram

Fiume

KUSTENLAND

Laibach

CARNIOLA

Cilli

Pola

Trieste

Venice

STYRIA

Gratz

Bruck

Odenburg

Vienna

LOWER
AUSTRIA

Danube

Pressburg

Lundenburg

Brünn

Olmütz

MORAVIA

Troppau

Teschen

Bielitz

Zwittau

BOHEMIA

Prague

Pilsen

Reichenberg

Tepliz

Dresden

Munich

Stuttgart

UPPER
AUSTRIA

Salzburg

SALZBURG

Lienz

CARINTHIA

Innsbruck

TYROL

Bozen

Trent

Belluno

Bologna

ITALY

Adriatic Sea

SWITZERLAND

slightly to the left, trying to entice socialist support. He enacted a few welfare measures. At the same time the Church, alarmed by the social unrest, relaxed its prohibition against Catholic participation in politics. From this, new conservative support for the regime might have developed, but there was no time. With its limited suffrage the regime rested on too small a segment of the population. Preoccupied with its own survival and with aggressive diplomacy, it ignored pressing internal problems. Popular agitation continued. Small rightist groups that formed around leading intellectuals like Gabriele d'Annunzio fomented violent demonstrations in the interests of authoritarian rule and an adventurous diplomacy. Socialists turned more and more radical and a significant syndicalist movement developed as well. Universal manhood suffrage was finally granted in 1912, but it was too late. It merely guaranteed that the various currents of protest would be brought into parliament.

Nationalist Conflicts in Austria-Hungary

The pressures on the Austrian government were different, but even more persistent. The minority Slavic nationalities had been bitterly disappointed by the *Ausgleich*, which subjected them to Magyar rule in Hungary and to German rule in Austria. The Czechs, the third largest ethnic group in the empire with 12.6 percent of the population, were particularly aggrieved. Czech nationalism spread widely in the Czech regions as industrialization, which centered in Bohemia, disrupted traditional patterns of life and moved many Czechs to the cities. In the 1890s, after a relatively calm period under Taafe's rule, more aggressive Czech nationalism developed. Nationalism also spread to other Slavic peoples, such as the Croats in Hungary. The Pan-Slav movement advocated the union of all Slavic peoples, while a more specifically "south Slav" nationalism was fomented by Serbia among the Serbs, Croats, and Slovenes in the empire. This nationalism spurred German and Magyar reaction. The Magyars reduced Croat rights in Hungary while raising new nationalist demands of their own. In 1905 the Hungarian parliament refused to vote money for the imperial army unless the Magyar language was spoken by all officers commanding Hungarian troops.

In Austria proper, parliament was paralyzed at the turn of the century, as clashes between German and Czech delegates often led to physical battles. The emperor and his ministers ruled by decree. In an effort to placate the Czechs, their language was placed on an equal basis with the German in courts of law and among government officials in Czech regions, but this measure brought such bitter German protest that it had to be withdrawn. The situation seemed hopeless. Nationalist passions were sincerely felt and they also conveyed some of the strains of a rapidly urbanizing, industrializing society. Many Austrians, including important government officials, believed the empire was doomed.

Yet the empire had some sources of strength. The emperor himself was not committed to any single nationalism, for his rule depended on some sort of accommodation. His office continued to command genuine reverence from many of the common people, even among the Slavic nationalities. In 1907 the emperor introduced universal manhood suffrage in Austria and assured adequate representation for the national minorities. Parliament remained unruly, but there was a chance that passions would be assuaged. The Social Democrats, who wanted to preserve the empire's unity, became the leading party. Industrialization was progressing steadily in Austria, which assured a solid economy and provided vital markets for agrarian Hungary. The government was efficient. It offered a social insurance program second only to the German.

The empire did perish after defeat in war. Its failure to resolve the nationalities disputes and the growing sense of hopelessness among some of its officials helped bring on the war. Possibly, as a multinational state, it could not have survived, being doomed by a failure of leadership that sought to remedy internal instability by means of an active foreign policy.

Revolution in Russia

Only Russia faced outright revolution in the prewar years. Unrest among peasants and workers had erupted many times in the late nineteenth century. The intellectuals, though divided as a group, were lost to the regime. Minority nationalities also were stirred up against Russian control. Finns and Ukrainians demanded cultural autonomy at least, while the Poles remained restive. Alone among the great powers the Russian government made no concession to compromise or even to the facade of compromise before compelled to do so by the Revolution of 1905.

Three political currents emerged in Russia in the 1890s. The heirs of the populists called themselves social revolutionaries, still hoping for a massive peasant rebellion that would lead to agrarian socialism. Liberalism spread among the professional people. Though not revolutionary, liberals hoped for a constitutional monarchy and sponsored illegal conferences and a newspaper. Finally, Marxism won adherents among revolutionaries who thought that the peasantry alone could not overturn the existing order. A party was formed in 1898, led largely by Russians living in the West. At a London conference in 1903 the party split between Mensheviks (minority) and Bolsheviks (majority). The Mensheviks believed that Russia had to develop a capitalist order before proletarian revolution was possible and therefore favored cooperation with the liberals. Let by Vladimir Ulyanov, better known as Lenin, the Bolsheviks insisted on tight central control of the party

The Revolution of 1905 and Its Aftermath: The tsar attempts a policy of repression.

PEACE REIGNS AT MOSCOW.

THE CZAR. *"NOW, I THINK, THE WAY IS CLEAR FOR UNIVERSAL SUFFRAGE."*

and maintained that a proletarian dictatorship should be imposed right after the revolution, with no collaboration with a liberal bourgeoisie. Despite their name, the Mensheviks represented most Russian Marxists and reflected something of the revisionist current that was developing elsewhere in Marxism. But the Bolsheviks would not yield control and expelled their opponents from the party in 1912. The Bolsheviks, committed to a revolution run exclusively by their own tightly organized party, had no counterpart in Europe before World War I. Their uniqueness corresponded to the inflexibility of the Russian government, but it owed much to Lenin's stern will.

Russia was defeated in a war with Japan in 1904–1905, a loss that surprised the world and inflamed opinion at home. The war followed several years of economic hardship, a combination that produced the Revolution of 1905. A demonstration on behalf of reforms by a huge crowd of workers in St. Petersburg was brutally repressed, and unrest quickly spread to many parts of the empire. Workers struck and peasants rioted; in October of 1905 a general strike paralyzed the whole nation. Tsar Nicholas II, forced to yield, issued a manifesto that promised freedom of speech, press, and assembly. A Duma, or parliament, elected by nearly universal manhood suffrage, was to have the right to approve every law before it was promulgated. Russia was to be a constitutional monarchy. Liberals were delighted, but radicals and the lower classes remained unsatisfied. Only military action restored order at the end of 1905.

Back in control, the government quickly eroded the power of the new parliament as the tsar continued in many of his autocratic ways. When he discovered that the first Duma was dominated, not surprisingly, by anti-government parties, he dissolved it and soon changed the election law to assure the domination of the landed gentry. The Duma thus became the tsar's rubber stamp.

Under the leadership of Peter Stolypin, the chief minister, the government took more fruitful steps to eradicate discontent among the peasantry. The hated redemption payments were abolished and peasants were freed from most village controls. They were encouraged to build up consolidated individual holdings, and a substantial minority of the peasantry took advantage of this opportunity. Rural riots declined.

Was Russia fated for another revolution? The nation was calm in the years before the war, in part because of the massive arrests and executions of radical leaders. Some historians argue that political and agrarian reforms satisfied key groups and that the steady development of the industrial economy would have reduced unrest among the others—if there had been time and if the war had not intervened. Others argue that World War I only hastened an inevitable collapse, at worst causing a more radical revolution than would otherwise have occurred.

The war did occur, destroying the regimes of Austria, Russia, and Italy. In no case was the destruction necessarily inevitable, but this is a moot point. Two things are certain: decades of unrest produced widespread uncertainty among statesmen within the three countries and among their allies, and this helped cause war. None of the three regimes was strong enough to withstand war.

DIPLOMATIC TENSIONS

Bismarck's alliance system began to unravel in 1890. One of the reasons for his dismissal was the widespread resentment within the German government against the complexity of his diplomacy and, particularly, against the alliance with Russia that many felt conflicted with obligations to Austria. After his departure the agreement with Russia was allowed to lapse, which gave France a chance to end its diplomatic isolation. France wooed Russia assiduously, offering funds for industrial investment and mutual protection against the German-Austrian alliance. In 1893 a loose agreement of mutual defense was concluded. This was a major change in the diplomatic balance, but it did not lead immediately to heightened tensions. Russia and France were highly suspicious of each other's regimes; the alliance between the most radical and the most conservative European powers was uncomfortable. Both were primarily interested in imperial gains—Russia in Asia and France in Africa—for which the alliance was little help.

It was in the imperial field that the most ominous developments occurred in the 1890s. In the first place, armaments programs were stepped up in the interests of empire expansion. France and several other countries built up their navies. In 1897, Germany embarked for the first time on a major naval program, inspired by the skillful politicking of Admiral Tirpitz, by the pressure of heavy industrialists seeking an outlet for their wares, and by William's own passionate interest in the sea. As an amateur yachtsman delighted with his new toy, William periodically boasted about Germany's great imperial future in a way that could only frighten the other powers. Britain grew increasingly hostile to Germany's bluster and her concrete competition in industry and on the sea. Thus imperial rivalries were beginning to color relationships within Europe.

It was in the 1890s also that imperialist propagandists and pressure groups made their great headway, and public opinion was becoming increasingly sensitive to developments in the empires. This was unfortunate, for in fact the easy days of imperialism were over.

In the first place, growing local opposition made further acquisitions difficult if not impossible. The British were hard pressed in the Sudan, the French in Madagascar. In 1896 an Ethiopian army defeated the Italians at Adowa, the first such loss since the advent of the new imperialism. The Boxer rebellion in China in 1900 was put down only after considerable violence to Europeans. The Boer War broke out in South Africa in 1899. British troops fought the Dutch settlers for three years and finally won out, but only after the greatest difficulty. Clashes of this sort took much of the fun out of imperialism; as a result, most of the powers had to reassess their policies.

Still more important was the fact that the great powers now ran into each other whenever they tried to expand their holdings. In 1898 expeditionary forces of France and Britain met at Fashoda in the Sudan. The French were seeking to complete an east-west empire, from Senegal to Somaliland; the British were attempting to unite Egypt with their colonies in the south. Public opinion was aroused in both countries and war threatened briefly until France backed down. With Africa having been almost completely divided, there was no further room for quick gains.

Asia offered more opportunity for the European powers to play, but even there the easy pickings had been taken. In 1904 war broke out between Japan and Russia. Japan had long and bitterly resented Russia's incursion into Manchuria. Russia, whose army was too inefficient and navy too inadequate, was decisively beaten. The defeat of a "white" power by a "yellow" one was considered shocking, but again a sign that times were changing.

No longer being able to expand safely in the Far East, Russia turned her attention toward her traditional goals in the Dardanelles and the Balkans.

The age of the new imperialism was over and the focus of diplomacy returned to Europe. Yet the decades of giddy expansion left their mark; new appetites had been whetted. However she might act, Germany no longer talked like a satiated power, while Italy and Russia longed to compensate for their failures in the imperialist game. Most governments had grown accustomed to using imperialist success to counter potential unrest at home. Whether they had to do so is open to question, for it is doubtful that lower-class discontent was really assuaged by the glory of empire. What matters is that many statesmen, fearful of even moderate socialism, thought or hoped it was so. With rising unrest after 1900, owing to socialist agitation and widespread inflation, it was hard for governments to lower their diplomatic sights. Finally, merely to preserve existing empires amid growing difficulties, several powers had to contemplate new alliances. Britain was forced to commit herself to the alliance system, a step that inevitably reduced Europe's diplomatic flexibility.

THE TRIPLE ALLIANCE VERSUS THE TRIPLE ENTENTE

During the Boer War, Britain's diplomatic isolation was clearly revealed as every other country rooted for the underdog Boers. William II publicly sided with them. In order to reduce her commitments, Britain made a defensive alliance with Japan in 1902 to guard against further Russian expansion in Asia. Through the Entente Cordiale of 1904, the British and French agreed to end their imperial rivalries, chiefly by setting recognized spheres of influence for each state in North Africa. The French ended their long if futile opposition to British control of Egypt; the British agreed to let France take over Morocco. France embraced the agreement as a supplement to its alliance with Russia, whose weakness was now apparent. Britain, too, looked on the entente as a factor in European policy: the British wanted to be free to concentrate more firmly on German ambitions in Europe and on the seas.

The Germans realized how much their position had been weakened by the alignment of two great powers with France. Germany tried to disrupt the Franco-British friendship in the first Moroccan crisis. France had long sought to control Morocco to prevent incursions into Algeria. The French had won Spanish and Italian as well as British consent, but in 1905 Germany objected and insisted on a conference. William II hoped to humiliate France and show the hollowness of British support. But all the powers, save Germany and Austria, supported France at the Conference of Algeciras, and the British were so antagonized by German bluster that they entered negotiations for defensive military arrangements with France.

In 1907 the British and Russians also agreed to end their imperial rivalries. Preoccupied with Germany, the British hoped to reduce Asian entanglements. Russia, now concentrating on the Balkans, regarded Austria as the chief enemy. The Russians were also concerned by Germany's economic penetration of the Near East, the first issue that brought the two countries into direct rivalry. France, naturally enough, encouraged the British-Russian entente. The agreement was a loose one and did not end all competition between the two powers, but it did stake out spheres of influence in Persia and central Asia. The prewar alliance system was complete.

German Belligerence

On paper the system seems evenly balanced, three against three. From the German standpoint, however, Italy was weak and untrustworthy. Germany alone was threatened on two sides, by Russia and by France. Germany's bluster, her sense of unfulfilled mission, had prompted this unfavorable balance. Nationalist groups like the Pan-German League continued to talk of uniting all Germans, which suggested the acquisition of Holland and other areas. Such talk, at the least, perpetuated British fears. Nor would Germany back down in its naval policy and its growing influence in the Near East, which inevitably created new antagonisms. Repeated British efforts to end the naval race failed, for Germany insisted on a strong fleet. Military policy increasingly influenced overall German diplomacy, if only because the weakness of the civilian statesmen and of parliament left the military officers a free hand.

After World War I many people argued that Germany had been primarily responsible for the conflict, and many historians have taken up this theme. It is simplistic to offer moral judgments about guilt and innocence, but it is still important, if only to understand Germany, to determine whether German policy was exceptionally belligerent.

There is little question that the European ambitions of the German nationalists were more inflated than those of their counterparts in France and Britain; moreover, in the Kaiser, the Germans had a most irresponsible leader. Perhaps these problems reflected basic tensions in German society and the unusually authoritarian political structure. Yet they could also stem from a recognition that Germany, though a great power, did not have the imperial trappings of Britain or even France and in fact had little chance of obtaining them outside Europe. Such recognition, however reprehensible, might point to a nationalist fervor that was common throughout Europe at this time, rather than to a distinctively German ambition.

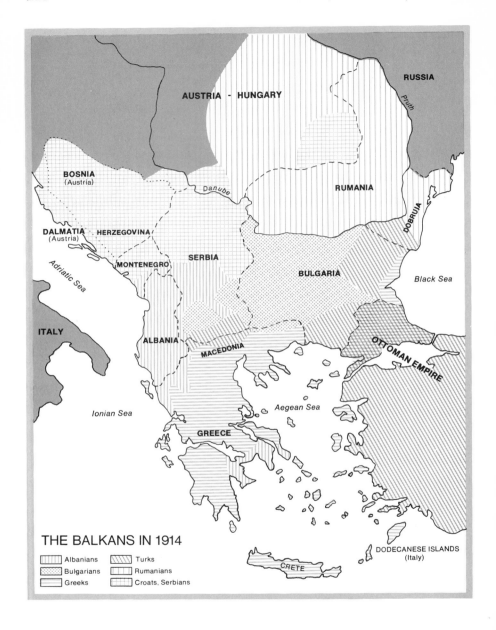

THE BALKANS IN 1914

	Albanians		Turks
	Bulgarians		Rumanians
	Greeks		Croats, Serbians

Germany's rise to great power status produced tensions, which were displayed by the new imperialism and were painfully evident by 1914. Yet the tensions need not be attributed to Germany alone. It is easy to say that Germany rejected a naval agreement with Britain, but note that the British were insisting on a fleet twice as large as the German. Britain in no sense started World War I, but British resistance to diplomatic decline, a decline compelled by Germany's new power and Britain's economic lag, played a role. Most important, Germany had a real reason, from 1907 onward, to feel encircled.

A curious mood prevailed in many countries during the last years before World War I. Almost every power was on the defensive. France and Britain were intimidated by Germany. The French, particularly, recognized their inferiority in population and economic resources. Russia and Austria thought they could endure no further setbacks lest their regimes collapse. The more stable western powers thought that any damage to their weaker allies was a direct threat to them. As a result, most states enlarged their military forces. First Germany and then France and Russia extended conscription and terms of service. Each move provoked new fears. At the same time, aggressive nationalism increased. French opinion had not been so aroused against Germany in several decades. Was this the product of France's improved diplomatic position or was it a curious expression of a heightened fear of attack? The sense that war was inevitable spread in many countries. Some people rejoiced.

THE BALKANS AND WAR

Tension in the Balkans triggered World War I. Most of the great powers were dabbling, in an imperialistic fashion, in Balkan affairs. They vied for the rights to build railroads and advise armies. They encouraged internal Balkan rivalries, which were already intense. But Austria and Russia were the only powers intimately involved in the area. Russia was eager to gain access to the Mediterranean by controlling the Straits of the Dardanelles. Russian nationalists felt their kinship to the Balkan Slavs; Russian agents constantly incited the Serbs and others. Austria feared Slavic nationalism because of its impact on national disputes within the Hapsburg monarchy. Both powers saw the Balkans as an area of possible expansion, to win glory that might reduce internal pressure.

The first step toward conflagration came in 1908, when Austria annexed Bosnia-Herzegovina, which previously it had only administered. The Austrian foreign minister, Lexa von Aehrenthal, was convinced that the fate of his country was tied to diplomatic success. He believed that Austria was near collapse from internal nationalities disputes and that an annexationist foreign policy might restore unity. Austria's minister also wanted to humiliate Serbia, which was actively encouraging South Slav nationalism in the Dual Monarchy. Bosnia was inhabited by the Serbs, and the Serbians were indeed infuriated by the action. Russia was angered as well since Aehrenthal had agreed to give Russia a sphere of influence in the Straits in return for the annexation. This would have been a triumph for Russian diplomacy. By making his own move first he tricked the Russians before they were ready to act. Serbia mobilized its army as war threatened.

The next step in the crisis had more remote origins. The cause in fact was the continued interest in imperialism. In 1911 France acquired Morocco against German opposition. To win Italian approval, the French had promised that Italy could take over Tripoli. Italy had long wanted North African territory, and to claim their prize Italians declared war on the Ottoman Empire. Riotous agitation by authoritarian nationalists at home further impelled the Italian government to take this action.

Italy's war quickly stirred the Balkans. With Turkey engaged in conflict with Italy, the Balkan states saw an opportunity to annex other Turkish territories for themselves. Nationalists in most of the Balkan states had spent decades trying to rouse the inhabitants of Ottoman-ruled Macedonia to their own advantage. Now was the time for direct action. Greed was heightened by a fear that the Ottoman government, long in disarray, was becoming more efficient under the impulse of reformist Young Turks who seized power in 1907.

Urged on by Russian diplomats, Serbia, Greece, Montenegro, and Bulgaria formed a Balkan League to attack Turkey in 1912. All wanted parts of Macedonia, but Serbia wanted more. The Serbs hoped to trigger a war between Austria and Russia which would allow them to seize Austria's South Slavic regions. This was the tragic Balkan formula: intense nationalisms fanned by powerful nationalist organizations and exploited by opportunist monarchs. All the states hated the Turks; Serbia also hated the Austrians; and the states could barely conceal their mutual rivalries. Russian prompting was the final ingredient giving everyone a sense of great-power sponsorship.

Fearful of war, Austria and even Russia tried to prevent aggression, but it was too late. The League won handily over the hard-pressed Turks. Now the great powers moved in forcefully. Austria could not tolerate Serbian gains and contemplated war, but Germany withheld support in case of trouble with Russia. Russia itself was concerned about Bulgaria's advance toward the precious Dardanelles. Austria finally agreed to the division of Macedonia but insisted that her friend Rumania be given a share and that a free Albania be created to block Serbia from the Adriatic Sea. Serbian frustration mounted, for Serbian troops had occupied much of Albania during the war.

The Second Balkan War broke out in 1913 when Bulgaria attacked Serbia and Greece for refusing to hand over the bulk of Macedonia. Rumania and Turkey seized the opportunity to declare war on Bulgaria. The Bulgars, who had done most of the actual fighting in the first war while their "allies" had seized undefended territory, were quickly defeated. In the Treaty of Bucharest of August 1913, Serbia and Greece acquired most of

Macedonia. Rumania also gained territory while Turkey recovered part of Thrace. Bulgaria was left with small portions of Thrace and Macedonia.

Austria had been the main loser in the Balkan wars, apart from Turkey, because of Serbia's expansion and growing nationalism. But Serbia remained unsatisfied. Her victories had merely whetted nationalist appetites, for what she really wanted was an outlet to the sea plus the Austrian-held South Slav lands. Defying Austria, Serbian troops reentered Albania. Russia and France supported the Serbs, Russia because it had gained nothing in the region and could only hope for further confusion, France because it believed gains for Russia were essential to the Franco-Russian alliance that was in turn essential to French security. Further trouble in the Balkans was inevitable. Several great powers now believed that their vital interests were involved.

On June 28 1914, the Austrian Archduke Francis Ferdinand was assassinated in Sarajevo, the capital of Bosnia. The archduke's visit inevitably stirred Serbian resentment, so it was not surprising that the assassin was a young Bosnian aroused by Serbian propaganda. Austria now resolved on war with Serbia at all cost. Russia, hoping to avoid a clash, made Serbia apologize, but Austria pressed on, this time supported in its strong stand by the German government. The Germans realized that Austria was unstable and needed a diplomatic victory; this was, after all, their only reliable ally. The German military, which controlled negotiations with Austria for many crucial days in the month of tension before the war, believed that world war was inevitable and that this was the best time for it—before French and Russian military improvements had been fully carried out. Austria was willing to risk a general war. Aehrenthal believed that the empire was doomed unless Serbia was crushed; if it fell in a general war at least its death would be glorious. An important segment of the German government wanted war, and the Germans gave the Austrians a free hand until the last moment.

Russia realized that any abandonment of Serbia would erase Russian influence in the Balkans. Hence Russia began to mobilize when Austria declared war on Serbia on July 28. This frightened Germany. German strategic plans called for a quick victory over France before Russia's slow mobilization had been completed. Again the military dominated German diplomacy. Germany thus declared war on France and Russia on August 1. France, which had backed Russia throughout the crisis, naturally responded to the German declaration by mobilization of its own. Britain in no way wanted war. Edward Grey, the foreign minister, hesitated and tried to negotiate, which may have misled the Germans into thinking that Britain would not intervene. But Britain was tied to France. Even their naval policies were closely linked, with the French fleets defending the Mediterranean and the British, the North Sea. Germany's invasion of neutral Belgium, another long-standing part of her strategic planning, facilitated Britain's declaration of war on August 4.

CATASTROPHE

The war, a horrible conflagration, changed many facets of European life. What caused it? Serbia, Austria, and Russia were clearly willing to risk world war in defense of what they judged to be their rights and interests in the Balkans. The Germans were also willing, and some Germans thought war was essential. In playing the game of who's to blame, perhaps the Serbs and the Germans come off worst, but everyone else tagged along.

The more interesting question is: how deeply must one probe to explain the war? We know that the war was catastrophic, but few in 1914 expected it to be. There was virtually no protest against the war. Frenchmen and Germans lightheartedly boarded trains for the front. Everyone expected a short war. Everyone expected victory. French and German strategy alike called for quick offensive thrusts into enemy territory that would bring the foe to its knees. With such attitudes, however wrongheaded, need one look beyond purely diplomatic jockeying to explain the war? War was a natural part of European diplomacy. In this as in many other ways the outlook of states remained highly traditional. Diplomatic entanglements—some new but some of long standing, such as Russia's interest in the Straits or Britain's fear of a dominant continental power—may help to explain the great powers' actions. A truism worth stating: small causes produce great events; mighty wars from little diplomats grow.

It is possible also to see the war as the product of a deep crisis in European society and culture, which the diplomats merely reflected. Decades of cultural glorification of violence and actual experience of violent class struggle may have encouraged the lightheartedness toward going to war. Some undoubtedly found war a welcome release from the boredom and tension of industrial life—a life that had imposed new restraints on human impulses. Men were regulated by factory whistles and time clocks. The rise of sports and aggressive nationalism may suggest that Europeans had been seeking an outlet for several decades. Yet, while the popular reaction to the war's outbreak is fascinating, it should not be pressed too far. Men had joyfully gone to war before; this phenomenon is not necessarily the result of the society that had developed in Europe. Furthermore, the spread of belief in humanitarianism and progress may itself have been responsible for some of the initial reaction, for many people could not imagine how horrible war could become. They may have wanted action, but few of them thirsted for violence. Finally, however the popular reaction is explained, it followed from the declaration of war; it did not cause it. The men who declared war did not do so in direct fear of being removed from office if they had found some other recourse.

The war inevitably was tied to economic problems. Big business needed new markets. It might have sought them by rapidly expanding purchasing power at home, but this would have threatened the social hierarchy by allowing the masses to ascend to too high a level. Big business looked to state and empire, encouraging a dizzy spiral of armaments and empires that had to lead to war. German industrialists cast covetous eyes on the iron fields of eastern France and the coal mines of Belgium. Far more than the populace in general they may have contributed to a mood that made war seem desirable. But even the big businessmen were not in on the decisions that actually led to war. The "crisis of capitalism" explanation cannot be pushed too far.

The impact of social crisis on the diplomacy of Italy, Austria, Russia and the Balkan states needs no additional emphasis. The relationship between social tensions and diplomacy in Britain, France, and Germany cannot be so easily determined. The solution depends less on the severity of the tensions—they were, even in Britain, far less acute than those of eastern and southern Europe—than on the response of the political elite. Policy, particularly foreign and military policy, was still being set by aristocrats and others who had assimilated much of the aristocratic outlook. Some of them were distressed not just by labor agitation but by the whole direction of industrial society, with its class-based disrespect for established status. Elements of the German elite, particularly in the military, felt seriously threatened. The upper class in Britain and France was more flexible, but it too felt insecure and confused. It was understandable that statesmen drawn from this group were inclined, perhaps subconsciously, to reach for the more traditional, better-understood forms of glory. They paid dearly, for the war undercut the remnants of the aristocratic order.

A sense of crisis in the ruling elite is suggested also by the undoubted decline in the quality of statesmen right before the war. The people who made the key decisions were not diplomats of the top rank. Indeed many shied away from decision at all, for the month that passed between the assassination and the war saw few basic initiatives. There have, of course, been many periods of history when the diplomats were mediocre, so the prewar deterioration may have been just an accident. But it may also have resulted from the ruling elite's battle against industrial democracy, a symptom of its loss of grip.

The war did not, then, spring from a fundamental collapse of European society or cultural values. Its causes were more superficial. But it was not simply the result of traditional diplomacy either, though this played an important role. Europe's rulers were beleaguered and uncertain, which is why they followed the lead of countries that were in fact locked in intense social crisis. Finally, if Europe as a whole was not on the edge of chaos in 1914 it was in no position to endure the kind of war that occurred. The war exacerbated every tension and weakness that existed in 1914. It produced a crisis that was unquestionably profound.

8 WAR, REVOLUTION, AND THEIR AFTERMATH

World War I, a war so blithely entered into, was one of the most traumatic events of human history. Quickly it turned into a bloodbath, and before the fighting stopped, some four years later, almost ten million men had lost their lives and another twenty million had been wounded.

BATTLEFRONTS OF THE WAR

The most dramatic conflict came early. Germany and France had both planned quick, decisive strikes against each other. The Germans hoped to knock France out early in order to concentrate on Russia, where they expected the fighting would be more prolonged. Their strategy, based on a plan drawn up in 1905 by Count von Schlieffen, called for them to sweep through neutral Belgium and encircle Paris. It was a bold scheme, but Germany reduced her chances for success by withdrawing some troops to meet the slow-moving Russians in East Prussia and others to parry the French invasion of Germany from Lorraine. Even so, they almost achieved success.

Germany's Thrust to the West

German troops sped through Belgium and routed the French in eastern France. The French troops were sent to attack the Germans in open formation, almost as if they were on parade, and were mowed down by German

Gaily to War, 1914: French troops ready to entrain for the German frontier.

machine guns. The road to Paris lay open. The French government fled to Bordeaux.

Yet as the Germans reached the Marne River, they began to make mistakes. The French rallied under the command of General Joffre. The entire fleet of Paris taxis was mobilized to carry soldiers to the front. After a week of heavy fighting in the battle of the Marne (September 1914), the Germans retreated to take a new stand on the Aisne river. Never again would they advance so far. Amid constant attack and counterattack, which claimed hundreds of thousands of lives, the battle line did not change by more than ten miles for the next three years.

The western front saw German troops pitched against French and British armies in an unprecedented kind of warfare. Each side faced each other from trenches, with an unbroken line of improvised fortifications stretching for more than 300 miles. At some points the lines were five miles apart; at others the opposing forces were within shouting distance of each other. At Christmas in the first winter of the war, a spontaneous truce was declared

in some sectors, and soldiers exchanged gifts with their "enemies." The scene was not repeated, for trench warfare ground down men's spirits and created an atmosphere of constant fear. During 1915 the French, backed by the British, tried to break through the German trenches. They were slower than the Germans to understand the nature of the new warfare, and they were fighting to regain their own land. First they tried a series of frontal attacks, carefully prepared by deadly artillery fire. A spring offensive in Artois cracked the German lines for three miles before the gap was closed. During this campaign the French lost 400,000 men; a fall offensive had similar results.

In 1916 the Germans tried to mount a decisive offensive, attacking the

French at Verdun after the greatest artillery bombardment yet known in human history. The French held on during weeks of desperate fighting. Then the British staged an offensive along the Somme River. In the first day alone they lost 60,000 men, including more than half the officers engaged in the combat. The western front had reached a stalemate. The Germans lost 850,000 men along it in 1916, the French 700,000, the British 410,000—all for naught.

The Eastern Front

The Germans' eastern front was more fluid but no less bloody. It did not turn into a trench war and was therefore less intense. Also it had not captured the imagination of contemporaries to the extent that the war in the west had, in part because the west, still regarded as the center of civilization, produced more writers to memorialize the ghastly fighting. But if the war in the east was more conventional, the slaughter and chaos were nevertheless immense. The weather killed as many troops as did bullets. Russian armies had first pressed into East Prussia, but the Germans, under the command of two of their ablest generals, Paul von Hindenburg and Erich Ludendorff, rallied. Late in August, they routed the Russians at the battle of Tannenberg, and captured 120,000 men out of an army of 200,000. The Russians moved successfully against the weak Austrian troops, however, which required another German counteroffensive. During 1915 German and Austrian troops captured much of Poland. The Russians tried a final offensive in 1916 and met with some success against Austria, but from then until the Revolution they declined steadily.

There was a third front in the Balkans. Austria and Serbia battled inconclusively, while each side tried to lure the other Balkan states into the war with lavish promises of territorial gain. In 1915 Bulgaria entered on the side of the Central Powers. In 1916 Rumania entered on the side of the Allies— quite stupidly, as it turned out, since Russia collapsed shortly thereafter leaving Rumania defenseless. An Austro-German force combined with a Bulgarian offensive to overrun the whole Balkan peninsula north of Greece, including Rumania. Greece, in the meantime, tried to stay neutral, but an Anglo-French expeditionary force landed near Thessalonika anyway and finally forced the country to declare war on the Central Powers in 1917.

Turkey, in the meantime, had joined the Central Powers late in 1914 as a result of her close military ties with Germany. This action forced the British to keep large numbers of troops in the Near East to protect the Suez Canal and also prevented the shipment of supplies to Russia through the Black Sea. A British force tried to capture Constantinople in 1915 but failed. Only in 1917 did British forces in the Near East, supported by desert Arabs led by the dashing T. E. Lawrence, make headway against the Turks.

Finally there was Italy. Having refused to honor the Triple Alliance, Italy remained neutral until 1915, waiting to see which side would offer the most for her services. The Central Powers had little inducement, since Italy coveted Austrian territory that could hardly be tossed into the kitty. They could only promise big slices of French holdings in North Africa. The western powers were not so encumbered. In the secret Treaty of London, of April 1915, the Allies promised Italy big chunks of Austrian and Turkish territory—some of which they had already committed to other countries. The Italians, once in the war, accomplished little. They opened up a narrow front against Austria near Venice, and during two years of repeated attacks, advanced ten miles. Then in 1917, having mopped up Serbia and Rumania, Germany sent six divisions against the Italians and on the first day of attack regained all the territory the Italians had won in two years. A new front was stabilized for the Italians with emergency Franco-British reinforcements; advance was resumed only in the last weeks of the war when the Austro-Hungarian monarchy was collapsing.

War Outside Europe

War was not confined exclusively to the mainland of Europe. German colonies in Africa quickly fell to the Allies, while in the Far East Japan, which had declared war on Germany in August 1914, seized German holdings in China and occupied the German Pacific islands, the Marshalls and Carolines.

On the high seas, the vaunted German fleet remained bottled up during most of the war—the government that had spent so much time and money in building it seemed reluctant to risk losing it. Only German submarines ranged widely, a distinct innovation in naval warfare. The Germans tried to blockade Britain and sank many civilian vessels, including the liner Lusitania in which 1,200 lives were lost. Because of American opposition Germany briefly restricted her submarine warfare, but resumed it in 1917, thus impelling the United States into the war. At the same time the British navy developed convoy techniques and began destroying German submarines faster than they could be built.

THE WAR'S END

In 1917, after three years of fruitless combat, the deadlock began to break on many fronts. March 1917 saw the overthrow of the Russian monarchy. The liberal provisional government tried to continue the war, but the governmental machinery had broken down, resulting in renewed defeat. The Germans agreed to transport Lenin and other exiled Bolshevik leaders from Switzerland to Finland. The Bolsheviks made their way to St. Petersburg in April and by November had torpedoed the provisional government—which was what the Germans hoped would happen when they granted Lenin and his company safe passage. The Bolsheviks immediately began negotiations with Germany, while many nationalist elements seized the opportunity to declare their independence. Poland, Finland, Estonia, Latvia, the Ukraine, and Bessarabia all broke away for a time. Faced with this pressure and a general civil war within Russia, the Bolsheviks were compelled to sign the Treaty of Brest-Litovsk in March 1918, which gave huge chunks of Russian territory to the Germans and the new states, while subjecting additional Russian land to German administration. The eastern front was closed, though the Germans had to leave a substantial force there to safeguard the new acquisitions.

America's Entry into the War

Germany's bid to bring Britain to her knees by indiscriminate submarine attacks had the ironic result of bringing the United States into the conflict. Most Americans had hoped to stay out, and President Wilson had tried a number of times to negotiate a war settlement. But when several American ships were sunk in February and March of 1917, public opinion veered toward intervention. The United States declared war on April 6 1917, but given America's unpreparedness, the declaration had little military impact for a year.

The German General Ludendorff, now virtual dictator of Germany, launched a make-or-break offensive in the west in March, 1918, before the Americans could reach the front lines in any large numbers. Backed by an unprecedented artillery barrage and extensive use of poison gas, he pressed within striking distance of Paris. But then the offensive stalled because of the exhaustion of German troops and the arrival of fresh American soldiers.

In the second Battle of the Marne, July 15 to August 7 1918, the Germans were decisively routed and the Allies proceeded to take, and keep, the offensive. At the same time an attack in the Balkans, launched from Albania and Greece, forced Bulgaria and Turkey to capitulate; the Serbs pressed on into Hungary, and riots by the Slavic minorities tore the Hapsburg lands asunder. The Austro-Hungarian government sued for peace on November 3 1918. In Germany a new liberal government had tried to arrange an armistice in October. Riots broke out in many German cities and William II was forced to abdicate. The Allies required the German leaders to agree to a virtual unconditional surrender. The guns were silenced on November 11 1918.

THE IMPACT OF THE WAR

The horror of World War I can be seen in the staggering numbers of men who were killed and the numbing impact the war had on those who survived. Never had the power of industrial technology been more awesomely displayed. Heavy artillery became devastatingly precise—Paris, for example, could be shelled from 40 to 50 miles away. The machine gun greatly increased the effectiveness of small arms fire. Toxic gases added their own toll. Toward the end of the war the introduction of tanks and military aircraft gave a foretaste of military-industrial power that was yet to be fully unleashed.

Particularly on the western front World War I was a battle fought in trenches. Soldiers lived for months in the ditches, immobilized by artillery and machine gunfire. The noise, the fear, the futility marked many of them for life—if they lived. For the only thing worse than the trenches was the attempt to advance from them. The German effort to capture the French positions around Verdun, in 1916, cost each side 350,000 lives. When the French under General Nivelle tried yet another offensive early in 1917, the troops simply refused to leave their trenches. They had been deceived too often, lured by promises of victory only to be crushed with horrible losses that the human imagination could scarcely grasp.

During the war, Germany lost 2 million people and France 1.7 million —a full twentieth of her total population. Serbia was even harder hit, and Italy and Britain each lost a million. Russian war losses numbered in the millions—ultimately 17 million people lost their lives from war, revolution, and famine. Few families in any belligerent country did not have a death to mourn. And, of course, it was the young men in each country, the source of vitality and leadership for the future, who bore the brunt of the slaughter. Hardest hit were those from the ranks of the educated and the aristocracy, the men who served as officers and had to lead the fruitless charges; proportionately, their casualties were far higher than the military's in general. The overall losses and their impact on the surviving population were the war's key legacy to the next two decades.

Exposed to shellings, often forced to flee their homes, civilian populations in many areas tasted war directly. There was also immense property damage, as cities were leveled and farmlands torn up. The overall losses have been estimated at more than 300 billion dollars in the purchasing power of the period.

The war created hatred and bitterness that only led to further violence. The taste for massive slaughter had been pretty well bottled up since 1815. Now millions of people were exposed to the sight of violent death and the fear of it as well. Many were revolted, but some seemed to believe that violence was normal. And, as the war revealed, modern technology allowed such slaughter from afar. It was not always necessary to see the victims. Increased crime and political violence followed the war directly, and the war helped create the atmosphere in which advocates of large-scale violence could come to power in Germany and elsewhere.

WARTIME GOVERNMENT

The war revealed the power of modern governments as well as the power of modern machines. In the extreme, controls imposed by wartime governments foreshadowed outright totalitarianism. Lenin, who learned much from the activities of the German military regime, was not the last to draw lessons from this experience.

Governments immediately mobilized their scientific resources. The Germans had the greatest need to spur discoveries in chemistry, not only for use on the battlefields but to supply artificial products, such as synthetic rubber, to replace goods normally imported from overseas. The few countries that had not already installed compulsory military service soon did so; Britain introduced it in 1916, the United States a year later.

The governments took over large sectors of the economy. France intervened the least, though its economy was hard-pressed because much of its industrial zone had been occupied. The government encouraged the rapid buildup of industry in other areas, but by improvisations rather than set formulas. Nonetheless, the French, like all the combatant nations, had to ration strategic materials and many consumer goods. Most governments also set price controls and attempted to handle labor problems through war industry boards that included state, business, and trade union representation. The British and Germans allocated labor directly, carefully exempting vital manufacturing labor from military service while filling as many positions as possible with women, foreigners, and prisoners. Under government guidance, British agricultural production forged ahead for the first time in decades.

The German government set the standard for war controls. The state, despite its military leadership, had taken no economic precautions before the war. There were few stockpiles, and as a result of the British naval blockade, shortages appeared everywhere. The government appointed the talented industrialist Walter Rathenau as "Organizer of German Trade and Industry"; he quickly formed compulsory cartels under mixed state and private control in the major branches of manufacturing, ruthlessly weeding out uneconomic small business. Manpower controls were imposed simultaneously. The Auxiliary Labor Law at the end of 1916 in theory mobilized all males between 17 and 60.

Governments mobilized public opinion as well. All nations imposed censorship. Even Britain, the traditional champion of liberties, in effect imposed martial law on the country through the Defense of the Realm Act. Such measures were not entirely new—Britain had done much the same during the Napoleonic Wars. But governments could now be more efficient in their guard against subversion. Each nation also engaged in positive propaganda to convince its own people as well as neutral nations that it was fighting for justice, while its opponents were committing all sorts of atrocities. All the European governments argued that they had gone to war in self-defense and were innocent of any aggressive act. They supplemented this approach with nationalist appeals designed to persuade the citizenry that the nation, though blameless, would certainly come out ahead now that it had been forced into war. The entry of the American government changed the nature of the propaganda. The Americans tirelessly trumpeted and doubtless believed that they were warring to end war and to make the world safe for democracy. Aided by the death of the tsarist regime in Russia and eager to please their new American ally, France and Britain began also to talk in terms of a more perfect postwar world.

The vast strengthening of government authority inevitably weakened the power of parliaments, particularly as the war dragged on. Parliamentary representatives showed a genius for putting themselves in a bad light. In France they were exempt from military service, a sensible enough measure but one which made them suspect to a beleaguered population. They tended to pose as military experts, trotting up to the front with gratuitous advice and putting pressure on generals to win quick victories; this pressure was one of the reasons for the disastrous Nivelle offensive in 1917. Many past parliamentary squabbles were forgotten during the first years of the war as coalition governments embraced both socialists and conservatives. But under the pressure of bitter war and as disillusionment mounted on the front and at home, parliamentary maneuvering resumed.

In Britain Lloyd George took over the government at the end of 1916. Bent on winning the war as effectively as possible, he paid little attention to the Labour Party or any political opposition; rather, he consorted with big businessmen and ran the war in a personal and capricious fashion. By 1917 the coalition in France between super-patriotic conservatives and the socialists had become impossible. Here too the answer was a strongman, Georges Clemenceau, who jailed many of his opponents and bullied and cajoled the French people into one last effort until victory was won. The two leaders, Clemenceau and George, shared similar goals for personal power. Both stemmed from a radical political background, which both had completely forgotten. From victory they sought to attain the narrowest and most selfish of national aims, including territorial gains and massive reparations from Germany.

By the end of 1916 the German government, under General Ludendorff, had been virtually taken over by the military. In July 1917, the German Reichstag passed a Peace Resolution calling for a compromise settlement that would make neither side a victor. Ludendorff was completely opposed to democracy and parliamentary rule and vowed to achieve total victory with huge annexations in both east and west. The parliamentary initiative was ignored.

Results of State Activities

The changes in government form and functions had huge implications. They encouraged some groups in all countries to distrust parliaments and favor efficient authority and glamorous military leadership. Government economic controls set an obvious precedent that would be taken up in many countries during the next two decades and practically everywhere when a world war broke out again. The tendency toward economic rationalization could be continued under private auspices even earlier. World War I greatly encouraged the trends of economic organization that had developed in the later nineteenth century. Most obviously it favored an extension of big business and nonpolitical combinations. Almost as important was the encouragement it gave to trade unions as it brought them—as big organizations in their own right—into the rationalization process.

Military conscription, economic mobilization, and the constant propaganda din involved the whole population of the combatant countries in the war. Many believed in the sweeping gains their leaders promised; others wanted only an end to the war. All, however, were actively caught up in the war effort and excitement. All would be marked by these four frenzied years and their constant frustrations.

For all their powers, governments refrained from certain activities and tried to minimize the impact of war on the existing social structure. Germany still favored aristocrats for the leading military positions and refused to appoint Jews as army officers, even though it was a Jew, Rathenau, who ran the economy. This discrimination cost much in military efficiency. None of the combatant countries tried to limit war profits consistently, and, except to a limited degree in Britain, the European states did not increase their levels of taxation, even as their expenses mushroomed. They feared that they would antagonize the citizenry—particularly the wealthy, who would have to bear the major burden. So instead they borrowed money abroad, abandoning their investments and becoming debtors for the first time in modern history. They also borrowed money at home: the German national debt rose from 4 billion to 99 billion marks, while France's debt soared from 34 to 144 billion francs. Finally, they simply printed new money and tried to hold prices down as best they could through controls. Inevitably inflationary pressures developed as prices rose 150 percent in Britain, 250 percent in France and Italy by 1917. More important, the financing of the war guaranteed massive economic problems when peace returned, for with price controls removed further inflation was virtually inevitable.

The self-imposed limitations on state interference aroused discontent both during and after the war. It was easy to believe—and it was partially true—that the few were protected while the many suffered. By 1917 the frustrations of the military stalemate and growing hardship at home, combined with a bitter winter, led to a revival of protest. Germany suffered most severely from a shortage of coal and from a lack of food, her people living on a meager diet of turnips and synthetic foods. Left-wing socialists in most countries, who had never agreed with their parties' acceptance of war, stepped up their agitation for peace. Strikes and riots hit many cities, along with some military mutinies. There was a certain democracy in this bitterness and suffering, which most classes endured to some degree, but class antagonisms heightened as remaining injustices stood out ever more starkly. Except in Russia, wartime controls were adequate to put down the protest but not to stem the hostility. More and more people, in various classes and of various political persuasions, grew disillusioned with their governments' constant efforts to conceal the truth with a barrage of lies and promises. Here, too, the war sowed the seeds of postwar problems.

THE RUSSIAN REVOLUTION

The Russian government could not stand up under the strains of total war. Some historians have argued that the revolution was inevitable anyway. Certainly liberals strongly resented the emasculation of the Duma, while workers in the growing factories protested their material conditions and their lack of an effective political voice. On the other hand the existence of the Duma divided the liberals and the Stolypin reform contented an important segment of the peasantry. More and more peasants pulled their land out of village control, consolidated their holdings, and worked to improve their production for the market. This very process aggrieved the smaller landowners who were left behind or even pressed to sell out, but peasant rioting declined between 1906 and 1914. Possibly, without war, the regime could have survived. There is no question that war brought out its worst features.

The Impact of War

Many Russians initially greeted the war enthusiastically, but their enthusiasm crumbled as inept leadership at home and on the front led to crushing defeats and enormous casualty lists. Tsar Nicholas, a stupid but stubborn man, relied for advice on his hysterical wife and on the unordained monk Gregory Rasputin, an illiterate Siberian peasant. Rasputin was openly immoral, but the empress came to believe that God had sent him to guide Russia; his initial power over her resulted from his supposed ability to stop the hemophiliac bleeding of the heir to the throne. Under pressure from the empress and Rasputin, the tsar constantly shuffled ministers about while corruption and inefficiency reached new heights. High aristocrats, fearing revolution, begged the tsar to dismiss the monk; when he refused, a small group of them assassinated Rasputin in December, 1916. But the tsar and his wife grew still more obstinate on their own and government approached complete paralysis.

Even without the government's mismanagement, the war would have brought severe economic dislocations to Russia. The country raised a gigantic army of 15 million men at a great cost to manpower in the factories and fields. Much of Russia's output had to be turned over to the military, while imports of manufactured goods dwindled. Scarcity of goods plus the government's fiscal irresponsibility produced galloping inflation. Like all great European revolutions of the previous century and a half, the Russian revolution was preceded by a rapid increase in food prices: by early 1917 the cost of living had risen almost 700 percent. During 1916 strikes and bread riots increased in intensity and frequency. On March 8 1917 (February 23 according to the Julian calendar that was used in imperial Russia), strikes broke out in the capital, whose name had recently been changed to Petrograd, replacing the German-sounding St. Petersburg. The strike assumed revolutionary proportions only gradually, but as it spread steadily troops joined the demonstrators and gave them weapons. On March 12 leaders of the workers and soldiers, along with representatives of socialist parties, formed a council (called a soviet) of Workers' and Soldiers' Deputies, as in the 1905 revolution. The soviet arrested the government ministers and took control of the city.

The February Revolution

On March 12 a committee of the Duma, which had previously shunned disorder, decided to establish a provisional government headed by the liberal Prince George Lvov and dominated by members of the liberal Constitutional Democratic party. The new government persuaded the tsar to abdicate. With almost no bloodshed, the long reign of the Romanov dynasty had ended.

The new regime quickly introduced the usual range of liberal political reforms, proclaiming freedom of speech, press, and religion. It announced plans for sweeping social reforms and land distribution and promised to call a constitutional assembly to decide on Russia's permanent form of government.

At this point in Russian developments there was more than a suggestion

of the historic pattern of western revolutions. Urban lower classes, goaded
by hunger, provided the muscle on the streets while a government that
had lost confidence in itself gave way easily. The beneficiaries were the
liberals, who had not made the revolution but knew what to do with it.
But the liberals in Russia, weaker in numbers than their western counterparts of a century before, could not hold on. More important, the workers
in Petrograd and elsewhere would not yield control to the liberals. They had
been cheated out of genuine gains in a revolution only 12 years before.
They had organizational experience and a political consciousness far greater
than those of any western artisans in 1848. If this were not enough, the
liberals themselves made a decision that sealed their fate: they continued
the war. They wanted support from the western democracies, which indeed
quickly recognized the new regime and, believing in Russia's national mission, they could not resign themselves to a prudent withdrawal.

So the war went on and with it economic hardship. The Petrograd soviet
built up its strength. For several months it had been controlled by moderate
socialists who supported the government and the continuation of the war,
claiming that Russia was not yet ready for outright socialism. Even so they
kept the soviet free from the government's control.

The Bolsheviks

In April, Vladimir Ilyich Ulyanov arrived: pen-name Lenin, profession
revolutionary. The son of an ennobled school director, Lenin had been a
scholarly, idealistic youth who was deeply shocked when his older brother
was hanged for terrorist activities. He turned to Marxism and to revolutionary propaganda. Like most Russian revolutionaries he spent several years
in Siberian exile and many years in exile abroad. Europe had produced
many professional revolutionaries during the nineteenth century, but Lenin
was something new. His willpower and dedication were unrivaled. He
bullied his fellow Marxists into submission by literally living the revolution
24 hours a day. He was severely practical. He had mastered Marxist theory,
but unlike most Marxists he was not interested in it for its own sake. Hence
as early as 1903 he modified Marxist theory to read that a socialist revolution
could occur in Russia despite the fact that industrialization was only beginning there; it was on this belief that the Bolshevik party was based. Finally,
like very few other Marxists, Lenin studied revolution as a science. He
knew that rigid organization and dedication maintained by centralized
authority were essential. This was no Marxist of western variety, devoted
to revolution in theory but tolerant and law-abiding in practice.

The Bolsheviks were weak in 1917, outnumbered by the more moderate
Marxists. Lenin had been in exile for years and was unknown in Russia.
When he arrived in April, the Bolsheviks had not decided whether or not

to support the liberal government. Lenin made the decision. Quickly assuming control he announced his complete hostility to the existing regime and promised that the proletarian revolution was imminent. Perhaps more importantly he urged Russia's immediate withdrawal from the war. The Bolsheviks thus capitalized on the popular war-weariness, and by the end of April their membership had risen from less than 30,000 to 76,000.

Popular discontent, goaded by Bolshevik propaganda, erupted in July when soldiers and workers in Petrograd tried to overturn the government. Several Bolsheviks were arrested and Lenin fled to Finland. But growing socialist pressure forced the provisional government to replace Prince Lvov with a moderate socialist, Alexander Kerensky. This in turn created right-wing opposition to the regime. Liberals and other nonsocialists looked to the army's new commander in chief, General Kornilov, for support. In September Kornilov tried to march on Petrograd. As always, civil war helped turn revolution to the left. Kerensky appealed to the Bolsheviks for help, freeing their imprisoned leaders and giving them arms. The Bolsheviks spread propaganda among the advancing troops, which, combined with a general demoralization, led the soldiers to refuse to fight. Meanwhile the Bolsheviks had won a majority in the soviets of Petrograd and Moscow and in most of the provincial soviets. Lenin returned secretly from Finland and, convinced that the time had come, urged his followers to get ready for armed insurrection.

The October Revolution

During the night of October 24 (November 6 in the western calendar) armed workers known as Red Guards, together with sympathetic regular troops, occupied railroad stations and other strategic points in Petrograd. The next day they stormed the Winter Palace where the government was located and arrested many officials. Kerensky had already fled. Lenin formed a new government called the Council of Peoples' Commissars.

This was merely a beginning. It took four long years before the Bolshevik Revolution was truly won, years of civil strife and appalling loss of life, for the Russian Revolution, like all the great revolutions of the past, was opposed both from within and without. The vast majority of the people were not Bolsheviks. The revolution shocked the world's major powers, though the Russian revolutionaries were fortunate in that the exhaustion from World War I prevented massive intervention. Furthermore, benefiting from the example of Robespierre and others before him, Lenin knew what had to be done to hold power. Marx himself had stressed the need for a proletarian dictatorship. Lenin might agree with Marx that the dictatorship was only transitional, but for the moment he was not hampered by scruples about authoritarian rule.

The Bolsheviks stayed in power by introducing a drastic program called

The Bolshevik Revolution: Leninists firing on a crowd in Petrograd.

War Communism that included some nationalization of manufacturing, confiscation of land for distribution among the peasants, and a new legal system. The keynote was a single-party dictatorship and what Lenin called "unsparing mass terror." In December 1917, the government set up a secret police force called the Cheka to combat counterrevolutionaries. At the same time, the long-awaited constitutional assembly was elected, with Socialist Revolutionaries—non-Marxist agrarian socialists—in a large majority. In January 1918, Lenin sent troops to dissolve the assembly after a single session, branding the Socialist Revolutionaries and all other opponents of the Bolsheviks as counterrevolutionaries. When the Socialist Revolutionaries reverted to their traditional tactic, political assassination, the Bolsheviks countered with a massive police effort that wiped out great numbers of their political opponents. All opposition newspapers were suppressed. Bolshevik control was now unchallenged, and in March 1918, they moved the central government to Moscow.

Lenin quickly ended Russia's participation in the war. The government recognized the independence of Poland and Finland and was also forced to accept the independence of the Baltic states—Lithuania, Estonia, and Latvia. The Treaty of Brest-Litovsk gave Germany large parts of the Ukraine and Transcaucasia—great sacrifices for Russia, but the government was in no position to continue fighting either the Germans or the borderland nationalist movements.

In fact, even with its greatly reduced territories, Russia still faced military opposition on the borders. Anti-communist "White" armies formed in the Cossack lands in the south and in eastern Russia and Siberia. Early in 1919 two more White armies were organized in the north and northwest. At the same time the allied nations sent troops in. At first, in 1918, they were concerned with preventing the Germans from seizing war materials that had been supplied to Russia. Only Japan sent a large contingent, 60,000 men, while Great Britain and France sent about 1,000 each, and the United States 8,500. The troops skirmished with the Red army, but their major contribution to counterrevolution was giving military supplies to the Whites and blockading the Russian coasts. The Allies, pressed by war weariness at home, withdrew in 1920, except for the Japanese who stayed in western Siberia until 1922. Their main accomplishment was to make the Russians suspicious of other powers and to embitter relations with them for many years.

The fight against the White armies continued until the end of 1920. There were three reasons for the ultimate Red victory. First, the White generals could not coordinate their efforts, each jealously guarding his own authority, and they were spread out on the Russian periphery; the Red army on the other hand controlled the central lines of communication. Second, the Red army itself was the product of the genius of Leon Trotsky. Trotsky won revolutionary fame in 1905 and was far better known than Lenin, with whom he joined forces only in 1917. As war commissar he combined the enthusiasm of worker volunteers with the vital technical knowledge of former tsarist officers. Finally, the White generals steadily antagonized the people. They had great popularity at first, and they committed no more atrocities than did the Red army—though no less either. Gradually they became associated with restoration of the old regime, which hastened their defeat.

Thus political, military, and foreign enemies had been beaten. But what was won? Even Lenin had been hesitant in his policies beyond direct defense of the revolution. Marx had scorned as "utopian" making plans for putting socialism into practice, and Lenin, though eminently practical, had focused on seizing power, not on what to do with it. The Bolsheviks immediately abolished private property, which in effect invited peasants to seize land from their landlords—something they were doing anyway. In the cities the Bolsheviks were more uncertain. They seem to have assumed that major companies would remain under their old management with only some vague kind of supervision to ensure they would be run in the people's interest. When the managers resisted, branches of manufacturing were nationalized, but then the question arose: should the workers run the factories directly or should more efficient professional managers be introduced? In June 1918, the government finally decreed the nationalization of basic industry, but this did not answer the real problem of how to manage production. During the years of civil war, the government's principal economic policy was dictated by the need to survive. Workers were conscripted into labor battalions, while peasants were forced to submit to requisitions by these bat-tallions. Only by such drastic means were the Bolsheviks able to provide the cities and the Red army with a minimum ration of food.

War Communism was thus a series of expedients, many of which bore no relation to socialist theory. It created some durable institutions, notably the Red army and the dreaded secret police. But it did not create a viable economy. Russia, exhausted in 1917, was prostrate by 1920. Industrial pro-duction had dropped to a mere 16 percent of its 1912 level. A third of the urban population had returned to the countryside in search of food. Regular trade and communications had almost ceased, and many sections of the country reverted to a barter economy. Wide stretches of the country-side had been laid waste by war and civil war, while peasants who could farm saw no point in bringing their crops to market since there was nothing to buy. In 1921 the wheat crop failed in the Volga basin, and for the next two years the eastern and southern regions of Russia were gripped by a dreadful famine in which three million people died. Also in 1921 the sailors of the Kronstadt naval base, long devoted to the Bolshevik cause, mutinied. The time for reconstruction had come. Gradually the government realized that the peasantry held the key to the situation. Only the peasants—whom Marxist theory had always neglected—would break through the vicious economic circle. As Lenin put it to the Tenth Congress of his own party: "Only an agreement with the peasantry can save the socialist revolution in Russia."

Although the establishment of a new state and society in Russia had only begun, the Russian Revolution had already had a major impact beyond its borders. It played a major role in the peace settlement of World War I and was one of the reasons the settlement failed. Despite Russia's weak-ness, owing to economic dislocation and civil war, despite the resolution of the other powers to treat the Bolshevik regime as a pariah, the Revolu-tion stirred new hopes and new fears in Europe that contributed to the growing division in society. It is in fact impossible to separate the echoes of the Russian Revolution from the effects of the war itself.

VERSAILLES

As Marxism followed its swift course in Russia, the rest of Europe was gripped by nationalism. Nationalists ruled the established nations of the west and were busy setting up new nations in the east. When the repre-sentatives of the victorious Allies met in Paris in January 1919, to decide the fate of Germany and its defeated partners, there was little doubt that national self-interest would govern the settlement. Ironically, the interna-tionalist American president, Woodrow Wilson, representing a country that appeared to be the strongest on earth, contributed mightily toward making the peace settlement both nationalist and selfish.

VERSAILLES SETTLEMENT
World War I Losses

- by Germany
- by Austria Hungary
- by Bulgaria
- by Russia

Wilson and the European Allies

Some months before the end of the war Wilson issued his famous Fourteen Points to clarify his own war aims and to rally support for them in the allied nations. He was also eager to compete with Bolshevik efforts that were rousing Europe to revolution. Wilson wanted to prove that he too sought a new and just order in Europe. He advocated such general aims as freedom of the seas, disarmament, and an international association to maintain the peace, but his main emphasis was on national self-determination. France was to regain Alsace-Lorraine, while Italy could adjust her frontiers "along clearly recognizable lines of nationality." Poland was to gain independence "with free and secure access to the sea," while "the peoples of Austria-Hungary, whose place among nations we wish to see safeguarded and assured, should be accorded the freest opportunity of autonomous development."

Wilson was not deeply informed about Europe's situation, particularly economic issues which he ignored almost entirely. He assumed that democracy could spread throughout the continent, apparently unaware that east of Germany it had never existed. There is no question of Wilson's sincerity: he believed that national self-determination was the key to peace and progress. But even in his own terms he made a crucial mistake: he forgot to consider the national interests of the defeated powers.

The representatives of the other great powers at the peace conference were out for revenge and maximum national gains. Vittorio Orlando, Prime Minister of Italy, demanded vast territorial acquisitions at the expense of the old Hapsburg and Ottoman Empires, as Italy had been promised in 1915. Clemenceau wanted revenge against Germany—for 1870–1871 as well as for the recent war—seeking reparations for the heavy costs of the war and absolute security against further German aggression. Both Clemenceau and Orlando were pressed by nationalist public opinion. France, for example, was about to elect a new parliament made up of returning veterans eager for national glory. Lloyd George of Britain was personally more moderate, but he too was hampered by a public opinion that his own wartime propaganda against the Germans had stirred up. His coalition government had won a recent election with promises to punish German leaders and to make Germany pay for the war. Minor allies like Belgium and Japan demanded gains of their own, while nationalists in eastern Europe not only sought independence but also squabbled among themselves for territory.

Reasons for Failure

The Versailles settlement was a disaster. There are many reasons for this and possibly no better solution could have been found at that time. What was missing was the traditional belief in balance of power that made the Vienna settlement 100 years before so successful. Russia was barred from the conference for ideological reasons. Germany was barred because it had lost the war and, according to the new nationalist thinking, would have to accept whatever was imposed. In contrast to 1815, the desire for punishment outweighed the desire to reconstruct. Of all the diplomats, Clemenceau came closest to a careful calculation of future balance of power. His hope was to remove Germany altogether from the major power status, but he was not allowed to accomplish this; as a result, even victorious France was dissatisfied and insecure. Finally, power considerations were completely absent from the settlement in east Europe. Under the banners of nationalism a dangerous new vacuum of power was created.

Eastern Europe had broken up before the peace conference began. During the war Austrian statesmen had failed to conciliate the Slavic nationalities, with the result that new nationalists emerged who insisted on independence. Led by the scholarly Thomas Masaryk, Czechs in exile won support from Britain and the United States, and Czechoslovakia became an independent nation ten weeks before the war ended. Rumanian and especially Serbian leaders were promised gains at Austria's expense. Rumania took over Transylvania while Serbia proclaimed the union of its country with the lands inhabited by the Croats and Slovenes—a Yugoslav state based on Serbian supremacy. Hungarians themselves lost faith in the old empire and welcomed independence. Meanwhile, to the north, Polish and Baltic nationalists were confident that their nations could be reconstituted with Germany defeated and Russia distracted. The Paris Peace Conference could only ratify these developments, which created a new belt of small states from the Balkans to the Baltic.

The German Settlement

Hence the diplomats in Paris concentrated mainly on what to do with Germany. The armistice had already compelled the Germans to renounce the Brest-Litovsk Treaty and to evacuate not only areas conquered in the war but the Rhineland itself, which the Allies had occupied. It also forced them to turn over a great deal of equipment and most of the navy to aid the Allies' reconstruction and to guarantee that Germany could not resume war. All these provisions were incorporated in the new treaty. Furthermore, while negotiations proceeded in 1919, the Allies appeared to be maintaining their blockade of Germany. Suffering and outright starvation continued through the severe winter. Actually the Allies were not to blame; German shipowners had refused to donate their vessels for humanitarian purposes, and relief shipments arrived only in April. To the German people, who did not know this, it seemed that the Allies were bent on bringing them to their knees. The actual peace terms, which the new German government had no choice but to accept, confirmed this impression.

The Versailles Treaty deprived the Germans of about a tenth of their prewar territory and population. France regained Alsace-Lorraine and occupied the coal-rich Saar valley; the treaty provided for a Saar plebiscite after 15 years to determine the wishes of the inhabitants. Belgium received a bit of territory. Wilson blocked a French proposal for a separate buffer state in the Rhineland, but the Rhineland was to be demilitarized and occupied by the Allies for 15 years. Posen and West Prussia went to Poland; East Prussia remained German but was separated territorially by Poland's new "corridor to the sea," while German-speaking Danzig was made a free city within the Polish customs frontier. Poland also won the richest part of Upper Silesia. The Allies took over all German colonies.

The Allies tried to prevent future German aggression by limiting the nation's war-making potential. In addition to the Rhineland, a belt 30 miles wide east of the Rhine was demilitarized. The German army was restricted to 100,000 men, while the General Staff was to be abolished. Germany could possess no tanks, heavy artillery, poison gas, military aircraft, or submarines. The navy was to be severely limited and the naval base at Helgoland was to be razed. Germany was also to turn over all her big merchant ships, plus much coal and other raw materials. Germany's power to impose tariff barriers was restricted. Finally, Article 231 of the treaty stipulated:

> The Allied and Associated Governments affirm and Germany accepts the responsibility of Germany and her allies for causing all the loss and damage to which the Allied and Associated Governments and their nationals have been subjected as a consequence of the war imposed upon them by the aggression of Germany and her allies.

This "war guilt" clause saddled Germany with the entire moral blame for the war and allowed the Allies to impose heavy reparations on the country. The war guilt notion was based on inexact history, and if history is to be invoked in peace treaties it ought to be sound. Above all, it burdened the new German government with a stigma it did not deserve, while its unfairness encouraged many Germans to believe that the rest of the Versailles settlement was just as invalid.

Many of the nonterritorial provisions were difficult to enforce, and Germans quickly found ways to circumvent some of the military clauses. The General Staff remained intact. Reparations payments were agreed upon only later, in 1921. Britain, France, and Belgium wanted Germany to pay for the whole cost of the war, not just for damages to civilians. The American government opposed these claims but insisted on repayment of the loans it had extended to the Allies during the war, which virtually forced these countries to press for German reparations at least to this amount. In point of fact, Germany could pay very little, and like it or not, Germany was essential to the international economy. Again, in their desire for revenge and an easy way out of their own troubles, the Allies guaranteed instability in Germany and ultimately far graver problems for their own economies. The level of reparations was finally set, not in terms of the absolute cost of the war, but at the maximum the Allies decided they could possibly extract: 33 billion dollars, a sum several times larger than Germany's annual national income.

Settlement in the Former Hapsburg Lands and the Balkans

Treaties with Austria and Hungary essentially recognized the new nation-states that had been carved from the Hapsburg empire. The Austrian emperor had abdicated on November 1 1918, and Austria, like Germany, was now a republic. By the treaty of Saint-Germain the new Austrian government was forced to pay reparations on behalf of the old empire. Austria itself was now a truncated state of less than eight million people, cut off from her traditional economic hinterland. The Austrians would have preferred union with Germany, but here too national self-determination was not allowed to apply to the losers. In Hungary a Communist revolt led by Bela Kun overthrew the new republic in 1919 and plunged the country into war with Czechoslovakia and Rumania. The Communists were defeated and in March 1920, Admiral Nicholas Horthy proclaimed Hungary a monarchy with a vacant throne and named himself regent and chief of state. Hungary at this point signed its own treaty, the Treaty of the Trianon, which sheared off three-quarters of the territory of the historic kingdom of Hungary to the benefit of Yugoslavia, Rumania, and Czechoslovakia. Bulgaria, in yet another treaty, was forced to concede small bits of its prewar territory.

This settlement in eastern Europe created automatic grievances among the defeated powers. Equally important it did not satisfy the new states in the area. Since it was impossible to draw strictly national boundaries, all the states had important national minorities. Over two million Magyars lived in Rumania, Czechoslovakia and Yugoslavia. Over three million Germans lived in Czechoslovakia and smaller numbers in other new states. Here was an obvious source of friction. Moreover awakened nationalists clamored for territory apart from clear ethnic justifications. Italy gained the town of Trieste from Austria, which angered Yugoslavia. The two countries disputed the possession of Fiume and the Dalmatian coast until 1924 when they reached an uneasy compromise. Bulgaria and Yugoslavia were natural enemies and there were persistent problems with border raids between the two countries. Poland and Czechoslovakia conducted a brief border war in 1919–1920. Poland won its part of Upper Silesia in the Versailles Treaty by occupying the area despite the plebiscite that voted overwhelmingly for reunion with Germany. The diplomats could not determine Poland's eastern boundary since Russia was not present. In 1920 the Poles, with help from a White army and ultimately from the French, invaded the western Ukraine and White Russia, claiming that these territories belonged to Poland. They insisted on their historic boundaries of 1772. The Russians finally sued for peace, and the Treaty of Riga of March 1921, conceded the Polish demands —which meant that over four million Russians now lived in Poland. The Poles also quarreled with Lithuania.

There is one way to describe the whole frightful situation in eastern

Europe. Even with the best of will, lines could not be drawn by nationality, and the best of will was lacking as Germans and Russians particularly were simply handed over to the new states. The weakness of so many small states was greatly increased by the fact that almost all of them had quarrels to pick with one or more of their neighbors.

Settlement in the Near East

The Allies were unable to impose their will on Turkey, the last of the defeated powers. They stripped away the remaining Arab sections of the Ottoman Empire, forming mandates of Syria and Lebanon (under France) and Iraq, Palestine, and Jordan (under Britain). Large parts of Turkey itself were to be given to Greece and Italy, but the Turkish Nationalist movement led by Mustapha Kemal—later known as Kemal Atatürk, the "Father of the Turks"—deposed the Sultan and fought off the Greeks and Italians. The goal was a nationalist Turkish state on the western model. By the Treaty of Lausanne in 1923 the Turks abandoned all non-Turkish territory but retained all the Turkish lands that the Ottomans had possessed, except a number of Mediterranean islands. So deep were the nationalist passions in this case that the treaty provided for the "repatriation" of over a million Greeks whose ancestors had lived in Asia Minor since ancient times, while a smaller number of Turks in Greece returned to Turkey.

The League of Nations

The peace settlement in Paris was capped, or so it was hoped, by the establishment of the new League of Nations. This was Wilson's fondest dream, and the other Allies went along to retain American friendship. Wilson believed that the League could rectify any inequities in the treaties and viewed it as a "permanent process" to keep the peace. The League was a voluntary association that did not infringe the sovereignty of any nation; it had no powers of coercion. It was a logical outgrowth of a liberal theory of international relations and as such depended on good will. Unhappily, even aside from this doubtful dependence, the League was flawed from the start. Its establishment as an integral part of all peace treaties made it seem the creature of the Allies—which indeed it turned out to be. Germany and Russia, the new pariahs, were not invited to membership at all. And the United States, the champion and sponsor of the League, refused to join.

The League was able to set up some important subsidiary agencies such as the International Labor Office. Wilson managed also to convert all the German colonies seized by the various allies into mandate territories under League supervision. The main point here was that the mandates, though in practice run like colonies, were promised ultimate independence. To this extent European imperialism, which reached its fullest territorial extent by the peace settlement, was modified. But the League itself did little but talk—and talk and talk. It was a negligible factor in postwar international relations. Furthermore, America's refusal to join the League left Britain, and particularly France, to defend a principle in which they did not believe. The French had agreed to the League for one main reason: America promised aid against potential German aggression to allay Clemenceau's fears. This promise was now nullified. France would have to assure her own security against Germany as the United States retreated into isolation.

The Paris settlement thus fell between two stools. It did not reconcile the European states but it was not severe enough to restrain the aggrieved parties. The Germans and the Russians could not be held down forever under the treaties' terms, yet they would inevitably seek a revision of these terms. The victorious powers, especially France, realized the fragility of the settlement and promptly made things worse by trying to ride roughshod over the Germans. Never had so many treaties created so little peace.

POSTWAR UNREST

After the dubious intoxication of four years of war, Europe had a prolonged hangover, compounded by the Russian Revolution and the continuing brushfire wars.

Million of veterans returned home only to discover quickly that any hopes they cherished for a better society or even an improvement in their personal positions were unrealistic. Here too the politicans had lied. Many of the veterans had difficulty adjusting to peacetime—large numbers were wounded, others psychologically scarred. Many flocked to veterans' organizations, like the German *Stahlhelm*, which helped maintain their bitterness against civilian society and against a diplomacy that seemed to render their wartime sacrifices meaningless. The veterans' anger would be a factor of great importance in years to come.

People drifted about in the years after the war, particularly in eastern and central Europe. By the end of the civil war, up to 1,750,000 Russians had fled to other parts of Europe. Nearly a million Germans, including 100 thousand from Alsace-Lorraine who had been satisfied with German rule, moved from territories now assigned to other countries into the shrunken fatherland. Four hundred thousand Magyars migrated into the new Hungary, burdening its agrarian economy. Such dislocations guaranteed long-term economic problems and fed diplomatic tensions. In the shortrun, they added greatly to the chaos.

For a brief moment the economy boomed in the western countries as consumers and producers tried to make up for wartime shortages. Inflation was a problem everywhere but working-class wages remained stable. But as soon as immediate reconstruction needs were met a severe though brief depression set in during 1920–1921. Only by 1922 did the economy begin to revive even in the most stable countries.

Social Unrest

Workers reacted to the end of the war and the subsequent confusion with an unprecedented burst of protest. Often led by returning veterans, workers were excited by the Russian Revolution, which to them was proof positive that the proletariat could overturn the existing order. Hardships of the war encouraged protest, as did the boom of 1919–1920 and the new hopes to be gained from it. At the same time, socialists and labor organizations had won new respectability through participation in wartime governments.

There were many reasons for the labor unrest, some of which tended to cancel each other out as soon as the first enthusiasm died down. Workers flocked to trade unions; French unions had more than doubled their membership by 1920. Strikes reached unheard of intensity from Germany to Spain. In Italy and elsewhere workers took over some factories outright. Many workers moved their political allegiance to the left, which meant an increase in the socialist vote. This was particularly important in Britain where the Labour Party quickly displaced the Liberals as one of the two principal parties in the country. On the continent the same movement to the left gave support to the new Communist parties that formed in most countries.

Throughout western and central Europe left-wing socialists rallied to the Russian Revolution. They had long objected to the timidity of mainstream socialists and especially to their sell-out to the war effort. The Bolsheviks for their part were eager to lead a general European revolution, for even Lenin believed that the revolution needed a secure proletarian base, which could only be found in the advanced industrial nations of the west. In this spirit they founded the Third International, or Comintern, in 1919. Within a year it became clear that Lenin intended to impose the same rigid orthodoxy on this group that he had on the Bolshevik party in Russia. Hence by 1921 most socialist parties and unions split with the wing that favored the revolution and accepted the Comintern calling themselves Communists.

Workers' agitation quickly faded after 1920. Their great hopes had not been realized; the depression forced them to fear for their jobs. Trade union membership fell off drastically and the strike movement ground to a halt. A general strike in France, called by revolutionaries for May 1 1920, failed dismally. Politically the moderate socialist parties regained their ascendancy and became still more moderate. They had been shaken by Communist secession, which in some cases robbed them of almost half their leadership. But by 1920 it was clear that only a small minority of voters had followed the Communists. Socialist strength was secure, while the secession left them freer from radical influence than ever before.

Chaos in Germany

Not surprisingly Germany was far more troubled in these years than the nations of the west. Defeated in war, Germany was forced to change its form of government if only because President Wilson refused to agree to an armistice so long as the emperor was on the throne. There was also a fear of left-wing demonstrations in Berlin. All in all it seemed safest to proclaim a republic. Officially this was a revolution, but of the most peaceful sort. The Social Democrats (moderate socialists) who ran the new regime intended orderly change.

Order was hard to maintain, however. Many returning veterans, including officers who lost their army jobs because of imposed army cutbacks, formed paramilitary groups called the "Free Corps," which were hostile to parliamentary rule. At the other extreme Communists, as well as an independent radical socialist group, tried repeatedly to seize power. They set up a regime for a short time in Bavaria and staged an immense demonstration in Berlin two months after the war's end; to put down this demonstration the government called in the army and the Free Corps. The talented left-wing leader Rosa Luxemburg was killed during a repression ordered by the socialist government. Against rightist coups, on the other hand, the government appealed for a general strike; this defeated the most serious rightist attempt, the Kapp putsch of 1920. Even in Germany the greatest threats from right and left had ended by 1921, if only for a time. Although Communist efforts continued until 1923, they commanded little popular support in the last years and became more and more contrived and conspiratorial. A rightist named Adolf Hitler tried a *putsch* in Munich in 1923, but this too was a hollow farce, easily suppressed. After a shaky start the new German regime seemed to have taken hold. The republican form of the regime was decidedly novel; it remained to be seen if it could create a genuinely new political culture in Germany.

The postwar disorders were important. In Italy and Spain worker unrest unintentionally helped install new authoritarian governments. Everywhere the disorders had produced new institutions, notably the Communist parties, which were of immense potential importance. Yet most people, and certainly most governments, hoped for a return to normalcy defined in largely prewar terms. If nothing else they were too tired, too drained emotionally to maintain the postwar excitement.

WORLD WAR I:
A WATERSHED?

The war and its aftermath virtually guaranteed that normalcy could not be preserved. The problem was one of economics: property destruction and wartime fiscal policies were complicated by the complete disregard for economic stability in the peace settlement. In addition to the disruption of the German economy, the Austro-Hungarian empire, which for all its faults had given economic unity to the Danube basin, was destroyed without any thought to the consequences. The proliferation of small agrarian states, cut off from their markets in Austria and Bohemia, did not augur well for the prosperity of the region.

The war also painfully altered the economic relationship between Europe and the world. The United States, Japan, and other non-European countries captured many of Europe's traditional foreign markets, and this was hard to undo even after the war's domination of the European economy ended. Europe also lost shipping and banking income abroad, again particularly to the United States. Many foreign investments were exchanged for needed war materials or, in Germany's case, confiscated; France and other countries lost huge holdings in Russia when the Soviet regime refused to recognize past debts. The United States, on the other hand, became a creditor nation, instead of a debtor, because of its large loans to the Allies.

The population losses of the war could not easily be made up. Two "hollow generations" had been created—one among the age group that served in the armies, the other among the babies they would normally have sired but did not. Birth rates rose right after the war, in the usual pattern, and most countries quickly restored their previous population levels. But the high incidence of mortality among leadership groups long left a mark. The scars of slaughter and mourning left by such a brutal, frustrating war would not soon be erased.

For it was Europe's morale that was most heavily damaged. Violence in war had often been followed by violence in civil society. The shock of World War I was particularly great both because its violence had no precedent in human history and because it so contradicted the optimistic assumptions of many European people, visible even at the start of the war itself. The optimism of the middle class was particularly damaged. The middle class was harmed by the economic dislocation of the war, above all by the inflation. They were shocked by the Russian Revolution. The damage to their morale set the embittered tone for the next two decades.

In a variety of ways, then, the war and its faulty settlement made it likely that Europe was in for a bad time. The two decades after the war were indeed horrible. But was the war a fundamental break in European history, comparable, say, to the French revolutionary era? Many contemporaries thought that it was. The war jolted them into a belief that the

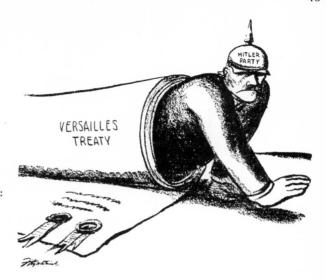

Versailles in Retrospect:
Did the Treaty make
Hitler's rise inevitable?

whole nature of civilization had changed and, undoubtedly, greatly deteriorated. The "decline of the West," the title of a new interpretation of world
history by the German Oswald Spengler, became a common phrase.

What had the war fundamentally changed? For Russia, a great deal,
but no other European state had undergone a real revolution. There were
many new regimes in eastern and central Europe but most of them left the
social structure untouched. Life for most people in Poland or Hungary had
changed very little. Nationalist grievances were channeled in somewhat different directions but they were not new, and just as before the war they
made the region inherently unstable. In the mature industrial countries the
war did not induce a new economic or social structure, but greatly heightened preexisting economic problems and social tensions. The fundamental
economic problem remained the recurrent imbalance between production
and consumption. The fundamental social problem remained the relationship between workers and the middle class. The new fears of the middle
class made this problem much more difficult to solve, but they did not
alter the social framework that had developed with the second stage of
industrialization after 1870. Nor was Europe's intellectual life altered in a
fundamental way. Earlier pessimism and relativism were greatly heightened,
not newly created.

The war did signal the beginning of the end for Europe's traditional
dominance of the rest of the world, though this was a long, gradual process
that had begun earlier and thus far had left Europe still with great power.
It vastly heightened the power of governments, as we have seen; and the
totalitarian regimes that arose after the war were new.

Any student of history has to make his own decision about where the
major breaks occur. The interpretation of the war requires a judgment of

the previous decades and the subsequent course of twentieth-century history. The war's impact can be seen as an intensification of the tendencies of the later nineteenth century, even with regard to the growth of governmental power—a great intensification, to be sure, for Europe was not doomed to paralysis before the war occurred. The demographic weakness of western Europe had been developing before; so had symptoms of economic decline and the nervousness of intellectuals. In this sense the two decades after the war were the end of an era, which the war itself made particularly complicated. The major break in recent European history was still to come.

There is no question, of course, that the war left a bitter legacy that overshadowed the next two decades. The very fact that so many people believed that the world had fundamentally changed is proof of this.

There is also no question that the judgment of the war and the next two decades is of great importance. If the war did alter the direction of European history, if the two decades after the war are representative of the new Europe, then our judgment of the contemporary world must be extremely bleak. Are the forces that created Nazism, for example, permanent forces in contemporary society? Or was Nazism the monstrous product of a particular situation in the waning years of the second stage of industrialization in a country particularly disoriented by the war? Were there, during the two decades of decay, signs that Europe could turn in yet another new direction?

9 DEMOCRACY PARALYZED: WESTERN EUROPE

1920–1939

Four major European countries and a host of minor ones began the decade of the 1920s as parliamentary democracies. Within two decades only two major countries, France and Britain, retained this form of government and they seemed incapable of taking initiative either at home or abroad. Only a few smaller democracies, mostly in Scandinavia where the war had not seriously touched, showed signs of health. Elsewhere the initiative lay with authoritarian and totalitarian regimes.

The history of the western democracies in the interwar decades is a dismal tale, but one that deserves attention: first, because the democracies' weakness helped bring on renewed world war and second, because that very weakness taught some lessons that were remembered in the brighter days following World War II. There were in fact a few hopeful signs even before 1939, amid the pervasive gloom.

STABILITY AND DEPRESSION

The history of the democracies between the wars falls naturally into two subperiods. The first was concerned with regaining stability after the postwar chaos. The second saw the onset of the depression. With economic collapse the democracies, with a few important exceptions, found themselves virtually immobilized and often wracked by class conflict. Cultural activity continued, but it was subordinated to the problems of economics and politics.

The Rich, the Poor, the Angry: A drawing by George Grosz depicting social conditions in Germany after World War I.

The 1920s offer no simple, overriding theme. We have already seen that politics had begun to polarize, that political stability was already questionable. But there may be too great a temptation to see in the 1920s the prefigurations of the paralysis of the 1930s. Once again we face the question of inevitability, a question that is particularly important for Germany. Germany did not establish any new political institutions in the 1920s, but in taking on the normal apparatus of a parliamentary democracy the country assumed something quite novel in its own experience. Germany had its years of success—indeed the democracies generally seemed to be in relatively good shape in the mid-1920s. While their new weaknesses are important, their achievements should not be ignored.

Judgment of the politics of the 1920s is closely bound to an evaluation of economic trends. There was a period of prosperity as industrial economies proved surprisingly resilient. But the war left a fatal legacy to these economies, which could have been remedied only by major reform. Such reform was impossible, however, for the ruling classes were on the defensive and could not escape a sense of foreboding. The war scared them, as did Communism and inflation, which the war had made inevitable. They could only think of preserving the existing order, which meant among other things keeping the purchasing power of the lower classes relatively low. In this situation a depression could not be avoided. Thus the economic history of the 1920s largely continued along prewar trends, including an increased concentration of business. The depression itself bore some resemblance to prewar slumps, but the war had exacerbated many weaknesses of the economy, and as a result the collapse was far more severe than ever before. With economic collapse, the fragile political stability of the decade collapsed too. Only the few democracies that had not been involved in World War I were capable of a really creative response to the depression. This again forces us to look at the major democracies with great care, to see what had changed in their politics despite superficial stability.

Cultural Trends

The culture of the 1920s is also related to politics and the economy. Again the war exaggerated a number of preexisting themes. Cultural pessimism and anti-rationalism became popular, which may in turn have weakened the strength of the democracies, as intellectuals shunned the political arena or supported anti-democratic movements. Mass culture, too, stepped up its prewar addiction to faddish fashions, sports, and the like. This was in part escapism, reflecting a sense that the world had gone haywire. The cultural frenzy of the 1920s was an obvious reaction to the strain of war; it also seems to have anticipated the new crises of the 1930s.

Yet there was more to it than this. In formal culture, perhaps even more in popular culture, the 1920s was a genuinely creative decade. This raises an interesting possibility about the relationship of cultural creativity to economic and political well-being: when innovation is blocked in one sphere it seems to flow to another. In any event, trends in art and literature established in the 1920s had lasting importance. So did new kinds of popular behavior, including a keen interest in sports, new courtship patterns, and a new spirit of freedom among women. The depression interrupted some of these trends, but they foreshadowed at least a new consumer culture.

ECONOMY AND SOCIETY

After the slump of 1920–1921 the French economy resumed its rapid advance. Germany, though less stable, moved forward as well. Only Britain obviously lagged. The British government returned to the gold standard—which all the European states had abandoned in the press of war—in the

1920s; the British currency was in the process of being deflated. Britain thus avoided damaging inflation, but by the same token its internal purchasing power fell behind. Britain was also hardest hit by the international shifts in trade as its overseas trade reached only 75 percent of prewar levels. Hence during the 1920s British production advanced only slowly and there was substantial unemployment.

Economic Rationalization

The interwar years saw no radical breakthroughs in technology, but there was steady technical advance. Particularly promising were the many new products for consumers such as artificial cloth fibers. Electric power spread widely, even to some rural areas. No prosperous home was without a radio, and movies came to be a part of Europe's popular culture. The new means of communication, together with the growth of air transport, bound Europe more closely with the rest of the world. In 1927 Europe was connected by telephone to the United States, and by the eve of World War II there was regular air service across the Atlantic. In general, these technological changes foreshadowed a new era of abundance, the advent of a consumer society. Unfortunately the rest of the economy would not keep pace.

The rationalization of economic organization continued, aided by the technical advances and also by the experiences of the wartime economy. A few new processes were introduced, notably the electric furnace for treating light metals. More important was the "scientific" reorganization of factory work, which set workers' tasks by careful calculations of their every motion. Increasing standardization of parts facilitated the spread of assembly-line methods. A new type of skilled and semi-skilled worker took over the factories. Rationalization affected office work too, and the widespread use of typewriters and accounting machines helped speed the pace of clerical work.

Rationalization, the slogan of the 1920s, was also taken to mean the concentration of economic units, which went steadily forward, particularly in Germany. Giant new combines arose, like the *Vereinigte Stahlwerke*, which controlled almost half of German steel production. Cartels proliferated, some of them crossing national boundaries. But by no means were all these combinations rational. Horizontal combinations, that is, companies that extended over a variety of different industries, were often based on sheer speculation. Encouraged by inflation, many investors poured their money into giant enterprises whose *raison d'être* was simply to receive investments. They brought no gains in efficiency and they greatly overheated the stock markets.

Nevertheless, the progress of the industrial countries was impressive during the 1920s. By 1928 Germany, despite her territorial losses, had increased total production by 40 percent over prewar levels. Nevertheless, Europe's share in world production was down. Germany had produced 17 percent of the world's industrial total in 1909, but managed a bare 11 percent in 1928. Europe was now importing most of the new techniques and procedures from the United States. Moreover, the relatively small size of even the major European countries prevented full development of industrial rationalization on the American model. But these problems, though perceived at the time, were left for later decades to solve. Europe had more immediate economic worries.

The Impact of Inflation

Inflation dogged the continent through the early 1920s, with central Europe being particularly hard hit. The obligation to pay reparations encouraged governments to persist in fiscally irresponsible actions, such as printing new money. In Austria the cost of living was 2,645 times higher in July 1922, than it had been in 1914. Prices rose to astronomical heights in Germany until 1923, a condition that made money almost valueless. A less severe inflation hit France in the middle of the decade. Governments could and did end the inflation by reducing the value of currency. In 1923 the new Stresemann government in Germany pegged the value of the mark at the rate of one new unit to one trillion old units, which stabilized the mark but at great cost. More modestly, the French government, in 1928, stabilized the franc at one-quarter of its previous value.

These massive inflations and the attempted settlements created great scars. During the height of the German inflation people had to carry suitcases full of money to make simple purchases, and because prices increased from hour to hour one might often be forced to go home for another suitcase. Anyone might lose faith in an economic system that could go so berserk. But it was the middle class that was hardest hit. Many workers managed to keep their wages on a par with prices. Peasants, who were debtors, actually benefited for a short time. Big businessmen, accustomed to borrowing money, plunged into speculative investments that increased their financial strength at least in the short run. But the people in the middle—those on a fixed income—were caught. Bureaucrats and teachers on pensions came close to starvation as precious savings, investments and property were wiped out. Creditors were hurt, for with inflation the value of a loan fell to nothing. By 1925 over 50 percent of the capital of the lower middle class in Germany had been destroyed. The incalculable blow to morale was just as important as the great material suffering. The middle class had always been a possessing class, its status based on ownership. This was now challenged.

Structural Weaknesses

Inflation was only the most obvious sign of disruption during the 1920s. It could be cured, and though its cure confirmed the damage to the middle classes and left them extremely nervous there was no sign of persistent rebellion so long as overall prosperity advanced. In fact, the prewar problem of inadequate markets was heightened during the decade.

Two major traditional sources of demand were now limited. In western Europe population growth ground to a halt. British and Scandinavian birth rates were only slightly higher than death rates, while in Germany population growth slowed up considerably. In France birth rates actually fell below death rates, and French population would have declined except for massive immigration from Italy and eastern Europe. The demographic slowdown was not new: it reflected the decline of religion and the desire to improve material well-being by limiting the number of children in the family. But in this period these obvious motives were overshadowed by the fear and insecurity that the war had produced. To many, particularly in the middle classes, it simply did not seem safe to have more than one child. Ironically, the decline in population growth heightened the feeling of insecurity; in France, for example, it reduced economic vitality and confirmed fears of being threatened by larger neighboring states such as Germany. Thus, fearful families risked still fewer children and the cycle continued.

Other areas of Europe and certainly much of the non-European world advanced rapidly in population, but this did not greatly boost the markets for Europe's industrial goods. In addition to American and Japanese competition, Europe suffered from a proliferation of tariff barriers. The small states of eastern Europe sought to protect infant industries—some of which had yet to be born—with massive tariffs, and the advanced industrial states followed the same policies with less reason. Even Britain passed a major tariff at the decade's end. Finally, in 1926–1927 a collapse in the price of raw materials reduced export markets still further. Countries of eastern and southern Europe as well as non-European areas that depended on the export of food, ores, and other nonmanufactured products had been encouraged to increase their production substantially, both during and after the war. The industrial countries could not absorb all this production, so the prices of these goods fell. Only in the short run did Europe benefit, for soon lower incomes in the raw-materials areas reduced their capacity to buy. Here was another vicious circle.

Market deficiencies at home could be remedied more easily, but no remedies were offered in the 1920s. The wages of many workers advanced, and some were able to take advantage of new consumer products, but there were still important limitations of their purchasing power. Most important, several traditional industries were sick. Shipbuilding declined because of the sluggishness of international trade. The textile industry faced overwhelming competition from cheap-labor areas, many of them outside

Europe. Coal production fell everywhere because oil provided cheaper and more efficient fuel; but the oil industry could not provide alternate employment for European coal miners, for oil was produced almost exclusively in non-European areas. Thus, some of the biggest employers of labor were declining, which in Britain led to virtual depression even during the 1920s. Overall levels of unemployment stood at 10 percent even in the best years, and at 16 percent in mining and textiles. Continental countries suffered similar problems to a lesser degree.

Agricultural Crisis

Conditions in agriculture deteriorated to the point of tragedy. The war and postwar dislocations encouraged peasants and landlords to increase their production wherever they could, and during the period of inflation many had borrowed money for further technical improvements. There were signs of great change in the countryside. For the first time there were reports that German peasants were abandoning traditional religion. As radios, movies, and bus lines came to be part of daily life, peasants were in much closer touch with the cities. They began to develop a new assertiveness, new expectations. Their attempt to take advantage of new economic opportunities was part of this, but for the time being it brought disaster. By 1924 the wartime dislocation of agriculture had been eliminated, but many regions in Europe and abroad were producing more than they had before the war. Agricultural prices plummeted, while many farmers were heavily in debt. By 1930 French peasants' purchasing power had fallen 10 percent from 1913 levels. As with the workers, hardships for an important segment of the population reduced the strength of the whole economy. Depression, when it came in 1928, was no surprise; it had begun some years before for many people.

Class Conflict

Class tensions increased in the 1920s, a foretaste of the bitter conflict of the depression years. A minority of peasants experimented with new forms of protest. Some voted Communist and joined Communist unions, notably in France, while others flirted with authoritarian movements on the right that promised to protect rural values. A minority of workers remained wedded to Communism after 1920 while others relied on more traditional protests such as striking and voting socialist. British workers, particularly miners and others afflicted by massive unemployment, launched the largest strike movement in British history in 1926, when two-and-a-half million workers protested the intransigence of mine owners.

But the heightening of social tension did not come primarily from the lower classes. After 1920 the rate of strikes fell to prewar levels in most years and in most countries. Socialist parties became increasingly tame. Workers were either satisfied, as some benefited from the prosperity of the mid-1920s, or restrained from protest by unemployment and other factors. What was new was the insecurity of the middle and upper classes.

These groups were now on the defensive—shocked by the war, the Russian Revolution, and the rise of Communism—and their economic problems did not end with the inflation. Aristocrats suffered from the agricultural crisis. Junkers in eastern Germany survived the last years of the decade only with state subsidies. Important segments of the middle classes suffered unemployment even during the prosperous years. Despite the expansion of middle-class jobs that accompanied the growth of business and government bureaucracies, more people, ironically and tragically, sought more work than the economy could support. In Germany, for example, over half a million workers were looking for white-collar employment right after the war. New competition, combined with the inflation, forced many white-collar workers into the factory labor force and reduced average earnings. By 1929 four million white-collar workers in Germany earned no more than factory labor—again a traditional status distinction was eroding.

Higher on the middle-class scale, professional people continued to be in superabundance. In 1926 14,000 of 48,000 trained physicians in Germany were unable to practice medicine and were engaged in clerical or other lower-middle-class professions instead. Problems of this sort were greatest in Germany but everywhere complaints about limited mobility proliferated. Managerial positions, for example, tended to pass within the families of existing managers; in Britain the number of managers who had risen from the lower middle class declined by 50 percent. In other words, virtually all the cornerstones of middle-class life were crumbling: property, security, status, advancement. Some members of the class were driven to outright misery. Newspaper advertisements in Germany before the depression expressed the extremes of despair: "30 years old, married, 3 children. Nothing earned for 3 years. Future? Poor house, madhouse, or the gas jet."

Rising suicide rates reflected the agonies of some members of the middle and upper classes. So did their flirtation with extremist political movements. In France, a mood of *incivisme* spread—a strong reluctance to fulfill the duties of citizenship. Businessmen, from small shopkeepers to large industrialists, made it a matter of pride to avoid paying taxes. Most important, during the 1920s, was the growing inflexibility toward lower-class demands. A "Red scare" swept through western and central Europe in the early 1920s. Conservative parties found it easy to win votes with posters showing a red hand holding a dagger dripping with blood. Fear and resentment of workers spread as hard-pressed shopkeepers and clerks believed that governments were doing too much for labor while offering nothing for them. This middle-class mood was expressed in the attitude toward strikes. Strike failures increased dramatically as businessmen took a tougher stand than before the war. In Britain the general strike of 1926 illustrated middle-class hostility to labor; students and lawyers, as well as aristocratic landlords, pitched in to keep the economy going, running trains and loading goods. Naturally this defensive stance extended to politics. In 1927 the British government passed legislation forbidding sympathetic strikes, thereby weakening labor's bargaining power. More generally, few new welfare measures were introduced during the 1920s, in contrast to the prewar decades. Some legislation was passed in the years immediately after the war; Britain, for example, extended unemployment insurance to cover most categories of workers. Germany passed an unemployment insurance act in 1927, but otherwise none of the industrial countries extended their welfare programs after 1920.

The inflexibility of the middle and upper classes, bred by their insecurity, could only increase when depression struck, while workers sought more radical forms of protest. But even before this, class tension threatened to poison the political atmosphere. Indeed, it added yet another cause to the depression itself, for its net result was to keep the incomes of the lower classes low. Caught up in their own problems, the middle classes could not afford to encourage a great surge in mass consumption standards, for this would further threaten their own shaky status. Tragedy was unavoidable. Not surprisingly, an undercurrent of foreboding underlay the frenzied culture of the 1920s.

EUROPEAN CULTURE BETWEEN THE WARS

The interwar decades, particularly the years before the depression, were marked by unprecedented cultural outpouring. Experimentation and innovation were the order of the day, in marked contrast to the caution that dominated the political and economic sphere. Though trends varied greatly from one field to another, artists and scientists had a common disdain for the Victorian era. They judged the nineteenth century, even at its height, as narrow, prudish, materialistic and dull.

Scientific Developments

In physics the ground-breaking work of Albert Einstein and Max Planck gained ever wider attention. The big theoretical discussions of the 1920s concerned the behavior of radiation units. Niels Bohr in 1913 formulated a theory to explain the movement of electrons, but in 1925 it was discovered that his explanations did not account for all the observable phenomena in the hydrogen spectrum. Several diverse, complex theories were developed: some physicists spoke of particles, others of waves. The revolution in physics was complete: long the source of certain truth, the science was now dominated by discontinuity and indeterminacy. To many educated laymen these developments were extremely troubling. Not a few returned to religion in their search for certainty.

At the same time there was an important drawing together of the major sciences. Biology made increasing use of the theory of physics, and the sciences of biochemistry and biophysics arose. Genetic theory was greatly refined. By treating the gene as a basic, indivisible unit, biologists confirmed the physicists' new belief that nature proceeded by jumps rather than through continuous, smooth processes of change as nineteenth-century scientists had assumed.

All the sciences, even when their theoretical bases seemed uncertain, produced a steady stream of practical applications. Chemists identified vitamins and by the 1930s their analysis permitted the artificial synthesis of these substances. There were major discoveries in the field of endocrinology, notably with regard to the functions of hormones. Production of antibiotics began with the almost accidental discovery of penicillin in 1928. All this added up to the greatest period of medical progress in history.

The practical applications of physics were less obvious. Analysis of the constituent particles of the atom, particularly the identification of the neutron in 1932, led physicists to begin the intense bombardment of basic matter that culminated, during World War II, in the discovery of the atom bomb.

Changes in the Social Sciences

In the social sciences the major new development was psychology's rise to the center of attention. As in physics, basic discoveries in psychology antedated World War I. Freud continued to write, and he and his followers continued to train a group of psychiatrists in the psychoanalytic method. There were many challenges to the Freudian approach. Freud's heir apparent, Carl Jung, stressed the importance of religion. He believed in the existence of a "collective unconscious" that produced the same myths and symbols in different times and places; he urged on his patients the therapeutic value of a return to faith.

Other social sciences supported the implications of psychology. Anthropology progressed through the systematic study of primitive peoples and emphasized the importance of unconscious motivation through tribal ritual. The heirs of Max Weber in Germany concentrated particularly on the sociology of knowledge, stressing the dependence of intellectual activity on sociological milieu—in yet another way suggesting relativism, the absence of intellectual absolutes.

Trends in Philosophy

The irrational found exponents in formal philosophy as well. Many writers, such as the poet-philosopher Gabriele d'Annunzio, professed to disdain rational activity and hailed "thinking with the blood," thus contributing to the rising fascist movement. Existentialism also developed after the war, winning a substantial audience among German intellectuals who rejected rationalism and the traditional concern with philosophical categories in favor of penetrating the heart of human experience. The existentialist Martin Heidegger found the central meaning of human existence in dread, despair, and death.

In England and the United States a quite different movement was taking shape. Led by Bertrand Russell and Alfred North Whitehead, logical positivists hoped to convert philosophy to the unambiguous language of mathematics. They argued that any parts of traditional philosophy, such as ethics and metaphysics, that could not be thus converted were not worth considering. Logical positivists tended to reduce philosophy to a set of abstract propositons comprehensible only to initiates. On the other hand, they turned to careful empirical studies of language itself, coming closer to the interests and techniques of social scientists.

Literature and the Arts

In the arts the keynote, aside from sheer, bewildering diversity, was symbolism. Novelists sought to use physical details as symbols to evoke new levels of emotional and esthetic perception, instead of contenting themselves with realistic portrayals. Marcel Proust developed an elaborate analysis of hidden motives and of the mysterious meaning of seemingly insignificant memories. Franz Kafka portrayed a world of inexplicable, menacing necessity in which the individual was helpless. James Joyce and others pioneered the stream-of-consciousness technique. In his novel, Ulysses, an extraordinary and complex account of a single day in Dublin, Joyce combined puns, parodies, scraps of recollection, fragments of foreign languages—any and all elements to convey the workings of the unconscious of the author himself. Joyce defied the bounds of traditional literary language as well as the conventional theme and substance of the novel. Some critics wondered whether the novel as a literary form could survive further experimentation.

Like the novelists, many poets portrayed a dreary, meaningless world through symbols. In *The Waste Land* T. S. Eliot expressed the doubt and

Dada Art: *The Persistence of Memory* by Salvador Dali (1931).

torment of his age, while experimenting with new poetic forms. Paul Valéry carried on the Symbolist tradition in French poetry, while Luigi Pirandello, who wanted to convey a psychological rather than literal reality, brought new dramatic methods to the theater. His plays defied dramatic conventions in their effort to deal with problems of emotional despair, and they also placed great demands on their audience. In his *Six Characters in Search of an Author,* two sets of characters appeared simultaneously on stage, each offering its own version of the truth; the audience was left to draw its own conclusion.

Thus the symbolism and personalism already visible in poetry before the war were extended to other fields—heightened by the awareness of Freudian psychology and by the despair of the interwar years. More than before, writers also attacked the hollowness of bourgeois values and morality, urging an individual ethic that could be truly genuine. In the same spirit, many, like André Gide in France, a self-professed homosexual, widely publicized their own deviations from conventional morality. Writers in all fields felt free to experiment with new forms of expression, defying conventions of grammar and language as well as the standard forms of poetry or drama. Some saw experiment as desirable for its own sake, for aesthetic reward. Far more saw it as essential to convey the irrationality of man and man's world.

Defiance of convention was also apparent in music and painting. Arnold Schönberg devised a new twelve-tone scale—a highly mathematic scheme that stressed atonality. In painting Picasso and other cubists turned away from austere, geometrical designs toward experimentation with a whole range of styles. Picasso's work increasingly featured grotesque shapes and the use of strong colors. A new group called the Dadaists painted ordinary objects in weird settings and combinations to portray the starkness and horror of life. On the other hand, artists like Paul Klee and Piet Mondrian turned toward completely nonrepresentational abstract art.

The interwar years established a new architectural style, led by Walter Gropius and the Bauhaus school in Germany. The new style owed much to abstract art and tried to capture the same cleanness and severity of line. The architects sought to challenge tradition. They eschewed copying styles from the past, a practice that had been sacred since the Renaissance; instead they wanted their buildings to be functional, each to serve the specific purpose for which it was intended.

Leading Cultural Trends

It is not enough to sketch the outlines of the major trends in the arts and sciences. We must ask: what do they add up to?

First, the interwar years did not see basic departures from the more fundamental innovations of the previous intellectual generation. Belief in relativism was merely sharpened in the arts as in science. No new syntheses were worked out. The division of philosophy was in this sense particularly revealing. There were stark anti-rationalists, like the existentialists, whose approach prevented them from working out a general system. There were stark rationalists, the logical positivists, whose approach turned them either toward abstract mathematics or to empirical linguistics. There was no philosopher of genius capable of dominating an intellectual generation as Kant or Hegel had a century before. There was scant innovation in political theory. The divisions in ideas, together with the overriding belief in relativism—aside from pure mathematics—seemed to have killed philosophy in the traditional sense. Outside of philosophy the quarrel between rationalists and irrationalists continued. Freud and his followers were fundamentally rationalists, but many of the writers who used Freud neglected this element in their embrace with man's unconscious.

Second, there was a distinct tone of despair in much of the culture of the interwar years. The fascination with the purely irrational was one sign of this. Another, perhaps, was the absence of fundamental new departures despite the proliferation of new styles and fads. There was a frenzy to the culture of the 1920s that at times came close to superficiality. The causes of the despairing tone were twofold. The war itself and subsequent disorder played a major role, but so did the increasing realization of the implications of the ideas developed before the war—relativity and the unconscious, to cite just two examples.

Two historians captured much of the decades' mood, as their wide popularity attests. Oswald Spengler frankly stated that western civilization was in decline, entering a barren era like the last centuries of the Roman Empire. Arnold Toynbee agreed that western culture had broken down, but he hoped for a revival through a return to religious faith.

The insecurity of the time, based on the belief that western civilization had perhaps gone wrong long ago, combined with the desire for a certainty that science no longer seemed to offer, led many intellectuals back to the churches. To explain Europe's decline historians like Toynbee and Huizinga pointed to the Enlightenment's preoccupation with rationality and materialism; they were thus tempted to reject the heritage of the previous two centuries. Echoing this mood was a revived interest in religion and theology. The Protestant theologian Karl Barth sought to strip away liberal interpretations of dogma to get back to original Protestant orthodoxy. He believed that the churches were in large part deserted because of the compromises the clergy had made with religious truth. Man was sinful. Hell and damnation could not be wished away. Religion could explain why the world was in such a mess.

Finally, in addition to its note of despair and in spite of its lack of fundamental innovation, the culture of the interwar years had two immensely promising aspects. First, most intellectuals themselves modified or abandoned the self-conscious rejection of society that had characterized the mood of the later nineteenth century. They wanted to help. They sought contact with a broader public. The Bauhaus hoped to reintegrate the artist and society. The Dadaists, though immensely individualistic and delighting in shock effects, wanted to build a new and better society. The depression and the rise of Fascism greatly heightened the intellectuals' commitment to society. They took sides, mostly on the political left. The same commitment spread to the theologians. Barth and others were firm anti-Fascists and urged the churches to work for a new social order. Pope Pius XI, in his 1931 encyclical *Quadragesimo Anno*, confirmed the church's social mission by castigating the heartlessness of the capitalist order.

A second promising aspect of the interwar culture was the fact that the intellectuals found a new audience. Modern art shocked many traditionalists, including Adolf Hitler, who railed against the perversion of good Teutonic styles, such as sloping roofs on houses. The artists' defiance of conventional forms and language no doubt bewildered people who were still taught the conventions in school. For them the gap between popular culture and "high" culture widened and added to the confusion of the period. But the new styles, particularly in the visual arts, began to win converts. Knowledge of at least the catchwords of psychology and even physics spread widely. This meant that many people shared the uncertainty and despair of intellectuals themselves, but it also indicated that the gap between intellectuals and a part of society was closing and that many people were developing a new aesthetic appreciation.

The philosopher Alfred Whitehead, writing in the 1930s, did not share the deep pessimism of some of his contemporaries. He believed, however, that western civilization had unduly neglected the arts during the previous two centuries, and in so doing had ignored an important aspect of man's personality. Possibly, as Whitehead himself hoped, the interwar years would begin to remedy this deficiency. The development of a new architectural style was a striking achievement, for architecture is the most "social" of all the fine arts in that it depends on wide public backing. The imitative, showy, status-conscious architecture of the nineteenth century was indicative of the mood of the wealthier classes. The development of a new style suggested an important and healthy change in this mood. Finally, art reached a still wider public through the new medium of the film. Particularly in the 1930s, when the decade's socially conscious temper encouraged directors to treat themes of general importance, films of great esthetic subtlety gained wide popularity.

There was another point in which popular culture corresponded, if only indirectly, to some of the leading intellectual trends. The middle classes continued their emancipation from the rigid work and sexual ethic of the mid-1800s. The war heightened the independence of women by drawing them out of the home and into the war factories. Arranged marriage and chaperoned courtship declined rapidly in the middle classes after the war; women now felt free to smoke and drink in public and fashions became still less formal and restrictive. The quest for pleasure led to the establishment of new outlets for entertainment such as night clubs.

The Vitality of Popular Culture

Popular culture displayed some of the same frenzy that characterized formal culture, until the depression restored a more sober mood. Fad after fad gained attention in the 1920s as people sought to escape their nagging fear that the world had gone wrong. Newspapers, finding that their frivolous articles attracted wide readership, provided intensive coverage of particularly juicy crimes, the activities of the socially fashionable, and other diversions ranging from nudist movements to tales of the Loch Ness monster. Virtually all sports soared in popularity. Soccer football, both amateur and professional, drew huge crowds, as did tennis, automobile racing, bicycle racing, and every other type of athletic contest. There was a new passion for record-breaking. Pioneering airplane flights, such as Alan Cobham's flight to Australia from Capetown, as well as speed records on air, land, and sea, aroused great excitement. The interest in sports and achievements was not just from the spectator's standpoint. More Europeans than ever before actively participated in sports. Swimming, for example, which previously had been reserved for the upper classes in the cities, became a normal skill for middle- and working-class youths.

Fashions changed as new substances like rayon gave rise to new and less expensive clothes. Faddishness was the keynote in fashion, for leading designers changed their styles every year. But the general trend was toward greater looseness and sexuality. The popularity of glamorous movie stars added to the impression of a new interest in or new definition of the sexy female. Skirts were shorter, swimming suits more revealing, and cosmetics came into wide use—all of which allowed more and more women to approximate the new image of beauty. Without question there was now less difference between the upper-class and popular projection of female beauty than ever before, at least since Europe emerged from a tribal system. Relatedly, a new passion for the slim look developed among the middle classes.

This new popular culture was exceedingly important. Its hedonism was obviously a reaction to wartime tension and continuing insecurity. Since the tensions of the 1930s cut down the eager experiments and the search for pleasure, the culture of the 1920s must be understood as part of the history of a brief period. But it carried the seeds of something more durable, and many of its themes would reemerge after World War II. Europeans were groping toward a new kind of adaptation to the problems and possibilities of an advanced industrial society. Hedonism was part of this adaptation. Europeans sought new kinds of pleasure in sports, in diverting entertainment and news, and in fashions. A new interest in sex was also suggested, though there were few signs that actual sexual behavior had yet changed, apart from a new elite of freewheeling artists and movie stars. The new culture involved an interest in further development of the human personality, of which the mania for record-breaking and the increasing freedom allowed to women, particularly in recreational activities and dress, were symptomatic. For all the faddishness of the new culture, the interests of many Europeans were broadened as a new device, called the radio, exposed them in increasing numbers to regular contact with music and drama. This was an important change, even if radio, the most popular "art," bore little resemblance to the formal arts. Boredom, a pervasive if unmeasurable part of the lives of most people throughout human history, probably declined.

POLITICS AND DIPLOMACY IN THE 1920s

The politicians displayed little of the creativity apparent among artists and intellectuals. The politicians were tired and stale; so, apparently, were the traditional isms. Since the liberals could find no new issues, they had no message and their strength declined. This tended to push the political spectrum to extremes, for the liberals constituted the central grouping around which consensus could most easily be formed. The liberals' decline left most democratic governments, most of the time, in the hands of conservatives who now represented property owners of all sorts, both urban and rural. The conservatives faithfully reproduced the timidity of their constituents, the people made desperate by inflation and terrified by the revolutionary left. Typically, the conservatives campaigned on a "Red scare" platform and when in power diligently did nothing at all.

Inadequacies of Economic Policy

Neither conservatives nor liberals could master the economic problems of the decade. In Britain the tradition of classical education and proud amateurism of the elite now served the country badly. As a remedy for mounting unemployment the Conservative party offered the dole, a system of relief payments inadequate to support the families of the unemployed and, smacking of outright charity, damaging to human dignity as well. Led by Winston Churchill as chancellor of the exchequer, the Conservatives in 1925 took their one bold initiative of the decade: they returned to the prewar gold standard, which reduced the purchasing power of the working classes and with it the vitality of the economy. French liberals tried to ignore the economy while stressing more traditional issues such as the power of the Catholic Church; they failed to solve the inflation in 1924 just as they would fail to meet the depression eight years later.

The most surprising deficiency was found among the socialists, who were not wedded to the existing economic order. In almost every country the socialists lost their nerve. They had more power than ever before and they loyally supported parliamentary democracy, but their new responsibility frightened them. Confused by the existence of Communist groups to their left, they thought they owed it to democracy to prove they were respectable by not pressing hard for major reforms. When in power in 1924, the leader of the British Labour party, Ramsay MacDonald, did nothing on the home front, thus showing how mild his party was; he made the bold move of recognizing the Soviet Union, but this did little for the British economy. German socialists returned to power in 1928 but they had no program left at all. To complete the tragedy, despite the fact that socialists had completely forsaken any longing for revolution, the socialist parties still frightened a considerable part of the electorate. Their strength neither produced vital reforms nor served to build a new political consensus.

Politics in Britain and France

The British and French governments stumbled along with apparent success in the 1920s, but this should not conceal their fundamental caution and conservatism. Britain eliminated two prewar problems: women gained

New Political Currents in Weimar Germany: Demonstration for peace in Berlin, 1921.

the vote, as did those adult males who had previously been unenfranchised; Ireland (except Protestant Ulster) gained virtual independence in 1922 after two years of violent struggle between British troops and the nationalist Sinn Fein ("We ourselves") party that had arisen in 1918. Ireland declared itself a republic only during World War II, but for Britain the distraction of the age-old Irish question seemed ended. There was little to trouble political harmony, aside from the massive general strike in 1926. One decisive change did take place: the Liberal party declined dramatically and by 1922 had been replaced by Labour as the second major party. British politics were more polarized than they had been for decades, as campaigns between Labour and Conservative candidates took on overtones of class struggle. But both major parties accepted the political system. Britain's problem was not strife but the absence of strife, for the problems of the economy begged for attention. Conservatives retained power with only brief interruptions, providing an image of saneness but little more.

Polarization in French politics was more serious. The leading republican party, the Radicals, could no longer win elections on its own; after 1924 its strength declined further with each election. To form a government the Radicals sought the support of socialists, in the traditional united left approach. But the Radicals were opposed to any social or economic reform, and once in power they invariably split from the socialists and united with outright conservatives. It became increasingly difficult to form a political coalition that could agree on any positive policy. On both right and left there were new groups that rejected the existing political system altogether. The Communist party used its few parliamentary votes to try to discredit the government. More important, it took to the streets, sending bands of its followers to disrupt opposition political meetings. Several groups on the right, some of them fascist, replied in kind. In 1924 a new organization, the "Patriotic Youth," rose with the crest of the depression, appealing to the middle classes and to veterans to resist the Communist threat and replace parliament with authoritarian rule. The French republic tended to resolve its worst crises by appealing to a strong leader, on the model of Clemenceau during the war, to run a national ministry composed of representatives from various parties. The inflation question, for example, was settled on this basis. After the government elected in 1924 failed to solve the problem, the conservative leader Raymond Poincaré formed a coalition ministry and ultimately stabilized the currency. As a result the conservative coalition won the election of 1928. But this pattern was troubling, for it suggested that the normal party system could not solve major problems. Moreover Poincaré himself resolutely avoided dealing with any of the other pressing difficulties facing France.

The Weimar Experiment

The big political question mark was Germany. The Weimar Republic, so called because its constitution was drawn up in the small town of Weimar, had an unhappy birth. It was associated with defeat in war, for the German military regime had refused to sign even the armistice, leaving this to the new civilian authorities. Many Germans believed that their country had been "stabbed in the back" by Jews or socialists or politicians in general, causing her to lose a war that the military could have won. Then too the new regime had to sign the inglorious Versailles treaty. The political strife of the republic's early years left its mark. Could a regime launched amid near–civil war and repeated political assassination easily root itself among the German people?

During the tumultuous years right after the war, particularly when the socialists controlled the government before the new constitution was drawn up in 1919, the government failed to bring about any meaningful reforms. In essence there was a political revolution—a republic replacing a monarchy

—without a social revolution. Weimar achieved only minor land reform, leaving the Junker landlords untouched in the east. The army's high command, closely linked to the Junkers, was intact; the socialists needed the army to put down riots and, moreover, they were afraid to incur further nationalist criticism by attacking this bastion of German strength. Big business was similarly untouched. The civil service was not purged, and many bureaucrats resented the new regime and tried to sabotage its decrees. Most of these traditional forces learned to live with the republic, but their primary loyalties were elsewhere. An attack on any of these forces would have involved revolution—something the socialists shied away from in Germany as they did in all the democratic countries. Did they thereby doom their own democracy?

No one can prove with certainty that Germans were so inexperienced with democracy and so attached to firm authority that Weimar's ultimate failure was inevitable. But the balance of evidence is against this proposition. The republic's constitution was the most advanced of any major European power. It provided for women's suffrage and for popular referenda on major issues. Reversing prewar German practice it made the ministers responsible to parliament. The three-class voting system was abolished in Prussia, and the Prussian state government remained firmly democratic, normally under socialist control; its police force, for example, was purged of elements disloyal to the republic. By 1924 the republic had won at least passive loyalty from most Germans. Communists and rightist groups, notably the National Socialist (Nazi) party, had earlier rejected the regime altogether and tried to hamper it in parliament and in the streets. Their strength was limited, however, after the immediate postwar confusion ended. German conservatives were represented primarily by the Nationalist party, which, unlike the conservative groups in France, retained strong monarchist loyalties as well as great resentment against the Versailles treaty. But by 1924 the party was brought into a government coalition and had tacitly accepted the new regime.

Apart from the Nationalists, the German political spectrum in 1924 was not unlike the French—which was its main problem. The political center was weak. A variety of small parties maintained a fundamentally liberal tradition, hoping for minor social reforms while preserving the new regime. They could rule only with the help of socialists or conservatives, yet when they leaned on one they automatically antagonized the other. Forming and preserving governments required great skill and it was difficult to decide on major initiatives.

Yet the republic functioned. Under the leadership of Gustav Stresemann, who served as prime minister or foreign minister from 1923 to 1929, the government settled the problem of inflation, achieved some minor but rewarding revisions in the Versailles settlement, and regained a place as a major power. But there were no exciting gains. The dullness characteristic of all the democracies during the 1920s was positively dangerous in Germany, for many groups were not actively loyal to the regime. In 1928 the Nationalist party again began to pull away from the regime, allying with the Nazis. Would the republic have collapsed from nationalist pressures alone? There is no reason to assume so, but no way of proving the contrary. What is certain is that the regime did not have enough solid support to survive a catastrophe and, as in other democratic countries, divisions within the government prevented economic reforms, thus making catastrophe likely.

German Diplomacy

At a time when the government should have been concentrating on domestic problems, it had to work for diplomatic changes. Even socialist governments ignored the provisions of the Versailles treaty limiting the size and weaponry of the German army. In 1922 Germany signed the Rapallo pact with Russia, Europe's other pariah, which promised friendship and neutrality and secretly allowed the German army to maneuver and to develop new weaponry in Russia in exchange for industrial and technical aid. Stresemann continued to follow this tactic but added to it. France had initially tried to enforce the Versailles treaty as rigorously as possible, believing that her security depended on German weakness. When the Germans lagged in their reparations payments, the French in 1923 occupied the entire Ruhr. The move failed, and both Germany and France sought to reconcile their differences. Under the Dawes plan, France agreed to a revision of the annual reparations payments and pulled out of the Ruhr.

In 1925 the major powers signed a series of treaties at Locarno that guaranteed the integrity of the Franco-German and German-Belgian frontiers, with Italy and Great Britain serving as additional guarantors. Stresemann did not make the same commitments about Germany's eastern boundaries but signed arbitration treaties with Poland and Czechoslovakia. Germany was in turn admitted to the League of Nations. Four years later Stresemann accepted the Young Plan that called for a reduction in reparations payments and put an end to the allied occupation of the Rhineland, which had been stipulated by the Versailles treaty.

Stresemann's policy was clear: he would fulfill Germany's treaty obligations but he would press steadily for their revision, knowing full well that the German army was gaining strength, in part through the pact with Russia, in case negotiation failed. Germany, in other words, did not take defeat lying down. Indeed the Nationalist party bitterly opposed the Young plan because it confirmed Germany's obligations to pay any reparations at all. Many historians have argued that Germany's pressure to revise Versailles reflected a fundamental aggressiveness that would inevitably lead to Hitler.

Given the terms of the treaty, only a revolution in diplomatic posture, far greater than any European power had yet undergone, could have brought Germany into tame submission.

The Spirit of Locarno

The Locarno spirit, a mood of international harmony that lasted through 1929, also reflected the western powers' second thoughts about the Versailles treaty. The British were not sure they had treated the Germans properly and they grew suspicious of the French. The French remained fearful of Germany, but after the failure of the Ruhr occupation, caused in part by the people's refusal to tolerate the strain and expense required, France adopted a defensive mood. The French formed defensive alliances with Poland, Czechoslovakia, Rumania, and Yugoslavia—a pale imitation of the prewar alliance system that had distracted Germany on the east. They also began building the Maginot line—a massive string of forts to defend France from German attack. Here was the epitome of France's retreat to a defensive stance. The line was an absurd undertaking, however, since it was designed only for use against weapons and tactics of the last war. In essence French policy depended on normal relations with Germany.

The Locarno spirit encouraged such pious gestures as the Kellogg-Briand pact of 1928, which outlawed aggressive war and was dutifully signed by the nations of the world. There was a large dose of unreality in the diplomacy of the 1920s. The German problem was the only major one being tackled. Russia was largely ignored, although most countries recognized the revolutionary regime. The American problem was also ignored, as the American government stuck stubbornly to isolation, emerging only for initiatives like the Kellogg pact and for an endless round of abortive disarmament conferences. Nevertheless American capital was pouring into Europe, particularly into Germany, as was American culture.

Yet the European states behaved as if the rules of the diplomatic game were unchanged from prewar years. Both Britain and France had colonial troubles. France faced repeated rebellions in Morocco and in its new mandate of Syria. In India the Congress party, led by Mahatma Gandhi, took shape and conducted a series of acts of civil disobedience while avoiding outright violence. In the later 1930s Britain began to prepare for India's independence. Also in the 1930s Japan's invasion of China revealed the dramatic decline of Europe's power in the Far East. But in Europe the merry dance continued, as if Europe were still the center of the world. There was just enough truth in that assumption for Europe to start another world war.

Stresemann died in 1929, worn out by his efforts to win acceptance for the Young Plan in Germany. The spirit of Locarno, which meant fundamentally a policy of negotiation to align Germany's diplomatic position with her actual power in Europe, may have been dying a natural death. Like the political stability of the 1920s it seems in retrospect shallow, perhaps doomed to failure. Certainly it could not survive the shock of the depression.

ECONOMIC COLLAPSE

The German economy began to falter in 1928, largely because of declining sales to eastern and southern Europe where the plunge of raw materials prices had caused an economic slump two years before. Germany's problems were heightened by the withdrawal of American capital as American investors sought to take advantage of the soaring stock market at home. Many American investments in central Europe had been for unproductive projects like fancy new town halls. Given their reparations obligations, Germany and Austria could repay American loans only by taking out new American loans. In 1928 this process was interrupted and in 1929, with the stock market crash, it was doomed.

Banks failed, first in Austria and Germany, soon after the American crash. Credit was restricted everywhere and, coming so close on the heels of inflation, faith in the economic system was severely shaken. Both developments rapidly reduced purchases of industrial goods, and with sales down production levels tumbled despite massive reductions in prices. In Germany production had fallen 39 percent by 1932. Profits declined, wages fell and unemployment increased enormously. Germany was hardest hit, but Britain, already in economic doldrums, suffered severely. France and Italy seemed immune for a brief time, but by 1932 France was in serious trouble; the French had never managed to recover predepression levels of production or employment before World War II. The depression touched even fascist Italy and hit hard at the more industrial states of Scandinavia and the Low Countries.

Impact of the Depression

All major social classes suffered from the depression. Peasants found their meager earnings further reduced by the collapse of urban purchasing power. The living standards for French peasants fell almost a third. The middle class was hit by declining profits and the loss of stock market investments. Shopkeepers suffered as their clients' purchasing power dropped. White-collar workers and professional people were thrown out of work. Seven thousand German engineers lost their jobs. Thousands of teachers were unemployed—40 thousand in Germany alone—as governments cut their payrolls. New university graduates could not find work at all. The proportion of unemployment in the salaried middle class was almost as high as in the working class. Coming soon after the disastrous inflation and the long-standing employment problems of professional people, the depression seemed to seal the doom of many segments of the middle class.

Workers suffered most severely. In Britain 22 percent of the working class was unemployed by 1932, while almost six million workers lost their jobs in Germany. France, suffering much less, still had 850,000 unemployed. Sheer numbers tell only part of the story. Many workers endured months, even years of unemployment. They survived on some insurance payments, on charity, or on the earnings of their wives (for sometimes women, whose salaries were lower, found it easier to keep jobs than men), but they could do no more than survive. Their standard of living—and their morale—collapsed. Unemployment or the threat of unemployment reduced many workers to sullen apathy while stirring others to new anger.

The very magnitude of the depression made recovery difficult. Depressions were supposed to cure themselves, as prices fell low enough to permit a rise in consumption. But so many people were out of work and confidence was so severely shaken that this pattern was slow to develop. The depression reached its depth in 1932–1933, except for France where it occurred a bit later. Production then started to rise and by 1938 the British economy was turning out more goods than ever before. But in none of the major democracies was the depression fully cured by 1939. In Britain, for example, there were still over a million and a half workers unemployed. The depression's long duration, as well as its intensity, made it by far the worst in industrial history.

Government Policies

Governments reacted badly to the deepening crisis. If it is true that politicians often approach new problems with the same set of old solutions, then Europe's leaders between the wars had a peculiar genius for this. For example, remembering their governments' irresponsibility in financing World War I and what damage it did to property and the propertied classes, the leaders set about to prevent inflation and to balance their budgets. With rapidly falling tax revenues, an inevitable result of the production collapse, expenditures were strictly curtailed. In Britain the unemployment insurance program ran out of funds under the impact of depression, but the government refused to commit tax revenues to it until 1934, and even then the duration of assistance was severely limited. During the first years of the depression no government took new measures to help the unemployed; understandably, workers' suffering increased and their anger became intense. Budget-balancing forced governments to dismiss thousands of state employees, which deepened the crisis for the middle class. And, perhaps most difficult to fathom, some governments actually increased taxation. The German government raised taxes on shopkeepers already hard hit and angered by what they believed was the state's use of their money to help workers. All these measures left many segments of the population in misery. They also deepened the depression, for by reducing purchasing power governments only exacerbated what had been the real problem in the first place.

Governments also turned to nationalist economics: they raised their protective tariffs and abandoned any pretense of financial cooperation. Germany suspended reparations payments. France, for a time the strongest power financially, refused any assistance to her neighbors. All European countries except Finland stopped payment on their war debts to the United States, which gave American nationalists a topic of conversation for many decades thereafter. Britain and the United States abandoned the gold standard. Many countries developed export subsidies and tried to find ways to save themselves at the expense of other countries. These policies did little good. International monetary chaos and new trade barriers simply impeded trade. It was a sorry performance.

POLITICS IN THE DEPRESSION

The depression exacerbated all the symptoms of political sickness visible in the 1920s. The democracies were paralyzed, incapable of positive action. Their economic policies were only one sign of this; diplomacy was affected as well.

Politics was the only outlet for the massive grievances the depression provoked, and everywhere political polarization increased. To publicize their plight French peasants engaged in demonstrations and French workers conducted an unprecedented national strike in 1936. These were important developments but they mainly supplemented political action. In countries where unemployment was more severe, strikes were pointless and union membership declined since workers lacked money for union dues. Workers therefore focused on politics. Because they wanted to express their rising protest, many of them turned from their normal politics to something new— usually the left. In most industrial countries on the continent a substantial group of workers abandoned socialism for Communism.

Some elements of the peasantry and the middle classes also turned to Communism, an indication that there is no perfect correlation between social class and politics. But most showed their protest by turning to the right. Radical rightist groups, including Fascists, talked to the peasants about the need to protect agriculture and the virtues of rural life. Peasants saw in Nazism and other rightist movements not only assistance in the current economic crisis but also restoration of the values of the peasantry against the corrupting influence of urban life. Not surprisingly the most traditionalist villages in Germany, those which had made the least adaptation to commercial agriculture, turned most solidly Nazi after 1928. Shopkeepers and clerks were wooed by rightist condemnations of the evils of big business and the labor movements alike. Artisans were told that their skills were important, that small-shop production should be protected against the industrial giants, and that guilds should be restored in some fashion. In other words the depression tempted many people in the peasantry and middle classes to turn back the clock, to protest against the institutions and values of modern society. The rightists were there to tell them it could be done. The rightists also appealed vigorously to nationalism and usually to anti-Semitism. In most continental countries substantial segments of the middle classes and peasantry abandoned traditional liberal and conservative parties and embraced the radical right.

Politics, then, became increasingly enmeshed in class conflict. Every action produced a reaction. A Communist surge scared the good burghers and drove more of them to the radical right, which in turn, scared the workers.

The Results of Polarization

Political polarization made positive government action almost impossible in many countries; any effort to please one group aroused another to new fury. Government inaction increased despair on all sides, thus feeding polarization and contributing to the vicious circle. Only one of the new democracies, Czechoslovakia, could withstand the pressure. Austria, Germany, and Spain succumbed to the dubious delights of authoritarian rule, as Italy had during a less severe crisis a decade earlier. The western democracies, better established, survived. Britain was indeed immune to the extremes of polarization. Belgium and to a lesser degree Holland were deeply affected, though in both countries Fascism reached its peak around 1936 and then subsided. In Belgium and Czechoslovakia the depression intensified nationalities disputes. French-speaking Walloons were increasingly challenged by Flemings in Belgium and many riots broke out. Germans in Czechoslovakia formed a Nazi-inspired party following Hitler's takeover in Germany. Finally, France was virtually torn asunder by political strife.

In Britain the Conservatives retained power through most of the 1930s. A weak Labour government took office in 1929 and had to face the first onslaught of depression. It did very badly, striving for a balanced budget at the expense of the workers. Not surprisingly, most workers abandoned the Labour party in the 1932 election, but unlike their continental counterparts few of them went further left. Hence the Conservatives were in charge, though Labour began to pick up growing support during the decade as economic conditions remained bleak. The Conservatives did take some important economic initiatives: they put tax revenues into unemployment relief;

developed programs to retrain workers and encouraged technical improvements in export industries; and sponsored a substantial housing program.
In other words, the Conservatives began to modify the hands-off policy
with which the government had first greeted the depression. But essentially
the Conservatives merely tinkered instead of experimenting boldly. They
did not come close to ending unemployment and were unable to boost national morale. Apathy and discouragement were Britain's counterpart to
political polarization and were almost as damaging. British diplomacy in
this decade faithfully reflected the timidity of the government and the confusion of the population.

Paralysis in France

Beginning with the election of 1932, the center of the French political
spectrum rapidly eroded. The Radical party had no solution to the depression; like the British Conservatives the Radicals wanted to weather the
storm without making any significant changes in government policy. As
the depression deepened, French voters turned away from the Radicals.
Ironically the Radicals had held office more than any other party during
the decade, but this was because French politics was so divided that only
a do-nothing government could be agreed upon. Socialist and Communist
strength increased steadily through the elections of 1936, and the Communists continued their rise thereafter. On the right a variety of groups arose
advocating an authoritarian regime and a nationalist solution to class conflict. These rightist groups used the streets as their arena and disdained
parliament altogether. They organized uniformed bands—each with distinctively colored shirts—to break up opposition meetings and to demonstrate. In
February 1934, France came close to civil war when the rightists seized on
a rather minor government scandal to attack the Chamber of Deputies.
Riots and clashes occurred periodically thereafter, as the socialists and
Communists armed to meet the rightist threat.

The French had one last chance for salvation. In 1936 the Popular Front
government took office under the socialist Léon Blum. Properly frightened
by Hitler's success in Germany, the Communists, under a directive from Russia, everywhere professed their willingness to cooperate with reformist parties. They joined with the Radicals and socialists for an overwhelming
election triumph; for the first time the socialists were the strongest party in
France. To confirm this victory, over a million French workers conducted
sit-down strikes to shut their factories; without violence, they were telling
the government that major reform was necessary. Blum acted quickly. He
brought employers and union leaders together in the Hôtel Matignon to
settle the strike. The resulting Matignon agreements laid the foundation
for the welfare state in France. Employers granted labor a 40-hour week,
paid vacations, a minimum wage scale, and the right to collective bargaining.

But after this great step forward everything then went wrong. The social reforms were expensive and some of them inappropriate for the depression situation. With a reduction in the number of hours worked, productivity did not rise to match the wage gains. Furthermore Blum was restrained by the uncertain nature of his coalition. The Communists had refused to enter his government—they would not tie themselves this closely to reformism— and so they were free to peck away at the socialists' left flank. They made striking gains in the trade union movement, wresting control of the main national federation from the socialists. Given the Communists' policy and the fact that the socialists were still a minority party, Blum depended on the cooperation of the Radicals. But the Radicals were frightened by the Matignon reforms and refused to countenance further steps. They pressed Blum to keep France on the gold standard—the middle-class symbol of financial orthodoxy—despite the fact that it weakened France's export position. Blum finally abandoned the gold standard, but too late. On the right the Popular Front government aroused massive hostility: many property owners were frightened by the government's reforms; many nationalists were offended by the fact that Blum was Jewish.

Blum resigned after little more than a year in office. The depression was still unresolved and political polarization continued unabated. Weak coalitions between radicals and various conservative groups produced stand-pat governments while the Communists, already a major factor, gained strength in local elections. The Radical rightists, though unrepresented in parliament because they had boycotted the 1936 elections, increased in number and ferocity. Outright Fascist groups arose, claiming over a million supporters. A sinister political assassination society, the Cagoulards, took shape as well. The radical right began to chant the slogan "Better Hitler than Blum," a sign that political polarization had overcome even traditional French nationalism.

Defensive Diplomacy

Political and economic tensions inevitably dominated the diplomacy of the major democracies. Every diplomatic issue had ideological implications. For the conservatives Russia was the logical enemy and even British conservatives were tempted to compromise with the Fascist powers in order to concentrate on the Communist threat. The leftists had a strong pacifist streak that reduced their willingness to support traditional diplomatic and military measures even against the Fascists. In such a situation the easiest course for a government to follow was to do nothing; in that way, no one would be offended. The democratic powers were constantly on the defensive in the 1930s. They never acted, only reacted to diplomatic initiatives. Typically their reaction was to pretend that nothing had happened.

French diplomacy was completely paralyzed from 1936 onward because of internal stresses. France depended on Britain's taking the lead, but Britain was also incapable of firm action. The blind led the blind.

TOWARD A BRIGHTER FUTURE

Europe's democracies were able to resolve the social and economic problems of the depression—but only after the trauma of another world war. Despite the picture of gathering gloom, some bases of their action were suggested before the war began.

The Scandinavian Welfare State

Led by Sweden, the Scandinavian countries began to build a new welfare state during the 1920s. Reform-minded socialist parties governed these countries for most of the interwar years, though often in coalition with liberals and conservatives. The progressive labor and welfare legislation they enacted during the 1920s enabled these governments to meet the depression head-on. During the 1930s Sweden boasted the lowest rate of unemployment in western Europe. Because the government also launched a large-scale housing program, the Swedish population was the best-housed in the world. Collective bargaining was encouraged so that labor strife was kept to a minimum, and Sweden and the other Scandinavian countries largely avoided the paralyzing political strife that afflicted most of the democracies to the south. Pressures on the far right and the far left were mild. Workers had no reason to abandon reformist socialism that was bringing them so many gains.

Perhaps more notable was the flexibility of the propertied classes, which could tolerate if not actively welcome new state welfare programs. The Scandinavian countries had the advantage of small size and ethnic cohesion. All except Finland had a well-established parliamentary and democratic tradition and, a factor not to be minimized, they had also escaped the ravages and strains of the war. Their marked successes suggest the distortions the war caused elsewhere, particularly among the middle classes.

Achievements of the Popular Front

The Popular Front government in France was not a complete failure. It placed social legislation on the books that served as the basis for the French welfare state less than a decade later. It also provided ideas and leaders for the wartime resistance against Nazism that played such an important role in renewing French society. There were other hopeful signs in France. The vigor of working-class protest and the signs of peasant discontent added to the troubles of the 1930s but also suggested a new level of lower-class expectation that was sorely needed. Workers in their 1936 strikes were demanding a fairer share of the national product and unprecedented leisure time. The economy badly needed this push from below if consumption power were to be spread. At yet another level, among elements of the middle class and peasantry, new types of Catholic organizations were taking hold that sought to come to grips with social and economic problems. They stressed the importance of technological advance and the reduction of social tension by positive action on behalf of the lower classes. Here was the genesis of the progressive Christian Democratic movement in France that blossomed in the wartime resistance.

Keynesian Economics

From John Maynard Keynes in Britain came a new economic theory, an alternative to orthodox liberal economics short of socialism. His message, proclaimed in 1936 in his *General Theory of Employment, Interest, and Money,* called for government manipulation of the economy. The government could use its power to tax and to spend and, through its control of the money supply, it could heat up the economy or cool it down. He blasted the abstractions of the classic liberal economists and urged instead practical action, here and now, to cure the depression. Few in Europe listened to Keynes before World War II. His lessons in part gave theoretical support to the measures that had already been devised to meet the depression; they were most clearly applied in programs of the American New Deal, which tackled the economic problems of the decade more successfully than any European government outside Scandinavia. Keynes' advice was gradually absorbed in Europe, however, and was widely applied after World War II.

These developments were admittedly just straws in the wind. They help explain why European democracies could gain a new lease on life, but this lease had yet to be signed. Until 1940 the major democracies wallowed in fear. Their inability to resolve the depression or to take diplomatic initiatives nurtured more fear. Political polarization increased. The dynamism of the interwar years came not from the leading democracies but from a much newer kind of political organization: the totalitarian state. The rise of totalitarianism heightened the despair of the democracies. By 1938 the policies of the totalitarian states gave rise to a new fear, then a mournful certainty, that war was inevitable.

10 THE AUTHORITARIAN REGIMES

Totalitarianism emerged as a form of government for the first time in the two decades between the wars. It had been suggested before at the city-state level and propounded many times in political theory, but never applied on a large scale. The reason for this was that totalitarianism depended on modern technology. It needed high-speed communications to inform the central police apparatus and to allow the central government to reach individual citizens regularly with its message. Totalitarian regimes are bent on commanding all of society's resources to achieve an overriding goal. In a sense they represent the culmination of many centuries of governmental centralization in Europe and as such, their motives may not be as new as their means. Would Napoleon I or even Louis XIV have instituted totalitarian regimes if they had possessed the appropriate technology? The question is worth asking even if it cannot be answered precisely.

THE NATURE OF TOTALITARIANISM

Totalitarian regimes vastly extended the functions of the central state, and in this regard there can be no doubt of their newness. Moreover they went well beyond traditional dictatorships or authoritarian monarchies in seeking to command active loyalty, not just passive obedience, from their subjects. Totalitarianism reflected modern expectations and political awareness as well as modern technology. It developed unprecedented police controls and strove to conquer the minds of its subjects because traditional deference to authority could no longer be relied upon.

Totalitarian political organizations, which sprang up as Fascist or Communist parties in many democratic countries, had distinctive characteristics: they were firmly controlled from the center; they relied heavily on propaganda and group loyalties; they were intolerant of parliamentary processes and of other political groups; and they worked persistently to transform the state into their own version of what it should be. With their firm party hierarchy and their intense discipline, they had already established the outline for such a state.

It would be convenient if we could carry generalizations further and elaborate on an overall definition of totalitarian states and parties and then recount what happened in individual cases. But totalitarianism quickly becomes an abstraction and the actual behavior of most totalitarian states raises some questions about the accuracy of any definition. Furthermore there is very little similarity in the causes of totalitarianism from one state to the next.

Students of politics have spent considerable time seeking types of people likely to respond to totalitarian politics. The effort may be useful but it does little to explain the actual origins of the totalitarian states. Communism, where it gained an inroad, appealed primarily to workers. Fascism won few workers. Even when it was in power Nazism failed to win the active loyalty of most manufacturing workers; its strength lay with the middle classes and the peasantry. Furthermore only the Nazi regime came to power with anything approaching mass support. At best the search for authoritarian personality types or generalizations about a desire to escape the uncertainties of individual freedom only explain why totalitarian regimes remained in power so easily. They do not get at the causes of totalitarianism.

Regional explanations are a bit more helpful. Totalitarian regimes took power in countries lacking a liberal or democratic political tradition as strong as that of Britain or France, or in countries accustomed to an active central state. At the same time, apart from Russia, most of the totalitarian states arose in new nations where the existing regimes lacked traditional legitimacy; thus although Germany, through Prussia, had a strong state tradition, it was itself a new nation. Totalitarianism also arose where nationalism remained unsatisfied, in countries that had recently been defeated or disappointed in war. In these states industrialization had not dislodged a traditional social order headed by a powerful aristocracy. It was certainly no accident that the new regimes gained power in countries dominated by landed estates, where peasants had been repressed for centuries and prevented from developing an independent political voice. There was more natural hostility to industrialization which a totalitarian movement could seize upon, than there had been in the west. At the same time supporters of industrialization, accustomed to heavy reliance on the central state, might turn to totalitarianism as the only way to cut through resistance. The regional explanations are perforce very general. They do not explain why totalitarianism arose in Germany—an advanced industrial country with at least a limited liberal tradition—as well as in Russia, where industrialization was only beginning.

Varieties of Regimes

Three kinds of new regimes developed between the wars, all proceeding from different sets of causes. At one extreme was Russian Communism. Totalitarianism followed naturally from the Russian Revolution for two related reasons. A successful revolution invariably produces an authoritarian regime to defend itself from enemies both at home and abroad. With the technology available to them, the Communists made this authoritarian phase totalitarian and were able to perpetuate it on this basis. Furthermore real totalitarianism, as it has been defined above, is revolutionary. Any effort to remake human loyalties and redirect society's resources to a single goal has to attack existing social and even familial relationships. The Communists were ideologically committed to precisely this goal.

At the other extreme was authoritarianism as it emerged in Poland or Spain in the 1920s. The authoritarian regimes were new. They had wide police powers. Although they tried to appeal to mass loyalties, they were committed to defending the existing social order. They were in fact called to power not by the masses but by the upper classes, above all the landlords who wanted the state to defend their interests against democratic pressures. These regimes were not really totalitarian, though they had some of the same trappings.

Finally there was Fascism. Fascist doctrine had revolutionary implications but it envisaged quite a different kind of revolution from the Communist model. Ideally suited for the construction of a totalitarian regime, Fascism stressed the primacy of the state, the need for authority, and the impotence of the individual. Yet in actual practice Fascism was often more authoritarian than totalitarian, because it, too, was bent on the defense of the existing social order. Franco's Spain used only the merest trappings of Fascism to decorate an authoritarian state. The Italian regime, more genuinely Fascist, never managed to construct a totalitarian state. Even Nazi Germany fell short of any abstract definition of totalitarianism. It did not, for example, mobilize all its resources for a higher goal, even the goal of war; it was in many ways less efficient in war than the German government during World War I.

All the new regimes were anti-liberal and all vastly extended the police power of the state. But to go beyond this we need more precision than the general labels of totalitarianism, authoritarianism, or even Fascism allow. One further point. Both the Communist and authoritarian systems that de-

veloped between the wars have proved immensely successful: they continued to flourish in Europe after World War II and have been exported to
other areas of the world. Nowhere has the Fascist form lasted more than
25 years. Was Fascism the product of a temporary combination of forces or
is it inherent in certain regions of Europe? Was Fascism part of a transient
stage of modernization or is it a permanent possibility in modern industrial
society? It is ironic that the least durable of the new political forms raises
the most questions.

COMMUNISM IN RUSSIA

Victorious in the civil war but faced with massive economic problems,
Lenin decided on a policy of relaxation in 1921. He replaced "War Communism" with a "New Economic Policy" (NEP), which he called "a step backward in order to go forward." The NEP was a radical departure from War
Communism and even represented a limited return to capitalism. The free
market was stressed, particularly in agriculture. Peasants were assessed a
special tax in kind, instead of being subjected to irregular requisitions, and
could sell their surplus at free-market prices. Small businesses were returned to private hands, while foreigners were encouraged to invest in new
industries. The state continued to own and operate all large-scale industries,
as well as banking, transportation, and foreign trade. It launched a variety
of programs including the training of engineers and rural electrification.

Under this relatively loose guidance the Russian economy surged forward once more. Agricultural production rose far more rapidly than industrial production; the latter reached 1913 levels only in 1926. Still, given the
vast dislocations of the revolution, this was no small achievement. In the
countryside the NEP encouraged a minority of the peasants, the substantial
kulaks, to acquire more land at the expense of the majority in order to produce more for the market. It thus furthered the growth of peasant capitalism that had begun with the Stolypin reforms before World War I.

Russia in the mid-1920s was in an anomalous situation. It had an authoritarian political apparatus, complete with a strong political police and
one-party rule that had been established right after the revolution. Its economic structure, which was far looser, functioned adequately though not
spectacularly; certainly it was a long way from achieving socialist ideals.
The country was almost completely isolated in diplomatic terms. The hoped-
for spread of revolution had not materialized, yet many Bolsheviks continued
to devote thought and effort to the international advance of Communism. A new leader, Joseph Stalin, resolved most of these anomalies and constructed a totalitarian state.

Stalinism

In 1922 Lenin suffered a stroke; he died two years later without providing for his successor. Lenin had held no high state office; in the Communist party he served as one of five members of the Politburo, which formulated policy for the party and through this guided the Soviet state. Lenin was a dictator, but he owed his rule to his ability consistently to persuade his fellows on the Politburo.

Stalin was a different sort altogether. His rise to power was based on his party position. An old-line Bolshevik, faithful to Lenin since 1903, Stalin became secretary of the Central Committee of the party in 1922; a post he held until his death in 1953. Stalin lacked Lenin's intellectual gifts, but was a skillful political manipulator. He had three formidable rivals for power after Lenin's death, among them the popular Leon Trotsky. Through shifting alliances among the rivals Stalin eliminated them one by one. Trotsky was exiled, finally settling in Mexico where Stalin, always on guard, had him assassinated in 1940. Other rivals for the time being were cast aside more gently. Stalin was completely in control by 1930, with supporters in all the principal party positions.

There was much of the opportunist in Stalin. He switched positions frequently in his fight for power, and in this he had much in common with the

Leaders of Soviet Russia:
Lenin and Stalin
in 1922.

Fascist dictators. But his victory was more than a personal triumph. It assured a renewal of the effort to revolutionize Russia.

Against Trotsky, who was a leading internationalist, Stalin asserted the principle of "socialism in one country." Most of the prerevolutionary Bolsheviks found it impossible to build a socialist society in Russia until the revolution took hold in the advanced industrial countries. Stalin disagreed. He proudly asserted Russia's ability to construct socialism on its own—an argument that appealed to Russian patriotism.

The principle of "socialism in one country" attracted a new generation of party managers and organizers, men who were impatient with ideological speculation and dependent for their own advancement on the party's role in Russia. These were the men Stalin was raising in the party machine. This principle also enhanced Stalin's own distrust of the outside world and echoed another theme in Russian history, resentment against the west.

The "socialism in one country" slogan had one very definite flaw however: there was precious little socialism in Russia. Stalin's next step, as he consolidated his power, was to replace the NEP with a policy of vigorous collectivization. He saw that Russia needed rapid industrialization if she was to stand firm against the outside world. Even more immediate was the crisis in the countryside. Peasants, particularly the kulaks, slowed their effort to increase agricultural production after 1925. Their reason was simple: industrial goods, whose output lagged, were so expensive that it seemed pointless to try to earn more money by market sales. To resolve this crisis, which reflected the power and the capitalist mentality of the kulaks, Stalin resolved on a collectivization of agriculture.

In 1928 the government began to force peasants to merge their land holdings into large collective farms. In this way Stalin hoped to end the power of the kulaks and create a rural social structure that would be more egalitarian and more efficient—and also easier for the government to control. When the kulaks resisted, they were attacked not only by government agents but by the poorer peasants as well. In their despair the kulaks killed their own livestock and smashed farm machinery. As a result famine returned to Russia and possibly as many as five million people died. By the end of 1933 the government had finally won. The kulaks were gone—killed, starved, or driven off to Siberia. Collective farms embraced the bulk of the Russian land; by 1939 95 percent of the farms had been collectivized. Peasants in the collectives were allowed to cultivate small plots of their own, but the basis of Russian agriculture was now a farm of 1000 acres or more, run by 60 to 200 peasant families, sometimes with a professional or party manager. The state encouraged steady improvements in techniques and set up tractor stations to rotate scarce farm machinery among the collectives.

The collectivization program was not a complete success, for it did not eliminate rural inequality. Some collectives were far more prosperous than others. Incentives were introduced that enabled good workers to receive far more than the less productive. More important, many peasants disliked the collectives and continued to hold their production to traditional levels. Hence the problem of supplying the cities with food remained, and the peasants' resistance to collectivization was the chief weakness of the Soviet economy.

Nevertheless, though agriculture advanced less rapidly than the government hoped, new machinery and new work arrangements had some effect. Agricultural productivity gradually improved and millions of excess farm hands became available for industrial work. This was fundamental to Stalin's unambiguous success in spurring industrialization.

The Five-Year Plans

A few months after the decision to collectivize the land, Stalin launched the first of three Five-Year Plans to industrialize Russia rapidly and systematically. The state took over the entire economy and guided it through a planning commission (*Gosplan*) that had been created in 1921. The Five-Year Plans set output goals for all manufacturing units; the commission allocated supplies, capital, and labor. Regional planning units actually served as large-scale, concentrated industrial firms. Labor unions, under strict party control, were called upon to preserve discipline, prevent strikes, and encourage productivity. The emphasis of the first Five-Year Plan, as well as the second, was on heavy industry, basic to industrial expansion and military equipment. Consumer goods were given little attention. Although some of the goals proved hopelessly optimistic, output in heavy industry soared, and by the end of the 1930s Russia was the world's third greatest industrial power.

Forced industrialization, a fundamental feature of Russia's totalitarianism, was successful but only at great human costs. Workers were deprived of the freedom to choose their jobs and were without any outlet for protest. Yet we must remember that industrialization under other systems had also involved compulsion and hardship. Moreover Russian workers, unlike their western counterparts, were given certain protections. The state inspected factories for safety and health conditions, provided old-age pensions and recreational facilities, and, most important, afforded guarantees against unemployment. Through local party and union activities, however hollow they may seem, workers gained some sense of participation and sociability. Without question, in Russia it was the state that guided and impelled workers to industrialize, rather than private capitalists as earlier in the west. It is not clear whether this factor made the process more painful or even less free for the workers involved in these early stages of industrialization.

Cultural Controls

To achieve full totalitarianism, the Communist state had to seek control of intellectual life. The Communists were militant atheists, hostile to religion. Rather than arouse needless opposition, they proceeded cautiously against the powerful Orthodox Church. Even Stalin did not try to abolish the Church, but he tightened state control over it, in order to make sure that the hierarchy did not undermine his rule. Formal intellectuals were kept in check more directly. After allowing an initial period of considerable intellectual freedom, the Communist party, under Stalin, set firm lines. Party loyalty was essential, as was avoidance of modern styles in art and literature. "Socialist realism" was bent toward the glorification of men of toil—a stereotype that doubtless stifled much creativity, especially in the fine arts. Like the Fascist regimes, the Communist state favored massive, grandiose styles in architecture, painting, and sculpture.

The key to the battle for men's minds lay not in restrictions but in education, to which the government devoted great attention and supplemented with a variety of youth groups. Education reduced illiteracy from 55 percent in 1914 to 20 percent by 1939. It provided the means for rapid advancement. Between 1933 and 1938 the state sent a million young people, many from the lower classes, into courses of higher education, thus producing a vast array of professional people. Education also provided the means to convert Russian youth to loyalty to the new regime. It stressed ideological indoctrination, while the youth groups directly trained future members of the Communist party.

In all its efforts, economic and ideological, the regime was backed by the powerful secret police. This did not mean that most Russians lived in constant terror, but police tactics could threaten ordinary people, as happened in the campaign against the kulaks and again in the great purges of 1934–1938. In 1934 one of Stalin's deputies was assassinated. Stalin, shaken by this, insisted on questioning the murderer himself. He then resolved on a brutal housecleaning. His old rivals of the 1920s were tried for treason and executed and all branches of the government were purged. Only a handful of the pre-1914 Bolsheviks, those completely loyal to Stalin, remained alive. The purge reached far down in the ranks of the Communist party and beyond—as many as eight million people were arrested, most of them subsequently deported to forced labor camps. Psychological pressure induced most of the prisoners to confess to treason they had not committed.

Why the purges? Stalin was a despot obsessed by unreal fears. As he got older he trusted fewer and fewer people. There was no one to stop him. The purges themselves, followed by a campaign of glorification of Stalin, created a mixture of fear and sycophancy that assured orthodoxy.

The formal political system was largely a facade for one-party rule, the party ruled in turn by Stalin. The constitution of 1936 set up a parliament based on universal suffrage and guaranteed all the traditional civil liberties.

From the parliament (the Supreme Soviet) came smaller executive commit-
tees, which in turn chose a president and a prime minister. The country had
also been divided into nominally independent republics—there were 11 of
these by 1936—to give at least a suggestion of autonomy to the many non-
Russian peoples.

In organization the Communist party, which actually held all power,
paralleled this constitutional structure. It was the only legal political party
and nominated all candidates for elective office. The party, the "vanguard
of the revolution," consistently tried to keep itself trim by admitting only
2 or 3 percent of the population as members. This was sufficient to guide
policy, to watch for deviations, and to provide a party member for all major
organizations, such as collective farms and local trade unions.

At the same time the party at the local levels encouraged a certain sense
of participation. Lenin had intended to guard against abuses of the central
state by vigorous self-criticism by leaders of their own mistakes and by
what he called "democratic centralism," through which each party echelon
elected the one above it, thereby ensuring democracy at the base of the
political pyramid. Stalin distorted both these safeguards. Democracy became spurious, as the party leadership selected the candidates for the lower
levels. Self-criticism was directed not to the leaders but to local bureaucrats. But there was an impression of some discussion, of some outlet for
popular participation. Party members often apologized for their mistakes,
which reassured the people that the regime was trying to build a new society, and occasionally remedied the mistakes.

One can express horror over the abuses of police power in Russia—eight
million people arrested in the purges!—while at the same time wax ecstatic
over Russia's achievements—a society industrialized, illiteracy almost completely wiped out! Russia created a totalitarian regime and used it, among
other things, to accomplish such goals as industrialization that invariably
involve considerable compulsion. Despite Stalin's paranoia the regime was
not simply bent on maintaining itself. It was not dependent on an aggressive foreign policy and it paid some heed to the principles of Marx and
Lenin. In these respects it differed from Fascist totalitarianism. For these
reasons also it has proved vastly more successful.

THE AUTHORITARIAN
REGIMES

Except for Finland and Czechoslovakia, which hung onto democratic
forms with difficulty, eastern Europe quickly yielded to authoritarian regimes after 1918, as did Spain and Portugal for roughly the same reasons.
After bitter unrest in 1920, including massive labor strikes, General Primo
de Rivera seized dictatorial power in Spain, though the monarchy was offi-

cially maintained. In 1926 Marshal Joseph Pilsudski staged a *coup d'etat* in Poland and established a military dictatorship. In the same year a military coup overthrew the recently formed republic of Portugal; the new government was soon taken over by Antonio Salazar, who was to rule for more than 30 years. Yugoslavia, torn by ethnic disputes among Serbs, Croats, and Slovenes, was converted to a monarchical dictatorship under King Alexander after 1928; parliament was dissolved and the constitution suspended. King Carol II of Rumania assumed dictatorial powers in 1930. Greece and Bulgaria remained constitutional monarchies in name, but they experienced constant conflicts between dictatorial kings and reactionary military cliques. Albania, Hungary, and the new Baltic republics turned to dictatorial governments outright.

The precise forms of the new regimes varied. Monarchies played an important role in several east European countries. Under Salazar Portugal moved closer to a Fascist model. Rather than abolish parliament and a constitution, the government founded a single party designed to instill loyalty and discipline among the people. Still, there were many common elements among the new regimes. They stressed one-man rule and glorification of the leader. They vigorously supported the established church—Catholic in some cases, Orthodox in others—and tried to enforce religious orthodoxy. They strengthened the government's police power and arrested all conceivable political enemies.

Causes of Authoritarianism

On the surface the authoritarian governments resulted from the wrangling and divisions of parliaments, to which none of the eastern and southern countries was really accustomed. In most cases the countries themselves were newly created; in almost all, parliamentary democracies were novel. A multitude of political parties quickly formed. Coherent policy was almost impossible. Hence an individual or a group, usually from the military, resolved to end the chaos.

Beneath this political surface the key problems in this eastern zone of Europe were land and economic development. Large estates predominated in most of these countries, and everywhere the majority of the population was rural. In Hungary .7 percent of the population owned 48.3 percent of the land; in Poland .6 percent owned 43 percent of the land. Parliamentary governments after World War I introduced very little land reform, except in Rumania where by 1922 only 7 percent of the land represented large holdings. Even in Rumania, the peasantry remained desperately poor while the erstwhile landlords received sufficient monetary compensation to maintain their traditional eminence. In all these areas rapid population growth added to the peasants' woes. In most cases rural unrest had been substantial before World War I; after 1918 it tended to take political forms, as peasant parties demanding land reform arose in most east European countries. There was unrest in the cities too, as the first steps of industrialization created an angry labor force.

Everywhere the traditional ruling class was threatened. Landed aristocrats disliked new political forms, but when their land itself was attacked they had to fight back. Military officers, drawn from the landlord class, naturally led the attack. The regimes they formed were primarily designed to defend the status quo. Hence, though they wielded great police powers and sometimes set up a Fascist facade, they differed substantially from more modern totalitarian governments. They could not support rapid economic development or the extension of education, for both might boomerang. They were not strong enough to engage in diplomatic adventures either; they might talk a strong nationalist game but they were normally cautious in practice. Their goals were conservative in an almost Metternichean sense—indeed the social structure of these countries differed little from that of a century before in central Europe. Their methods and the political forms they used were new. Where they were not forcibly overturned by war, they proved durable. Greece was to return to a regime of of this type in the later 1960s.

The Spanish Civil War

For a brief moment Spain, which had a definite if recessive liberal gene, seemed able to break the pattern. Unrest chased both Primo de Rivera and the monarchy in 1931 and a republic was established. The government was deeply divided, however. Middle-class liberals firmly supported the new regime and favored moderate land reform. Socialists, supported by industrial workers in Madrid and Bilbao, wanted more sweeping changes and hesitated to cooperate with the liberals at all. The anarchist movements to the left, which commanded much worker and peasant support, refused to participate in the political process, holding that all government was immoral. This deprived the government of vital backing, while individual anarchists poisoned the political atmosphere by numerous assassinations. Against the new regime were arrayed the landlords, who dominated southern Spain particularly, the Church, and the military. In 1936 General Francisco Franco led a revolt against the government. The bloody civil war that followed revealed that the opposing forces were very nearly equal, with a large but inefficient army opposed by the numbers and zeal of reformers and revolutionaries (including the anarchists). Substantial assistance from Germany and Italy finally tipped the scales to Franco. When the civil war ended in 1939, Spain returned to the roster of authoritarian states.

A Fascist movement, the Falange, had arisen during the republican years. It was very small, very idealistic. Franco reorganized the Falange into a government party in 1938, keeping many of the slogans and retaining the stress on youth groups and other uniformed organizations, but little else. His regime was devoted to defense of the status quo and repression of disorder. It forbade all other political parties. It created government trade unions that prevented strikes. It actively supported Catholicism but did not support economic change or diplomatic adventures—Franco cleverly stayed out of World War II despite his debts to Hitler. The Franco state endured.

FASCIST THEORY

It is common to call Franco's regime Fascist, but here we face another problem of definition as we did with earlier isms. We can define Fascist doctrine to an extent, but Fascism was weak on doctrine, preferring actions to words. We can define the Fascist appeal, though on this basis Franco's regime is definitely not Fascist, for it explicitly relied on traditional ruling groups, including the Church. Fascism in practice blithely ignored much of its background. It still is desirable to differentiate Fascism from conservative-authoritarianism typified by Franco, but the division is fuzzy.

Fascist theory was profoundly anti-rational and therefore hard to pin down. As Mussolini said of his doctrines, "The spirit of Fascism is will and action, not intellect." The Fascists claimed that man is fundamentally irrational and based their educational systems on this premise. They attacked political systems that assumed rationality, notably liberal democracy. According to Fascists democracy was absurd because individual men could not know what they needed. Liberalism was equally absurd because it treated people as individuals. Hence the product of liberalism, parliaments, were hopelessly divided and incapable of action because they reflected the narrowness and selfishness of people left to run themselves. Fascists also attacked the results of industrialization. Class war was just another form of selfishness. Individual greed and prevasive materialism were signs of a society gone wrong.

It is easy, then, to list what the Fascists opposed: liberals and all liberal institutions, Communists, socialists, and all manifestations of class conflict. They also opposed big businessmen, and in the case of German and French Fascists, but not Italian, they were against Jews. What were they for? What remedies did they propose?

The Fascists vaunted the absolute supremacy of the state. The state in their view was no mere sum of the individuals within it, no mere servant of the people. It was, as an Italian theorist put it, "a spiritual and moral fact in itself," which should be headed by a single leader. Its main purpose was war, the noblest human activity. Under the state Fascists promised to reorganize society along corporate lines, to replace both capitalism and socialism. It would unite owners and workers in corporations that would subordinate both to the higher interests of the state.

Fascist theory was vague, often was ignored, and much of it was penned after the fact. For example, after Mussolini had seized power, he employed the philosopher Giovanni Gentile to spin out Fascist philosophy. But there were intensely idealistic Fascists who saw Fascism as a genuine solution to society's problems, as a genuine vehicle of social reform. Fascist ideology —and the Nazi version developed by Hitler was very similar with the important anti-Semitic addendum by which the state itself was to serve German racial purity—offered genuine appeal to a variety of groups. It attracted intellectuals conditioned by the anti-rationalism of the last several decades, as well as disgruntled professionals, artisans, and shopkeepers hostile to big business and unions, and many peasants. It did not appeal to the traditional ruling class. Landowning aristocrats might make deals with fascists but they were rarely converted from their conservatism. Fascism was in theory revolutionary, but in its appeal largely reactionary, a reaction of the middling elements in society who felt bypassed by the modern world.

Fascists took power spontaneously in only two countries, Italy and Germany, though important Fascist parties developed in France, Austria, and elsewhere. In power, Fascists followed their ideology in certain respects, notably in foreign policy and in education. They worked toward constructing a totalitarian state, for which their theory was admirably designed, but were held back by traditional conservative elements. They made a few gestures toward those who gave them their reactionary support, but military and political interests impelled Fascists to advance industrialization rather than reform or retard it. Mixed in with all their policies was a huge dose of sheer opportunism. The successful Fascist valued power—he wanted to get it, to keep it and to enhance it. His ideology reflected his fascination with power, but he would never let it get in the way of power itself.

Fascism in Italy

Italy after World War I was not unlike a defeated country. Her armies had performed badly, her share of the spoils of war seemed hopelessly inadequate, her aroused nationalists were demanding a stronger government. Italy was also rocked by a huge wave of strikes and rural riots. The government, headed by liberals accustomed to the prewar politics of compromise, seemed impotent to act. The programs they did propose were inadequate to meet social disorder, as they had been in the 1890s when similar disorder led to a military regime for several years. The political scene was vastly complicated as a result of universal suffrage, which had been passed in 1912; now in parliament were radical socialists and radical nationalists who refused to play the parliamentary game.

Benito Mussolini had been an ardent socialist before the war, but during the conflict he was converted to an equally ardent nationalist. After the war, he toyed with the idea of regaining his position in the socialist movement; rebuffed by his former comrades, he formed an anti-socialist group called the *fascio de combattimento*. The term *fascio* was derived from the Roman *fasces,* the bundle of sticks with an ax projecting from them that was used as a symbol of authority. Mussolini picked up support from some ex-soldiers and unemployed youths and received financial backing from rich businessmen who found his strong-arm groups useful for breaking strikes. Mussolini dressed his toughs in black shirts and subjected them to military discipline, interspersed with frequent parades and elaborate rituals. Fear of Communist revolution swelled his support from property owners and devout Catholics; by 1921 his party had 300,000 members and 35 deputies in the parliament.

Although Italian socialists, like other socialists of the period, threatened revolution, they did little to carry it out. In 1922 they called a general strike. It failed, but the Fascists used the abortive strike as an excuse to attack socialists. They took over many socialist city governments by force. The government, frightened of the socialist threat itself and unsure of the loyalty of the army officers, did not oppose the Fascists. When Mussolini threatened a march on Rome, the king named him prime minister. His accession to power was technically legal, but Mussolini immediately set about to create a new state.

Consolidation of the Regime

Mussolini obtained a year's grant of dictatorial powers from the cowed parliament. He proceeded cautiously during this year, allowing some political liberty, but in 1924 he conducted a new election in which he freely employed violence and intimidation to produce a massive Fascist majority in parliament. Socialists and liberals resigned in protest and in 1926 Mussolini was sufficiently confident to dissolve their political parties. Opponents of the regime had to keep quiet or emigrate; those who refused to do either were arrested by Mussolini's political police. In addition to the secret police, squads of Fascist Blackshirts were used to intimidate the people. Parliament was reduced to a rubber stamp for the party. The press was tightly censored and the Fascists controlled the other mass media directly.

As in Russia power was in the hands of the party, which both ruled and checked the state. It named all candidates for political office and supervised regular government officials in the performance of their duties. Mussolini kept the party small, about 5 percent of the adult population, so it could serve as a loyal, elite group.

To consolidate his power further Mussolini signed the Lateran treaty with the Catholic Church in 1929, which ended the 70-year dispute between the pope and the Italian government. Mussolini recognized papal sovereignty over Vatican City, promised financial support, and gave the Church a large measure of educational control. In return the pope promised not to interfere in politics and to obtain government approval for the appointment of bishops, who also had to swear loyalty to the state. By bestowing the pope's implicit moral approval on the regime, the treaty won Mussolini considerable support at home and abroad.

Along with opposition political parties, Mussolini suppressed the independent trade unions and naturally the right to strike. In principle he replaced unions with new corporations, but actually workers were forced to enroll in Fascist-led organizations that represented them in the corporations. The other representatives came from the employers and the state, and they had little trouble cooperating. In 1925 Mussolini formally agreed to give the leaders of Italian industry free rein in return for their support of his regime. He kept his promise. The institutions of the corporate state were sham, a veneer over unrestrained capitalism, under which profits rose steadily. Mussolini similarly refrained from any significant land reform. The government supported public works and a large armaments program, but there was no social reform. Indeed, Italy suffered severely from the depression.

Having constructed his Fascist regime and having eschewed social reform, Mussolini turned in the 1930s to the only thing there was left to do: diplomatic adventures. While not severely pressed by an opposition, he squabbled with the Church over educational rights in the 1930s and he faced hostility from young idealists in his own party. He was also spurred by rivalry with Hitler. Although he had promised a glorious foreign policy, Mussolini's Italy was in no position to take an independent course. His regime in practice had not revolutionized the country, which remained poor and industrially backward; nor had he actively mobilized the support of the people. For all its Fascist trappings the Italian state resembled the conservative-authoritarian governments that arose elsewhere. It protected roughly the same interests using roughly the same means. The big difference was Mussolini's switch to a bold foreign policy—a difference that brought down the regime.

NAZISM

Adolf Hitler was named chancellor of Germany on January 30, 1933. The son of a minor Austrian civil servant, Hitler had a troubled childhood and an unsuccessful youth. Before World War I he eked out a living as a third-rate artist in Vienna, and he relieved his sense of failure by becoming a bitter anti-Semite. He enlisted in the German army during the war and was deeply shocked by Germany's defeat. In 1919 he joined a small but fanatical nationalist party in Munich, and soon afterwards the party's name was changed to the National Socialist German Workers' Party, or Nazis for short. The party made little headway. The abortive effort to overthrow the

Bavarian state government in 1923 convinced Hitler that direct revolutionary efforts were impossible. A year in jail gave him the chance to write *Mein Kampf* (My Struggle), a confused exposition of his hatreds and plans. The Nazi party maintained a shadowy existence during the next years; it was near collapse in 1928.

During the depression, however, the party's fortunes soared. Unemployed workers and students joined the party's brownshirted storm troopers, who in turn gave an impression of great strength as well as serving to break up political meetings of other groups. In 1932 the party won 37 percent of the vote in the national election, making it the largest party in the Reichstag. It drew votes away from liberal, middle-class parties, particularly attracting shopkeepers and professional people who were bitter about their economic decline. The Communist vote rose at the same time, reducing the socialist strength. Political polarization inevitably fed itself; Communist gains impelled still more moderate and conservative voters to seek protection at the hands of the vigorously anti-Communist Nazis.

Causes of Nazism

What really caused Hitler's rise to power? Obviously the depression, coming on the heels of inflation and defeat in war, triggered the rise. Germany's depression was the most severe in the world, which helps to explain why its political reaction was the most severe. But Hitler's subsequent actions proved so monstrous that historians, particularly those outside Germany, have often sought more monstrous causes. Some talk of the pressures of modern industrial society, which impel people to abandon their freedom to a totalitarian leader. The problem with this argument, however, is that only in Germany, among the advanced industrial countries, were so many people so impelled. More commonly, historians seek factors deep in the German political character. They note a peculiar German conception of liberty, stemming perhaps from Lutheranism, that holds freedom to be internal, within one's own mind, and therefore consistent with a strong state. They talk of Prussia's authoritarian military tradition—though this argument is complicated by the fact that Nazism was weakest in Prussia; it had its greatest strength in areas like Thuringia where industrialization was less advanced and there were more traditional peasant and middle-class property owners. Proper assessment of the explanation of Nazism through aspects of German character demands careful consideration of German history. When and why did German political and intellectual traits diverge dramatically from those of her neighbors? It must be remembered also that success came to the Nazis a full decade after the formation of the party, which raises questions about how many national characteristics drew Germans to the movement. The comparative point is important as well. Strong

The Power of Nazi Ritual: A Party rally in Nuremberg, 1936.

Fascist parties arose elsewhere, as in France, after the depression became severe.

Popular support was a basic element in Hitler's success, but it was not the only one. Hitler was a masterful leader in many ways. A great orator, he carefully staged his performances to appeal to the emotions of his audience. He preferred speech to writing as a propaganda vehicle, so that people would have less opportunity for individual, critical thought. He held meetings in the evenings rather than in the morning, for a tired audience would be more easily swayed. Among most of his immediate followers he commanded great devotion and loyalty, and after 1930 he was also able to make deals with big businessmen; these won him vital financial support in return for his pledge to protect hig business despite his rhetorical attacks on capitalism. As Nazi strength increased Hitler received indirect assistance from still other quarters. The Communists favored his taking power, erroneously believing that this would facilitate their own revolution. Aristocrats and military men, though not Nazis, began to believe that Hitler could be used for their own purposes and would serve to end political chaos and the threat of revolution; they therefore helped to arrange his legal takeover. Finally, the Weimar government was collapsing, incapable of positive action against the depression or against the political extremes. Even moderate political parties yielded to despair and played a role in Hitler's advance.

Gleichschaltung

Once chancellor, Hitler immediately called for a new election and outlawed the Communist party in hopes of assuring a Nazi victory. Even with these pressures the Nazis failed to win a majority in the Reichstag; however, with the moderates intimidated by storm troopers surrounding the Reichstag, the Communists expelled, and the Nationalist party unified, Hitler forced through the Enabling Act in March that gave him emergency dictatorial powers for four years. There was little resistance. Other political groups were too divided and bewildered to lead a protest. Even the socialists, who loyally voted against the Enabling Act, did not try to foment strikes or other direct action to defend the republic. Hitler made sure that there would be no chance for afterthoughts as he systematically destroyed all rival groups. Within a year Hitler had proclaimed the Third Reich with himself a *Fuehrer* and *Reichskanzler* (leader and imperial chancellor).

Typical of authoritarian leaders, Hitler banned all political parties save his own and forced other voluntary associations, including the trade unions, to dissolve. Accompanying these measures was a steady stream of arrests of potential dissidents. Within a few years, half a million non-Jewish Germans were held as political prisoners in the newly established concentration camps.

Hitler worked steadily to bring the state apparatus under his command. He dismissed more than a quarter of the civil servants, replacing them with his own men. In key branches of the government he also organized parallel Nazi units even more firmly under his control. For example, he put his deputy Hermann Göring in charge of the nation's police forces and at the same time set up a special police division, the Gestapo, with almost unlimited powers. Later, Nazi diplomatic and military units were formed to check on and compete with the regular government services. Hitler ousted elected officials of the state and local governments and then eliminated the traditional units outright, establishing local *Gauleiters*, or district leaders, appointed by the central government, usually from the Nazi party. Judiciary and university personnel were also reorganized and screened for loyalty.

Very quickly, then, Hitler had subjected all branches of the state to the process called *Gleichschaltung*, in which they were brought into line under rigorous central Nazi control. He was never completely successful in controlling the army or the diplomatic corps, which were indispensable to him but in which aristocratic traditions were particularly strong. There were a few efforts to resist Hitler, notably by several generals in 1938. These

Hitler put down easily, and there was no question of his mastery of the state.

Gleichschaltung extended beyond the state, monopolizing education and propaganda. To instill active loyalty to the regime, the government used the radio and held mass meetings, while all other public meetings were forbidden. Special youth groups indoctrinated children in the Nazi ideology. The curriculum of the school system was changed: academic subjects, including science, were reduced in importance, while sports and propaganda rose to fill the gap. Hitler was trying to raise new generations according to his image of man.

The regime inevitably clashed with the churches in its quest for absolute loyalty and complete control over the youth. Several Protestant groups yielded tamely, and a Nazified church was created whose bishops were appointed by the state and whose Christ was magically transformed from Jew to Aryan. Hitler closed most Catholic schools and directed a stream of vicious propaganda against the Church; the pope replied with a thorough condemnation of Nazism. But there was no complete break, and the papacy did not try to turn German Catholics into opponents of the state. Hitler did not succeed in bringing the churches fully into line—in fact, a strong minority of Protestant pastors constituted the most courageous opposition to his regime.

Hitler quickly moved against the Jews. He was deeply committed to anti-Semitism and the Jews provided a vital scapegoat, "somebody to hate," that would cement loyalty to the Nazi state. He barred Jews from government service and progressively restricted their economic rights. Jews were forbidden to marry or to have sexual relations with "Aryans." Many fled the country. In 1938 the campaign became more intensive: outright violence was directed against Jews, while the state seized their property and began to arrest them. Then, in 1942, Hitler arrived at the appalling "final solution" to the "Jewish Question," which brought death to six million Jews throughout Europe.

Economic Policies

Within five years of coming to power Hitler had ended unemployment. His remedy was a massive public works program, stressing a modern highway system, and soon an even more massive rearmament effort. Wages were kept low but German workers, assured of jobs, had a security that no democratic nation could offer during the 1930s. They also benefited from an organized vacation program and various new state welfare payments, particularly for large families. At the same time they were robbed of their unions and their right to strike, and were forced into a Nazi-dominated Labor Front.

The second pillar of Nazi economic policy was national self-sufficiency in preparation for war. Synthetic products were developed to eliminate dependence on imports. The state's trading policy was manipulated to give Germany virtually complete control over the foods and raw materials of eastern Europe and the Balkans.

The government interfered very little with big business. It made a few bows to artisans and peasants, forming new guilds and favoring peasant costumes as part of its encouragement of national folk culture. But most of this was mere rhetoric. The regime supported the ongoing process of consolidation in manufacturing and agriculture by helping to eliminate small firms and small farms. To assure maximum growth to the armaments industry, the Nazis set some limits on the movement of capital, but otherwise left big businessmen free to run the economic show. As in Italy corporate bodies were set up to govern the various branches of the economy, but industrialists controlled them easily.

Nazism in power was thus a political revolution without a social revolution. In 1934 Hitler purged the Nazi group that had wanted major social reform. The personnel of government changed somewhat. The percentage of aristocrats serving as army officers, for example, dropped below 50 for the first time in German history. Individual Nazis, many of them from the lower classes, made huge fortunes. But there were no dramatic shifts in social structure. The recruitment of university students scarcely changed, remaining predominantly upper-class. Even at the height of World War II, when Germany's resources were strained to the utmost, a million and a half women were allowed to continue as household servants to the upper classes —a measure of how little Hitler sought to change the established social order.

This lack of genuine social change complicates a judgment of the political regime. Hitler wanted to create a totalitarian state but his reluctance to touch key groups, such as the big industrialists, meant that the state's power was incomplete. Moreover the Nazi state was inefficient. It tended toward a top-heavy bureaucracy, which was complicated by its penchant for creating competing agencies. The regime could not command all the nation's resources, and it is doubtful that it commanded all the nation's active loyalties. For all its propaganda apparatus it did not radically change the lives of all ordinary Germans, until it brought war upon them. In only one area—the police—were the Nazis supremely efficient.

With the possible exception of two incidents, there was little resistance to Hitler. During World War II a group of Munich university students made a courageous attempt to overthrow the Fuehrer, and in 1944 various army officers and others tried unsuccessfully to kill him. Why were there not more efforts? Economic security, the suppression of voluntary organizations, and the pervasive police terror add up to a thus far irresistible formula. A special German docility to authority may have contributed as well, but Germany's lack of resistance was not really unusual in the totalitarian states save where war and invasion occurred. In none of the firmly established totalitarian or authoritarian regimes was there serious protest in this period. The regimes that ultimately fell owed their failure to defeat in war. Where they avoided defeat they have proved an unusually successful form of government, if measured in the traditional terms of stability and growing power.

THE ORIGINS OF
WORLD WAR II

Hitler, like Mussolini, believed his own rhetoric about the warlike purpose of the state. He desperately wanted to reverse the Versailles treaty and had a broader vision of Germany's expansion to the east against the Slavic peoples, whom he considered racially inferior. Soon after consolidating his power, he began, therefore, to gear the state and the economy for war. His actual diplomatic moves were often planned on the spur of the moment—such as the invasion of Poland that triggered World War II. Hitler did not have a clear master plan, nor did he insist on a world war, being quite content to make gains more cheaply. In all probability he did not expect the war to come precisely when it did. But along with his Italian partner, he rocked the diplomatic boat from 1933 on. The causes of World War II in Europe thus consist of Hitler's actions and the other powers' reactions—or, tragically, their lack of reaction.

The Breakdown of
Diplomatic Power

Hitler repudiated the treaty limitations of German armaments in 1935 and reintroduced universal military service. The League of Nations—from which Germany had withdrawn the previous year—bitterly denounced this violation but it did nothing. In 1936 Hitler remilitarized the Rhineland. Again there were protests, but no action. France was paralyzed by the internal crisis of that year and, moreover, her relations with Britain were shaky. The French were moved to seek an alliance with Russia, which was also frightened by Germany's revival, but this alliance proved to have no practical effect.

Even before this, the diplomatic status quo was upset in Asia and Africa. Japan invaded China in 1931. Italy invaded Ethiopia, the one independent native state in Africa, in 1935. Here was a venture in the old imperialist style, particularly appropriate to reverse the blow to Italian nationalism caused by the Ethiopians' defeat of the Italian army in 1896. In both these cases the League rained condemnations and sanctions, but to no avail. Britain and France also feared to antagonize the aggressors unduly and thereby closed off any effective resistance.

Germany and Italy moved quickly to aid Franco during the Spanish Civil War, seeing this as a fine opportunity to extend their war against liberalism and to reveal the weakness of the western powers. Both powers, but particularly Germany, used the war as a means of testing new weaponry. Spain served as a bloody dress rehearsal for civilian bombings—a tactic applied more widely four years later.

Weapons and troops from the Fascist powers ultimately turned the tide for Franco and enabled him to crush the republicans. The western powers again were paralyzed. Under the Blum government France longed to aid the republicans but feared to act without British approval; moreover, conservative factions in France favored Franco, making it dangerous for Blum to decide on any positive policy. The British were divided in somewhat the same manner and feared to get involved. Although large numbers of volunteers from the western countries, including the United States, fought on the republican side, official policy remained neutral. Negotiations produced firm nonintervention resolutions, but Germany and Italy defied them while France and Britain feared to enforce them. The Civil War helped draw Germany and Italy closer together. More important, the Soviet Union became disillusioned with the western powers. Russia alone officially aided the republican side, supplying military advisers and equipment. Russia had counted on western support in a common anti-Fascist cause, but such support did not come. Russia now realized that the western powers were almost as afraid of Communism as they were of Fascism. Since they could not be counted upon, Russia would have to protect herself in other ways. Despite repeated negotiations over the next years, Russia and the west could not become allies and the most natural barrier to German expansion remained unbuilt.

The Axis Powers

In 1936 Hitler and Mussolini signed a formal agreement. Italy had feared German designs on Austria but when Hitler promised to respect Austrian sovereignty that objection was mitigated. The two countries had every reason to ally, as both sought mutual support for further diplomatic adventures. This Rome-Berlin "axis" was supplemented by an agreement with Japan, a loose alliance ostensibly directed against the spread of international Communism. Within the European axis, Germany quickly assumed ascendancy over Italy; Germany's superior power and Hitler's personal dominance of Mussolini gave the Germans virtually a free hand.

In 1938 Germany launched her new annexationist policy by taking over

Austria, a prime target because Hitler sought to unite all German-speaking peoples. He had pressed the country several times before; now he insisted that the Austrian government admit Nazis to its ranks. When the government sought to circumvent his command he first sent the German army in and he himself followed the next day, laying a wreath on the tomb of his parents. The local boy had at last made good.

Hitler proclaimed the formal union (*Anschluss*) of the two countries and quickly repressed political opposition and the Jews in Austria. A plebiscite under Nazi supervision produced a 99.7 percent vote in favor of the union.

Because this move had proved so easy Hitler decided to act quickly against another small neighbor. Czechoslovakia had a large German population and the country was a constant reminder of Germany's defeat in World War I. Having spurred the Czech Germans to demand self-determi-

Before and After the Nazi-Soviet Pact: Hitler and Stalin move from denunciation to uneasy cooperation.

"IN AN ATMOSPHERE OF MUTUAL TRUST"

nation and then union with the Third Reich, Hitler prepared for invasion in May 1938.

For a moment resistance threatened. The Czech government refused to back down and France, their ally, supported them. But the French were too weak to stand alone, while the British were unprepared to act. Many Britons wanted to avoid war at all costs; some agreed with Hitler's arguments that Germany had been unfairly treated at Versailles. Moreover, they wanted to believe that Hitler would be satisfied with a few revisions—after all, he said he would be. The British prime minister, Neville Chamberlain, took the lead in negotiating a settlement. In September he, the French premier Edouard Daladier, Mussolini and Hitler met in Munich and agreed to the partition of Czechoslovakia. Czechoslovakia was not consulted. Neither was Russia, which still had a defensive agreement with France.

Chamberlain went home to greater popular acclaim for having saved "Peace in our time." Our time lasted slightly over a year. Munich proved to be a futile gesture of appeasement. In addition to dismembering Czechoslovakia it whetted Hitler's appetite and reinforced his belief that the weaker powers would back down if pressed. Russia, alarmed at the German advance, began to think of appeasement also, which further weakened the opposition to Germany.

Having annexed the German portions of Czechoslovakia, Hitler encouraged Poland and Hungary, also rivals of the Czechs, to chip off additional portions of the country while he supported other ethnic minorities against the Czechs. In March 1939 he incorporated the bulk of what was left of the country into Germany and made the rest a protectorate. The democracies were still unprepared for action, but at least they knew Hitler's goals were limitless. Britain, particularly, began to arm.

Hitler next moved against Poland, another country that had a German minority and traditional German territory. France and Britain pledged to support the Poles and tried to negotiate an alliance with Russia. The Russians were too suspicious to agree. Instead, on August 23, 1939, they signed a nonaggression pact with Germany that set the stage for a new partition of Poland.

Germany attacked Poland on September 1. Motorized columns swept rapidly through the country while bombers reduced large sections of Poland's cities to rubble. This was *Blitzkrieg*, lightning war that proved to be devastatingly effective. Polish resistance crumbled in a few days. France and Britain declared war against Germany on September 3, but they could not help Poland directly. Within a few months they were battling for their own lives, for the weakness of the western powers extended particularly to their military forces. Totalitarianism and democracy were about to be measured on the battlefield.

11 WORLD WAR II AND THE DECLINE OF EUROPE

Europe entered the new war in a mood far different from that of 1914. There was no eagerness, no rejoicing, except possibly in Germany, and even there the people were calm until they tasted the excitement of Hitler's first victories. The French and the British, knowing what suffering lay ahead, faced the prospect of war reluctantly, indeed sullenly.

The war, horrible in the extreme, cost millions of lives and left still more millions homeless and starving. It caused intense mental anguish to prisoners enslaved in labor battalions, to civilians crouched night after night in shelters during bombing attacks, to the fighting men themselves.

Unquestionably the war severely weakened Europe's position in the world, yet it did not leave Europe so dangerously demoralized as had World War I. In fact, developments both during the war and in the years of confusion immediately afterwards helped produce a decisively new stage in European history. Twenty years after World War I Europe experienced disastrous inflation and depression. Class tensions paralyzed the democracies while new, often warlike regimes had been installed elsewhere. Twenty years after World War II, Europe enjoyed unprecedented economic advance. Social tensions declined and new diplomatic initiatives reduced the likelihood of war. Problems abounded but they proved less crippling than those of the interwar years.

Any account of World War II must take into full account the horror and dislocation it caused. But another, more hopeful strand should be pursued as well. In a sense, the war served as a cathartic to Europe, a bloody cleansing. World War I had produced two unhappy decades of European history. World War II revolutionized Europe for generations to come.

AXIS VICTORIES

The Axis powers advanced steadily during the first two years of the war. During the fall and winter of 1939–1940, there was little activity on the western front as the French dug in behind their presumably impregnable Maginot line, expecting a replay of World War I. Britain took a more constructive stance by building up its supply of armaments. Newspapermen dubbed the war a "Phony War" or *Sitzkrieg*.

Russia, shocked by Germany's rapid conquest of western Poland, took steps to assure her own gains. Russian armies invaded eastern Poland where they quickly met the German columns. Poland was thus divided between the two powers. Russia assumed control of the Baltic countries, Lithuania, Latvia, and Estonia, and also invaded Finland, gaining important territory after bitter fighting. The Russians were clearly bent on regaining the areas they had lost after World War I, a policy that brought them directly to Germany's new borders. This fact, combined with Hitler's disdain for the Slavs and the ideological clash between Nazism and Communism, made conflict likely—but not yet. Some hoped that Germany and Russia would turn against each other, but Hitler wanted to avoid a two-front war and planned to mop up the west before turning to Russia. The Russians, unprepared for major war, were content to remain neutral.

Invasion of the West

Any illusions in western Europe about Hitler's intentions were dispelled in April 1940. Germany attacked and quickly overran Denmark, a country he had signed a nonaggression pact with just the previous year. Norway was next. The Norwegians had more chance to prepare than had the Danes and there was fierce fighting for a month. In both countries German conquest was facilitated by local Nazi sympathizers, such as the Norwegian Vidkun Quisling who later headed the German puppet regime in Norway and whose name came to mean "traitor."

In May the Germans invaded the Low Countries, including the neutral Netherlands. The *Luftwaffe* mounted a massive air attack; using incendiary bombs it practically leveled Rotterdam and inflicted huge civilian casualties. The Dutch soon had to yield. The Belgians, backed by French and British troops, held out a bit longer, but they too were forced to surrender by the end of the month. French and British troops were cut off, but some 300,000 of them were rescued from the French port of Dunkirk by a heroic band of British ships—yachts and fishing boats as well as naval vessels. But 30,000 troops were killed or captured and vast stores of equipment had to be abandoned.

France fell almost as readily as the smaller countries—a collapse that

WORLD WAR II—
WESTERN FRONT

→ German advances
⇨ Allied advances
✈ Major aerial conflict

capped the nation's tragic disarray during the 1930s. France was unquestionably a poor match for Germany. Less populous and less industrial, France had more difficulty recovering from the physical and demographic damage caused by World War I, which after all had been fought on French soil, not German. It was not surprising that the French could not repeat their performance of 1914–1918, but their rapid defeat should not be considered as inevitable. Political divisions played a major role. Those on the extreme right, including out and out Fascists, favored Germany. At the other end were Communists, reluctant to join a war against a country with which Russia had signed a pact. In the middle stood the prime minister, Paul Reynaud, and other politicians who, scarred by a decade of confusion and impotence, were unaccustomed to bold initiatives.

The military was equally ill-prepared. France had not built up significant air power or armored divisions despite the example of Germany and the warnings of younger French officers like Charles de Gaulle. Their defensive Maginot line could not hold against the German weaponry; ignoring the example of 1914, the French had not extended the line to the Belgian border, so the Germans were able to enter easily. They met little resistance as the swift invasion completed the demoralization of troops and civilians alike. The government fled to Bordeaux, its members arguing fiercely about whether to fight on or sue for peace. On June 16, Marshal Henri Pétain, the aged hero of Verdun, replaced Reynaud as premier and immediately requested an armistice.

Hitler was in his glory. He traveled to the town of Compiègne, the site of the 1918 armistice, and in the same railroad carriage in which Germany surrendered he personally dictated the truce terms. He compelled the French to disband their armed forces and turn over all military equipment. Germany was to occupy more than half of France, including the major industrial regions and the whole Atlantic coast. Pétain's government, which moved to the town of Vichy, assumed dictatorial powers. It abandoned the republican structure, abolished free trade unions, encouraged Catholic education—in sum, attempted to create yet another authoritarian regime with Fascist trappings. The government sought to protect French interests in negotiations with Hitler and maintained an official neutrality in the war, but above all it was careful to avoid offending the Nazi conqueror.

Resistance Efforts

In all the invaded countries there were elements that refused to yield. The Dutch and Norwegian monarchs fled to England and set up governments in exile. Charles de Gaulle of France, royal in bearing if not in title, did the same. He claimed legitimacy for his government by virtue of a post he had held under Reynaud, but his real argument was the necessity of preserving

A Plan That Failed: Cartoonist's conception of Hitler's blueprint for the invasion of England.

France and French honor. He organized the thousands of French troops who had fled to Britain and immediately began beaming radio messages of hope and encouragement to France. Within the French borders and in the other occupied countries small resistance groups soon arose to harass the Germans and supply information and other services to those who fought on.

Those who fought on meant, for the moment at least, only the British. Winston Churchill became prime minister as soon as the Germans invaded the Low Countries. Throughout the 1930s he had excoriated the policy of appeasement. It was ironically fitting that he was now called upon to lead the war that policy had failed to prevent. A superb speaker, Churchill personified the stubbornness of the British bulldog, to which he bore a not so remote resemblance. Under him an all-party government was formed, which minimized political bickering throughout the war.

Hitler was determined to crush his last rival in the west. His only problem was getting there—a feat last successfully accomplished by a continental warrior in 1066. An invasion of Britain would require mastery of the air, and in 1940 Hitler was confident he could achieve that. The Battle of Britain took place in the sky. The *Luftwaffe* mounted massive fighter and bomber attacks. Coventry and portions of other industrial cities were leveled as the Germans tried to destroy British industrial strength and sap civilian morale. But the Royal Air Force, aided by volunteers from many countries, held its own. From August through October, three months of the most intense fighting, the British shot down almost 2,500 German planes while losing fewer than 1,000 of their own.

When the Luftwaffe failed to bring Britain to her knees, Hitler was left without an alternative strategy. Had the Germans crossed the Channel and invaded directly in the autumn of 1940, they might have succeeded. But the German high command had overestimated British reserves of supplies and trained manpower. Hitler himself had not actually planned to invade, for he assumed that his great air attacks would prompt British leaders to seek a truce. When they did not, he toyed with the idea of an invasion, but as winter approached his attention turned to the riper opportunities of expansion in the east. Meanwhile British military strength steadily increased, aided by military supplies from the United States, which the American government granted on Churchill's direct appeal.

Invasion of the Balkans and North Africa

Hitler's success during the tumultuous autumn of 1940 extended to the Balkans. Without the need for outright invasion, he imposed his will on the governments of Hungary, Bulgaria, and Rumania, which were already economically dependent on Germany. Rumania was forced to give up territory to the other two.

In October 1940, however, the Balkan situation was disturbed by Hitler's ally Mussolini. The Duce had watched his mighty ally's success with growing dismay, for it cast his regime into near-oblivion. Moreover Italian armies that attacked in the south of France (when the French were already collapsing), had gained little success, while Hitler added insult by refusing to let the Italians occupy southern France or the French African Empire. Mussolini therefore decided to win his own laurels. During 1939 he had established a protectorate in Albania, and from this base he now invaded Greece. After a brief advance the Italians were repulsed and the Greeks invaded Albania.

Hitler was furious at Mussolini's folly but he had to protect the German flank. During the spring of 1941 the Germans overran Yugoslavia and Greece, bringing new conquests for Germany but also new areas to occupy and defend.

Mussolini had also moved against British territories in Africa, hoping for spectacular gains while the British were fighting for survival. The British successfully counterattacked, however, and Mussolini failed again.

The Germans had to come to the rescue once more, though with far less reason than in the Balkans. Under General Erwin Rommel the Germans forced the British North African Army back into Egypt. There were thus more conquests for Germany, more proof of German superiority in military organization and tactics, but still greater dispersion of strength. Hitler had mastered western and central Europe, but outside this zone had failed to drive on to total victory in any single area. He now opened yet another front.

THE INVASION OF RUSSIA AND WAR IN THE PACIFIC

Hitler ordered preparations for an invasion of Russia during the fall of 1940. He had planned an early spring offensive to take maximum advantage of the summer weather, but this strategy was postponed by the Balkan and North African adventures. Hitler insisted on pressing forward, however, ignoring his military advisers who urged a decisive contest in the Mediterranean against Britain. The Germans, supported by Rumanian, Hungarian, and Finnish troops, moved into Russia on June 22, 1941. The Russians, although not unprepared for this violation of their pact with Germany, were quickly pushed back.

Hitler expected to conquer Russia during the summer, and he might have accomplished this if the invasion had begun on schedule. The German armies conquered southern Russia, encircled Leningrad, and pushed to the outskirts of Moscow before the bitter winter set in. The winter gave the Russians a chance to reorganize their defenses. They spurred production of war goods in industrial centers well away from the fighting, such as in the Urals, and they also began to receive substantial supplies from Britain and the United States. Even so, the Germans made further gains in southern Russia during the summer of 1942, pushing to Stalingrad, a strategic point on the Volga river. This was the invasion's high point, and indeed the high point of Hitler's military success. By this time the German supply lines were greatly overextended and troops were committed at too many different points on the vast Russian plains. For four months the battle raged around Stalingrad but during the winter the Germans were forced to pull back, beginning a long and costly retreat. By mid-April 1943, the Russians had regained all the territory the Germans had won during 1942.

History teaches some lessons, one of which is that would-be conquerors are advised to finish off Britain completely before turning to Russia. As in the Napoleonic wars the British were able to abet Russian resistance with

money and supplies; in both cases they also compelled the Germans to commit troops to various peripheral areas. Conquerors are further advised that the invasion of Russia itself is most risky—usually signaling the beginning of the end of a conqueror's otherwise successful career.

War in the Pacific

The United States' entry into the war hastened Germany's now inevitable defeat. Hitler had hoped for prolonged American neutrality, but events quickly moved out of his control. Germany had encouraged Japan to harass France and Britain in Asia, an area where there were no vital German interests. Eager to take advantage of the European powers' distraction, the Japanese assumed a virtual protectorate over French Indochina and increased its pressure on China. They saw the United States as the only obstacle to their complete domination of the Orient and accordingly sought to remove the obstacle. On December 7, 1941, Japanese planes attacked Pearl Harbor, the main American naval base in the Pacific, plunging the United States into war.

During the next six months the Japanese pressed invasions of all western-held Pacific territory, not only the American Philippines but also British Hong Kong, Burma, Malaya and Dutch Indonesia. In almost all these areas the Europeans were forced to pull out.

Mid-1942 was unquestionably the Axis powers' finest hour. Even before the Germans' retreat from Stalingrad there were signs that the tide was turning. Because the United States was far better prepared for war in 1941 than in 1917, the American entry had immediate impact. Military supplies to Britain and Russia increased rapidly, and by the end of 1943 there were enough American troops in Europe to have direct effect on the European war. In November a joint Anglo-American force landed in French Morocco and Algeria and pressed on against the German and Italian troops. Germany had to withdraw some troops from the Russian front to meet this threat, which in turn facilitated the Russian counterattack. Allied bombings were at the same time beginning to interfere with the German economy. The pincers were beginning to close.

EUROPE'S PEOPLE AT WAR

Governmental controls increased in all the belligerent countries during the war. Most of the trends that had appeared in the previous conflict were now enhanced. Governments carefully allocated labor and raw materials and rationed most consumer goods. Tight censorship was imposed. Official propaganda in Britain was more restrained than in World War I—there was little need to embellish the image of a nation fighting for its life—but in the totalitarian countries propaganda knew no bounds. The German people, in particular, were given a consistently rosy view of the war and its purposes. To assure satisfaction at home, Hitler long attempted to maintain his program of public works as well; urban renewal and other projects continued into 1943, at some cost to the war effort.

Civilians were brought more directly into this war than in any previous one in history. Aerial bombing made every town and city potentially part of the war zone, no matter how remote from the front lines. On the continent, Nazi policies intensified the new horrors of war.

The "New Order"

At his height Hitler controlled more of Europe than had any previous European conqueror and there was some possibility he could consolidate his power. To many non-Germans he suggested a welcome measure of authority and efficiency after two decades of chaos; disillusioned with the welter of fragmented nation-states, they were open to a new system. Many national minorities, such as the Ukrainians in Russia, had special reasons to welcome release from their traditional masters. But Hitler had nothing to offer. In this he differed markedly from Napoleon, who had just as great a thirst for power but who brought a rationalizing ideology in his wake. Hitler brought only force and German dominance. The poverty of the Nazi ideology was strikingly revealed.

Hitler talked vaguely of a "New Order" for Europe in which each nation would gain a fitting role. But in fact he extended German control over all the occupied areas, not only to defend against local resistance but to force them actively into the war effort. Germany needed labor. Manpower was desperately short following the invasion of Russia. Hitler pulled all able-bodied Germans from field and factory and drafted foreign labor to take their place. Workers were forced into labor bands and treated abominably. This was outright slavery, and by the war's end it involved millions of people, from "allies" such as Italy as well as from conquered territories. Young men who fled from forced labor became the chief source of recruitment for the resistance organizations that sprang up everywhere.

The Nazis also imposed their racial theories fully. They treated the Nordic peoples best and even invited the Danes, Dutch, and Norwegians to join the master race in the New Order. The French and Belgians, whom the Nazis considered mixed people, came next, followed by the Slavs, who were so brutally treated that any initial interest in the New Order, such as the Ukrainians expressed, quickly vanished. Jews and gypsies, at the bottom of the racial heap, were to be exterminated. In the spring of 1942 Hitler decided on a "final solution" to the Jewish question, and in the next three years his faithful SS detachments slaughtered six million Jews in the gas chambers and crematories of the concentration camps. Three quarters of all the Jews in Europe thus perished during the war.

This policy was as incredibly stupid as it was insanely criminal, for many non-Jews were revolted by Hitler's racial attacks. They sought to protect the Jews, often at great personal risk. More and more people actively turned against the Nazis, and at the war's end only a few genuine collaborationists remained. By 1943 even the Italians were rising up against German control.

Resistance Movements

Small resistance movements had already been organized before the character of Nazi rule became clear, simply in reaction to foreign conquest. These spread steadily. Even in Germany a small but determined Resistance developed when by 1944 defeat seemed inevitable. Traditional conservatives, including many army officers, Christian clergymen, and some surviving labor leaders, were appalled by Nazi excesses and joined in a plot to assassinate Hitler. They failed in their purpose when, on July 20, the bomb planted in a staff conference room merely injured but did not kill the Fuehrer. Almost all the plotters were arrested and killed. With the country left to Hitler's increasingly erratic will, the war went on until German forces were totally defeated. Thus Germany was deprived of the flowering of political leaders and of ideas that provided new directions for other countries after the war's end.

In the conquered territories as well as in Italy, the Resistance was important for many reasons. It harassed the Germans and forced them to divert significant manpower simply to maintain the occupation. In France, for example, the movement at least modified the sense of national shame that inevitably followed crushing defeat. Because almost all countries participated to some degree in their own liberation, they had a basis for high morale after the war was over and also for demanding a role in postwar Europe, in the face of American and Russian domination.

The Resistance involved many social and political groups, although most movements were small until the war neared its end. Joining the Resistance were upper-class conservatives, motivated by a belief in national honor and a taste for adventure, as well as many young peasants who were fleeing from labor conscription. But young intellectuals and workers predominated, which helped give the Resistance, not surprisingly, a distinctly leftist political tinge. Indeed a Popular Front mentality revived in many countries and persisted for a few years after 1945, loosely allying socialist, Communist, and Christian reformers in the effort to expel Nazis and collaborators and build a new society.

Communists played a vital role in the Resistance. As soon as Hitler attacked Russia their confusion gave way to sure purpose: now both allegiance and ideology commanded them to resist Fascism. Given their vital assets of discipline and loyalty, they everywhere gained new recruits and prestige. The Yugoslavian leader Josip Broz, better known by his revolutionary nickname Tito, gained control of the leading Resistance movement. By playing down Communist doctrine, by preaching reconciliation among

Yugoslavia's diverse peoples against Hitler's effort to divide them by race, and above all by fighting hard against the Germans in battle, he won support in his own country and from the western Allies. Nowhere else did the Communists win control of the Resistance on their own, but in France and Italy they demonstrated enough strength to assure themselves a major role after the war.

In France, and later in northern Italy, Catholics played an important part in the Resistance. They continued or revived the kind of socially conscious Catholicism visible in Italy after World War I and in France in the later 1930s. Catholic Resistance appealed to more than Christian tradition: it called for a thorough restructuring of European society. It was also anti-Communist.

Non-Communist resisters in France found a natural leader in Charles de Gaulle. De Gaulle was a nationalist and a conservative, though he could exhibit some interest in limited social reform. With his great strength of character and his important following, he had much to offer the French Resistance. Backed by Churchill, de Gaulle was gradually able to rally support from many of France's colonies. By 1942 he controlled Equatorial Africa, Syria, and France's Pacific islands, and he was recognized by most of the Resistance organizations in France as their leader. From this point onward French Resistance combined internal attacks on the German occupation with de Gaulle's organization of a Free French army and government.

The Resistance thus proved most important in providing much of the basis of postwar governments, both in terms of individual leaders and broader political movements. In France, Italy, Yugoslavia, and the Low Countries, it colored political life for the next generation. Only in Poland was the Resistance crushed. Here, because of the Poles' traditional hatred of Russia, Communists had not been involved, but the Resistance was nevertheless extremely strong, maintaining contact with the Polish government-in-exile in London. When the Russian army moved into Poland, Stalin chose to ignore both the local Resistance and the London-based government. Instead he set up a regime of Moscow-trained Communists and let the retreating German army kill off most of the Polish Resistance fighters.

Although divided between Communists and non-Communists, the Resistance produced something akin to an ideology. Resistance spokesmen talked of European unity and of social justice. They sought a new structure for Europe, eliminating the petty nationalism that had brought the continent to two world wars. They also advocated a modification of the capitalist system, whereby the government would introduce greater economic equality and security. To this end they wanted to renew and purify the political process. The idealism set forth by the Resistance was rather vague and much of it was to be unfulfilled. But almost all segments were firm in their desire not to restore Europe to its prewar conditions. Their efforts help to explain the subsequent changes that did take place in Europe.

Reforms in Britain

During the war years Britain underwent a renewal of morale comparable in some ways to the Resistance spirit. Pride in Britain's heroic war effort helped to bring hostile social classes closer together. Many members of the upper classes, grateful for the wartime steadfastness of the common people, vowed not to return to the inequities of the previous decades. More than pious rhetoric was involved here, for the government had already begun planning for a better society. It sponsored reports on housing, health, and other issues. The most famous of these, the Beveridge report, urged the expansion of social insurance, the prevention of unemployment, and even the redistribution of income. The government definitely pledged a major expansion of educational facilities. Beyond this, the conditions of the common people improved during the war itself, and there was none of the profiteering that went on in World War I. High income taxes assured that the rich would pay their way. Consumer goods were allocated on a "fair share" basis, with the result that poor people received more milk and meat than ever before. Workers' wages rose; infant mortality dropped to the lowest level ever known.

Here for Europe's people was the irony of this horrible war. Out of the war's suffering emerged new political movements and attitudes in many classes of society. Changes were planned—and in Britain already introduced —to relieve a number of the social tensions of the previous decades. Unquestionably the death and suffering of millions of people left an indelible mark. But outside of Germany, there was a far more hopeful outlook in 1945 than in 1939. The new Europe would be forged from diverse elements.

GREAT-POWER DIPLOMACY AND THE WAR'S END

In August 1941, even before America's entry into the war, President Franklin Roosevelt and Prime Minister Churchill drew up the Atlantic Charter to lay the basis for an enduring peace. In the Charter Britain and the United States declared that they had no territorial ambitions and that after the war boundaries would be drawn in accordance with the principles of national self-determination. This document, though at the time a rather empty declaration, foreshadowed the later United Nations Charter; its terms played a definite role in the ultimate peace settlement.

Allied leaders had a number of subsequent conferences, particularly during 1943, but for the most part these dealt with strategic questions. At the December 1943, conference in Tehran, for example, an agreement was reached to open a second front in France against Germany, thus complementing the growing Russian offensive in the east. No firm decisions about a postwar settlement were made.

Russian Interests

It was clear, nevertheless, that the principles of the Atlantic Charter would be complicated by other interests. As the Germans pressed into Russia, Soviet diplomats informed their new British allies that in any post-war settlement they expected to keep the territories they had won during their pact with the Nazis—that is, the Baltic states and parts of Finland and Poland. The British refused to acknowledge these claims but they were in no position to oppose them outright. Roosevelt and his advisers, who in any event were less fully informed about Russian plans, insisted that all boundary questions be settled in one piece after the war was over. Churchill, as an experienced diplomat and staunch anti-Communist, urged greater vigilance against Russia, but Britain was the junior partner in the Anglo-American alliance and his advice was usually ignored. Hence the Tehran conference barely hinted at a settlement for Poland and left all other eastern European questions entirely open, in accordance with Roosevelt's wishes. Stalin had no reason to disagree: a later settlement could only mean that more territory would be in the hands of the Red army now that the Germans were being pushed back. Similarly Churchill's urgings against an invasion of France were ignored; he favored a strike in the Balkans, which could more directly challenge Russia's role in eastern and central Europe. Russia wanted a massive second front and Roosevelt heeded the pleas of his military advisers to strike at the Germans as directly and quickly as possible. The decision not to outline a precise European settlement facilitated cooperation with the Russians during the war itself, but it left the way open for profound misunderstanding later.

Russian aims were not the only problem. The United States, while sincere in its disclaimers of territorial ambitions in Europe, had plans of its own. Roosevelt and his advisers were not disposed to let Europeans devise their own postwar structure. He was convinced that Europe needed to be set straight and that the United States had the right and ability to do the setting. He long resisted de Gaulle's claims to head the French government, for example, because he believed that the United States should reorganize French political life. These plans were vague and many of them were abandoned before the war was over—de Gaulle was recognized as head of the provisional government in 1944. But the Americans intended to play a major role in Europe, which was in many ways more novel than the Russian territorial ambitions.

Finally there was the question of Germany. At their conference in Casablanca in January 1943, the Allies agreed to insist on an unconditional surrender. Moved by their horror at Nazi aggression, they may have discouraged some of Hitler's opponents and missed an opportunity for a negotiated settlement with them—always assuming these opponents could have dislodged Hitler from power. The Allies certainly took on the obligation of conquering the whole of Germany and of arranging Germany's postwar structure. Though the Atlantic Charter had spoken of natural self-determination, the insistence on unconditional surrender negated the principle with regard to Germany, as the Germans realized. Yet the actual disposition of Germany once conquered, was left unclear.

The Invasion of Western Europe

The Allies pressed their military offensive. By the spring of 1943 American, British, and some French troops had driven the Germans from North Africa. In the summer they invaded Sicily. This spurred the Italian Resistance to topple Mussolini and negotiate an armistice with the Allies. The Germans, in turn, took over the defense of Italy and reinstalled Mussolini as a puppet ruler. The Allies ground slowly and painfully north, taking Rome, in 1944. The Germans were not completely expelled from the peninsula until 1945, at which time Italian partisans seized and executed Mussolini.

On June 6, 1944, a huge Allied amphibious force landed in Normandy and began to fan out into France. By August the Allies neared Paris and a French armored column took over the city, installing a provisional government under General de Gaulle. American and British troops moved on toward Germany, though at the end of the year Hitler attempted a massive counteroffensive, the Battle of the Bulge, which threw them back for a time. All the while Allied bombers steadily pounded German industrial centers and some cities, such as Dresden, were virtually destroyed in retaliation for earlier German raids on England.

During 1944 Russian forces completed the liberation of Russian territory and advanced toward Germany along an 800-mile front. They moved into Eastern Prussia and parts of Poland, into Rumania and Bulgaria. Prodded by Resistance movements, the Germans pulled out of Greece and retreated into Yugoslavia. They held firm for several months against Russian troops in Hungary, but the Russians successfully shifted their focus to Poland. With Hitler's forces deliberately concentrating against the western Allies in the Battle of the Bulge, Russian troops swept into Warsaw and 300 miles further into Germany itself. They paused in the bitter winter only when they reached the Oder River, 40 miles from Berlin.

Yalta and the War's End

By this time plans for a postwar settlement became imperative. In October 1944, Churchill had approached Stalin directly concerning a settlement in eastern Europe. He sought to use his scanty bargaining power in a classic spheres of influence agreement, and Stalin agreed. The formula essentially conceded Rumania and Bulgaria to the Russian sphere, Greece to the British-American sphere, with great-power influence in Yugoslavia and Hungary to be divided. When the leaders of the Big Three met at Yalta in February 1945, they were less candid but followed somewhat similar principles in practice. Roosevelt, Churchill, and Stalin issued a Declaration on Liberated Europe, pledging to assist the nations newly freed from Nazi tyranny to establish sound democracies. But Roosevelt and Churchill allowed Stalin a virtually free hand with Poland. They persuaded him to admit four non-Communists to the puppet government he had established as his troops moved into Poland, but that was all. They agreed to Stalin's demands for a new Russian frontier with Poland far to the west of the prewar boundary, along the frontier contemplated by the western powers in 1919 before the Polish attack on Russia in 1920. Poland was to be compensated by annexations of German territory. In sum, then, the Yalta conference ratified what existed in fact. Russian troops controlled eastern Europe except for Greece and Yugoslavia. Roosevelt, and to a lesser extent Churchill, realizing they could not change the facts, accepted them publicly hoping to preserve good relations with Russia. There were signs that this policy might pay off, for the Russians did not support Greek Communists in their revolt against the new government that the British had installed in Athens.

Moreover the Yalta conference agreed to strengthen France and preserve Germany. Churchill led the battle here, seeking two strong continental countries against Russian influence. France was granted great-power status, with equal rights in the future occupation of Germany. A variety of proposals were put forth to punish Germany harshly and possibly to divide it into a number of tiny states, but these plans were abandoned or quietly shelved.

Three months later the European war was over. Victorious in the Battle of the Bulge, British, French, and American troops were able to cross the Rhine without resistance. The Russians forced the Germans out of Hungary and in April captured Vienna, enhancing their claims for a strong voice in central as well as eastern Europe. The remaining question was who would first reach Berlin. The American commander, Dwight Eisenhower, worried about his overextended supply lines and not fully aware of the political significance of the capture of Berlin, held his troops back at the Elbe river. On April 16, the Russian Marshal Grigori Zhukov began the final offensive against the mass of rubble that Berlin had become. Hitler, immured in an air raid bunker, vowed that the German people should be destroyed with him in the final battle. But when Russian tanks smashed into the city he knew the end had come and shot himself. On May 9 the German high command surrendered at Eisenhower's headquarters in France. All that remained was a slight mopping up operation, notably in Czechoslovakia where the Resistance had risen and invited American troops to enter. Again, the Americans held back in a desire to preserve good relations with Russia, and Russian troops moved into yet another key central European state.

The war in the Pacific also moved rapidly to a close. American forces

The End of World War II: American and Russian soldiers meet at the Elbe, 1945.

began to reconquer key Pacific islands from the Japanese in 1943. They seized the Philippines in the autumn of 1944. With the European war over in the spring of 1945, thousands of bombers were turned against Japan in an aerial offensive greater than that against Germany. On August 6 an atomic bomb was dropped on Hiroshima, flattening half that industrial city and killing over 50 thousand people. Two days later the Soviet Union rushed to declare war against Japan, as had been promised at Yalta. On August 9 a second atomic bomb was dropped. On August 14 the Japanese surrendered.

It was time to pick up the pieces, or try to. Europe was devastated, its economy a shambles, millions of its people homeless—millions, in fact, fleeing conquerors old and new. Dislocation and hardship dominated the immediate postwar years. No previous war had created such widespread material disruption. Furthermore, no previous war had been so genuinely global. Even as it faced massive problems of rebuilding, Europe had to deal with the problem of reestablishing a relationship with the rest of the world, notably with the traditional colonies. Finally, no previous war had left Europe so decisively at the mercy of peripheral powers. World War II seems to have been the final outburst of conventional nation-state diplomacy in Europe, with the superpower rising in its stead. Making the peace was thus no longer a matter for a conference of European states. The key to peace lay in the hands of the two giants, Russia and the United States. They proved unequal to the task, and a formal peace has yet to be signed in Europe.

ECONOMIC COLLAPSE

Europe's economy was virtually paralyzed at the war's end. Areas occupied by Germany—which included most of the continent—had been systematically stripped of resources. Vital train service, for example, had been disrupted everywhere, not only by bomb damage to rail facilities but by the fact that most rolling stock had been moved to Germany.

Highways, ports, and factories had all suffered from bombardment, and housing had been damaged even more seriously. In Germany about 40 percent of prewar housing units were destroyed or rendered unfit for habitation. The transportation problems caused by damaged bridges, roads, and canals were further complicated by the fact that civilian truck production had virtually ceased during the war.

Labor was also in short supply. Outside the Soviet Union some fifteen million people died as a result of the war: more than six million soldiers, almost six million Jews, and more than two million other civilians. Losses were particularly great in central and eastern Europe. For France and Britain World War II was less costly to life than its predecessor, but everywhere massive death rates were an inescapable reality, a blow to morale as well as to the economy.

Furthermore, millions of people were on the move: east Europeans and Germans fled the advance of the Russians; labor conscripts and concentration camp inmates gradually drifted out of Germany. Within a decade or so, a million of Europe's surviving Jews emigrated to the new state of Israel. These movements of people added to economic dislocation but in some areas provided the means for recruitment of an adequate labor force.

Finally, millions of people were hungry. The war had drastically reduced standards of food consumption on the continent. Agricultural production lagged for years after the war because of labor shortages, inadequate supplies of fertilizer and equipment as well as the disruption of transportation. Industrial workers were ill-fed, often far below the minimum necessary to sustain an active life. Understandably, this reduced their own production. Europe seemed trapped in a vicious circle.

Europe's manufacturing capacity was not damaged as severely as had been expected, indeed as had been planned by the wartime airforces. Bombing was clearly more successful against civilian housing than against factories, for only 10 percent of the latter were completely destroyed. But manufacturing production dropped rapidly, by over 50 percent in western and central Europe, primarily because of labor shortages and transportation bottlenecks.

In many countries, particularly Germany, a barter economy returned for a few years as people tried to assure themselves of subsistence in any way they could. Inflation was everywhere a serious threat. With manufacturing and agriculture disrupted, prices soared.

The most severe economic dislocation lasted until 1947 or 1948 and

A Bombed City: Berlin in May, 1945–The Kaiser-Wilhelm Church.

confirmed many Europeans in a more radical political stance than they had adopted before the war. Italian and French Communists, for example, solidified their hold over a larger segment of the lower classes who sought to protest their misery. Massive strikes and violent demonstrations were another common feature of these years, in Britain as well as on the continent. These developments were comparable to the aftermath of World War I.

More novel was the impact of economic dislocation on Europe's governments as a wave of new regimes followed the war's end. In eastern and central Europe, including Italy, prewar rulers were forcibly swept away. A new republic was proclaimed in France, slightly different at least from the prewar version. Even Britain had a strong Labour government for the first time, though its political system was not changed. The new governments were born with an inescapable commitment to place first priority on economic and social reconstruction. This confirmed the rethinking of commitments undertaken by Resistance movements and wartime governments. It contrasted strongly with the business-as-usual outlook of most governments after World War I.

Economic dislocation and the European governments understandable preoccupation with it confirmed one other development that the war had already revealed. Europe's place in the world had to shrink. Europe could no longer maintain its colonial holdings against growing resistance, and European diplomacy itself was dominated by the two superpowers. The ramifications of these developments extended over the next 15 years, but they were part of the war's aftermath. For diplomacy especially, the war served as a watershed in European history.

THE POSTWAR SETTLEMENT

American influence in Europe was far more novel than the Russian, though in the three years after the war Russian influence was more pervasive, both in central Europe and the Balkans, than during its nineteenth-century heyday.

American troops remained in Europe, particularly as occupation forces in Germany and Austria, and American economic dominance was overwhelming. The Europeans had no means of acquiring on their own the goods they needed. Their merchant marine was decimated and their overseas financial holdings had been swept away in the war. They had lost overseas markets to North American companies and even to firms newly established in previously backward areas.

The United States quickly moved into the breach. Even before the war's end American troops distributed food and medical supplies to civilians. From 1944 to 1947 the United Nations Relief and Rehabilitation Administration dispensed over a billion dollars' worth of supplies, mainly to eastern Europe and to China, with the United States bearing two-thirds of the cost. Ironically, American diplomatic influence did not extend as far as American-supported relief operations, for eastern Europe quickly moved into the Russian orbit. But Americans and west Europeans alike talked freely of an enduring "dollar gap,"—Europe's permanent dependence on American assistance. The concept revealed the new power relationships.

Russia's power in its zone of Europe was more direct, its intentions clearer and more traditional. With the exception of Finland it had regained the territory lost after the Revolution, but it wanted a buffer zone of loyal states to prevent a recurrence of the prewar vacuum of power around its borders, and to eliminate any possibility of renewed German aggression.

Both Russia and the United States wished to avoid conflict. Unhappily their new juxtaposition brought them into direct confrontation. Before the Cold War between the two superpowers began, however, there were two years of flux in which postwar Europe began to take shape.

The wartime Allies met for the last time in Potsdam, Germany, in July 1945. Here they decided on a four-power occupation of Germany, but postponed a final settlement. They granted Poland "temporary administration" over Germany east of the Oder and Neisse rivers, in return for ceding much of its prewar territory to Russia. They set up a committee to prepare peace treaties with Germany's former allies. This was about the extent to which an overall postwar settlement was planned and agreed upon.

Treaties were signed with Rumania, Bulgaria, Hungary, Finland, and Italy in February 1947. Rumania gained some territory from Hungary but also ceded some to Russia and Bulgaria, while Hungary gave up a bit to the reestablished Czechoslovak state. All three countries had to pay reparations, mainly to Russia, which were fairly modest by World War I standards. Finland also gave up some territory and was required to pay reparations to Russia. The treaty with Italy required surrender of its colonial empire, some territorial concessions to Greece and Yugoslavia and small reparation payments.

Austria was occupied by Britain, France, Russia, and the United States until 1955. A coalition government of Catholics and Social Democrats was elected in 1945 and enjoyed substantial autonomy in internal affairs, but Russia long blocked a formal peace treaty while drawing large reparations in the form of petroleum and machinery. The treaty of 1955 restored Austrian sovereignty, pledged Austria to perpetual neutrality guaranteed by the great powers, and prohibited reunion with Germany.

Germany was treated, not surprisingly, as a power to be punished. The country was administered in four zones by the allied powers; Berlin, though deep in the Soviet zone, was similarly divided. Initially no German governments were established beyond the local level. Twenty-two Nazi leaders were put on trial in Nuremberg before an Interallied Tribunal, and most were sentenced to imprisonment or death. Individual occupying powers, particularly the United States, tried and sentenced many lesser officials.

The Potsdam conference had authorized the dismantling of German heavy industry and exaction of reparation payments. Soviet authorities moved many German factories to Russia, but the western powers quickly abandoned any such policy because they wanted to revive the German economy in order to support the German people and assist the economic recovery of western Europe. To encourage economic development the United States and Britain united their occupation zones in 1946 and France later joined in. In May 1949, the western zone was proclaimed the German Federal Republic and allowed to set up its own government. The Russians matched this by establishing the German Democratic Republic. In both cases allied military forces remained, though their purpose shifted from occupation to Cold War.

In 1945 the Allied powers established the United Nations, which in

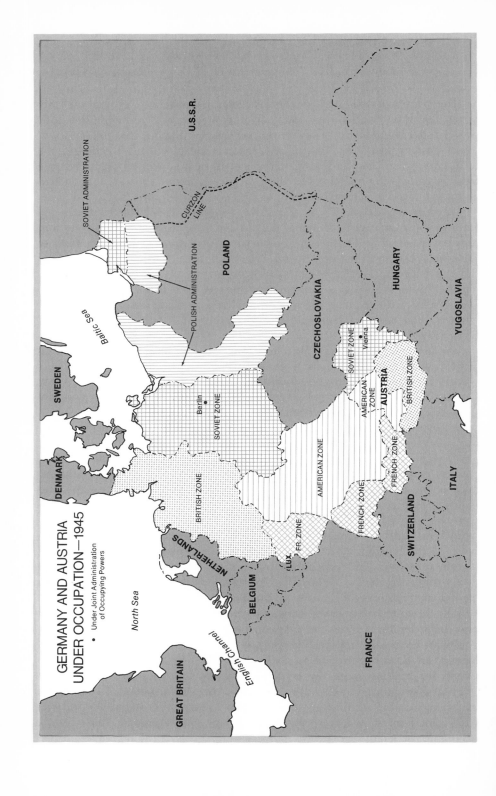

GERMANY AND AUSTRIA
UNDER OCCUPATION—1945

• Under Joint Administration
  of Occupying Powers

GREAT BRITAIN

North Sea

English Channel

NETHERLANDS

BELGIUM

LUX.

FRANCE

DENMARK

SWEDEN

Baltic Sea

SOVIET ADMINISTRATION

POLISH ADMINISTRATION

CURZON LINE

POLAND

U.S.S.R.

BRITISH ZONE

Berlin

SOVIET ZONE

AMERICAN ZONE

FR. ZONE

FRENCH ZONE

FRENCH ZONE

SWITZERLAND

ITALY

CZECHOSLOVAKIA

SOVIET ZONE

Vienna

AMERICAN ZONE

AUSTRIA

BRITISH ZONE

FRENCH ZONE

HUNGARY

YUGOSLAVIA

structure and hoped-for purpose largely resembled the old League. Unlike the League, however, the United Nations was not dominated by the traditional western European powers and played only a slight role in strictly European diplomatic problems. Russia and the United States quickly converted the organization into a forum for their world-wide quarrels. By the 1960s the United Nations came under the growing influence of the new states of Asia and Africa. Both these developments mirrored the changes in Europe's diplomatic posture.

The Nature of the Settlement

It is difficult to compare the peace settlement of World War II with earlier settlements, if only because it developed so sloppily. Russia was obviously the big winner in traditional terms, acquiring territory and some reparations, and largely behaved like a "satisfied" power in Europe, concerned with consolidating its new influence rather than undertaking new gains. There were relatively few territorial changes compared to previous treaties, aside from Germany's uncertain status. Shifts in the Balkans alleviated some traditional quarrels. Few new disputes were opened up. Italy had minor difficulties with Yugoslavia, which were ironed out in 1955, and with Austria. Germany was the big loser: occupied, punished, implicitly saddled with war guilt in the trials of Nazis (though the Allies insisted that Nazis, not Germans in general, were to blame for the war), divided, and above all despoiled of territory in the east. No treaty has yet confirmed Poland's control of what was traditionally east Germany, but the Poles quickly expelled the German inhabitants, replacing them with Poles, and the "temporary administration" has thus far proved permanent. In traditional terms, then, Germany was left an aggrieved power, the only major one in Europe. Traditional terms have not really applied, however, because of superpower influence over European affairs, and German diplomacy has not been motivated by revenge. Though sometimes precariously, the postwar settlement has kept the peace in Europe for 25 years. Among the many reasons for this is the fact that the settlement, however sloppy, was designed with peace-keeping in mind and it cannot be interpreted as unusually selfish or largely punitive in intent.

DEVELOPMENT OF THE COLD WAR

Popular Front governments were established in most east European countries soon after the war. Under the protection of Soviet troops, the Moscow-trained Communists in the governments of Rumania, Bulgaria, and

The boundaries shown on this map
date from the beginning of World War II.

POSTWAR EUROPE

Axis nations after World War II

Lands which changed hands after World War II

Hungary had little difficulty disposing of their liberal, socialist, and agrarian collaborators, after which they established peoples' democracies along Russian lines. A similar regime emerged in Albania. Under Marshal Tito,

Yugoslavia also established a Russian-type constitution and a one-party state, but in this case refused to accept dictation from the Soviet Union; Yugoslavia publicly broke with Russia and its satellites in 1948. Along with Finland and later Austria, Yugoslavia alone preserved a precarious neutrality in east-central Europe.

Poland retained a coalition government until 1947, when the Communists ousted their partners and assumed complete control. Czechoslovakia fell to Communist control the next year. In relatively free elections, held in 1946, the Communists had polled a third of the votes and their leader, Klement Gottwald, became prime minister. But other parties had genuine strength and the president, Eduard Beneš, was the liberal who had headed the state before the war. A Communist coup in March 1948, forced Beneš' resignation; this, combined with the mysterious death of the Foreign Minister Jan Masaryk and the expulsion of other non-Communist leaders, caused widespread revulsion in western Europe and the United States.

Tensions had been developing between east and west long before this. In 1946 civil war broke out in Greece, with Communist guerrillas attacking the restored monarchy with support from the neighboring Communist states. Britain, which still occupied the country, was too hard-pressed by the demands of domestic recovery to continue the struggle. The United States stepped in and, under the Truman Doctrine, offered extensive military and economic assistance to Greece, Turkey, and by implication, to any other nation threatened with Communist subversion.

In 1947 Russia encouraged Communist parties in Italy and France to mount a wave of strikes and civil disorders in order to paralyze and possibly topple the governments of these countries. In response the governments expelled Communist ministers who had participated in Popular Front regimes after the war. In retaliation Poland, Hungary, Rumania and Bulgaria purged non-Communists from their official ranks.

American Initiatives

The United States also moved in at this point to bolster the western Allies. Through the Marshall Plan (enunciated by Secretary of State George Marshall) the United States distributed billions of dollars in loans and grants to aid European recovery. Aid went principally to France, West Germany, Great Britain, and Italy. The United States also pressed its most threatened allies, notably Italy, to curtail Communist voting strength.

Russia termed the Marshall Plan a new instrument of capitalist imperialism, and in response reestablished an international Communist organization, known now as the Communist Information Bureau (Cominform) to promote and control Communist parties throughout the world. Russia also forbade Finland and Czechoslovakia to receive Marshall Plan aid, which both countries at least wanted to discuss, and soon took over the latter country.

The Cold War was on. Russia, by seizing eastern Europe, was most obviously to blame for it. The Russians had undoubtedly hoped and worked for the collapse of capitalist regimes in the west; they certainly interfered in the Greek civil war, though this country was beyond the "sphere of influence" they had recognized during the war. But the United States, urged on by traditional anti-Communists like Winston Churchill who first coined the term "iron curtain" to describe the borders of Russia's satellites, solidified its own sphere of influence and talked at least of dabbling in east European affairs. The "who's to blame" approach to the Cold War is as complicated and possibly as sterile as was the same approach applied to the causes of World War I. Judgment is further complicated by our nearness to events. Only recently have some American diplomatic historians seen the Cold War as anything but virtue (USA) versus evil (USSR); perhaps, in reversing the simplistic view, they move too far in the other direction. What is certain is that from 1948 onward both great powers played the Cold War game vigorously and their conflict dominated European diplomacy for over a decade. When Russia exploded its first atomic bomb in 1949, Europe indeed seemed trapped between two giants with unparalleled powers of destruction.

The Impact of the Superpowers

In Europe the Cold War focused on Germany. The western Allies resolved to build up the German economic and political strength to counter Russian power. The Russians were sincerely afraid of a revived Germany and in retaliation Soviet authorities closed off all land transportation to West Berlin. The allies, led by the United States, airlifted masses of supplies into the beleaguered city, causing the Russians to lift the blockade in 1949.

That same year most western European countries joined the United States and Canada in the North Atlantic Treaty Organization (NATO), pledging themselves to mutual assistance in the event of armed aggression against any one of them. Far-reaching military collaboration followed, including the formation of an allied military command under an American general. West Germany joined this effort in 1955. In retaliation—the challenge-response pattern was now the basis for the continuation of the Cold War, with each side firmly convinced that it was being challenged—the Soviet Union set up the Council for Mutual Economic Assistance (COMECON) to coordinate the economies of the east European countries. After West Germany entered NATO, Russia and its satellites signed the East European Mutual Assistance Treaty, commonly called the Warsaw Pact, a 20-year agreement of friendship, military assistance, and collaboration in international affairs.

The Cold War spilled well beyond the borders of Europe. For the most part, however, Europe's contribution to the worldwide dimensions of the conflict was limited to votes in the United Nations, supporting one or the other of the superpowers, and to token gestures of collaboration in other efforts—when as several western countries committed small numbers of troops to back the United States during the Korean War. Here again Europe had renounced major action on a world scale—it could not compete with the superpowers.

The Cold War set the framework for internal European diplomacy. The peak of the conflict passed after the mid-1950s, but subsequent European diplomacy has only mildly modified the division of Europe into two separate camps. European morale was profoundly shaken by the dominance of the continent by two peripheral great powers. It suffered and suffers still from the threat of the bomb. The prospect of renewed warfare in which Europe would be obliterated was strong through the early 1950s and it has not disappeared. Yet the Cold War did not destroy European diplomacy—it helped redirect it. In western Europe, most notably, there were efforts to achieve greater unity, prompted at first by the United States and reinforced by fear of Russian aggression. Under the shadow of the two giants, who increasingly neutralized each other's power, European countries could undertake modest new initiatives.

DECOLONIZATION

Far more rapidly than she had gained them, Europe lost her colonies after World War II. Arab and Asian nationalism had risen in the decades before the war, which foreshadowed a growing challenge to European rule. The war made the challenge irresistible. Japan took more Asian colonies away from Europe's control, and even after Japan's defeat it was difficult to reestablish the old dominance. Other colonies were left largely to their own devices during the war because of the distraction of the colonial powers. Some declared their independence outright, as did Syria and Lebanon after the fall of France. Others witnessed the rise of powerful new independence parties. Wartime slogans of liberty and democracy from the Allied nations encouraged this movement and raised new doubts in Europe about the propriety of retaining colonies. The United States nominally favored national independence movements, which also encouraged the imperial powers to relinquish their hold. Above all, Europe's preoccupation with postwar reconstruction precluded the forceful measures needed to retain the colonies.

From a European standpoint, decolonization was really part of the war-induced reduction of Europe's position in the world. Like the emergence of the superpowers, it may well have been inevitable, but the war accelerated the process and heightened its impact. Even so, decolonization was a painful process, and while Europe's empire crumbled fast, great efforts by the colonial peoples themselves were required. Obviously, decolonization was far more than a phase of European history. It was a major chapter in the history of Africa, Asia, and the Near East. But the relationship of the decline of empire to the development of a new Europe was vital as well.

British Policies

Most of the imperial powers voluntarily granted independence to their colonies, though often they acted reluctantly and under great pressure from local nationalists. They typically tried to exert considerable influence after they left. Britain quickly abandoned her Arab colonies, including Egypt, while retaining some oil sheikdoms on the Persian Gulf until the late 1960s. Iraq's independence, initially granted in 1930, was confirmed in 1947; Jordan became a nation in 1946. Britain pulled out of Israel in 1948; she had also agreed to the demands of Indian nationalists, led by Mohandas Gandhi, for complete independence. The British left in 1947, after which the nations of India and Pakistan were formed. Burma gained independence the following year. Britain remained in Malaya for several years, successfully battling Communist guerrillas; the Federation of Malaysia was established in 1963.

African independence was also slow to come, but the British began to prepare for it soon after the war, granting African colonies more local autonomy, opening the civil service to Africans, and establishing more schools and universities. Led by Kwame Nkrumah, nationalists in the Gold Coast threatened revolt in the mid-1950s, and Britain quickly yielded; the new state of Ghana became independent in 1957. Nigeria followed three years later, and Britain soon was entirely out of West Africa. The British clung more firmly to its East African colonies, both because of their greater economic stake and because of the presence of white minorities in the area. They resisted Mau Mau terrorism in Kenya in the 1950s, but by 1965 Britain had granted independence to all the East African colonies except white-ruled Southern Rhodesia, which declared independence unilaterally.

Britain was thus almost completely out of the business of empire. Most of her former colonies remained in the British Commonwealth, whose members continue to meet periodically to discuss issues of common concern and share some special economic ties.

Policies of Other Nations

Holland and Belgium abandoned their holdings with less grace. The Dutch forcibly put down Indonesian nationalists after the war, but they had to grant considerable local autonomy and even so encountered steady resistance. In 1949, under pressure from the United States, they granted Indonesia full independence. Belgium, which had made no preparations for independence, faced rioting in the Congo in 1958. After stalling for a year amid mounting unrest, they yielded in 1960.

France's withdrawal from empire was more painful still. French politicians and military men yearned to compensate for their dismal performance against the Germans in 1940 and saw the maintenance of the colonies as essential to the national honor. Soon after the war a revolt in Madagascar was put down with great brutality. In 1946 fighting broke out against nationalists in Indochina. Finally defeated, in 1954, the French granted independence to the area the following year. The final troublespot was North Africa. France granted increased autonomy to Tunisia and Morocco and then yielded to nationalist demands for virtually complete independence in 1956, rather than face another war like that in Indochina.

Algeria was a different story. The French insisted on treating it as part of France and the large minority of European settlers pressed the government to maintain this policy. A guerrilla war broke out in 1954, marked by frequent acts of terrorism by the Algerian nationalists and by the French army. The agony of conducting yet another war took its toll on French morale. Finally, in 1962, the government of Charles de Gaulle decided to withdraw. De Gaulle also had resolved to risk no similar conflicts with France's colonies in Black Africa. In 1958 he offered them the choice of complete independence or autonomy within a newly established "French Community." Guinea chose independence; 14 other countries entered the Community. These countries received full independence in 1960, though a looser Community was retained between them and France, providing cultural exchanges and offering the new nations special privileges in trading with France.

Of all the European powers only Portugal has refused to give up its colonial holdings. It still continues to battle nationalist guerrillas in Angola and, to a lesser extent, in Mozambique.

Europe's Position

The end of outright European imperialism is one of the seminal developments in modern world history. Europe's influence did not recede as rapidly as the colonial independence movement might suggest. After several years of bitterness, Belgian advisers and businessmen returned to the Congo. France in 1970 was still sending thousands of teachers, a great deal of financial and technical aid, and in some cases military advisers to many former French colonies. Europe's greatest success in preserving cordial relations occurred with the new nations of Africa, though there were important exceptions even here. Having granted independence before any major nationalist protests erupted, Europe had already made a good start in this area. The new nations' dependence on European markets and the absence of interference from the superpowers, who have dabbled in African affairs only sporadically, are factors that also explain Europe's success. But European influence is modest in Asia; Britain's decision in 1968 to pull out all or almost all its military forces from Asia capped Europe's steady retreat. Still more notable was Europe's lack of control over events in the Middle East, Europe's own doorstep. During the 1956 Suez crisis, Britain and France had a final fling at old-fashioned imperialism. Their efforts to discipline Egypt failed because of opposition at home but above all because of the hostility of the superpowers.

The profound transformation of diplomacy since 1945 is only part of Europe's story. Europe's position in world affairs has greatly declined and, correspondingly, diplomacy has receded in importance in European history proper. The end of empire strikingly reveals the new situation: a sign of Europe's weakness, it was also a sign of the reorientation of Europe's politics and society. Admittedly Europe was prodded into abandoning its empire and the process caused much internal bitterness. Nationalists, among them many former colonists and many military men, were outraged. Yet from a European standpoint the process went amazingly smoothly. Europe did not seriously try to make the decision that most former imperial powers have done when threatened—namely, to move toward a military dictatorship in order to preserve the empire at all costs. This temptation, visible in ancient Athens and still more so in Rome, was avoided in part because of the exhaustion of war and the pressure of the superpowers, but also because Europe was discovering a new and positive set of priorities. This process, if still incomplete, is the essence of Europe's history since 1945.

12 POLITICS
AND THE STATE
IN CONTEMPORARY
EUROPE

There is no point in concealing the pitfalls that beset anyone who tries to treat contemporary European history, or any contemporary history for that matter, in textbook form. The historian's biases are unusually obtrusive—in this case the author's enthusiasm for the course Europe has pursued in the last 20 years. We are so close to the events that it is difficult to be sure leading trends are correctly interpreted. One may be unduly tempted to exaggerate comparisons with the past or to venture some prediction of the future course of events; indeed, correctly identifying trends involves predicting to a certain extent, though there is no guarantee that unforeseen factors might not divert the trends. It is always safest to offer only a brief factual narrative. But a more speculative approach is necessary if one is to make any sense out of the facts as we now know them.

THE NEW EUROPE

The major thesis of these two final chapters is that along with its decline in world diplomacy, Europe entered a decisive new period. The contrast with Europe's recent past is vivid. In the welfare state Europe developed an unprecedented definition of state functions, with a decided shift in the political spectrum as well. Above all, Europe entered a new stage of industralization, the stage of consumer affluence, and every social class was changed in the process. Indeed the class relationships of the first stages of industrialization, which had soured so bitterly after World War I, were decisively altered. Links with the past were preserved, but insofar as the historian can judge any society "new," there was a new Europe.

The new Europe in many ways resembled other countries in a comparable stage of industrialization, most notably those in North America. But Europe changed more decisively, in part because it shed many traditional diplomatic responsibilities but also because of the marked differences in its social classes. To an extent, then, Europe was developing a distinctive model for the affluent society.

There was no single Europe after 1945. As has been the case since the beginning of industrialization, and even before, Europe must be considered in the light of a variety of distinctions. One distinction divides political forms between non-Communist and Communist states, with remaining authoritarian regimes a differentiated group in the first category. Another distinction, at least as important as the first, is between those areas of Europe in the most advanced stages of industrialization, mainly the northwest, those in an intermediate state, such as Russia and Czechoslovakia, and those in a rather preliminary stage, including Communist and non-Communist countries in southern Europe. Most of the Communist areas of Europe underwent a profound social as well as political transformation after World War II, which accompanied their extensive development of industrialization. A leading question, unfortunately unanswerable, is whether still further economic development would take the eastern European states into an age of affluence, whether the gap between them and the more advanced zones of Europe, which long antedated the "iron curtain," would diminish.

THE AUTHORITARIAN STATES

The defeat of Fascism in World War II did not touch the conservative regimes of Spain and Portugal, both of which had remained carefully and cleverly neutral. The subsequent Cold War benefited these countries, for since they were not Communist they were automatically put in the "free-world" category. Portugal was a charter member of NATO. Spain was not so readily accepted, for socialists and others in northern Europe harbored bitter memories of the Civil War. But the United States granted military and economic assistance to Franco's government in return for American bases on Spanish soil. Spain's diplomatic position within Europe improved as well, though it remained isolated from any formal alliances.

The basic nature of the two states did not alter. Both continued to rely heavily on the Church. Both maintained powerful political police and normally restricted freedom of the press. State-controlled labor unions inhibited working-class protest. Elections were carefully staged to limit opposition, and no elected body had any significant authority. The survival of the founders of the two regimes, Salazar in Portugal and Franco in Spain, was more than symbolic; neither man would countenance real political change.

The diplomatic situation encouraged occasional modifications of political tone, for both regimes wanted to please the democratic states with which they were now allied. Salazar periodically relaxed his control of the press. In 1953 a semi-free municipal election was held in which opposition candidates won 20 percent of the vote. But these were sporadic gestures, and opposition groups—led mainly by elderly politicians—were generally tame.

Franco made somewhat more durable concessions to freedom of the press during the 1960s, but recurrent political arrests testified that in Spain, as well as in Portugal, authoritarianism was essentially unchanged. Traditional conservative forces gained greater predominance in Spain, continuing a trend that began virtually with Franco's seizure of power. The Falange party, with its Fascist trappings, lost most of its authority. Franco himself abandoned any effort to play the role of Fascist leader, preferring to work quietly instead of arousing the masses. In this situation the army, the Church, and the landlords—Spain's conservative trinity—found their interests well served.

Economic Policies

Both Spain and Portugal faced major problems of economic development. Despite their conservatism the regimes could not continue to ignore the poverty and backwardness of their countries. During the early 1950s Portuguese economic expansion failed to keep pace even with its population growth. Appalling poverty prompted the conservative Catholic hierarchy to sound an alarm. In 1955 Salazar launched an economic development plan, which increased annual economic growth to about 5 percent. But in the early 1960s, revolt broke out in the African territory of Angola. The Salazar government resolved to maintain its colonies at all costs—thus rejecting the flexible policy that every other European imperial power had adopted by this time. Military expenses quadrupled, drastically reducing funds for economic growth, and to forestall dissent at home repressive policies were tightened.

The Spanish economy followed a different pattern. Spain had few colonies left, and several pockets of territory in Africa were turned over to newly independent states such as Morocco without great difficulty. The Spanish economy also benefited from American aid and from a vast influx of tourists from northern Europe. As the power of the Falange party waned, its role in the government was partly taken over by a Catholic group called the *Opus Dei,* which advocated economic development along with strictly conservative politics. From the *Opus Dei* came a number of cabinet minis-

ters with a technocratic bent, who increased the pace of Spanish industrialization. Spain remained a backward country by general European standards,
but economic growth quickened and the usual signs of industrialization, including rapidly expanding cities, showed up in more and more regions. To
be sure, the countryside was still impoverished, as the hold of great estates
was unshaken and the landlords continued to be disinterested in agricultural
improvements. Spain was attempting the difficult trick of industrialization
without political or social reform.

Signs of Change

Two decades of weary apathy followed the Civil War, after which
Spain's political calm began to be challenged. At the end of 1955 labor
unrest developed in Barcelona and in the Basque provinces, both centers
of traditional autonomist sentiment. Lengthy strikes broke out, particularly
in the mines, despite the government control of trade unions. Students also
grew restive and several demonstrations occurred. At the same time a segment of the Catholic Church became critical of the regime. A minority of
bishops as well as many younger priests sought to dissociate the Church
from Franco's policies and also preached the necessity of thorough social
reform. This movement received considerable support from the Papacy
after the accession of the liberal John XXIII in 1958. Franco remained in
power, however. Since it was still difficult for formal opposition to develop,
unrest was sporadic rather than persistent. Massive arrests and harsh court
sentences, for example, ended the 1955 outburst. But major strikes broke
out again at several points during the 1960s and protest by university students crested once more at the end of that decade. Separatist sentiment in
the Basque provinces also gained strength, causing unrest during 1970.

In both Spain and Portugal, under their aging leaders, the problem of
succession loomed large. Because the conservatives who supported Franco
were mainly monarchists, it was not surprising that Franco promised, as
early as 1947, that on his death or retirement a king would once again rule
Spain. From 1955 onward the young prince, Juan Carlos, was groomed for
the job and gained increasing popularity. By the end of the 1960s, when
Juan Carlos was allowed a more independent voice, he suggested that the
restored monarchy might be more liberal than Franco's regime. It seemed
possible, certainly, that the transition to monarchy might be easy and practical. In Portugal, Salazar made fewer plans for the future. Incapacitated
by a stroke in 1969, he was succeeded by a long-time aide, Marcello
Caetano, a simple enough transition. Caetano sought to modify the tone
of the Salazar regime, relaxing press censorship and allowing opposition
politicians to speak, but in substance the regime did not change. Political
activity was still severely limited; colonialism in Africa was maintained.

The future of the authoritarian states remains unclear. The succession of new leaders may force major changes, but more fundamental the question asked is whether the authoritarian regimes can modernize their economies to keep pace with developments elsewhere in Europe. If they fail, unrest may broaden, for it is apparent that new expectations are developing in the Iberian peninsula, if only because so many Spanish and Portuguese workers have sought jobs in industrially advanced areas like France and Germany. If economic change goes too far, it might undermine the conservative base of the regimes.

The Greek Regime

Yet it would be a mistake to underestimate the durability of the authoritarian regimes or to dismiss them as Iberian anachronisms. Similar regimes spread in many parts of the world after World War II, and even in Europe authoritarianism made a comeback. In 1967 a military coup abolished democracy in Greece and, when the young King Constantine tried to take an independent role, he was exiled by the new leaders. Greece was another impoverished country, with deep divisions between the very wealthy few and the poor masses. The parliamentary regime, restored after the war and the defeat of Communist guerillas, proved unstable and ineffective. By the 1960s leftist political agitation revived, which frightened the military. After the coup, parliament was dissolved and political opposition rigorously repressed. There were many arrests and Colonel Pappadopoulos ruled as virtual dictator. His aim, he claimed, was not only to unite Greece but to uplift Greek morality. Legislation favoring religion and banning "indecent" attire and behavior soon followed the takeover.

As with Spain and Portugal, the future of the Greek regime cannot be foretold. An equally important question, though no easier to answer, is whether authoritarian government might spread further in Europe, in countries without a firm democratic tradition or with a tradition of unstable democracy.

THE COMMUNIST STATES: STALINISM

During the war, Communist discipline had relaxed somewhat in Russia as ideological conformity took a back seat to the military effort. Stalin made concessions to Russian patriotism and even to religion in order to achieve national unity. With victory, however, the old controls returned. In 1946 Stalin reasserted his supremacy by purging the armed forces. Successful generals who had gained popularity during the war were demoted, while troops contaminated by contact with the west were weeded out. Ministers of state were also purged, primarily because Stalin feared they were disloyal to him. The labor camps in Siberia were filled with minority peoples of the Crimea and the Caucasus whom Stalin accused of collaboration with the Germans.

Rigorous orthodoxy was imposed on all cultural life. Prokofiev and other noted composers were accused of betraying "bourgeois" influences in their music; most confessed their "guilt" and promised to reform. A party line was established in biology, which insisted that Mendelian genetics, which pointed to random inheritance, was incorrect and stressed instead the possibility of inheriting acquired characteristics. This theory, far more optimistic about human progress than Mendelian genetics, did little to advance Soviet biology. Cultural life in general was stultified as the last years of Stalin's rule were dominated by his near-paranoia. More massive purges seemed to threaten, while Stalin's suspicions of those around him created constant turmoil.

Economic Advances

Russia's economic reconstruction proceeded rapidly despite the political confusion. The fourth Five-Year Plan, which went into effect in 1946, stressed heavy industry and military production, including atomic energy. Russia made extensive use of reparations from defeated countries and of the resources of the new Communist states of eastern Europe. Rapid economic development designed to bolster military strength became a characteristic of the Stalinist system. Stalin's fearful mood extended to diplomatic relations; the United States' Cold War policies and its leadership in atomic weapons convinced the dictator that war was more than possible. America's intervention in the Korean War in 1950 heightened his apprehension, for if the "imperialists" would fight for so small a cause as Korea, what would prevent them from assaulting European Communist states as well? Hence a military orientation pervaded Russia's economic development, which meant that despite rapid economic growth severe shortages of consumer goods and housing continued.

The Satellite States

The Stalinist system was fully extended to the Communist states of eastern Europe. Communist seizure of control in Rumania, Bulgaria, Albania, Hungary, Czechoslovakia and Poland was followed by a three-stage suppression of organized opposition. Democratic political leaders were attacked first, followed by a series of trials of prominent churchmen. Then the Communists began to purge their own ranks, as "Muscovites" loyal to Stalin battled home-grown Communist leaders accused of "nationalist" deviations. The first two stages cleared the way for a totalitarian state, having made organized opposition virtually impossible. The third reflected the ambiguities of Communism outside Russia, for revolutionary fervor might not prove compatible with acceptance of Russian control.

Opposition politicians were disposed of rather easily. Some escaped abroad; others, like Imliu Maniu, a veteran peasant party leader in Rumania, were imprisoned for life; still others were tried and hanged. In the countries of Orthodox faith, religion offered little resistance. The Orthodox churches were accustomed to state authority and the clergy were neither forceful nor well educated; as a result, they either acquiesced or actively supported the new regimes. Roman Catholicism presented a more serious problem: religious faith was strong and the Church enjoyed active support from Catholics elsewhere and from the Papacy. The Communists avoided a frontal attack; instead they limited the Church's role in education and struck at the chief religious figure in each country in order to frighten the clergy into submission. In Hungary, for example, Cardinal Joseph Mindszenty was tried in 1949 and was forced to confess to a series of most unlikely crimes. By the early 1950s the Church had been terrified into submission everywhere save in Poland, where religious feeling was unusually intense and where the Communist regime had to move far more cautiously.

The Yugoslavian Experience

Yugoslavia under Tito followed a roughly similar pattern until 1948. Non-Communist leaders and parties were brought to heel, the Church was bullied into submission. But Tito had come to power without Russian help, and Stalin believed he was too independent. Tito, in turn, resented Stalin's domineering tone and complained of the tendency of Russian secret police to treat Yugoslavia as its own preserve. When Tito discussed a South Slav federation with Bulgaria, he was roundly rebuked, for Stalin wanted no secondary groupings in the Communist camp. Soon after this, in June 1948, the newly formed association of Communist parties, or Cominform, expelled the Yugoslav party.

Tito was shaken by this act. Hostile propaganda from neighboring states further challenged his authority. But the Yugoslav party and his own secret police remained loyal, and Tito's popularity as a Resistance hero won him still wider support. Soon the regime began to make a virtue of necessity. Tito groped toward a definition of his position by stressing the Leninist purity of his doctrine against Stalin's perversions of it. He began to liberalize his regime and reopened contacts with the west.

Consolidation of Communism

Tito's break prompted tighter Russian control in the other Communist states. Russia sought a purge of each Communist party in order to eliminate those with a "nationalist" or Titoist bent. The purge went on from 1949 to Stalin's death in 1953. Everywhere older leaders, trained in Russia, won out over the younger men who had risen during the war and postwar years. As in Russia during the purges of the 1930s, the winnowing process stifled talent and independent initiative in the Communist parties and a dull bureaucratic uniformity resulted.

At the political level, the consolidation of Communist rule may seem largely a matter of petty if brutal manipulation. In broader terms, however, the Communist takeover had truly revolutionary effects on the eastern European countries. The old ruling class was destroyed and upper-class politicians and churchmen were attacked. But more important was the Communist seizure of the large estates. The long-dominant landlords were swept away as each regime began a collectivization of agriculture along Russian lines. By 1951 Bulgaria had collectivized half the land. Elsewhere the process moved more slowly, but the peasant world was being shaken. The regimes rapidly extended educational facilities. Literacy increased quickly, and some talented children from the lower classes gained access to higher education. Each government, finally, pushed for rapid industrialization—again a profound change for all the new Communist countries save Czechoslovakia. Basic industry was nationalized and almost all countries embarked on five-year development plans. By 1953 the area's steel production had doubled, and most sectors of industry, particularly of heavy industry, expanded rapidly. Other trappings of industrialization, including rapid urban growth, were visible as well.

As with early industrialization elsewhere, widespread hardship existed in the new factories and growing cities. Workers were forced into long hours and severe factory discipline. In a few sectors of the economy forced labor was used. Urban overcrowding was a massive problem as the industrial labor force increased by about a third. Communist policies in some respects heightened these common problems. The collectivization of agriculture was resisted by many peasants and did not quickly result in increased production. This in turn limited the quality and sometimes the quantity of food available to urban workers. The stress on heavy industry kept other consumer goods in short supply. Russia's dominance of the east European zone forced economic specialization in some countries that benefited Russia but not necessarily themselves. All the new Communist countries maintained large military forces that further drained their already limited resources.

RUSSIAN COMMUNISM AFTER STALIN

Stalin died in March 1953. As was immediately evident in the battle for succession that followed his death, the system he had built up could not continue unchanged, either in Russia or the other Communist countries. Political and military leaders jockeyed for power until a triumvirate emerged, headed by Georgi Malenkov, a party bureaucrat, and including V. M. Molotov, a foreign affairs expert, and Lavrenti Beria, the chief of secret police. This group quickly fell apart. Beria was stripped of his authority and executed. His fall marked a decline in the almost unlimited powers the secret police had exercised during Stalin's last years. The police continued to exist, but it resorted less often to arbitrary arrest and loomed less large in the life of the ordinary Russian citizen. Malenkov also tried to modify Stalin's economic policies by emphasizing consumer goods and trying to reorganize agricultural production. Writers and artists were granted greater freedom of expression, and conditions in the forced labor camps were slightly improved. A revolt in East Berlin and other East German cities in 1953 and rioting in a Russian forced labor camp brought quick military repression, but thereafter the Russian government continued its cautious retreat from Stalinist practices. A new five-year plan for 1956–1960 sought to double Russian consumption levels and provide housing for 17 million new city dwellers. Concessions were also offered to the peasantry to cope with the enduring problem of low agricultural production. Abroad, Malenkov relaxed Russian economic exploitation of the east European states.

These changes dismayed orthodox Stalinists and the military. In 1955 Malenkov was forced to resign, admitting his inability to deal with the problems his partial abandonment of Stalinism had created. The military dominated the new government, which had Marshal Nikolai Bulganin as its nominal head. Emphasis on armaments and heavy industrial equipment was restored. At the same time Russia reconsidered its relations with the east European countries. The Warsaw Pact was formed in response to the rearmament of West Germany. Russia remained dominant in the alliance, but the links were defined in terms of greater equality.

The Rise of Khrushchev

Throughout these months a little-known party figure, Nikita Khrushchev, had been advancing in the government. He became first secretary of the

Communist party after Stalin's death and a member of the triumvirate after Beria's execution. He allied himself with the military when Malenkov was dismissed, and under this cover steadily consolidated his own power. As was the case with Stalin a generation before, control of the party machinery proved the most direct path to control of the Soviet state. Unlike Stalin, however, Khrushchev merely pushed his rivals out, rather than having them executed. Late in 1955 Molotov, the last of the Old Bolsheviks, confessed his errors and resigned the following year. Khrushchev was now master of the state. When Bulganin resigned in 1958, all pretense of collective rule was abandoned.

At the Twentieth Communist Party Congress in February 1956, Khrushchev dramatically set the tone for his regime. He denounced Stalin as a brutal, almost insane tyrant who had ordered the slaughter of countless innocent people, who had brought great suffering to his country, and who had caused the government to lose touch with the people. One by one he detailed the "crimes of the Stalin era" and denounced Stalin's self-glorification. In his long, rambling speech Khrushchev also claimed that there were several possible ways to reach "socialism" besides Communist orthodoxy. Supposedly secret, the speech was allowed to leak both to the Communist and the non-Communist press, causing great ferment in the Communist movement everywhere. The confirmation of the evils of Stalin's regime repelled many. On the other hand Khrushchev's promise of a better future won him considerable support and inspired a new vitality in a number of Communist parties.

Within the Soviet Union, Khrushchev followed his speech by extending the relaxations begun under Malenkov. An official program of de-Stalinization was launched, which included removing his pictures and statues from public places, rewriting official histories, and removing Stalin's body from the Lenin Tomb in Moscow's Red Square. Conditions were again improved in the forced labor camps. Contacts with the west increased. Khrushchev launched a program of cultural exchange and made a number of official visits to western countries. Selected Russians traveled and studied abroad, foreign visitors were welcomed to Russia, and writers and artists were held under looser controls. In 1955 Ilya Ehrenburg published a story called "The Thaw," which referred to the changes that had taken place since Stalin's death.

Nonetheless there were limits still. Writers could criticize Soviet life but they had to point out that any shortcomings were being overcome. In 1957 Boris Pasternak was forbidden to publish *Dr. Zhivago* in Russia, for the novel questioned certain values of Soviet society. Khrushchev's economic policies had ambiguities as well. He talked of the importance of improving the standard of living and without question the availability of consumer goods increased. Yet emphasis on heavy industrial goods remained, and the growth rate of this sector was by far the most rapid. Khrushchev was fond of boasting that Russia would soon overtake the United States in heavy industrial production. He did make major efforts to improve Russian agriculture, which persistently suffered because the peasants disliked the lack of incentive on the collective farms and concentrated on their own small plots of land. Though these plots constituted only about 3 percent of Russian cultivated land, they produced a fifth of the country's milk and a third of its meat. In 1954 Khrushchev launched a "virgin lands" project to bring the vast area of Soviet Asia under cultivation. He also tried to increase the production of corn and in 1957 began a drive to overtake the United States by 1961 in the per capita production of milk, butter, and meat. But Russian agriculture still faltered. Despite frequent dismissals of agricultural officials, food shortages continued and the Russians were forced, despite the needs of advancing industrialization, to keep nearly half the population in the countryside in order to assure food for the cities.

Khrushchev was a tinkerer, and no brief survey can do full justice to the shifts of his policy. He radiated optimism and energy. He enjoyed intervening in the economic planning apparatus. First he stressed local initiative in factory management, then he returned to central control. His shifts annoyed many bureaucrats, and he was not always able to claim success. Khrushchev's standing was seriously weakened by the failure of his agricultural policies—a failure made strikingly visible by a disastrous harvest in 1963 that forced the Russians to buy wheat abroad.

Khrushchev's Decline

Khrushchev's foreign policy also had erratic qualities. He normally sought to be conciliatory toward the west, but he periodically became truculent. In 1961 he authorized the East German government to build a wall between the Communist and western sectors of Berlin in order to cut off the flow of escapees to the west. The following year he installed medium-range missiles in Cuba. Though he pulled off the first venture, he was forced to withdraw the Cuban missiles. At the same time, although his periods of conciliation notably relaxed Cold War tension, they produced few concrete gains for Russia. From 1960 onward, Khrushchev was also involved in an ideological battle with the Chinese Communists, who accused him of deviating from revolutionary purity in dealing with the west. Though most European Communists supported Khrushchev's vigorous rebuttal—only Albania sided with the Chinese, in response to which Khrushchev severed diplomatic relations—many were unhappy with the rift.

By the mid-1960s, Khrushchev's troubles mounted. He was finding it difficult to point to clear successes either at home or abroad, and his personal style—impulsive, sometimes boorish—annoyed many Russians. He was resented not only by the old-line Stalinists, but by the newer Communist bureaucrats as well. In 1964 Khrushchev was forced out, replaced by colorless party bureaucrats. Alexei Kosygin became premier, while Leonid Brezhnev held the more influential post of party first secretary. This time the collective approach to leadership seemed to work. Brezhnev's ascendancy gradually increased over the more moderate and internationally minded Kosygin. By the Twenty-fourth Party Congress in 1971 some effort developed to glorify Brezhnev as first leader, but no new personality cult developed and key decisions seemed to emerge from the leadership as a whole.

The New Rulers

The new leaders generally maintained Khrushchev's policies. They continued to advocate co-existence with the west, but suspicions remained deep and the effort to expand Russian armaments accelerated. Despite the softer tone they adopted toward China, the rift remained. Internal policy became somewhat tougher. In reaction to Khrushchev's departure there was a partial rehabilitation of Stalin's reputation, which was more than purely symbolic. Restrictions on writers and artists were tightened, but all this merely modified the post-Stalinist relaxation—there was no return to the old-style police state. A mounting series of protests against arrests of dissident intellectuals, from prominent scientists and authors, confirmed the ambiguous situation. Undoubtedly there was repression, but there was some room for agitation against it.

The new leaders produced no experiments in agriculture to compare with Khrushchev's, but agricultural production did improve. The rate of industrial production, though substantial, still lagged, and Russian officials blamed unduly rigid central planning for some of the difficulties. They cited problems in assuring adequate supplies to factories and bemoaned the temptation of factory managers to falsify production figures. At the same time widely noted difficulties with the labor force, particularly excessive drinking and even alcoholism, affected production as well. In an attempt to meet the structural problems of industrial production, a number of Russian economists urged some decentralization of planning; they further recommended the adoption of a market-based accounting system for individual factories that would clearly reveal profit and loss and would provide real incentives for factories to improve their operations. The main remedies put forth against alcoholism were extensive propaganda and vigorous efforts at disciplining offenders. In the Party Congress of 1971, Brezhnev returned to a familiar post-Stalin theme in promising rapid improvements in the consumer sector under the next five-year plan. Indeed the Congress had been delayed a year while the government discussed this new tack, presumably encountering stiff opposition from the military. It remained unclear to what extent the economy would take a really new direction.

POST-STALINIST COMMUNISM:
THE SMALLER STATES

Between 1948 and 1954, Yugoslavia developed something of an alternative to the Russian brand of Communism. It stood alone in the Communist world in advocating a diplomatic policy of neutrality between east and west. Tito encouraged economic and cultural contacts with western Europe and the United States and aligned himself with new countries in Africa and Asia, which also sought neutrality in the Cold War.

Titoism was far more than a diplomatic policy, however; it offered a distinctive model for the construction of a socialist society. Tito halted the program of agricultural collectivization and compulsory delivery of crops; instead, Yugoslav agriculture continued to be based on peasant plots producing for a market system. Industrial planning and direction were decentralized. While there was no independent trade union movement, workers' councils in the larger factories had an important voice in management decisions. Tito was less innovative in the political sphere. He recognized the rights of individual citizens in the courts and before the secret police, granted freedom of speech to a limited extent, and relaxed his conflict with the Catholic Church. But basically there was little structural change in the authoritarian system, and by 1954 Tito moved to restrict freedom of expression. He bitterly condemned the effort of a former colleague, Milovan Djilas, to form a liberal socialist party to compete with the communists. Djilas was ultimately jailed, and the Communist monopoly of power reaffirmed. Titoism, then, meant a relatively flexible diplomatic and economic policy under an authoritarian political structure.

The other Communist countries were firmly in the Stalinist orbit and most survived his death and the ensuing confusion in Russian leadership without great change. Because of the completeness of the recent purges, many states were more Stalinist than Russia for a number of years. The Stalinist model for the countries of eastern Europe involved complete loyalty to Russia in diplomatic policy, which the Warsaw Pact confirmed. In dealing with western Europe and the United States, the countries of eastern Europe acted as one with Russia. Internally they promoted rapid collectivization of agriculture and also stressed the development of heavy industry over consumer goods production. These programs required firm control over the citizenry. The east European countries mounted extensive propaganda efforts to encourage loyalty and established an elaborate secret police to enforce it. Dissent was not tolerated. The Communist party controlled the government and it in turn was usually controlled by a single leader—often one who had been trained in Russia before 1945.

East Germany proved to be one of the most durable "Stalinist" states. Walther Ulbricht, backed by numerous Russian troops and a large army of his own, ruled with an iron hand. Dissent was sternly repressed, while the regime began a rapid program of agricultural collectivization and heavy industrial growth. In Czechoslovakia, Albania, Rumania, and Bulgaria similar regimes easily maintained their sway for years after Stalin's death. In two countries, however, the apparent changes in Russian policy prompted a swift reaction.

Agitation in Poland and Hungary

Poland and Hungary each had a tradition of hostility toward Russia and of openness toward western Europe, but both countries had leaders who were willing to steer a new course. Wladislaw Gomulka was the only major national Communist to survive the final Stalinist purge in Poland, while in Hungary Imre Nagy was a rather liberal Communist who served as prime minister in the Malenkov era and gained considerable popularity. Khrushchev's anti-Stalin speech in 1956 caused widespread ferment among intellectuals and articulate urban workers of both countries. There seemed to be hope for more freedom, yet at the same time the existing regimes seemed immune to change. Literary discussion groups were formed, and they soon made contact with some of the workers. Ironically, halting efforts at de-Stalinization added fuel to the fire. Some political prisoners, including Gomulka, were released, but there was no substantive reform. All that resulted was a chance for dissidence to spread, even among younger Communists.

In June 1956, Polish workers rioted in Poznan. Russian troops had to use force to suppress them, which merely proved that Polish Stalinists no longer had control of the country. Agitation by intellectual groups continued, and gradually the Stalinist leaders were forced to resign. By October Gomulka reentered the government. Frightened by the prospect of dissidence, Khrushchev rushed to Warsaw and the Russian army began moving toward the capital. But Gomulka and his colleagues stood fast, and the Russians accepted Gomulka's election as party first secretary. In return Gomulka promised to remain in the Warsaw Pact and to keep dissidence under firm control.

Inspired by events in Poland, a vast crowd of demonstrators gathered in Budapest on October 23, calling for the resignation of the government. When the secret police opened fire, outright revolution burst forth. Nagy became premier, but he lacked control of events and was forced to promise free elections and withdrawal from the Warsaw Pact. At this point the Russians decided to intervene. Soviet tanks brutally beat down the revolutionaries. Tens of thousands of Hungarians fled abroad and the old Stalinists were returned to power. Nagy was later executed, a grim warning to Communist leaders who might be tempted to deviate from orthodoxy.

The Hungarian Revolt: Funeral procession for a patriot killed in the first days of the uprising.

The suppression of the revolution created worldwide shock. The western powers were preoccupied with their own problems: the United States with a presidential election, Britain and France with an expedition against Egypt over the control of the Suez Canal. Consequently Russia had a free hand. But western Communists were dismayed by the brutal act and many intellectuals abandoned the party. Nevertheless, with the exception of Poland, experimentation in eastern Europe came to an end for many years. Even Tito approved of Russia's action.

Massive anti-Russian demonstrations occurred in Poland, but Gomulka kept his people under control; in this he had support from the Church, which regarded his rule as the best Poland could hope for. A new regime began to take shape in 1957. Partially free elections returned a minority of non-Communists to parliament, and genuine debates took place in that body thereafter. As in Yugoslavia, agricultural collectivization came to an end. Workers' councils, which had arisen during earlier agitation, were recognized and allowed to represent workers in their grievances against the factories. Political prisoners were released and the secret police curbed. Ferment among intellectuals increased as censorship virtually collapsed.

Then, in the second half of 1957, Gomulka partially reversed the tide of change as he gained full control of the party and state. Police spying resumed, the powers of the workers' councils were reduced, and the campaign against the Church was revived. Poland did not return to Stalinist policies but, as happened in Yugoslavia, the process of liberalization had been limited and many intellectuals were profoundly disillusioned with the result. Peasants were relatively free from state interference and workers had some individual and collective rights. Intellectual activity was not forced into a single mold; rather there was considerable creativity in Polish literature and social sciences.

New Pressures for Change

Thus matters stood for four or five years. The Russian orbit seemed intact, with only Yugoslavia outside it, while within only Poland offered any significant variation of the essentially Stalinist model. But in the early 1960s a new but modest push for independence emerged. Intellectuals sought looser controls, encouraged both by the partial relaxation in Russia under Khrushchev and by some contacts with new trends in the west. Response to such pressures varied. In Czechoslovakia and East Germany, the old-line Stalinist policies continued, but under Janos Kadar the Hungarian government began to curtail police controls by the mid-1960s. Cultural exchange with the west expanded. By 1971 some genuine electoral contests were permitted, particularly at the local level; Communist candidates did not always win, though all candidates were required to pledge loyalty to the regime. Rumania, too, embarked on liberalization though on a more modest scale than Hungary.

Still more pervasive were pressures for economic reform. Agriculture was a problem everywhere, though less in Poland and Yugoslavia where collectivization ceased and production expanded. Elsewhere stagnation threatened, for by 1960 agriculture had been almost completely collectivized. Governments did little to conciliate the hostile peasantry and did not allot funds for agricultural development. The main emphasis was on industrial expansion, but here, too, there were problems. As in Russia, growth rates were beginning to slacken and centralized planning frequently created bottlenecks. The working class showed signs of dissatisfaction. Absenteeism increased as did thefts from factories. Generally, workers lacked incentives for diligent labor, for with the slow expansion of consumer goods production there was little left for them to buy.

A number of Communist states partially decentralized economic management. In the 1960s Yugoslavia, which had led the way, resumed the effort to reform economic organization. Workers' councils were created in major factories to participate in decisions about plant management and the allocation of resources. In at least some instances increased productivity resulted. No other state went so far. But in 1964 Czechoslovakia introduced "market relations" and an ordinary price mechanism into the state-controlled economy. Planning authorities issued long-term rather than annual directives to individual factory managers. In general, Czechoslovakia and other states moved farther in economic reforms than Russia did, though most of the problems were the same. Economists in several countries talked of the need for still further change. They hailed the effort to introduce market prices as the most efficient means of exchanging resources and talked also of the need for a profit system to provide some incentives for greater efficiency on the part of the managers and workers in individual factories.

Economic problems triggered new conflicts with Russia. It was widely recognized that greater coordination was needed among the Communist states in order to utilize the largest possible economic market. But there was widespread fear that Russia would use such coordination to her own advantage. An effort by Khrushchev to offer specific investment plans in 1962 brought widespread dissension. Rumania, particularly, claimed that the Russians sought a permanent division between industrial and agrarian nations in the Communist world. The Rumanians insisted on their own industrialization and were not content merely to provide grain and oil for more advanced areas. Building on this economic disagreement, they steadily assumed greater independence of action in the late 1960s. New contacts with the west and with China were opened, while the young Rumanian leader, Nicolae Ceausescu, regularly lectured the Russians on the need to respect national autonomy.

Though no other east European state went so far toward diplomatic independence, it was obvious by the late 1960s that each Communist state made most of its own decisions and had something of its own style. Only Bulgaria and East Germany, the latter guided by Ulbricht's stern hand and the belief that Russian protection was needed against West Germany, showed little change. Elsewhere there was no automatic deference to Soviet wishes.

At the same time, however, limitations remained. Russia could tolerate Rumania's gestures because the Rumanian party kept firm control of internal developments. But in 1968 a more genuine challenge erupted and brought renewed reprisal.

The Crisis of 1968 and Its Aftermath

The halting economic reform begun in Czechoslovakia had proved inadequate. Production continued to be slack and worker dissatisfaction mounted. At the same time, a limited relaxation of restrictions on intellectual life whetted the appetite for more. Nationalist disputes between the Czechs and the Slovaks, with the latter demanding greater autonomy, added further to the unrest. In 1968 a reformist regime came into power, under the leadership of Alexander Dubcek. It promised extensive liberalization and won widespread support from burgeoning groups of workers and intellectuals throughout the country. Old-line Communists were alarmed and appealed for Russian aid. Response came quickly, and in August Russian troops moved into the major cities. This time there was no bloodbath, for the Czechs held back from a futile attack on the Russians. The reformist leadership was eased out, not executed, but the experiment had ended, amid profound disillusionment.

By the early 1970s, the smaller Communist states, like Russia itself, had staked out a limited range of experimentation around a totalitarian model. Opposition parties and open political discussion were ruled out. Only in Yugoslavia, as preparations began for a successor to Tito, and to an extent in Hungary, was there a suggestion of a more open political process. Secret police and censors enforced the political peace, and contact with the west was limited. At the same time no regime extended repression along Stalinist or Nazi lines. Changes in economic organization were widely discussed, both within the Communist parties and outside.

None of the regimes, however, at least outside of Russia, had yet won widespread popular enthusiasm. Czechoslovakia revealed the passions that could still burst forth after 20 years of Communist rule. Russia remained in a position to curb excessive unrest or deviation in any of the states on her borders. Many people doubtless accepted the Communist state out of disillusionment or simple indifference. But where a certain amount of flexibility had been introduced, as in Kadar's Hungary, there were some signs of more than passive acquiescence. Even critical intellectuals professed pride in many achievements of Communism and, though advocating change, sought to remain within a Communist framework.

Nevertheless, the problem of maintaining loyalty remained. Even those regimes that were initially flexible became more rigid as leaders grew older and less responsive to the mood of their people. Late in 1970 a series of massive strikes broke out in many Polish cities. Economic problems had prompted the regime to raise prices on food and some other consumer items. The strikes were in response to this action and also to efforts to speed up work on the docks and in some factories. The strikes were quelled with considerable bloodshed, but not before the now inflexible and aging Gomulka had been forced out of power and the price increases rescinded.

Clearly this new agitation raises many questions about the future of

Communist regimes. Recurrent protest has occurred despite police controls, and it often has made some gains. The problem of meeting consumer expectations is real and possibly growing; as needs are unfulfilled the zeal for work perhaps diminishes. There is little doubt that the Communist states are economically capable of meeting many consumer demands if they choose to do so. The question is whether they can do so without unforeseen changes in the political structure. The traditional association of Communist regimes with heavy industry has encouraged other features of the Communist state—control of workers in large industrial units, a powerful military, centralized planning. The Communist state has already evolved away from any simple totalitarian model. Despite Russian preeminence in Communist Europe, some interesting diversity among Communist states has developed. If their future course is unclear, some of the leading problems are not. Will the Communist states be able to enter what some call the postindustrial or consumer society, and if so with what effect? Or will an alternative economic stage be found? The Polish revolt suggests the desire for consumer advance and the Russian party congress in 1971 points toward some fulfillment of this desire. Both guarantee further change in the Communist states.

WESTERN EUROPE:
THE POLITICAL SPECTRUM

Most of the countries of western Europe faced a painful task of reconstruction after 1945. Economic rebuilding was the primary problem after the devastation of war, but new political arrangements were needed as well. In many of the areas that had been occupied by the Germans, old regimes could not automatically be restored. Many had been sullied by defeat; some political leaders had been discredited because of their collaboration with the Germans. In France, the Low Countries, and Scandinavia leading collaborators were tried and many executed or imprisoned. The process created considerable bitterness, but it helped open the way for a new regime. At the same time Resistance leaders had demanded a new political order and their active entry into postwar politics prompted some changes.

In Italy the collapse of the Fascist regime necessitated a new constitution. Many of the Fascist leaders were killed by Resistance partisans with or without benefit of a trial. West Germany was able to begin its political rebuilding in 1948 when the French zone of occupation was joined to the British and American zones and a federal government was formed.

None of the regimes in western Europe was entirely new. All preserved elements of the past. In Germany, for example, political leadership was assumed by Konrad Adenauer, a major local politician of the late Weimar years, while the revived Socialist party also harked back to its Weimar traditions. In France and elsewhere, restoration of prewar political trends and the prominence of elderly politicians profoundly disappointed Resistance idealists. But there was change and an indication of it was the spectrum of major political parties.

Political Trends: The Decline of the Radical Right

Political characteristics varied from one country to the next, and they changed frequently during the quarter century after 1945. Following an initial leftist surge, most countries turned more conservative in the 1950s. The 1960s saw a resurgence of the moderate left. Still, despite important variations, the lineup of political parties that emerged in 1945 tended to persist, and it was different from that of the interwar years. The rightist extreme was largely eliminated; the political center broadened and moved left. Polarization was greatly reduced.

The Fascist and authoritarian right was discredited. In the years immediately after the war it was dangerous to avow rightist sentiment, for trials of collaborationists continued. In Germany the Nazi party was outlawed. But even after memories of the war faded there were a few signs of a rightist revival. Both a neo-Fascist and a monarchist party existed in Italy, drawing some electoral support from the economically backward south. Small groups of neo-Fascist students occasionally rioted, particularly in response to leftist agitation. In 1970 there were rumors of a rightist coup.

The Fascist movement was not large and showed little indication of growing in strength, but it could not be entirely discounted. In France a rightist party briefly flourished in the mid-1950s when the country was politically unstable and the battle to retain rebellious colonies created further pressure. The Poujadistes, named after their leader, Pierre Poujade, drew support from small shopkeepers and peasants and frequently disrupted parliament by rowdy tactics. Though it elected 50 deputies in 1956, the movement was shortlived. In Germany the German Nationalist Party contained some neo-Nazi elements and adopted a strident nationalist program. In the mid-1960s, after a moderate economic recession, it picked up some voting strength in regional elections. Again, however, the movement quickly receded. In other words, the authoritarian right could still evoke memories and fears but it seemed to have lost any basis for durable strength.

Postwar Conservatism: The Rise of Christian Democracy

The leading conservative parties believed in parliamentary democracy and became more open to programs of social reform. They also became more complex. Most of them embraced a wider array of elements than had been true in the past, which on the whole helped moderate political dispute by reducing fragmentation and drawing the more flexible conservatives toward the center.

In Britain the Conservative party lost the easy predominance it had enjoyed between the wars. To win new support it began to advocate moderate welfare reforms or at least to accept those the socialists had introduced. The Conservatives retained their distinctiveness by cautioning against socialist extremes, including excessive nationalization, and by promising encouragement to private enterprise. They also were more nationalistic, critical of the dismemberment of the British Empire and eager to see Britain play an important role in world diplomacy. In the late 1960s some Conservative politicians seized on widespread concern about the influx of West Indian and Pakistani immigrants to advocate discriminatory policies, but the party as a whole disavowed outright racism.

On the continent, the rise of Christian Democratic parties constituted the most striking addition to the political spectrum. In Germany, Christian Democracy had some precedent in the traditional Catholic Center party, but it now broadened its base to include a substantial Protestant element. In France and Italy the new parties had their immediate origins in the Resistance movement, which therefore gave them a stronger reformist bent than the German party. But they drew substantial conservative support as well because of their association with religion; moreover, with the decay of the authoritarian right, conservative voters sought a new home. In Italy the Christian Democrats quickly became the largest party and controlled the government either outright or in coalition with other parties from 1945 onward. In Germany the party lost majority status only at the end of the 1960s. The French party (called the *Mouvement Républicain Populaire,* or MRP) rose to prominence immediately after the war; it later declined but continued to serve in most government coalitions.

Christian Democracy accepted the parliamentary system, republicanism, and universal suffrage. The old battle between Church and democracy was now over. As moderates, the Christian Democrats still maintained some conservative traditions. They defended private property against socialist or Communist systems and, while accepting religious liberty, they advocated state encouragement to religion. In most German states the Christian Democrats gave support to religious training in the public schools; in Italy the party backed Church policies on birth control and, until its legalization in 1971, divorce. But the rise of Christian Democratic parties involved considerable innovation in traditional European conservatism, even apart from their unambiguous commitment to democracy. They played down nationalism and provided most of the initiatives for European unity, particularly in France. In Germany Adenauer led his party away from a nationalist reaction to the division of the country by subordinating German reunification to a firm alliance with the United States and the nations of western Europe.

The Christian Democrats also favored moderate social reform. Like the British Conservatives they could live with the institutions of a welfare state and indeed often played a significant role in creating these institutions. Although the parties, particularly in Italy, often made positive action difficult, Christian Democracy was a more flexible form of conservatism than had ever before been developed on the continent.

The Nature of Gaullism

In France Gaullism to some extent took the role that Christian Democracy did elsewhere. As the leading figure in French Resistance, Charles de Gaulle served as head of the government until 1946, when he resigned. The following year, disgusted by the weaknesses of the parliamentary regime, de Gaulle founded his own party, the Rally of the French People (RPF), which emerged as the strongest single party in the elections of 1951. But the party declined thereafter. Upon de Gaulle's seizure of power in 1958, a new Gaullist party was founded, the Union of the New Republic (UNR), which has since maintained control of the government and parliament, usually in coalition with other groups including the Christian Democrats.

Gaullism differs from Christian Democracy in several respects, for it bears the unique stamp of its founder. De Gaulle was profoundly suspicious of parliamentary rule and party divisions, and his movement undoubtedly drew support from advocates of authoritarian rule. The UNR, however, has emphasized the importance of parliament, occasionally against de Gaulle himself. In its insistence on the grandeur of France Gaullism represented a revival of nationalism. Many Gaullists sought to retain France's colonial empire; still more objected to France's subservience to American diplomacy and to undue European integration. But the Gaullists have not made nationalism their principal platform and, like de Gaulle, they have proved flexible on most nationalist issues. Hence they acquiesced on the question of decolonization.

In most other respects, the Gaullists resemble Christian Democrats. They favor some aid to the Church, and the Gaullist regime extended financial assistance to Church schools. They embrace a wide spectrum of opinions on social questions and include a minority of ardent reformers. They have thus maintained, and in some ways extended, the institutions of the welfare state.

Intermediate Parties

A variety of small parties fell between the moderate conservatives and the left. Most of them, like the venerable Radical party in France, maintained the liberal tradition. They defended free enterprise and were uncomfortable with major social reform; but at the same time they vigorously supported individual freedom and in many cases remained hostile to state and to religion. In France, Italy, and even Germany, the parties were able to play a role in government coalitions because of their position in the center. The Radicals were prominent in most of the coalition ministries in France between 1948 and 1958. But the position of these liberal groups continued to erode, for the issues on which they concentrated were no longer paramount.

Changes in Socialism

Socialist parties comprised the second large political group in western Europe. They continued to dominate in the Scandinavian countries, while in Britain, Germany, and Austria they were the other element in what was practically a two-party system. The British Labour party won unprecedented control of the government from 1945 to 1951, and returned to power in 1964. German socialists long had to content themselves with an opposition role but in 1969 they, too, won control of a coalition government.

Socialists in France and Italy faced a powerful Communist party to their left, which limited their importance and encouraged some oscillation in policy. French socialists, defending the republic against a possible Communist takeover, frequently participated in coalition governments as a minority partner or supported such governments, even when they did not join, in the interests of political stability. Italian socialists split over a similar problem, with the Democratic Socialists willing to serve in coalition governments and the larger group, under Pietro Nenni, cooperating with the Communists in local governments and in national elections. In the late 1960s Nenni himself switched policies and entered a coalition government with the Christian Democrats, which displeased many of his followers. In France during the same years, socialists, excluded from the government of Charles de Gaulle, occasionally made agreements with the Communists to bow out in favor of the candidate with the best chance in close elections.

The socialists found it difficult therefore to maintain a constant policy or even to develop a clearly independent stance. French and Italian socialists risked appearing merely negative in policy and splitting the working class when they resisted the Communists, or seeming to be helpless fellow travelers when they cooperated too closely. Nevertheless, even in these two countries the socialist parties retained substantial strength; in France they played a key role in several governments of the Fourth Republic.

Initially socialist policies changed little from those of the interwar years. In France even the leadership was the same, which contributed to the impression of a rather tired, aging party. German socialists were eager to avoid some of the mistakes made under Weimar. In particular they tried to steer a more nationalist course and were more critical of allied occupation and, later, American diplomatic influence than were the Christian Democrats. In this way they hoped to avoid the stigma of betraying the nation.

During the 1950s socialists in many countries picked up a bit of nationalist caution. Fearful that socialist strength would be buried in a conservative union, they were leery of schemes for European integration, which their rival, the Christian Democrats, sponsored. French socialists even failed to carry through their theoretical opposition to colonialism. In 1956–1957 France was treated to the odd spectacle of a socialist-led coalition steadily widening the war against Algerian rebels, in defense of French empire and the minority of European settlers in Algeria. The British Labour party, on the other hand, was more consistently willing to dismantle the empire than were their Conservative opponents. By the 1960s socialists generally had returned to a more internationalist position and favored measures for European integration. In France they opposed de Gaulle's efforts to develop a nationalist mission for France, while in Germany the government of Willy Brandt began in 1969 to open new contacts with the Communist states of eastern Europe.

Socialist domestic policy shifted during the 1950s. For Britain this meant abandoning nationalization as the chief party platform. Since its inception early in the twentieth century, the party had stressed nationalization of key industrial sectors as an economic and social panacea. In power after 1945, it undertook extensive nationalization, but the results were somewhat disappointing. It was hard to modify tradition; but during the 1950s, with the Conservatives in power, the Labour party specifically renounced further significant nationalization and broadened its appeal. During the same decade the German socialists explicitly eschewed Marxism as the basis of party platforms. Since early in the century, Marxism had been little more than a theoretical embellishment to German socialism, yet its renunciation signaled a significant shift. Like the British movement, the German socialists had to win votes beyond the working class if they were to succeed in gaining a national majority. Thus they played down dogma and stressed their flexibility. Genuine differences between socialists and conservatives remained, but increasingly the socialists were promising minor reforms of the existing order and an ability to run the welfare state more efficiently and humanely than the conservatives.

The Communist Parties

Communism, the final ingredient of the political spectrum, was important only in France and Italy, but there it loomed large. As leaders of the resistance, Communists emerged from the war with great prestige and considerable funds, and in both countries they were able to take over the main trade union movement. Russian support, including financial aid, was a continuing boon. French Communists regularly won upwards of 20 percent of the national vote, while their Italian counterparts neared 25 percent. In both countries their strength in parliament was less than their share of the vote, as their opponents arranged election laws to limit their effectiveness; but the Communists had substantial blocs in parliaments and controlled a large number of local governments.

In France and in Italy the Communists made a fairly explicit decision, toward the end of World War II, to work primarily through the political process rather than to attempt overt revolution. The reasons for this decision were many, including guidelines from Russia while Russia was still interested in cooperating with the western Allies. Reaction to the wartime Fascist threat was another factor that prompted Communists to maintain some contact with other anti-Fascist parties. The institutional power of Communism, with its elaborate trade union as well as party apparatus, convinced some leaders that control of the country could be achieved through the political process and dissuaded others from taking undue risks that might jeopardize existing gains.

Communist policy was not constant. Like the socialists they moved back and forth from a popular-front approach. Immediately after the war they entered government coalitions. In 1947, having been expelled from the coalitions in both France and Italy, they began to disrupt parliamentary meetings and to mount repeated street demonstrations and political strikes. This policy in turn subsided by the mid-1950s. The shock of Russia's suppression of the Hungarian revolution in 1956 dampened party activity still further. In these post-Stalinist years, the Italian Communists, with the French following at a slower pace, began to convert themselves into reformists willing to cooperate with other reform-minded elements and where possible to share power with reformist governments. By the 1960s the Communists cooperated with other groups in local and regional governments, particularly in Italy.

At the end of the decade the twin results of this evolution were becoming evident. On the one hand, western Communists were taking an increasingly independent line toward Russia. The Italian party vigorously condemned the invasion of Czechoslovakia and insisted that each national Communist movement had the right to choose its own path to a Communist society. There was no break with Russia, and French Communists were muted in their criticism, but an interesting shift had taken place. At the same time, Communists began to have trouble on the left. The French Communist party, true to its evolution, played an essentially moderating role in the revolt of 1968, seeking to hold the workers back from revolution. This policy, combined with the heavily bureaucratic nature of the Communist movement and compounded by the example of Chinese attacks on the conservatism of Russian Communism, led to dissent. Small groups, mainly of intellectuals and students, began to form Maoist organizations that criticized mainline Communism. Communist leaders condemned such deviations but they could not prevent them. At the same time the dissenting groups remained small and there was no sign that the Communist parties would be diverted from their reformist policies. The situation bore some resemblance to the conversion of socialist parties to revisionism a half century before, though no Communist leader would appreciate the analogy. The Communist parties maintained distinctive policies. They advocated extensive domestic reform and escape from American-oriented diplomacy. In no sense were they fully accepted by other political elements, but they had won a place in the political system and seemed bent on working within that system.

A New Consensus?

The new political spectrum in Europe was by no means entirely stable. In Italy and in France, until 1958, ministries continued to shift with bewildering frequency. Political partisanship could be intense, but there was a wide area of political consensus. Pragmatism and flexibility were the order of the day, as political passions and even political idealism were on the wane. The type of government that resulted, relatively undistracted by sniping from the extremes, was capable of great achievement. It built the welfare state, ended the colonial empires, and began the integration of Europe. But the political spectrum could also seem depressing. It provided little outlet for new kinds of political dissent and encouraged the political manipulator and the party bureaucrat. If by the 1970s no major shifts in the spectrum had yet taken shape, there was some dissatisfaction with its limitations.

NEW REGIMES

Western Europe returned to parliamentary democracy after the war. Governments-in-exile resumed control in Norway, Denmark, and the Netherlands, with their parliamentary systems unchanged. Controversy over King Leopold of Belgium, who was accused of collaboration with the Germans, delayed a return to order until 1950, when Leopold abdicated in favor of his son. Increasing strife developed between the country's two main ethnic groups, the Flemings and Walloons, but parliamentary democracy was itself not in question. Britain, of course, preserved her form of government unchanged.

Despite this continuity, however, there was a gradual shift in the nature of parliamentary rule even in the countries where it had long been established. The power of the executive branch, both professional civil servants and ministers chosen by parliament, increased at the expense of the legislature. Relatedly, government decisions steadily became more centralized. As the government expanded its functions, particularly in complex economic matters, it was difficult for parliamentary politicians, normally amateurs in economics, to follow what was going on in great detail. At most parliaments provided general guidelines that were then filled in by the executive branch. In this situation, several states during the 1960s experimented with new controls over the bureaucracy. In Scandinavia and Great Britain the ombudsman was introduced to deal with citizen complaints about bureaucratic mistreatment.

Constitutional Changes

France, Germany, and Italy were not exempt from these trends; indeed they tried to deal with some of them through their new constitutions developed after the war.

The French sought to avoid the weaknesses of the Third Republic. A popular referendum in 1945 revealed overwhelming sentiment for a new institutional framework. In the subsequent Constituent Assembly, socialists and Communists sought a single parliamentary body with predominant power; de Gaulle and the Christian Democrats wanted a strong executive and a reduction of parliamentary controls. A leftist constitution was voted down. What was finally approved was a regime very close in nature to the Third Republic. There was a new procedure for designating the prime minister; this was intended to make his tenure more secure but it turned out to make his appointment more difficult. Ministerial instability was greater in the new Fourth Republic than it had been in the Third. The new constitution enfranchised women for the first time, but their voting patterns proved as varied as men's and political stability was not enhanced.

Italy also needed a new constitution to replace the one that was nearly a century old, and that had been suspended for the previous two decades. A popular referendum in 1946 abolished the monarchy and a Constituent Assembly was elected. Its republican constitution, produced after nine months of debate, was a massive document specifying a variety of human rights, many of which proved unenforcable in practice. Institutionally, the document reproduced most of the features of the pre-Fascist regime. A president was substituted for the king as titular head of state, with substantially reduced powers; the senate became elective instead of appointive; and women were granted suffrage.

The lack of genuine innovation in France and Italy was surprising, given the idealism of the Resistance and the widespread desire for change. Disagreements among the leading parties tended to force the constituent assemblies back to familiar institutions as a lowest common denominator. Both countries left their highly centralized bureaucratic structure intact while creating a powerful parliament and a weak executive. The result, combined with the multifold political divisions in each country, was recurrent political instability. Each regime proved capable of important initiatives; neither was paralyzed as the French Third Republic had been during the 1930s. The reduction of political polarization made changes in governments less traumatic, while some of the instability was largely superficial.

In France single parties and even single individuals controlled key ministries through a number of successive coalition governments. For years the MRP, for example, provided the foreign minister, usually either Robert Schuman or Georges Bidault, thus ensuring a certain consistency in foreign policy. From this in turn came a variety of major proposals for European integration. The predominance of Christian Democrats in the Italian government, whether ruling outright or in coalition, mitigated the effects of instability and provided considerable continuity in policy.

But the instability was still troubling, and from the start there was widespread concern about the not-so-new institutions. De Gaulle, unable to deal with the demands of a resurgent parliament, resigned in January 1946, as the new constitution was being debated. A large segment of the electorate voted against the new constitution or abstained and as a result the document was accepted by little more than one-third of the citizenry. There was little overt protest against the new Italian and French republics, but there was widespread apathy.

The New Republic in West Germany

The West German constitution was drawn up in 1949 by an elected Parliamentary Council meeting in the university town of Bonn, which became the capital of West Germany. The Germans for the most part reestablished the institutions of the Weimar republic. They introduced two innovations, however, that were designed to eliminate the obvious institutional weakness that had developed under Weimar. The emergency powers of the president, which had been the device under which Hitler was able to seize control, were dropped, and the German president became a ceremonial figure, as he was in most European countries. At the same time the chancellor was assured of a more stable tenure through an ingenious device that allowed parliament to vote no confidence in the chancellor only when the opposition had already agreed on a candidate for the succession. Combined with the essentially two-party system that developed in the new republic, this provision resulted in an unusually small number of chancellors —four to be exact—from 1949 to 1971. Konrad Adenauer, a powerful personality, held the position for 14 years, causing many to wonder if the chancellorship had been made too secure. Under his strong leadership the voice of parliament became progressively less effective, and the bureaucracy was really responsible to him alone. But with his retirement in 1963 one-man rule came to an end, and both parliament and the cabinet gained new responsibility.

Under pressure from the Americans, the formulators of the German constitution also departed from the Weimar pattern by giving more powers to the individual states, in matters of education, for example, thus creating a genuine federal system.

Like the new regimes in France and Italy, the Bonn Republic was not greeted with great popular enthusiasm nor did it flow from a compelling ideology. It was pragmatically conceived. Memories of the Nazi takeover prompted observers to wonder how deep-rooted the new democracy was. Some wonder still, pointing out that Bonn has not yet faced major economic or diplomatic crises that would truly test the allegiance of the citizenry. The regime has endured thus far, without serious challenge and with few pressures for important constitutional revision.

Only in France, in fact, has there been a real change in the parliamentary democracies since their restoration or establishment after World War II. This in turn reflects the relative political consensus of the postwar decades and the absence of acceptable alternatives even to those people disenchanted with parliamentary democracy. The relative stability is in marked contrast to developments not only during the interwar years but also during many parts of the nineteenth century.

The Fall of the Fourth Republic

Despite bewildering changes in governments, the Fourth Republic had made advances in many spheres. It had established a welfare state and guided the French economy out of postwar chaos into rapidly advancing prosperity. It had initiated European integration as an imaginative way to deal with Germany's revival—in marked contrast to the heavy-handedness of the Third Republic after the previous world war. At considerable cost it had begun the process of decolonization. Following World War II the French attempted to reassert authority in all their colonies, including Indochina which the Japanese had captured. Encountering Indochinese resistance, the French launched a war that dragged on for seven years, draining France's military strength and morale. After a major defeat in 1954, the French, under the leadership of Pierre Mendès-France, the most courageous of the Fourth Republic's leaders, decided to cut their losses and make peace. Indochina was divided and the French withdrew. Soon thereafter the French accepted the independence of Morocco and Tunisia. It is evident, therefore, that the Fourth Republic was not incapable of action or doomed to failure. Many observers believed that, for all its faults, it suited French political character and provided ample outlet for political divisions.

The French Republic foundered, finally, on the Algerian war. When the Algerian revolt broke out in 1954, four months after the Indochinese settlement, the French government resolved on resistance. Military leaders, and many politicians, could not contemplate another defeat, for they recalled not only Indochina but also the loss to Germany in 1940. Algeria's proximity to France and the existence of a sizable and extremely vocal European minority there were other reasons for the decision to hold out. The war dragged on, involving hundreds of thousands of reluctant French recruits and resulting in great cruelty on both sides. The government responded to critics at home by some arbitrary arrests and periodic censorship of the press. Finally, when in 1958 Pierre Pflimin, a leader of the MRP, tried to organize a government that would favor conciliation with the Algerian rebels, yet another revolt broke out. A combination of European settlers, semi-Fascist organizations, and the local army command seized control of the Algerian administration. With the bulk of the French army in Algeria, the French position was tenuous and a response difficult; moreover, there was support for the coup among nationalists and conservatives in France. As the government's power slipped away, Charles de Gaulle emerged from retirement and proclaimed himself ready to form an alternative regime. De Gaulle, the conservative nationalist, appealed to certain elements in France; de Gaulle, hero of the Resistance and one who disliked the tactics of a *coup d'etat*, was acceptable to most other political groups. With the French mainland defenseless against the mounting threat of attack from the Algerian-based French army, parliament bowed to the inevitable and selected de Gaulle as prime minister. Parliament then disbanded after granting full power to de Gaulle's government to rule France as it saw fit for a period of six months, and to draw up a new constitution for the Fifth Republic.

The Fifth Republic

The constitution was approved by 80 percent of the French people, with only the Communists and a few devoted democrats dissenting. It called for a mixed parliamentary-presidential structure, with the powers of parliament curbed and its sessions shortened. Parliament still selected a prime minister (whom it could also dismiss) to conduct day-to-day business and be the liaison between the executive branch and parliament. Real power was now centered in the presidency, with the president elected by an electoral college made up of local officials. In December 1958, de Gaulle was elected first president of the Fifth Republic. This, combined with the victory of the newly formed Gaullist UNR in the parliamentary elections, set the stage for the evolution of the new regime.

De Gaulle determined his own foreign and colonial policy. His first prime minister, Michel Debré, was content to act as his faithful lieutenant.

Leading ministers were chosen from the ranks of professional bureaucrats and technicians rather than eminent politicians. Key political freedoms were largely preserved, though there were—as under the Fourth Republic—some political arrests and occasional censorship. Government control of radio and television was vigorously used to promote loyalty to the regime. For a time normal political activity waned, and many of the established parties were divided and confused.

By 1960, however, political pressures resumed. De Gaulle had been unable to end the Algerian war. He alternately pressed for military action, which angered French leftists now adamantly opposed to the war, and for conciliation, which angered French nationalists. Controversy spilled into the streets; rightists planted plastic bombs against people known to favor conciliation of Algerian Moslems, while socialists, Communists, and others organized demonstrations of students and workers against the war.

Amid this confusion de Gaulle managed to establish the permanency of his regime. In 1962 he ended the war on the rebels' terms. Through a popular referendum he altered the constitution to provide for direct election of the president by the people; he feared that, in the event of his death, the officials previously responsible for the election might choose an old-style politician who would yield power to parliament. This move infuriated the parliamentary deputies, save those in the Gaullist party, who overthrew the new prime minister, Georges Pompidou, who had prepared the amendment. De Gaulle responded by dissolving the parliament and calling for new elections. In these elections the Gaullists won a virtual majority—a full half of the deputies elected had never served before. They, and the people who had voted for them, were tired of the old party maneuvers and the traditional parliamentary leadership. The Fifth Republic, now firmly installed, had its own roots in French political tradition, which from Napoleon onward periodically resorted to one-man rule to give the nation respite from instability.

De Gaulle did not succeed in uniting France. His dream of establishing a two-party system, with Gaullists the majority and Communists a permanent minority, was not realized. Nor was social unity achieved. Problems of university crowding, and archaic curricula and teaching methods triggered a massive student uprising in May 1968. Workers, spurred by inflationary prices, followed with an extensive general strike. Order was restored, but de Gaulle wanted more. He asked again for a vote of confidence through a referendum, but this time he was defeated. In April 1969 he resigned, having ruled France longer than any man since Napoleon III. Without question most Frenchmen were tired of his aloofness and his authoritarian rule, but they elected as his successor Georges Pompidou, who was committed to maintenance of the Fifth Republic. Although he modified some of de Gaulle's authoritarian ways, he preserved the strong presidency.

Thus France, too, seemed to have found a durable regime, which actually embodied and extended certain common trends in the parliamentary democracies. The presidential system, at one time unique in Europe, developed almost everywhere; with it came a concentration of power in the executive branch at considerable expense to parliamentary authority. This tendency, in turn, was part of the most profound political development after World War II—the rise of the welfare state.

THE FORMATION OF
THE WELFARE STATE

Governments had long made provision for certain welfare measures. Even before industrialization many European states gave some aid to the poor, particularly in times of famine. The aid was quite limited, however, and its purpose was primarily to preserve order; by the eighteenth century many states also tried to promote the wealth and population of the nation in order to enhance the state's military strength. With industrialization the state's welfare activities increased, particularly in the fields of factory legislation and social insurance. Except in Scandinavia, the democratic countries made few advances in welfare legislation between the wars, but there was considerable precedent for such activity. Nevertheless, insofar as a type of state is ever really new, the welfare state was decidedly so in its definition of the functions and purposes of government.

The British Model

In Britain the welfare state was a direct product of the war, during which time party frictions abated and members of different social classes gained greater contact with each other. Many people realized that new policies were needed to cure the unhealthy social situation of the interwar period and to provide the sense of purpose needed to guarantee national unity during the war itself. Concrete measures taken during the war aided the lower classes, particularly the provision that supplied rations of milk and meat to all thereby ensuring better diets. After the war the coalition government had plans for further social reforms. The Beveridge plan, drawn up in the spirit of middle-class humanitarianism, urged the expansion of social insurance measures to prevent unemployment and even to redistribute income. Other plans called for extension of educational facilities for the poor. These programs reflected new social concern on the part of the upper classes and stimulated the expectations of the lower classes.

The triumph of the Labour party in 1945 can be traced to a general desire for the government to assume new and greater responsibilities in the economy. Housing was a key issue. A large minority of the middle class joined most of the working class in voting for the Labour party as the best means of assuring an activist government. During the following six years the party, under the leadership of Clement Attlee, built the basic institutions of the welfare state.

Existing social insurance schemes were elaborated, the unemployment insurance program was extended, and for the first time in British history no unemployed person had to rely on a dole. A national system of health care was instituted, giving virtually free medical attention to all citizens, with the bulk of the funds coming from tax sources. This measure obviously increased the medical facilities for the poorer classes and, in relying on tax support, it provided a means of redistributing income.

Housing programs were greatly expanded. Designed partly to compensate for wartime damage and neglect, they resulted in better housing than many citizens ever had before. By 1960 more than a quarter of the entire population resided in government-built housing. The government also established direct financial aid to large families.

Two of the principal programs of the Labour government were intended to raise economic levels and to alter the existing system of class relationships. Education facilities were greatly expanded and particular attention was given to the secondary schools, where attendance was required until age 15 (later raised to 16). At the same time new university facilities were created and scholarships were increased. Even now, only a small minority of the population could go to the universities, but the earlier stratification of education was modified. Lower-class youths, a rarity at universities before the war, now passed unnoticed. The government also nationalized several major industries, including mining, steel, and the railroads. The purpose was to spur economic growth but above all to make public interest predominate in these key sectors. Worker groups were given a voice in the direction of the nationalized industries.

The Conservatives, returning to power in 1951, left the essentials of the welfare state untouched. However, they played down further public housing, instituted some changes in the National Health Service, and denationalized the steel industry. When Labour returned to power in 1964, they in turn reversed these policies and also proposed further democratization of the school system. But they were essentially talking of embellishing the existing welfare state, not of major new initiatives, and economic problems ultimately consumed most of the government's attention.

Welfare States in Western Europe

In France and Italy, both of which had long lagged in welfare measures, the impetus to the welfare state came immediately from the Resistance.

Coalition governments formed after the war included Communists, socialists, and Christian Democrats, all of whom agreed on the need for social reform despite huge differences over the nature of this reform. The Italian state extended a variety of social insurance measures and instituted health insurance. It undertook a partial land reform, dividing some though not all of the large estates in the south. State-run concerns directed not only the railroads, which had been nationalized earlier, but also the nation's petroleum industry. A decade later electric utilities were nationalized. Development of a complete welfare state was inhibited by Italy's economic backwardness, but there was a clear beginning nevertheless.

The postwar French government, prior to the expulsion of the Communists in 1947, introduced a wide array of welfare measures. A full social security program was established. Hospital costs were insured, and coverage was provided for old age and unemployment. Workers in both industry and agriculture were required to participate in these programs and to pay part of the cost, but employers paid a substantial percentage and the state also contributed. Supplementing these measures was a large program of family aid, the size of the payment increasing with the size of the family. Though payments were given to all families regardless of income, they allowed some redistribution of income in favor of the poor, since the payments were drawn from tax revenues and the poor families had more children on the average. A laborer with low earnings and a large family could increase his income by as much as 40 percent with the family aid he received. The program provided a minimum of material well-being and promoted rapid population growth as well. By the early 1950s about 16 percent of the French national income was being devoted to the various social security programs.

In addition, the French state participated actively in educational reform. The age at which children could leave school was raised from 14 to 16, and the curriculum of secondary schools was altered to meet the needs of a larger segment of society. Classical subjects, though still important, gave ground to science, modern languages and social studies.

Finally, the French government introduced several measures to alter the control of industry. Experiments were made with a system of comités d'entreprise, joint labor-management councils that regulated working conditions and shaped general industrial policy. The government also encouraged collective bargaining, extending direct aid to unions for training programs, including training in union management. Above all, the government increased its own direct role in the economy, nationalizing several industries. Railroads were taken over entirely, the government operating on the premise felt throughout Europe generally that transportation links were too vital to be left in private hands. Coal mines were nationalized because of their economic importance and the hardships of mine labor. The government assumed control of the large Renault auto works. A general agency, the Office du plan, was established to set basic standards for economic development. Through government funds and tax benefits, as well as a program of education and persuasion, the office tried to stimulate the economy and maintain full employment.

Germany and Scandinavia

Germany required no such drastic transformation to the welfare state, for an elaborate social insurance program had long since been developed and key sectors such as the railroads were already nationalized. But the government did increase its activity. It took a major role in housing construction, a vital necessity since 40 percent of German dwellings had been destroyed during the war. Compensation for those who had suffered severe wartime damage was provided through taxing the more fortunate, which permitted some redistribution of income. The German states extended educational facilities, building new universities and granting increased scholarship aid. There were also experiments with worker-management councils in several industries. The German government, though committed like the French to rapid economic growth, did not develop an elaborate economic planning system. The Christian Democratic economic minister, Ludwig Erhard, believed in free enterprise and he made his system work.

The Scandinavian countries had earlier established the essentials of a welfare state but they steadily elaborated insurance programs, particularly in the field of health. They also extended the state's role in collective bargaining and economic planning.

THE NATURE OF
THE WELFARE STATE

The welfare systems developed in western and central Europe varied considerably in detail. Britain possessed the most complete medical program, France the most extensive system of family aid. One of the keynotes of the welfare state was a certain pragmatism and flexibility, but certain common ideals underlay the various programs.

First there was a belief that society had the responsibility for banishing poverty. A clear effort was made to set minimal conditions in factory work, minimal income levels for the lower classes in both industry and agriculture, and minimal standards for the whole population in such matters as medical care. There was an interest in limiting, though not eliminating, inequalities of wealth by funding the welfare programs through a system of graduated taxes, with the state serving as the agent for redistribution. The state was also pledged to promote economic growth and limit unemployment to a bare minimum.

In addition to the material goals, the welfare state sought to remove class barriers to opportunity by extending educational facilities. It hoped to give the lower classes, particularly the workers, greater participation in the direction of their own affairs. Hence the spread of mixed governing boards, as well as active encouragement of collective bargaining.

The welfare programs obviously represented a great extension of the power of the state in the interest of the public good. The size of government bureaucracies increased substantially. Regulatory action was extended to cover minimum wages and even the conditions under which workers could be dismissed. The government's role in industrial ownership, housing, and the like increased dramatically. The welfare state required individual participation in insurance programs, set doctors' fees, and in some cases even stipulated that certain elderly people live in state-run old-age homes. Taxes were raised at all levels to pay for the new programs.

Welfare principles—as well as benefits and controls—penetrated society as a whole, not just factory labor. Insurance programs were fully applied to clerical and agricultural workers and even to many of the self-employed. Medical plans and new educational facilities had a far-reaching effect on society generally while protective legislation regulating hours of work, vacations, and wages affected almost all categories of employees. Thus the welfare state was involved in many aspects of daily life. But this did not necessarily mean rigid or complete domination by the government; to a great extent the welfare state relied on persuasion and private initiative. After setting certain minimum standards and some guidelines for general economic development, the welfare state intended to leave society with more opportunities for effective initiative than ever before.

The establishment of the European welfare state both annoyed and disappointed many people. Its controls offended some traditional liberals and certain elements of the upper class; its failure to effect a profound social revolution dismayed those on the far left; while its materialism and pragmatism repelled many intellectuals. Yet the welfare state drew on a number of key political traditions in Europe, among them the steady expansion of secular government. By no means liberal in the classic sense, it nevertheless used the state mainly for those purposes that individuals could not satisfactorily fulfill themselves, leaving them free in other matters. It was by no means socialist either, though it accepted much of what socialists claimed was society's responsibility. Thus, while winning unqualified admiration from few, the welfare state proved to have wide appeal. Despite its failure to fulfill its own goals completely and some new problems it has created, the welfare state faced no serious challenge as Europe entered the 1970s. Most political debate centered around modifying it or extending it; few people clearly proposed an alternate definition of state functions.

A Conservative View of Popular Culture and the Welfare State, 1964: Shakespeare looks at a tawdry England four centuries after his birth.

EUROPEAN DIPLOMACY

A strictly European diplomacy scarcely existed between the war's end and the mid-1950s. The European states were subsumed under the Cold War interests of the two superpowers, while decolonization commanded any remaining diplomatic energies. The welfare state itself had significant implications for traditional diplomacy. It has proved difficult for European countries to maintain the expenditures of the welfare state and at the same time aspire to be world powers. The same Labour government that built the welfare state in Britain in 1945, not only kept the British promise to pull out of the Indian subcontinent, but also withdrew from Jordan and Israel and declared Britain impotent to defend Greece and Turkey against the Communist threat. Obviously these decisions were made in light of war weariness and the tremendous burdens of economic reconstruction, but they suggest a more durable reorientation of government's purposes. It may be more than accidental that the leading European diplomatic initiative after World War II, the partial integration of Europe through the Common Market, was directly related to economic expansion, one of the key functions of the welfare state.

Most west European states tried to keep military expenditures at a low level. Again, these policies were encouraged not only by a sense of impotence against the superpowers and a reliance on American protection but also by the imperatives of the welfare state. During the height of the Cold War military conscription was reinstituted, only to be drastically limited (in Britain, abandoned altogether) as tensions eased in the mid-1950s. France bucked the trend to some degree. Because of the Algerian war, widespread conscription was retained into the 1960s, and then reduced. De Gaulle, in his quest for French greatness, began to build an atomic striking force, the *force de frappe,* at vast expense. To be sure, the British had developed atomic weaponry earlier, but with American aid. The French effort to go it alone caused far greater strain, and its real military usefulness was contested.

In general, however, the importance of military expenditures and the military itself declined in Europe. Most significant was the relatively modest and tightly controlled army that West Germany developed. There was little effort to revive the old-style officer corps or defy allied-imposed limitations on German armaments, which included prohibitions on nuclear weaponry. In Germany and elsewhere, considerable disenchantment with military activity developed, particularly among the young.

The Suez Fiasco

None of this means that European diplomacy changed completely. The British Labour government pulled out of many colonies, but it launched a war against Communist guerillas in Malaya, delaying independence there. Major gains by conservatives during the early 1950s—the triumph of the Conservative party in Britain in 1951, the rise of Gaullism and other conservative movements in France—suggested a more vigorous defense of empire. This was encouraged by the return of many embittered Europeans from the colonies already abandoned, who urged an attack on Asian and African nationalism.

The climax occurred in 1956. The British had withdrawn from the Suez Canal the year before, but the Conservative government was outraged when the Egyptian nationalist leader, Gamal Abdel Nasser, seized possession of the canal itself from its European stockholders. They resolved to punish Nasser and, symbolically, other nationalists from formerly colonial areas. The French gladly cooperated because Egypt was aiding the Algerian rebels. In November, a British and French parachute force attacked the Suez Canal and moved toward Cairo. But worldwide indignation—ranging from complete disapproval by the United States to threats from Russia—forced a retreat. Within a month the last of the invaders had sailed for home. The process of decolonization continued.

Toward New European Institutions

Long before this futile episode, however, the central issues in European diplomacy had begun to change. Initially developed within the Cold War framework, European diplomatic initiatives ultimately helped to free western Europe from the worst of these pressures.

Resistance leaders in many countries had hoped for a reduction of nationalism and a reorganization of the European states system, a dream that many people had indeed shared long before. Following the war, American economic aid provided vital experience in cooperative economic endeavor among most non-Communist states. The Marshall Plan required recipients to coordinate their economic policies in order to use the aid to best advantage. The beginning of the Cold War impelled both Americans and west Europeans to consider further joint action against the Communist threat. The North Atlantic Treaty Organization was one result of this thinking. So, in part, were purely European diplomatic moves. Finally, the revival of Germany, which the Cold War decisions by the western Allies promoted, encouraged a new diplomatic framework. Many countries had reason to fear a resurgent Germany. Led by France, however, those in western Europe determined to avoid the fearful defensiveness that had characterized their policy toward Germany after World War I. If Germany became part of a larger European unit it would have no motive to use its growing power for aggressive ends.

In May 1950 the French foreign minister, Robert Schuman, issued the first call for a "European" institution above the national level. In what has come to be known as the Schuman Plan he proposed a European Coal and Steel Community, which involved the pooling of heavy industrial resources and the elimination of tariffs in the "core" nations of western Europe—France, Italy, West Germany, and the Low Countries. The Schuman Plan had wide appeal. It promised more efficient use of resources and suggested a "European" control of Germany's heavy industry, which was rapidly reviving and which had played such a great role in earlier German militarism. To those who sought a European alternative to the limits of the national state, the Schuman Plan seemed a sound first step—as indeed it proved to be. In less than a year the treaty establishing the Community was signed and a half decade of transition was allowed for heavy industrial firms to adjust to the new competitive situation. Offices were established in Luxembourg to monitor the Community, which had authority not only to oversee trade but to phase out uneconomic operations, particularly in coal mining. In other words the Community was given some governmental powers.

Germany obviously stood to gain from the new arrangement. Chancellor Adenauer had resolved to revive his country but was convinced that it could make no major diplomatic gains through a nationalist policy. Though rankled by the division of Germany, Adenauer realized that nationalist protest would merely arouse fear and antagonism. He was convinced that Germany's best hope was to cast its lot with western Europe and the United States. A firm alliance might induce Russia to relax its hold on East Germany; if it did not, West Germany could make its own way, though never officially abandoning hope for reunification. The Schuman Plan encouraged Adenauer to steer his country on the new course.

Belgium, Holland and Luxembourg had already moved toward considerable economic integration to reduce the disadvantages of their small size. For France, the turn to economic integration marked a more obvious departure. France had always been a high tariff country, its industrialists fearful of foreign competition. That this policy was now modified showed France's determination to find some new framework that would encourage economic growth and, even more, avoid the diplomatic tensions that had so long divided the national states of western Europe. Italy too had a tradition of high tariffs and was economically backward compared to its new partners; its decision to "go European" was a major departure.

Britain and Scandinavia were left out for a variety of reasons, including their peripheral geographic positions to the rest of western Europe. The Scandinavian countries were developing some economic integration among themselves. Sweden's vigorously defended neutrality, both in World War II and in the Cold War, discouraged thoughts of alliance with the major west European powers. Britain was approached concerning the Schuman Plan, but preferred to remain aloof. The Conservatives, returning to the government in 1951, believed that Britain could hold her own as a world power, in close alliance with the United States. Traditional wariness of continental entaglements remained strong and many feared that new European arrangements would weaken Britain's ties with the Commonwealth.

An Abortive Effort: The EDC

The next step in European integration was a direct product of the Cold War, and it misfired. The Korean War aroused great fear that conflict might spread to Europe. The United States professed its concern lest NATO prove inadequate to withstand a Russian attack on Germany; it insisted that the West Germans be armed for their own defense. This raised a difficult problem for western Europe, particularly France, so recently overrun by German armies and yet eager to avoid offense to the United States, which was still providing vital economic and military aid. The solution seemed to be a European army, which would prevent a national German military force but allow Germans to rearm under international command.

The founding treaty for the European Defense Community, proposed by the French, was signed in 1952 by the six states already involved in the Coal and Steel Community. It was a bold step, for although it allowed all its members except Germany to retain national forces in addition to those contributed to the European command, it involved internationalization of one of the most vital arms of the nation-state. The EDC suggested a European army before a European state existed; advocates of a united Europe pleaded for ratification of the EDC, though some feared that the idea was premature. In fact, after two years of debate, the plan fell through, as Europe's political climate in the early 1950s turned increasingly conservative. In France the rise of the first Gaullist party symbolized the new mood—it was the French parliament that finally rejected the EDC. But Christian Democratic parties in other countries also adopted a more conservative tone. For them as for France the EDC was too radical; it offended too many nationalist sensibilities.

Despite this failure, the six nations of "Little Europe" proceeded to organize still more economic organizations. In 1957 they pooled their nuclear energy resources in "Euratom" and in the same year they established the European Economic Community—quickly labeled the Common Market—through the treaty of Rome that was quickly ratified by all the member states.

The Common Market

As a first step, the Common Market involved the progressive elimination of all tariff barriers among the member states. From the start, however, the new organization aimed to be more than a customs union. A supranational executive organization was established, ultimately located in Brussels. Though responsible to a council of ministers of the member states, this executive had wide-ranging functions. One of its principal charges was preserving free competition. While its powers to bring suit against monopolies were limited, it could make recommendations to member governments. Among its other responsibilities were: coordinating policies toward foreign labor in an attempt to ease the movement of workers from one member country to another; managing a complicated system of support for agricultural prices, which after long debate was standardized for the member states; and encouraging economic development in backward areas, such as southern Italy. The budget and bureaucracy of the organization steadily expanded. In 1966 Euratom and the Coal and Steel Community were merged with the Common Market executive.

By creating an economic unit of 170 million people, the Common Market was an immediate success in promoting economic prosperity. Trade within the member countries increased dramatically and overall economic growth was the most rapid in Europe. Buoyed by these results, the tariff-cutting functions of the Common Market were allowed to proceed ahead of schedule. The French, initially fearful of new competition, dropped their reservations. Agricultural policy raised other problems. France insisted on high support prices because of her abundant agricultural production. This meant that the more industrial countries, notably Germany—which ironically had an inefficient agricultural sector—paid substantial support to French farmers. Nevertheless agreements on agricultural policies were regularly renewed, though often at the last minute.

Politically the Common Market moved ahead only slowly if at all. In addition to the economic institutions, a court of justice and an international assembly, drawn from representatives of the parliaments of the member states, had been created. But the assembly had no real powers; it was merely a discussion body. Moreover proposals to convert the Common Market executive into a genuine government made little headway. The Gaullist regime in France, though it fully honored the Fourth Republic's commitment to the Common Market, would not tolerate infringements on national sovereignty.

The French insisted, for example, that agreements of the council of ministers, the overseeing body for the Common Market executive, had to be unanimous. All the other member states advocated majority rule, which would convert the Common Market into something like a real federation. De Gaulle retained his veto, however.

From the first the Common Market acted as a unit in economic negotiations with outsiders. It set a common tariff on all goods imported into the Market and made special arrangements with former colonies as they gained their independence. In particular it gave favored treatment to products from the former French colonies in Africa. It also negotiated some special tariff arrangements with other European states, including Greece and Yugoslavia, many of which involved complicated issues.

Setting general tariffs brought the Common Market into repeated conflict with the United States, which feared discrimination against its products, especially foodstuffs. Negotiations that began in 1962 resulted in some tariff reductions, but the problem was not resolved. The arrangement with the former French colonies aroused resentment from other "third world" countries that exported similar products. But by far the most difficult diplomatic problem the Common Market faced involved other European countries, notably Great Britain.

The Common Market and the Rest of Western Europe

In November 1959, seven nations on the European periphery—Britain, Denmark, Sweden, and Norway, Switzerland, Austria, and Portugal—signed an agreement for the reduction of trade barriers. The "Outer Seven," as they were called, were frightened by the Common Market, for they depended heavily on exports to the member states. Their European Free Trade Association was designed to compensate, or at least to buy time, while the Common Market actually developed. The effort met with only limited success, however, in part because it was merely a tariff arrangement that lacked the governing apparatus and the broader purposes of the Common Market. Economic growth in the "Outer Seven" countries was barely half that of the Common Market members.

After three years of hesitation, the British government in 1961 applied for Common Market membership. Several other "Outer Seven" states indicated they would do the same if Britain was admitted. Denmark, for example, which exported a great deal to Britain, had everything to gain from participation in a Common Market that included Britain. Most Common Market members welcomed the prospect of British membership; the Low Countries, in particular, traded extensively with Britain and also valued Britain's commitment to an orderly democracy. But the British tried to enter on terms of maximum benefit to themselves. They sought to modify the Common Market's agricultural support policy, which differed from their own, and they wanted to preserve their Commonwealth trading ties along with their Common Market membership.

After several months of silence, de Gaulle voiced his opposition to British membership. He mentioned Britain's efforts to make a one-sided bargain, but he had more general objections to Britain as an Anglo-Saxon power. His war experience had taught him to resent Britain's patronizing attitude, and he specifically criticized Britain's special diplomatic relationship with the United States, which made the country, in his opinion, unready for participation in a truly European organization. It was not surprising, therefore, that in 1963 he vetoed Britain's application.

But the matter did not end there. Because of the Common Market's continued economic progress and Britain's own economic lag, the British pursued their interest in becoming a member state. Labour party leaders, long skeptical of membership, were now convinced, and after de Gaulle passed from power in France they renewed their country's application. This time the French government indicated approval in principle, while the other members were more enthusiastic than before, seeing British membership as a desirable counterweight to France in the organization. Details once again proved troublesome, particularly with regard to agricultural policy and the length of transition time to be allowed for Britain's full conversion to Common Market operations. France made it clear that British entry, though possible, should not be easy. At the same time opinion in Britain had cooled. In 1971, however, negotiations were successfully completed and the British Parliament voted to approve Britain's membership in the Common Market. As before, a number of other countries have indicated their desire to follow Britain into the Market, when Britain enters.

Though the existence and success of the Common Market were well established, its future was not clear as Europe entered the 1970s. If confined to the original six members, its progress toward further integration, particularly political integration, raised many questions. The impact of expansion, if expansion occurred, clouded the issue still further. Despite these problems, the Common Market has greatly changed the traditional framework of European diplomacy and its creation marked the central diplomatic achievement of postwar Europe.

Broader Diplomatic Initiatives

By the early 1960s, Europe was emerging from the immediate diplomatic control of the two great powers. The principal reasons were the relaxation of the Cold War after Stalin's death and the growing sense of stalemate between the United States and Russia; but Europe's growing economic strength, to which the Common Market contributed, played a role as well. France, under de Gaulle, was the first to take advantage of the new situation. Once the Algerian War was over, de Gaulle determined to make France a world power once again. He talked, somewhat contradictorily, of two goals: first, Europeans must rely on themselves, drawing closer together in the process; second, they should preserve their separate national identities and defer to France's leadership. Within Europe, de Gaulle relied on a close alliance with Germany, which Adenauer was happy to provide, and

Reassertion of European Power: Adenauer and de Gaulle reduce their reliance on the United States.

"IS IT SHRINKING YET, KONRAD?"

in 1963 they signed a special treaty of friendship. De Gaulle also courted Communist countries, notably Czechoslovakia, Hungary, and Rumania, opening cultural and economic exchanges. Relations with Russia were also improved. At the same time de Gaulle built up French strength, developing an atomic striking force, and opposed further steps toward European integration. His resistance to British participation in Europe may have hampered Europe's diplomatic revival.

De Gaulle missed few opportunities to thumb his nose at the United States. During his first year in power he sought to improve France's role within NATO, suggesting close and equal cooperation among Britain, the United States, and France in leading the alliance. When these suggestions were ignored, he pulled French military forces out of NATO, retaining only nominal membership. Here was a graphic illustration of the independence now possible to diplomacy in western Europe. On the larger world scale de Gaulle tightened diplomatic and cultural relations with Latin America and with the Arab nations of the Middle East—ultimately renouncing traditional ties to Israel. He even wooed the French population of Canada.

Only de Gaulle's commanding personality gave importance to some of these ventures. He did not succeed in bringing France to world-power status, nor did his nationalistic appeals catch hold with most of his own countrymen. Furthermore he was not able to retain close ties with Germany after Adenauer passed from the scene. Franco-German relations remained cordial but not intimate. Germany increasingly went her own way and German diplomatic strength steadily grew in comparison with that of France. French predominance even within western Europe became increasingly questionable. De Gaulle's successor, Georges Pompidou, dropped most of the General's grandiose diplomatic pretensions. He played down France's world role, and concentrated on developing good relations with African and particularly Arab nations.

Two of de Gaulle's policies, however, continued in modified form and even spread to other nations. American diplomatic influence declined. NATO survived and western Europe still depended on American military support, but interest in the alliance waned, owing in part to American concentration on Asian problems. Key diplomatic decisions in Europe were now made without reference to the United States.

Relatedly, ties with east European countries continued to improve. In West Germany the government of Willy Brandt reversed his country's postwar policy of nonrecognition of Russia's satellites, which had been justified in terms of hostility to any nation that had recognized East Germany. Beginning in 1969 he established relations with a number of east European countries, improved existing relations with Russia, and even negotiated with East Germany. He rather explicitly acknowledged the validity of the postwar diplomatic settlement that was still not ratified by a formal peace treaty. Most notably, in arranging diplomatic relations with Poland, he accepted Polish sovereignty over much former German territory. Brandt's policy, following de Gaulle's earlier efforts, modified the Cold War barriers between east and west Europe. They were supported by the growing diplomatic independence of some east European states, particularly Rumania. It is likely that there will be further developments in this area.

Despite the great strides it had made in the two preceding decades, Europe in the early 1970s was still overshadowed by the superpowers. The integration it had achieved was not sufficient to make Europe or any part of it a superpower of its own. Most diplomatic decisions were made on a national basis. Britain, which had most pretensions to great-power status still, continued to scale down its world role. The Labour government in the late 1960s pledged on the grounds of economy to pull British troops completely out of the Far East and the Persian Gulf, where token forces had remained. The next Conservative government, in the name of nationalism, promised to reverse this decision but in fact continued the pullout. Yet the European nations retained a modified world role through extensive economic aid and cultural exchanges. Their influence in Africa was particularly strong. Within Europe itself great power controls had obviously loosened, particularly in the non-Communist countries. It was by no means clear what Europe would do with its new freedom. The Common Market pointed in one direction, yet there were possibilities that some traditional diplomatic patterns would be revived. Efforts like Willy Brandt's recalled pre-Hitlerian German interest in eastern Europe. The growing strength of West Germany had yet to be fully assimilated in the postwar diplomatic structure, which recalled another familiar problem. Europe's diplomacy had changed, but the extent and direction of the change had yet to be worked out.

POLITICS AND DISSENT
IN WESTERN EUROPE

The establishment of new regimes and the more fundamental creation of the welfare state had been accomplished by the early 1950s. The revival of conservatism in the 1950s reduced the chances of further domestic reform, though the construction of the Common Market during the conservative decade revealed genuine diplomatic flexibility.

The 1960s saw a revival of the political left. Gaullist control, even after de Gaulle's retirement, made France immune to the trend. Victory by the Labour party in Britain and, later, by the Social Democratic party in Germany constituted the most important political changes. But socialists also gained in Italy, as the Christian Democratic leaders "opened to the left," admitting socialists into the governing coalition as minority members and promising a planned economy and urgent social reforms. Yet most of the new governments in western Europe departed but little from the policies of their conservative predecessors. Willy Brandt took major diplomatic initiatives but, at least up to 1971, delayed any major domestic reforms. In Britain, Harold Wilson's Labour government committed most of its energies to grappling with Britain's balance of payments problem. Britain, with a sluggish economy, tended to import more than it exported, which left the country in debt and threatened the stability of the British pound. The Labour government thus tried to hold back consumer prosperity in the interests of defending the currency. With the aid of one devaluation, it won modest success; but its policies were understandably unpopular, which led to its defeat at the hands of the Conservatives in 1970.

The Italian reformers had perhaps the least success of all. They too were bogged down in economic problems, in this case a fight against inflation that began to assume disturbing proportions in 1963. Italy was left, by the early 1970s, with an outdated, cumbersome government bureaucracy, an underdeveloped south, and rising social pressure from workers and students. Government instability increased by the end of the 1960s, as most socialists pulled out of the government coalition once more. Faced with this near-paralysis in politics, massive strikes and demonstrations became commonplace and armed groups formed on both right and left.

Italy's troubles were unique, and even in Italy the extent of the crisis was unclear, but a certain political malaise became evident as Europe approached the 1970s. In France political unrest continued to simmer after the end of the 1968 uprising, particularly among university students. Swedish socialists, firmly entrenched since the 1930s, faced unprecedented agitation by workers and others.

For the most part, dissent did not take the form of political upheaval. Swedish socialists suffered a loss of votes in the 1970 elections, but they retained control of the government. In France and Italy small groups arose to the left of the established Communist party; drawing particularly on students, these groups claimed allegiance to Maoist Communism or anarchism. Neo-Fascism also gained strength in Italy. For the most part, however, the political spectrum developed after World War II remained valid.

Because of the vagueness of political dissent and uncertainty about its extent, governments were not yet compelled to take major new initiatives. Some attention was given to providing new university facilities and to modernizing curriculums, particularly in France and Germany. The Italian government embarked on a process of decentralization, creating new regional units with considerable power. France also considered a revitalization of local governments. But the basic framework of the welfare state remained intact, and most major political parties talked mainly in terms of improving it. A new set of governmental tasks had yet to emerge.

13 SOCIETY AND CULTURE IN CONTEMPORARY EUROPE

Europe entered a new stage of social development after World War II. Eastern Europe, to be sure, was preoccupied with completing a basic industrial revolution. The Communist method of achieving this goal was distinctive, but the society that emerged had some parallels with that achieved earlier by western Europe.

In the west, Europe approached a period that has variously been called affluent, post-industrial, or even post-modern. There had been no such comparable change since the development of a mature industrial society in the 1870s. Class structure was significantly modified. The nature of protest changed. The character of the economy shifted. The typical economic problem of the previous period, depression, gave way to the problem of inflation. The issue now was not to arrange consumption to meet the levels of possible production, but rather to lift production to meet constantly rising consumer expectations. Europe saw the development of a new outlook as well, though it had been building for some time. Secular, materialistic, imbued with a belief in progress—the new European was shifting his values.

In dealing with the immense destruction and dislocation of the war years, Europeans did not simply rebuild what they had known in the past. They established a far stabler economy than had existed since the industrial revolution began, without sacrificing a rapid growth rate. Social strife was eased as class tension lost its bitterest edge. Even personal relationships became smoother, particularly between husband and wife. Postwar Europe was not only new; it was successful. Problems still existed, and by the end of the 1960s there were signs that new discontents and protests were being generated. But as Europe entered the 1970s the successful innovations still seemed to predominate. Most Europeans were better adjusted to their industrial society than ever before. Their success was a contrast to their own recent past and, for a time at least, to the more chaotic society that had developed in North America.

A number of ingredients combined to produce the new Europe, including some lessons from history that the war brought home to many Europeans. Many vowed not to repeat previous mistakes. British industrialists, for example, seeing how close their country had come to complete collapse, realized they had to treat their workers better and pay more attention to their wishes. The result was no utopia, but a far less authoritarian atmosphere on the job. The need to rebuild after the war added to this sense of purpose. In Germany and elsewhere the focus on reconstruction was easily transformed into a continued devotion to economic growth. The welfare state played an obvious role in changing Europe. By protecting workers against the worst fluctuations in income, it resolved one of the longstanding concerns of the lower classes. Most people no longer had to fear unemployment or the economic effects of old age. This reduced lower-class grievances and also encouraged more positive demands for a greater share of well-being.

Political and economic changes thus played the greatest role in creating the new Europe. Several other factors, which had loomed large in earlier shifts in European society, were now less prominent. A shift in European population growth suggested for a time that the continent might be entering a new stage of demographic development, but it had little long-term effect. There was no basic alteration of the intellectual climate either. No new unity developed in the various strands of intellectual activity and, more important, there were few fundamentally new departures—no new isms, no major new artistic schools. In most respects artists and scholars elaborated forms and tendencies that had begun between the wars or even before. The new Europe put most of its energies elsewhere. The main intellectual trends had only limited impact on the lives and thinking of most people. Indeed the uneasiness with which many intellectuals still viewed modern society was further removed than ever from the growing optimism of popular culture.

IDEAS AND STYLES

Intellectual activity crested in the years immediately after the war and the sense of creativity and excitement has not been recaptured since. Philosophers and filmmakers, each in their own way, seemed to distill the confusion of the postwar years and find in it some elements of hope. They also advanced the now-traditional debate over man's rationality to a new plateau.

Years of depression and war paved the way for the new intellectual climate. The war and Resistance killed off many leading intellectuals; others were imprisoned while still others—including large numbers of Jews—fled from Europe to the United States. These losses were serious and reduced Europe's intellectual vitality, but they opened the way for a new generation of intellectuals who unleashed the initial burst of creativity that seemed more novel than it actually was. Many intellectuals had made a definite political commitment during the 1930s, which brought them closer to the leading social problems of the day, and during the war they participated in the resistance to Fascism. They retained their sense of commitment, but less to specific political goals than to a hoped-for renewal of Europe's humanist tradition.

Literary Trends

Novels of the Resistance, written during and immediately after the war, combined an understanding of the harsh realities of war and oppression with a belief that ethical progress was possible. A number of Italian writers preached this message. The Italian Ignazio Silone, writing in exile in the 1930s, chronicled the struggles of Italian peasants to resist political and economic exploitation. Carlo Levi, exiled by Mussolini to a village in southern Italy, published *Christ Stopped at Eboli* in 1947, which revealed an impoverishment unknown to cultivated northerners. The book helped stimulate a widespread demand for social and economic reform. In Germany, where cultural activity was more limited after the war, a number of writers recounted the horrors of concentration-camp life, citing examples of courage as well as degradation.

In France, the novels of Albert Camus heralded human struggle. *The Plague*, published in 1947, was an allegory of man's fight against disease and death, carrying overtones of Camus' Resistance activities against Nazi barbarism. Camus was no moralist; he believed that no single individual could do much more than bear witness against evil. But he also felt that he was serving as a representative of a new generation of Europeans born during World War I, whose whole youth had been overshadowed by social chaos and who now sought to recreate a purpose and solidarity in human life.

The new novelists shared many of the characteristics of prewar literature. Camus, for example, was influenced by André Gide's fascination with the absurdities of existence. But the new novelists were more compassionate, more eager to find meaning.

Existentialism

The same was true of the leading philosophical current to emerge from the war. Existentialism was not new—its origins could be traced to the nineteenth century—but it now received a distinctly new formulation and an unprecedented following. Jean-Paul Sartre was responsible for giving existentialism a new twist during the 1940s, and he became the most prominent intellectual in France and probably in the whole of Europe after the war.

As formulated in Germany in the 1920s, existentialism was a profoundly anti-rational philosophy that sought to go directly to the heart of human experience. Martin Heidegger broke completely with conventional philosophical categories, trying to create a new kind of discourse to deal with what he saw to be the central questions of human existence: dread, despair, and death. Karl Jaspers was more concerned with the meaning of history and moral principles. Sartre redefined this approach to existentialism, focusing on human problems, which the experience of war, collaboration, and resistance had brought to general attention. Sartre emphasized extreme moral dilemmas, the responsibility of every human being to make his own choices in ambiguous situations where right and wrong were far from clear. Sartre was also a Marxist, and urged the necessity of ideological commitment as well. The new existentialism claimed to be a philosophy of action. Many of its proponents, including Sartre, recognized no God and most saw no meaning in the universe. The notion of the rationality of nature was dead. But Sartre professed optimism: he found a spark in man, though not necessarily the spark of reason.

The Nature of Postwar Culture

In films, which became an increasingly important cultural outlet after the war, a neo-realist school developed some of the same themes that the novelists and philosophers were expounding. Particularly in Italy, film-makers sought to show the reality of poverty and at the same time to tinge it with poetry and hope. Working with severe budget restrictions, often using amateur actors, directors Roberto Rossellini, Vittorio de Sica, and others produced a series of masterpieces that captured the life and the dignity of the poor both in the countryside and the city.

This postwar cultural outburst, while bringing little that was really new, was extremely important. Realism in novels and even in films had abundant antecedents, as had existentialism. But the postwar intellectuals did seem to break the pattern of despair and pessimism that had dominated so much of cultural activity between the wars. They turned away from a primary concern with form and tried to understand humanity. In dealing with people, in capturing some of the confusion of the postwar years, in urging political commitment, the intellectuals suggested that a new relationship between themselves and society might be developing.

New Divisions Among the Intellectuals

The new mood did not last, however. Existentialism continued to dominate philosophy faculties in western Europe, though not in Britain, but its popularity among intellectuals more generally declined. Sartre himself contributed to the decline by pushing his desire for political commitment to the extreme. Camus, for example, broke with him in 1950 when Sartre refused to speak out against the Soviet concentration-camp system. He revealed the extent to which his insistence on choice could defy standards of reason and humanity.

Furthermore, as postwar chaos yielded to conditions approaching normalcy, the existentialist position proved less appealing. The existentialists painted an alien, meaningless world. Only man brought meaning and he had to assert himself. Camus portrayed Sisyphus, condemned everlastingly to roll his rock to the mountain's top only to see it roll down again. "The struggle itself towards the heights is enough to fill a man's heart. One must imagine Sisyphus happy."

The existentialists had not really bridged the gap between philosophy and the broader public. Their optimism had only a shaky base. Most people wanted to base their happiness on more than struggle. Nor had the existentialists firmly united the strands of rationalism and romanticism. They took over a bit of the language and purposefulness of the rationalists, but remained fundamentally in the nonrationalist camp. Small wonder that Europe's intellectuals split apart once again.

Although the neo-realist spirit withered in a few years, it helped to undermine the postwar mood. It declined in the Italian films by the early 1950s because of widespread public apathy and attacks by the Church and the government which feared its political implications. Neo-realism was most clearly carried on in Britain after 1950 by the school of "angry young men," including many writers of lower-class origin who were enraged at continued class distinctions and injustice. Novelists like Alan Sillitoe, the author of *Saturday Night and Sunday Morning*, and films like *Room at the Top* portrayed the continued frustrations of working-class life. But the "angry young men" were also depressed by the drabness of the welfare state and partly angry at workers themselves for accepting this state and devoting themselves to materialistic goals. While many intellectuals shared these sentiments, they turned away from realism and, often, from political commitment as a result. Artists and writers went back to stylistic experiments and to statements of individual experience. They continued to react to their society, but they saw themselves in flight from it, not working within it.

Finally, it can be suggested that the limitations on Europe's intellectual activity were becoming clearer by the 1950s. With the exception of the physical sciences and music, most creative activity was stifled in eastern Europe. Artists were locked in the socialist-realist mold that required triumphant depictions of happy workers and peasants and shunned western art as decadent. Novelists and filmmakers faced similar restrictions.

Germany in the 1950s was not yet ready to participate in intense cultural activity. In films, for example, the Germans produced almost nothing to rival their work of the 1920s. The confusion and slaughter of the Nazi period and the war were overcome only slowly because attention had to be directed to economic reconstruction. In Europe generally, advances in the sciences and to an extent in other realms of intellectual life were often overshadowed by work in the United States—not infrequently work by refugees from Europe. Money talked, and even with Europe's remarkable economic resurgence money was easier to find across the ocean. Europe's intellectual achievements were not insignificant, but with one or two major exceptions they largely represented elaboration or consolidation of previous trends.

THE ARTS

The most striking development in the arts after the war was the widespread public acceptance of "modern" styles. Here the gap between intellectuals and society seemed definitely to have narrowed. The welfare state playd some role in this, for example, in subsidizing films and in sponsoring theaters—in provincial towns as well as in capital cities—in which both modern and classical works were performed.

Modern Architecture

In architecture, always the most sensitive barometer of the relationship between intellectual and public taste, the modern style won a resounding victory throughout western Europe. In the Communist countries the heavy classical style continued to predominate, but even there some experiments were encouraged by the 1960s. In the western countries, almost all the massive rebuilding after the war was done in modern lines. The association between architecture and engineering became increasingly close. Here American leadership was important, but ironically, if only because of the amount of reconstruction needed, more Europeans were exposed to modern styles than their American counterparts. European architects such as Pier Luigi

Nervi, Oscar Niemeyer, and Le Corbusier, achieved international recognition.

Many of the buildings thrown up immediately after the war were haphazard and unimaginative, but where reconstruction was delayed, more genuine innovation was possible. Various architects contributed to an experimental residential section of West Berlin. The Scandinavian countries built dramatic apartment units for workers outside the major cities. To absorb the overflow from the cities, the British also constructed a variety of "satellite towns" as self-contained units rather than conventional suburbs. Furthermore, stylistic innovation continued. Swedish architects experimented within the modern style by using rough building materials and breaking up plain wall surfaces. Italian designers specialized in industrial design and in the use of reinforced concrete. Nervi, particularly, developed a whole range of new possibilities by using concrete slabs, beams, and shell domes.

Painting and Music

The "modern" was incorporated in the fine arts and music during the same period. American composers and Europeans living in America guided west European musicians toward bold experiment. The influence of Arnold Schönberg, the pioneer in atonal music, peaked after World War II. At the same time Russian composers won a wide audience too. Dmitri Shostakovich emerged as the leading composer in the Soviet Union. Having twice fallen into official disfavor, Shostakovich curbed his more experimental effects. Aram Katchaturian stuck to safe ground as well, working folk melodies into instrumental form, which had great popular appeal.

A number of major modern artists, including Pablo Picasso, continued their work after the war, concentrating for the most part in the abstract vein. Abstractionism received an important boost from younger American artists, such as Jackson Pollock, who were well received and widely imitated in Europe. The result was a great variety of styles, largely nonrepresentational, but there was little striking originality and few pronounced changes of direction.

In several cases, however, there was a slight retreat from the abstract. The French painter Bernard Buffet won widespread recognition for still lifes and nudes presented in somber colors with a stark linear quality. A number of Italian painters, using warmer colors than Buffet, moved still further toward figurative art. In sculpture, Marino Marini's remarkable series of horses and riders won great acclaim; these too defied the general trend to the abstact. The English sculptor Henry Moore achieved major importance after the war. He dealt mainly with human forms but treated them in an unusual way, hollowing the forms and piercing them with holes to bring a sense of space into the figure itself. By the 1960s Moore was turning to more abstract, though suggestive, forms.

Modern Sculpture: *Family Group* by Henry Moore.

There was, therefore, little definable unity in art or in music. Experimentalism was firmly established outside the Communist countries but there were periodic moves to reconcile the very new with more traditional values. Public acceptance of modern styles undoubtedly increased, but in music especially a considerable gap remained between the most avant-garde work and general public taste.

Novels, Drama, and Films

Something akin to the themes of modern art gained ground once again in literature and the theater after the short-lived popularity of neo-realism. By the late 1950s a "new wave" of novelists and filmmakers emerged in France and other countries. They stressed surrealistic forms and meditation on individual experience; many became increasingly interested in fantasy. The French novelist Nathalie Sarraute conveyed feeling and emotion without invoking psychological explanations or other "realistic" effects. On a more popular level Françoise Sagan portrayed the interactions of small numbers of people through the eye and emotions of a single individual. Younger

Italian novelists like Italo Calvino similarly turned away from realism and toward more fanciful themes.

A similar approach came to dominate films by the end of the 1950s and through most of the following decade. The Swedish director Ingmar Bergman produced unstructured films to express a vague and rambling philosophy. But at his best, in *Wild Strawberries* and *The Seventh Seal,* for example, his work had a haunting, evocative quality. He quickly won wide acclaim. Young French and Italian directors—Alain Resnais, François Truffaut, Federico Fellini, Michelangelo Antonioni—had a less abstruse philosophy to express but they shared other elements in common with Bergman. They were not concerned with direct expressions of reality or with clear story lines but used special effects and bewildering shifts of time-sequence to convey a new and more profound sense of emotional reality.

In drama, a number of powerful plays with themes of social protest dominated the immediate postwar years. Bertolt Brecht went back to Berlin—East Berlin—to write his major social commentary, *Mother Courage,* and to assemble an exciting repertory company. Jean Anouilh in France alternated light comedies with plays of intense moral earnestness dealing with the theme of human innocence pitted against arrogance and cruelty. His vogue passed by the 1950s, however, and the serious theater in its turn passed to the hands of experimenters.

Two foreigners who had spent much of their life in France and wrote in French became the new leaders. The Rumanian Eugène Ionesco wrote a number of short plays in a surrealist vein. Samuel Beckett, who had once served as secretary to James Joyce, applied the stream-of-consciousness technique to the dramatic stage in *Waiting for Godot.* These playwrights and others—including Jean Genêt, Fernando Arrabal, and the American Edward Albee—produced a series of powerful expressionistic plays, which collectively have been described as the "theater of the absurd." These dramatists defy normal dramatic conventions and play down the importance of language in favor of strong visual images. Their message follows from their style. Human life is meaningless, and the plays are intended to convey a metaphysical anguish at the absurdity of the human condition. Ionesco defined his perception: "Absurd is that which is devoid of purpose. . . . Cut off from his religious, metaphysical and transcendental roots, man is lost; all his actions become senseless, absurd, useless."

Due weight must be given to the diversity of production in the arts and literature. There was no agreement on form or content. Postwar literature suggested the possibility of oscillation between neo-realism and what might be called neo-romanticism, which was itself not new. Nevertheless several general conclusions can be drawn. First, while new terms were applied to some postwar cultural movements, there was little fundamental innovation. Even the theater of the absurd had its roots in the drama and literature of the early twentieth century. Second, there were virtually no limits, at least of the traditional sort, on stylistic experiments in any of the art forms. A leading composer, Igor Stravinsky, tried to explain the lack of definition: "In the absence of identifying rules and conventions, and at a time when an aesthetic object may be anything at all, the limits of art are not only not airtight but indefinable."

Some artists, most particularly in music, experimented for aesthetic effect alone. But in most cases new modes of expression were seen as vital in expressing an emotional understanding of life, usually specifically of modern life. The leading trends in the arts and literature advanced the anti-rationalist view of man, just as the new styles continued the rebellion against convention begun by the early Romantics. Man was emotion, action, feeling. Neither he nor the world around him could be described in terms of reason. In many works, particularly in certain aspects of existentialism and in the theater of the absurd, there was also a cosmic pessimism, a sense of futility that had been assuming a growing role in the anti-rationalist tradition since the late nineteenth century. Finally, there was a specific revulsion against the conditions of modern life, which the films picked up most specifically. Fellini's *La Dolce Vita* described the emptiness, materialism, and essential loneliness of urban life in Italy. The widespread attention to emotion and individual perception can be seen as a protest against the depersonalization of modern society.

While the general tone of the arts was exceedingly important, it does not describe the whole of intellectual activity. The rationalist tradition, which had given ground in some fields, still remained strong; the gap between formal culture and popular taste, which had closed primarily in the visual arts, still remained wide in other areas. Perhaps for this reason the "new wave" films gained greatest popularity among the productions that involved the written or spoken word. Yet even as crowds of young people, particularly students, flocked to see the new films, television gained its hold on mass taste. What most people read, if they read at all, was not the introspective novel. What they went to see, if they went to see anything, was not the theater of the absurd. In other words, the artists' perceptions about society may or may not have been correct, but they cannot be accepted automatically. Without question the artists themselves were affected by the profound gulf they sensed between their work and the general culture. The problem of the role of intellectuals in modern society had not been resolved.

SCIENCE AND SOCIAL SCIENCE

Intellectuals working in the rationalist tradition failed to accomplish a number of things, though their failure had begun to be apparent earlier, between the wars. They did not produce a new philosophy and offered little to challenge existentialism, for those who were interested in philosophy at all. Nonexistentialist philosophers, particularly in Britain and the United States, turned increasingly toward a study of linguistics and fields that belonged essentially to the social sciences. Scientists produced no unifying views of the physical universe to displace the uncertainties that Einstein had created, and this was a fundamental limitation on the possibilities of a new rationalist philosophical view. In a sense the rationalists tacitly recognized that there were more things they did not know than their nineteenth-century counterparts had acknowledged. Nor was a new rationalist political theory propounded—in fact little work was done in this field at all, for the anti-rationalists were not interested in it either.

The scientists and social scientists were not concerned with providing a rational world view, but they did believe that rational investigation of man and the physical environment would produce useful knowledge and, often, important practical applications. Their findings continued to have significant implications about human nature.

Growing specialization in the sciences and social sciences further inhibited the production of a new rationalist overview. But in smaller ways some new interconnections were made. The boundary line between biology and chemistry became even shakier, for example, as geneticists advanced their understanding of the chemical composition of reproductive cells. Steady progress was registered in atomic physics, medicine, astronomy, and other sciences. For the first two decades after the war, European scientists found themselves lagging behind their counterparts in the United States and the Soviet Union. Many of them were restricted by the laboratory and team research facilities available in their own countries and had to be trained abroad to keep abreast of the latest advances. There was in fact a troubling "brain drain" to the United States that affected the sciences particularly. But Europe made its own advances too and in some fields, such as microbiology and genetics, it could rival the United States by the late 1960s.

With the theory of relativity, science had lost its claim as an intellectual panacea. No longer was it looked to for sweeping, certain judgments about the functioning of nature. Indeed this was now a dead issue, for most scientists and scientifically aware laymen no longer sought this kind of truth. With the awesome practical applications of science more and more visible, the impact of science changed. Many renewed their faith in science as a solver of practical problems and a key ingredient in human progress. At the same time, the link between science and new methods of warfare and a potentially dehumanizing technology raised many new fears. Few could quarrel with the steady advances in medical knowledge, but the applications of nuclear physics and the potential applications of new discoveries in genetics had at best ambiguous implications.

American scholars overwhelmed the Europeans in a number of social sciences, with their larger numbers and their more elaborate research facilities. In economics and sociology, particularly, the United States emphasized teamwork and quantitative methods for empirical research. The Europeans tended to stress a more discursive, theoretical approach. At the same time Europeans took the lead in certain of the social sciences, both in method and in overall approach.

From the anthropologists Claude Lévi-Strauss and Michel Foucault in France came the "new philosophy" known as structuralism, which attempts to classify societies and cultural systems. The structuralists seek to quantify as many social characteristics as possible—to develop formulas for myths, languages, and social structure, and to convert the study of society into an exact analytical science. This association of social science with some of the methods and goals of the physical sciences was not new. But with the range of materials and particularly the methods of quantification now available the structuralists predicted steady advance in the classification of human behavior. Aspects of the structuralist approach affected the study of history, and again French scholars took the lead. Attention focused increasingly on social history, the attempt to understand social structures and the behavior patterns of ordinary people in the past. Vast efforts were undertaken to develop precise histories of factors that shaped past human behavior, such as climate, sexual habits, and family patterns.

Social scientists were concerned with understanding human behavior rather than with generalizations about human nature. Yet their work had philosophical implications. Some critics accused the structuralists of taking an unduly mechanistic view of man since they always sought to categorize human behavior and to explain it in terms of predictable results from general causes. This could be viewed as an attack on man's free choice. Hence the structuralists were in bitter conflict with the existentialists, who did not care about a rational study of man but insisted on individual choice.

In psychology, where most of the leading work was done in the United States, the hold of Freudianism waned, which suggested still other changes in the view of man. Erik Erikson and others relaxed Freud's focus on the determinism of the early years of life, finding psychological turning points at other stages, notably the identity crisis at the end of adolescence. The implications of this new approach were not fully clear, but it was possible that there were more periods of choice in a person's life than Freud had allowed.

Scientists and social scientists sought primarily to explain natural and human phenomena and to apply their findings. They largely shunned moralism just as they ignored political theory and philosophy. They steadily widened the gap between their approach to the world and that of the artists and writers who saw man primarily in emotional terms. The scientists were not rationalists in even the nineteenth-century sense, but with their interest in specialized, applied knowledge and their avoidance of judgments about human nature, the division between their "culture" and that of the anti-rationalists followed from the more clear-cut rationalist-Romantic split.

As the scientists and social scientists won growing power in the universities and in government research projects they introduced an institutional element into the debate. They were "the establishment" in intellectual life. Many in fact were political radicals, in no sense content with the status quo. But most accepted the premises of industrial society, which they helped to advance by their technical discoveries. Even when they criticized society, their lack of a sweeping philosophy made them better at a careful dissection of social problems than at offering sweeping alternatives.

New Trends and Problems

By the mid-1960s European intellectual life troubled many observers. The rift between scientists and nonscientists removed any hope of intellectual unity or even useful cross-fertilization between different approaches. The abandonment, on the scientific side, of any effort at philosophy could be seen as a weakness; certainly it was a major change from the eighteenth and nineteenth centuries when science's role was that of handmaiden to philosophy. Science and social science had largely abandoned ideology. Yet their opponents, including the existentialists who urged moral judgments and emotional commitment, were too skeptical of human reason to formulate any general counterprograms or beliefs. They resented also the indifference of the general public, which seemed either to have no clear ideas or actually to share some of the assumptions of the scientists about the utility of applied knowledge.

By the late 1960s the malaise of the artists and writers spread to many students of the social sciences as well. The students were aroused by a number of factors, including a concern about their professional future and the inadequacies of university life. But they had important intellectual motivation as well. Many found the objective approach sought in the social sciences too cold and remote; they wanted commitment, not the careful dissection of man in society. Thus students of sociology, history, and related subjects were most often found leading dissent.

Tentatively, the young dissenting intellectuals groped toward a new political philosophy. They found a hero in Herbert Marcuse, a German-born professor who fled from Nazi persecution to the United States. Marcuse wrote his leading political works—most notably *One Dimensional Man*—in the mid-1950s, but they won wide attention only a decade later. Marcuse railed against the dominance of modern technology and the entrenchment of political stability that create a limited society in which men can develop only one dimension of their being. Class and political conflict has ceased to be really effective; real life is stifled by affluence and tolerance. Marcuse urged rejection of the administered good life in favor of new or revived values of contemplation, enjoyment, fantasy. In this he appealed to the neo-Romantic tradition and to values that writers and filmmakers had promoted during the 1950s and 1960s.

Was a response by rationalists possible? Would the terms of intellectual debate decisively change? No final answers were possible by the early 1970s, but it seemed clear that the postwar confinement of the neo-Romantic tradition to the arts and philosophy, and of the rationalist tradition to the sciences, and social sciences, was being challenged. Young intellectuals were trying to put new pieces together. Marcuse briefly helped here, though his popularity was waning by 1970. What the new synthesis, if any, would be remained to be determined. Also it was not clear if the crisis among intellectuals foreshadowed a broader social crisis. The dissenting intellectuals sought new contacts in the broader society. They tried to reach across the broad gap that had developed between formal culture and popular ideas. In a sense they sought a restoration of the roles that formal ideas and intellectuals had played two centuries before, and that scientists still played.

ECONOMIC DEVELOPMENT AND POPULATION GROWTH

Economic development provided a striking contrast to the intellectual activity of postwar Europe. Here there was massive change, though many specific features that had immediate impact upon society as a whole had begun taking shape before World War II. Economic change was the prime cause of changes in the social structure, even in personal values, yet it did not occur in a vacuum. A new kind of businessman arose who thought in terms of planning and coordination. In addition a new peasant mentality sparked rapid agricultural development, while new working-class expectations spurred consumption and encouraged workers to seek new skills.

The Population Boom

One of the first indications that basic changes were occurring in Europe came with the population spurt following World War II. This in turn encouraged economic expansion and a new sense of dynamism and progress.

The war had had a devastating effect on population levels in many countries. A million and a half Germans were killed in action, and at the war's end another two million were missing. Many east European countries suffered still more heavily. In France, Britain, and Italy war deaths were far lower than they had been in World War I, but here too there had been extensive suffering. Everywhere civilians as well as the military shared in the casualty figures, and there were permanent injuries and psychological scars from the bombardments of cities in addition to many deaths. Furthermore millions of people on the continent had been displaced. During the first three and a half years of the war, 30 million Europeans had fled or been driven from their homes. A million and a half Poles were deported from Polish territories annexed by Germany. Two and a half million French men and women had been held in captivity in Germany as prisoners of war or forced laborers; in all, there were eight million foreign workers in Germany by 1944. Some 12 million Russians had fled to the interior of their country.

During the immediate postwar period the confused movement of peoples increased. Millions of displaced people, often physically debilitated and injured in spirit, sought to go home, while millions more sought to avoid going home. Many east Europeans, for example, wanted no part of the new regimes in their countries, and most of the surviving European Jews sought a new homeland. Despite the appalling wartime slaughter, a substantial Jewish population remained in Poland, Rumania, and the Soviet Union. Russia generally refused to let its citizens emigrate, but elsewhere in eastern Europe the policy was more flexible; within a decade after the war about half a million European Jews had made their way to Israel. Finally, the war's de facto settlement put millions of Germans on the move. Some had fled the Red armies; others moved west because of Polish control of former German lands; still others moved farther west to escape the Communist regime in East Germany—an exodus of hundreds of thousands that effectively ended only with the building of the Berlin Wall and the stabilization of the East German regime.

Such suffering and confusion convinced many, right after the war, that Europe could never recover, and that Europe's morale was irreparably harmed. Demographically, however, the impact was short-lived.

Germany and the countries of eastern Europe soon made up their wartime losses. Poland resumed its especially high birth rate. Despite government encouragement, population growth was slower in Russia. Furthermore all these countries suffered a "hollow generation" like that which had afflicted Europe generally after World War I. A generation that normally would have been born during the early 1940s, coming to maturity in the 1960s, simply did not exist. This, combined with outright war losses, disrupted normal patterns of leadership recruitment. Some of the problems the Communist regimes faced by the 1960s,—bureaucratic rigidity and lack of innovation— owed much to the war's disruption of normal demography. Nevertheless the sheer birth rate, ultimately the most important traditional measure of a country's demographic vitality, bounced back quickly in eastern and central Europe. Population growth in West Germany exceeded the rate during the interwar years.

The same was true of western Europe, where the decline or outright cessation of population growth between the wars had acted as a powerfully depressing force. Britain's population rose from 45 million to 47 million during the war itself and by 1960 had passed 52 million; the growth rate was a steady .5 percent a year. Scandinavian population increased at similar rates. The Netherlands, another highly urbanized country, jumped to first place in population growth in western Europe. But the greatest surprise was France, Europe's traditional demographic laggard. In 1945, for the first time in a decade, France registered an excess of births over deaths. During the next nine years the country gained three million people, which represented the most rapid rate of population increase since early in the nineteenth century.

Some demographers speculated that the industrial nations were entering a third stage of modern demography. First came massive population growth, then a pronounced downturn, then renewed growth. They argued that the age of affluence brought a desire for more children. By the 1960s this argument became harder to maintain. Growth rates slowed once again, though they did not reach the stagnant levels of the interwar years.

A certain amount of demographic compensation is normal after wartime loss and confusion, though it is notable that the post-World War II gains were much more extensive than those after World War I. A number of factors accounted for the population spurt. First, the welfare state encouraged population growth. In France, family assistance was the most obvious reason for the reversal of prewar demographic trends. Welfare protection and, within a few years after the war, advancing prosperity encouraged people in many social classes to have an extra child. Another factor was that morale in western Europe had improved. Political and economic changes made people less fearful, despite Cold War tensions. Rising population rates in turn encouraged further economic growth.

Within 15 years, however, western Europe largely reverted to the slower demographic increase that had been normal for industrial nations for almost a century. Rising expectations in many social groups, increasing mobility into the middle classes, and growing interest in education convinced many people that they should limit family size more rigorously. As in the late nineteenth century, one must wonder whether this decision also reflected a new fearfulness about the future that presaged the rising social tension visible by the late 1960s. At the same time, Italy and Russia, countries which were maturing industrially for the first time, witnessed a more pronounced reduction in population growth even before 1960. Most of Europe seemed to be in a comparable demographic situation, though interesting national variations remained. The result, again, was slow, undramatic growth, and

Europeans seemed largely content with the demographic situation. The gloom of the interwar years was absent and it was clear that continued economic growth was quite compatible with a roughly stable population.

Economic Development

Western Europe decisively entered a new stage of economic growth as the problems that had produced the depression and had defied solution for a decade were now resolved. In many countries average annual growth rates exceeded those of any previous decade in the century, while France and Italy increased their output more rapidly than at any point since the industrial revolution had begun. The transformation of the economies of eastern Europe was almost as dramatic, but in this case what was achieved was a mature industrialization, not an affluent society. The gap between east and west narrowed but it did not disappear.

Problems of Reconstruction

Until 1948 confusion was rampant in the European economy. People in many areas were near starvation. French miners, for example, were unable to work regularly because they did not have enough food. Much agricultural land and animal stock had been destroyed, while loss of transportation facilities and equipment made it difficult to distribute what food was produced. France had lost three quarters of her railroad rolling stock and many other countries were similarly depleted. Loss of workers because of death and dislocation added to production difficulties, as did interruption of the regular supply of raw materials.

In every area the lag in production was reflected in massive inflation as people tried to buy goods that simply were not available. Excessive demand was heightened in many cases by the inflationary measures introduced by governments seeking to increase investment, often at the expense of balanced budgets. Germany suffered from rampant inflation until 1948, when the government stabilized the mark. For a time the Germans had returned to a near-barter economy, using goods like cigarettes as means of exchange because money was almost worthless. Italy stabilized its currency only in 1952 on the basis of a devaluation of the lira to one-fiftieth of its previous value. French inflation persisted until the latter part of the 1950s, although successive devaluations reduced the franc to less than one-twenty-fifth of its earlier worth. British inflation continued until about 1950, and it too was cured only by substantial devaluation.

The inflationary problem did not prevent some economic advance. Government investment programs helped restore transportation facilities and some manufacturing equipment. In France, production levels began to rise well before the currency was stabilized. Generally, however, the massive postwar inflation inhibited major economic gains and caused extensive political unrest. Savings were lost, while entrepreneurs questioned the future of the economy. Workers were disgruntled as prices rose more rapidly than wages.

Inflation also weakened the ability of the European countries to sell, and therefore to buy, abroad because European goods in effect were overpriced on the world market. This really reflected the fact that European production was below its traditional levels. It could not meet demands at home, much less produce for export, but precisely because of the production lag, exports were vitally necessary. To rebuild, Europe needed equipment from abroad, particularly from the United States. In this early period, however, it was impossible to earn the dollars for these purchases. Real progress seemed impossible, and many people on both sides of the Atlantic spoke of a permanent "dollar gap," that is, permanent economic dependence of Europe on the United States.

In this situation American aid after 1947 was of vital significance. The United States had assisted Europe before, but mainly in the form of relief rather than aid for reconstruction. Spurred by genuine concern for Europe's future and more specifically by the dynamics of the growing Cold War, the United States undertook a comprehensive program of aid. With the Marshall Plan, American funds began to close the dollar gap, thus allowing European purchases of modern equipment; government and intergovernmental economic planning was encouraged. Nations that received aid first, notably Germany, rebuilt most rapidly, but all western countries were ultimately aided, and began to advance with extraordinary speed.

By the early 1950s it was obvious that much wartime damage had been superficial. In Germany, for example, although the destruction of transportation linkages had paralyzed the economy for a time, almost 90 percent of factory productive capacity had remained intact despite massive bombing. When the currency stabilized and transportation facilities were restored, the German economy was ready to rise. Its recovery has been dubbed an "economic miracle," but like many miracles it was not inexplicable. Postwar economic advance was not simply based on the previous industrial economy, or even on the addition of American aid. Something new was afoot, a more vigorous desire for economic change. The very intensity of the postwar crisis encouraged new ways of thinking. Government planning and other forms of state assistance encouraged new methods, in agriculture as well as industry. Population growth acted as a powerful spur through the 1950s.

Economic Strength

Beginning in Germany in 1948, and in France and Italy in the early 1950s, an economic advance of vast proportions began that continued

A City Rebuilt: Contemporary West Berlin—modern structures surround the Kaiser-Wilhelm Church, retained as a memorial of the horrors of World War II.

through the 1960s. It was not completely uninterrupted and there were years of reduced growth. But in contrast to previous industrial history there were no real recessions. Even recessions in the United States merely resulted in a slower pace of growth, not in a cessation. State guidance helped channel resources to points of actual need and prevented speculative over-development. The provision of minimal standards for all classes and the maintenance of full employment opened a new mass market for many goods. Thus economic growth was unprecedentedly steady as wartime damage was repaired and production soared to new heights.

Growth was also rapid in most countries, exceeding the rates of the inter-war years and also the decades before World War I. It also exceeded the rates of the more troubled American economy from the mid-1950s onward. The German economy expanded at an annual rate of 6 percent during much of the 1950s. During the early part of the decade significant unemployment persisted, tolerated by the trade unions in the interest of using resources for new investment. But by the end of the 1950's German industry was crying out for more workers and growth continued at a high rate during most of the 1960s.

France attained an 8 percent annual growth by the end of the 1950s.

Expansion continued at a somewhat slower pace during the 1960s, rising again in the early 1970s to over 7 percent a year. By 1959 the Italian economy expanded at the rate of 11 percent a year, propelling Italy into the ranks of advanced industrial nations. Growth rates in Scandinavia and particularly in Britain were somewhat lower. The British economy grew at a rate of about 4 percent a year in the 1950s. British workers and entrepreneurs both seemed more resistant to technological change than their counterparts on the continent; as a result, the British standard of living declined in relation to France and Germany. But even in Britain there was significant advance, in contrast to the stagnation of the interwar years.

New Industries

Certain traditional industries continued to decline throughout western Europe. Textiles and particularly mining suffered. Some mines were completely closed, unable to compete with petroleum fuels. On the whole, however, this decline was more than balanced by the advance of petrochemicals, electronics, and heavy consumer goods such as automobiles and appliances. There was a marked increase as well in the service sector of the economy, as the need for teachers, sales personnel, and the like expanded.

These shifts in turn altered the regional balance of national economies. Italian industry continued to be centered in the north, despite the location of a few important firms elsewhere. In France and Britain, however, the coal regions, the traditional centers of manufacturing, declined. Many of the newer industries preferred to locate in regions free from the grime of the mining areas. Service industries, such as insurance, and many company bureaucracies tended to settle in the capital cities or other financial centers. Paris, London, and Frankfurt, and the regions around them, expanded rapidly. Southern England, long eclipsed by the industrial north, was now reversing the process. A few traditional factory areas in Britain and the coal districts of Belgium were afflicted with noticeable levels of unemployment. But generally the expansion of the economy more than sufficed to compensate for lagging areas and industries. All this meant greater geographical as well as social mobility.

A Dynamic Agriculture

Agriculture participated strongly in economic growth. Increasing numbers of peasants abandoned the countryside for the city where industrial growth assured them of jobs. The result was less rural poverty and more efficient farm units. Governments encouraged more productive methods on the farms, providing better training and information on new techniques.

They promoted the consolidation of small plots into larger, more efficient holdings and they actively backed the cooperative movement. Improved equipment, including tractors and other agricultural machines, spread widely, resulting in a sharp increase in crop yields. West Germany, cut off from the agricultural east, raised agricultural productivity rapidly; by 1952 West German wheat yield per acre was 1.2 tons, compared to .4 in the United States. French agricultural gains were in many ways still more dramatic, and output rose rapidly. European farmers were not as efficient as those of North America where farming was far more mechanized. Their increased output added to the problem of excessive agricultural production in the industrial nations of the world and this output could be maintained only by tariff protection and subsidies. Nevertheless agriculture was not the invalid it had been during the previous half century. It was less of a drain on the economy as a whole and provided better quality food to Europe's cities.

Rising Living Standards

Growth in most major sectors of the economy rapidly advanced general prosperity. The European middle classes enjoyed high rates of profits and salaries. Continuing a well-established trend, the size of businesses grew steadily. The Common Market encouraged the formation of international business combines. Small wonder then that earnings rose, sometimes more rapidly than wages. Because of government encouragement to private enterprise and labor's surprising acquiesence in modest earnings, German profits climbed faster than wages until the later 1950s. French government programs of anti-inflationary wage restraint in 1958–1959 allowed profits to rise more rapidly than working-class income. But the earnings of the lower classes increased overall, and this was one of the key results of the new economic setting.

Unemployment was virtually eliminated after the economic boom began, though there was a lag in Germany where more than two million workers were out of work as late as February 1954. After the mid-1950s, rates of no more than 2 percent unemployment were maintained in France and Germany, which meant that most of the unemployed were simply in transition from one job to the next. Both countries, along with Switzerland, Belgium, and other areas, relied extensively on immigration to fill the soaring demand for workers created by economic growth. Large numbers of Italians, Spaniards, and Turks were brought in to work in Germany; several hundred thousand Algerians found employment in France; close to two million Pakistanis and West Indians poured into Britain. Many of the new workers were badly treated, if only because they filled the most unskilled positions. In Britain, where unemployment was higher than on the continent though far lower than it had been in the 1920s, serious racial hostilities developed. But some of the immigrants benefited from their work and there were other, clearer gains as well. Emigration, along with rapid industrialization, significantly reduced Italy's traditional pool of unemployment. Immigration combined with full employment also allowed growing numbers of workers to rise to higher-paying jobs in the most prosperous countries. Finally, growing numbers of women found employment, which boosted family income. In Britain the number of working-class women with jobs rose six times over the level of the 1930s. Never, in fact, since the population explosion of the eighteenth century had such a high percentage of the adult population been regularly employed over such an extended period of time.

Full employment and the steadily rising demand for workers naturally produced a rise in wages. Demands by individuals and unions for new raises met little resistance. By the early 1960s wage rates were rising fast, which helped ultimately to bring a renewed threat of inflation. Before this point, wage rises brought the urban lower classes in western and central Europe unprecedented affluence. This was not mass consumption of the limited sort developed before World War I; rather it involved not only improvement in diet and clothing but also mass purchase of large and expensive consumer goods. Television sets and refrigerators were now normal household items for the majority of the people, and the average family in the wealthy countries possessed a motor vehicle—either a scooter or an automobile. Recreational opportunities increased as work hours were lowered and most workers were legally guaranteed two or three weeks of paid vacation.

Economic Problems

Despite the remarkable economic advances, there were weaknesses in Europe's new economic structure. Because of its slower growth rate and dependence on massive imports of food and other goods, Britain faced a chronic balance of payments problem that dominated national policy by the 1960s. The British, bent on improving their consumption levels, bought more imported goods, but did not export enough to earn the necessary foreign exchange. In order to produce more for export and adjust the payments' balance, the government periodically imposed restrictions not only on imports and travel abroad but on consumer spending at home. France more briefly faced a similar problem after the social unrest of 1968. Both Britain and France undertook another devaluation at the end of the decade in order to improve the payments situation. Germany, on the other hand, regularly exported more than was imported and so faced periodic pressure to revalue the mark upward. In general, however, European currencies remained strong and relatively stable into the early 1970s.

Few countries managed to maintain the growth rates developed around 1960, when reconstruction efforts were still continuing and the population boom was in full force. Although rates remained relatively high, there was some question about the future stability of Europe's economy. Despite the activities of the welfare state, income inequality was great. In Britain, less than 7 percent of the population owned over 84 percent of all income-producing assets and property. Five percent of the population garnered 68 percent of all earnings from private property, compared to 79 percent in the 1930s. In other words, the relative wealth of the upper class was diminished a bit but it remained high. At the other end of the scale many groups were still very limited in what they could afford to buy. Although the peasants' general lot had improved, their situation remained well below urban living standards; some urban workers in turn were unable to purchase refrigerators and other items. Many Europeans deplored these great income inequalities on moral grounds. The inequalities also raised doubts about the ability of most consumers to continue to expand their purchases to maintain a high economic growth rate. With declining population growth this question could become acute. But it must be emphasized that the problem, by the early 1970s, was still a potential one, for growth rates remained high.

International Competition

In 1969 a French politician and journalist, Jacques Servan-Schreiber, published a book called *The American Challange*, which quickly won wide attention. Though directed primarily toward France, he pointed to problems that affected other countries as well. His claim was that despite impressive economic gains, including a growth rate far more rapid than that of the United States, Europe had not achieved a level of technology or of business organization comparable to American standards. European firms were too small, their willingness to innovate still too limited.

The argument was difficult to assess. It was true that large American firms had moved into the prosperous European market in increasing numbers, setting up subsidiaries and buying European firms outright. This development disturbed many Europeans and some halting limitations were imposed, particularly by the Gaullist government. Yet it was difficult to resist the ample investment funds and the technical expertise the Americans could provide. Undoubtedly something of a "lag" probably existed, though it was exaggerated by the peculiar position of the dollar as a world currency, which European governments had to defend in order to protect their own currencies—this, despite the weak balance of payments situation of the United States. In effect American businessmen could invest vast sums abroad because the European governments would underwrite the value of the currency. But to the extent that a real lag existed, its economic significance remained unclear. American penetration worried Europeans politically, but it helped spur further economic advance. In terms of employment and economic growth levels, Europe remained in considerably better shape than the United States by the early 1970s. Most European countries were also more successful in export sales than their American rival. One wondered who was lagging behind whom.

The most important problem in the European economy by the later 1960s was a renewed bout of inflation that affected even stable, secure Germany. Some blamed the flood of unwanted dollars from American investors and speculators, which increased the money supply and contributed to price rises. Other factors were also involved. Consumer expectations were rising steadily, despite continuing income inequality and some outright poverty. It was not so easy to expand production in order to meet these demands. France and Germany already suffered from a shortage of labor, which limited production gains. Workers there and also in Britain resisted undue pressures to step up the pace of work or introduce rapid technological change. At the same time many groups of workers and others pressed for massive wage increases. When they won, they contributed to the formula for inflation. Price increases did not get totally out of hand, but wages and earnings for many groups failed to keep pace after 1965.

Europe thus had not achieved economic utopia. No one could be sure that serious dislocations might not develop in the future. But Europe's formula for economic success had worked for over 20 years, and this success dominates postwar history. Inevitably it changed the way most people lived, even the way they thought. Some changes indeed had to precede the economic boom, for new motives were essential for new kinds of economic behavior. The key question, then, is what kind of new society grew up around the new economy.

SOCIAL STRUCTURE

Bolstered by rising prosperity and the benefits of the welfare state, the major social classes seemed to be drawing closer together in a number of respects. Consumption patterns became more similar, and there was increasing mobility from one class to the next. Large numbers of workers—30 percent of the French working class, for example—moved into middle-class jobs within two decades after the war. Class antagonisms were reduced, and the bitter social tensions of the interwar years did not reappear in postwar Europe. Increasing flexibility in the outlook of the middle and upper classes and growing satisfaction among the lower classes added up to greater social stability than Europe had achieved since the beginning of industrialization. By the 1960s European stability contrasted vividly not only with the European past but with North America. The theme of stability extended to more personal aspects of life as well, such as relationships within the family.

While social differences declined, a distinct class structure remained. Each major social group maintained its own outlook and life style, but each changed considerably in comparison with the interwar years. At the same time a class structure took shape in the Communist countries that bore some marked resemblances to that in western Europe.

Finally, new forms of protest developed, indications that Europe's stability was not complete. At the end of the 1960s a new unrest surfaced that threatened to disrupt the relative social peace that had prevailed for two decades.

The principal focus of a survey of postwar social developments must rest on the growing adaptation that most social classes made to an advanced industrial society. The nature of the adaptation varied with the class. In some cases it involved protest as well as new satisfactions. But only as Europe neared the 1970s did protest threaten to become the dominant theme.

The Upper Class

The upper class throughout Europe changed notably following World War II, becoming far more receptive to economic and political change. There was no question that an upper class still existed, at least in the non-Communist countries. The hold of a small minority on the bulk of private wealth defied the higher taxes that the welfare state imposed. From this upper class were drawn the bulk of high government officials. Indeed one important part of the political elite, the parliamentary representatives, became more solidly middle- and upper-class than it had been between the wars. The percentage of lower-class parliamentary deputies—an important minority in democratic countries in the 1920s and 1930s—decreased in number. But the composition and outlook of the upper class altered considerably.

One of the most striking developments across Europe was the virtual disappearance of the aristocracy. Long declining, the aristocracy had continued to play a significant economic and political role after World War I, forming an influential part of the upper class. In Germany and elsewhere it resisted democracy and social reform and often contributed to the rise of rightist movements. More subtly, the continued deference given to aristocratic values in France and elsewhere encouraged elements of the middle classes to adhere to rightist parties and to scorn undue devotion to business success.

The most decisive blow to the aristocracy was the advance of Communism across eastern Europe. In Poland, Hungary, and eastern Germany the aristocracy had maintained its strongest base, including ownership of most of the land. This was now destroyed. Aristocrats lost their land, their titles, their distinctive political influence. The aristocracy in western Europe retained a certain identity—indeed in Spain and Portugal their economic and political power was considerable. Elsewhere, however, the spread of democracy virtually eliminated any special aristocratic political influence. The civil service in Britain, for example, was filled largely by people of middle-class origin, with a significant minority from the working classes. The high property taxes imposed by the welfare state hit hard at the remaining landed estates. Some aristocrats ingeniously hung on, opening their homes to gawking, but paying, tourists or even converting ancestral grounds into open-air zoos. They still had their titles and a certain sense of common identity; they still received public attention and some deference. But their role was no longer distinctive. For better or worse, the aristocratic influence on general culture was gone as well. Businessmen no longer aspired to titles. They were free, also, from aristocratic disdain for commerce.

Some of the great industrial families slipped from power. Nationalization of coal and other industries hit some of the great magnates; others, while retaining ownership of huge industrial combines, turned direction of the enterprise over to specially trained managers. The giant Krupp concern, for example, revived after the war, but direction was in the hands of a new manager, Berthold Beitz. Upper-level civil servants were given more technical training, which was necessary for the management of the welfare state. Hence, both in and out of government, the specialized technocrat became a vital adjunct of the upper class. The technocrats thought in terms of long-term planning and efficiency. They were less concerned than traditional European big businessmen with high short-term profits and with defense of the prerogatives of ownership. They played an important role, particularly in France, in spurring unprecedented economic growth. They could accept the institutions of the welfare state, including extensive government involvement in the economy.

The upper class thus received new blood from below, from people with advanced managerial training. The extension of the mass media created many new opportunities for wealth and influence, and the directors of newspapers and television were most likely to be "new men." Whether new or not, members of the upper class were better trained than ever before. They contained no large element, which, like the aristocracy in earlier decades, felt threatened by modern society. The upper class did run the risk of being somewhat cut off from the rest of society, for even new entrants to the class had essentially the same education and values as the older members. With its growing devotion to centralized planning and efficiency, this contributed to a sense of impersonal rule, both in government and in the economy.

The Middle Classes

As opportunities in bureaucracy, professional life, and the service industries increased, the middle classes expanded rapidly in numbers. Some aspired to rise into the upper class, but most remained far more modest in wealth and influence; in most non-Communist countries only 5 percent of the population reached real upper-class status. But the middle classes were changing rapidly in their own right, resolving several traditional problems and significantly modifying their outlook.

The welfare state benefited the middle class greatly. Although middle-class families remained smaller than those in the lower classes, the aid distributed to children was a great help; inexpensive medical care was another. Still more important was the expansion and updating of the secondary school system and the increased scholarship support for university education. Educating the child, still a special concern of the middle classes, was far less burdensome than ever before. The welfare state also provided jobs for many professional people, along with the general expansion of the economy; as a result, until the later 1960s, the perennial problem of overproduction of professional people did not reappear.

Certain aspects of the welfare state troubled the middle classes; they had a sense of constraint, a belief that freedom for individual advancement had been limited. Doctors under the state health plans, for example, felt constraint directly. Their reactions ranged from grumbling in Britain to periodic strikes in Belgium and Italy. But for most elements in the middle classes the benefits outweighed the disadvantages, as the standard of living improved rapidly. Previously the middle classes had looked on welfare measures with suspicion, fearing they would only help the lower classes. Their acceptance of the full-fledged welfare state was a key element in the social harmony of postwar Europe.

At the same time, the middle-class definition of success and security changed. A minority clung to independent property ownership as the key, and particularly in France a large group of small shopkeepers tried to resist the growing competition of supermarkets and chain stores. They and their families worked up to 15 hours a day to survive; they used political pressure and even street demonstrations to fight for tax advantages and other aid. But the bulk of the middle classes, from sales clerks through technicians to managers, no longer depended on property ownership to measure their success in life. The amount of salary and the level of education were now far more important.

All these changes help to explain the growing flexibility of middle-class political outlook. Most members of the middle classes were still nonsocialists, certainly non-Communists. But defense of ownership rights no longer prevented them from making concessions to the lower classes and from seeing advantages for themselves in some "socialistic" measures. Many voted socialist on occasion and most could tolerate socialist rule; some even viewed the Communist party as an acceptable element of the political system, though they did not want Communist rule.

The middle classes could afford to be tolerant, for most of them had never had it so good. Their standard of living was far higher than that of the lower classes, for taxes did not redistribute much of their income. Their hold on education was confirmed. Examinations that determined at age 11 whether a child would be able to go to the best secondary schools excluded all but the most talented children from the lower classes; children with a middle-class cultural background, on the other hand, had an excellent chance.

The middle classes learned to have fun. They still enjoyed their work, but the old compulsion for work was gone. Ample leisure time and regular annual vacations of at least three weeks created a new life style. Clerks as well as bankers became continental travelers. Most significantly, the middle classes discovered the sun. Every year millions of middle-class Germans, Britons, Scandinavians, and Frenchmen pour into the south of France, into Italy, and into Spain. New attention to leisure activities altered middle-class spending patterns. No longer did house and furnishings loom so large. These were still considered important, but increasing numbers could accept pleasant but not showy row houses and apartments, often because they knew they could escape them frequently. Not only formal vacations but weekend drives to the country, which packed the roads around every major city, became a regular part of middle-class life.

The new outlook was reflected also in family relationships. With property less important, there was no need to arrange marriages and provide abundant dowries. The middle classes now married for love. Their sexual practices became more varied and probably more interesting, within marriage as well as outside it; certainly their sexual tolerance increased. There was little outcry against the growing sexual license of films and theater. Indeed there was considerable evidence that the middle class was now less sexually repressed than the lower class. There was marked change, also, in the general attitude of men toward women. Partly from economic necessity in the hard days after the war, more and more middle-class women took jobs outside the home. A larger number also went to the universities and prestigious secondary schools. Finally, there was noticeable relaxation in the treatment of children. Fathers became less severe; toilet training and other disciplinary measures were eased, in favor of more permissiveness.

The middle classes were still identifiable and still maintained some traditional values, but they had made a major adjustment to the society of abundance. They had moved farther in certain respects than their American counterparts.

A "New Class" in the Communist States

A middle class was taking shape in eastern Europe as well. Less affluent than the western middle classes, less fully weaned from a work ethic, yet it developed a number of recognizable middle-class characteristics, some of which were quite comparable to contemporaneous developments in the west.

The middle class in eastern Europe was not based on possession of property, since state ownership of industrial and commercial concerns was almost complete. It was a managerial-professional class, drawn initially from a variety of groups that had taken advantage of expanding educational opportunities. Its members received relatively high incomes. They sought some distinctive consumption patterns, such as small country houses, and they served as one of the principal sources of pressure for greater production of consumer goods and improved urban housing. Above all, seeing the benefits they derived from superior education, they tried to assure educational opportunities for their children. They struggled to prepare their children for entrance examinations to the higher schools and used all their influence to place them well. Not surprisingly, therefore, they displayed a conventional middle-class attachment to status. Correspondingly the new middle class limited its birth rates severely, in order to improve material standards and to make it easier to assure middle-class success to the children it did have. Women often had jobs of their own and did not want the distraction of too many children.

The new middle class had substantial political influence—some achieved their first gains as local Communist party leaders—as well as a leading role in management of the economy. Their existence and their close ties with the Communist party dismayed idealists, like Milovan Djilas in Yugoslavia. But they could be seen also as a logical component of an increasingly industrial society. Like their western counterparts, they advocated efficiency, rational planning, and ambition. Their own lives were built in large part on these values and they preached them, often through Communist party directives, to the rest of society.

The Working Classes

The working classes in western Europe seemed in many ways increasingly bourgeois, and the theme of working-class *embourgeoisement* was picked up, in praise or lament, by many observers. The decline of political radicalism and even of political interest, at least until the mid-1960s, was one symptom of a major change in working-class life. There was important political agitation right after the war, but then came greater calm. The increasing moderation of both socialist and Communist parties reflected and encouraged workers' new political outlook. Only a minority of French Communist voters displayed real ideological concern, and increasing numbers of workers did not bother to vote at all. Attendance at party and trade union meetings dwindled in many areas. Since the early twentieth century Danish socialists had maintained a party brewery, which they used among other things to train young leaders in management techniques. By the late 1950s they found that workers no longer bought the party beer, so they had to develop other training methods. In a variety of ways, then, even when voting patterns did not change, worker attachment to traditional class symbols was declining.

Most noticeable was the workers' interest in new items of consumption. They began to give as much attention to their housing as the middle classes did, and, with public housing, they frequently lived in the same areas; class-based residential districts declined in importance. Workers became property owners for the first time since industrialization began, as they bought refrigerators, television sets, cars, and motor scooters. Here was one source of new political attitudes. Workers were too busy working overtime in order to pay for their new possessions, or spending time actively enjoying them, to come to party meetings. Other aspects of behavior changed also.

Workers eagerly sought better jobs, often in distant areas, to satisfy their new expectations. Along with their new buying interests they devoted themselves to a variety of hobbies at home. Their lives became more private off the job as group recreation, even gatherings in bars, declined. Family interests increased by the same token. Relations between husband and wife became more equal, in part because growing numbers of the wives worked and contributed to the family income. The divorce rate stabilized in most of the advanced industrial countries for the first time since the late nineteenth century. A number of studies revealed that most workers talked of their mates and their marriage in terms of satisfaction and affection.

A new working-class outlook was thus developing. Dependence on sweeping ideologies lessened, just as religion had earlier declined. The worker became more dependent on individual satisfactions, material in large part but also familial. He had a stronger belief in steady material progress, which had still been somewhat hesitant in the interwar period even in the leading industrial countries. A poll taken in 1954 among unskilled Italian workers—many of them Communists—revealed that the vast majority did not believe that durable progress was possible. By the late 1960s even this group had been converted.

But for all their changes, workers were still workers. They shared more middle-class habits and beliefs than before, but they had not merged with that class. Their earnings were still lower, their leisure activities more modest. A few single workers managed vacations abroad, but most married workers, though they had at least three weeks' annual holiday, could only travel locally if at all. Their outlook differed as well, in many ways revealing a persistence of class traditions. They were still less likely to save; their sense of looking to the future was less developed. They aspired to middle-class jobs for their children and when asked they talked of law or medicine. But they did not give their children active support and coaching in their school work. In other words, they were unable fully to connect aspiration and reality. Hence most working-class children went to vocational schools; few entered the prestigious secondary schools; and still fewer entered the universities, despite the scholarship system. In France by the mid-1960s, only 4 percent of the university student body came from below the middle classes. Most important, workers took no pleasure in work and lived their lives outside it. They viewed their job, which they found dull and depressing, as an instrument, a means, solely as a source of money.

It is not surprising therefore that they did protest. Strike rates varied from one country to the next in non-Communist Europe; after the bitter postwar strike wave subsided, many observers predicted that the strike would decline as a protest form, as workers became more respectable and more willing to submit their grievances to bargaining procedures. But in most industrial countries strike rates remained high even in prosperous times. The most important agitation occurred in state-run industries, where governments, worried about inflation, tried to keep wages below the level of private industry. Strikes by transportation workers became almost commonplace in France and Italy. Most of the strikes were calm and well-organized and many general strikes were called just for a day or so to demonstrate labor's strength without disrupting the economy unduly. The workers' declining ideological concern, combined with the greater tolerance of the middle classes, prevented strikes from threatening the political system.

Workers did not use most strikes to protest work conditions or discontent over their jobs. Consistently they asked for more wages, which expressed their rising expectations but did not get at the problem of work directly. In other words, part of the moderation of the working class depended on the deliberate bifurcation of their existence on and off the job, and their focus in protest on what was easiest to grant in an expanding economy. But this should not conceal the important change in the nature of protest: workers were for the first time using strikes regularly to express a demand for more.

Workers in eastern Europe, pehaps more obviously than the new middle class, were in a different stage of development from that of their western counterparts. Their standard of living lagged and prospects for greater consumption developed more slowly. At the same time, given Communist party control of the trade unions, there were no regular protest outlets. Individual workers could improve their lot by rising through the educational system or through party service. The mass of workers were insured against illness and unemployment, and were provided with important recreational and vacation facilities. But increasingly there were signs of dissatisfaction. Collective protest perforce was rare. When it occurred it took a political or nationalistic focus or, as in Poland in 1970, it seized on a deterioration in living conditions in the traditional fashion of lower-class unrest. More important, however, were signs of individual discontent: theft in the factories, alcoholism, resistance to changes in work methods and to an increased pace of work. It was not clear when or even whether these workers would move into a new kind of adaptation to industrialization, as their western counterparts had done.

Peasants

Some of the most important shifts in outlook occurred among Europe's peasantry after World War II. The class was dwindling in size but remained an important minority of the population everywhere. The peasant's situation changed most dramatically in the Communist countries, with the elimination of the aristocracy and the attack on religion. New educational opportunities and new methods of work, generally imposed through the collective farms, continued this process. But resistance to the new system, expressed primarily through low levels of production, suggested that peasant values were changing more slowly than the institutions around them.

Peasants in western Europe maintained some of their traditions too. They were more religious than their urban counterparts and they had larger families. A French survey in 1970 showed that only peasants continued to define a successful family in terms of the number of children it had. Peasants in many areas remained attached to age-old but now inefficient customs such as scattered plots of land. Government encouragement to consolidate family holdings made only slow headway. Peasants continued to find safety in a variety of small fields scattered around the village, even though they wasted a great deal of time traveling from one to the other and often could not efficiently use new equipment on any one plot. Peasant traditionalism was heightened by the continued exodus of many younger, ambitious peasants to the city.

Nevertheless great changes came to the countryside. Religion and family size both declined significantly. Material conditions improved. Welfare-state aid, such as family assistance and medical care programs, provided significant benefits.

With government encouragement, peasants themselves showed a growing interest in economic change. In particular, observers noted a real revolution in the attitudes of younger French peasants. Their interest in technical development was most striking and tractors became a more important status symbol than land itself. Some peasants whose plots were too small to use tractors still bought them to display in their front yards. The cooperative movement continued to spread, aided by government subsidies. Peasants were exposed to a variety of new organizations, and elections for the leadership of cooperatives and of local state agencies changed the nature of village politics. Political contests became a subject of lively, even bitter debate, as traditional village leaders were pushed aside by younger, more forward-looking ones. Peasants' understanding of national politics also changed and their voting rates increased markedly.

The new peasant outlook was extremely conducive to protest. In France and Italy there were signs of new dissatisfaction shortly after World War II as a minority of peasants began to vote Communist. In the early 1960s a more direct protest movement developed in France, led by peasants who had adopted the most advanced technical improvements. These peasants knew that their conditions were still inferior to urban standards and they looked to the government for remedies. They demonstrated repeatedly to call the attention of government and the urban public to their hardships. A favorite tactic was an invasion of a provincial administrative center by thousands of tractor-driving peasants, or disruption, again by tractors, of major highways during the vacation period. These protests had limited success, though they undoubtedly helped maintain government agricultural support. They were most interesting in revealing the new peasant mentality.

STABILITY AND PROTEST

Europe by the mid-1960s was in no sense free from tension and unrest, but the new kind of peasant and worker protest seemed to be containable. The lower classes worked for gains within the existing system, and in asking for a greater share, they showed that their protests had been significantly modernized. Thus peasant agitation was in many ways less troubling than that which developed between the wars. Then many peasants were still protesting the whole nature of industrial society and turned to Fascist or other rightist movements that purported to seek a return to traditional ways. Workers' protest, largely depoliticized, could be met as long as the economy expanded. After a century and a half of industrialization all the major social classes for the first time agreed that economic advance was desirable, possible, and important.

Social stability reflected growing personal stability. Despite important class differences, the emotional importance of the family generally increased. In the middle- and working-classes, husbands and wives interacted on the basis of growing equality. In this they seemed to resemble their counterparts in the United States, yet the European divorce rates were comparatively low and stable. European families achieved a different balance between tradition and change. The same was true in relations between parents and children. Parental authority was loosened; tensions in French middle-class families, for example, diminished as children found fewer reasons to rebel against control. Since they were freer, they were able to form closer alliances among members of their own age group. As a result, something of a youth culture developed by the later 1950s, stressing an interest in jazz and new dance forms, and giving young people an alternative to parental values that they had lacked before World War II. At the same time, parental control did not collapse; new cultural interests did not add up to rebellion. Reasonably small apartments, if nothing else, required continued interaction between parents and children. Hence there were few problems in general with juvenile delinquency and with drug taking in France, even in the early 1970s.

There were signs of personal dislocation, however, after World War II. France suffered from high rates of alcoholism, which numerous sobriety campaigns barely dented. Scandinavia and Austria had high suicide rates. Some observers claimed that this indicated the pressure of modern life or the dullness of the welfare state. But the problems did not affect all the advanced areas of Europe equally and most of them were not new. France had maintained high drinking rates for at least two centuries, while Scandinavia and Austria had led Europe in suicides for at least as long.

Crime was a more genuinely novel problem. European crime rates remained far below American standards, and crimes of violence were particularly rare. But crime increased during the interwar years and rose still more after 1945. Juvenile delinquency rose particularly; in Britain, crimes by teenage males advanced almost 50 percent between 1953 and 1960. Most of the hardcore offenders were from the working classes, many of them products of broken homes. But by the 1960s a significant minority of British young people were accused at least once in their lives of committing some kind of crime. Signs of maladjustment were less obvious among their elders. But many Europeans were finding some new ways to express aggressive urges and sometimes kill each other in the process. Sports events often prompted riots by partisan crowds. Automobile drivers reveled in speed and bitterly resented any effort to limit their freedom; as a result highway death rates were significantly higher than in the United States.

Yet in terms of most measures of social stability, Europe seemed to have reached a new and relatively successful level of adjustment to the continuing process of industrialization by the mid-1960s.

NEW STRESSES IN SOCIETY

It would be dramatic to claim that this stage of adjustment has been superseded in the years since 1965, that purely individual protest like juvenile delinquency foreshadowed a more sophisticated unrest to come. This is possible but in no sense certain. New stresses have arisen in European society, but it is not clear that Europe has entered a decisively new or troubled stage of social development.

Peasant unrest has continued and its geographical extent has increased. As evidence of this, in 1970 there was a vigorous demonstration in Brussels by almost 100,000 peasants from all over the Common Market countries, in which considerable violence occurred. Such agitation has remained sporadic, however, and has not taken clear political forms. Similarly the crime rate has continued to increase in most European countries, though it remains low by American standards.

The most significant changes in protest activities have come from workers, salaried employees, and students primarily. The working-class strike rate began to increase rapidly after 1965. Workers in Germany and Sweden, long relatively quiescent, began to conduct vigorous strikes for higher wages, despite efforts by unions and government to maintain traditions of conciliation. Strike rates soared even higher in Italy, France, and Britain. In France a massive general strike, in which several million workers occupied their factories, formed a major part of the May 1968, rebellion. Italian workers produced no comparable single effort, but they struck repeatedly at the end of the decade and in the early 1970s, often paralyzing the economy. British workers staged a number of major strikes for higher wages and also a bewildering series of wildcat strikes, often directed against moderate unions as well as management, over local issues.

A large part of the working-class protest fit into the pattern already suggested by rising expectations. Inflation after 1965 reduced real wages in many instances, and workers fought back. But they wanted more than compensation for their losses. Never before had they consistently struggled for such great wage gains. The French workers found themselves, in 1968, the second lowest paid working class in the Common Market, after several years of decline in real wages. They rejected a settlement that offered increases of 10 to 35 percent, which far more than made good their losses. Their rejection flew in the face of the urgent recommendation of the leading Communist union. Ultimately they accepted a similar offer; ultimately, too, many of them apparently voted to support de Gaulle's regime, which indicated that they were not clearly revolutionary. But they, and the workers who pressed for massive wage gains in other countries, were seeking raises far higher than price increases or potential productivity gains. In many instances they were successful, which fueled further inflation and therefore set the stage for new demands.

Some workers began to seek more than wage gains in their protest. Many of the British wildcat strikes, for example, concerned human relations on the job. The German trade unions embarked on a major campaign to win co-determination between workers and management in making important industrial decisions, and not just those that directly affected working conditions. In other words, some workers were thinking about new, far-reaching kinds of participation in their own governance, and there were signs of similar interests in some Communist countries as well. In Czechoslovakia in 1968 worker councils quickly formed and asked for a direct voice in management. Nowhere had the movement advanced very far by the early 1970s, but it suggested a significant new line of working-class protest.

Unrest Among Employees

Large numbers of salaried white-collar workers, particularly government employees, participated in similar kinds of protest. There was precedent for this, but never had unionization and strike activity among these workers gone so far. Court clerks, bank tellers, postal workers—all demanded higher wages and other gains, and their strikes disrupted many European countries. Large numbers of clerks and civil servants joined the May 1968, strike in France. These people, too, found their expectations outrunning their actual earnings in a period of inflation. They may also have been protesting a decline in enjoyment of their work, which in many cases was almost as monotonous as labor in the factory. Other segments of the middle class protested or at least grumbled about what they felt was a squeeze on their standard of living.

What is important to emphasize, however, is that none of the protests was directed explicitly at the existing system. Italy was most seriously troubled, for here economic advance had not been accompanied by corresponding gains by the lower classes, and here too political instability limited social reforms. But the protesters were for the most part asking for a greater share within the system, not for a radically new system. The new protest nonetheless had serious implications. Workers who wanted their incomes to rise faster than prices and productivity were implicitly asking for a redistribution of income in their favor. The middle-class elements (and governments as well) who condemned their agitation as inflationary were implicitly saying that they proposed to resist such redistribution. The possibility of a new round of class conflict, drawn on rather new bases, certainly existed, and the recognition by many white-collar workers that they were essentially proletarian enhanced the possibility.

Student Revolts

Student protest burst forth in 1967 at the Free University of Berlin, where students and a few of the younger faculty attacked inadequate and anachronistic academic structures. During the following winter Italian students occupied several universities in sit-in strikes, while agitation of Spanish students forced the closing of the University of Madrid for part of the

Student Revolt: Paris, May, 1968.

academic year. A student revolt in Paris precipitated the general strike in France in 1968, which nearly toppled the Fifth Republic. Agitation continued thereafter in many French, German, and Italian institutions. Student unrest, which played an important role in the Czechoslovakian reform movement in 1968, also developed in Belgrade and to a limited degree in Moscow. This was in fact the only kind of protest that clearly jumped the Iron Curtain; except for a few qualifications regarding workers, the other protest activities that developed in western Europe were not possible in the Communist countries, where both government repression and public expectations were of a different order.

Student protest most directly concerned the university itself. Interestingly enough, little protest developed in British universities, which had a high teacher-student ratio and much informal contact between the two groups. Universities on the continent were traditionally impersonal, and their growing size after World War II greatly strained existing facilities. Almost all teaching occurred in large lecture halls. Student-professor contact was otherwise limited to examinations after four or five years, which large numbers of students not surprisingly failed. Some students also feared they would not be able to find appropriate jobs, given the rising number of university graduates, while many young instructors resented a rigid university hierarchy that subordinated them to older professors. On a more general level, university students sensed the new importance of youth, which because of the postwar population boom had risen to a significant percentage of the total population.

Concerns about the university structure led to broader social protest. The university was part of a rotten system; its rigid bureaucracy was symptomatic of the excessive institutionalization of society generally; its selectivity was part of an overall discrimination against the lower classes. Student protest also undoubtedly had direct ideological inspiration, reflecting the protest against modern industrial society that Herbert Marcuse and others had outlined. One French student group proclaimed: "We believe that the university is an essential element supporting society. We are convinced that the sole way of solving the problems at all levels is to take part in the destruction of the system."

Student protest was not new in Europe. Previous peaks of agitation, as in the 1840s and the 1890s, bore many interesting resemblances to the outburst at the end of the 1960s. They too resulted from increasing student enrollments, inflexible university systems, and concerns about jobs, combined with a largely anti-rationalist, action-centered ideology. Earlier student agitation had not always been successful in arousing a popular response and when it was, as in 1848, it often turned out that the lower classes sought different, even contradictory goals.

There were some signs that the student protest of the 1960s might find popular backing. The strike of ten million workers and employees that followed the Parisian student rising could not be ignored. Some young workers fraternized with the students. In Italy as well as France the staid Communist parties displayed obvious concern lest student radicalism spread to the ranks of their supporters. Insofar as workers showed an interest in new systems of participation and control, it suggested common ground with the students. But for the most part, by the early 1970s, such a juncture had not been made. In the eyes of workers, students were a privileged elite to be distrusted. Students, for their part, tended to scorn the materialistic goals that continued to dominate worker protest. Much of student protest was anti-organizational, even anti-industrial in tone, against the structures and discipline that industrialization had depended upon since its inception. Workers had learned the power of organization in their own right and were increasingly interested in demanding benefits within the industrial system. Student sloganeering, which often smacked of self-indulgent wit, had little appeal. "Imagination has seized power"; "Be realistic, demand the impossible"—these were the slogans that adorned the walls of the University of Paris in 1968 and evoked delight from sophisticated observers. The question was whether they corresponded to what workers or any other large group of potential agitators had learned about the style or purpose of protest.

Political Response
to Unrest

Finally, the welfare-state governments did respond to the new wave of protest. New funds were poured into university expansion, young instructors were upgraded, and undergraduates were exposed to more small classes under their guidance. Germany led the way in giving students and young faculty equal voice with senior professors in most major university decisions. France modified a 150-year-old tradition by granting individual universities wide autonomy to govern their own affairs. It was not clear whether reforms of this sort would reduce student discontent, but they led to at least a temporary subsidence in Europe in the early 1970s.

Worker protests also won new gains. Wages increased rapidly in most countries, usually surpassing prices. The French government undertook more unusual measures, notably the encouragement of "mensualisation," a monthly payment scheme for workers that increased their security and ability to plan ahead and, it was hoped, would increase their output and loyalty as well. Contracts were signed with workers and employees in government concerns, which provided profit-sharing and wage increases proportionate to national economic development and to prices—a measure that at least partially answered peoples' rising expectations and diminished the pay differential between workers and white-collar employees. The result, in France, was a notable diminution of working-class protest.

By the early 1970s it was not clear whether the various new strands of protest would join together, or whether most of them would persistently demand more than the system could give. If Europe was entering a truly new stage of social development, it had only felt the first sharp birth pangs.

POPULAR CULTURE:
THE MODERNIZED EUROPEAN

The history of industrial Europe since 1815 revealed that each new stage of political and economic development produced new discontent, some of which would call the principles of industrial society into question. From the mid-nineteenth century onward intellectuals in the anti-rationalist tradition constantly returned to the attack on materialism and disciplined organization. At times they struck a popular chord, for industrialization did not produce a uniform outlook within the masses of the population. But more often they failed, for popular culture was generally moving in a different direction. Intellectuals themselves were divided, for the rationalist tradition remained strong.

Most of the directions of popular culture had been set in the previous century, but they advanced significantly after World War II. The continued spread of education helped alter the outlook of the lower classes, and changes in curricula affected all groups. With expanding student bodies, particularly in the secondary schools, classical subjects were deemphasized in favor of science and contemporary subjects. New forms of entertainment, notably television, helped to spread new values. State control of television and limited daytime broadcasting hours reduced some of the problems television raised in the United States, particularly in terms of children's viewing, but there was no question of the impact of the new medium. Some observers were worried that television would downgrade the written word and rational thought. More probably it served as a convenient diversion, promoting a belief in science, in material progress, even in happy endings— all of which were part of the modern mentality. Most important, new attitudes were promoted by the growing prosperity and the increasing margin that even the lower classes had over subsistence and the insecurities of joblessness, illness, and old age. There was no single European outlook. Eastern Europe lagged behind the west or, possibly, was developing a different version of the modern man. Important differences in the culture of the leading social classes, even in western Europe, could not be ignored, but on the whole the key trends were clear.

Religious and Secular Currents

Modern European culture was most decidedly secular. Important developments took place in the Christian churches after World War II, in part in response to the overwhelming secularization. Protestantism gained a new vigor in Germany, after its unhappy compromises with Nazism. Catholics made a definite attempt to come to terms with the modern world, Christian Democracy being one expression of this. In France after the war a worker-priest movement sent priests into the factories, in ordinary laborer's clothes, to undertake missionary activity. The movement was soon condemned, in part because many of the priests became Communists, but the interest continued. John XXIII, who became pope in 1958, was bent on bringing the Church up to date. He reduced the influence of aristocratic Italian cardinals in the Church; he issued a series of social pronouncements, particularly urging the advanced industrial countries to share their wealth with the world's poor; and he called the first Church council since 1870, which came to be known as Vatican II.

In autumn sessions stretching over four years, 2500 cardinals and bishops, dominated by "progressives" from France, Germany, the Low Countries, North America, and the underdeveloped world, met in Rome and dealt with a massive agenda. With the death of John and the accession of the more conservative Paul VI the mood of the council changed somewhat, as did the overall direction of the Church, but spirited debate continued. The council authorized the use of vernacular languages in the liturgy and voted acceptance of the principle of religious liberty, a major new step intended to heighten understanding with non-Catholics. Controversy continued among Catholic clergy and laymen after the council ended, demonstrating the new vitality within the Church. At the same time major problems remained. Pope Paul refused to rescind the Church's ban on the use of contraceptives and spoke out against some of the new ideas and rituals with which Catholic radicals in Holland and elsewhere were experimenting. Many priests and bishops opposed the pope in turn. Large numbers of priests in Holland, France, Germany—even in the United States—continued to challenge the pope on questions of priestly celibacy, birth control, and other issues.

These developments, whatever their ultimate outcome, were exceedingly important, for they revealed the continued ability of the Church to seek compromises between the new and the old. By the same token they revealed the extent to which modern ideas were penetrating Catholic ranks. Most significant of all, the advance of outright secularism continued, though more rapidly in Protestant than in Catholic countries. England and Scandinavia were almost entirely de-Christianized—only 5 percent of England's population even belongs to a church. In Austria, where 86 percent of the population is Catholic, only 20 percent attend church, while in Belgium and in the cities of West Germany, about a quarter of all the Catholics attend. In France approximately 20 percent of all middle-class Catholics and 5 percent of working-class Catholics hear Mass on a regular basis. The number of Italian communicants dropped by half between 1938 and 1948. Despite important differences in degree, the pattern is clear: European culture has become profoundly secular. Polls indicated that a majority of people—though not a large majority in England and Scandinavia—still believed in God, but the issue was no longer very important.

Key Values

The decline of many of the new ideologies after World War II suggested that, at least for the time being, many Europeans were dispensing with organized belief and institutionalized group loyalties altogether. Not only Marxism but also nationalism served less and less as substitute religions. The modern European was not valueless, but his key beliefs were not embodied in any explicit creed.

What the modern European believed in, though somewhat hesitantly, was progress. The horrors of the war and the uncertainties of the Cold War undeniably encouraged a "let's live for today" mood, but they were gradually counterbalanced by advancing prosperity. New forms of working-class protest expressed a belief in future progress, for the gains that were sought had no reference to past standards. Belief in technological advance even spread to the peasantry. Individual behavior also reflected a belief in progress. Encouraged by the welfare state, the bulk of the citizenry began to consult doctors regularly for the first time, thus acting on a belief that their health could be improved. The significant improvements in levels of health, particularly among infants and children, helped confirm the belief.

The modern European believed in the individual. This was not a classic liberal formulation, for obviously extensive state activities had been accepted. Many observers claimed that conformity was rising, and certainly instruments of mass culture were more important than ever before. Yet despite the impossibility of measuring individualism with any precision, the modern European probably experienced more individual choices and options in his daily life than ever before. Without any question the masses were far freer from pressures of conformity than their ancestors had been— at least 150 years before—when tightly knit village and family life set the standards for most people's lives. The life styles of the leading social classes involved individual decisions and satisfactions. Within the family, the growing freedom and equality accorded women and, to a lesser degree, children, reflected the importance of individualism in another respect.

The Quest for Pleasure

The modern European was a hedonist. He actively sought pleasure as an individual, sexual pleasure among other things. At the very beginning of the modernization process in Europe in the latter eighteenth century, new sexual interests had developed as part of the new definition of the individual ego. In the 1960s there were signs that a new stage in this evolution was taking shape. The greater sexual frankness of films and advertisements may have been part of this development, although sexual culture can differ from actual behavior. More indicative were the developments in popular fashion. The advent of the mini-skirt was a landmark in a variety of ways. It stemmed from lower-class designers, though their income did not remain lower-class very long, and was adopted by most of the urban classes at about the same rate. It was one of the first important changes in twentieth-century popular fashion to start in Europe rather than the United States. It expressed, along with a less striking relaxation in men's styles, a new sexual interest. In the 1960s, for the first prolonged period since 1870, illegitimacy rates began to rise in western Europe, which, combined with the growing use of contraceptives, suggested a significant increase in sexual activity, corresponding to the growing search for pleasure in other areas.

Prospects for Change

The various beliefs and structures of modern Europe were not entirely compatible. Individualism could easily clash with another historic modern trend, the growth of large organizations and the centralized state; by the early 1970s there were intimations of a skirmish, if not an actual clash. The search for individual satisfaction may also be interpreted as betraying more than a bit of uncertainty about progress in general. In other words, Europeans probably believed that greater individual pleasure could be achieved more readily than social or political advance.

The beliefs of the modern European were certainly not unchanging. They had been evolving steadily since the eighteenth century, and developments in the 1960s presaged still further change. The main lines of the evolution still seemed clear, despite the fact that no single movement or institution expressed the whole of the modern outlook. Europeans had moved far from the traditional beliefs that had been virtually unchallenged, at the popular level, just two hundred years before. They had elaborated values not just of material and scientific advance but also of humanitarian progress and individual romantic love. The modern values would doubtless not last forever, but basic views of life alter slowly in human history. The new outlook took shape as part of the revolution to modernity. Its elaboration is more important to the understanding of modern man than the more easily defined revolutions in the economy and in politics.

Modernization has involved constant change, which has accustomed people to the fact of change and encouraged facile statements about the increasing pace of change. It is, after all, fashionable to talk of the confusion in the modern world. The modern outlook accepts and incorporates change, which means it is in fact less unsettling than it was in the superficially more sedate past. At the same time, the modern era is still young and its implications remain to be fully worked out. Popular values continue to move away from traditional norms. The process continues.

APPENDICES

APPENDIX I

CHRONOLOGICAL TABLES—MAJOR DEVELOPMENTS
IN THE EUROPEAN EXPERIENCE SINCE 1815

POLITICAL

DIPLOMATIC

1814–1848 Metternich's influence in
central Europe
1814–1830 France—Restoration
Monarchy
1815–1848 Conservatism at its height

1815 Congress of Vienna

1817 Burschenschaften Congress

1819 Carlsbad Decrees
1819 Peterloo Massacre and the Six
Acts
1820 Revolution—Spain and southern
Italy

1820 Congress of Troppau

1821–1830 Greek war of independence

1822 Congress of Verona

1825 Decembrist revolt in Russia
1830 Revolution—France, Belgium,
Poland, and Italy

1830 France captures Algiers

1830–1848 France—July Monarchy
1832 English Reform Bill
1833 Guizot Law in France

1833 Convention of Münchengrätz

1839–1846 Chartism in England

1848 Revolutions throughout Europe
1848–1852 Second French Republic

SOCIAL AND ECONOMIC	INTELLECTUAL
1811–1816 Luddism	
1815–1848 Commercialization of western European agriculture 1815 English Corn Laws	1815–1848 Romanticism at its height
1818 Prussian tariff	
1820s Initial industrialization in France and Belgium	
1830–1833 Lyons weaver riots	1830 *Hernani* by Victor Hugo 1830–1848 *Course on Positive Philosophy* by Auguste Comte
1834 English Poor Law reform	
1840s Initial industrialization in Germany 1844 Silesian weaver revolt 1846 Repeal of English Corn Laws	
	1847 First law of thermodynamics 1848 *Communist Manifesto*
1850 English industrial maturity	1850–1870 Influence of Positivism and Realism

POLITICAL   DIPLOMATIC

1852–1870 Second Empire—Napoleon
    III
                                                   1854–1856 Crimean War
1855–1881 Tsar Alexander II of
    Russia

1860 Italian unification

1861 Abolition of serfdom—Russia
1862–1890 Bismarck's rule in Germany

1864–1876 First International   1864 Prussia and Austria defeat
                                                  Denmark
1866–1871 Unification of Germany   1866 Seven Weeks War (Austro-
                                                  Prussian)
1867 *Ausgleich* in the Hapsburg
    Monarchy (dual monarchy)
1867 English electoral reform

1870 England—civil service reform and   1870 Franco-Prussian War
    the Education Act
1870–1940 Third French Republic

1871 Paris Commune
1871–1918 German Empire
1871–1883 *Kulturkampf*
1875 Formation of German Socialist
    party (SD)
1878–1890 Germany—anti-socialist   1878 Congress of Berlin
    laws
                                           1879 Dual Alliance—Germany and
                                                 Austria
                                           1880–1914 "New" Imperialism

1881 Tsar Alexander II assassinated
                                           1882 Triple Alliance—Germany,
                                                 Austria, and Italy

SOCIAL AND ECONOMIC

INTELLECTUAL

1857 *Madame Bovary* by Gustave
Flaubert
1859 *The Origin of Species* by Charles
Darwin
1859 *On Liberty* by John Stuart Mill
1860 Cobden treaty
1860s Mendeleev—Periodic Table of
Chemical Weights

1863 *The Life of Jesus* by Ernest Renan
1864 Proclamation of Pius IX—*Syllabus
of Errors*

1867–1894 *Das Kapital*

1869–1870 Vatican I: promulgation of
Papal infallibility
1870–1914 Growing union of
aristocracy and upper middle
classes
1870s Initial industrialization in Italy
and Austria
1870s Populism and Nihilism in Russia
1870–1900 Emergence of distinct
social sciences

1879 German agricultural tariff

1880–1914 Strikes become normal part
of industrial life
1880–1930 Influence of symbolism
1880–1914 Emergence of lower middle
class

1883–1889 Social insurance laws—
Germany

POLITICAL

1886 Irish Home Rule

1889 Boulanger Affair

1894–1906 Dreyfus Affair

1901–1905 France—laic laws
        (separation of Church and state)

1905 Formation of unified French
      Socialist party (SFIO)
1905 Revolution—Russia
1906 Formation of English Labour
      Party

1917 Bolshevik revolution in February
      and October
1918 Dissolution of German and
      Austro-Hungarian Empires
1919 Comintern
1919–1933 Weimar Republic
1920 Kapp *Putsch*

1922 Mussolini "marches" on Rome

DIPLOMATIC

1887 Reinsurance Treaty—Germany
      and Russia

1890 End of German-Russian alliance

1894 Sino-Japanese War

1904–1905 Russo-Japanese War
1904 *Entente Cordiale*

1907 Anglo-Russian Entente

1914 Assassination of Francis
      Ferdinand
1914–1918 World War I
1914 Battle of Marne
1917 United States enters war

1918 Treaty of Brest Litovsk

1919 Treaty of Versailles

1920 League of Nations

1922 Rapallo Pact

1923 French occupation of the Ruhr
1925 Locarno treaties

SOCIAL AND ECONOMIC   INTELLECTUAL

1889 London dock strike
1890–1914 Anarcho-syndicalism
1890s Initial industrialization in Russia

                              1891 Encyclical of Leo XIII—*Rerum*
                                          Novarum

1892 Méline tariff

                              1898 Discovery of radioactivity—Pierre
                                          and Marie Curie
1900 German industrial maturity   1900 *The Interpretation of Dreams* by
                                        Sigmund Freud

                              1905 Einstein's Theory of Relativity

                              1908 *Reflections on Violence* by
                                        Georges Sorel
                              1908 *Creative Evolution* by Henri
                                        Bergson
                              1910–1913 *Principia Mathematica* by
                                        Bertrand Russell and Alfred North
                                        Whitehead
1914 French industrial maturity

1921 New Economic Policy—U.S.S.R.
                              1922 *Ulysses* by James Joyce
                              1922 *The Wasteland* by T. S. Eliot

POLITICAL   DIPLOMATIC

1927–1953 Stalin

                                       1928 Kellogg Briand Pact

1933–1945 Hitler
1936–1937 French Popular Front   1936 Remilitarization of the Rhineland
1936–1939 Spanish Civil War

                                       1937 Rome-Berlin-Tokyo axis
                                       1938 Anschluss—movement for union of
                                             Germany and Austria
                                       1938 Munich agreements
                                       1939 Russo-German non-aggression
                                             pact
                                       1939–1945 World War II

                                       1941 Pearl Harbor
1945–1951 Labour government in   1945 Yalta and Potsdam conferences
           Britain   1945 Hiroshima
1945–1951 Fourth French Republic   1945 Founding of United Nations
                                       1945–1970 Decolonization

                                       1948 Start of Cold War
1949–1963 Chancellorship of Konrad   1949 Founding of NATO
           Adenauer in West Germany

                                       1950–1953 Korean War
                                       1951 European Coal and Steel
                                             Community
1953–1964 Rule of Nikita Khrushchev
           in U.S.S.R.

                                       1955 Warsaw Pact
1956 Revolts in Poland and Hungary   1956 England and France invade
                                             Egypt
                                       1957 European Common Market

1958–1969 Presidency of Charles de
           Gaulle in France
                                       1961 Berlin Wall erected
1962–1963 Beginning of ideological   1962 Cuban missile crisis
           split between China and U.S.S.R.

SOCIAL AND ECONOMIC	INTELLECTUAL
1926 English General Strike	1926 *Decline of the West* by Oswald Spengler
1928 First Five Year Plan—U.S.S.R.	1928 Discovery of penicillin by Sir Alexander Fleming
1928 Onslaught of worldwide economic depression	
	1931 Pius XI encyclical—*Quadragesimo Anno*
1936 Matignon agreements—French labor reform laws	1936 *General Theory of Employment, Interest and Money* by John Maynard Keynes
1940s Initial industrialization of Communist East Europe	
1945–1950 Formation of welfare states in western and central Europe	
1947–1951 Marshall Plan	1947 *The Plague* by Albert Camus
	1949 *Mother Courage* by Bertolt Brecht
1950–1970 Economic boom	
	1954 *Waiting for Godot* by Samuel Beckett
	1956 *Being and Nothingness* by Jean Paul Sartre
	1957 *Doctor Zhivago* by Boris Pasternak
	1962–1965 Vatican II—ecumenism and *aggiornamento*

POLITICAL

DIPLOMATIC

1963 Ludwig Erhard heads West
Germany

1964 Brezhnev and Kosygin supplant
Khrushchev

1967 Military coup in Greece

1968 Massive unrest in France

1968 Russian invasion of
Czechoslovakia

1969 Willy Brandt elected president of
West Germany

1971 Britain admitted to the Common
Market

SOCIAL AND ECONOMIC

INTELLECTUAL

1964 *One Dimensional Man* by Herbert
Marcuse

APPENDIX II

SUGGESTIONS FOR FURTHER READINGS

DEVELOPMENTS TOWARD MODERNIZATION IN THE EIGHTEENTH CENTURY

*Alfred R. Hall, *The Scientific Revolution, 1500–1800* (1954, Beacon); *Herbert Butterfield, *The Origins of Modern Science, 1300–1800*, rev. ed. (1962, Free Press).

AGRICULTURAL CHANGE

B. E. Slicker van Bath, *The Agrarian History of Western Europe, 500–1850* (1963, St. Martin's); Robert Trow-Smith, *Life from the Land: The Growth of Farming in Western Europe* (1967, Intl. Pubns. Serv.).

THE POPULATION REVOLUTION

*Carlo Cipolla, *The Economic History of World Population, 1705–1918* (1962, Penguin). For suggestions on the outlook of the urban classes, see *Elinor Barber, *The Bourgeoisie in 18th Century France* (1955, Princeton University Press) and Gwyn A. Williams, *Artisans and Sans Culottes* (1969, Norton); *Phyllis Deane, *The First Industrial Revolution* (1965, Cambridge University Press) outlines the vital early stages of industrialization in Britain. *Peter Laslett, *The World We Have Lost* (1966, Scribner) tries to capture the very different society and culture of Europe before modernization really took hold. *Phillippe Ariès, *Centuries of Childhood: A Social History of Family Life* (1962, Vintage), deals with changing attitudes toward children.

PREREVOLUTIONARY POLITICAL CHANGE

*Geoffrey Bruun, *The Enlightened Despot*, 2nd ed. (1967, Holt, Rinehart & Winston).

THE FRENCH REVOLUTION

The best account is Georges Lefebvre, *The French Revolution*, 2 vols. (1961–

* indicates paperback

436

1964, Columbia University Press). The same author provides an excellent, succinct analysis in *Coming of the French Revolution, 1789* (1947, Princeton University Press). A reassessment of the revolution's "revolutionary" impact is *Alfred Cobban, *The Social Interpretation of the French Revolution* (1964, Cambridge University Press). Worldwide revolutionary tendencies are traced in *R. R. Palmer, *Age of the Democratic Revolution, 1780–1800,* 2 vols. (1959–1964, Princeton University Press). On Napoleon and Europe, see *Geoffrey Bruun, *Europe and the French Imperium, 1799–1814* (1938, Harper).

IMPORTANT NATIONAL HISTORIES

In general, political history is best followed through national histories that deal with this period as part of a general survey.

For Britain: David Thomson, *England in the Nineteenth Century, 1815–1914* (1964, Penguin); John W. Derry, *Reaction and Reform, 1783–1868* (1963, Humanities). For France: Paul A. Gagnon, *France Since 1789* (1964, Harper); *Alfred Cobban, *A History of Modern France,* vols. II and III (1966, Penguin). For Germany: K. S. Pinson, *Modern Germany: Its History and Civilization* (1966, Macmillan) is a good survey; *A. J. B. Taylor, *The Course of German History* (1962, Putnam) is a stimulating book on the subject.

Other important national surveys are: A. J. B. Taylor, *The Hapsburg Monarchy, 1809–1918* (1965, Harper); D. Mack Smith, *Italy: A Modern History* (1959, University of Michigan Press); *René Albrecht-Carrié, *Italy from Napoleon to Mussolini* (1950, Columbia University Press); *H. V. Livermore, *A History of Spain* (1968, Minerva). For Eastern Europe: L. Stavrianos, *The Balkans Since 1453* (1958, Holt, Rinehart & Winston) is an extraordinarily coherent summary; O. Halecki, *History of Poland* (1956, Regnery) is useful. For Russia: *Lionel Kochran, *The Making of Modern Russia* (1962, Penguin) is an excellent survey. See also Michael Florinsky, *Russia: A History and an Interpretation,* 2 vols. (1954, Macmillan) and Hugh Seton Watson, *The Russian Empire, 1801–1917* (1967, Oxford University Press). M. V. Nechkina, *Russia in the Nineteenth Century,* 2 vols. (1953, Am. Council of Learned Societies) is the translation of a standard Soviet treatment.

ABOVE THE NATIONAL LEVEL

E. N. and P. R. Anderson, *Political Institutions and Social Changes in Continental Europe in the Nineteenth Century* (1967, University of California Press) deals with the development of the modern state. René Albrecht-Carrié, *Diplomatic History of Europe Since the Congress of Vienna* (1958, Harper) provides a factual overview.

CHURCH HISTORY

*E. Hales, *Catholic Church in the Modern World* (1960, Image) is a very pro-Catholic account, while J. B. Bury, *History of the Papacy in the Nineteenth Century* (1964, Schocken) is a very hostile treatment; J. N. Moody, *Church and Society* (1953, N.Y. Arts, Inc.) provides a more balanced view. A good survey is *J. J. Altholz, *The Churches in the Nineteenth Century* (1967, Bobbs-Merrill).

CONSERVATISM AND THE CONSERVATIVE FORCES

There are several studies of conservatism, a number of which go beyond the 1815–1848 period. E. L. Woodward, *Three Studies in European Conservatism:*

Metternich, Guizot, and the Catholic Church in the 19th Century (1963, Frank Cass) is excellent. °Gordon Craig, *The Politics of the Prussian Army* (1955, Oxford University Press) and °Hans Rosenberg, *Bureaucracy, Aristocracy, and Autocracy* (1958, Beacon) deal with conservative forces in Germany. René Remond, *The Right Wing in France* (1969, University of Pennsylvania Press) and Paul M. de la Gorce, *The French Army* (1963, Braziller), trace the conservative tradition in France.

THE PERIOD 1815–1848

E. J. Hobsbawm, *The Age of Revolution: Europe from 1789 to 1848* (1969, Mentor) is a fine analysis by a Marxist historian. See also °F. B. Artz, *Reaction and Revolution, 1815–1832* (1935, Harper).

For the French Restoration: G. de Bertier de Sauvigny, *The Restoration* (1967, University of Pennsylvania Press). For Germany: °T. S. Hamerow, *Restoration, Revolution, Reaction: Economics and Politics in Germany, 1815–1871* (1958, Princeton University Press). Arthur J. May, *The Age of Metternich, 1814–1848* (1933, Holt, Rinehart & Winston) deals with Austria. For Russia: Leonid I. Strakhovsky, *Alexander I of Russia* (1947, Greenwood) sketches a complex personality, while Sidney Monas, *Third Section: Police and Society in Russia Under Nicholas I* (1961, Harvard University Press) treats the rise of one of the key instruments of tsarist repression. For the Congress of Vienna and its aftermath: °Harold G. Nicolson, *Congress of Vienna: A Study in Allied Unity, 1812–1822* (1946, Compass; also available as Harbinger Book, Harcourt Brace Jovanovich) and L. C. B. Seaman, *From Vienna to Versailles* (1958, Harper). H. G. Schenk, *The Aftermath of the Napoleonic Wars: The Concert of Europe—An Experiment* (1947, Fertig) deals with basic concepts of diplomacy in the period. Early revolutionary stirrings are analyzed in Mikhail Zetlin, *The Decembrists* (1958, International University Press). George T. Romani, *The Neapolitan Revolution of 1870–1921* (1950, Northwestern University Press); C. M. Woodhouse, *The Greek War of Independence* (1952, Hutchinson University Library).

IMPORTANT STUDIES OF NINETEENTH-CENTURY INTELLECTUAL HISTORY

Beginning with the age of Romanticism the best general survey is George Mosse, *The Culture of Western Europe* (1962, Rand McNally); for more detail, see John T. Merz, *History of European Thought in the Nineteenth Century*, new ed., 4 vols. (1924, University of Chicago Press). For political theory and for economic theory, see respectively G. H. Sabine, *A History of Political Theory*, 3rd ed. (1961, Holt, Rinehart & Winston) and the excellent C. Gide and G. Rist, *History of Economic Doctrines from the Physiocrats to the Present Day* (1948, Heath).

General surveys of the history of science include J. Jeans, *The Growth of Physical Science* (1948, Cambridge University Press); Carl T. Chase, *The Evolution of Modern Physics* (1947, D. Van Nostrand); and T. M. Lowry, *Historical Introduction to Chemistry* (1936, Macmillan & Co., Ltd.). Two fine surveys are Charles Singer, *A Short History of Scientific Ideas to 1900* (1959, Oxford University Press) and Charles Gillispie, *The Edge of Objectivity* (1960, Princeton University Press).

For the arts, see °E. H. Gombrich, *The Story of Art* (1956, Praeger); Hugo Leichtentritt, *Music, History and Ideas* (1950, Harvard University Press).

On Romanticism: *Jacques Barzun, *Classic, Romantic and Modern* (1961, Anchor) treats the movement very empathically. *Hans Kohn, *The Mind of Germany* (1960, Harper) deals with the relationship between Romanticism and political ideas. On various aspects of Romanticism see *Kenneth Clark, *The Gothic Revival* (1950, Penguin); E. Newton, *Romantic Rebellion* (1964, Schocken); Kathleen M. Tillotson, *Novels of the Eighteen-Forties* (1954, Oxford University Press). *Charles Gillispie, *Genesis and Geology* (1951, Harper) deals with the impact of science on religion before Darwin.

THE INTELLECTUAL HISTORY OF LIBERALISM

*G. de Ruggiero, *The History of European Liberalism* (1927, Beacon); *Harry K. Girvetz, *The Evolution of Liberalism* (1963, Collier); Donald G. Rohr, *The Origins of Social Liberalism in Germany* (1963, University of Chicago Press); Leonard Krieger, *The German Idea of Freedom* (1957, Beacon Press). On utilitarianism: Leslie Stephen, *The English Utilitarians*, 3 vols. (1900, Kelley); John P. Plamenatz, *Mill's Utilitarianism Reprinted with a Study of the English Utilitarians* (1949, Humanities); and *Elie Halévy, *The Growth of Philosophical Radicalism* (1955, Beacon). On conservative thought: *Peter Viereck, *Conservatism Revisited: The Revolt against Revolt, 1815–1949* (1949, Free Press). Hans Kohn, *The Idea of Nationalism: A Study of Its Origins and Background* (1961, Collier) and *Boyd C. Shafer, *Nationalism: Myth and Reality* (1955, Harcourt Brace Jovanovich) are the best introductions to nationalism. G. D. H. Cole, *Socialist Thought: The Forerunners, 1789–1850* (1935, St. Martin's) and *Frank E. Manuel, *The Prophets of Paris* (1962, Harper) treat the utopian socialists.

ECONOMIC HISTORY

*David Landes, *The Unbound Prometheus: Technological Change and Industrial Development in Western Europe from 1750 to the Present* (1969, Cambridge University Press) is outstanding. *W. W. Rostow, *The Stages of Economic Growth* (1960, Cambridge University Press) is controversial and thought-provoking. A comprehensive though more conventional treatment can be found in Witt Bowden, Michael Karpovich, and A. P. Usher, *An Economic History of Europe since 1750* (1937, Am. Book Company) and *J. H. Clapham, *The Economic Development of France and Germany, 1815–1914* (1937, Cambridge University Press). More specifically on the early industrial period are *T. S. Ashton, *The Industrial Revolution, 1760–1830* (1948, Oxford University Press) (on Britain), Arthur C. Dunham, *The Industrial Revolution in France* (1935, Exposition), and William O. Henderson, *Britain and Industrial Europe, 1750–1870* (1954, Humanities). Rondo Cameron, ed., *Banking in the Early Stages of Industrialization* (1967, Oxford University Press) fills an important gap. Kingston Derry and Trevor I. Williams, *A Short History of Technology* (1961, Oxford University Press) is very useful.

SOCIAL HISTORY

*Peter N. Stearns, *European Society in Upheaval: Social History since 1800* (1967, Macmillan) is a general survey. Barrington Moore, *The Social Origins of Dictatorship and Democracy* (1966, Beacon) is an important synthesis, drawing on non-European as well as European social-political patterns. *Charles Morazé, *The Triumph of the Middle Classes* (1967, Anchor) traces the rise of this vital group. *Reinhard Bendix, *Work and Authority in Industry: Ideologies of Management in* *the Course of Industrial Labor* (1956, Harper) is an excellent treatment of this aspect of social history. °Ernest Bramsted, *Aristocracy and the Middle Classes in Germany* (1964, University of Chicago Press) treats his subject in terms of the literature of the nineteenth century. °E. P. Thompson, *The Making of the English Working Class* (1964, Vintage) is a vital if partisan treatment. Neil Smelser, *Social Change in the Industrial Revolution: An Application of Theory to the Lancashire Cotton Industry, 1770–1840* (1959, University of Chicago Press) takes a rather different view of workers' problems. See also Eric Hobsbawm, *Labouring Men* (1964, Doubleday) and M. C. Buer, *Health, Wealth, and Population in the Early Days of the Industrial Revolution* (1968, Fertig). Jurgen Kuczynski, *A Short History of Labour Conditions Under Industrial Capitalism: Germany, 1800 to the Present Day* (1945, F. Muller, Ltd.) is an interesting Marxist account. On demographic history: E. A. Wrigley, *Population and History* (1969, McGraw-Hill) and *Industrial Growth and Population Change* (1962, Cambridge University Press). On urban development: Adna Weber, *The Growth of Cities in the Nineteenth Century* (1963, Cornell University Press).

On the nature of early industrial protest, see °George Rudé, *The Crowd in History* (1964, Wiley) and °Eric Hobsbawm, *Primitive Rebels* (1959, Norton). Rudé and Hobsbawm coauthor another fine study, *Captain Swing* (1969, Pantheon). °Jerome Blum, *Lord and Peasant in Russia from the Ninth to the Nineteenth Century* (1965, Atheneum) and °Traian Stoianovich, *A Study in Balkan Civilization* (1967, Knopf) deal with peasant societies into the nineteenth century.

APPROACHES TO POPULAR CULTURE

See William Boyd, *The History of Western Education*, 8th ed. (1967, Barnes & Noble) and Brian Simon, *Studies in the History of Education, 1780–1870* (1960, Lawrence & Werhart, Ltd.). See also Richard D. Altick, *The English Common Reader: A Social History of the Mass Reading Public, 1800–1900* (1957, University of Chicago Press).

PROTEST AND REFORM IN BRITAIN

°E. P. Thompson, *The Making of the English Working Class* (1964, Vintage); °Asa Briggs, *The Age of Improvement* (1959, Harper); Asa Briggs, ed., *Chartist Studies* (1959, St. Martin's); Norman Gash, *Reaction and Reconstruction in English Politics* (1965, Oxford University Press); Maurice Thomas, *The Early Factory Legislation* (1948, Greenwood).

REVOLT ON THE CONTINENT

Two good biographies suggest the outlook of the continental revolutionary: Elizabeth Eisenstein, *The First Professional Revolutionary, Felippe Michele Buonarroti* (1959, Harvard University Press) and Leo Loubère, *Louis Blanc* (1960, Northwestern University Press). On Louis Philippe's reign: see Douglas Johnson, *Guizot: Aspects of French History, 1787–1874* (1963, University of Toronto Press) and T. E. B. Howarth, *Citizen King: The Life of Louis Philippe* (1961, Verry).

THE REVOLUTION OF 1848

°Priscilla Robertson, *Revolutions of 1848: A Social Study* (1957, Princeton University Press) is a general survey. François Fejtö, ed., *The Opening of an Era, 1848*, 2 vols. (1948, Fertig) offers a variety of interpretations. On France: the best study is George Duveau, *1848: The Making of a Revolution* (1966, Pantheon). Donald L. McKay, *The National Workshops* (1965, Harvard University Press) treats the role and condition of the lower classes. On Germany: *Louis Namier, *1848: The Revolution of the Intellectuals* (1946, Anchor) looks to ideological causation. Viet Valentin, *1848: Chapter in German History* (1965, Anchor) offers a liberal interpretation. Paul Noyes, *Organization and Revolution: Working Class Association in the German Revolution of 1848–1849* (1966, Princeton University Press) examines the lower-class role. On Italy: see D. Mack Smith, *Garibaldi* (1956, Knopf). On Austria: see R. John Rath, *The Viennese Revolution of 1848* (1957, Greenwood).

A useful general work is William L. Langer, *Political and Social Upheaval, 1832–1852* (1969, Harper). See also the political histories listed in Suggested Readings—Chapter 1.

ON WAR AND DIPLOMACY

Theodore Ropp, *War in the Modern World* (1959, Macmillan) is a comprehensive treatment. A. J. B. Taylor, *The Struggle for Mastery in Europe, 1848–1918* (1954, Oxford University Press) offers a sweeping interpretation. More specific works include G. B. Henderson, *Crimean War Diplomacy* (1947, Jackson, Son & Co.); T. W. Riker, *The Making of Rumania* (1931, Oxford University Press); and Gordon A. Craig, *The Battle of Königgratz* (1964, Lippincott). *Michael Howard, *The Franco-Prussian War* (1961, Collier) is excellent.

ON THE SECOND EMPIRE IN FRANCE

*J. M. Thompson, *Louis Napoleon and the Second Empire* (1954, Norton) is a good political biography. A. Guérard, *Napoleon III: An Interpretation* (1943, Knopf) considers the regime as a forerunner of modern totalitarianism. See also Theodore Zeldin, *The Political System of Napoleon III* (1958, St. Martin's) and David Kulstein, *Napoleon III and the Working Class* (1969, California State Colleges). The watershed of 1870 is described in *Roger L. Williams, *The French Revolution of 1870–1871* (1969, Norton).

ON THE COMMUNE

E. S. Mason, *The Paris Commune* (1968, Fertig) is the most balanced treatment; Alistair Horne, *The Fall of Paris* (1965, St. Martin's) is also useful. On the formation of the Third Republic, see David Thompson, *Democracy in France: The Third Republic* (1952, Oxford University Press).

ON ITALIAN UNIFICATION

A number of books deal with different aspects of Italian unification. D. Mack Smith, *Cavour and Garibaldi in 1860* (1954, Kraus Repr.) is critical of Cavour. K. Roberts Greenfield, *Economics and Liberalism in the Risorgimento: A Study of Nationalism in Lombardy, 1814–1848* (1934, Johns Hopkins Press) is a brilliant interpretation. E. E. Y. Hales, *Pio Nono* (1954, P. J. Kenedy) offers a sympathetic judgment of the pope. See also D. Mack Smith, *Garibaldi* (1956, Knopf); Raymond Grew, *A Sterner Plan for Italian Unity: The Italian National Society in the Risorgimento* (1963, Princeton University Press) and S. W. Halperin, *The Separation of Church and State in Italian Thought from Cavour to Mussolini* (1937, Octagon).

ON GERMANY

An important recent survey is Theodore S. Hamerow, *The Social Foundation of German Unification, 1858–1871: Ideas and Institutions* (1969, Princeton University Press). See also Hajo Holborn, *A History of Modern Germany, 1840–1945* (1969, Knopf). On the Prussian constitutional conflict, see E. N. Anderson, *The Social and Political Conflict in Prussia* (1954, Octagon). The best biographies of Bismarck are Erich Eyck, *Bismarck and the German Empire* (1950, Norton) and Otto Pflanze, *Bismarck and the Development of Germany: The Period of Unification* (1963, Princeton University Press).

ON BRITAIN

There are several excellent studies of Britain in this period. G. M. Young, *Victorian England: Portrait of an Age* (1953, Oxford University Press) deals with society and culture. G. Kitson Clark, *The Making of Victorian England* (1962, Harvard University Press) and Asa Briggs, *Victorian People: A Reassessment of Persons and Themes* (1954, University of Chicago Press) offer interesting interpretations. Two good specific studies are F. B. Smith, *The Making of the Second Reform Bill* (1966, Cambridge University Press) and J. H. Hanham, *Elections and Party Management: Politics in the Time of Disraeli and Gladstone* (1959, Humanities).

ON RUSSIA

E. M. Almedingen, *The Emperor Alexander II* (1962, Bodley Head, Ltd.) is a good biography. More important is W. E. Mosse, *Alexander II and the Modernization of Russia* (1958, Macmillan). On land reform, see Terence Emmons, *The Russian Landed Gentry and the Peasant Emancipation of 1861* (1968, Cambridge University Press) and the classic by G. T. Robinson, *Rural Russia under the Old Regime* (1932, Macmillan).

ON THE HAPSBURG MONARCHY

Robert A. Kann, *The Multinational Empire: Nationalism and National Reform in the Hapsburg Monarchy, 1848–1918,* 2 vols. (1951, Octagon) deals with the overriding problem of internal conflict. For a survey of the period in general, see °Robert C. Binkley, *Realism and Nationalism, 1852–1871* (1935, Harper).

IMPORTANT ECONOMIC STUDIES

There are several books that focus primarily on the decade after 1850. Rondo E. Cameron, *France and the Economic Development of Europe, 1800–1914* (1961, Princeton University Press) and H. Feis, *Europe, the World's Banker, 1870–1914: An Account of European Foreign Investment and the Connection of World Finance with Diplomacy Before the War* (1930, Kelley) are important contributions. Jacob Riesser, *The German Great Banks* (1911, Washington, Gov't. Printing Office) and W. O. Henderson, *The State and the Industrial Revolution in Prussia* (1958, Liverpool University Press) deal with some special features of German economics. Charles Kindleberger, *Economic Growth in France and Britain, 1851–1950* (1964, Clarion) is a valuable comparative study. A. L. Levine, *Industrial Retardation in Britain* (1967, Basic) deals with some of Britain's special problems in this period. For Italian and Russian development, Alexander Gerschenkron, *Economic Backwardness in Historical Perspective* (1962, Harvard University Press) is immensely valuable. See also John P. McKay, *Pioneers for Profit: Foreign Entrepreneurship and Russian Industrialization, 1885–1913* (1970, University of Chicago Press).

ON TECHNOLOGY AND THE CITIES

*Sigfried Giedion, *Mechanization Takes Command* (1948, Norton) and Lewis Mumford, *Technics and Civilization* (1934, Harcourt Bace Jovanovich) are important general essays. Ludwig Haber, *The Chemical Industry in the Nineteenth Century* (1958, Oxford University Press) deals with a vital new industry. On agriculture, see Michael Tracy, *Agriculture in Western Europe* (1964, J. Cape, Ltd.). Two good introductions to modern urban history are *Constantinos A. Doxiadis and T. B. Douglass, *The New World of Urban Man* (1965, United Church) and W. E. Cole, *Urban Society* (1958, United Church). Asa Briggs, *Victorian Cities* (1965, Harper) is an important specific study.

ON GENERAL MATERIAL CONDITIONS

See John Burnett, *Plenty and Want, A Social History of Diet in England from 1815 to the Present Day* (1966, Nelson); Lawrence Wright, *Clean and Decent: The Fascinating History of the Bathroom and the Water Closet* (1960, University of Toronto Press); *Shops and Shopping* (1961, Hutchinson University Library); Nathaniel Faxon, ed., *The Hospital in Contemporary Life* (1949, Harvard University Press); and *Charles Wilcocks, *Medical Advance, Public Health and Social Evolution* (1966, Pergamon).

ON ALL CLASSES

On the upper classes, Alexander Gerschenkron, *Bread and Democracy in Germany* (1943, Fertig) and Lysbeth Muncy, *The Junkers in the Prussian Administration Under William II, 1888–1914* (1944, Fertig) are important studies for Germany. For Britain, see F. M. L. Thompson, *English Landed Society in the Nineteenth Century* (1963, University of Toronto Press) and Roger Kelsall, *Higher Civil Servants in Britain from 1810 to the Present Day* (1955, Humanities).

The best study of the lower-middle class is David Lockwood, *The Blackcoated Workers: A Study in Class Consciousness* (1966, Unwin University Books). See also *P. G. J. Pulzer, *Rise of Political Anti-Semitism in Germany and Austria* (1964, Wiley). Joseph Banks, *Prosperity and Parenthood: A Study of Family Planning Among the Victorian Middle Classes* (1954, Humanities) deals with another vital development.

Most studies of the peasantry for this period focus on eastern and southern Europe. See *Eric Hobsbawm, *Primitive Rebels* (1959, Norton) on Italy and Spain. G. T. Robinson, *Rural Russia Under the Old Regime* (1932, Macmillan) is vital. See also David Mitrany, *The Land and the Peasant in Rumania* (1930, Greenwood) and Jozo Tomasevich, *Peasants, Politics, and Economic Change in Yugoslavia* (1955, Stanford University Press).

Studies of the workers concentrate on protest movements. For a general survey, see *Harvey Mitchell and Peter N. Stearns, *Workers and Protest* (1971, Peacock). K. G. J. C. Knowles, *Strikes—A Study in Industrial Conflict* (1952, Philosophical Library) is an important general analysis. Hugh Clegg, *et al.*, *A History of British Trade Unions Since 1889* (1964, Oxford University Press) is a fine, detailed study. Two books deal with protest movements on the Continent from the standpoint of workers themselves: Guenther Roth, *The Social Democrats in Imperial Germany:*

A Study in Working Class Isolation and National Integration (1963, Bedminster) and Peter N. Stearns, *Revolutionary Syndicalism and French Labor: A Cause Without Rebels* (1971, Rutgers University Press).

On women and their protest, see J. A. and Olive Banks, *Feminism and Family Planning in Victorian England* (1964, Schocken); and William L. O'Neill, *Woman Movements: Feminism in the United States and England* (1969, Barnes & Noble). See also Suggested Readings—Chapter 2.

DEVELOPMENTS IN THE SCIENCES

John C. Greene, *The Death of Adam: Evolution and Its Impact on Western Thought* (1959, Iowa State University Press); P. B. Sears, *Charles Darwin: The Naturalist as a Cultural Force* (1950, Scribner); *Leopold Infeld, *Albert Einstein: His Work and Its Influence on Our World* (1954, Scribner); E. Zimmer, *The Revolution in Physics* (1936, Faber & Faber, Ltd.); L. Barnett, *The Universe and Doctor Einstein* (1952, Sloane).

DEVELOPMENTS IN THE SOCIAL SCIENCES

H. E. Barnes, ed., *An Introduction to the History of Sociology* (1948, University of Chicago Press); H. Alpert, *Émile Durkheim and His Sociology* (1939, Columbia University Press); B. P. Bapkin, *Pavlov: A Biography* (1949, University of Chicago Press); *Ernest Jones, *The Life and Works of Sigmund Freud* (1961, Anchor); Walter Hollitscher, *Sigmund Freud: An Introduction* (1947, Routledge & Kegan Paul, Ltd.); *Benjamin N. Nelson, ed., *Freud and the 20th Century* (1958, Meridian).

DEVELOPMENTS IN THE ARTS

Nikolaus Pevsner, *Pioneers of the Modern Movement* (1936, Faber & Faber, Ltd.); *Alfred H. Barr, Jr., *What Is Modern Painting?* (1968, Mus. of Modern Art); *H. and A. Gernshem, *A Concise History of Photography* (1965, Grosset and Dunlap). François Mathey, *The World of the Impressionists* (1961, Praeger), *John Rewald, *The History of Impressionism* (1946, Mus. of Modern Art), and *Post-Impressionism from van Gogh to Gauguin* (1956, Mus. of Modern Art) are exceptionally detailed and well illustrated. *Herbert E. Read, *Concise History of Modern Painting* (1959, Praeger) is a convenient summary.

ON MARX AND MARXISM

*G. Lichtheim, *Marxism: An Historical and Critical Study* (1961, Routledge & Kegan Paul, Ltd.); I. Berlin, *Karl Marx: His Life and Environment* (1948, Oxford University Press); M. Bober, *Karl Marx's Interpretation of History*, rev. ed. (1948, Norton); Bertram O. Wolfe, *Marxism: 100 Years in the Life of a Doctrine* (1965, Dial).

THE INTELLECTUAL SPIRIT OF THE AGE

A number of books deal with larger aspects of intellectual history: J. Barzun, *Darwin, Marx, Wagner: Critique of a Heritage* (1941, Doubleday); *H. Stuart Hughes, *Consciousness and Society: The Reorientation of European Social Thought, 1850–1930* (1958, Vintage); *Gerhard Masur, *Prophets of Yesterday* (1961, Harper); *G. L. Mosse, *The Crisis of German Ideology: Intellectual Origins of the*

Third Reich (1964, Grosset and Dunlap). More specific studies of the new intellectual currents are: Michael Curtis, *Three Against the Third Republic: Sorel, Barrès, and Maurras* (1959, Princeton University Press); H. A. Reyburn, *Nietzsche: The Story of a Human Philosopher* (1948, Macmillan); R. Humphrey, *Georges Sorel: Prophet Without Honor* (1951, Harvard University Press). °Fritz Stern, *Politics of Cultural Despair* (1965, Anchor) deals with links between intellectual anti-Semites and popular culture. °James Joll, *Three Intellectuals in Politics: Blum, Rathenau, Marinetti* (1960, Harper) is another approach to the intellectual history of this period. F. K. Ringer, *The Decline of the German Mandarins* (1969, Harvard University Press) discusses the problem one kind of intellectual had in industrial society; S. R. Tomkins, *The Russian Intelligentsia* (1957, University of Oklahoma Press) sketches another important group.

ON POPULAR CULTURE

°Carl Cipolla, *Literacy and Development in the West* (1969, Pelican) is a vital survey of popular culture. Studies that reveal the people's reading habits include: Eda Sagarra, *Tradition and Revolution: German Literature and Society, 1830–1890* (1971, Basic Books); °Lee Lowenthal, *Literature, Popular Culture, and Society* (1961, Pacific Books); Henry N. Smith, *Popular Culture and Industrialism, 1865–1890* (1967, Anchor); °Richard O. Altick, *The English Common Reader: A Social History of the Mass Reading Public, 1800–1900* (1957, Phoenix); and Richard Hoggart, *The Uses of Literacy* (1957, Oxford University Press). Popular culture can be approached more generally through °Raymond Williams, *Culture and Society, 1780–1950* (1958, Harper) and *The Long Revolution* (1961, Columbia University Press). Also °Bernard Rosenberg and D. M. White, eds., *Mass Culture* (1957, Free Press).

Studies of "Victorianism" offer broad insight into popular culture: °G. Kiston Clark, *The Making of Victorian England* (1962, Atheneum); W. E. Houghton, *The Victorian Frame of Mind, 1830–1870* (1957, Yale University Press); °W. L. Burn, *The Age of Equipoise: A Study of the Mid-Victorian Generation* (1964, Norton).

ON EDUCATION AND THE PRESS

H. C. Barnard, *Short History of English Education* (1947, University of London Press); E. H. Reisner, *Nationalism and Education Since 1789* (1923, Macmillan); C. J. H. Hayes, *France: A Nation of Patriots* (1930, Columbia University Press); C. F. Carr and F. Stevens, *Modern Journalism* (1931, Sir I. Pitman & Sons, Ltd.).

ON SPORTS

Peter C. McIntosh, *Sport in Society* (1963, Pub. Service); *Physical Education in England Since 1800* (1969, Soccer).

ON RELIGION

Adrien Dansette, *Religious History of Modern France* (1961, Herder and Herder); K. S. Inglis, *Churches and the Working Class in Victorian England* (1963, University of Toronto Press); °S. A. Burrell, ed., *The Role of Religion in Modern European History* (1964, Macmillan).

ON ANTI-SEMITISM

See *P. Pulzer, *The Rise of Political Anti-Semitism in Germany and Austria* (1964, Wiley); Robert Byrnes, *Anti-Semitism in Modern France* (1950, Rutgers University Press); J. W. Parkes, *The Emergence of the Jewish Problem, 1878– 1939* (1946, Oxford University Press); N. W. Ackerman and M. Jahoda, *Anti-Semitism and Emotional Disorder* (1950, Harper); P. F. Bernstein, *Jew-Hate as a Social Problem* (1951, The Philosophical Library); Jules Isaac, *The Teaching of Contempt: Christian Roots of Anti-Semitism* (1940, Holt, Rinehart & Winston).

POLITICAL DEVELOPMENTS AS SEEN IN NATIONAL STUDIES

On Germany: J. A. Nichols, *Germany After Bismarck* (1958, Harvard University Press) and J. C. G. Röhl, *Germany Without Bismarck: The Crisis of Government in the Second Reich* (1967, University of California Press) deal with Germany's political problems. General interpretations are W. M. Simon, *Germany in the Age of Bismarck* (1968, Barnes & Noble) and Arthur Rosenberg, *The Birth of the German Republic* (1931, Russell), the latter a vigorous denunciation of imperial Germany.

On Britain: R. C. K. Ensor, *England, 1870–1914* (1936, Oxford University Press) is a good survey. For the main political trends, see R. B. McDowell, *British Conservatism* (1955, Hillary) and Colin Cross, *The Liberals in Power, 1905–1914* (1962, Dufour). On the Irish question, see J. C. Hammond, *Gladstone and the Irish Nation* (1938, Shoe String). George Dangerfield, *The Strange Death of Liberal England* (1961, Capricorn) is a stimulating account of social unrest before 1914, but see also Henry Pelling, *Popular Politics and Society in Late Victorian Britain* (1968, St. Martin's).

On Italy: see Christopher Seton-Watson, *Italy from Liberalism to Fascism, 1870–1925* (1967, Barnes & Noble); A. W. Salomone, *Italian Democracy in the Making* (1945, University of Pennsylvania Press).

On France: E. M. Earle, ed., *Modern France* (1951, Russell) contains many essays on society and politics in the Third and Fourth Republics. On the Dreyfus affair, see Guy Chapman, *The Dreyfus Case* (1955, R. Hart-Davis, Ltd.) and D. B. Ralston, *The Army of the Republic: The Place of the Military in the Political Evolution of France, 1871–1914* (1967, MIT Press).

On Austria: Austria's decline has engendered a number of studies. A. J. May, *The Habsburg Monarchy, 1867–1914* (1951, Harvard University Press) argues against the inevitability of collapse while O. Jaszi, *The Dissolution of the Habsburg Monarchy* (1929, University of Chicago Press) argues for it. Edward Crankshaw, *The Fall of the House of Hapsburg* (1963, Viking) is very readable. See also C. A. Macartney, *The Hapsburg Monarchy, 1790–1918* (1968, Macmillan). On Hungary, C. A. Macartney, *Hungary, A Short History* (1962, Aldine).

On the Balkans: See C. and B. Jelavich, eds., *The Balkans in Transition* (1963, University of California Press).

On Russia: R. F. Byrnes, *Pobiedonostsev, His Life and Thought* (1968, Indiana University Press) and Theodore Von Laue, *Sergei Witte and the Industrialization of Russia* (1963, Columbia University Press) deal with major trends within the government. See also *Bernard Pares, *The Fall of the Russian Monarchy* (1939, Vintage) and *Hugh Seton-Watson, *The Decline of Imperial Russia, 1855– 1914* (1952, Praeger). On dissent and protest see L. A. Owen, *The Russian Peasant Movement, 1906–1917* (1937, Russell); *Franco Venturi, *Roots of Revolution*

(1960, Grosset & Dunlap); Avraham Yarmolinsky, *Road to Revolution: A Century of Russian Radicalism* (1959, Collier); E. Lampert, *Sons Against Fathers: Studies in Russian Radicalism and Revolution* (1965, Oxford University Press); L. H. Haimson, *The Russian Marxists and the Origins of Bolshevism* (1955, Harvard University Press).

INTERPRETATIONS OF IMPERIALISM

J. A. Hobson, *Imperialism: A Study*, 3rd ed. (1938, Allen & Unwin, Ltd.); V. I. Lenin, *Imperialism, The Highest Stage of Capitalism* (1916, Int. Pubs.); J. A. Schumpeter, *Imperialism and Social Classes* (1955, Kelley). W. L. Langer, *The Diplomacy of Imperialism, 1890–1902* (1935, Knopf) is a detailed and balanced study. Good recent surveys are Stewart L. Easton, *The Rise and Fall of Western Colonialism* (1964, Praeger); C. J. Lowe, *The Reluctant Imperialists* (1969, Macmillan); E. M. Winslow, *The Pattern of Imperialism: A Study in the Theories of Power* (1948, Columbia University Press); and D. K. Fieldhouse, *The Colonial Empires* (1966, Weidenfeld & Nicolson, Ltd.).

National studies also include D. J. Dallin, *The Rise of Russia in Asia* (1949, Yale University Press); M. E. Townsend, *The Rise and Fall of Germany's Colonial Empire* (1930, Macmillan); H. I. Priestley, *France Overseas, A Study of Modern Imperialism* (1938, University of California Press).

Ronald Robinson and John Gallagher, *Africa and the Victorians* (1961, St. Martin's) offer a political interpretation of British imperialism. See also E. J. Hobsbawm, *Industry and Empire* (1968, Pantheon) and D. C. M. Platt, *Finance, Trade, and Politics in British Foreign Policy, 1815–1914* (1968, Oxford University Press). On internal views see Bernard Semmel, *Imperialism and Social Reform: English Social-Imperial Thought, 1895–1914* (1960, Harvard University Press); Jeffrey Bulter, *The Liberal Party and the Jameson Raid* (1968, Oxford University Press); and A. P. Thornton, *The Imperial Idea and Its Enemies* (1959, St. Martin's). For the reaction of the colonized see *Frantz Fanon, *The Wretched of the Earth* (1965, Grove).

SOCIALISM IN INDUSTRIAL EUROPE

Carl Landauer, *European Socialism*, 2 vols. (1959, University of California Press) is the most comprehensive survey. Shorter treatments include *Alexander Gray, *The Socialist Tradition: Moses to Lenin* (1946, Harper); H. Edmund Wilson, *To the Finland Station* (1946, Anchor); and George Lichtheim, *The Origins of Socialism* (1969, Praeger). On revisionism, see *Peter Gay, *The Dilemma of Democratic Socialism* (1952, Collier). On national movements, see Henry Pelling, *Origins of the Labour Party, 1880–1900* (1954, Oxford University Press). Also Harvey Goldberg, *The Life of Jean Jaurès* (1962, University of Wisconsin Press); Vernon Lidtke, *The Outlawed Party: Social Democracy in Germany, 1878–1890* (1966, Princeton University Press); *Carl Schorske, *German Socialism, 1905–1917* (1955, Wiley); Richard Hostetter, *The Italian Socialist Movement* (1958, Van Nostrand). See also bibliography on labor movements, Suggested Readings—Chapter 5.

ON RIGHTIST POLITICS

*Hans Rogger and Eugen Weber, eds., *The European Right* (1965, University of California Press); *Eugen Weber, *Action Française* (1962, Stanford). See also bibliography on anti-Semitism, Suggested Readings—Chapter 6.

THE DEVELOPMENT OF THE ALLIANCE SYSTEM

William L. Langer, *European Alliance and Alignments* (1950, Knopf); also R. J. Sontag, *Germany and England: The Background of Conflict, 1848-1894* (1938, Russell). On the Balkans, W. N. Medlicott, *The Congress of Berlin and After* (1938, Shoe String); B. H. Sumner, *Russia and the Balkans* (1937, Clarendon Press); and Hans Kohn, *Pan Slavism* (1953, Vintage).

THE CAUSES OF WORLD WAR I

L. C. Robbins, *The Economic Causes of War* (1939, Macmillan) and Alfred Vagts, *Defense and Diplomacy* (1956, Columbia University Press) discuss economic and military factors respectively. Classic older works include L. Albertini, *The Origins of the War of 1814*, 3 vols. (1952–57, Oxford University Press); S. B. Fay, *The Origins of the World War*, 2 vols. (1930, Macmillan); and Nicholas Mansergh, *The Coming of the First World War* (1949, Longmans, Green and Co.). G. P. Gooch, *Before the War*, 2 vols. (1936–1938, Longmans, Green and Co.) focuses on the leading statements of the great powers. Fritz Fischer, *Germany's Aims in the First World War* (1967, Norton) has reopened the whole question of responsibility for the war. See also Emanuel Geiss, *1914: A Documentary Survey* (1918, Scribner). Some of the main issues are discussed in "1914," *Journal of Contemporary History*, Vol. I, 3 (1966, Harper & Row) and in the very readable book by Laurence Lafore, *The Long Fuse: An Interpretation of the Origins of World War I* (1965, Lippincott).

MILITARY DEVELOPMENTS

The best short surveys are: *Cyril Falls, *The Great War, 1914–1918* (1936, Capricorn); R. H. Liddell Hart, *The War in Outline, 1914–1918* (1936, University Pub. & Dist.); and H. W. Baldwin, *World War I: An Outline History* (1962, Harper & Row). See also L. Stallings, *The First World War: A Photographic History*, new ed. (1964, Simon & Schuster) and A. J. P. Taylor, *Politics in Wartime* (1964, Hamilton). The opening of the war is narrated in Barbara Tuchman's *The Guns of August* (1967, Macmillan). *Alistair Horne, *The Price of Glory: Verdun, 1916* (1963, Harper) is an excellent study of a single campaign.

INTERNAL DEVELOPMENTS

See F. P. Chambers, *The War Behind the War, 1914–1918* (1939, Harcourt Brace Jovanovich). On economics, J. C. King, *Generals and Politicians* (1951, University of California Press) deals with French politics. On Germany see H. W. Gatzke, *Germany's Drive to the West* (1950, Johns Hopkins Press) and H. C. Meyer, *Mitteleuropa in German Thought and Action* (1955, The Hague). On social changes, Gerald D. Feldman, *Army, Industry, and Labor, 1914–1918* (1966, Princeton University Press) deals with Germany, as does A. M. Bartholdy, *The War and German Society* (1938, Fertig). See also *Arthur Marwick, *The Deluge: British Society and the First World War* (1965, Norton); A. Fontaine, *French Industry During the War* (1962, Yale University Press). On Austria, Z. A. B. Zeman, *The Breakup of the Hapsburg Empire, 1914–1918* (1961, Oxford University Press) and A. J. May, *The Passing of the Hapsburg Monarchy*, 2 vols. (1966, University of Pennsylvania Press).

Suggestions for Further Readings

THE RUSSIAN REVOLUTION

The best study is E. H. Carr, *History of Soviet Russia*, 7 vols. (1950–, Macmillan), the first three volumes of which deal with the revolution. Shorter surveys include *William Chamberlin, *The Russian Revolution*, 2 vols. (1935, Grosset & Dunlap); B. O. Wolfe, *Three Who Made a Revolution* [Lenin, Trotsky, Stalin] (1964, Delta); *John Reed, *Ten Days That Shook the World* (1919, Modern Lib.). See also the provocative analysis of Theodore Von Laue, *Why Lenin? Why Stalin? A Reappraisal of the Russian Revolution, 1900–1930* (1964, Lippincott). Important biographies include Louis Fischer, *Life of Lenin* (1964, Harper & Row) and Isaac Deutscher's three-volume biography of Trotsky (1954–1963, Random House). Arno Mayer, *Political Origins of the New Diplomacy* (1970, Fertig) suggests the immediate impact of the revolution on wartime diplomacy. The impact elsewhere is discussed in Ruth Fischer, *Stalin and German Communism* (1948, Harvard University Press); M. D. Carroll, *Soviet Communism and Western Opinion, 1919–1920* (1965, University of North Carolina Press); and Robert Wohl, *French Communism in the Making* (1965, Stanford University Press). See also Franz Borkenau, *The Communist International* (1938, Faber & Faber, Ltd.). For a brilliant analysis of why the Bolsheviks failed outside of Russia see J. A. Schumpeter, *Capitalism, Socialism, and Democracy* (1950, Harper & Row).

ON VERSAILLES

The standard work is H. W. V. Temperley, ed., *History of the Peace Conference*, 6 vols (1920–1924). *H. G. Nicolson, *Peacemaking, 1919* (1939, Grosset & Dunlap) is a good brief account. Arno Mayer, *Politics and Diplomacy of Peacemaking: Containment and Counterrevolution at Versailles, 1918–1919* (1968, Knopf) shows the role of fear of Bolshevism. J. M. Keynes, *Economic Consequences of the Peace* (1920, Harcourt Brace Jovanovich) condemns the economic clauses of the treaty; Paul Mantoux, *The Carthaginian Peace* (1952, University of Pittsburgh Press) attacks Keynes. Stephen Bonsal, *Suitors and Suppliants: The Little Nations at Versailles* (1946, Kennikat) is useful. See also I. J. Lederer, *Yugoslavia at the Paris Peace Conference* (1964, Yale University Press); R. Albrecht Carrié, *Italy at the Paris Peace Conference* (1938, Shoe String); and N. Almond and R. H. Lutz, *The Treaty of Saint-Germain* (1935, Stanford University Press). Paul Birdsall, *Versailles–Twenty Years After* (1941, Shoe String) appraises the far-reaching effects of the settlement.

ON THE LEAGUE

F. P. Walters, *History of the League of Nations*, 2 vols. (1960, Oxford University Press).

STUDY OF THE LITERATURE OF THE WAR

See Bernard Bergonzi, *Heroes' Twilight* (1966, Coward).

NATIONAL STUDIES OF THE PERIOD

C. L. Mowat, *Britain Between the Wars* (1955, University of Chicago Press) is an excellent survey of England in the interim period. See also A. J. P. Taylor, *English History, 1914–1945* (1965, Oxford University Press). *Robert Graves and

Alan Hodge, *The Long Weekend: A Social History of Great Britain, 1918–1939* (1941, Norton) is a valuable book on the spirit of the age.

On France see Alexander Werth, *The Twilight of France, 1933–1940* (1942, Fertig). David Thomson, *Democracy in France Since 1870* (1964, Oxford University Press) surveys the whole period. Important special studies are P. J. Larmour, *The French Radical Party in the 1930s* (1964, Stanford University Press); John T. Marcus, *French Socialism in the Crisis Years, 1933–1936* (1958, Praeger); Henry W. Ehrmann, *French Labor from Popular Front to Liberation* (1947, Oxford University Press); C. A. Micaud, *Communism and the French Left* (1962, Praeger); Joel Colton, *Léon Blum* (1966, Knopf); and C. A. Micaud, *The French Right and Nazi Germany* (1943, Octagon). Adolph F. Sturmthal, *The Tragedy of European Labor, 1918–1939* (1943, Columbia University Press) deals with the misfortunes of socialist parties in several countries, including France.

On Weimar Germany, °Richard Greenberger, *Germany, 1918–1945* (1964, Harper) is a brief survey. °Erich Eyck, *A History of the Weimar Republic*, 2 vols. (1963, Atheneum) is more detailed. On early agitation see Werner Angress, *Stillborn Revolution: The Communist Bid for Power in Germany* (1963, Princeton University Press) and R. G. L. Waite, *Vanguard of Nazism: The Free Corps Movement in Postwar Germany* (1952, Norton). See also Henry A. Turner, *Stresemann and the Politics of Weimar Germany* (1963, Princeton University Press).

On the Scandinavian welfare state see Franklin Scott, *The United States and Scandinavia* (1950, Harvard University Press) and Marquis W. Childs, *Sweden: The Middle Way* (1947, Yale University Press).

ECONOMIC DEVELOPMENTS

See Paul Alpert, *Twentieth Century Economic History of Europe* (1951, Schuman); Gustav Stolper, *German Economy, 1870–1940* (1940, Reynal & Hitchcock); and H. V. Hodson, *Slump and Recovery, 1929–1937* (1938, Oxford University Press).

LEADING INTELLECTUAL DEVELOPMENTS

See George Gurvitch and W. E. Moore, eds., *Twentieth Century Sociology* (1945, Philosophical Library); Morton White, *The Age of Analysis* (1955, New Am. Library). Two important specific studies are H. Stuart Hughes, *Oswald Spengler* (1952, Scribner) and R. F. Harrod, *The Life of John Maynard Keynes* (1951, St. Martin's).

On German thought and culture see Walter Kaufmann, ed., *Existentialism from Dostoyevsky to Sartre* (1956, Meridian); Istvan Deak, *Weimar Germany's Left-Wing Intellectuals* (1968, University of California Press); and Peter Gay, *Weimar Culture* (1968, Harper & Row).

On France see Julian Park, ed., *The Culture of France in Our Time* (1954, Cornell University Press); Henri Peyre, *The Contemporary French Novel* (1955, Oxford University Press); and H. Stuart Hughes, *The Obstructed Path: French Social Thought in the Years of Desperation, 1930–1960* (1966, Harper & Row).

ON LITERATURE AND THE ARTS

Barbara M. Lane, *Architecture and Politics in Germany, 1918–1945* (1968, Harvard University Press); Hans M. Wingler, *The Bauhaus* (1969, Adler); Béla Balázs, *Theory of the Film: Character and Growth of a New Art* (1952, D. Dobson);

and °H. L. Bacharach, ed., *The Music Masters*, Vol. IV: "The Twentieth Century" (1948–54, M. Fridberg). On new literary trends see Edmund Wilson, *Axel's Castle* (1931, Scribner). On painting and sculpture, Emile Langu, *Fifty Years of Modern Art* (1959, Thames and Hudson, Ltd.); Hans Richter, *Dada* (1967, Abrams); °Patrick Waldberg, *Surrealism* (1965, McGraw-Hill).

On popular culture see Robert Graves and Alan Hodge, *The Long Weekend: A Social History of Great Britain, 1918–1939* (1941, Norton). Also Ronald H. Coase, *British Broadcasting* (1950, Longmans, Green and Co.). Herman Lebovic, *Social Conservatism and the Middle Classes in Germany, 1914–1933* (1969, Princeton University Press) is useful on intellectual history but not, as its title implies, on social development.

ON AUTHORITARIANISM IN GENERAL

°Elizabeth Wiskemann, *Europe of the Dictators, 1914–1945* (1966, Harper) is a good factual survey. See also Alfred Cobban, *Dictatorship: Its History and Theory* (1939, Scribner); G. W. F. Hallgarten, *Why Dictators?* (1954, Macmillan); C. J. Friedrich and Zbigniew Brzezinski, *Totalitarian Dictatorship and Autocracy* (1956, Praeger). °Erich Fromm, *Escape from Freedom* (1941, Avon) argues that modern men cannot bear the burden of freedom and escapes into mass movements. Seymour Lipset, *Political Man* (1959, Doubleday) discusses authoritarian personality types and specifically studies Nazi voters. °Hannah Arendt, *Origins of Totalitarianism* (1950, Meridian) also deals mainly with fascism. °Barrington Moore, *The Social Origins of Dictatorship and Democracy* (1966, Beacon) tries to suggest why modernization led to democracy, fascism, or communism in different cases.

ON RUSSIA AND COMMUNISM

°Massino Salvadori, *The Rise of Modern Communism* (1963, Holt, Rinehart & Winston); K. E. McKenzie, *Comintern and World Revolution* (1964, Columbia University Press); and R. N. C. Hunt, *Theory and Practice of Communism* (1950, Macmillan). A good survey is °Hugh Seton-Watson, *From Lenin to Khrushchev: The History of World Communism* (1960, Praeger). More specifically on Russia, E. H. Carr, *A History of Soviet Russia*, vols. IV–VII (1954–1964, Penguin); Isaac Deutscher, *Stalin: A Political Biography* (1949, Oxford University Press) and the *Unfinished Revolution: Russia, 1917–1962* (1967, Oxford University Press); Zbigniew Brzezinski, *The Permanent Purge: Politics in Soviet Totalitarianism* (1956, Harvard University Press); and Barrington Moore, *Soviet Politics: The Dilemma of Power* (1950, Harvard University Press). On economics, see Alexander Baykov, *The Development of the Soviet Economic System* (1947, Macmillan).

On military affairs: John Erikson, *The Soviet High Command* (1962, St. Martin's). On diplomacy: George F. Kennan, *Soviet Foreign Policy, 1917–1941* (1961, Van Nostrand). On the purges: Robert Conquest, *The Great Terror: Stalin's Purge of the Thirties* (1968, Macmillan). On opposition to Stalin: R. V. Daniels, *The Conscience of the Revolution: Communist Opposition in Soviet Russia* (1960, Harvard University Press).

ON FASCISM IN GENERAL

See Ernst Nolte, *Three Faces of Fascism* (1966, Holt, Rinehart & Winston); F. L. Carsten, *The Rise of Fascism* (1967, University of California Press); S. J. Woolf, ed., *The Nature of Fascism* (1968, Random House); and "International Fascism, 1920–1945," *Journal of Contemporary History*, Vol. I, 1 (1966, Harper & Row).

FASCISM IN ITALY

See Sir Ivone J. A. Kirkpatrick, *Mussolini: A Study of a Demagogue* (1964, Odhams Books); H. Finer, *Mussolini's Italy* (1935, Shoe String); Federico Chabod, *A History of Italian Fascism* (1963, Weidenfeld and Nicolson); R. A. Webster, *The Cross and the Fasces: Christian Democracy and Fascism in Italy* (1956, Stanford University Press); Danti L. Germinio, *The Italian Fascist Party in Power* (1959, University of Minnesota Press). On foreign policy: Elizabeth Wiskemann, *The Rome-Berlin Axis* (1949, Oxford University Press). A fine short survey is °W. S. Halperin, *Mussolini and Italian Fascism* (1964, Van Nostrand Reinhold). See also Benito Mussolini, *My Autobiography* (1928, Scribner).

NAZISM

See Edward Crankshaw, *Gestapo* (1956, Viking Press) and °Eugen Kogon, *The Theory and Practice of Hell* (1950, Medallion), the latter on the concentration camps. The regime's more positive accomplishments are studied in °David Schoenbaum, *Hitler's Social Revolution* (1966, Anchor). On economics, see °Franz Neuman, *Behemoth: The Structure and Practice of National Socialism* (1944, Harper); C. W. Guillebaud, *The Social Policy of Nazi Germany* (1914, Cambridge University Press); and Jürgen Kuczynski, *Germany: Economic and Labor Conditions Under Fascism* (1945, N.Y. International Publishers). Daniel Lerner, *et al.*, *The Nazi Elite* (1951, Stanford University Press) deals with the new ruling class. A fine collective survey is M. Baumont, J. H. E. Fried, and Edmond Vermeil, *The Third Reich* (1955, Weidenfeld and Nicolson). On propaganda, see Z. A. B. Zeman, *Nazi Propaganda* (1964, Oxford University Press).

The best biography of Hitler is °A. L. C. Bullock, *Hitler, A Study in Tyranny* (1964, Harper). W. S. Allen, *The Nazi Seizure of Power* (1955, Quadrangle) is a valuable case study of a small German town. °William L. Shirer, *Rise and Fall of the Third Reich* (1960, Crest) is a popular narrative.

ON SPAIN

°Gerald Brenan, *Spanish Labyrinth* (1960, Cambridge University Press) gives vital background to the Civil War. On the war itself, see °Hugh Thomas, *The Spanish Civil War* (1961, Harper); °Gabriel Jackson, *The Spanish Republic and the Civil War, 1931–1939* (1965, Princeton University Press); and °Stanley Payne, *The Spanish Revolution* (1970, Norton). On fascism, °Stanley Payne, *Falange: A History of Spanish Fascism* (1961, Stanford University Press).

OTHER AUTHORITARIAN REGIMES

See Charles Gulick, *Austria, From Habsburg to Hitler* (1948, University of California Press); Hugh Seton-Watson, *Eastern Europe Between the Wars* (1945, Shoe String); and °C. A. Macartney and A. W. Palmer, *Independent Eastern Europe* (1962, St. Martin's).

CAUSES OF WORLD WAR II

°A. J. P. Taylor, *Origins of the Second World War* (1962, Premier) is a controversial treatment. See also Cyril B. Falls, *The Second World War, A Short History* (1950, Methuen) and especially °Lionel Kochan, *The Struggle for Germany,*

1914–1945 (1963, Harper). On Munich, see J. W. Wheeler-Bennett, *Munich: Prologue to Tragedy* (1948, Meredith). A more general diplomatic survey is Gordon Craig and Felix Gilbert, *The Diplomats, 1919–1939* (1953, Atheneum). Laurence Lafore, *The End of Glory: An Interpretation of the Origins of World War II* (1970, Lippincott) is a useful recent analysis.

WARTIME POLICIES

See Arnold and V. M. Toynbee, eds., *Hitler's Europe* (1954, Oxford University Press) and Alexander Dallin, *German Rule in Russia, 1941–1945* (1957, St. Martin's). On France's collapse: Marc Bloch, *Strange Defeat* (1968, Octagon Books). On the Vichy regime: °Robert Aron, *The Vichy Regime, 1940–1945* (1958, Beacon); see also Alexander Werth, *France, 1940–1955* (1956, Beacon). On Russia: Alexander Werth, *Russia at War, 1941–1945* (1964, Dutton). On Italy: F. W. Deakin, *The Brutal Friendship: Mussolini, Hitler, and the Fall of Italian Fascism* (1962, Harper & Row) and Charles F. Delzell, *Mussolini's Enemies: The Italian Anti-Fascist Resistance* (1961, Princeton University Press).

On resistance within Germany, see H. C. Deutsch, *The Conspiracy Against Hitler in the Twilight War* (1968, University of Minnesota Press) and Hans Rothfels, *The German Opposition to Hitler* (1962, Regnery). On the fall of the Nazi Reich, H. R. Trevor-Roper, *The Last Days of Hitler* (1947, Collier).

ON WAR AND POSTWAR DIPLOMACY

The best overview of World War II is °Gordon Wright, *The Ordeal of Total War, 1939–1945* (1968, Harper). See also Herbert C. O'Neill, *A Short History of the Second World War* (1950, Praeger) and the highly readable °Winston Churchill, *The Second World War*, 6 vols. (1949–1952, Bantam).

Peter Novick, *The Resistance Versus Vichy* (1968, Columbia University Press) deals with the purge of collaborators after France's liberation. See also John L. Snell, ed., *The Meaning of Yalta* (1956, Louisiana State University Press); Herbert Feis, *Churchill, Roosevelt, Stalin: The War They Waged and the Peace They Sought* (1957, Princeton University Press) and *Between War and Peace: The Potsdam Conference* (1960, Princeton University Press). Hajo Holborn, *The Political Collapse of Europe* (1951, Knopf) offers a postwar assessment. See Wilfred F. Knapp, *A History of War and Peace, 1939–1965* (1967, Oxford University Press); °Arnold J. Toynbee, *The World and the West* (1953, Meridian); °George Lichtheim, *The New Europe: Today and Tomorrow* (1963, Praeger); Jacques Freymond, *Western Europe Since the War* (1964, Praeger); Robert C. Mowat, *Ruin and Resurgence, 1939–1965* (1966, Humanities). See also °Raymond Aron, *The Century of Total War* (1954, Beacon). On the Cold War specifically, see John Lukacs, *A New History of the Cold War* (1966, Doubleday); Louis J. Halle, *The Cold War as History* (1967, Harper & Row); °David Rees, *The Age of Containment: The Cold War* (1967, St. Martin's). On NATO, H. F. Haviland, Jr., *The Atlantic Community: Progress and Prospects* (1963, Praeger) and Lord Ismay, *NATO: The First Five Years* (1955, NATO).

DECOLONIZATION

The most useful introduction is John Strachey, *End of Empire* (1960, Praeger), which deals mainly with British withdrawal from India. On France's colonial wars: Ellen Hammer, *The Struggle for Indochina* (1954, Stanford University Press); Richard and Joan Brace, *Ordeal in Algeria* (1960, Van Nostrand); and Dorothy

Pickles, *Algeria and France* (1963, Praeger). On sub-Saharan Africa: Lord Hailey, *An African Survey: A Study of Problems Arising in Africa South of the Sahara* (1966, Oxford University Press); Crawford Young, *Politics in the Congo: Decolonization and Independence* (1965, Princeton University Press). On the Suez crisis, see Hugh Thomas, *The Suez Affair* (1966, Harper & Row). A general interpretation, in part an anticipation, is Eric Fischer, *The Passing of the European Age* (1948, Harvard University Press).

GENERAL STUDIES OF POSTWAR POLITICAL DEVELOPMENTS

Walter Laqueur, *Europe Since Hitler* (1970, Weidenfeld & Nicolson, Ltd.) is an excellent general survey. T. H. White, *Fire in the Ashes: Europe in Mid-Century* (1953, Sloane) appraises the first decades of recovery. Mario Einaudi, J-M. Domenach, and Aldo Garosci, *Communism in Western Europe* (1951, Shoe String) is useful. On Christian Democracy: Mario Einaudi and François Goguel, *Christian Democracy in Italy and France* (1952, University of Notre Dame Press) and especially Michael Fogarty, *Christian Democracy in Western Europe* (1957, University of Notre Dame Press).

NATIONAL STUDIES OF POSTWAR POLITICAL DEVELOPMENTS

On eastern Europe, Hugh Seton-Watson, *The East European Revolution* (1950, Praeger) deals with events between 1945 and 1949. See also Josef Korbel, *The Communist Subversion of Czechoslovakia* (1959, Princeton University Press). F. W. Neal, *Titoism in Action: The Reforms in Yugoslavia After 1948* (1958, Harvard University Press) is useful. Zbigniew Brzezinski, *The Soviet Bloc: Unity and Conflict* (1964, Harvard University Press) deals with the consolidation of the bloc and post-Stalinist tensions. W. E. Griffith, ed., *Communism in Europe: Continuity, Change, and the Sino-Soviet Disputes* (1964, MIT) and Stephen Fischer-Galati, ed., *Eastern Europe in the Sixties* (1963, Praeger) offer essays on a variety of trends. On the Hungarian revolt, see F. A. Váti, *Rift and Revolt in Hungary* (1961, Harvard University Press) and P. E. Zinner, *Revolution in Hungary* (1962, Columbia University Press). On Czechoslovakia: R. R. James, ed., *The Czechoslovak Crisis, 1968* (1969, Weidenfeld & Nicolson, Ltd.). Also useful are °Robert L. Wolff, *The Balkans in Our Time* (1967, Norton); Ghita Ionescu, *Communism in Rumania, 1944–1962* (1964, Oxford University Press); Andrzei Korbanski, *Politics of Socialist Agriculture in Poland, 1945–1960* (1965, Columbia University Press) and David Childs, *East Germany* (1969, Praeger).

On Russia, Merle Fainsod, *How Russia Is Ruled* (1963, Harvard University Press) deals with changes since Stalin. Robert C. Tucker, *The Soviet Political Mind* is good on ideological issues; see also Richard Löwenthal, *World Communism: The Disintegration of a Secular Faith* (1964, Oxford University Press). On politics: Edward Crankshaw, *Khrushchev: A Career* (1964, Viking). °Leonard Schapiro, *The Communist Party in the Soviet Union* (1960, Vintage) has a good section on postwar developments.

On the authoritarian regimes see °Herbert L. Matthews, *The Yoke and the Arrow: A Report on Spain* (1957, Braziller); Stanley Payne, *Franco's Spain* (1967, Crowell); and Kenneth Young, *The Greek Passion* (1969, Simon & Schuster).

On Britain: Francis Boyd, *British Politics in Transition, 1945–1963* (1964, Praeger). On the welfare state's development see Francis Williams, *Socialist Britain* (1949, Viking Press) and E. S. Watkins, *The Cautious Revolution* (1950, Farrar Straus). See also David Thomson, *England in the Twentieth Century, 1914–*

1963 (1964, Penguin). Max Nicholson, *The System: The Misgovernment of Modern Britain* (1967, McGraw-Hill) is a critical view. On the principles of the welfare state, with reference mainly to Britain, see Richard M. Titmuss, *Essays on "The Welfare State"* (1959, Yale University Press) and other works. Also Alvin Schorr, *Social Security and Social Services in France* (1965, Washington, Gov't. Printing Office).

On France, Gordon Wright, *The Reshaping of the French Democracy* (1948, Reynal & Hitchcock) deals with postwar changes. On the Fourth Republic see Philip M. Williams, *Politics in Post-War France* (1954, Longmans, Green and Co.) and °Herbert Lüthy, *France Against Herself* (1955, Meridian). On the Gaullist takeover: Stewart Ambler, *The French Army in Politics, 1945–1962* (1966, Ohio State University Press) and J. H. Meisel, *The Fall of the Republic: Military Revolt in France* (1962, University of Michigan Press). On the Fifth Republic: Philip M. Williams and Martin Harrison, *De Gaulle's Republic* (1960, Longmans, Green and Co.); °Dorothy Pickles, *The Fifth Republic* (1960, Praeger); and °Jean Lacouture, *De Gaulle* (1966, Discus). On foreign policy see Alfred Grosser, *French Foreign Policy Under De Gaulle* (1965, Little, Brown). Three important specialized studies are François Fejtö, *The French Communist Party and the Crisis of International Communism* (1967, MIT); H. G. Simmons, *French Socialists in Search of a Role, 1956–1967* (1970, Cornell University Press); and, on local government, Mark Kesselman, *The Ambiguous Consensus* (1967, Knopf).

On Italy: Guiseppe Mammarella, *Italy After Fascism: A Political History, 1943–1963* (1964, University of Notre Dame Press); Muriel Grindrod, *The Rebuilding of Italy* (1955, Royal Institute of International Affairs); H. Stuart Hughes, *The United States and Italy* (1965, Harvard University Press); and Serge Hughes, *The Fall and Rise of Modern Italy* (1967, Funk & Wagnalls).

On Germany: Alfred Grosser, *Western Germany from Defeat to Rearmament* (1955, Allen & Unwin) and *The Federal Republic of Germany: A Concise History* (1963, Praeger). On the founding of the republic see J. F. Golay, *The Founding of the Federal Republic of Germany* (1958, University of Chicago Press) and G. A. Almond, ed., *The Struggle for Democracy in Germany* (1949, Russell). On foreign policy: K. W. Deutsch and L. Edinger, *Germany Rejoins the Powers* (1959, Stanford University Press); Hans Speier and W. P. Davison, *West German Leadership and Foreign Policy* (1957, Row, Peterson); and Ferenc A. Váli, *The Quest for a United Germany* (1968, Johns Hopkins Press).

THE COMMON MARKET AND RELATED DEVELOPMENTS

Leon Lindberg, *The Political Dynamics of European Economic Integration* (1963, Stanford University Press); Miriam Campo, *European Unification in the Sixties: From the Veto to the Crisis* (1966, McGraw-Hill); Louis Lister, *Europe's Coal and Steel Community: New Experiment in European Union* (1960, Twentieth Century).

POSTWAR CULTURE AND SOCIETY IN EUROPE

The arts and sciences are sketched in A. Pryce-Jones, ed., *The New Outline of Modern Knowledge* (1956, Simon and Schuster). See also R. Richman, ed., *The Arts at Midcentury* (1954, Horizon Press). On existentialism: R. Harper, *Existentialism: A Theory of Man* (1949, Harvard University Press). °L. R. Lippard, *Pop Art* (1967, Praeger) is concerned with one of the most recent trends in art.

On cultural activities in Russia see E. J. Simmons, ed., *Through the Glass of So-*

viet Literature (1962, Columbia University Press) and Harold Swayze, *Political Control of Literature in the USSR* (1962, Harvard University Press).

On postwar economic history, °M. M. Postan, *An Economic History of Western Europe, 1945–1964* (1967, Barnes & Noble) is the best survey. See also Andrew Shonfield, *Modern Capitalism* (1967, Oxford University Press).

°Stephen Graubard, ed., *A New Europe?* (1963, Beacon) offers a series of essays on postwar European politics, culture, and society, with emphasis on the use of technocracy in class structure and education. °Judith Ryder and Harold Silver, *Modern English Society, History, and Structure, 1850–1970* (1970, Methuen) is very useful. Stanley Hoffman, ed., *In Search of France* (1963, Harvard University Press) deals with recent political and social developments. On Germany: Ralf Dahrendorf, *Society and Democracy in Germany* (1968, Doubleday). On demography right after the war see Gregory (Grzegorz) Frumkin, *Population Change in Europe Since 1939* (1951, Allen & Unwin, Ltd.). Milovan Djilas, *Land Without Justice* (1958, Harcourt Brace Jovanovich) and *The New Class* (1957, Praeger) discuss and condemn social changes in communist Europe. There are several fine studies of French peasants: °Laurence Wylie, *Village in the Vaucluse* (1957, Harper); °Gordon Wright, *Rural Revolution in France* (1964, Stanford University Press); and °R. T. and B. G. Anderson, *Bus Stop for Paris* (1966, Doubleday).

°David Riesman, *et al.*, *The Lonely Crowd* (1950, Yale University Press) discusses implications of modern mass society, but from an American view.

SPECIAL STUDIES OF INTEREST

See O. R. McGregor, *Divorce in England* (1947, Fernhill) and Herbert Hendin, *Suicide and Scandinavia* (1964, Grune). John Ardagh, *The New French Revolution* (1968, Harper & Row) is an excellent discussion of changes in French society and culture. R. V. Clements, *Managers, A Study of Their Careers in Industry* (1958, Allen & Unwin, Ltd.) is useful on the new middle classes. °T. B. Bottomore, *Classes in Modern Society* (1966, Pantheon) outlines the contemporary upper and middle classes.

On Italy, see Joseph A. Martellaro, *Economic Development in Southern Italy, 1950–1960* (1965, Catholic University of America Press). There are also a number of fine contemporary studies on the Balkans: J. M. Halpern, *A Serbian Village* (1958, Columbia University Press); I. T. Sanders, *Balkan Village* (1949, University of Kentucky Press) and *Rainbow in the Rock: The People of Rural Greece* (1962, Harvard University Press); and E. Friedl Vasilika, *A Village in Modern Greece* (1962, Holt, Rinehart & Winston). On Russian peasants see Nicholas Vakar, *The Taproot of Soviet Society* (1962, Harper).

On labor movements: Val R. Lorwin, *The French Labor Movement* (1954, Harvard University Press) and D. L. Horowitz, *The Italian Labor Movement* (1963, Harvard University Press). Ferdynand Zweig, *The British Worker* (1952, Penguin Books) and *The Worker in an Affluent Society: Family Life and Industry* (1962, Free Press) deal with important changes in workers' behavior. °J. H. Goldthorpe, *et al.*, *The Affluent Worker in the Class Structure* (1965, Cambridge University Press) takes a different, less optimistic view.

On youth revolt see °Tarig Ali, ed., *New Revolutionaries: Left Opposition* (1965, Apollo) and °Paul Jacobs and Saul Landau, eds., *The New Radicals* (1966, Vintage). On the French revolt of 1968 see °H. Bourges, ed., *The Student Revolt* (1968, Hill and Wang).

INDEX

INDEX

PAGE NUMBERS IN ITALICS INDICATE ILLUSTRATIONS.

459